CHINESE PAINTING

LEADING MASTERS AND PRINCIPLES

PART I

THE FIRST MILLENNIUM

Vol. I. Early Chinese Painting. Vol. II. The Sung Period

Vol. III. Plates

PART II

THE LATER CENTURIES

Vol. IV. The Yüan and Early Ming Masters

Vol. V. The Later Ming and Leading Ch'ing Masters

Vol. VI. Plates

Vol. VII. Annotated Lists of the works of Chinese Painters of the Yüan, Ming and Ch'ing Periods

Osvald Sirén

Chinese Painting

LEADING MASTERS AND PRINCIPLES

PART II

The Later Centuries

VOLUME VII

ANNOTATED LISTS OF PAINTINGS

AND REPRODUCTIONS OF PAINTINGS

BY CHINESE ARTISTS

THE RONALD PRESS COMPANY, NEW YORK

LUND HUMPHRIES, LONDON

These Annotated Lists have been printed with contributions from *Kungafonden* and *Humanistiska Fonden* in Stockholm.

MADE AND PRINTED IN GREAT BRITAIN BY
PERCY LUND, HUMPHRIES AND COMPANY LIMITED
LONDON AND BRADFORD

TABLE OF CONTENTS

Introduction to the Annotated Lists of the Later Centuries

WHEN AT A certain stage in the development of the present publication it was found that the originally planned six volumes could not offer the space necessary for the inclusion of the Annotated Lists of works by painters of "the later centuries", and when many of these proved to be of essential importance for the scope and general usefulness of the whole publication, it became necessary to add a special seventh volume in which the Annotated Lists of the Yüan, Ming and Ch'ing dynasties could find place. By its general plan and composition, this new volume thus became a direct continuation of the section of earlier Lists inserted in Vol.II, a fact also emphasized in the consecutive pagination by which the two widely separated portions of the Annotated Lists are tied together into a framework for the present survey of Chinese Painting. The historical and stylistic problems connected with the composition of the Lists were briefly indicated in the Introduction to the earlier section and need not be repeated in detail at this place, but it should be noted that the problems shift and vary in accordance with the characteristics of the artistic material available from each successive period.

This, indeed, as is well known by every student, is very uneven in quantity as well as in quality or, to put it differently, the number of paintings preserved from "the later centuries" is infinitely larger and more representative from an historical as well as an artistic point of view than the paintings traditionally ascribed to "the first millennium". While the former to a large extent may be accepted as authentic creations by the artists who signed them or whose names are mentioned in the colophons or attestations, the latter are more often imitations or transpositions of famous models of earlier date, executed at later epochs. Their iconographic and historical interest may be considerable, but their importance as examples of a certain individual or periodic style is often conditioned or blurred by their later execution. There are many variations and degrees among the examples of this kind, and they have often occupied us in our historical discussions of the successive stages in the stylistic development. But, on the other hand, it must be admitted that such examples, however interesting, are not conducive to the establishment of what we have called Annotated Lists. The problems connected with them are of various kinds, referring not only to the actual quality of each picture, but also to its derivation from earlier designs, its time of execution, state of preservation, etc., not to mention a number of other questions difficult to explain in a few words. Our endeavour to find a way out of these difficulties led to the application of a system of classification which could be conveniently abbreviated by the addition of ciphers or letters to the descriptions on the Annotated Lists.

This system, which was further explained in the original Introduction (in Vol.II), does not offer exhaustive answers or explanations to each and all of the problems inherent in the paintings under discussion, but it contains suggestions or pointers, which, at the time of study, seemed most useful for the sorting out and classifying of the material according to individual, periodic, or other criteria.

The usefulness of a system like this varies naturally from case to case; to the compiler, it has proved most serviceable in the classification of works commonly ascribed to "the first millennium", *viz.* the Sung and pre-Sung periods, as may be seen in Vol.II of the present publication. It has also been applied in the listing of works by some painters of the Yüan period, but only exceptionally in the catalogues of paintings by leading masters of the Ming and Ch'ing dynasties; their works being more often provided not only with seals and signatures, but also with other criteria for critical classification.

The source-material for our Lists may be said to fall into two different classes or categories, *i.e.* the original paintings, and (secondly) reproductions of paintings. These two groups or classes are by no means of equal value to the student, yet they complete each other and are both necessary for the establishment of all-inclusive Lists which may serve as a framework for the study of the development of Chinese painting. There can be no doubt that one original painting by a great master is more important as a source for study and appreciation than a hundred reproductions, but since so much of the Chinese material is still practically inaccessible to Western students, it seems evident that systematized indexes or *catalogues raisonnés* of an inclusive kind have to be based on reproductions as well as on original works of art.

The Lists are supplemented by special Bibliographies referring to publications in which some of the listed pictures are reproduced. Whenever the reproductions have served as starting points or main supports for the descriptive notes, the titles of the respective publications are indicated in abbreviated form at the head of each entry, but when the descriptions are based on original pictures, the references to the books are added in the form of short notes. It is hoped that these distinctions in the arrangement of the Lists together with the principles of chronological and geographic division, described in our earlier Introduction, will make the Lists serviceable to students, even though they may leave much to be desired in the way of completeness and exactness.

The examples described in the present catalogues form, indeed, only a minor section of the total mass of Chinese scroll-paintings still preserved. They cover a period of about 1200 years – from the sixth to the eighteenth century – and represent works by more than 1360 recorded painters and a few that are unrecorded. The number of paintings *per capita* is very unequal, some of the painters are represented by only two or three examples, while the listed works by others run up to 200 or 300 and might easily have been increased still more, if completeness had been a principal aim of our catalogues. But limitations of space as well as considerations of the artistic quality made it necessary to make selections from the still preserved works by some of the most popular and officially most highly appreciated painters of the K'ang-hsi and Ch'ien-lung eras. If all the works by these men were entered, they would outweigh in size and volume all the earlier catalogues, a disproportion which would hardly correspond to the general aim and character of the present publication.

The work on these Annotated Lists has been spread over a number of years and passed through various stages, briefly recorded in our earlier Introduction, but has not as yet reached a final state. They still represent more of a project or a sketch-map than a completely surveyed or mapped out field of exploration, but in spite of this they may prove useful to students and amateurs who are venturing into the same field of research, though no less convinced than the author that all-inclusive Lists of the whole body of still existing Chinese paintings can never be accomplished completely by any one man, however well equipped he may be. It requires the co-operation of a number of specialists trained for the purpose and willing to follow the same principles in their work.

Thus, in repeating my thanks to precursors, friends and colleagues, named in earlier Introductions and Prefaces, who during the long drawn out preparation of the present publication have supplied some additional information or support, I cannot but reiterate my hopes that some of them may find it possible to get together and organize a group or body of compilers who could bring the task here partly outlined closer to completion.

The printing of these gradually extended Lists, now forming a volume of more than 450 pages, would hardly have been possible at this time, had it not been for grants from *Kungafonden* and *Humanistiska Fonden* in Stockholm, for which the author takes this welcome opportunity of expressing his sincere thanks.

O. S.

Additional Bibliography for the Lists

This Bibliography was concluded at the end of 1956

Ku-kung ming-jên hua-chu chi 故宮名人畫竹集, part II. Published by the Palace Museum, Peking, 1936.

Pao-yün 寶蘊, 3 vols., published by the National Museum, Peking, 1930.

Chung-kuo ming-hua, vols.25–40 (not previously indexed).

T'ai-shan Ts'an-shih lou, Series II–IV (ten individual albums in each series).

T'ien-ch'i shu-wu ts'ang-hua 田溪書屋藏畫, 1 vol., Chung-hua Book Co., 1939 (corresponds to the Ho Kuan-wu collection, Hongkong).

Hsü-ching chai so ts'ang ming-hua chi 虛靜齋所藏名畫集. One vol., Commercial Press, 1934 (Hsü-ching chai).

Ku-kung shu-hua lu 故宮書畫錄, 3 vols. (8 *chüan*), published by the Palace and National Museum, Taiwan. This catalogue, which was received at the end of 1956, has served for the identification of some pictures, not published elsewhere and not reproduced.

Kokka 國華, Nos.607–770 (not previously indexed).

Bijutsu Kenkyū 美術研究, Nos.170–186 (not previously indexed).

Osvald Sirén. A History of Later Chinese Painting. I–II, pl.1–242, London, 1938. (Sirén, *Later*).

Y. Yonezawa: Painting in the Ming Dynasty. Published by Mayuyama & Co., Tōkyō, 1956 (Yonezawa).

Chinese Paintings from King Kwei Collection, 2 vols., published by Benridō, Kyōto, 1956 (J. D. Ch'ên Catalogue).

M. Kitano: Yang-chou School of Painters in Ch'ien-lung Period, China. Heibonsha, Tōkyō, 1957.

Ausstellung Chinesische Malerei, Museum für Ostasiatische Kunst der Stadt Köln, 1955.

Kung Hsien and the Nanking School. Some Chinese Paintings of the Seventeenth Century (A Loan Exhibition). Chinese Art Society of America, New York, 1955.

Loan Exhibition of Chinese Paintings, The Royal Ontario Museum of Archaeology, Toronto, 1956. Catalogue by Hsien-ch'i Tsêng (Toronto).

IV

Painters of the Yüan Dynasty

A-chia-chia	阿加加
Chang Chung	張中
Chang Fang-ju	張芳汝
Chang Hsün	張遜
Chang Kuan	張觀
Chang K'ung-sun	張孔孫
Chang Mêng-k'uei	張夢奎
Chang Shên	張紳
Chang Shou-chung	張守中
Chang Shun-tzŭ	張舜咨
Chang Wu	張渥
Chang Yen-fu	張彥輔
Chang Yü	張雨
Chang Yü-ts'ai	張羽材
Chang Yüan	張遠
Chang Yüeh-hu	張月壺
Chao Chung	趙衷
Chao Hsi-yüan	趙希遠
Chao Lin	趙麟
Chao Mêng-fu	趙孟頫
Chao Mêng-yü	趙孟籲
Chao Yung	趙雍
Chao Yüan	趙元
Ch'ên Chên	陳貞
Ch'ên Chien-ju	陳鑑如
Ch'ên Chih	陳植
Ch'ên Chung-jên	陳仲仁
Ch'ên Li-shan	陳立善
Ch'ên Lin	陳琳
Chêng Hsi	鄭禧
Ch'êng Ch'i	程棨
Ch'i-tsung	啓宗
Chieh-hsi Ssŭ	揭傒斯
Ch'ien Hsüan	錢選
Chou Chih	周砥
Chou Tung-ch'ing	周東卿
Chou Yüan	周淵
Chu Shu-chung	朱叔重
Chu Tê-jun	朱德潤
Chu Yü	朱玉
Chuang Lin	莊麟
Fang Chün-jui	方君瑞
Fang Ts'ung-i	方從義
Fang-yai	方崖
Ho Ching	郝經
Hsia K'ao-ch'ang	夏考昌
Hsia Ti	夏迪
Hsia Yung	夏永
Hsieh Po-ch'êng	謝伯誠
Hsien-yü Shu	鮮于樞
Hsüeh-chien	雪澗
Hu T'ing-hui	胡廷暉
Huang Chin	黃溍
Huang Kung-wang	黃公望
Jên Jên-fa	任仁發
Jên K'ang-min	任康民
Jên Tzŭ-chao	任子昭
Kao Jan-hui	高然暉
Kao K'o-kung	高克恭
K'o Chiu-ssu	柯九思
Ku An	顧安
Ku K'uei	顧逵
Ku Tê-hui	顧德輝
Kuan Tao-shêng	管道昇
Kuo Min	郭敏
Kuo Pi	郭畀
Kuo Tsung-mao	郭宗茂
Lai-an	賴菴
Lêng Ch'ien	冷謙
Li Hêng	李亨
Li Jung-chin	李容瑾
Li K'an	李衎
Li K'ang	李康
Li Shêng	李升
Li Shih-hsing	李士行
Li T'i	李倜
Liang-ch'üan	良銓
Lin Chüan-a	林卷阿
Liu Fang	劉枋
Liu Kuan-tao	劉貫道
Liu Min-shu	劉敏叔
Liu Tzŭ-yü	劉子輿

LIU YIN	劉　因
LO CHIH-CH'UAN	羅稚川
LU KUANG	陸　廣
MA YÜAN	馬　琬
MÊNG YÜ-CHIEN	孟玉澗
NI TSAN	倪　瓚
PÊN-CH'ÊNG	本　誠
PIEN WU	邊　武
PO TZŬ-T'ING	柏子庭
PO-YEN PU-HUA	伯顏不花
P'U-KUANG	溥　光
P'U-MÊN	普　門
P'U-MING	普　明
SA TU-LA	薩都拉
SHANG CH'I	商　琦
SHANG CHU	商　璹
SHÊN HSÜAN	沈　鉉
SHÊNG HUNG	盛　洪
SHÊNG MOU	盛　懋
SHIH CHIANG	史　杠
SHIH CH'ING	時　清
SUN CHÜN-TSÊ	孫君澤
SUNG K'O	宋　克
SUNG-T'IEN	松　田
TAI SHUN	戴　淳
T'AI PU-HUA	泰不華
T'AN CHIH-JUI	檀芝瑞
T'ANG TI	唐　棣
T'AO FU-CH'U	陶復初
T'AO HSÜAN	陶　鉉
TING CH'ING-CH'I	丁清溪
TS'AI SHAN	蔡　山
TS'AO CHIH-PO	曹知白
TSOU FU-LEI	鄒復雷
TS'UI YEN-FU	崔彥輔
WANG CHÊN-P'ÊNG	王振鵬
WANG CH'ÊN	王　臣
WANG I	王　繹
WANG KUEI	王　珪
WANG LIANG-CH'ÊN	王良臣
WANG MÊNG	王　蒙
WANG MIEN	王　冕
WANG TI-CHIEN	王迪簡
WANG YÜAN	王　淵
WEI CHIU-TING	衛九鼎
WU CHÊN	吳　鎮
WU T'AI-SU	吳太素
WU T'ING-HUI	吳廷暉
YANG WEI-CHÊN	楊維楨
YAO T'ING-MEI	姚廷美
YAO YEN-CH'ING	姚彥卿
YEN HUI	顏　輝
YÜ-WÊN KUNG-LIANG	宇文公諒
YÜN-KANG TAO-SHIH	雲岡道士
YUNG-T'IEN	用　田

A-CHIA-CHIA 阿加加.
Probably a nun; active in the Yüan period. Not recorded in Chinese books but in *Kundaikan Sayuchōki* (No.185).

Shimbi, XI (Count Sakai). Kuanyin Seated on a Rock by a Stream; the boy Shan-ts'ai standing on a lotus petal. Attributed. *Cf.* Tōyō, IX; Tōsō, p.144.

CHANG CHUNG 張中. See Chang Shou-chung.

CHANG FANG-JU 張芳汝.
Yüan period. Landscapes and figures. Unrecorded in Chinese books but mentioned in *Kundaikan Sayuchōki* (No.40).

Kokka 246 (Ueno collect.). Misty River Landscape. Album-leaf. Attributed.

Sōgen Meigashū 49, 50 (Baron Dan). A pair of pictures each representing A Herd-boy with a Buffalo in a Sketchy Landscape. Attributed. *Cf.* Shimbi, VIII.

Kawasaki cat. 27. A Buffalo Feeding from the Branches of a Tree. Attributed.

Mutō cat. 23. A Winding Stream in Mist and Rain; large trees on the banks. Album-leaf. Attributed.

CHANG HSÜN 張遜, *t.* Chung-min 仲敏, *h.* Ch'i-yün 溪雲.
Native of Suchou. Studied bamboo with Li K'an; also painted landscapes after Chü-jan. H, 5. M, p.463.

C. T. Loo Successor, N.Y. Bamboo painted in outline, pine and rocks. Handscroll. Signed and dated 1341.

CHANG KUAN 張觀, *t.* K'o-kuan 可觀.
From Sung-chiang, Kiangsu. Active at end of Yüan and beginning of Ming dynasty. Followed the Ma-Hsia tradition. N, 6, p.2. H, 5, p.11. M, p.464.

Hui-hua kuan. A Landscape Study. Ink on paper. Mounted together with paintings by Shên Hsüan, Liu Tzŭ-yü and Chao Chung. A.

S.c.t.k. hsü-pien, V. High Mountains, Winding Road and Stream. In the style of Ma Yüan. Signed.

Freer Gallery (16.36). A Man with his Servant in a Small Boat, at the Foot of a Cliff under an Overhanging Willow-tree. Attributed.

CHANG K'UNG-SUN 張孔孫, *t.* Mêng-fu 夢符.
From Lung-an, Chi-lin. B. 1233, d. 1307. Served as a censor in the reign of Kublai Khan. Landscapes. I, 37, 53. L, 24. M, p.463.

Sōgen 75 (Chang Shan-tzŭ collect.) Two Men in a Straw-covered Hut at the Foot of Misty Mountains. Signed and dated 1306.

CHANG MÊNG-K'UEI 張夢奎.
Unrecorded. According to the label, active in the Yüan period (probably also early Ming).

Princeton University (Du Bois-Morris collect.) Nine Egrets, Reeds and Lotus Plant. Signed.

CHANG SHÊN 張紳, *t.* Shih-hsing 士行 and Chung-shên 仲紳, *h.* Yün-mên Shan-ch'iao 雲門山樵.
From Chi-nan. Served as Governor of Chekiang in the Hung-wu period (1368–1398). Bamboos. I, 54. L, 25. M, p.465.

K.-k. shu-hua chi, V. An Old Tree and Bamboos by a Rock, painted together with Ni Tsan and Ku An. Poems by Ni Tsan (dated 1373) and by Yang Wei-chêng. *Cf. K.-k. ming-jên hua-chu chi*, p.6.

CHANG SHOU-CHUNG 張守中, or 張守忠. Also named Chang Chung, *t.* Tzŭ-chêng 子政 (正) and Yü-chêng 于政.
From Sung-chiang, Kiangsu. Active middle of the 14th century. Landscapes, flowers and birds. H, 5. M, p.464.

H. C. Wêng, Scarsedale, N.Y. Lotuses, Sea-grass and Crabs. Signed and dated 1347. Handscroll (?)

S.c.t.k. hsü-pien, III. Man Fishing by a Waterfall. Signed and dated 1350. C.

K.-k. shu-hua chi, XX. A Cock under Flowers. Signed and dated 1351. Colophon by Chang Shên. *Cf.* Chinese cat., London Exhibition, p.162. C.

Sōraikan, II, 39. Two Swallows on a Willow Branch. Ink on paper. Signed and dated 1352. Inscription by Yang Wei-chên (1296–1370) and others.

Peking National Museum cat. An album of twelve leaves representing Flowers and Birds. The last leaf is signed and dated 1356.

Shên-chou ta-kuan v.II. Two Wagtails by a Rockery. Handscroll. Signed and dated 1360.

K.-k. shu-hua chi, II. A Bird on the Branch of a Blossoming Peach-tree. Signed. Several poems by contemporaries. A.

Ibid. XLV. A Pair of Mandarin Ducks among Rushes. Signed. *Cf.* Nanking Exhib. cat. 77. A.

Sōgen 68 (Yeh Fan-yüan collect.) A Flowering Rose Bush, Birds and Butterflies. Handscroll.

CHANG SHUN-TZŬ 張舜咨. Also named Chang I-shang 張義上 or Chang Hsi-shang 張羲上, *t.* Shih-k'uei 師夔, *h.* Li-li-tzŭ 櫟里子.
From Hangchou. Active *c.*1330–1350. Landscapes. H, 5. M, p.463.

Ku-kung, XIV. Old Trees and Rocks by a Stream. Poem by the painter Yang I (Yen-ch'ang). Signed and dated 1347.

K.-k. shu-hua chi, VII. A Bare Tree by a Rockery. Signed and dated 1349. Two poems by contemporaries and three later ones. *Cf.* Chinese cat., London Exhibition, p.166. A.

CHANG WU 張渥, *t.* Shu-hou 叔厚, *h.* Chên-hsien-shêng 眞閒生 and Chên-ch'i-shêng 貞期生.
From Hangchou. Active *c.*1360. Figures, followed Li Kung-lin. H, 5. I, 54. L, 24. M, p.464.

Tōsō, p.164 (Huang Chih collect.) The Dragon King Issuing from Waves Saluting Kuanyin, who is seated on clouds. Handscroll. Signed and dated 1360. Sūtra copied by a Ming calligraphist.

Sōgen 53 (Chang Hsüeh-liang collect.) The Eight Immortals of the Wine Cup. Illustration to the poem by Tu Fu, which is copied on the picture. Portion of a long handscroll.

Sōgen 54. Wang Hui-chih on his Way to Tai K'uei on a Snowy Night. Signed. Poem by Ch'ien-lung. *Cf.* P'ang Yüan-chi Cat., Add. 1.

Pêng Hsi (Chên-ku chai) collect., Hongkong. Chung Kuei goes Hunting followed by a number of grotesque companions and servants. Handscroll; ink on gold-sprinkled paper. Signed.

C. C. Wang collect., New York. Illustrations to Ch'ü Yüan's Nine Songs. Ink drawings on paper. Text written in *li shu* by Ku Han.

Peking National Museum cat. The Eighteen Arhats, after Li Kung-lin. Long handscroll. Signed and dated 1366. Colophons by Wang Fêng, Ku Ying, Ts'ao Chih-po and Kao Shih-ch'i.

CHANG YEN-FU 張彥輔, *t.* Liu-i 六一.
A Taoist who lived in Peking about the middle of the 14th century. Landscapes and horses. H, 5. I, 54. M, p.464.

Nelson Gallery, Kansas City (ex-Chang Ts'ung-yü). Slender Bamboos and a Jujube Shrub by a Rockery. The picture was painted as a present for Shêng Mou; and another friend of the painter, called Wu Mêng-ssŭ, wrote an inscription in which he told about their meeting in the Taoist temple in 1343. Besides this there are seven more inscriptions by contemporaries.

CHANG YÜ 張雨, also named Chang T'ien-yü 張天雨, *t.* Po-yü 伯雨, *h.* Chü-ch'ü Wai-shih 句曲外史.
From Ch'ien-t'ang, Chekiang. B. 1275, d. 1348. A Taoist monk. Landscapes. I, 54. L, 24. M, p.464.

Nanga Taisei Introd. 4. A Wooded Hill rising to Shelter a Village by the Waterside. Signed and dated 1303.

Sōgen 55 (Chou Chih-ch'êng collect.) A Leafless Tree, Bamboos and a Rock. Signed and dated 1338.

K.-k. shu-hua chi, XXX. Pavilions under Trees on a River Shore in Autumn, after Chêng Ch'ien 鄭虔. Signed and dated 1344 (at 70). Poem by the painter. C.

Chêng Tê-k'un, Cambridge. Pavilion for listening to the Rain, *T'ing-yü lou.* River scenery in the mountains. Poem by the painter, dated 1348. Another inscription, signed by Ni Tsan and dated 1365.

P'ang Yüan-chi cat. 11. Bamboos. Album-leaf. Poem by the painter.

CHANG YÜ-TS'AI 張羽材, *t.* Kuo-liang 國樑, *h.* Wei-shan 薇山 and Kuang-wei-tzŭ 廣微子.
The 38th Taoist *T'ien-shih*. Yüan period. Bamboo and dragons. Biography in *Yüan-shih*. M, p.464.

C. T. Loo Successor, New York. Dragons in Clouds. Handscroll, on silk, much darkened. Signed.

CHANG YÜAN 張遠, *t.* Mei-yen 梅巖.
From Hua-t'ing, Kiangsu. Active *c.*1320. Landscapes and figures, followed Ma Yüan and Hsia Kuei. H, 5. M, p.463.

Kokka 256 (Shōkoku-ji). River Landscape. Short handscroll. Poem by the monk Chung-ching. Misleading traditional attribution.

Bijutsu II. A Solitary Cottage under a Pine-tree. Album-leaf.

Kawasaki cat. 31. A Pavilion under Willows by a Stream. Attributed. C.

CHANG YÜEH-HU 張月壺.
Active from the end of Sung into the Yüan period. Unrecorded in Chinese books but mentioned in *Kundaikan Sayuchōki* (No.36).

Kokka 153 (Ueno collect.) Bodhidharma Crossing the Yangtse on a Reed. Inscribed: Chang Yüeh-hu, the Han-lin Scholar of the Great Sung Dynasty.

Ibid. 533 (Baron Dan). Kuanyin Crossing the Sea on a Lotus Petal. Inscribed: Yüeh-hu.

Shimbi, XX (Daitoku-ji). White-robed Kuanyin Seated on a Rock by a Stream. Attributed. *Cf.* Tōyō, IX.

Kawasaki cat. 34. Kuanyin on a Rocky Shore Looking at the Moon in the Water. Attributed.

Mutō cat. 22. Kuanyin Seated on a Rock by a Stream, a Deva descending from the air. Attributed. B?

British Museum. Kuanyin Seated on a Rock by a Stream. Attributed. *Cf.* Ars Asiatica, IX, p.23.

CHAO CHUNG 趙衷, *t.* Yüan-ch'u 原初, *h.* Tung-wu yeh-jên 東吳野人.
From Wu-chiang. Active in the Yüan period as a doctor and calligraphist; painted figures in *pai-miao*. M, p.615.

Hui-hua kuan. Four Landscape Studies. Mounted together with some other paintings on a scroll: the first by Chang Kuan, second by Shên Hsüan and third by Liu Tzŭ-yü.

Shên-chou album, 1936 (together with a painting by Chang Yü-sou, Ming dynasty). Illustrations to the Nine Songs of Ch'ü Yüan. Signed.

CHAO HSI-YÜAN 趙希遠.
Landscapes in imitation of Wang Mêng. I, 54. L, 47. M, p.615.

K.-k. shu-hua chi, XXXII. Steep Wooded Mountains Divided by Deep Gullies. Signed and dated 1349. Poem by Wên Chia.

CHAO LIN 趙麟, *t.* Yen-chêng 彥徵.
Son of Chao Yung; active second half of the 14th century. Figures and horses. H, 5, p.1. M, p.615.

Freer Gallery (40.1). Tartar Horsemen. Painting in ink and gold ornaments on paper. Handscroll. Signed and dated 1360. Probably after an earlier original. A.

Yūrintaikan, I. Dressing a Horse by a Stream, after Li Kung-lin. Signed and dated 1365. Poem by the painter. *Cf.* Sōgen 35. B?

Ku-kung collect. A Man in a Red Coat seated at the Foot of a Tree in front of a Horse which is ready to lie down. Signed.

J. D. Chên collect., Hongkong. *Chuan-lan-t'ing*, after an original picture by Yen Li-pên, also copied by Chao Mêng-fu as seen in a picture ascribed to him in the Metropolitan Museum, dated 1298. Handscroll. Signed by the painter. Colophon by a friend. A?

CHAO MÊNG-FU 趙孟頫, *t.* Tzŭ-ang 子昂, *h.* Sung-hsüeh 松雪 and Ou-po 鷗波.
Also called Chao Wu-hsing after his native place in Chekiang. His posthumous titles were Wên-min 文敏 and Wei-kung 魏公. B. 1254, d. 1322. A descendant of the first Sung emperor. Summoned in 1286 to service at the Mongol court in Peking. Appointed 1316 Secretary of the Board of War, promoted several times and finally made director of the Han-lin College. Famous calligraphist and painter of horses, figures, landscapes and bamboos. H, 5. I, 53. L, 47. M, p.614.

Shên-chou 5. A River Between Steep Banks, a Man Seated on a Projecting Cliff. Signed and dated 1293.

Palace Museum scroll, 1933. The Ch'iao and Hua Mountains in Autumn. Short handscroll. Ink and colours on silk. Painted for his friend Chou Kung-chin. Signed and dated 1295. Colophons and poems by the painter, by Tung Ch'i-ch'ang and Ch'ien-lung. A.

Sōgen 31 (Ts'ao Yüan-tu collect.) Two Men Examining a Horse. Ink and colours. Signed and dated 1298. Poems by Hsien-yü Shu, Wu Chên, Lu Kuang, Shên Chou, Wên Chia and others. A?

Metropolitan Museum. *Chuan Lan-t'ing*, after an original picture by Yen Li-pên. Chih-yung, the owner of the Lan-t'ing manuscript, is seated on a high chair, while the envoy of T'ang T'ai-tsung is seated on a low stool; in another scene, the envoy is offered food by a servant. Short handscroll. Inscribed with the painter's name and the date 1298. B?

K.-k. shu-hua chi, XI. Leafless Trees by a Rock. Signed and dated 1299. Poems by Ch'ên Lin and K'o Chiu-ssŭ. A.

Shên-chou ta-kuan, vol.2. Playing the *Ch'in* under a Wu-t'ung Tree. Signed and dated 1299. Poems by Têng Wên-yüan (1258–1328) and Ch'ien-lung. *Cf.* P'ang Yüan-chi's catalogue. B?

A. Stoclet collect., Brussels. Two Horses on a River-bank; one drinking. Inscribed with painter's name and the date 1301. London Exhibition cat. 1116. C.

Del Drago collect., New York. Wên-chi departing from the Mongol Camp. Inscribed with the painter's name and the date 1301. London Exhibition cat. 1145. C.

Palace Museum. Winding Waters, Deep Bays and High Cliffs. Handscroll divided in sections. Signed and dated 1303. Colophons and poems by Yü Chi, Wu K'uan, Chou T'ien-ch'iu, Shên Chou, Wang Shih-chêng and others. *Cf.* Chinese cat., London Exhibition, pp.135–139. C.

Ku-kung collect. Looking at the Stream. Rocky design possibly after an earlier model. A small coloured picture, signed and dated 1309.

Chung-kuo, I, 100. A Homestead in the Mountains, Buildings and Bridges by a River which is winding between the Rocks. Blue and green colours. Inscribed with the painter's name and the date 1309. B?

Li-tai, VI (National Museum, Peking). T'ang, the First Emperor of the Shang Dynasty, Visiting I Yin. Inscribed with the painter's name and dated 1309. Inscription by Ch'ien Tsai (1299–1394). B?

Collotype scroll reproduction (Chi-hsiao chai 寂笑齋, Japan). The Eight Steeds. Sturdy Horses represented without bridle and trappings in lively postures against a neutral background. Handscroll. Colours on silk. Signed and dated 1309, but probably copy of later date. B?

British Museum. The Wang-ch'üan Homestead, after Wang Wei. Inscribed with the painter's name and dated 1309. *Cf.* Ars Asiatica, IX, p.26. C.

Ku-kung, IX. A Man Leading Three Horses. Signed and dated 1310. B?

Hui-hua kuan. Watering Horses in the Autumn Fields. Green and brownish colours on silk. Short handscroll. Signed and dated 1312. Same composition in Metropolitan Museum (said to be after P'ei K'uan).

Chung-kuo, I, 95 (Ti P'ing-tzŭ collect.) Verdant Hills and Ruddy Trees: Autumn in the Mountains. Signed and dated 1316. Probably after an old model. A?

K.-k. shu-hua chi, XLIV. The Abode of Immortals. High mountains rising through the clouds; buildings among trees on the terraces; musicians and immortals. Signed Tzŭ-ang and dated 1319. Resembling Shêng Mou's work. A?

Lo Chia-lun collect., Taipei. The Lan-t'ing Gathering. Handscroll. Signed, dated 1320. A?

C. C. Wang, New York. A Bare Tree and Bamboos by a Rock. Ink on silk. Signed and dated 1321. Colophon by Tung Ch'i-ch'ang. A.

Shên-chou, XIII. Two Men Examining Two Horses. Inscribed with the painter's name and the date 1342. Poem by Kao K'o-kung. *Cf.* Nanga Taisei, VII, 10. B?

Ku-kung collect. An Old Tree, Bamboo and Rocks. Short handscroll, signed. Mounted in the collected scroll of Yüan works called *Yüan-jên chi-chin.* A.

Ibid. A Dry Old Tree and some Bamboos by a Rock. Ink on silk. Signed. Two inscriptions by a man called Ch'ou-chai and by Ni Tsan (dated 1365). A?

Ch'ing-kung ts'ang, 62 (Manchu Household collect.) Two Mandarin Ducks. Album-leaf. Signed. *Cf.* Nanga Taisei. A.

Hui-hua kuan (Shên-chou ta-kuan v.13). A Split Rock, Dry Trees, some Bamboos and Brambles. Short handscroll. Signed. The inscription by the painter runs as follows: "The stones are like *fei pai* writing; the trees like *ta chuan.* In painting bamboos, the eight manners should be used. If there is a man who can do it all, he will certainly know that writing and painting developed from the same origin." Other colophons by K'o Chiu-ssŭ and contemporaries. A.

Ibid. A Woodpecker on a Bamboo Branch. Slight colour on silk. Short handscroll. Signed. Yüan painting, but probably not by the master. B.

Ibid. A Long Bamboo Branch Bending Down. Ink on paper. Handscroll. Inscription by the artist. Accompanied by a somewhat similar bamboo painting by Kuan Tao-shêng. A.

Ibid. A Dry Tree and some Bamboos Growing from a Rock. Signed. Very dark.

Chung-kuo, I, 94. Yang Kuei-fei Dressing her Hair with Flowers, attended by a Eunuch. C.

C. C. Wang, New York. A Hermit Seated in Meditation in a Pine Grove at the Foot of a Mountain Ridge. Handscroll. Archaistic picture in colour on silk. Colophons by Chao Yung, Tung Ch'i-ch'ang and others.

Chung-kuo, I, 96 (K'uai Li-ch'ing collect., now C. C. Wang). Two Pine-trees by a River. Handscroll. Signed. Colophon by the painter. A.

Another version of this picture is in the Art Museum at Cincinnati.

Ibid. I, 97. A Groom Feeding a White Horse Tied to a Pole. Short handscroll. Signed. Colophon by Sung Lien (1310–1381). A?

Ibid. I, 98. River Landscape in Autumn, Poets Assembled in a Pavilion on the Shore. Short handscroll. Signed. Colophons by Yang Wei-chên and Tung Ch'i-ch'ang. B?

Ibid. I, 99. A Groom with a Horse. Short handscroll. Reproduction indistinct. C?

Ku-kung, II. A Literary Gathering in the Western Garden. A free version of Li Kung-lin's famous composition. Signed. Inscription by Yü Chi (1272–1348). C.

K.-k. shu-hua chi, XII. Bamboos by a Rock. Short handscroll. Seals of the painter. *Cf.* Nanga Taisei. A.

Ibid. XXII. A Bird on a Withering Lotus Leaf. After Huang Ch'üan. Inscription by Tung Ch'i-ch'ang. Two poems by Ch'ien-lung. B.

Ibid. XLIII. Sprays of Bamboo and Bare Trees by a Rock. Signed. A.

Ibid. XLV. A Girl Seated on a Bench Playing the Flute. Poem by Sung Lien (1310–1381), Ch'ien-lung and six of his officials. C.

Liu, pl.28. The Top of a Slender Bamboo. Two characters by the artist; six colophons by contemporaries and later men. A?

S.c.t.k. hsü-pien, II. Men Departing in a Boat. Possibly Ming. C.

Ku-kung collect. (Nanking Exhib. cat. 391). A Groom Leading a Horse in the Wind. Short handscroll, mounted in an album. Signed. A?

Kokka 430 (Shimazu collect.) Two Horses under a Tree. Signed. B?

Ibid. 435 (Prince Matsukata collect.) Eight Horses, four of them with riders. Short handscroll. Signed. B?

Tōyō, IX (Nishi Honganji). T'ao Yüan-ming Standing under a Pine-tree on a Projecting Cliff. Attributed. B?

Nansō Ihatsu, II. Horsemen by a River in Autumn. Signed. Poem by the painter. B?

Sōraikan, II, 2. A Spray of Bamboo. Signed. Poem by Wu Mêng and Shên Chung. *Cf.* Bukkyō Bijutsu, 17. B?

Ch'ên Yung collect., Shanghai (1930). A Leafless Tree. Short handscroll. Colophon by the artist. A?

Tōsō, p.141 (Huang Chih collect., 1930). Ambulating Tea-vendors, after a composition by Yen Li-pên. Seal of the painter. *Cf.* Nanga Taisei. C.

J. D. Ch'ên collect., Hongkong. The Dragon King Paying Homage to Buddha. Signed. B.

Sōgen 30 (Ōkura collect.) Branches of Different Varieties of Chrysanthemums. Portion of a handscroll. Attributed. B?

Mutō cat. 27. Portrait of the Poet Po Chü-i. Full length, in scholar's dress and with a staff. Attributed. Poem by the Japanese monk Wu-hsüeh. C.

C. T. Loo's Successor, Frank Caro, New York. Bamboos and Orchids Growing from a Rock. Handscroll. Signed: Mêng-fu painted for Shan-fu. 29 colophons by scholars and painters of the Yüan and Ming periods. A.

Ibid. Epidendrum Growing in a Stone. Signed. Accompanied by a painting of a Slender Bamboo Branch by Kuan Tao-shêng. Ink on brownish paper. B.

Freer Gallery (31.4). A Goat and a Sheep. Ink on paper. Inscription by the painter, poem by Ch'ien-lung, and thirty collectors seals. A.

Ibid. (09.163). Three Horsemen Riding under Trees. Large picture in colour. B?

Ibid. (31.03). Fifteen Horses, Three of them with Grooms, Crossing a River. Handscroll. Signed. A fine picture executed with colours in *kung-pi* style. A?

Boston Museum (08.118). Two Horsemen under a Tree. In the manner of Chao Yung. B?

Ars Asiatica, I, p.20 (M. Alphons Kann). A Mongol Horseman Pursuing a Galloping Horse. Poems by Yang Ch'i and Chang Pi of Ming. Inscribed with the painter's name. B?

Sōraikan, II, 30. Fowls and Birds among Flowering Plants and Shrubs. Handscroll. Colour on silk. Signed and the painter's seal. C.

Ibid. II, 31. A Bamboo Branch. Ink on paper. Signed and the painter's seal. B.

Yūrintaikan, II. Scenes from the Life of T'ao Yüan-ming. Handscroll. Ink on silk. Inscribed with painter's name. C.

Peking National Museum cat. Feeding Horses under Pine-trees. Handscroll. Signed and dated 1309. Colophons by K'o Chiu-ssŭ, Ni Tsan and Ch'iu Yüan.

Ibid. Landscape in Spring with Figures. Handscroll. Signed. Colophons by Ni Tsan, Fang Ts'ung-i, Ma Yüan and Yang Wei-chên.

Ibid. Landscape in Spring: *Ch'i-shan shên-hsiu t'u.* Handscroll. Signed and dated 1309. Colophons by Têng Wên-yüan (1258–1328), K'o Chiu-ssŭ, Ch'iu Yüan, Tao-yen and Wu K'uan.

Ibid. Bamboo-garden and Waterfall: *Chu-yüan ming-ch'üan t'u.* Signed and dated 1309.

Ibid. Illustrations to the *Hsiao-ching*, the Book of Filial Piety. Long handscroll. Signed. The text copied by the painter.

P'ang Yüan-chi Cat. Two Bamboos. Signed. Colophons by Yang Wei-chên, Tan Chung-kuang and others.

Ibid. Epidendrums and Bamboos. Signed.

Ibid. Portrait of T'ao Yüan-ming. Signed and dated 1298. Colophons by T'ang Yin and others.

Ibid. A Man Playing the *Ch'in* under Wu-t'ung Trees. Signed and dated 1299. Poems by Têng Wên-yüan and Ch'ien-lung. *Cf.* Shên Chou ta-kuan, vol.2.

Ibid. 11. Men on Horseback. Album-leaf. Signed and dated 1315.

Ibid. 11. A Man Examining a Horse. Album-leaf. Seal of the painter.

CHAO MÊNG-YÜ 趙孟籲, *t.* Tzŭ-chün 子俊.

Younger brother of Chao Mêng-fu. Best known for his calligraphy, but also as a painter of figures and birds and flowers. H, 5. M, p.614.

Chêng Ch'i, Hongkong. A Duck on the Bank of a River, beneath a flowering bush. Painted in colours on paper. Signed and dated 1299. Seals and poem of Ch'ien-lung, perhaps spurious.

CHAO YUNG 趙雍, *t.* Chung-mu 仲穆.

Son of Chao Mêng-fu. B. 1289; served as prefect of Hu-chou. Landscapes in the manner of Tung Yüan. Figures, horses, bamboos and rocks. H, 5. L, 47. M, p.614.

Shina Kachō Gasatsu 33. Magpies Gathering around Trees, Quails on the Ground. Signed and dated 1319.

Sōgen 33 (M. Harada). The Washing of the Elephant; Buddha Seated on a Cliff Watching the Procedure. Signed and dated 1334. B?

Ku-kung collect. Houses under tall Pines on a River-bank; tall hills in the distance. Signed and dated 1342. A?

Ibid. Gathering Water-chestnuts. Colour on paper. Signed and dated 1342.

Chung-kuo ming-hua, XIV. Three Horses. Signed and dated 1345. Handscroll. A.

Hui-hua kuan. A Man in Red Coat on a Black-and-white Horse. Signed and dated 1347. B? *Cf.* I-shu ch'uan-t'ung, vol. VIII.

Freer Gallery (45,32). A Mongol in a Red Coat Leading a Black-and-White Horse. Handscroll, after one section of Li Kung-lin's *Five Horses* scroll. Signed, dated 1347. Inscription by Ch'ien-lung. A?

Ōmura, I, 12 (Chiang Mêng-p'in collect.) A Mynah Bird on a Rock and Some Bamboos. Signed and dated 1349. A?

Ku-kung collect. Horses on Pasture in a Wood. Colour on silk. Signed and dated 1352. Poems on the top by Liu Jung (of Ping-mên) and Wang Kuo-ch'i (of Wu-hsing). A?

Chung-kuo, I, 103 (Manchu Household collect.) River Landscape with an Angler on a Promontory. Signed. Poems by Yao Chih and Wang Shih-chên (1526–1590). *Cf.* Ch'ing-kung ts'ang, 63.

Ku-kung collect. A Man in a Red Coat on a White Horse under Leafy Trees. Colour on silk. Signed Chung-mu with one seal. Inscription by Tung Ch'i-ch'ang.

Ibid. Large Landscape in the manner of Tung Yüan. Slightly coloured.

Chang Ta-ch'ien cat., vol. IV. Mountain and Stream in Autumn; an old man riding on a donkey approaching a small bridge in the foreground. Signed. The picture is badly worn.

Hui-hua kuan. A Big Crowd of Horses on the Meadow. Painted in a minute manner in brownish and greenish colours on silk. A small handscroll. A.

Ibid. Fishing in a Mountain Stream under Large Pine Trees. A small picture mounted on the same scroll with Wang Mien's Plum Blossoms and Chu Tê-jun's Two Men in a Boat.

Ku-kung collect. *Chün-ma t'u.* Five Horses and a Groom under leafy trees by a river. Two or three colophons. A?

Liu, 29. Epidendrum and Bamboo. B?

Nansō Ihatsu, vol. 4. River Landscape with Tall Trees in the foreground; a boat on the water. Poem by Ch'ien-lung. *Cf.* Shina Meiga Senshū, III.

Takeuchi collect., Kyōto. Scholars in a Garden examining a Painting displayed. Colours on silk, somewhat damaged. Attributed. B.

Sōgen Meigashū, 58 (Hikkōen). A Monkey on the Back of a Horse Resting on the Ground. Album-leaf. Attributed. A?

Tōan 9 (Saitō collect.) River Landscape with Tall Trees and a Boat Moored by the Rocks. Signed. Poem by Ch'ien-lung. *Cf.* Bukkyō Bijutsu, 17.

Boston Museum (28.355). Portrait of the Ch'an Monk Yüan-miao. Biographical inscription at the top. Possibly an early copy. B.

National Museum, Stockholm. Old Trees on a Rocky Shore. Fan-shaped. Signed. A.

C. T. Loo Successors, New York (ex-Chang Ts'ung-yü). River Landscape with Two Fishermen in Boats. *Cf.* Sōgen, p.34. Cleveland Exhib. cat. 27. A.

Chang Ta-ch'ien cat., IV. Travelling in the Autumn Mountains. Signed. Much worn. B?

Peking National Museum cat. Feeding Horses: *Ssŭ-ma t'u.* Signed. Seals of the painter and of Ch'ien-lung.

P'ang Yüan-chi cat. 11. Men on Horseback. Signed.

CHAO YÜAN 趙原 or 趙元, *t.* Shan-ch'ang 善長, *h.* Tan-lin 丹林.

From Suchow. Active *c.*1370. Landscapes in the style of Tung Yüan. Executed by order of the emperor Hung-wu. N, I, 9. O, 2. M, p.616.

Yūrinkan, Kyōto. Buildings in a Bamboo Grove; Two Men Standing on a Bridge. Signed and dated 1361. An album-leaf. A?

Shanghai Museum. River Landscape with a Fisherman in a Boat and a Scholar in a Pavilion among Trees on the Low Shore. Signed and dated 1363. A.

Ku-kung collect. Pavilion by a Stream at the Foot of a Rocky Mountain. Signed by the painter. Poems by Yeh Mêng-hsien, Wang Ming-chi, Chang Chien and two others. *Cf.* Pageant, p.393. A.

Tōyō, IX. (Nanzen-ji, Kyōto). Bamboos in Rain. Seals of the painter. B?

C. C. Wang, New York (formerly Chang Ts'ung-yü collect.) Saying Farewell to Friends at Ch'ing-ch'uan. People are departing in a boat on a mountain river, their friends are standing on the shore. Inscription by the painter. A. The picture exists also in later imitations. *Cf.* Liu, 41; Cleveland Exhibition cat. 33.

Ku-kung collect. (Nanking Exhib. cat. 79) Lu Yü Preparing Tea. Short handscroll. Signed. Mounted in the collected scroll of Yüan works, *Yüan-jên chi-chin.* A.

Venice Exhibit. cat., p.217 (Low-Beer collect.) Buildings at the foot of a Range of low Mountains. Short handscroll. Signed. Seals of Ch'ien-lung. Colophons written by Wên Chia and others. A.

Honolulu Academy of Arts. Reading in the Summer Mountains, after Tung Yüan. Signed. Colophon by Hsieh K'ung-chao. *Cf.* Tōsō, 225. A.

P'ang Yüan-chi cat. Add. I. The Pavilion at Ho-ch'i. Signed. Poems by Ku Ying and Ch'ien-lung. *Cf.* Pageant, p.394. B.

Ch'ên Chên 陳貞, *t.* Li-yüan 履元.

From Ch'ien-t'ang, Chekiang. Active *c.*1350. Landscapes. L, 54. M, p.430.

K.-k. shu-hua chi, IX. The Study in the White Cloud Mountains. Signed and dated 1351. Poem by Ch'ien-lung.

Ch'ên Chien-ju 陳鑑如.

From Hangchou. Active *c.*1320. Famous as a portrait painter. H, 5. M, p.429.

Kokka 487 (The Prince Li Museum, Seoul). Portrait of Li Ch'i-hsien, a Korean Scholar. Signed. Colophon by Li Ch'i-hsien, dated 1319. *Cf.* Bijutsu Kenkyū, I.

Ch'ên Chih 陳植, *t.* Shu-fang 叔方, *h.* Shên-tu 慎獨.

From Suchou. B. 1293, d. 1362. Landscapes. H, 5. M, p.430.

Shên-chou ta-kuan, vol.3. Pavilions and Trees on a Mountain Slope in Mist. Poem by the painter. Colophon by Fang Ning, dated 1380, and by Ch'ên Ju-chih, dated 1377. *Cf.* P'ang Yüan-chi Cat. Add. I; Illustr. cat., IV.

Ch'ên Chung-jên 陳仲仁.

From Kiangsi. Active at the beginning of the 14th century. Chao Mêng-fu estimated him highly as a painter. Equally skilled in flowers, birds, figures and landscapes. H, 5. M, p.429.

Ku-kung collect. (Nanking Exhib. cat. 390). A House under Willows on a River Shore. Album-leaf. Signed and dated 1362.

K.-k. shu-hua chi, XLI. "The Hundred Sheep". Three children with them, one dressed as a prince. Signed.

Sōgen 41 (Mr. Etō, Tōkyō). Landscape after Chü-jan. Part of a scroll. Attributed.

Ibid. 42 (Lo Yüan-chüeh collect.) A Man Playing the Flute in a Boat at the Foot of a High Cliff. Seal of the painter. A?

Ch'ên Li-shan 陳立善.

From Hai-yen, Chekiang. Served in the Chih-chêng period (1341–1367) as a Censor in Chekiang. Reached great fame as a painter of plum-blossoms. I, 54. M, p.429.

K.-k. shu-hua chi, XVIII. Slender Branches of a Plum-tree in Bloom. Signed and dated 1351. Two poems by Ming writers. *Cf.* Chinese cat., London Exhibition, p.169. A.

Ibid. XXV. A Blossoming Plum-tree and Narcissi Growing from a Rock. Signed and dated 1356. Three poems by Ming writers. A?

CH'ÊN LIN 陳琳, *t.* Chung-mei 仲美.

From Hangchou. Lived *c.*1260–1320. Friend of Chao Mêng-fu. Landscapes, figures, flowers and birds. H, 5. M, p.42.

K.-k. shu-hua chi, XX. Chung K'uei Standing under some Leafless Trees on a Hill. Signed and dated 1300. C.

Ibid. VI. A Duck Standing on a River Shore. Dated 1301. Colophons by Chao Mêng-fu, Ch'iu Yüan and K'o Chiu-ssŭ. Poem by Ch'ien-lung. A.

Gems, II, 6. A Bare Tree Growing from Rocks. Inscription by Chang Pên (dated 1340) and another man. A?

Ku-kung, XXXIX. River Landscape with Old Trees on the Rocky Shore. Short handscroll. Seal of the painter. Poems by three Yüan writers. A.

Sōgen 22 (Chou Chih-ch'êng collect.) Two Small Birds in a Leafless Tree. Signed.

CHÊNG HSI 鄭禧, *t.* Hsi-chih 熙之 or 禧之.

From Suchou. Active *c.*1350. Landscapes after Tung Yüan, bamboos and birds. H, 5. M, p.640.

Ku-kung collect. Pavilion among Trees at the Bay-shore. Short handscroll. Signed and dated 1353. A long colophon of the period.

P'ang Yüan-chi cat. 7. River Landscape, man returning from fishing. Poem by the painter, dated 1351.

CH'ÊNG CH'I 程棨, *t.* I-fu 儀甫, *h.* Sui-chai 隨齋.

Second half of the 13th century. He was a contemporary of the writers Chao Mêng-yü and Yao Shih, but he is not recorded in the dictionaries of painters.

Freer Gallery (1954). *Kêng-tso t'u*, 21 pictures illustrating Rice-culture, now mounted in succession to form a long scroll. Each picture is accompanied by a poem written in seal characters. The poems as well as the pictures are copied after earlier originals by Lou Ch'ou of the Kao-tsung reign. The name of Liu Sung-nien has been added on later. At the beginning is an inscription by Ch'ien-lung, and at the end colophons by Chao Tzŭ-chün (Chao Mêng-yü), younger brother of Chao Mêng-fu, by Yao Shih, another contemporary, and several later writers.

Ibid. *Ts'an-chih t'u.* 24 pictures illustrating Sericulture mounted in succession to form a long scroll. The inscriptions on the pictures and the poems accompanying them are of the same kind as those on the *Kêng-tso t'u.* In fact the two scrolls are completing each other and have been reproduced in stone engravings (by the order of the emperor Ch'ien-lung in 1769) under the common name: *Kêng-chih t'u.* At the beginning are inscriptions by Ch'ien-lung and Chiang P'u and at the end colophons by Chao Tzŭ-chün and later men.

CH'I-TSUNG 啓宗.

A monk of the White Lotus temple near Suchou. Active *c.*1360. Unrecorded.

Ōmura, II, 4 (Ching Hsien). Portrait of Su Tung-p'o in Scholar's Dress with a High Cap. Colophons by Chang Chien, dated 1366, and by Miao-shêng. *Cf.* Chūgoku, vol.II.

CHIEH-HSI SSŬ 揭傒斯, *t.* Man-shih 曼碩.
From Lung-hsing, Kiangsi. B. 1274, d. 1344. Han-lin scholar, writer of historical works. Landscapes. L, 60. M, p.497.

I-shu ts'ung-pien, 14. A Cow, standing, turned inward. Signed and dated 1341.

CH'IEN HSÜAN 錢選, *t.* Shun-chü 舜舉, *h.* Yü-t'an 玉潭.
From Wu-hsing, Chekiang. *c.* 1235 – 1300. Figures after Li Kung-lin, landscapes after Chao Ling-jang, flowers and birds after Chao Ch'ang. One of the "Eight Talents of Wu-hsing". H, 5. I, 53. L, 18. M, p.679.

K.-k. shu-hua chi, XXXI. The Washing of the White Elephant, after Li Kung-lin. Signed and dated 1273. C.

Shên-chou, 12. A Branch of a Flowering Peach-tree. Signed. B?

Shên-chou ta-kuan, vol.7. An Aubergine Plant. Short handscroll. Colophons by Ch'ien Po, Chou Hsüan and others. Reproduction indistinct. C?

Chung-kuo, I, 104 (formerly P'ang Yüan-chi, now Freer Gallery). An Egg-plant with Two Fruits and some Flowers. Poem by the painter. B? A later copy of the picture in Laufer cat., p. 24.

Chung-kuo ming-hua, XI. Fisherman Returning in a Rain Storm. Colophon by Yün Shou-p'ing. An early Ming picture. B?

Ku-kung, III. Lu T'ung Preparing Tea on a Garden Terrace. Seal of the painter. Porm by Ch'ien-lung. C.

Ibid. VIII. The Trunk of a Tall Lichee-tree. Signed. Poem by Mo Hsien-chih. B?

Ibid. XXXVIII. A Mongol Groom Holding a Horse. Signed and dated 1342, *i.e.* fifty years after the death of Ch'ien Hsüan. Possibly a late copy after a T'ang painting. C?

Ibid. XL. Egg-plants, Melons, Turnips, Goosefoot and Cabbage. Short handscroll. B.

K.-k. shu-hua chi, XVI. A Melon Plant with Fruits and Flowers. Signed. Poem by the painter. *Cf.* Chinese cat., London Exhib., p.128. A.

Ibid. XXVI. A Squirrel on the Branch of a Peach-tree. Short handscroll. Seals of the painter. Poem by Ch'ien-lung. *Cf.* Chinese cat., London Exhib., p.129. A?

Ku-kung collect. Flowers and Leaves of two *Mutan* Plants, painted in the style of Hsü Hsi. Three seals of the master and his inscription. A?

Lo Chia-lun, Taipei. Two Mandarin Ducks under a *Fu-jung* Plant with Large Flowers. Signed. Possibly a late Sung picture. B.

K.-k. shu-hua chi, XL. Birds Perched on the Branches of a Blossoming Plum-tree in Snow. Short handscroll. The pattern is highly stylized also in colour. Signed. B.

Palace Museum Album, 1932. A Flowering Plant by a Rock and Swarming Bees. Signed and dated 1303. *Cf.* Chinese cat., London Exhib., p.105. B?

Formerly National Museum, Peking. Emperor Ming-huang Teaching Yang Kuei-fei to Play the Flute. Handscroll. Colophons and seals of the Yüan period. B.

Ibid. A Melon Plant with Fruits and Flowers. Poem by the painter. B?

P'u Ju collect., Peking. Three Strange Men Bringing a Tibetan Mastiff and its Puppy in Tribute. According to inscription by the painter, copied after a picture by Yen Li-pên. Seals of the painter.

Kokka 73. A Melon and Two Grasshoppers. Album-leaf. Seal of the painter. C.

Ibid. 238 (Murayama collect.) A Crab and a Radish. Seal of the painter. C.

Ibid. 259 (formerly Tuan Fang collect., now Chicago Art Institute). The Washing of the White Elephant. Short handscroll. Seal of the painter. B? A similar picture was in the former National Museum, Peking (1928).

Ibid. 390 (Marquis Asano collect.) A Sparrow and Some Peaches. Seal of the painter. C.

Ibid. 404 (Marquis Asano collect.) A Peony Flower. Seal of the painter. C.

Ibid. 482 (Suganuma collect.) White Plum-blossoms. Album-leaf. Seal of the painter. C.

Hikkōen, p.7 (Marquis Kuroda). Children at Play under a Banana-tree by a Garden Rock. Album-leaf. C.

Tōyō, IX, pl.100 (Count Sakai). A Bird on the Branch of a Plum-tree in Blossom, Watching a Bee. Album-leaf. C.

Ibid. IX, pl.101 (Marquis Kuroda). Two Birds on the Branch of a Pomegranate-tree. Fan-painting. C.

Nansō Ihatsu, II. The Red Cliff. River-landscape illustrating Su Tung-p'o's poem. C.

Tōsō, p.145 (Kuan Mien-chün). T'ao Yüan-ming Walking along Followed by a Servant who Carries a Wine-jar. Handscroll. Signed and three seals of the painter. C.

Ibid. p.146 (K. Magoshi). A Branch of an Apple-tree. Poem by the painter and three of his seals. C.

Ibid. p.147 (E. Takeuchi). Emperor T'ai-tsu of Sung Playing Football. Handscroll. After an earlier original. B?

Sōgen Meigashū 7 (Hikkōen, p.6). Four Rats Eating through a Melon. Album-leaf. Seal of the painter.

Ibid. 47 (Hompō-ji). A Cockscomb. Signed. Poem by the painter. *Cf.* Kokka 163. B.

Ibid. 48 (Nezu collect.) A Small Bird on the Branch of a Blossoming Pear-tree. Album-leaf. C.

Naitō, pl.67. Dwelling in the Mountains, River Landscape in archaic style. Handscroll, painted in colours on paper. Signed.

Nezu collect. A Pigeon on the Branch of a Pear-tree. *Cf.* London Exhib. cat. 919. C.

Ibid. A Bird on the Branch of a Peach-tree. Poem by the painter. *Cf.* London Exhib. cat. 916. C.

Kawasaki cat. 6. Huan Yeh-wang, the Flute-player of the 4th century, Cleaning his Nail. Seal of Ch'ien Hsüan. A?

Ibid. 25. A Branch of an Apricot-tree in Bloom. Seal of the painter. C.

Freer Gallery, Washington. Yang Kuei-fei Mounting on a Grey Horse in order to follow the Emperor Hsüan-tsung, who is seated on a White Horse. Eight grooms and four girl-servants assisting. Colours and ink on paper. Inscription by the painter. A?

Shên P'ing-ch'ên collect., Hongkong. Mice and Fruit. Signed. B?

Chang Ta-ch'ien cat., vol.IV. The Tipsy T'ao Yüan-ming is asking his two Guests to leave. Short handscroll. Inscription by the painter. Signed. B.

J. D. Chên collect., Hongkong. The Tartar King Shih Lo Asking the Way of Buddha. After Chao Po-chü. Handscroll. Signed. Four colophons. *Cf.* P'ang Yüan-chi cat. 2. B?

Ibid. A Bird on the Branch of a Blossoming Fruit-tree. Colours on paper. The attribution to Huang Ch'üan is misleading.

Detroit Institute of Fine Arts. Early Autumn; Insects among Rushes and Lotus Leaves. Handscroll. Signature and seals of the painter. *Cf.* R. Edward's article "Ch'ien Hsüan and Early Autumn" in *Archives of C.A.S. of America* 1953.

Cincinnati Art Museum. Two Doves on a Branch of a Blossoming Pear-tree. Short handscroll. Inscription by the painter and four of his seals. Partly retouched. Colophons and poems by more than twenty connoisseurs of the Yüan and later periods. A.

Freer Gallery (17.183). Branches of Blossoming Magnolia and Pear-trees. Two album-leaves mounted on a handscroll. Two seals of the painter. Colophons by Ch'eng-ch'in Wang, Chao Mêng-fu a.o. A.

Ibid. (52.25). A Lady Supervising Four Servants who are Spinning and Weaving. Short handscroll. Signed. A?

Ibid. (54.10). A Branch of Pear Blossoms. Colours on paper. Seal with the painter's *tzŭ*. B?

Ibid. Blossoming Shrubs and Plants, Birds and Butterflies. Handscroll. Inscribed with the painter's name. B?

Metropolitan Museum. Part of a scroll illustrating the *Kuei-ch'ü-lai* poem by T'ao Yüan-ming. Signed. Colours on paper. *Cf.* Toronto Exhibit. cat., No.12. A.

British Museum. A Youth in Red Cloak Seated on a White Horse Holding a Large Bow. Short handscroll. Poem by the painter, dated 1290. Several inscriptions of the Yüan and Ming periods.

C. C. Wang, New York. Wang Hsi-chih Admiring the Swimming Geese from a Pavilion. Handscroll. Colours on paper. Poem by the painter, and seals of Yüan and later periods. A.

Sir Percival David, London. Branches of a Blossoming Pear-tree. Short handscroll. Colours on paper. More than twenty colophons of the Yüan and later periods. A.

Shina Kachō Gasatsu. Two Cranes and Flowering Tree-peonies. Attributed.

Peking National Museum cat. The Sixteen Arhats Crossing the Sea. Long handscroll. Seals of the painter.

Ibid. The Eighteen Arhats. Long handscroll. Signed, and seal of the painter.

Ibid. Two Swans and Lotus flowers. Attributed.
Ibid. Three Wild Geese among Reeds. Attributed.
Ibid. Two Eagles and a Plum-tree in Blossoms. Attributed.
Ibid. A Peony Flower.
P'ang Yüan-chi cat. 2. Cottages on the Mountain of the Floating Jade. Short handscroll. Poem by the painter. Colophons by Ch'ien-lung, Ch'iu Yüan, Chang Yü, Huang Kung-wang and others.
Ibid. 11. The Washing of the Elephant. Album-leaf. Seals of the painter.

CHOU CHIH 周砥, *h.* Li-tao 履道, *h.* Tung-kao 東皐 and Chü-liu-shêng 匊溜生.
Native of Suchou; lived in Wu-hsi. Late 14th century. Landscapes after Wang Mêng and Huang Kung-wang. N, I, 8. O, 2. M, p.245.

Toronto, II (C. T. Loo Successor, N.Y.) Scenery of I-hsing. Short handscroll, mounted with a painting by Shên Chou. Poem by the painter. Signed and dated 1356. A.
Sōraikan, I, 26. Trees on a Rocky Promontory, Mountains beyond. Poem by the painter, dated 1365. A.

CHOU TUNG-CH'ING 周東卿. Active at end of Sung and beginning of Yüan. Friend of Wên T'ien-hsiang. Fishes. M, p.244.

Metropolitan Museum (47.18.10). The Pleasures of the Fishes. Colours and ink on paper. Handscroll. Signed and dated 1291.

CHOU YÜAN 周淵.
Unrecorded. Possibly Yüan period.

Freer Gallery. A Stag, a Doe and Red Camellias in Snow. Signed and dated the *ting-wei* year in winter.

CHU SHU-CHUNG 朱叔重.
From Lou-tung, Kiangsu. Active *c.*1365. Poet and painter, mainly landscapes. I, 53. M, p.93.

K.-k. shu-hua chi, XX. A Wooded Mountain Ridge Rising Through the Mist, in the manner of Kao K'o-kung. Signed and dated 1365. Poem by Ch'ien-lung. B.
Ibid. XXIX. Willows by a Stream in Spring. Signed and the painter's seal. Album-leaf. *Cf.* Chinese cat., London Exhibition, p.164. A?

CHU TÊ-JUN 朱德潤, *t.* Tsê-min 澤民.
From Sui-yang, Honan; lived in K'un-shan, Kiangsu. B. 1294, d. 1365. Imitated Kuo Hsi as a landscape-painter. H, 5. I, 53. L, 8. M, p.92.

Ōmura, I, 12 (Chang Chih-ho collect.) A Mountain Gorge in Snow; a Man on a Donkey Crossing a Bridge. Signed and dated 1339.
Kokka 620 (ex-K. Moriya collect.) Steep Cliffs and Bare Trees. Ink on paper. Signed and dated 1341. B.
Tōsō, p.150 (Seattle Art Museum). River Landscape with Willows in Spring. Signed and dated 1349. B.
Nansō Ihatsu, II. Mountains in Autumn. Signed and dated 1352. Poem by the painter. Indistinct reproduction. C?

Ming-hua lin-lang. A Tall Cliff with Pine-trees and a Waterfall. Signed and dated 1353. Inscription by Ch'ien-lung. C.

Ku-kung collect. Clouds and Waterfall on Sung-kang. Large album-leaf. Signed and dated 1353. A.

Nanga Taisei, Introd. 11. Mountain Rising from a Bay, Boats at Anchor. Signed and dated 1354.

Sōgen 39 (Han Tê-shou collect.) Five Scholars Assembled around a Table in a Garden. Signed and dated 1364. A?

Hui-hua kuan. *Hsiu-yeh hsüan.* The Pavilion of Flowering Fields. Two men are enjoying the view; hills in the background and trees on the shore. Ink and slight colour. Handscroll. A long inscription by the painter, dated 1364 (at 71), and later colophons. Another version of the same picture is in the Freer Gallery.

Shên-chou, X. A Scholar Seated under Two Tall Pine-trees. Signed and dated in the *jên-tzŭ* year of the Chih-chêng period (which did not exist). C?

Ibid. XX. River Shore with Some Sparse Trees and Buildings. Inscriptions by Sung K'o and the painter. C?

Ku-kung, IV. Mountains and Water in Autumn Mist. Ascribed to the painter in a colophon by Tung Ch'i-ch'ang. B?

Ibid. VII. Snow-covered Mountains and a Pavilion on the River-bank. Attributed. B?

K.-k. shu-hua chi, XII. River Landscape in Haze, Three Men Seated under Pine-trees, One Playing the *Ch'in.* Signed. Poem by Wang Fêng. *Cf.* Chinese cat., London Exhibition, p.154. B?

Chung-kuo ming-hua, XVI. A Steep River-shore in Snow, a Man Walking over a Bridge, Other Men in a Boat and a Pavilion on the Shore. Poem by Ch'ien-lung. B?

Hui-hua kuan. Two Men in a Boat Passing a Tiger-like Rock. A small picture mounted together with Wang Mien's Plum-blossoms and Chao Yung's Fishing in a Mountain Stream under Large Pine-trees. *Cf.* I-shu ch'uan-t'ung, vol.VIII. A.

Nanga Taisei, VIII, 23. A Leafless Tree and a Pine Overhanging a River; A Fisherman in his Boat. Fan-painting.

Sōgen, p.37 (Manchu Household collect.) High Mountains and Winding Waters. Short handscroll. Poems by Tu Mu and Ch'ien-lung. A?

Chūgoku, I. A Man in a Thatched Cottage under some Bare Trees by a River; two men in a boat. Short handscroll. Poem by the painter, and the painting dedicated to a man called Tê-ch'ang. A.

CHU YÜ 朱玉, *t.* Chün-pi 君璧.

From K'un-shan, Kiangsu. B. 1293, d. 1365. Boundary paintings and figures. Pupil of Wang Chên-p'êng. I, 54. L, 8. M, p.93.

Tōsō, p.148 (Chu Ch'i-ch'ien collect.) The Various Regions of Hell, represented by twelve tiers of figures. Signed. Colophon by Ch'ien-lung.

Chicago Art Institute. Figures Representing various Trades and Occupations. Possibly illustrations for a book. Signed.

CHUANG LIN 莊麟, *t.* Wên-chao 文昭.

A native of Chiang-tung; lived in Peking. Landscapes. Active at the end of the Yüan period. L, 32; *cf.* also *Shih-ch'ü sui-pi* 4, 16.

Ku-kung collect. (Nanking Exhib. cat. 79). A Scholar Crossing a Bridge toward a House. Signed. Colophon by Tung Ch'i-ch'ang, in which he states that this is the only surviving work by the artist. Mounted with other Yüan paintings in the collective scroll *Yüan-jên chi-chin.*

FANG CHÜN-JUI 方君瑞.

From Wu-chin, Kiangsu. Early 14th century. Grass and insects, followed the monk Chü-ning. I, 54. M, p.22.

Kokka 90. Two Butterflies and a Cabbage Plant. Album-leaf. Attributed.

Fang Ts'ung-i 方從義, *t.* Wu-yü 無隅, *h.* Fang-hu 方壺.

From Kuei-ch'i, Kiangsi. Active *c.*1340–1380. Taoist monk in the Shang-ch'ing temple, in Kiangsi. Landscapes; followed Mi Fei and Kao K'o-kung. H, 5. I, 54. L, 32. M, p.22.

Ku-kung collect. River-view in Mist with a Boat; Sharply rising Rocks on the Shore. Signed and dated 1348. Part of an album called *Mo-lin pa-ts'ui*. A later version of this picture dated 1378 is in the Yūrinkan collection, Kyōto. *Cf.* reproduction in Chung-kuo, I, p.106.

Ōmura, II, 5 (J. D. Chên collect. Hongkong). A River between High Cliffs, a Pagoda on a Promontory. Signed and dated 1349. Poem and colophon signed Wên Chêng-ming. Late imitation. B?

Kao Yen-yüeh, Hongkong. River Landscape; Grassy Mountains Rising through Clouds. Signed and dated 1355. A?

Chang Ta-ch'ien collect. (formerly Chang Ts'ung-yü collect.) An Overhanging Rock, Two Men in a Boat. Signed and dated 1359. B?

Sōraikan, II, 40. A Waterfall on a Steep Mountain; Large Trees in the foreground. Inscription dated 1360. C.

Shên-chou ta-kuan, vol.9. A Spray of Bamboo. Signed and dated 1361. Poem by Huang-fu Lien (1501–1564). A?

K.-k. shu-hua chi, VIII. A Sacred Mountain and Wonderful Trees. The water is running from a deep gully. Signed and dated 1365. Poem by Ch'ien-lung. A.

Tōsō, p.165 (Ch'ên Pao-ch'ên collect.) Clouds Circling around Mountains above a River. Signed and dated 1365. B?

Ōmura, I, 12 (Manchu Household collect.) Cloudy Mountains. Short handscroll. Signed and dated 1378. Colophon by the painter. A.

Liu, pl.38. A Mountain Brook crossed by a Bridge. Signed and dated 1379. A?

K.-k. shu-hua chi, V. Clouds and Snow on the Shan-yin Mountains, after Kao K'o-kung. Damaged and retouched. Signed. *Cf.* Chinese cat., London Exhibition, p.171. B.

Ibid. XIV. Pavilion on a Steep Terrace. Sketchy picture. Signed. Colophon by the painter. *Cf.* Chinese cat., London Exhibition, p.172. A.

Ibid. XLIV. A Pavilion on the Rocky Shore at the Foot of Rugged Mountains. Signed and dated the *hsin-wei* year of the Chih-chêng period (which did not exist). A.

Shina Nanga Taikan, vol.I. Autumn Winds over the Five Old Men Peaks. Signed. *Cf.* P'ang Yüan-chi cat. Add. 1; Pageant, p. 381.

Nansō Ihatsu, IV (Piacentini collect.) Cloudy Mountains. Poems by four contemporaries of the painter. In his manner. *Cf.* Shên Chou ta-kuan, vol.3. A?

Ibid. Pine-trees on Strange Rocks by a Misty River. Signed. *Cf.* Shên Chou, V. C.

Sōgen 56 (Yang Yin-pei). View over a Wide River; a Summer Retreat and Garden on the Shore in the foreground. Signed. B.

Chūgoku, II. Grassy Hills on a River Shore Rising through a Layer of Clouds. Album-leaf. Inscription by the painter.

Yūrintaikan, I. Ten Immortals. Handscroll. Ink on paper. Signed. Colophon by the painter. C?

P'ang Yüan-chi cat. 7. Mountains in Mist and Clouds; a Man in the foreground followed by a Boy carrying a *Ch'in*. Signed and dated 1378. Poems by four contemporaries and a colophon by Tan Shao, dated 1385.

Ibid. Cloudy Mountains. Signed and dated 1365.

Fang-yai 方崖.

Mentioned only by Li Jih-hua (*cf.* I, 54). The following information is contained in the inscriptions on his picture. Lived at the end of the Yüan period in Suchou. Ordained as a priest, a close friend of Ni Tsan. Painted trees, bamboos and stones; following the style of Su Tung-p'o's paintings.

Ku-kung, IV. Slender Bamboos by a Rockery. Seal of the painter. Poem and colophon by Ma Chih, dated 1382. *Cf.* K.-k. ming-jên hua-chu chi, 12.

HO CHING 郝經, *t*. Po-ch'ang 伯常.
From Ling-ch'uan, Shansi. Served as an official under the first Yüan emperor, he was sent as an envoy to the Sung capital and was there imprisoned. On his return to Peking he was made a teacher in the Central College. Equally skilled as a painter and a calligrapher. Noted in the Yüan history, but not in the records of painters. V, p.857.

Shên-chou ta-kuan, vol.7. A White-headed Bird on a Slender Branch. Six poems and an inscription by Wang Chien in which the attribution to Ho Ching is confirmed; but the picture is not signed.

HSIA K'AO-CH'ANG 夏考昌, *h*. Chiu-shan 九山.
Active *c*.1350. Landscapes. M, p.318.

P'ang Yüan-chi cat. Add. 1. The Fishermen's Pleasure. Signed and dated 1350.

HSIA TI 夏迪, *t*. Chien-po 簡伯.
From Wên-chou, Chekiang. Active in the Yüan period. Landscapes. H, 5. M, p.318.

Philadelphia Museum. Mountain Ridges and Bare Trees. Two lines of poetry. Attributed. C.

HSIA YUNG 夏永, *t*. Ming-yüan 明遠.
14th century? Mentioned in a book called *Hua-chien hsiao-yü* as having represented the Palace of the Prince of T'eng and the Yellow Crane Tower by embroidering with human hair "as fine as the eyelash of a mosquito". The identification of this man with the Hsia Ming-yüan mentioned in *Kundaikan Sayuchōki*, to whom various academic landscapes in Japan are attributed, is not certain.

Tōsō 210. Landscape with Palaces, in the manner of Chao Po-chü.

Hikkōen, pl.50 and 51. Two Landscapes with Buildings. Album-leaves.

Kokka 639 (Nezu Museum, Tōkyō). A Palace on the Bank of the Ch'ien-t'ang River. Album-leaf, fan-shaped. Considerable repainting.

HSIEH PO-CH'ÊNG 謝伯誠.
From Jen-yang. Friend of Yang Wei-chên (1296–1370). Landscapes in the manner of Tung Yüan. I, 54. M, p.704.

Ōmura, I, 11 (Pao Hsi, Peking). Two Men in a Pavilion under Leafy Trees. Signed. Four poems, one of them by the painter. *Cf*. Chūgoku, II.

Chang Ta-ch'ien cat., vol.IV. Looking at a Waterfall. An old man is seated on the river-bank under tall pine-trees. The inscription at the top of the picture is not signed. A?

HSIEN-YÜ SHU 鮮于樞, *t*. Po-chi 伯機, *h*. K'un-hsüeh-shih 困學氏, also Chih-an Lao-jên 直案老人.
From Yü-yang, Hopei. B. 1257, d. 1303. Famous as a calligrapher but little known as a painter. M, p.688.

Princeton University (Du Bois-Morris collect.) A River Winding between Wooded Mountains. After a T'ang picture. Signed: Po-chi. Dated 1303. Poem by the painter. Possibly a Ming-picture.

HSÜEH-CHIEN 雪澗.
A Ch'an monk active towards the end of the Yüan period. Unrecorded except in *Kundaikan Sayuchōki*, 112.

Kokka 410 (K. Magoshi). Mañjuśrī (Wên-shu), represented as a youthful monk with a mantle of plaited straw. *Cf.* Sōgen, 71.

Tōsō, p.220 (T. Ogura). Mañjuśrī as a youthful monk seated under a tree in a misty landscape.

Asano collect. Mañjuśrī as a youth (similar to the picture in the Magoshi collect.)

HSÜEH-CHUANG: see P'U-MING.

HU T'ING-HUI 胡廷暉.

From Wu-hsing, Chekiang. Active *c.*1300. Landscapes, highly admired by Chao Mêng-fu. I, 53. M, p.293.

Kokka 462 (Baron Kawasaki). A Vegetable Plant with Pole-root (radish or turnip?) Album-leaf. Attributed.

HUANG CHIN 黄溍, t. Chin-ch'ing 晉卿.

From I-wu, Chekiang. B. 1277, d. 1357. Han-lin scholar, official and a lecturer in the classics to the emperor. Recorded in *Jên-ming ta tz'ŭ-tien*, but not in the books on painters. Followed Huang Kung-wang and Wang Mêng. V, p. 1242.

K.-k. shu-hua chi, XVI. The Study in the Plum-tree Garden at the Foot of High Wooded Mountains. Signed and dated 1347. Colophons by the painter and by Li Yung, the latter dated 1454.

Photo (Huang Chih collect.?) Fishing Village by a River. Folded and terraced high mountains. Inscription by the painter dated 1341. The picture is dedicated to a man called I-hsi.

Chang Ta-ch'ien collect. Copy of Huang Kung-wang's Fu-ch'un scroll.

HUANG KUNG-WANG 黄公望, *t.* Tzŭ-chiu 子久, *h.* I-fêng 一峯, Ta-ch'ih 大癡 and Ching-hsi Tao-jên 井西道人.

From Ch'ang-shu, Kiangsu. B. 1269, d. 1354. Landscapes, followed Tung Yüan and Chü-jan. The earliest of the "Four Great Masters" of the Yüan period. H, 5. I, 54. L, 31. M, p.541.

Ku-kung collect. *Fu-ch'un shan-chü t'u*: Dwelling in the Fu-ch'un Mountain. A long handscroll with an inscription dated 1338 but no signature by the painter. Colophons by Tung Ch'i-ch'ang, Liu Chüeh (1410–1472), Tsou Chih-lin (early 17th cent.), K'ung O (early 15th cent.), Shên Tê-ch'ien (1673–1769) and Ch'ien Ch'ên-ch'ün (1686–1774), and a great number of inscriptions by the emperor Ch'ien-lung. *Cf.* Ku-kung album, 1935, and Chinese cat., London Exhibition, pp.143–147. B?

Ibid. The same composition as in the preceding picture but the introductory section is missing. According to the inscription by the painter, the picture was begun in 1347 and finished in 1350. It has also a lengthy inscription by Liang Shih-chêng (written on behalf of the emperor Ch'ien-lung), and colophons by Shên Chou (1488), Wên P'êng (1570), Wang Ch'ih-têng (1571), Tsou Chih-lin and Tung Ch'i-ch'ang. *Cf.* Scroll reproduction by Jurakusha, Tōkyō (?) A.

Tōan 10 (Saitō collect.) Wooded Mountains; a Man in a Pavilion Listening to a Waterfall. Signed and dated 1338. *Cf.* Nansō Ihatsu, III. Late imitation. B?

K.-k. shu-hua chi, XVII. The Heavenly Lake in the Mountains. Signed at the age of 73 (1341). Slightly coloured. Reproduction inadequate. *Cf.* K.-k. chou-k'an, vol.10, 217. B?

Ōmura, II, 4 (ex. Manchu Household collect.) The Orchid Studio at the Foot of Wooded Mountains. Large album-leaf. The painter's inscription on the accompanying leaf is dated 1342. Generally accepted as the master's work. A.

Freer Gallery (11.308). A View of Lu Shan; Mist in the Ravine. Inscription dated 1342. Ink and colours. Late copy. B?

J. D. Chên collect., Hongkong, 1951. Steep Grassy Mountains overgrown with Trees. Much worn soft greyish tone. According to inscription, painted 1343 for Yang Chêng (a Taoist) while stopping in a boat at Liang ch'i. A close imitation. B?

Shina Nanga, III, 5 (P'ang Yüan-chi collect.) Mountain

Village in Evening Mist. Album-leaf. Signed and dated 1343. *Cf.* Tōsō, p.170; Shên-chou ta-kuan, vol.8; P'ang Yüan-chi Cat. Add. 1. B?

Chung-kuo, I, 84 (Ti P'ing-tzŭ collect.) A Towering Mountain grown with Pines; a Pavilion by the River at its Foot. Signed and dated (probably) 1347. B?

Kokka 518 (Yamamoto collect.) *Chiang-shan shêng-lan t'u*: Far-reaching View over River and Mountains. Long handscroll. According to the inscription over the painter's name and the date 1348, the picture was done for his friend Ni Tsan. C.

Nansō Ihatsu, III (Ueno collect.) Mountains in Autumn. Fragment of a handscroll. Signed and dated 1348. Poem by Chou Chu. B?

Chang Ta-ch'ien collect. (1954). The Heavenly Lake in the Mountains. Terraced and topping mountains; buildings in the ravines, large trees and bridges below. Signed: I-fêng Tao-jên at the age of 79 (1348). Colophons by Tung Ch'i-ch'ang and Ch'ên So-yün dated 1608. B.

Chung-kuo ming-hua, XXII. The Heavenly Lake in the High Mountains. Dated 1348. Late imitation. C?

Hui-hua kuan. The Nine Peaks after Snowfall. Pale misty tone; the trees are rendered with deep black spots. Signed and dated 1349 (at 81). A?

Sōgen 62 (ex-Manchu Household collect.) Open Views over a Flat Marshy Beach. Short handscroll. Signed. Poem by Jao Chieh and Chang Yü, the latter dated 1349. A close early copy. B.

Tōsō, p.169 (Yamamoto collect.) Bare Mountains and Leafless Trees in Autumn. Signed and dated 1353. Imitation. C.

Ibid. 171 (Fang Jo). A Village in the Mountains by the Water. Seal of the painter. Poem and colophon by Yang Wei-chên, dated 1365. Imitation. C.

Shên Chou, XII. High Terraced Mountains in Layers. Signed. Indistinct reproduction. C?

Ming-jên shu-hua, 23. Cloudy Mountains and Winding River. Signed and dated 1335.

Ming-hua lin-lang. A Taoist Temple in the Misty Mountains. Signed. Inscription by the painter and by Ch'ien-lung. C?

Hui-hua kuan (ex P'ang Yüan-chi collect.) Clearing after Snowfall on the River. Misty atmosphere; sharp rocks and dry trees; pavilion on a terrace. Mounted on the same scroll as Hsü Pên's Rocks in Mist after Snowfall, and also a piece of writing by Chao Mêng-fu. B.

Shanghai Museum. *Hsien-shan t'u*. Sloping Hills with Rows of Trees; painted in the soft manner; now faded. Signed, and with the painter's seal. Dated 1338. Colophon by Ni Tsan 1359. *Cf.* Gems I, 11. B?

Ku-kung collect. Two Fishermen in Boats on the River; Old Trees and Rocky Shore. A high mountain on the further shore. Large album-leaf; damaged and repaired. Signed. B?

Ibid. Two Landscape Studies from an album called *Ming-hua hui-ts'ui*. Possibly late copies of the master's works.

Sōgen 63 (P'ang Yüan-chi collect.) Peaks of the Fu-ch'un Mountain and the Winding Road along the River. Signed. A?

Nansō Ihatsu, III. The Iron Cliff: a Misty Mountain Gorge with the Cottage of Yang Wei-chên. Signed. Poem by Chao I. A free imitation.

Sōraikan, II, 36 (Abe collect.) Pleasant Views of Rivers and Mountains. Terraced mountains with sparse trees, sails on the river, cottages on the shore. Handscroll. Signed, and seals of the painter. A skilful later imitation. Also published in a complete scroll-reproduction by the Hakubundō Co. B?

Nanga Taisei, XI, 16. A Wooded Hillside Rising gently from a River; a Pavilion built out over the Water. A bridge is leading over to the village on the farther shore. Large horizontal album-leaf or section of a handscroll. Interesting imitation. B.

Chang Ta-ch'ien cat., vol.IV. Cliffs in Autumn, a Village at their Foot. Short handscroll. Inscription by the painter. B?

Freer Gallery (16.566). Wooded Mountains. Ink only on silk. Signed. Free imitation. B?

P'ang Yüan-chi cat. 2. Trees in Autumn Mist. Short handscroll. Signed and dated 1342.

Ibid. 7. Landscapes. Signed and dated 1342. Poem by Hua Yen, dated 1417.

JÊN JÊN-FA 任仁發, *t.* Tzŭ-ming 子明, *h.* Yüeh-shan 月山.

From Sung-chiang, Kiangsu. Active in the first half of the 14th century, d. at 73. Vice-president of the River Conservancy Bureau. Horses and landscapes. I, 53. L, 39. M, p.86.

Tōsō, p.156 (Lo Chên-yü collect.) Five Horses, Three with their Grooms. Handscroll. Signed and dated 1304. A?

Fogg Museum, Cambridge, Mass. Horses and Grooms. Short handscroll. Partly the same horses as in the picture in Lo Chên-yü's collection. Signed and dated 1314. *Cf.* London Exhibition cat. 1320. A.

Hui-hua kuan (ex-Shimamura collect.) The Taoist Sorcerer Chang Kuo-lao before the Emperor Hsüan-tsung of T'ang, creating a Small Horse that speeds through the Air; several courtiers are watching him. Inscription by Ch'ien-lung. Signature retouched. A?

Ibid. Two Grooms Bringing out Four Horses to their Master, who is dressed in Red Gown. Colour on silk. Handscroll. A?

Ibid. Two Horses, one Strong and Fat, another Lean and Tired. According to the inscription by the master, they symbolize two opposite kinds of men, the nobles and the workmen. Colour on silk. Handscroll. A.

Shanghai Museum. Two Ducks on the Shore and a Small Bird in a Blossoming Tree with White and Pink Flowers. Signed. A.

Ming-jên shu-hua, 8. Two Horses; One led by a Groom and the Other rolling on the Grass. Signed.

K.-k. shu-hua chi, XXVI. A *Ch'in* Player Seated on a Cliff by a Mountain Stream. Poem by the painter. Probably a later picture, though marked with the painter's seal.

Kokka 323 (K. Murakami). A Saddled Horse. Album-leaf. C.

Ibid. 403 (Marquis Asano). A Horse Tied to a Pole. Seals of the painter. A.

Ibid. 412 (ex-Asano collect.) Two Horses under Willow-trees on a Shore. A fragment. B?

Tōyō, IX (The Art Academy, Tōkyō). A pair of pictures: one representing Playing the *Ch'in* and Practising Calligraphy; the other Playing Chess and Practising Painting. The pictures are badly worn, the traditional attribution misleading. *Cf.* Kokka 53, 57; Tōsō, pp.151, 152. C.

Bijutsu, XXX. A Basket with Fruits. Album-leaf. Attributed. C.

Hikkōen, pl.37. An Arhat Seated on a Cliff, Two Men Standing by. Album-leaf. C.

Ibid. pl.38. A high Official on Horseback, followed by Ladies on Foot and Men on Horseback. Fan-painting. B?

Ibid. pl.39. Branches of a Bean Plant in a Bowl. Album-leaf. C.

Kokka 636 (Marquis Lanza d'Ajeto; formerly Asano). A Caparisoned Horse. Album-leaf. B?

Tōsō, p.153. Emperor Yang-ti of Sui on Horseback followed by Court Ladies in front of a Palace. C.

Ibid. 154, 155 (Count Ōmura). A pair of pictures: A Man Playing the *Ch'in* to his Guests; Scholars Examining Paintings. Signed. Reproduction indistinct. C?

Nanga Taisei, IX, 41. A Man Seated on a Ledge under Gnarled Trees Overlooking a River. Signed.

Kawasaki cat. 5. A pair of pictures: One representing A Man Playing the *Ch'in* in a Hall; the other, A Bamboo Garden in Snow and a Man in a Pavilion. *Cf.* Kokka 321. B.

Victoria and Albert Museum. Feeding Horses. Inscribed with the painter's name. *Cf.* Ars Asiatica, IX, p.30; London Exhibition cat. 1119. B?

Musée Guimet. Two Horses and Two Men. Handscroll. Poem signed with the painter's name. B?

W. Hochstadter, New York. Five Princes Returning from a Drinking Party, Accompanied by Three Servants, all on Horseback. Colours on paper. Seal of the painter. Handscroll. A.

P'ang Yüan-chi Cat. 2. A Horse Rolling on the Ground, Two Grooms in Conversation. Handscroll. Poem by the painter.

Ibid. 7. Two Ducks, one pecking its wing, the other swimming in the water. Four small birds in a *hai-t'ang*-tree above. Seals of the painter.

JÊN K'ANG-MIN 任康民. Unrecorded in Chinese books, mentioned in *Kundaikan Sayuchōki, nr* 38, among the Yüan painters and said to have executed some wall-paintings, besides landscapes and figures.

Shimbi XVI (Count Matsudaira). a Pedlar, a Woman and Seven Children round his Stalls. Fan-painting. Attributed.

Hikkōen, pl.41. A Fragmentary Landscape. Badly worn. Album-leaf. Attributed.

JÊN TZŬ-CHAO 任子昭, *t.* Tzŭ-liang 子良.
From Sung-chiang, Kiangsu. Son of Jên Jên-fa. Active in the 14th cent. Figures and horses. M, p.86.

Chêng Tê-k'un, Cambridge. A Running Horse without Saddle. Album-leaf. Signed and dated 1348.

Hui-hua kuan. A Man in Red Cloak Leading a Grey Horse. Colour on silk. Signed.

KAO JAN-HUI 高然暉.
Unrecorded in Chinese books, mentioned in *Kundaikan Sayuchōki, nr* 71. Yüan period. Landscapes. Sometimes, though wrongly, identified with Kao K'o-kung. He may have been a Korean painter. *Cf. Bijutsu Kenkyū*. No.13.

Tōyō, 105, 106 (National Museum, Tōkyō). Two small Landscapes: one representing Spring; the other, Summer. Attributed. Both with inscriptions by Tu Kuan-tao, an official of the Hung-wu period. A?

Ibid. 104 (Akimoto). Summer Mountains with a Temple in Mist. Attributed. *Cf.* Kokka 211; Nanju, 3; Bijutsu Kenkyū, 13. A?

Ibid. 102, 103 (Konchi-in, Kyōto). Two Landscapes: one representing Summer; the other, Winter. Attributed. More likely to be by the master than any of the other pictures ascribed to him.

Tōsō, p.202 (T. Ogura). A Wooded Slope, a Herd-boy by the Stream and a Grazing Buffalo. Attributed. *Cf.* Bijutsu Kenkyū, 13. B.

KAO K'O-KUNG 高克恭 (according to *Ch'ing-ho shu-hua fang*, his original name was Shih-an 士安), *t.* Yen-ching 彥敬, *h* Fang-shan 房山.
From Ta-t'ung, Shansi. B. 1248, d. 1310 or later. The family had immigrated from Eastern Turkestan. Appointed by Kublai Khan to an official position and made President of the Board of Justice. Landscapes; followed Mi Fei and Mi Yu-jên. H, 5. I, 53. L, 20. M, p.331.

K.-k. shu-hua chi, XXXVII. Clearing after a Spring Rain over the Mountains. Colophon by Li K'an, dated 1299. A?

Ibid. XIII. Mountains Rising through Spring Clouds and Morning Mist. Signed and dated 1300. Damaged and retouched. A?

Ku-kung, XI. Cloud-encircled, Luxuriant Mountains. Colophons by Têng Wên-yüan (1258–1328), Li K'an (dated 1309), Wang To (1592–1652), and Ch'ien-lung. A.

Hsü Hsiao-p'u collect., Taipei. White Clouds Circling around Grassy Hills on a River-shore. A man on muleback is crossing a mud-bridge. Short handscroll. Poem by the painter, dated 1313. B.

K.-k. shu-hua chi, XXXIII. A Grove of Leafy Trees in Mist and Rain. Inscribed with the painter's name and the date 1333! Poems by Yü Ho (dated 1363), Wu K'uan (dated 1470) and Ch'ien-lung. *Cf.* Chinese cat., London Exhibition, p.142. C.

Ku-kung, IX. Mountains in Rain. Signed. Poem by Ch'ien-lung. *Cf.* Chinese cat., London Exhibition, p.141. C.

Shina Nanga Taikan, 4. Misty Landscape. Seals of the painter. B.

Nansō Ihatsu, II. Mist along a Mountain Ridge by a River; two men in a garden in the foreground. Short handscroll. B.

Ibid. II. "Coloured Mountains": Evening Mist along the River. Short handscroll. B.

Tōan, 8 (Saitō collect.) Mountain Landscape with a Man in a Pavilion and Circling Clouds in the Fissures. After Mi Fei. Signed. B?

Sōgen, 40 (N. Masaki). Low Buildings by a Beach, High Mountains in the background. Signed. Poem by the painter. Album-leaf. B?

P'ang Yüan-chi cat. 7 (Illustr. cat. 1940, II). Cloudy Mountains. Attributed. Colophon by Wang Chien.

K'o Chiu-ssŭ 柯九思, *t.* Ching-chung 敬仲, *h.* Tan-ch'iu 丹丘.

From T'ai-chou, Chekiang. B. 1312, d. 1365. Prominent connoisseur of paintings, writings and antiquities. He was ordered to examine the imperial collection in the T'ien-li era (1328–1330). Followed Wên T'ung as a painter of bamboos and old trees. H, 5. I, 53. L, 22. M, p.262.

Hui-hua kuan. Bamboos by a Garden Rock. Dated 1338. Poems by Ch'ien-lung. A.

Chang Ch'ün, Taipei. A Branch of a Phoenix-tailed Bamboo. Signed and dated 1338.

C. C. Wang, New York. A Branch of Bamboo. Ink on silk. Signed and dated 1343. *Cf.* Venice Exhibition, 1954. A.

K.-k. shu-hua chi, XXXVIII. River Landscape. Signed. Colophon by Yo Yü, dated 1344. B.

Sōgen 43 (Lo Chên-yü collect.) A Pavilion under Leafy Trees in Autumn. Poem and colophon by the painter. Signed and dated 1345. B.

K.-k. ming-jên hua-chu chi. A Tall Bamboo and a Chrysanthemum Plant by a Rock. Signed. Colophon by Yü Chi (1272–1348) and poem by Ch'ien-lung. A.

Ku-kung, V. A Bare Tree and Bamboos by a Rock. Signed. A.

K.-k. shu-hua chi, III. Bamboos by a Stone. Signed. *Cf.* K.-k. ming-jên hua-chu chi and Chinese cat., London Exhibition, p.155. A.

Ibid. XXV. Branches of a Blossoming Plum-tree. Signed. Possibly a Ming painting. B?

Ibid. XXXV. A Pavilion Built over a Stream at the Foot of High Mountains. Signed. B?

K.-k. chou-k'an, vol.7, 134. Bamboos Growing from a Rock. Fan-painting. Signed. Poem. A.

Sōraikan, II, 34. A Branch of Bamboo. Inscriptions by the painter and by Ch'ien-lung. A?

Mei-chan tê'-k'an. Bamboos and a Bare Tree by a Rockery. Signed.

Sōgen 44 (Shao Hou-fu). An Old Knotted Tree, Bamboos and Epidendrums by a Rock. Signed. B?

P'ang Yüan-chi cat., 2. Trees in Frost and Slender Rocks. Long colophon by the painter, dated 1342.

Ibid. 7 (Illustrated cat., II). Two Bamboos. Signed. *Cf.* Nanking Exhib. cat., 66. A.

Ibid. Add. 1. Bare Trees and Bamboos by a Rock. Signed.

Ku An 顧安, *t.* Ting-chih 定之.

From Yangchou, Kiangsu. Served as a judge in Ch'üan-chou in the Yüan-t'ung era (1333–1334). Bamboos, followed Hsiao Yüeh (of T'ang) and Wên T'ung. H, 5. I, 53. L, 52. M, p.736.

Chung-kuo, I, 113 (Ti P'ing-tzŭ collect.) A Spray of Bamboo. Signed and dated 1345. A.

Shên-chou ta-kuan, vol.4. Bamboo Groves along a River-bank. Short handscroll. Signed and dated 1349. Poem by Chang Yü. A?

K.-k. shu-hua chi, I. Bamboos on a Rock in Wind. Signed and dated 1350. A. *Cf.* K.-k. ming-jên hua-chu chi and Chinese cat., London Exhibition, p.159.

Ku-kung collect. *Ch'üan-shih hsin-huang t'u.* Rocks and Fresh Bamboo-sprouts. Large album-leaf. Signed and dated 1365. Inscription by Pu Chü-shih. A.

Ming-hua lin-lang. Fresh and Slender Bamboos on a Rock. Signed and dated 1365. Inscription by Mo Chin-kung and Ch'ien-lung. *Cf.* K.-k. chou-k'an, vol.I, 20. A?

K.-k. shu-hua chi, V. An Old Tree and Bamboos by a Rock, painted in co-operation with Ni Tsan and Chang Shên. Poem by Ni Tsan dated 1373. A. *Cf.* K.-k. ming-jên hua-chu chi and Chinese cat., London Exhibition, p.161.

Ibid. XXXVI. Bamboos in Wind. Seals of the painter. *Cf.* K.-k. ming-jên hua-chu chi. A.

Cincinnati Museum of Art. A Single Stem of Bamboo. Signed. Two inscriptions. A.

Private collect., Peking. Young Bamboo-shoots and Branches. Signed.

Peking National Museum cat. An album of eight leaves representing Narcissi.

Ku K'uei 顧逵 or Ku Ta 顧達, *t.* Chou-tao 周道.
From Suchou. Active first half of 14th century. Landscapes, figures, portraits. H, 5. L, 53. M, p.736.

National Museum, Stockholm. Chung K'uei Seated under a Tall Tree. Signed.

Ku Tê-hui 顧德輝 or Ku Ying 顧瑛, *t.* Chung-ying 仲瑛, *h.* Chin-su Tao-jên 金粟道人.
From K'un-shan, Kiangsu. B. 1310, d. 1369. Poet, connoisseur. L, 52. M, p.736.

K.-k. shu-hua chi, XXXIII. A Cabbage Plant. Album-leaf. Signature doubtful.

Chung-hua wên-wu chi-ch'êng, IV, 370. Two Mandarin Ducks under Some Reeds and Fu-yung Flowers. Poem by the painter. Colophon by Ch'ien-lung.

P'ang Yüan-chi cat., Add. 1. River Landscape with a Pavilion under Bare Trees on Shore. Poems by the painter, by Wên P'êng and Chü Chieh.

Kuan Tao-shêng 管道昇, *t.* Chung-chi 仲姬.
From Wu-hsing, Chekiang. B. 1262, d. *c.*1325. Wife of Chao Mêng-fu. Calligraphist and painter of bamboo, plum-blossoms, epidendrums and landscapes. H, 5. I, 54. L, 70. M, p.603.

T. Moriya collect., Kyōto. The Purple Bamboo Retreat; a small landscape. Two inscriptions by the painter, one dated 1296. A?

Chung-kuo, I, 101 (Abe collect.) Kuanyin with the Fish-basket, after Wu Tao-tzŭ. Signed and dated 1302. Poem by Chao Mêng-fu. Inscription by Chung-fên Ta-shih. *Cf.* Sōraikan, II, A.

Yūrintaikan, II. Two Branches of Bamboo. Ink on paper. Poem by Chao Mêng-fu. Signed and dated 1305. C.

Ku-kung collect. Bamboo Grove along a River-bank. Signed and dated 1308. Short handscroll, mounted in the collected scroll of Yüan works, *Yüan-jên chi-chin.* A.

Boston Museum. Sections of Bamboo Stems and Branches. Handscroll. Colophon and poem by Kuan Tao-kuo, sister of the painter, dated 1309. B?

Tōsō, p.142 (ex-Tokugawa collect, now National Museum, Tōkyō). Sections of Bamboo Stems and Branches. Long handscroll. Colophon by the painter, dated 1313. Poem by Chao Mêng-fu, copied by the painter. A later picture.

Preetorius collect., Munich. Mountain Landscape with a Bamboo Grove. On silk, much darkened. Poem by the painter, signed and dated 1315. A?

Laufer cat. 25. A Bamboo Grove on a River Shore at the Foot of Misty Mountains. Signed and dated 1322. Poems by Chao Mêng-fu, dated 1324. C.

Hui-hua kuan. A Long Branch of Bamboo. Handscroll. Accompanies a similar painting by Chao Mêng-fu. A.

Chung-kuo, I, 102 (Ti P'ing-tzŭ collect.) River Landscape, called Early Snow at Wu-hsing. Signed. B?

Chung-kuo ming-hua, II. A Man in an Open Pavilion on a River Shore amidst Bamboos. Album-leaf. Signed. B?

K.-k. shu-hua chi, XII. Slender Bamboos by a Rock. Seal of the painter. Colophon by Tung Ch'i-ch'ang. *Cf.* K.-k. ming-jên hua-chu chi, and London Exhibition, Chinese cat., p.140. A.

Tōan 7 (Saitō collect.) Tufts of Epidendrum. Signed. *Cf.* Kokka 555. A?

Ōgawa collect., Kyōto. Clumps of Small Bamboos among Rocks. Long handscroll, ink on paper. Attributed. B.

Ada S. Moore collect., New York. A River View with Bamboo Groves on the Rocky Shores. Handscroll. Signed. *Cf.* Laufer, cat. pl.XXVI and London Exhibition cat. 1038. B?

Seattle Art Museum. Bamboos by Garden Stone. Signed. B.

National Museum, Stockholm. The Slender Bamboos of Spring. Poem by the painter. Large album-leaf. B?

P'ang Yüan-chi cat. 2. A Lady Standing by Bamboos. Handscroll. Signed. Colophons by several Ch'ing writers.

KUO MIN 郭敏, *t.* Po-ta 伯達.

Yüan Dynasty. A native of Ch'i-hsien in Honan. Landscapes and figures, also flowers and ink bamboo. H, 5. M, p.398. also *Hua-shih hui-yao*.

J. Cahill, Wash. D.C. Wind and Snow in Pines and Firs. A house in a valley between towering mountains; three men drinking tea. Signed.

KUO PI 郭畀, *t.* T'ien-hsi 天錫 and Yu-chih 佑之, *h.* Pei-shan 北山.

From Ching-k'ou, Kiangsu. B. 1301, d. 1355; these dates are usually given for his birth and death, but they are probably about twenty years too late. Landscapes after Mi Fei. H, 5. I, 53. L, 60. M, p.398.

Yūrinkan (Shina Meiga Senshū, III). Mountain Landscape in the style of Mi Fei. Handscroll. Signed and dated 1327. A?

Nanga Taisei, IX, 35. Monastery in Mountains Lapped by Mist. Signed and dated 1330. A?

Kokka 412 (former Hayashi collect., now J. D. Chên, Hongkong). River Landscape after Rain. Signed and dated 1334. A?

Sōgen 70 (Chang Hsüeh-liang). River Landscape with Leafy Trees and Mountains Rising through Clouds. Signed and dated 1337. B?

K.-k. shu-hua chi, V. Mountains in Mist. Illustration to two lines of a poem by the T'ang poet Kao Shih. Signed and dated 1339. *Cf.* Chinese cat., London Exhibition, p.168. A?

K.-k. ming-jên hua-chu chi. A Bamboo Grove in Snow. Short handscroll. Signed. Poem by Ch'ien-lung. *Cf.* K.-k. chou-k'an, vol.6. A.

Liu, pl.42. River-landscape in Mist after Mi Fei. Handscroll. Signed. A.

Ueno collect., Ashiya. An Old Tree. Short handscroll. Signed. Colophon by Wang Fang. A.

K. Sumitomo collect., Ōiso. Mountains with Trees in Mist. Slightly coloured. Signed. A. *Cf.* Tōsō, p.198.

Tōsō, 199 (Chin Shou-shu). River Landscape in Mist. Handscroll. Signed. B.

C. T. Loo Successor, New York (ex-Chang Ts'ung-yü collect.) A Bunch of Bamboo Branches. Short handscroll. Signed. *Cf.* Toronto Exhibit. cat. nr 14.

KUO TSUNG-MAO 郭宗茂.

From Ning-po. 14th century. Flowers and birds. L, 60. M, p.398.

Chung-kuo, I, 116 (Ti P'ing-tzŭ collect.) Two Ducks on the River Shore. Attributed. C?

LAI-AN 賴菴.

Probably a priest. Yüan period. Specialized in painting fishes. Recorded only in *Kundaikan Sayuchōki*, *nr* 67.

Kokka 381 (Iwasaki collect.) A Fish. Short handscroll. Attributed. The seal on the picture reads Na-an 訥菴. A?

Ibid. 409 (Marquis Asano). Four Fishes among Weeds. Seal of the painter. A.

Hikkōen, pl.21. Three Fishes. Section of a scroll.

Ōgawa collect., Kyōto. Fishes among Weeds. Attributed.

Mutō cat. 21. A pair of pictures, each representing a fish. Attributed.

Nelson Gallery, Kansas City. A Large Carp (?) Swimming between Aquatic Plants. A?

LÊNG CH'IEN 冷謙, *t.* Ch'i-ching 啓敬, *h.* Lung-yang-tzŭ 龍陽子.

A legendary Taoist from Wu-ling, Hunan. In the Chih-yüan period (1335–1340) he is said to have been 100 years old, but became a Court musician in the Hung-wu period (1368–1398). Landscapes in the style of Li Ssŭ-hsün. His name has been used for the following pictures, which, however, do not represent the style of one single master. N, I, 10. O, 2. L, 49, 1. M, p.114.

Ku-kung, XXVI. The Po-yo Mountain. Signed and dated 1943. Colophon describing his journey to Po-yo with Liu Chi, who served as prime minister in the Hung-wu period.

K.-k. shu-hua chi, XLV. The Po-yo Mountain. Signed. Poem and colophon, dated 1343. Poem by Liu Chi. *Cf.* copy in the Chang Ta-ch'ien collect.

Ch'ing-kung ts'ang (2nd ed.) A Grove of Leafy Trees in a River Valley. Fan-painting. Signed. C.

Yūrintaikan, II. Clouds and Woods in the Purple Valley. Signed and dated 1359. C.

Freer Gallery (11.188). A Villa and a Garden by a River. Inscription of the Yung-lo period (1403–1424). C.

Peking National Museum cat. Taoist Immortals, after Li Kung-lin. Handscroll. Colophon by the painter.

P'ang Yüan-chi cat. 8. Cloudy Mountains. Painted in blue and green. Signed and dated 1407. Handscroll.

LI HÊNG 李亨, *t.* Ch'ang-shih 昌時.

Active *c.*1335–1340. Flowers and birds, pupil of Wang Yüan. Unrecorded in biographies of painters. The above information is offered by Ch'ien Ku in his inscription on this picture.

Ōmura, I, 11 (Chin K'ai-fan collect.) Shrubs and Plants Growing from a Vertical Rock. Insects swarming around. Signed. Colophon by Ch'ien Ku (1508–1572). Poem by Pien Yung-yü (17th cent.), the author of *Shu-hua hui-k'ao*. *Cf.* Tōsō, p.195. A.

LI JUNG-CHIN 李容瑾, *t.* Kung-yen 公琰.

First half of the 14th century. Specialized in boundary painting and followed Wang Chên-p'êng. H, 5. M, p.197.

K.-k. shu-hua chi, XXXVI. Imperial Palaces of the Han period built on cliffs projecting over a river. Signed.

LI K'AN 李衎, *t.* Chung-pin 仲賓, *h.* Hsi-chai Tao-jên 息齋道人.

From Chi-ch'iu, near Peking. B. 1245, d. *c.*1320. President of the Board of Officials. Trees and bamboos. Author of the *Chu-p'u* 竹譜. H, 5. I, 53. M, p.196.

Hui-hua kuan. Bamboos on Rocks. Ink-painting on paper. Handscroll. Colophon written in large characters by the painter, dated 1307. This picture is said to have formed one scroll with the picture now in the Nelson Gallery, Kansas City. A.

Nelson Gallery, Kansas City. Two Large Tufts of Bamboo with widely spreading branches. Signed. Painted for a friend called Hsüan-ch'ing, who recited a poem on the beauty of the bamboos. This is copied in the first colophon by Chao Mêng-fu, dated 1308. The second colophon is written by another friend called Yüan Ming-shan and dated 1309. A.

C. C. Wang, New York. Tall Bamboos Growing by a Garden Rock. Painted on two equal pieces of silk. Signed and dated 1318. A.

Gems, I, 9. Bamboos Growing by a Rock. Signed and dated 1319.

K.-k. shu-hua chi, XXI. A Pair of Tall Pine-trees and Some Jujube Shrubs. Seal of the painter. A.

Ku-kung collect. Three Thin Bamboos by a Stone. Ink on silk. Signed with two seals. A?

Hui-hua kuan. Bamboos on a Cliff in Rain. Ink and greenish colour on paper. A.

Ibid. Three Tall Bamboos. Ink and greenish colour on silk. Signed. A.

Chang Ta-ch'ien cat., vol.IV. Fresh Shoots of a Jade Bamboo. Greenish colouring. Signed.

Yūrinkan, Kyōto. Bamboo. Album-leaf, painted on silk. Inscription by Yang Kuo-ch'i. Attributed. B.

Lilly collect., Indianapolis. Three Dry Pine-trees and Small Bamboos on a Rocky Shore.

P'ang Yüan-chi cat. 7. Two Bamboos. Signed and dated 1310.

Li K'ang 李康, *t.* Ning-chih 甯之.
Native of T'ung-lu in Chekiang. Active *c.*1340–1360. Biography in *Yüan Shih*; also M, p.198.

Ku-kung collect. (Nanking Exhib. cat. pl. 76). Fu-hsi Seated on Rock holding Brush and Paper. Attributed.

Li Shêng 李升, *t.* Tzŭ-yün 子雲, *h.* Tzŭ-yün-shêng 紫篔生.
From Hao-liang. Active at the end of Yüan dynasty. Bamboos, rocks and landscapes. H, 5. M, p.197.

Shanghai Museum (Gems, II, 7). Mountain Landscape with Small Buildings on Hillocks among Pine-trees. Handscroll. Inscription by the painter, dated 1346. A.

Li Shih-hsing 李士行, *t.* Tsun-tao 遵道.
Son of Li K'an. B. 1282, d. 1328. Landscapes, bamboos and stones. H, 5. I, 53. M, p.197.

Preetorius collect., Munich. Mountain Landscape with Bare Trees. Signed and dated 1326. A.

Ku-kung, XI. A Knotted Old Pine-tree and Bamboos. Signed. *Cf.* Chinese cat., London Exhibition, p.157. A.

S.c.t.k. hsü-pien, I. Plum-tree. Inscribed and sealed. A.

Fogg Museum, Cambridge, Mass. Two Old Pine-trees on a Shore. Signed. A.

Hui-hua kuan. Topped Mountains Rising above a Stream. Signed. A.

Chang Ts'ung-yü cat. Two Intertwined Old Trees and Slender Bamboos. Signed. A?

Peking National Museum cat. River Landscape in Late Autumn. Short handscroll. Seal of the painter. A number of colophons by several contemporaries and later men.

Li T'i 李倜, *t.* Shih-hung 士弘, *h.* Yüan-ch'iao Chên-i 員嶠眞逸.
From T'ai-yüan, Shansi. 14th century. Served as a lecturer on the classics to the emperor. Followed Wên T'ung as a bamboo-painter. H, 5. I, 53. L, 43. M, p.197.

Sōgen 76 (Lo Chên-yü collect.) Bamboo Groves by a Rocky Shore. Part of a scroll. Attributed.

Liang-ch'üan 良銓, *h.* K'o-wêng 可翁, Wu-shih 無事 and Ssŭ-k'an 思堪.
Unrecorded, but according to *Shimbi, XII,* he went to Japan in 1299. There was also a Japanese monk with the name Liang-ch'üan (Ryōsen), who lived later and painted in Chinese style, as may be seen in two Arhat pictures, reproduced in Shimbi, XII.

Shimbi, XII (Baron J. Gō, Tōkyō). An Arhat and his Servant Standing on a Promontory in front of a Waterfall. A dragon appears in the clouds. Short handscroll. Attributed.

Lin Chüan-a 林卷阿, *t.* Tzŭ-huan 子奐, *h.* Yu-yu-shêng 優遊生.
Landscapes; followed Kuo Hsi. Recorded in Li Jih-hua's *Wei-shui-hsüan jih-chi*; also in K.

Ku-kung collect (Nanking Exhib. cat. nr 79). A Broad River-view with a Fishing-boat. Signed and dated *kuei-ch'ou* (1313?) Mounted in the collective scroll of Yüan works called *Yüan-jên chi-chin.*

LIU FANG 劉枋.
Unrecorded. Probably Yüan period.

Freer Gallery (09.164). Chung K'uei Making Demons do Acrobatic Feats. Signed. Ink and colours on silk.

LIU KUAN-TAO 劉貫道, *t.* Chung-hsien 仲賢.
From Chung-shan, Hopei. Active *c.*1270–1300. Taoist and Buddhist figures as well as portraits and landscapes. He was summoned to paint the portrait of Kublai Khan in 1279. H, 5. I, 53. M, p.659.

Sōgen 36 (Hêng Yung collect.) The Founders of the Three Religions with their Disciples under Trees. Signed and dated 1280. B?

Chung-hua wên-wu chi-ch'êng, IV, 356. Emperor Kublai Khan with a Party of Men on Horseback Hunting. Signed and dated 1280(?).

K.-k. shu-hua chi, VI. Two Arhats Seated under Palm-trees. Inscribed with painter's name and the date 1356(!)

Ibid. XV. Mountains and Pavilions in Snow by a River. Poem by Ch'ien-lung. Probably a Ming picture.

Tōsō, p.149 (Kuo Tsê-yün collect.) The Taoist Immortal Ko Hung Moving his Residence. Figures travelling through a landscape. Handscroll. A?

Nelson Gallery, Kansas City. A Man Resting on a Couch in the Open; behind him a painted screen, a table and some plants; two women stand at the foot-end of the couch. According to an inscription by Wu Hu-fan, the picture is signed Kuan-tao. A somewhat simplified version of the same design is in the Freer Gallery (11.232) ascribed to the Sung period.

Freer Gallery (16.110). Three Poets under a Pine-tree. A late Ming picture. C.

Peking National Museum cat. Immortals Celebrating the Birthday of Hsi-wang-mu. Handscroll. Signed and dated.

Ibid. A Meeting before the Ju-lai Buddha. Handscroll. Signed.

LIU MIN-SHU 劉敏叔.
Active in the Yüan period. Portraits. M, p.659.

Freer Gallery (16.584). Portraits of Three Scholars. The painter's name and title written on the margin. Possibly of the period.

LIU TZŬ-YÜ 劉子輿.
Active at end of Yüan and beginning of Ming dynasty.

Hui-hua kuan. A Landscape Study. Ink on paper. Mounted together with similar paintings by Chang Kuan, Chao Chung and Shên Hsüan.

LIU YIN 劉因, *t.* Mêng-chi 夢吉.
From Yung-ch'êng, Hopei. 1249–1293. Better known as writer and philosopher. Biography in the *Yüan Shih*.

Sōraikan, II, 35. A Fisherman in a Boat on the River; Bare Trees on the Rocky Shore in the foreground. Inscription by the painter.

Musée Guimet, Paris. A Mountain River. Seal of the painter.

Lo Chih-ch'uan 羅稚川.

A native of Ling-chiang in Kiangsi. Unrecorded in Chinese works on painting, but mentioned in Korean and Japanese record books as a scholar and as an associate of noted litterati of the time.

Sekai Bijutsu Zenshū, XIV, pl.72. Birds Gathering in Knotty Old Trees on a River-bank in Winter. Fragment of a handscroll?

Lu Kuang 陸廣, *t.* Chi-hung 季弘, *h.* T'ien-yu 天遊.

From Suchou. Active during second quarter of the 14th century. Landscapes. I, 54. M, p.417.

K.-k. shu-hua chi, VIII. Towers and Pavilions on the Mountains of the Immortals. Signed and dated in the T'ien-li era (1328–1330). Colophons by Li K'ai (1245–1320), Tung Ch'i-ch'ang, Li Jih-hua and Cha Shih-piao. Poem by Ch'ien-lung. A.

Shên Chou, VI. River Landscape in Mist. Album-leaf. Signed. C.

Chung-kuo, I, 92 (Manchu Household collect.) Spring in the Tan-t'ai Mountains. Signed. Poems by the painter and Ch'ien-lung; colophon by Tung Ch'i-ch'ang. *Cf.* Chung-kuo ming-hua, XXIII. *Cf.* Liu 39; Chūgoku, II. A.

Gems, I, 14. A Man in an Open Pavilion by a River. Colophon by Wu K'uan (15th cent.) attributing it to the master. A?

C. C. Wang, New York (ex-Yamamoto). Dawn over the Tan-t'ai Mountains. Poem by the painter. *Cf.* Chung-kuo, I, 93 and Ōmura, I, 2. A.

K.-k. shu-hua chi, XVI. The Five Auspicious Plants. Signed. Poem by Liu Chüeh (1410–1472). *Cf.* Chinese cat., London Exhibition, p.163. C.

Nansō Ihatsu, IV. River-landscape. Signed. Poem by Wang Lo-yü. C.

Nanga Taisei, XIV, 44. High Rocky Hills Sheltering a Temple, Two Men in a Boat. Signed. B?

W. Hochstadter, New York. A Pavilion among Rocks by a River on a Clear Autumn Day. Poem by the painter. *Cf* Tōsō, p.163. A.

Ma Yüan 馬琬, *t.* Wên-pi 文璧, *h.* Lu-ch'un 魯純, or Lu-tun 魯鈍.

From Nanking. Active *c.*1325–1365. Governor of Wu-chou in the Hung-wu period. Landscapes; followed Tung Yüan and Mi Fei. I, 55. M, p.339.

K.-k. shu-hua chi, XXXVIII. Cottages in the Mountains among Pine-trees. Signed and dated 1328. B.

Ibid. X. High Terraced and Deeply Crevassed Mountains in Snow. Signed and dated 1349. A.

I-shu ch'uan-t'ung, IX, 1. *Mu-yün shih-i t'u*: The Evening Clouds conveying Poetic Ideas. Mountain stream in clouds. Signed and dated 1349. A.

Shên-chou ta-kuan, vol.10. Bidding Farewell, the Boats are waiting at the Shore. Short handscroll. Signed and dated 1360. A.

Chung-kuo, I, 105 (Ti P'ing-tzŭ collect.) High Wooded Mountains with Cottages in Autumn. Signed and dated 1360. A?

Nansō Ihatsu, IV. Trees by a Stream in Mist, a Man Standing on the Shore. Signed and dated 1361. B.

Ku-kung collect. (Nanking Exhib. cat. 79). Clearing over Spring Mountains. Short handscroll. Signed and dated 1366. Mounted in the collected scroll of Yüan works, *Yüan-jên chi-chin*. A.

K.-k. shu-hua chi, I. An Angler in a Boat by the Shore in Autumn. Signed. Colophon by T'ao Tsung-i (Ch'iu-ch'eng). A?

Ibid. XLIII. Mountains in Autumn with Travellers. Inscriptions by Tung ch'i-ch'ang and Ch'ien-lung. B?

K.-k. chou-k'an, 431. A Man Seated under a tall Pine at a Bay. A boy stands behind. Signed.

Nansō Ihatsu, IV. Summer Mountains before Rain, Pavilions over the Stream. Signed. *Cf.* Sōraikan, II, 42. B.

Kyūka, I. An Immortal with a Gourd. Signed (at 69). C.

Kokka 492 (Manchu Household collect.) River Landscape with Grove of Leafy Trees. Handscroll. Signed. Poem by Ch'ien-lung. A.

Cincinnati Art Museum (ex-Chang Ts'ung-yü collect.) A Quiet River at the Foot of Misty Mountains. After a picture by Huang Kung-wang. Signed. Inscription by Tung Ch'i-ch'ang. A.

P'ang Yüan-chi cat. 7 (also in the Illustr. cat. 1940, I). Clouds and Mist on a Spring Morning. Signed. C.

Ibid. Add. 1. A Mountain Temple in Autumn, after Chü-jan. Signed. Poems by two contemporaries.

MÊNG YÜ-CHIEN 孟玉澗. Original name Mêng Chên 孟珍, *t.* Chi-shêng 季生, *h.* T'ien-tsê 天澤.
From Wu-ch'êng, Chekiang. Active at the beginning of the 14th century. Flowers, birds and landscapes in blue and green. H, 5. L, 57. M, p.225.

Tōsō, p.194 (T. Ogura). Two Mandarin Ducks on a Snowy River-bank. Signed and dated 1326.

Kokka 251 (Lo Chên-yü collect.) A Bird in a Loquat Tree. Signed.

Shimbi, XI (Count T. Tokugawa). River Landscape with Temple Buildings, Boats and Flocking Wild Geese. Album-leaf. Attributed. *Cf.* Tōyō, IX; Tōsō, p.193.

Moriya collect., Kyōto. Landscape: Mountains, Bridges and Trees. Seal of the painter.

Bijutsu, XII. Wooded Hills in Mist. Short handscroll. Poem by the painter.

Pennsylvania Museum, Philadelphia. The Red Cliff. Three philosophers in the boat. C.

P'ang Yüan-chi cat. 7. Four Quails. Signed and dated 1352.

NI TSAN 倪瓚, *t.* Yüan-chên 元鎮, *h.* Yün-lin 雲林, Yü 迂, Ching-ming Chü-shih 淨名居士.
From Wu-hsi, Kiangsu. B. 1301, d. 1374. Poet, calligraphist and painter of landscapes. One of the "Four Great Masters" of the Yüan period. H, 5. I, 54. L, 11. M, p.314.

Chang Ta-ch'ien cat., vol.IV. An Old Man in an Open Pavilion under Autumn Trees by a Stream; low hills on the opposite side of the water. Two inscriptions by the painter, the first one dated 1339. Four colophons by Wu K'uan and others. A?

Tōan, 12 (Saitō collect.) River Landscape with Tall Trees to the left in the foreground. Poem by the painter, dated 1341. Much worn. B?

Hakubundō album (Ueno collect.) Six double leaves with Studies of Barren Trees and Rocks; each accompanied by a poem. Last picture dated 1342. C.

Nansō Ihatsu, IV. Trees by a River in Autumn. Signed. Poem by the painter, dated 1342. Poem by Shên Chou and colophon by Tung Ch'i-ch'ang. B?

Freer Gallery (15.26). A Winding River; Topped Hills in the distance, spare trees around a straw-roofed pavilion. Poem and colophon by the painter, dated 1344. Probably seventeenth century. B?

Chung-kuo, I, 89 (P'ang Yüan-chi collect.) Six Trees on a Rocky Islet. Colophon by the painter, dated 1345. Poems by Huang Kung-wang and three other writers. *Cf.* Tōsō, p.182; P'ang Yüan-chi cat. 7. B?

Sōraikan, II (Abe collect.) River View with Scattered Trees and a Low Pavilion. Large album-leaf. Poem by the painter, dated 1348, and by two other writers. B?

Ku-kung collect. Sparse Trees and Distant Mountains. Ink on paper. Album-leaf. Signed and dated 1349. B?

Ming-hua sou-ch'i, I, 1. River Landscape; Spare Trees on the Cliffs. Poem by the painter, dated 1350. B?

Ch'ing-kung ts'ang, 61 (Manchu Household collect.) Two Cottages on a Hill-slope at the Foot of a Mountain by a River. Large album-leaf. Colophon by the painter, dated 1352. Poem by Hsü Pên. A?

J. D. Ch'ên collect., Hongkong. Two Leafless Trees and Slender Bamboos Growing by some Stones. Inscription by the painter dated 1353. Colophons by Wên Chêng-ming and Chang Ta-ch'ien. B.

K.-k. shu-hua chi, XVII. A Pavilion under Tall Trees by a River. Poem by the painter, dated 1354. Colophon at the top of the picture by Tung Ch'i-ch'ang. B?

Chung-kuo, I, 88 (Ti P'ing-tzŭ collect.) Bamboos and Bare Trees by some Strange Cliffs. Poem and colophon by the painter, dated 1360. C.

K.-k. shu-hua chi, II. Looking at the Waterfall. According to the inscription, painted with Wang Mêng, dated 1361. Colophon by Tung Ch'i-ch'ang. Probably imitation. B?

Nansō Ihatsu, IV (Tōkyō National Museum). River Landscape. Illustration to two lines of a poem by Tu Fu. Colophon by the painter dated 1361. Sketchy imitation. B?

Ku-kung collect. *Sui-chu chü:* The Water-Bamboo Hut. A small homestead in a bamboo grove on a river-shore. According to the inscription by the painter, which includes a poem, the picture was painted in 1362 for Wang Chung-ho who built the homestead by the South Lake in Sung-chiang. The picture is now blurred by washing, but the inscription seems authentic. Short handscroll, with some colophons. This picture is described in the new *Catalogue of the Palace Collection, chüan* IV, pp.195, 196 (1956).

The same inscription is repeated with only slight differences on another similar, though somewhat simplified painting, likewise a short handscroll, dated 1362, lately in private possession in New York. But it should be noted that the latter picture does not contain the homestead in a bamboo grove as described above.

National Museum, Stockholm. River Landscape. The further shore of steep mountains; a few trees and a pavilion to the right in the foreground. Signed and dated 1362. The top of mountain restored. *Cf.* Shina Nanga, III, 4. A?

Ōmura, I, 1 (Osaragi collect., Kamakura). River Landscape: Mountain Ridge on the Farther Shore; Spare Trees and low pavilion in front. Short handscroll. Retouched but probably genuine. Signed and dated 1362. *Cf.* Tōsō, p.181. A?

Freer Gallery (38.9) (ex-P'ang Yüan-chi). River View. Same design as in the preceeding picture. Short handscroll. Signed and dated 1362. Accompanied by a letter written by the painter.

Metropolitan Museum (18.124.6). River Valley with thin Pine-trees. Signed and dated 1362. Colophon by Wên P'êng. A late free imitation. B?

K.-k. shu-hua chi, XIX. River View: Two Steep Mountains Rising out of the Water. Poem by the painter, dated 1363. *Cf.* Chinese cat., London Exhibition, p.160. A.

Ku-kung, XXV. Fresh Bamboo and Dry Trees at a Stone. Dated 1363. A.

Sōgen 64 (Kuo Pao-ch'ang collect.) Portrait of Yang Chu-hsi in a Landscape. The figure by Wang I, the trees and stones by Ni Tsan. Short handscroll. Dated 1363. A.

C. T. Loo's Successor, Frank Caro, New York (ex Chang Ts'ung-yü collect.) Landscape seen from the T'ung-lu Pavilion. Signed and dated 1364. B?

S.c.t.k. hsü-pien, III. Bare Trees and Bamboo by Rocks. Signed and dated 1365. *Cf.* Nanga Taisei, I, 25. C.

Chung-kuo ming-hua, XXII. A Wu-t'ung Tree with some Climbing Plants and Bamboos by a Rock. Signed and dated 1365. B?

Lo Chia-lun collect., Taipei. A low Pavilion under Spare Trees; Tall Cliffs on the Opposite Shore. Inscriptions by the artist dated 1365, and by Sun Ta-ya dated 1382. A?

Chung-hua wên-wu chi-ch'êng, IV, 371. *Yü-hou k'ung-lin t'u*: Scattered Trees on a Rocky Shore after Rain. Painted in colours on paper. Inscription by the painter, dated 1368, and also colophons by four contemporaries. A.

C. C. Wang, New York. Low Straw-covered Pavilion and Five Thin Trees on a Rocky Ledge. Poem by the painter, dated 1368. Painted for his friend Shu-kuei. *Cf.* Cleveland Exhibition cat. 31. A.

Tōsō, p.184 (M. Katō collect.) Two Leafless Trees and Young Bamboo Sprigs. Poem and colophon by the painter, dated 1369. Also in Nanga Taisei. B?

Ku-kung, V. High Mountains by a River. Signed and dated 1371. Poem by Wang Ju-yü (beginning of 15th cent.) and Ch'ien-lung. Colophon by Tung Ch'i-ch'ang. A.

K.-k. shu-hua chi, XL. Leafless Trees and Young Bamboos by a Strange Stone. Signed and dated 1371. A.

Ku-kung collect. *Hu-yüeh hsien:* The Study of the Moon-pot. Low pavilion on the rocky ledge and mountains beyond. Short handscroll. Signed and dated 1371. Inscribed with ten poems. A?

Ibid. The Top-section of a Bamboo Plant. Ink on paper. Poem by the painter dated 1371. A number of contemporary inscriptions.

K.-k. shu-hua chi, XIII. "The Jung-ch'i Studio". Spare Trees and a Low Pavilion on the Shore; a

Rocky Promontory on the other side of the view. Poem and colophon by the painter, dated 1372. *Cf.* Chinese cat., London Exhibition, p.160. A?

K.-k. chou-k'an, 71. A River Landscape; a House on the near Shore. Painted for his friend Chang Yü. Signed and dated 1372. A.

Ōmura, II, 2 (Kikuchi collect.) A River Winding between Cliffs, Trees and a Pavilion in the foreground. Poem and colophon by the painter, dated 1372. This picture is probably destroyed, but another version of it in I-shu ts'ung-pien, 9. B.

Peking National Museum album: Ni Tsan, Wên Pi, Shên Chou, T'ang Yin and Two More. A Study by a Mountain Stream. Signed and dated 1372.

Photo by Yen Kuang, Peking (Manchu Household collect.) A High Mountain Ridge above a Bay. Large album-leaf. Poem by the painter, dated 1372. *Cf.* Chūgoku, vol.II. A.

P'ang Yüan-chi Illust. Cat., V. A Place for Fishing after Rain in Autumn. Poem by the painter dated 1372. Colophons by Tung Ch'i-ch'ang and two other men. *Cf.* Mei-chan t'ê-k'an. B?

Photo by Yen Kuang, Peking (Manchu Household collect.) Views from the Shih-tzŭ-lin (garden). Short handscroll. Inscription by the painter, dated 1373. Numerous inscriptions by Ch'ien-lung and colophons by officials, referring to the history of the place. A.

Ku-kung collect. Open River-view. Large album-leaf, much repaired. Signed and dated 1373.

K.-k. shu-hua chi, V. An Old Tree Trunk and Some Bamboos by a Rock. Painted together with Ku An and Chang Shên. The portions attributed to Ni Tsan are added later. Poem by Ni Tsan, dated 1373; by Yang Wei-chên and Chang Shên. *Cf.* K.-k. ming-jên hua-chu chi.

Ku-kung collect. (Chung-hua wên-wu chi-ch'êng, IV, 373). A slender Bamboo Branch. A long inscription by the painter, dated 1374, and colophons by Chang Shên, Wang Ju-yü and Miao-shêng. A.

Chiang Ku-sun, Taipei. River Landscape. An Open Pavilion under Three Trees in the foreground, and a Mountain with a Waterfall on the further Shore. Signed and dated 1374. Retouched. Three inscriptions and one colophon. A.

Ku-kung collect. *Su-lin yüan-yu t'u.* Scattered Trees and Far-away Mountains. Signed and dated 1372. Two more inscriptions by the painter, one dated 1374.

National Museum, Stockholm. Autumn Landscape. Poem by the painter, dated 1374, and by Yang Wei-chên. Possibly early seventeenth century. B?

Freer Gallery (11.299). Broad River, Rocky Shores with Spare Trees and a Pavilion. Inscriptions by the painter, dated Chih-chêng *i-mao* (1375?), by Shên Chou, Wên Chêng-ming (dated 1549) and Chang Ch'ung. Possibly seventeenth century. B?

Shên Chou, III. River View with Bare Trees. Inscription by the painter. B.

Ibid. VII. River Landscape with Spare Trees and a Pavilion. Signed. B?

Ibid. XI. A Tall Tree on a Rocky Shore. Signed. B?

Ku-kung, XXIII. Tall Spare Trees by a River; Hillocks farther away. Poem by the painter, by K'o Chiu-ssŭ and Sung K'o. Late imitation. B?

Ibid. XXXV. The "Pavilion of the Purple Fungus" on the River. Poem by the painter. A.

K.-k. shu-hua chi, XXIX. Leafless Trees on a Rocky Ledge in a River. Long colophon by the painter; poem by Ch'ien-lung. B?

K.-k. chou-k'an, vol.I, 1. Leafless Trees and Bamboos growing on Big Stones. Poem by the painter. C.

Ku-kung collect. The An-ch'u Study. Signed. Short handscroll, mounted with other Yüan paintings in the scroll called *Yüan-jên chi-chin.* A?

Hui-hua kuan (ex P'ang Yüan-chi collect.) A Few Bamboos and a Tall Wu-t'ung Tree by a Garden Rock. Inscription by the painter. A.

Ibid. Pavilion and Spare Trees in Autumn on a River Shore; mountains in the distance. Inscription by the painter and a poem to a friend. A.

Ibid. A Slender Branch of Bamboo. Short handscroll. Inscription by the painter in which he complains of great age and a feeble hand. A.

Shanghai Museum. *Wu-sung ch'un-shui t'u.* The mountain is cut sharply in terraces as in pictures by Huang Kung-wang, the water is rushing down; buildings among spare trees below. Inscription by the painter. A.

P'ang Yüan-chi Illust. Cat. III. Bare Trees and Bamboos by a Rock. Poems by the painter and by Chang Yü, Yang Wei-chên and Ch'ien-lung. Colophons by Tan Chung-kuang, Wang Hui and Wang Shih-chi. A?

Nansō Ihatsu, IV (Sasaki collect., Tōkyō). The Ch'an

Study in the Western Grove. Short handscroll. Signed. *Cf.* Tōsō, p.183. B?

Sōraikan, I, 24 (Abe collect., Ōsaka Museum). Three Trees on a Rocky Promontory. Poems by the painter, by Ch'ien-lung and three other writers. B?

C. T. Loo's Successor, New York. Two Leafless Trees and Slender Bamboos by a Rock. Marked "6 moon, 5 day" (no year) and dedicated to Lü-shui-yüan Chu-wêng (The Old Gentleman of the Green Water Garden). Colophons by Ts'ao Shu and Chu Shêng. *Cf.* Liu 35. A?

Ibid. (ex Chang Ts'ung-yü collect.) Four Leafy Trees growing on the Rocky Shore. Inscription by the painter. A.

C. C. Wang, New York. A Dry Tree by a Rock and a few Stalks of Bamboo. Inscriptions by the painter and four contemporaries. A.

Ibid. Two Trees, a High Stone and Some Bamboos around a House on the Shore; Mountain Silhouettes on the opposite Shore. Signed. A.

Ibid. (ex Chang Ts'ung-yü collect.) River View. Five Trees on the Shore, Large Rocks on the farther Shore; a narrow stretch of water. Inscriptions by the painter and by Ch'ien-lung. A.

Chang Ta-ch'ien collect. (1954). Two Leafless Trees and Small Sprays of Bamboo by a Large Stone. Inscription by the painter. Retouched. A?

Yūrintaikan, I. A Thatched Hut in the Mountains. Ink on paper. Colophon by the painter. C.

Peking National Museum cat. Ten Thousand Valleys; Pavilion in Autumn. Attributed.

Ibid. Bare Trees, Bamboos and Stones. Attributed.

Ibid. River Landscape with a Pavilion. Signed and dated 1367.

Ibid. Mountain Abodes. Poem by the painter, dated 1372.

P'ang Yüan-chi cat. 7. River Landscape. Signed and dated 1371.

Ibid. 7. River Landscape. Poems by the painter, dated 1364 and 1368.

Ibid. 7. Trees in Autumn, Hills in the Distance. Poem by the painter, dated 1372. Poems by Wu K'uan, Wên Chêng-ming, Chu Yün-ming, Shên Chou and others.

Ibid. 7. A Pavilion under Trees in Spring Mist. Colophon and poem by the painter, dated 1344.

Ibid. 7. The Wu-sung River in Spring. Poem by the painter. Colophons by Wang Chih-têng and Tung Ch'i-ch'ang.

Ibid. Add. 1. The Tan-shih Study. Short handscroll. Poems by the painter and three later men.

Ibid. Add. 1. Bamboos and Trees by a small Hill. Short handscroll. Poem by the painter, dated 1371, and by Ch'ien-lung. The *Nei-ching*, a Taoist canon, copied by the painter and mounted on the same scroll. Colophons by Tan Chung-kuang and later men.

Ibid. Add. 1. Old Trees and Bamboos. Colophon and poem by the painter, dated 1369.

PÊN-CH'ÊNG 本誠, *t.* Tao-yüan 道元, *h.* Chüeh-yin 覺隱.
A priest from Szechuan. Active *c.*1356. Landscapes, flowers and birds. I, 54. M, p.67.

Private collect., Japan. A Cabbage Plant, a Sparrow and Swarming Insects. Signed and dated 1356.

PIEN WU 邊武, *t.* Po-ching 伯京.
From Peking. Active first half of the 14th century. Followed Hsien-yü Shu (1257–1303) as a calligraphist. Flowers, birds, bamboos and stones. H, 5. I, 38, 53. M, p.720.

Berlin Museum (Shimbi, XX). Birds Gathering in a Tree on a Rocky Promontory. Fan-painting. Signed.

PO TZŬ-T'ING 柏子庭.
A Buddhist priest from Chia-ting, Kiangsu. Active first half of the 14th century. Stones and flowers. H, 5. I, 54. M, p.263.

Kokka 407 (Marquis Asano). An Iris Growing in the Crevice of a Stone. Short handscroll. Signed. A.
Ibid. 540 (K. Mutō). A pair of pictures representing Old Trees and Sprays of Bamboos. Signed. A.
Nansō Gashū, 3 (Prince Konoe, now Umezawa). Tufts of High Grass by a Rock. Poem by the painter. A. *Cf.* Bijutsu Kenkyū 180, article by S. Shimada.

PO-YÊN PU-HUA 伯顏不花, *t.* Ts'ang-yen 蒼岩.
A Mongol nobleman, distinguished himself as a military commander in fighting the rebel Ch'ên Yu-liang (d. 1363). Painted dragons and landscapes. H, 5. L, 61. M, p.112.

Ma Shou-hua, Taipei. Clumps of Trees on the Rocky Shore of a Bay enclosed by Steep Cliffs. Short handscroll. Signed and dated 1308. A.
K.-k. shu-hua chi, IV. Pines and Circling Clouds in a Mountain Valley. Signed. Colophon by Chiang Li-kang (15th century); poem by Ch'ien-lung.

P'U-KUANG 溥光. Family name Li 李, *t.* Hsüan-hui 玄暉, *h.* Hsüeh-an 雪菴.
From Ta-t'ung, Shansi. A priest, served as head of the Dhuta sect and as a professor in the Chao-wên College in the reign of Kublai Khan, who called him Yüan-wu Ta-shih 元悟大師. Active still in 1312. Landscapes, bamboos and Buddhist figures. H, 5. L, 64. M, p.556. See Pelliot's article in *T'oung Pao*, 1922, p.351.

Seikadō (Iwasaki collect.) A series of nineteen album-leaves representing Bodhidharma, Pu-tai and seventeen Arhats. Poems by the painter. *Cf.* Kokka 333.
Chung-kuo ming-hua, 40, An Arhat. Attributed. Colophon dated 1345.

P'U-MÊN 普門, h. Wu-kuan 無關.
From Hsin-chou, Kiangsi. A priest. B. 1201, d. 1281. Figures. Recorded only in *Kundaikan Sayuchōki*, *nr* 42.

Shimbi, IV (Viscount O. Akimoto). The Taoist Mao Po-tao on a Stag Speaking to his Servant-boy. Short handscroll. Attributed. *Cf.* Kokka 36.
Ibid. XV (Count N. Matsudaira). The Laughing Pu-tai. Attributed. Poem by Yüan-chao.
Tokugawa Museum, Nagoya. Bodhidharma Crossing the Yangtse on a Reed. A man on an ox and a man on a donkey at the sides. Attributed.

P'U-MING 普明. Family name Ts'ao 曹, *h.* Hsüeh-ch'uang 雪窓.
From Sung-chiang, Kiangsu. A priest of the Ch'êng-t'ien temple in Suchou. Active *c.*1340–1350. Specialized in epidendrums. H, 5. I, 54. L, 64. M, p.501.

Bijutsu, III. Epidendrums. Short handscroll. Inscription by the priest Ling-fêng, dated 1341. A.
Kokka 483, 484 (Imperial Household, Tōkyō). A set of four pictures representing Epidendrum and Sprays of Bamboo. Signed; one dated 1343. *Cf.* Tōsō, pp.214–217. A.
Seattle Art Museum. Epidendrums Grown on a Rock and Jujube Branches in Wind. Signed and dated 1345(9). *Cf.* Kokka 687 and Shina Meiga Senshū, II. A.
The Cleveland Museum of Art. Bamboo and Orchids in Wind. Signed. A.
Kokka 400 (Marquis Asano). Epidendrums and Jujube Shrubs by a Rock. Short handscroll. Signed. A. *Cf.* Bijutsu Kenkyū. Nr.XV.
Ibid. 630 (Nezu Museum). Two paintings of Orchids and Bamboo. Signed.
Hikkōen (J. Nakamura). A Tuft of Epidendrum. Album-leaf. A.
Tōsō, p.218 (Brooklyn Museum). Epidendrum and Bamboo in Wind. Short handscroll. Signed. A.

Sa Tu-la 薩都拉, *t.* T'ien-hsi 天錫, *h.* Chih-chai 直齋.
Born of a Mongol family which lived at Yen-mên, Shansi. Active *c.*1315–1340. Passed the *chin-shih* degree and became a provincial judge. Poet and calligraphist. *Cf.* K.-k. shu-hua chi, vol.I.

K.-k. shu-hua chi, XXXIV. Two Birds in a Plum-tree. Poem by the painter, dated 1315. A.

Ibid. I. The Yen Kuang (Tzŭ-ling) Cliff (of the Fu-ch'un Mountains) Projecting over a River. Poem by the painter, dated 1339. A.

Shang Ch'i 商琦, *t.* Tê-fu 德符.
From Ts'ao-chou, Shantung. Employed as a teacher at the court of the Emperor Ch'êng-tsung (1295–1307), and later on in the imperial library. Painted landscapes and bamboos. H, 5. M, p.376.

K.-k. shu-hua chi, XXVIII. A Lotus Stream in Summer at the Foot of Cloudy Mountains, after Chao Ling-jang. Signed and dated 1314. Poem by Wang Ta (end of the 14th century). A?

Ibid. VIII. Two Crows: one in a blossoming apricot-tree; the other splashing in the water below. Signed and dated 1315. A?

Ku-kung, XXXVI. A Wanderer Approaching a Taoist's Hut at the Foot of the Sung Mountain. Signed and dated 1342.

K.-k. shu-hua chi, XXIV. A Deep Mountain Gully; a pavilion built over a stream. Men are playing chess. Signed. A?

Hui-hua kuan. Spring Mountains. Ink and greenish colour on silk. Large handscroll. A.

Shang Chu 商璹, *t.* T'ai-yüan 台元, *h.* Sun-chai 遜齋.
Landscapes, in *p'o-mo* 破墨 manner. Also rocks. H, 5. L. M, p.376.

Chang Ta-ch'ien collect., Hongkong 1951. Moon over a Mountain Village. Handscroll; signed, dated 1342. A.

Shên Hsüan 沈鉉.
Active at end of Yüan and beginning of Ming dynasty. Followed Huang Kung-wang in landscape-painting. M, p.144.

Hui-hua kuan. A Landscape-study. Ink on paper. Mounted together with similar paintings by Chang Kuan, Chao Chung and Liu Tzŭ-yü. A.

Shêng Hung 盛洪, or Shêng Hung-fu 盛洪甫, *t.* Wên-yü 文裕.
From Hang-chou, lived in Chia-hsing, Chekiang. Father of Shêng Mou. Landscapes, figures and birds. H, 5. M, p.389.

P'ang Yüan-chi Illustr. cat. I, 3. Narcissus Plants. Signed and dated 1354. Inscriptions by Ch'en Chi-ju and Ch'ien-lung.

Shêng Mou 盛懋, *t.* Tzŭ-chao 子昭.
From Chia-hsing, Chekiang. Active *c.*1310–1360. Landscapes, figures and birds; followed Tung Yüan and Chü-jan as well as later Sung masters. H, 5. M, p.389.

Chung-kuo, I, 120 (Manchu Household collect.) Mountain Landscape, after Chang Seng-yu. Album-leaf. Signed and dated 1313. A.

Ku-kung, III. A Farmstead among Trees at the Foot of a Mountain Ridge in Snow. Poem by the painter, dated 1322. Poem by Ch'ien Wei-shan dated 1364, and by Ch'ien-lung. Reproduction indistinct. B?

Yen Kuang Co. (Manchu Household collect.) A Fisherman in a Boat by the Shore under Autumn Trees. Signed and dated 1344. A.

Hui-hua kuan. An Old Pine-tree Growing from a Split Rock. Ink on paper. Inscription by the painter, dated 1347 (?).

C. T. Loo Successor, New York (ex-Chang Ts'ung-yü). Enjoyment in Fishing. Signed and dated 1347.

Owen F. Roberts, New York (formerly). A River Valley Bordered by Cloudy Mountains. According to the inscription, painted by Shêng Mou at Wu-chin (in Kiangsu), dated 1348.

Chang Ta-ch'ien collect. Solitary Fisherman in an Autumn Forest. Album-leaf. Signed and dated 1349. A?

Ōmura, I, 5 (Yamamoto collect., now Art Institute, Chicago). River Landscape in Autumn with a Fishing-boat. Signed and dated 1350. *Cf.* Nansō Ihatsu, IV; Tōsō, p.192. A?

Freer Gallery (54.12). Waiting for the Ferry-boat on a River-bank in Autumn. The men are seated under a clump of trees. Ink on paper. Signed and dated 1351. Seven inscriptions. The same picture in a later execution in Yurintaikan, II.

Kao Yen-yüeh, Hongkong. River Landscape in the style of Wu Chên. Signed and dated 1351. Six inscriptions by contemporaries of the master.

Ku-kung collect. A Rocky Slope with Old Pine-trees; two boats on the water, and bluish mountains in the background. Effective colouring. Short handscroll. Eight inscriptions by contemporaries, the last one by Wei Chiu-ting, dated 1361.

K.-k. shu-hua chi, XVIII. Travellers in Cloudy Summer Mountains. Signed and dated 1362. C?

Ku-kung, V. Boating in the Moonlight under Pine-trees; a pavilion on the shore. Signed. Poem by Yao Shou (1423–1495). A?

K.-k. shu-hua chi, X. A Hermit Seated under Autumn Trees. High mountains rising through thick clouds. Signed. *Cf.* Chinese cat., London Exhibition, p.153. A.

Ibid. XIV. A Summer-day in the Mountains; River valley with numerous figures and pavilions. A.

Ibid. XXVIII. Swallow Soaring above the River in Spring. Signed. C.

Ibid. XXXVI. A Mountain Stream, Two Men in a Small Boat; Leafy Trees on the Shore, High Peaks in the background. Signed. A.

Ibid. XLIV. A Scholar with his Servant under Pine-trees and Two Cranes. Signed. A.

K.-k. chou-k'an, vol.6, 127. A Man Angling in a Boat on a Quiet Lake. Fan-painting. Seal of the painter. A?

Ibid. vol.6, 128. A Man Making a Barrel under Two Trees. Fan-painting. Signed. A?

Gems, I, 12. Autumn Scene: a Man in a Boat on the River. Attributed. B.

Hompōji, Kyōto. Two large Landscapes with Figures making Music under Trees. Signed. The pictures are damaged but possibly by the master.

Kokka 213 (K. Beppu). Liu P'u Seated under a Blossoming Plum-tree; a Servant-boy Bringing him Tea. Signed. A?

Ibid. 401 (Marquis Asano). The Immortal Chang Kuo-lao Riding on the Donkey through Clouds over the Sea. Fan-painting. B?

Hikkōen, Pl.44. River-landscape with a Fisherman in a boat. Signed. Large album-leaf. B?

Nansō Ihatsu, IV. A Boat in a Gorge; a Cart Travelling on the Road over the Rocks along the River. Short fragmentary handscroll. Signed?

Nelson Gallery, Kansas City. Enjoying the Mountain Air, a Scholar in a Pavilion among Leafy Trees at the Foot of High Mountains. Recorded in *Shu-hua chien-ying*. A.

Sōraikan (Abe collect.) Mountains Rising through Thick Clouds, a Man in a Pavilion under Large Trees. Fragment (?) B.

C. C. Wang, New York. Wooded Mountain Slope and River below. Colours on silk. Attribution by the owner.

Shina Kachō. Four Wild Geese among Reeds. C.

Ibid. Two Cats and a Falcon. C.

P'ang Yüan-chi cat. 11. Landscape in blue and green. Album-leaf. Signed and dated 1312.

Ibid. 11. Searching for Plum-blossoms. Album-leaf. Seals of the painter.

SHIH CHIANG (KANG) 史杠, *t.* Jou-ming 柔明, *h.* Chü-chai Tao-jên 橘齋道人.

From Yung-ch'ing, Hopei. First half of the 14th century. Figures, landscapes, flowers and birds. H, 5. L, 41. M, p.77.

S.c.t.k. hsü-pien, VI. Cock and Flowers. Inscription and signature by the painter.

Tōsō, 140 (Suda collect.) Demons Attacking a Tiger. Part of a scroll.

Sōgen, 77 (J. C. Ferguson collect.) The Meeting of Lao-tzŭ and Confucius. Short handscroll.

SHIH CH'ING 時清, *t.* (?) Jung-yang 榮陽.

Unrecorded. Presumably a Yüan dynasty priest-painter, close in style to T'an Chih-jui.

Hikkōen, Pl.26. Bamboos growing among Stones. Seals with the above names.

SUN CHÜN-TSÊ 孫君澤.

From Hang-chou. Active at the beginning of the 14th century. Landscapes with figures, and boundary paintings. Followed closely Ma Yüan and the Academy tradition. H, 5. M, p.346.

Tōyō, IX, pl.111 (G. Kikuya, Nagato). Cloudy Mountains with a Woodcutter and a Traveller on the Road. Signed. A?

Ibid. IX, pl.110 (Yōtoku-in, Daitoku-ji). Autumn Landscape: A man seated on a promontory in front of a pavilion overlooking a misty valley, a servant-boy standing behind with a *Ch'in*. Attributed. *Cf.* Kokka 191; Shimbi, II. A?

Ibid. IX, pl.112, 113 (Iwasaki collect.) Two pictures forming a pair: One representing a man on a Terrace in front of a Pavilion under a Twisted Pine; the other Two Men in a Pavilion under Pine-trees. Seal of the painter. *Cf.* Kokka 249; Shimbi, XII. A.

Kokka 282 (Count S. Tokugawa). Men Drinking Wine on a Terrace under Pine-trees. High mountains and temples beyond. B.

Ibid. 328, 381 (Viscount H. Akimoto). A pair of pictures, one representing A Filial Son; the other Lu Chi offering an Orange to his Mother. C.

Tōsō, pp.190, 191 (Nezu collect.) Garden Pavilions with Figures, built over a Stream. A pair of pictures. Partly coloured ink-paintings. Attributed. A?

Kokka 684. Winter Landscape, with a Man in a House. Attributed. B?

Musée Guimet. A House in a Bamboo Grove. Long inscription by the Yüan priest Li-t'ien. Attributed. *Cf.* Ars Asiatica, XIV, pl.7. A?

Kokka 689 (Y. Hagiwara). Landscape with Buildings. B?

SUNG K'O 宋克, *t.* Chung-wên 仲溫, *h.* Nan-kung-shêng 南宮生.

From Suchou. B. 1327, d. 1387. Poet; one of the "Ten Talents" of the time. Bamboos. N, I, 12. O, 7. I, 55, 1. M, p. 127.

Freer Gallery (58.18). Ten Thousand Bamboos, growing on the Hills by a River. Handscroll. Signed and dated 1369. *Cf.* P'ang Yüan-chi cat.; Tōsō, p.226. A.

Shên P'ing-ch'ên, Hongkong. Bamboos growing by a Stone. Signed.

SUNG-T'IEN 松田.

The painter is unrecorded in China, but mentioned in *Kundaikan Sayuchōki*, *nr* 114. He specialized in squirrel paintings, but should not be confused with Yung-t'ien 用田, who also painted squirrels.

Kokka 403 (Marquis Asano). Three Squirrels on the Branch of a Pomegranate-tree. Tall picture; ink only. Seal of the painter.

Moriya collect., Kyōto. Two Squirrels on a Bare Branch. Signed.

Mutō cat. 26. Two Squirrels on a Bamboo Stalk. Seal of the painter. *Cf.* Kokka 554.

Kokka 522 (Baron Dan). A Squirrel on the Branch of a Chestnut-tree. Attributed.

TAI SHUN 戴淳, *t.* Hou-fu 厚夫.
From Ch'ien-t'ang, Chekiang. Active *c.*1317. Landscapes. H, 5. M, p.714.

K.-k. shu-hua chi, XXXV. The K'uang-lu Mountain; a gateway at its foot, a temple at the top. Signed and dated 1318. Probably a later picture.

T'AI PU-HUA 泰不華, *t.* Chien-shan 兼善.
From T'ai-chou, Chekiang. B. 1304, d. 1352. Son of a Mongolian, who became naturalized. Minister of the Board of Rites. V, p.815.

Shên-chou ta-kuan, vol.9. A Tall T'ai-hu Stone. Poem and dedication to the Prime Minister by the painter. *Cf.* Chūgoku, II.

T'AN CHIH-JUI 檀芝瑞.
Early 14th century. Unrecorded except in *Kundaikan Sayuchōki*, *nr* 81. Painted bamboo.

Kokka 426 (Count T. Shimazu). Bamboos on a Rock. B.
Ibid. 468 (Count S. Tokugawa). Bamboos on a Rocky Shore by a Brook. Album-leaf. Poem by T'ung-ch'ê. *Cf.* Tōsō, p.207. A?
Tōyō, IX (Magoshi collect.) Bamboos and Rocks. Album-leaf. Poem by I-shan (1247–1317), a Chinese monk who lived in Japan. A.
Bijutsu, VI. Trees by a River in Mist. A?
Hikkōen pl.53. Bamboos in Mist. Album-leaf. A?
Tōsō, p.208 (Marquis Hachisuka). Bamboos on the Rocky Shore of a Mountain Stream. Handscroll. A.
Sōgen Meigashū, 54 (Nezu collect.) Wind-swept Bamboos Growing in a Rockery. Inscription by Ch'ing-cho. *Cf.* Kokka 664. A?
Seikadō (Iwasaki collect.) Spare Bamboos on a Rock. Inscription by the priest Lui-an.
Okazaki collec., Kyōto. Bamboo growing beside a Rock. Album-leaf, painted on paper. A seal perhaps belonging to the painter. A?
Freer Gallery (56.22). Bamboo growing in Snow beside a Stone. Album-leaf. Poem by I-shan. Attributed.

T'ANG TI 唐棣, *t.* Tzŭ-hua 子華.
From Wu-hsing, Chekiang. B. 1296, d. *c.*1364. Pupil of Chao Mêng-fu, followed also Kuo Hsi. Executed some wall-paintings in the palaces. H, 5. I, 53. M, p.326.

C. T. Loo's Successor, Frank Caro, New York. Dry Old Trees at the Foot of a Hill on the River shore; a man seated on a projecting cliff. Illustration to a poem by Wang Wei. Signed and dated 1323. *Cf.* Chung-kuo, I, 108. A.
K.-k. shu-hua chi, III. Fishermen Walking under Tall Trees along a River-bank. Signed and dated 1338. Another version of the same picture in C. C. Wang's collect., New York. A.
Ōmura, II, 2, 3, 5 (Chiang Mêng-p'in). Cliffs and Streams in Autumn; Travellers on Donkeys. Long handscroll. Signed and dated 1341. A.
Shên P'ing-ch'ên collect., Hongkong. Landscape, dated 1342. A.
Shên-chou ta-kuan, vol.16. Autumn Mist over the Hills. After Yen Su of the North Sung period. Signed and dated 1351.
Sōgen, 48 (Chang Wên-fu). A Quiet Day in the Mountains; Men in the Pavilions. Signed and dated 1361. Poem by Chou Chih (14th cent.) B?
Metropolitan Museum. River Valley with Thin Pine-trees. Signed and dated 1362. Colophon by Wên P'êng. C.
Ōmura, II (Chang Hsi-ts'un). A Misty Mountain-

gorge with a Pavilion. Signed and dated 1364. Poems by Ch'ien-lung and others. B.
Ku-kung collect. Travelling in Autumn Mountains, after Kuo Hsi. The bare trees and cloud-like rocks are seen through the mist. Signed. A.
Ku-kung, VI. A Boat on a Misty Stream. Pine-trees and a pavilion on the shore. Signed. B?
K.-k. shu-hua chi, XL. A Donkey-rider Travelling over Snow-covered Hills. Short handscroll. Seals of the painter. C.
Ch'ing-kung ts'ang, 28 (Manchu Household collect. Roses; after a Sung painting. Fan-shaped. Signed. A?
Musée Guimet. Homestead by a Winding Stream. Album-leaf. Accompanied by a writing by Tung Ch'i-ch'ang. A.
P'ang Yüan-chi cat. 7. Landscape. Signed and dated 1342.

T'AO FU-CH'U 陶復初, *t.* Ming-pên 明本, *h.* Chieh-hsüan Lao-jên 介軒老人.
From T'ien-t'ai, Chekiang. First half of the 14th century. Calligraphist. Followed Li K'an as a painter of bamboos. H, 5. M, p.394.

Kawasaki cat. 35. A Narcissus Plant and a Stone. Attributed.

T'AO HSÜAN 陶鉉, *h.* Chü-ts'un 菊邨.
From Chin-ling (Nanking), b. *c.*1280. Poet. Followed Li Ch'êng as a landscape-painter. H, 5. M, p.394.

C. T. Loo's Successor, Frank Caro, New York (ex Chang Ts'ung-yü). Leafless Trees on a Low Shore. A Ni Tsan motif. Signed and dated 1345. *Cf.* Toronto, 6.

TING CH'ING-CH'I 丁清溪.
A Taoist monk from 14th century. Native of Ch'ien-t'ang, Chekiang. Buddhist and Taoist figures after Li Sung, Wang Hui and Ma Lin. Also portraits. M, p.3.

Chêng Tê-k'un, Cambridge. Manju (Wên-shu) seated on a Crouching Lion. Album-leaf. Signed.

TS'AI SHAN 蔡山. Yüan period. Unrecorded except in *Kundaikan Sayuchōki*, *nr* 120.

Shimbi, XI (Tōkyō National Museum). An Arhat with a Staff Seated on a Rock. Ink and slight colours on silk. Attributed. *Cf.* Tōyō, IX. (Presented to a temple by Ashikaga Tadayoshi.)
Ibid. XIV (Myōshin-ji, Kyōto). A pair of pictures: An Arhat and a Priest Watching a Man Tickle the Nose of a Sleeping Indian; An Arhat and a Priest, two Devils Kneeling before them. Attributed.

TS'AO CHIH-PO 曹知白, *t.* Yu-yüan 又元 and Chên-su 貞素, *h.* Yün-hsi 雲西.
From Hua-t'ing, Kiangsu. B. 1272; possibly alive still 1362 (see below). Served in the reign of Kublai Khan as a professor in a government college, but resigned in order to devote himself entirely to Taoist studies and painting. Followed Li Ch'êng and Kuo Hsi as a landscape-painter. H, 5. I, 54. L, 21. M, p.404.

K.-k. shu-hua chi, VII. Two Pine-trees and some Shrubs. Signed and dated 1329. Colophons by Sung Lien (1310–1381), and two other men. *Cf.* Chinese cat., London Exhibition, p.148. A.

Ibid. II. A Pavilion among Sparse Trees. Signed and dated 1344. Poem by Chang Yü, Ni Tsan, Wang Mêng, Chou Chu and two more contemporaries. C.

Ibid. XV. Snow-covered Hills by a River. Signed. Colophon by Huang Kung-wang, dated 1350. Probably old copy.

Hui-hua kuan (ex-P'ang Yüan-chi). Landscape with Two Pine-trees. Signed and dated 1351 (at 80). Poems by two contemporaries. A.

Ku-kung collect. Spare Trees on a Rocky Ledge by a River. Signed and dated 1362. Part of an album called *Mo-lin pa-ts'ui.*

Ibid. A Man angling in a Boat under an Old Tree by a River. Large album-leaf. In the master's style, but not signed.

K.-k. shu-hua chi, XLII. A Hermitage among Pine-trees by a River; Misty Mountain in the background. Signed. Six poems, one of them by Wang Mien, another by Ch'ien-lung. *Cf.* Chung-kuo, I, 114. A.

Shên-chou, 8. A Pine-tree at a Waterfall. Signed and dated Chih-chêng, *kuei-ch'ou*, a year which did not exist. *Cf.* Shina Nanga, II, 11. A?

Ku-kung, XXIV. The Twelve Good News-bringers, *i.e.* Magpies in a Pine-tree. Inscribed with the painter's signature. C.

Chung-kuo, I, 125 (Manchu Household collect.) Two Pine-trees and some Shrubs on a Low Shore. Signed. Large album-leaf. A. *Cf.* Cleveland Exhibition cat., 32.

Ts'ao-hui Tung-yün (Shimbi Shoin, 1921). Eight Landscape Studies by Ts'ao Chih-po and eight poems by Tung Ch'i-ch'ang (dated 1632). Also published by I-yüan Chên-shang Shê. A?

Nansō, 2 (Yamamoto collect.) Two Pine-trees and a Rock on a River Shore; Mountains in the distance. Signed. Poem by Shên Chou. *Cf.* Ōmura, I, 3; Nansō Ihatsu, III; Tōsō, p.160; Chūgoku, I. B.

Nansō Ihatsu, III. A Man with a Staff Walking in a Forest. Colophon by Wang Hui. A?

Tōsō, p.161 (Ch'ên Pao-ch'ên). River Landscape with Bare Trees and a Man in a Boat. Poems by the painter and by Huang Ch'ien. A.

Ibid. 162 (Chang Ying-hua). Sparse Trees on Rocky Islets in a River. Signed. Poem by Wu K'uan (1435–1504). A?

Sōgen, p.52 (Chang Hsüeh-liang). Strange Cliffs forming Islets in a River; a Pavilion in the centre. Handscroll. Poem by the painter. B?

Gems, I, 13. Landscape with Two Fishermen in Boats on a Lake. Signed. Colophon by Ni Tsan dated 1362. A.

C. C. Wang, New York. Dry Trees growing in a Rockery. Fan-shaped. Signed. A.

P'ang Yüan-chi cat. 7. A Study in the Mountains. Colophon by the painter, dated 1337.

TSOU FU-LEI 鄒復雷.

Poet and painter, active about the middle of the 14th century. Said to have lived as a hermit. Followed in his plum-blossom paintings Chung-jên. I, 54. M, p.567.

Freer Gallery. The Breath of Spring. A long branch of a plum-tree laden with flowers. Handscroll. Poem by the painter, dated 1360. Colophon by Yang Wei-chên, dated 1361. *Cf.* Chung-kuo, I, 118; Tōsō, p.120.

TS'UI YEN-FU 崔彥輔, or Ts'ui Yen-hui 崔彥輝, *t.* Tsun-hui 遵暉, *h.* Yün-lin 雲林.

From Ch'ien-t'ang, Chekiang. Active *c.*1340. A nephew of Chao Mêng-fu. I, 54, L. 12. M, p.388.

K.-k. shu-hua chi, XXI. A Deeply Crevassed and Folded Mountain rising above a River. Signed and dated 1342. Poem by Ch'ien-lung.

WANG CHÊN-P'ÊNG 王振鵬, *t.* P'êng-mei 朋梅.

Emperor Jên-tsung (1312–20) bestowed on him the *hao*, Ku-yün Ch'u-shih 孤雲處士, The Hermit of Lonely Clouds. From Yung-chia, Chekiang. Most prominent as a boundary painter, but painted also other landscapes and figures. H, 5. I, 53. M, p.35.

Chung-kuo, I, 110 (Ti P'ing-tzŭ collect.) A Toy-pedlar and a Man and a Woman with their Child. Signed and dated 1310.

Ku-kung collect. Dragon-boat Festival in the Han Period. A handscroll executed in very fine *kung-pi* manner on silk. Signed and dated 1310. A.

Ibid. The Dragon-boat Festival on the Chin-ming Lake. Handscroll. According to the inscription, the original of this picture was presented to the emperor in 1310. Twelve years later when the elder sister of the emperor asked for a similar picture, the painter made the present one, but apologized in writing for the poor execution due to his old age. Signed and dated 1323. Inscriptions by Yüan Chüeh and Liu Chi.

Sōgen, 46 (Chou Chih-ch'êng). The A-fang Palace. High buildings and trees rising over a misty river. Signed and dated 1321. A.

Ch'ing-kung ts'ang, 10 (Manchu Household collect.) A Man Seated on a Cliff overlooking a Misty Gorge. Fan-painting. Signed.

Chung-kuo, I, 111 (Ti P'ing-tzŭ collect.) A Hermit under a Tree with Two Attendants Receiving Peaches from a Monkey. Signed. C.

K.-k. shu-hua chi, XXIII. The Abode of the Immortals in the midst of a Misty Sea. A large coloured picture on silk. C.

Boston Museum. The Imperial Dragon Boat. Fan-painting. Attributed. *Cf.* Kokka 270. A.

Ibid. Hariti Nursing a Baby. Handscroll. Signed. A.

Ibid. The Palace of Prince T'êng in the time of T'ang T'ai-tsung. Album-leaf. The poem by Wang Po of T'ang, describing the palace, is copied by the painter Hsia Ming-yüan 夏明遠 of Ming who, according to a Chinese tradition, made a minutely executed design for an embroidery of this palace. The same composition is reproduced in a later picture (?) in the Freer Gallery (15.36) and also in a somewhat extended form in a picture in Laufer cat., pl.XXVII.

Nelson Gallery, Kansas City. An Elaborate Palace Building on a Terrace; misty Mountain Silhouettes. Album-leaf. Signed.

Indianapolis Art Institute (ex Chang Ts'ung-yü collect.) Demons Attacking the Glass Bowl Containing Hariti's Son. Handscroll. Signed. A.

Peking National Museum cat. The Imperial Dragon Boat. Handscroll. Seals of the painter, Hsiang Mo-lin and later collectors.

P'ang Yüan-chi cat. 2. An Imperial Summer Palace. Long handscroll. Signed and dated 1312. Colophons by two Yüan writers and a Ming writer.

WANG CH'ÊN 王臣, *t.* Wu-yün 五雲.

Unrecorded. Yüan, or possibly South Sung, period.

P'ang Yüan-chi cat. Add. 1. Bamboos. Poem by the painter.

WANG I 王繹, *t.* Ssŭ-shan 思善, *h.* Ch'ih-chüeh 癡絕.

Lived in Hangchou. Active *c.*1360. Portraits and landscapes. Author of a book on portrait-painting and on coloured paintings translated by Herbert Franke in *Oriental Art Magazine*, vol.III, No.1. H, 5. I, 54. L, 28. M, p.36.

Shên-chou, 5. High Mountains Rising along a River, after Tung Yüan. Handscroll. Signed and dated 1362.

Sōgen, 64 (Kuo Pao-ch'ang). Portrait of Yang Chu-hsi, in a landscape. The figure by Wang I, the trees and stones by Ni Tsan, dated 1363. A.

WANG KUEI 王珪, *t.* Chün-chang 君璋, *h.* Chung-yang Lao-jên 中陽老人.

From K'ai-fêng, moved to Ch'ang-shu, Kiangsu, in the Ta-tê era (1297–1307). Landscapes. I, 54. L, 28. M, p.36.

Tōsō, 149 (Lo Chên-yü collect.) The Hundred Buffaloes Grazing along the River. Part of a scroll. A?

WANG LIANG-CH'ÊN 王良臣, *h.* Yen-hsia Chu-jên 煙霞主人.
Unrecorded. Date uncertain.

Freer Gallery (16.240). A Long Hanging Branch of a Grape Vine Swayed by the Wind in the Moonlight. Signed. A.

WANG MÊNG 王蒙, *t.* Shu-ming 叔明, *h.* Huang-hao Shan-ch'iao 黃鶴山樵.
From Wu-hsing, Chekiang. B. *c.*1309, d. 1385 in prison. Nephew of Chao Mêng-fu; one of the "Four Great Masters" of the Yüan period. Landscapes. Learned from his uncle but followed mainly Tung Yüan and Chü-jan. H, 5. I, 54. L, 28. M, p.36.

K.-k. shu-hua chi, XXVII. Tung Shan Homestead at the Foot of High Mountains by the Water. Signed and dated 1343. *Cf.* Chinese cat., London Exhibition, p.158. C.

Tōsō, p.180 (Hsiao Fang-chün). A Rock from the Sung Mountains. Colophon by the painter, dated 1343. Two poems by Ch'ien-lung. C.

Ku-kung, XXIX. A Deep Gully Between Wooded Cliffs; Two Men on the Bridge in the foreground. Slight colours on silk. Signed and dated 1344. Poem by Ch'ien-lung. A?

Ku-kung collect. *Lin-ch'üan ch'ing-ch'ü t'u.* Mountain Gully with Tall Trees. Much repaired. Poem by the painter, dated 1346. Inscription by Wang To. Probably original, though in bad state.

Shên-chou ta-kuan, vol.16. Pavilions on the Mountain of the Immortals. Signed, dated 1348. Poems by Ni Tsan and Chang Yü. Reproduction blurred.

Sōraikan, I, 25 (Abe collect., Ōsaka Museum). A River Winding between Ridges of Wooded Mountains. Long handscroll. Signed and dated 1349. *Cf.* Kokka 556; Shōman. B?

Ōmura, II, 3 (Kikuchi collect.) A Hermit's Cottage under Pine-trees at the Foot of High Mountains. Signed and dated 1349. B?

Ibid. I, 1 (Takashima collect.) Two Men in a Cottage under Pine-trees by a Stream in the Mountains. Signed and dated 1350. Poems by Shên Chou, Ch'ien-lung and others. *Cf.* Chūgoku, II. B?

Ku-kung collect. *Yu-lin ch'ing-i t'u*: Enjoying the Beauty of the Forest. A scholar's abode at the foot of a mountain. Painted in light greyish tone. Signed and dated 1350.

Chūgoku, II. A Waterfall between High Mountains; a Clump of Pine-trees below. Signed and dated 1350. C?

Shina Nanga, I, 3. Steep Cliffs with a Waterfall; a Man in a Pavilion by the River. Handscroll. Signed and dated 1351. A.

K. Takashima collect., Kugenuma. Mountains with Waterfall; open pavilions below under leafy trees. Soft colours set off by spots of dark ink. Poem by the painter, dated 1351, and two other colophons. *Cf.* Liu, pl.34. A?

Chang Ta-ch'ien collect., 1954. The Summer Retreat in the Mountains: View over a Broad Stream with a Large Mountain-cone Rising in the Centre. Pavilions built over the water. Signed and dated 1354. A?

Tōan, II (Saitō collect.) A Retreat among Cassia-trees at the Foot of High Mountains. Long colophon by the painter, dated 1357. *Cf.* Nansō Ihatsu, IV, and Shina Meiga Shenshū, II. B.

K.-k. shu-hua chi, XIX. The Ya-i Study of Ch'ên Wei-yün, under Pine-trees in front of Steep Mountains. Signed and dated 1358. A?

Nansō Ihatsu, III. A Scholar's Retreat in the Mountains. Signed and dated 1360. B.

I-shu ts'ung-pien, 12. A River Winding through a wooded Mountain Valley. Fishermen in a Boat. Signed and dated 1361. A?

Chicago Art Institute. Quiet Life in a Wooded Glen. A man in his study under leafy trees at the foot of high mountains. Signed and dated 1361. A.

K.-k. shu-hua chi, II. A Man by a Mountain Stream Looking at the Waterfall. Painted together with Ni Tsan. Poems and colophons by both painters, Ni Tsan's dated 1361; and by Tung Ch'i-ch'ang. C.

Kuan Po-hêng collect. Wooded Mountain Ridge;

Buildings in the Gorge and a Man Seated by the Stream under Tall Pines. Signed and dated 1361. A?

Ku-kung collect. *Ch'iu-shan hsiao-ssŭ t'u.* A Mountain Ridge is rising steep, Tall Pine-trees below. Ink painting executed for Tsou Fu-lei, a Taoist priest. Signed and dated 1362.

Wang Shih-chieh, Taipei. The Study Pavilion of a Scholar in a Pine-grove near a rocky shore; the water is forming a cascade over the mountain wall in the background. Short handscroll. Inscription by the painter dated 1365.

Chung-kuo, I, 85 (Ti P'ing-tzŭ collect.) A Hermit's Abode in the Ch'ing-pien Mountains. Signed and dated 1366. Poem by Ch'ien-lung; colophon by Tung Ch'i-ch'ang. *Cf.* Shina Nanga, I, 2; Tōsō, p.172. A?

P'ang Yüan-chi Illust. cat., vol.III. Clumps of Bamboo Growing on the Hills by a Stream; a Scholar Seated in Contemplation. Signed and dated 1367. B?

Shina Nanga, III, 3. Hermits Gathering by a Stream under Pine-trees in the Mountains. Signed and dated 1367. A. *Cf.* Chūgoku, II. Another version of the picture in Shên Chou, 5.

Chang Ta-ch'ien collect., 1951. Landscape. Slightly coloured. Signed and dated 1367. A?

Kao Yen-yüeh, Hongkong. Pavilions under Large Pine-trees at the Foot of High Mountains. Signed and dated 1367. The picture is grey and worn.

Hui-hua kuan (ex-P'ang Yüan-chi). Staying in the Mountains on a Summer Day. Painted for Tung Hsüan. Signed and dated 1368. Poems by Lin Han and Ch'ien-lung. *Cf.* Tōsō, p.178, and P'ang Yüan-chi's Illust. cat., IV. A.

Ku-kung collect. *T'ao-yüan ch'un-hsiao t'u*: Spring Morning in the Peach-grove Temple. A fisherman in a boat. Slightly coloured. Poem and inscription by the painter, dated 1370. A?

Chung-kuo, I, 86. Ko Hung Moving his Residence; he is standing on a bridge which spans the stream between steep terraced rocks. Inscription with title of the picture by the painter. *Cf.* Shina Nanga, III, 6. A.

Ibid. I, 87 (formerly Ti P'ing-tzŭ collect.) A Deep Gully; the water rushes down from the ridge into a stream spanned by a bridge. Colophons by Ma Han-chung and Cha Shih-piao. *Cf.* Tōsō, p.173. B?

K.-k. shu-hua chi, XXXII. *Ch'iu-shan ts'ao-t'ang t'u.* The Autumn Mountains form a Ridge around the Bay; the scholar's straw-covered pavilion is shaded by a tree; a fisherman in a boat is lifting his net. Signed. Poem by Ch'ien-lung. A. Another version of the painting, dark in tone and without the Ch'ien-lung inscription, in the same collection.

Ku-kung collect. *Chu-shih liu-ch'üan t'u.* A Bamboo-grove. Bluish in the background and dark in the front. Excellent brushwork. Poems by the painter and by Yao Kung-shou. A?

Ibid. *Hua-ch'i yü-yin t'u.* A Fisherman in a Boat at the lower edge; a large bay between curving mountains. Soft silvery tone. Poem by the painter, and inscriptions by Shên Mêng-lin, dated 1393, and by another man. Photo by the Yen Kuang Co., Peking. A.

Ibid. Fantastically Hollowed and Split Mountains; two Pavilions with Scholars and large Pine-trees. Signed. The painting is much worn, but may be right. A?

Ibid. *Hua-ch'i shu-wu t'u.* A Mountain Village by a Stream. Inscription by the painter and by Chang Na. Part of an album called *Ming-hua hui-ts'ui.* A?

Chung-kuo ming-hua, 10. Small Pavilions at the Foot of Lofty Mountains, Two Men on the river-bank. Signed. C.

Wên-hua album, 1922. River View with Friends Meeting in a Pavilion. A saddled horse prepared for a journey. Short handscroll. Signed. C.

K.-k. shu-hua chi, XIV. Tilling the Soil in a Mountain Valley. Poems by the painter, by Ch'ien-lung and three other men. Colophon by Tung Ch'i-ch'ang. *Cf.* Chinese cat., London Exhibition, p.159. B?

Ibid. XXXIV. A Scholar's Pavilion by a Mountain Stream under Leafy Trees. Signed. Painted in colours on silk. A?

K.-k. chou-k'an, vol.1, 3. Misty Mountain Landscape. Album-leaf. Signed. B?

S.c.t.k. hsü-pien, VII. High Wooded Mountains. Signed. B?

Hui-hua kuan. The Lan-tien Village. The water is rushing down the hills; a man is seated in the pavilion on a terrace. Inscription by the painter. Much repaired. A.

Ibid. *Hsi-chiao ts'ao-t'ang t'u*: The Straw-covered Cottage in the Western Field. A man in a pavilion under budding trees; view over a river between rocky shores. Signed. A.

Mei-chan t'ê-k'an. Bamboo and an Old Tree by a Rockery. Signed; colophon by Yang Wei-chên.

Shanghai Museum (ex-Chou Hung-sun). A Scholar's Study in the Spring Mountains. Two pavilions under the large pines at the foot of a steep mountain. Long inscription by the painter. *Cf.* Tōsō, p.179. A.

Freer Gallery. A Homestead in a Fantastic Garden with Hollowed Rocks; Leafy Trees and Waterfalls by a River along a Mountain Ridge. Signed and dedicated to a man called Chang Chih. Short handscroll. B.

Ernest Erikson, New York. River View; Tall Bamboos on the near Shore and distant Mountains. Inscription by the painter in which he refers to Wên T'ung of the Sung period. *Cf.* Shên-chou ta-kuan, VII. Another version of the same picture is in the Ku-kung collect. A?

E. Lilly collect., Indianapolis. A Scholar's Retreat on a Rocky Promontory at the Foot of the Wei Mountain. Short handscroll. Signed. A.

Pageant, 348 (formerly Shao Fu-ying collect.) A Homestead in the Gorge of a steep Mountain. Signed. B?

Kokka 441 (Yamamoto collect.) Fishermen in Two Small Boats at the Foot of a Mountain Ridge. Album-leaf. Signed. Poems by Chang Yü (1333–1385) and four other contemporaries. *Cf.* Ōmura, I, 2; Nansō Ihatsu, IV; Tōsō, p.176; Bukkyō Bijutsu, 17. B.

Nansō Ihatsu, IV. An Old Man and a Crane in a Small Boat on a Mountain River. Signed. Poem by Ch'ien-lung. C.

Tōsō, p.174 (Kuan Mien-chün, now C. C. Wang, New York). The Homestead of Mr. Su-an under Pine-trees at the foot of towering mountains. Signed. A.

C. C. Wang, New York. Fishing in the Ching-i River; a homestead by a river at the foot of a mountain ridge. Poem by the painter and two other men. *Cf.* Cleveland Exhibition cat. 30. A.

Ibid. Large Bending and Twisting Pines along a Steep Mountain-path. A pavilion below and two men approaching. Signed and dedicated to I-yün Shang-jên. A?

Chêng Tê-k'un, Cambridge. Rocky Mountain with Waterfalls and Tall Pine-trees at the lower edge, surrounding the scholar's pavilion. Poem by the painter. A?

Tōsō, p.175 (Shên Jui-lin). A Temple in a Mountain-gorge. Signed. Poem by Ch'ien-lung. B?

Ibid., p.177 (formerly Shao Fu-ying collect.) A Solitary Angler in a Boat on the Stream near some Pine-trees. Signed. C.

Chūgoku, II. A Mountain Stream with Fishermen in Two Boats; a Grove of Pine-trees on the Shore. Large album-leaf (?). Inscription by the painter. Six poems. A?

Ibid. II. Thatched Cottages of Ts'ui Yen-hui by a Stream in the Mountains. Handscroll. Signed. Long inscriptions by the painter and by two contemporaries.

J. P. Dubosc, Lugano. The House of Fragrant Orchids, *Chih-lan shih*. A scholar study between old trees in a mountainous landscape. Ink and slight colour. Short handscroll. Painter's name written in seal characters. Colophons by K'o Chiu-ssŭ and four other contemporaries. Calligraphy by Wên Chia and Tung ch'i-ch'ang.

Peking National Museum cat. Tall Pines and Waterfalls. Said to be signed and dated in the first year of the Ta-tê era (1297), *i.e.* before the birth of the painter.

Ibid. Ten Thousand Valleys; Pines in Wind. Signed.

Ibid. T'ai Looking at the Waterfall, after Tung Yüan. Signed.

P'ang Yüan-chi cat. 2. The I-ch'ing Hall. Handscroll. Signed. Colophons by Hu Yen, dated 1405.

Ibid. 7 (now N. P. Wang, Hong-kong). A Temple in the Mountains in Autumn. Signed, dedicated to Ch'ên Ju-yen.

Ibid. 7. Bare Trees and Bamboos by a Rock. Signed. Poems by two contemporaries.

Ibid. 7. A Temple in the Mountains in Autumn. Two poems by the painter.

Ibid. Add. 1. The Island of the Immortals. Handscroll. Signed. Poems by two contemporaries.

WANG MIEN 王冕, *t.* Yüan-chang 元章, *h.* Lao-ts'un 老村, Chu-shih Shan-nung 煮石山農.
From K'uai-chi, Chekiang. B. 1335, d. 1407. Specialized in plum-blossoms. I, 55, 1. L, 28, 2. M, p.36. N,I, 5–7. O,7.

Hui-hua kuan. Three Bamboos in outline. Colophon by the painter, dated 1349.

Ibid. Branch of a Blossoming Plum-tree. Poem by the painter. Mounted on the same scroll as Chao Yung's

Fishing in a Mountain Stream and Chu Tê-jun's Two Men in a Boat. *Cf.* I-shu ch'uan-t'ung, 9.

Ku-kung collect. Plum-blossoms. Poem by the painter, dated 1353; another poem by T'ang Su.

Chung-kuo, I. Plum-blossoms. Signed. Five poems by the painter. one dated 1355. Later poetic inscriptions by Chu Yün-ming, Wên Chêng-ming, Wang Ch'ung, Hsü Lin, T'ang Yin and Ch'ên I. A.

Chung-hua album. Plum-blossoms. Handscroll. Signed and dated 1355. A.

Tōsō, p.196 (Shao Fu-ying collect.) A Branch of Plum-tree over the Water. Signed. Colophon and poem, dated 1355. A.

Nanga Taisei, XVI, 30, 31. Widely Spreading Branches of a Blossoming Plum-tree. Long handscroll. Signed and dated 1355.

Ku-kung collect. *Nan-chih ch'un-tsao t'u.* A Long Branch of Blossoming Plum-tree, hanging down in a double curve. The background is tinted and the flowers white. Poem by the painter, dated 1357. (The year *ting-ping* should be read *ting-yu*, *i.e.* 1357.)

Ku-kung collect. A Branch of Plum-blossom combined with a Branch of Bamboo painted by Wu Chên. The painters have added their own poems to these records of their brushes. *Cf.* K.-k. chou-k'an, 118. A.

Po-mei chi. Plum-blossoms. Signed. Poem by the painter. Colophons.

Kokka 302. A Branch of Plum-tree. Signed. Poems. A.

Shimbi, XVI. A Blossoming Plum-tree. Part of a scroll.

Tōsō, p.197 (Nelson Gallery, Kansas City). A Branch of a Plum-tree. Poem by the monk Fu-yüan. A?

Kao Yin-yüeh, Hongkong. Plum-blossoms. Signed. A.

C. C. Wang, New York. A Hanging Branch of Plum-blossoms. Ink on silk. Poem by the painter. Writing at the top by Ku Ta-tien. *Cf.* Nanga Taisei. A.

WANG TI-CHIEN 王迪簡, *t.* T'ing-chi 庭吉, *h.* Chi-yin 蕺隱.
From Chekiang. Yüan period. Narcissi. H, 5. M, p.35.

Nansō, 4 (Prince Konoe collect.) A Narcissus Plant. Poem by the painter and his seals.

WANG YÜAN 王淵, *t.* Jo-shui 若水, *h.* Tan-hsüan 澹軒.
From Hang-chou. Active *c.*1310–1350. Pupil of Chao Mêng-fu. Flowers, birds and landscapes. H, 5. I, 53. M, p.35.

Peking National Museum. Scroll-reproduction. River Landscape. The trees along the shore bending over the water; two egrets on a stone in the foreground. Handscroll. Signed and dated 1310. B.

Sōgen 49 (Shanghai Museum). Two Turkeys on a Rockery. Signed and dated 1344. A.

Yūrintaikan, II (formerly Yamamoto). A White Cock under Peony Flowers. Signed and dated 1345. Poem by Ch'ien-lung. B?

K.-k. shu-hua chi, XXXV. A Bird on a Young Peach-tree and some Bamboos; Ducks sleeping below. Signed and dated 1346. A.

C. C. Wang, New York. Bamboos and a Blossoming Gardenia Growing by a Rock. Two mandarin ducks in the water. Signed and dated 1347. A.

C. T. Loo Successor, Frank Caro, New York (ex Chang Ts'ung-yü collect.) Two Quails at the Foot of a Rock; Bamboos and Dry Brambles behind; Small Birds Soaring above. Signed and dated 1347. *Cf.* Toronto, 7.

Lilly collect., Indianapolis. Flowers, Bamboos and Small Birds. Signed and dated 1347. Poem by Hsü Chin. A.

Chang Ta-ch'ien cat., vol.IV. Peonies. Album-leaf. Four poems written at the top of the painting; the longest one is copied by Li Shêng and dated 1347.

Ku-kung, XVI. Two Wild Geese among Reeds on a Shore. Dedicated to a friend by the painter. A?

Former National Museum, Peking. A Hawk Chasing a Thrush. Signed. Colophons by Ch'ên Chi-ju and others. *Cf.* Chinese cat., London Exhibition, p.156. B?

Hui-hua kuan. A Large Pheasant on a Rock; Blossoming Magnolia, Bamboos and other Plants. Bright colours on silk. Signed.

Mei-chan t'ê-k'an. Cock in a Rockery. Signed. Poem by a contemporary. B.

Kokka 56 (Ueno collect.) Birds in a Flowering Tree by a Stream; a Pheasant on the opposite Shore. B.

Ibid. 157 (Marquis Kuroda). A Dragonfly on a Pea-vine. Album-leaf. *Cf.* Hikkōen. B.

Ibid. 173 (K. Magoshi). A Branch of Wild Camellia. Album-leaf. B.

Ibid. 337 (Baron Kawasaki). Two Pheasants and Rose-mallows. *Cf.* Kawasaki cat., 21. C.

Ibid. 579 (Katō collect., Tōkyō). A Spring Landscape. Fan-painting. B.

Shimbi, XI (Shokoku-ji). Pheasants, Bamboo and Rose-mallows. B?

Hikkōen, pl.56. Two Wagtails on a Lotus Plant. Album-leaf. B.

Boston Museum. A Small Bird on a Thin Branch. Ink-painting of later date. The poem is signed by the painter Yo Tai (active in the 16th cent.) C.

Shina Kachō Gasatsu. Mandarin Ducks on a River and Birds in a Willow; Pheasants on a Rockery and Mynah-birds in a Tree. A pair of pictures. C.

Ibid. Chrysanthemum Flowers. Album-leaf. C.

Ibid. Three White Herons on a Wintry Day. Two standing on the river bank, the third in an old tree. C.

Chūgoku, I. A Man Reading in a Thatched Cottage on a River-bank; cloudy mountains on the other side of the river. Short handscroll. Signed and dedicated to a man called Tê-ch'ang.

S.c.t.k. hsü-pien, VII. Waterfowl on a Flowery Bank. Part of a handscroll. Signed.

Ibid. IX. Fisherman on a Flooded Bank. A bush swept by the water just off the bank. B.

Metropolitan Museum, New York (50.157). The Hundred Flowers. Handscroll. Painted in colours on silk. Signed. B?

Sōraikan, I, 21 (Abe collect.) Sparrows Gathering at a Tuft of Bamboo, Two Quails on the ground. After Huang Ch'üan's picture of Bamboos and Birds. Signed. Poem by Ch'ien-lung. *Cf.* Sōgen 50. A.

Tōsō, p.159 (Kuo Pao-ch'ang collect.) Two Mynah Birds on a Blossoming Plum-tree. Signed. Poem by Ch'ien-lung. B?

Nezu collect., Tōkyō. Peach-tree and a Parrakeet. *Cf.* London Exhibition cat. 1120. C.

Peking National Museum cat. Birds Playing in a Lotus Pond. Album-leaf, mounted on a handscroll. Signed. Colophons by Ch'iu Yüan, K'o Chiu-ssŭ and later men.

P'ang Yüan-chi cat. 7 and Illustr. cat. 1940, vol.V. A Hen with Five Chickens; Lilies, Bamboos and Rocks. Signed. Colophons by Yang Wei-chên and later men.

Ibid. 11. Hibiscus Flowers. Album-leaf. Seal of the painter.

Ibid. Add. 1. A Cock, a Hen and Three Chickens by a Rockery. Signed. Poems by contemporaries.

WEI CHIU-TING 衛九鼎, *t.* Ming-hsüan 明鉉.

From T'ien-t'ai, Chekiang. Active *c.*1350–1370. Landscapes and boundary paintings. Followed Wang Chên-p'êng. H, 5. M, p.671.

Ōmura, I, 11 (Manchu Household collect.) River-landscape; divided by a mountain ridge; temples and minor buildings on the shores. Album-leaf. Signed and dated 1352. Poem by Ch'ien-lung. *Cf.* Chūgoku, II.

Ku-kung, IV. The Nymph of the Lo River Walking on the Waves. Poem by Ni Tsan, dated 1368.

WU CHÊN 吳鎮, *t.* Chung-kuei 仲圭, *h.* Mei-hua Tao-jên 梅花道人.

From Chia-hsing, Chekiang. B. 1280, d. 1354. One of the "Four Great Masters" of the Yüan period. Prominent as a poet and calligraphist, particularly in *ts'ao-shu* style. As a landscape painter, he followed Chü-jan and in his bamboo paintings, Wên T'ung. H, 5. I, 54. L, 7. M, p.160.

K.-k. shu-hua chi, IX. Two Old Pine-trees on a Stony Beach. Signed and dated 1328. *Cf.* Chinese cat., London Exhibition, p.150. A.

Kao Yen-yüeh, Hongkong. River Landscape with Fishermen in a Boat; Hills beyond. Signed and dated 1336.

Ku-kung collect. A Landscape with Rounded Mountain Peaks. Short handscroll. Signed and dated 1336. Part of the scroll called *Yüan-jên chi-chin.* A?

C. C. Wang, New York. A Dry Tree and Some Bamboos by a Stone. A large ink painting on silk. Inscription by the painter, dated 1338. *Cf.* Cleveland Exhibition cat. 29. A?

K.-k. shu-hua chi, XI. A Lonely Fisherman on the Tung-t'ing Lake. Poem by the painter, dated 1341; another by Ch'ien-lung. *Cf.* Chinese cat., London Exhibition, p.152. B?

Ibid. XLI. View over a Broad River between Low Hills; Two Men in a Fishing-boat. Poem by the painter, dated 1342. In the manner of Chü-jan. A.

Ming-hua lin-lang. Returning in a Boat on a Mountain Stream. In the manner of Chü-jan. Signed and dated 1342. Poem by Ch'ien-lung. *Cf.* K.-k. chou-k'an, vol.2, 32. A.

Ku-kung collect. Returning Boat on a Stream; grassy mountain slopes. Large album-leaf. Signed and dated 1342. A?

Freer Gallery (11.495). A Steep Rock by the Water, Two Men in a Boat. Signed and dated 1342. Sketchy album-leaf. B?

Tōsō 189 (Kuan Mien-chün). A Bamboo Stem and a Bamboo Shoot. Signed and dated 1343. B?

Kokka 500 (Lo Chia-lun, Taipei). Eight Views from the Chia-ho district: Misty Waters, Mountains and Villages. Long handscroll. Signed and dated 1344. Part of the picture in Sōgen 60. A.

Nansō, I (Prince Konoe). Bamboos by a Rock. Poem by the painter, dated 1344. A?

Ōgawa collect., Kyōto. A River Valley Overshadowed by Trees; a Man in a Boat. Signed and dated 1344. B.

Tōsō p.188 (Yang Hêng). A Sailing-boat on the River, a Two-storied Pavilion behind; trees in the foreground. Signed and dated 1344. Poem by T'ang Yin. C.

Ibid. p.187 (Huang Chih). Willows on the Low Banks of a River below the Hills. Colophon by the painter, dated 1345. C.

Ku-kung collect. A Branch of Bamboo combined with a Branch of Plum-blossom painted by Wang Mien. Both painters have added a poem to their respective pictures. Wu Chên's inscription dated 1346. *Cf.* K.-k. chou-k'an, 120. A.

K.-k. shu-hua chi, II. Two Slender Bamboos by a Stone. Colophon by the painter, dated 1347. *Cf.* Chinese cat., London Exhibition, p.151; K.-k. ming-jên hua-chu chi. A.

Freer Gallery (ex-Ti P'ing-tzŭ collect.) A Slender Branch of Bamboo in Wind. Colophon by the painter, dated 1350. *Cf.* Chung-kuo, I, 91 and Shina Nanga, II, 1. A.

Wu Chên mo-chu p'u (Palace Museum album, 1936). Twenty studies of Bamboo. Signed. Poems and colophons by the painter, dated 1350. A.

K.-k. shu-hua chi, VII. A Slender Branch of Bamboo. Poem by the painter, dated 1350. *Cf.* K.-k. ming-jên hua-chu chi. A.

C. T. Loo's Successor, Frank Caro, New York. A Branch of Bamboo. A long poem by the painter, dated at the age of 71, *i.e.* 1350.

Ibid. (ex-Chang Ts'ung-yü). A Thin Bamboo Spray Growing from a Rock. Long inscription by the painter. *Cf.* Toronto, 9. A.

Freer Gallery. The Fishermen's Pleasure. The men are all placed in small separate boats; the river is winding between rocky islets and mountainous shores. At the end of the scroll some high buildings. Each scene accompanied by a short poem. The colophon at the end is dated 1352, but the picture was done ten years earlier. A.

Hui-hua kuan (ex-P'ang Yüan-chi). A Fisherman in his Boat among Reeds near the Shore; Alighting Wild Geese. Ink on silk. Poem by the painter. A?

Ibid. The Top of a Bamboo Branch; a Stone below. Long inscription in running style by the painter. A.

Shanghai Museum. Tops of Two Bamboo Branches. Long inscription by the painter. A.

Shên-chou, II. An Old Pine-tree. Signed. B?

I-shu ts'ung-pien, 23. Bamboos in Wind Growing in a Rockery. Signed. B.

Chung-kuo, I, 90 (Ti P'ing-tzŭ collect.) Rapids in the Mountains; Tall Trees and Small Buildings along the Mountain Stream. Poem by the painter. *Cf.* Shina Nanga, I, 1 and Tōsō, p.185. B?

K.-k. shu-hua chi, XXIII. A Lonely Fisherman on an Autumn River below a Steep Cliff. Poems by the painter and by Ch'ien-lung. A.

K.-k. chou-k'an, vol.1, 2. A Mountain River. Album-leaf. Signed. A?

Chung-hua wên-wu chi-ch'êng, IV, 365. *Ch'ing-chiang ch'un-hsiao t'u*: The Clear River on a Spring Morning. A very large picture, in the manner of Chü-jan. Signed. Colophon by Tung Ch'i-ch'ang. *Cf.* Nanking Exhib. cat. 58. A?

Hakubundō album, 1917. An album of eight sketches of Rocks and Trees. The last one in Mi-style. Seal of the painter. *Cf.* Tōan, pp.13–15. B?

Shina Nanga, III, 7 (P'ang Yüan-chi, later J. D. Chên, Hongkong). Mountains after Rain, Large Trees and a Cottage. Inscription by the painter. *Cf.* Shên-chou ta-kuan, vol.8; Tōsō, p.186. B?

S.c.t.k. hsü-pien, III. Two Birds Asleep on a Bough. Poem by Wu K'uan. B?

Ōmura, II, 1 (Wang Shih-yüan). Two Dragon-pines with Intertwined Stems. Poem by the painter. A different version in Shên Chou, II. Possibly later.

Nansō Ihatsu, III. Pavilions and Temples in a Mountain-gorge. Poem by the painter and dedicated to Hsü I, who served as a censor about the middle of the century. A?

Nansō Ihatsu, III. A Dry Shrub and some Bamboos Growing through a Garden Rock. Signed. A?

Sōraikan, I, 22 (Abe collect.) Two sections of a scroll, each with Men in a Boat. Much damaged. B?

Sōgen 61 (P'ang Yüan-chi). Mountain Landscape after Rain. Poem by the painter. *Cf.* P'ang Yüan-chi Cat. 7. B?

Chūgoku, II. Village in the Mountains; a wanderer approaching on the path below. Poem by the painter. B.

Musée Guimet. Bamboos. Album-leaf. Signed. C.

Boston Museum. Bamboos in Wind. Poem by the painter. B.

Chang Ta-ch'ien Cat. I, p.13. Fisherman in a Boat near the Shore under Overhanging Trees. Poem by the painter. Sketchy album-leaf. A?

Ibid. vol.IV. A Slender Bamboo and Orchid by a Rock. Long inscription by the painter. B.

P'ang Yüan-chi Cat. 2. Bamboos. Long handscroll. Poems and colophons by the painter, dated 1351.

WU T'AI-SU 吳太素, *t.* Hsiu-chang 秀章, *h.* Sung-chai 松齋.

A native of K'uai-chi, Chekiang. Yüan period. Painted plum-blossoms and wrote a treatise on this subject, *Sung-chai mei-p'u*. L, 7, 1. M, p.160.

Sekai Bijutsu Zenshū, 14, pl.77 (Daisen-ji, Yamanashi). Branches of Blossoming Plum and Pine. Painted on silk, much damaged. Two seals of the artist.

Bijutsu-shi, 18 (1955). A Branch of a Blossoming Plum-tree. Poem and seals of artist.

WU T'ING-HUI 吳廷暉.

From Wu-hsing, Chekiang. 14th century. Landscapes in blue and green; flowers and birds. H, 5. M, p.160.

Ku-kung, XV. A Dragon-boat Race on a River below a Misty Temple Hill. *Cf.* Chinese cat., London Exhibition, p.167.

YANG WEI-CHÊN 楊維楨, *t.* Lien-fu 廉夫, *h.* T'ieh-ya 鐵崖.

From Chu-chi, Chekiang. B. 1296, d. 1370. Best known as a calligraphist; wrote colophons on many pictures by contemporaries. I, 39.

Chung-kuo, I, 107 (Ti P'ing-tzŭ collect.) Drinking Tea among Bare Trees by a Stream. Poem by the painter, dated 1342.

K.-k. shu-hua chi, III. A Knotted Old Pine. Poems by the painter and two of his pupils.

Ibid. XXII. A Crowing Cock Standing below a Tree on a Rock. Signed.

Suchiku (Oguri). Sailing Boats on a Lake; a Temple on the Shore. Album-leaf. Poem, signed. A?

YAO T'ING-MEI 姚廷美.
From Wu-hsing, Chekiang. According to the inscription on the following picture he was active about the middle of the 14th century.

C. T. Loo Successor, New York. The Scholar's Leisure. The little study is seen between two trees on the river-bank. Short handscroll. Poem by the painter dated 1360, and an inscription by Ch'ien-lung. *Cf.* Cleveland Exhibition cat. 34.

YAO YEN-CH'ING 姚彥卿.
From Wu-hsing, Chekiang. Active at the end of 13th century. Followed as a landscape-painter the style of Kuo Hsi. H,5 M, 286.

Hui-hua kuan. Dry Trees on a Rocky River-bank; Fishing Boats on the Water. Ink only. Short handscroll. A?

Boston Museum. Temples in a Mountain Rivine; Rushing Water and Leafless Trees. Inscribed with the painter's name. Darkened. B.

YEN HUI 顏輝, t. Ch'iu-yüeh 秋月.
From Chiang-shan, Chekiang. 14th century. Buddhist and Taoist figures, landscapes. H, 5. I, 53. M, p.710.

Chêng Tê-k'un, Cambridge. Men in Boats Fishing with Cormorants, while others are Drawing their Nets. Handscroll. Ink and slight colour. Signed and dated 1339. Colophon by Yeh Kung-cho.

K.-k. shu-hua chi, IV. Winter Landscape. Yüan An (of the Han dynasty) lying in the Snow; the mayor approaching in an ox-cart. *Cf.* Chinese cat., London Exhibition, p.165. C.

Ibid. XXXV. Two Monkeys on the Branch of a P'i-pa-tree. Signature incomplete. A.

Tōyō, IX (Chion-ji, Kyōto). A pair of pictures, one representing the Taoist Li T'ieh-kuai watching his *anima* mounting on high, and the other his companion Liu Hai-chan with the three-legged toad. The former picture with the seal of the painter. A. *Cf.* Kokka 29; Shimbi, II; Tōsō, pp.166, 167.

Kokka 207 (Count Matsudaira). Three Immortals, Liu Hai-chan, Li T'ieh-kuai and Lü Tung-pin. C.

Ibid. 231 (Marquis Inoue). The Priest Wên-yen Sewing his Mantle; a servant is seated before him. Poem by Yün-an. C.

Ibid. 279 (R. Murayama). Two Arhats from a series of sixteen. One is Seated under a Cliff, attended by a monk; the other meditating in a Cave. B.

Ibid. (Count M. Tanaka). A Hermit Standing on Billowing Water. C.

Tōyō, IX (National Museum, Tōkyō). A pair of pictures representing Han-shan and Shih-te. *Cf.* Kokka, 298; Kawasaki cat. 1. A?

Sōgen Meigashū, 6. A Splashing Wave and the Moon Rising behind a Mountain. Album-leaf. *Cf.* Kokka 164; Hikkōen. B.

Hui-hua kuan. The Taoist Immortal Li T'ieh-kuai as a Beggar Seated on a Stone. Ink and colour on silk. Very dark. A?

Kao Yin-yüeh, Hongkong. A Monk Seated on a Projecting Rock; a Monkey in a Tree above reaches down a Ring. Colours on silk. Signed. B.

Nelson Gallery, Kansas City. White-robed Kuanyin Seated on a Rock by a Waterfall. B. *Cf.* Tōyō, IX; Kokka 298.

C. T. Loo Successor, New York (ex-Chang Ts'ung-yü collect.) Chung K'uei Riding on a Donkey, returning from the Hunt (?). He is preceded by a number of devils with falcon and eagle and a large tiger, while others are fighting with spears, bows and swords. Handscroll. Several colophons with the painter's name; the first dated 1358.

YÜ-WÊN KUNG-LIANG 宇文公諒, *t.* Tzŭ-chên 子貞.

From Ch'êng-tu, Szechuan; moved to Wu-hsing, Chekiang. *Chin shih* in 1333 and became a Han-lin member. *Cf.* Note in *K.-k shu-hua chi*, XXXVIII.

K.-k. shu-hua chi, XXXVIII. Wooded Mountain Landscape, in Wang Mêng's manner. Poem by the painter, dated 1346.

YÜN-KANG TAO-SHIH 雲岡道士.

A Taoist monk; friend of Ni Tsan. *Cf.* Note on the following picture.

Chung-kuo, I, 117 (Ti P'ing-tzŭ collect.) Two Magpies on a Rock and some Bamboos. A poem and a colophon by a writer of the Ming period, dated 1466.

YUNG-T'IEN 用田.

The painter is unrecorded in China, but mentioned in *Kundaikan Sayuchōki*. He is not the same person as Sung-t'ien, though both painted squirrels of similar kinds.

Kokka 413 (Marquis Asano). A Squirrel on a Pine Branch. Album-leaf. Attributed.

Kokka 460 (Kawasaki cat. 30). Two Squirrels on Pine Branches. Seal of the painter.

Tōsō, p.219 (Makita collect.) Two Squirrels on the Stem and the Branch of a Bamboo. Seal of the painter.

Anonymous Paintings of the Yüan Period

1. *Taoist and Buddhist*

K.-k. shu-hua chi, XXIII. An Indian Monk Seated on a Rock explaining a Sūtra, flowers falling down upon him.

Ibid. XXXII. The Three Taoist Patriarchs (San Ch'ing) Seated under Trees, and some Devotees.

Ibid. XXXVI. Two Arhats in Conversation by a Rockery.

Ibid. XXXVII. A set of three pictures: the middle picture represents A Buddha Enthroned between Two Monks. Each side-piece Four Bodhisattvas.

Ibid. XXXVII. Bodhidharma Seated on a Rock. Poems by Chang Yü (1277–1348), by Ch'ien-lung and four others.

Kokka 126. Mañjuśrī as a Youthful Monk, in a Mantle of Plaited Straw. Half length. Inscription by the monk Tsu-ming, dated 1353.

Ibid. 286 (Ryūko-in, Kyōto). Five pictures from a series of the Sixteen Arhats. Inscription by Ichinei (1247–1317).

Ibid. 311 (Tokai-an, Kyōto). Five pictures from a series of the Sixteen Arhats, some of the Arhats are attended by servants.

Ibid. 337 (Private collect., Japan). The Fourth Arhat as a White-bearded Man Seated in a Root-chair. Dated 1345.

Ibid. 387 (Marquis Asano). Yün-fang and Lü Tung-pin.

Ibid. 526 (Baron Dan). Two pictures from a series of twelve: one representing a Bodhisattva; the other, a Taoist female Deity followed by two Women Attendants.

Sōgen 80 (S. Yamaoka collect.) Manjusri on the Lion. Poem by Chi-an.

Ibid. 85 (P. Inoue collect.) Han-shan and Shih-tê.

Sōgen Appendix 17 (Daitoku-ji). Kuanyin at the Sea-shore (sometimes attributed to Wu Tao-tzŭ).

Ars Asiatica, I, pp.4,5 (Collect. Goloubew). The Immortal Lü Tung-pin. Full length.

Freer Gallery. Hsia-ma with his Toad under a Large Tree in the Moonlight. *Cf.* Amer. collect., p.116.

Boston Museum. Kuanyin with the Fish-basket. Inscription by Mu-an, dated 1315. *Cf.* Amer. collect., 129.

Ibid. Han-shan under a Large Willow-tree. *Cf.* Amer. collect., p.146.

Freer Gallery. Šakyamuni as an Ascetic. *Cf.* Amer. collect., p.147.

Boston Museum. Šakyamuni Seated on a Chariot, Drawn by a Bullock among the Stars and Constellations. *Cf.* Amer. collect., p.159.

Ibid. Buddha Expounding the Law, Surrounded by Bodhisattvas and Devas. *Cf.* Amer. collect., p.160.

Ibid. Mañjušrī Seated on a Lion. Style of Chang Ssŭ-kung; mentioned under his name. *Cf.* Amer. collect., p.179.

Freer Gallery. The Buddha Enthroned and Preaching; Eight Bodhisattvas. *Cf.* Amer. collect., p.185.

Ibid. A Bodhisattva and two Attendants. *Cf.* Amer. collect., p.186.

Kyōto Museum. Mañjušrī in a Chariot, Drawn by the Elephant; Two Grooms are leading the Animal. Replica in private collect., Stockholm.

Boston Museum. Šakyamuni and two Bodhisattvas Standing on Clouds.

Ibid. An Arhat Attended by a Maid who offers him some Peaches.

Ibid. An Arhat Holding a Reliquary.

Ibid. Arhats Assembling in a Garden, attended by Servants.

Revue des Arts Asiatiques, tome XI, fascicule 2. Wall-paintings in Kuang-sheng ssŭ, Shansi, representing Taoistic subjects and theatrical scenes. Dated 1326.

Louvre. A Judgement Scene: The Sixth King of Hell Surrounded by Attendants; below, Scene of Torture.

National Museum, Stockholm. Kuanyin with the Fish-basket. *Cf.* picture in the Boston Museum, dated 1315.

Ibid. A Taoist Immortal Seated on the Ground Holding a Small Gilt Casket in his Raised Hand.

Cincinnati Museum of Art (formerly Chang Ts'ung-yü). Portraits of Four Scholars. Handscroll, colour on paper. Colophon by Su Ch'ang-ling, dated 1354.

Chung-kuo, I, 122. Bodhidharma Meditating in a Cave in the Snowy Mountains.

2. *Figure Compositions and Portraits*

Ku-kung, XXI. Two Men under one Umbrella Passing a Bridge leading to a Garden Gate where a Woman is Standing.

Ibid. XXXII. Seven Boys Performing a New Year's Play on the House Porch.

K.-k. shu-hua chi, XIII. Scholars Studying and Practising Calligraphy in a Garden.

Ibid. XV. Scholars Examining Paintings in an open Pavilion. Servants gathering.

Ibid. XVIII. A School for Small Children. Some in the house, others playing in the garden.

Ibid. XXIX. Shooting Wild Geese. Huntsmen on Horseback Passing through a Mountain Defile in Snow. *Cf.* Chinese cat., London Exhibition, p.174.

Ibid. XXXIX. A Bird-merchant with his Stand Offering his Goods to a Lady with two Children on a Garden Terrace in Spring.

Sōgen 82 (G. Harada). Chao-chün Mounting a Horse with the Aid of some Servants to start her Journey to Mongolia.

Ars Asiatica, I, p.17 (Collect. Rivière). Portrait of a Priest.

3. *Palaces and Buildings*

Ku-kung, XVII. A Portion of the Emperor Han Wu-ti's Gorgeous Palace Compound, known as Chien-chang. Handscroll.

Ibid. XVIII. The Palace of Prince T'eng. Poem by Ch'ien-lung.

K.-k. shu-hua chi, XXII. A Two-storied Pavilion by a Broad River. *Cf.* Chinese cat., London Exhibition, p.173.

Ars Asiatica, I, p.32 (Collect. Goloubew). Palatial Pavilions on a High Terrace. Album-leaf.

4. *Dragons and Fishes*

Kokka 381 (Baron Iwasaki). A Perch. Handscroll.

5. *Landscapes*

Chung-kuo, I, 115 (Ti P'ing-tzŭ collect.) An Old Scholar in a Boat, Paddled along the Shore.

Ibid. I, 123 (Ti P'ing-tzŭ collect.) Fantastic Mountains in Snow; Poet on Donkey Crossing the Bridge.

Ku-kung, XIV. Li Po in a Boat Enjoying the Moonlight. Short handscroll. Seals of K'o Chiu-ssŭ and Mi Wan-chung.

Ibid. XX. Two Fishermen in Boats; their Homes on the Promontory; Mountains in the background.

Ibid. XXX. Scholars Enjoying themselves in a Pavilion by a Mountain Stream.

K.-k. shu-hua chi, III. Cloudy Mountains, after Mi Fei. Poem by Ch'ien-lung.

Ibid. VI. Blue Mountains and White Clouds. A misty valley at their foot. Short handscroll. Poem by Ch'ien-lung.

Ibid. IX. Leafless Trees on the Rocky Shore of a River.

Ibid. XI. Mountain in Spring. A temple at the bottom of a gorge. Poem by Yang Wei-chên.

Ibid. XVII. A Richly Wooded Mountain in Autumn. A homestead by a river. Handscroll.

Ibid. XIX. Buildings with Figures by a River. Large mountains covered by snow filling the field.

Ibid. XXXI. Homeward Bound in Wind and Rain. A boat with two men steering towards the pavilion on the shore.

Ibid. XXXIII. River Landscape and Garden Scenery in Snow.

Kokka 108. Pavilion on a Cliff, a Man and his Servant Walking under Overhanging Pines. Album-leaf.

Ibid. 260 (ex-Tuan Fang collect.) Mountains by a River in Spring.

Ibid. 273 (Marquis Inouye). Winter Landscape. Poem by the monk Ching-tz'ŭ (1280–1361).

Sōgen 79 (Prince Chichibu). River Landscape, Two Men Seated in a Pavilion Surrounded by Chrysanthemum Flowers.

Ibid. 83 (Chin K'ai-fang). Hsiao I and the Lan-t'ing Manuscript: landscape with a man on horseback approaching a temple.

Ibid. 84 (Jên Chên-t'ing). A Wooded Mountain in Summer, after Chü-jan.

Freer Gallery. A Mountain Gorge in Winter, Many Travellers. *Cf.* Amer. collect., p.143.

Nelson Gallery, Kansas City. A River View with Fishing-boats. Pointed mountain peaks in the background. Handscroll.

6. *Animals*

Ku-kung, XXXIV. A Taoist Fairy with a Basket of Fungi Seated between a Lion and a Tiger.

K.-k. shu-hua chi, XLIII. A Tartar on Horseback by a River.

Sōgen 81 (Masaki). A Groom Leading a Lean Horse.

Ars Asiatica, I, p.23 (Collect. Doucet). A Horse called "White as Frost". Album-leaf.

Boston Museum. A Dog. Album-leaf. Attributed to Mao I. *Cf.* Amer. collect., p.115.

Freer Gallery. A Dodging Horse led by a Mongol. *Cf.* Amer. collect., p.120.

7. *Flowers and Birds*

Ku-kung, XIII. Two Wild Geese under a Willow

Ibid. XXII. A Branch of Autumn Hollyhock with Two Flowers.

K.-k. shu-hua chi, II. Two Wild Geese among Reeds and a Heron.

Ibid. IV. Three Herons on the Shore and Small Birds in a Plum-tree in Snow.

Ibid. V. Ten Crows in an Old Tree.

Ibid. XI. A Tuft of Giant Rice.

Ibid. XXI. Six Quails by a Rock and Small Birds on Stalks of Millet. *Cf.* Chinese cat., London Exhibition, p.175.

Ibid. XXVII. Two Ducks among Peony Flowers.

Ibid. XXX. Lotus Flowers and Bamboos in a Vase, Fungi in a Pot, "Buddha's Hands" and Peaches on a Plate.

Ibid. XXXI. A Cock, a Hen and Chickens under Peony Flowers.

Ibid. XXXVI. Flowers of the New Year's Day in a Vase, Fruits in a Plate and Toys.

Ibid. XLIII. Doves, Sparrows and Early Spring Flowers. Poem by Ch'ien-lung.

Ibid. XLIV. A Cassia-tree.

Chinese cat., London Exhibition, p.176. Two Pheasants and Small Birds in a Bamboo Grove.

Shimbi, IV (Hompōji). A pair of pictures representing Lotus Flowers. *Cf.* Tōsō, pp.211, 212.

Sōgen Meigashū, 63, 64 (Koto-in). A pair of pictures representing Peony Flowers. *Cf.* Tōsō, pp.209, 210; Sōgen Appendix, 5, 6.

Sasagawa collect., Ōsaka. A Bird Pecking an Insect. Album-leaf.

Ibid. Four Magpies Pecking a Mantis. Album-leaf.

Boston Museum. A Dragon-fly on a Bamboo Spray. Album-leaf. Formerly attributed to Ch'ien Hsüan. *Cf.* Amer. collect., p.149.

V

Painters of the Ming Dynasty

Ch‘ai Chên	柴楨
Chan Ching-fêng	詹景鳳
Chan Ho	詹和
Chang Ch‘êng-lung	張成龍
Chang Ch‘i-tsu	張啓祖
Chang Ch‘ung	張翀
Chang Fu (*t.* Fu-yang)	張復(復陽)
Chang Fu (*t.* Yüan-ch‘un)	張復(元春)
Chang Ho	張翮
Chang Hsüan	張萱
Chang Hui	張翬
Chang Hung	張宏
Chang Jui-t‘u	張瑞圖
Chang Ling	張靈
Chang Lu	張路
Chang Lung-chang	張龍章
Chang Ning	張甯
Chang Tsê-chih	張則之
Chang Yen	張彥
Chang Yu	張祐
Chang Yü	張宇
Chang Yü-ssŭ	張宇思
Chang Yüan-chü	張元舉
Chang Yüan-shih	張元士
Ch‘ang-ying	常瑩
Chao Chê	趙浙
Chao Hsün	趙洵
Chao Hsün	趙珣
Chao Ju-yin	趙汝殷
Chao Pei	趙備
Chao Tso	趙左
Ch‘ên Chên-hui	陳貞慧
Ch‘ên Chêng	陳正
Ch‘ên Chi-ju	陳繼儒
Ch‘ên Chia-yên	陳嘉言
Ch‘ên Ch‘ing	陳清
Ch‘ên Hsien	陳賢
Ch‘ên Hsien-chang	陳獻章
Ch‘ên Huan	陳煥
Ch‘ên Hui	陳惠
Ch‘ên Hung-shou	陳洪綬
Ch‘ên I	陳沂
Ch‘ên Ju-yen	陳汝言
Ch‘ên Kua	陳括
Ch‘ên Lien	陳廉
Ch‘ên Lo	陳裸
Ch‘ên Lu	陳錄
Ch‘ên Shao-ying	陳紹英
Ch‘ên Shun	陳淳
Ch‘ên Tsun	陳遵
Ch‘ên Tzŭ-ho	陳子和
Ch‘ên Yü	陳遇
Ch‘ên Yüan	陳遠
Ch‘ên Yüan-su	陳元素
Chêng Chih-yen	鄭之彥
Chêng Chung	鄭重
Chêng Shih	鄭石
Chêng Tien-hsien	鄭顛仙
Chêng Yao-nien	鄭堯年
Ch‘êng Chia-sui	程嘉燧
Ch‘êng-i	誠意
Chi Chên	紀鎮
Chiang Ai	蔣藹
Chiang Ch‘êng-tsung	姜承宗
Chiang Ch‘ien	蔣乾
Chiang Li-kang	姜立綱
Chiang Ssŭ-chou	姜思周
Chiang Sung	蔣嵩
Chiang Tzŭ-ch‘êng	蔣子成
Chiang Yin	姜隱
Ch‘ien Hsü	錢旭
Ch‘ien Ku	錢穀
Ch‘ien Kung	錢貢
Chin Shêng	金聲
Chin Shih	金湜
Chin Wên-chin	金文璡
Ch‘iu Shih	仇氏
Ch‘iu Ying	仇英
Chou Ch‘ên	周臣
Chou Chih-mien	周之冕
Chou Ch‘üan	周全
Chou Fan	周蕃

Chou-hsien Wang .. .. .. 周憲王
Chou Hsin .. .. 周璕
Chou K'ai .. .. 周愷
Chou Kuan .. .. 周官
Chou Lun .. .. 周綸
Chou Lung .. .. 周龍
Chou Shih-ch'ên .. .. .. 周時臣
Chou T'ien-ch'iu .. .. .. 周天球
Chou Tsung-lien .. .. .. 周宗濂
Chou Wei .. .. 周位
Chou Wên-ching .. .. .. 周文靖
Chou Yung .. .. 周用
Chu Chih-fan .. .. 朱之蕃
Chu Ch'ing-yün .. .. .. 朱慶雲
Chu Chu .. .. 朱竺
Chu Fei .. .. 朱芾
Chu Hsün .. .. 諸勛
Chu Lang .. .. 朱朗
Chu Ling .. .. 朱陵
Chu Lu .. .. 朱鷺
Chu Ming .. .. 朱明
Chu Nan-yung .. .. .. 朱南雍
Chu Pang .. .. 朱邦
Chu Tuan .. .. 朱端
Chu Wei.. .. .. 朱蔚
Chu Yo-chi .. .. 朱約佶
Chü Chieh .. .. 居節
Chü Chih-p'u .. .. 璩之璞
Chü Mou-shih.. .. .. .. 居懋時
Chung Hsing .. .. 鍾惺
Chung Li .. .. 鍾禮
Fan Ching-wên .. .. .. 范景文
Fan Li .. .. 范禮
Fang Chin-shih .. .. .. 方矜式
Fang Hsiao-ju.. .. .. .. 方孝孺
Fang Pi .. .. 方弼
Fei Ch'êng .. .. 費澄
Fu Tao-k'un .. .. 傅道坤
Ho Ch'êng .. .. 何澄
Ho Lung .. .. 何龍
Hou Mou-kung .. .. .. 侯懋功
Hsia Ch'ang .. .. 夏昶
Hsia Chih .. .. 夏芷
Hsia K'uei .. .. 夏葵
Hsia Ping .. .. 夏昺
Hsiang Shêng-mo .. .. .. 項聖謨

Hsiang Tê-hsin .. .. 項德新
Hsiang Yüan-pien .. .. 項元汴
Hsiao-an.. .. .. 曉菴
Hsiao Hai-shan .. .. 蕭海山
Hsieh Ch'êng .. .. 謝成
Hsieh Chin .. .. 謝晉
Hsieh Huan .. .. 謝環
Hsieh Shih-ch'ên .. .. 謝時臣
Hsien-tsung, of Ming .. .. .. 明憲宗
Hsing T'ung .. .. 邢侗
Hsing Tz'ŭ-ching .. .. 邢慈靜
Hsü Chên .. .. 許震
Hsü I .. .. 許儀
Hsü Lin .. .. 徐霖
Hsü Mou-wei .. .. 徐懋緯
Hsü Pên .. .. 徐賁
Hsü Wei .. .. 徐渭
Hsü Yüan .. .. 徐奫
Hsüan-tsung, of Ming .. .. 明宣宗
Hsüeh Su-su or Hsüeh Wu .. 薛素素
Hsüeh-yai .. .. 雪崖
Hu Chêng-yen .. .. 胡正言
Hu Ching .. .. 胡靖
Hu Kao .. .. 胡皐
Hu Tsung-hsin .. .. 胡宗信
Hu Tsung-jên .. .. 胡宗仁
Hu Yü-k'un .. .. 胡玉昆
Huang Ch'i-min .. .. 黃起溟
Huang Chüan .. .. 黃卷
Huang Jui .. .. 黃瑞
Huang Shih-fu .. .. 黃石符
Huang Tao-chou .. .. 黃道周
Huang Wên-li .. .. 黃文立
I Ch'ang-wu .. .. 易昌武
Ju Wên-shu .. .. 汝文淑
Ju-t'ai .. .. 如泰
K'ang Hai .. .. 康海
Kao T'ing-li .. .. 高廷禮
Kao Yang .. .. 高陽
Ko Chêng-ch'i .. .. 葛徵奇
Ko I-lung .. .. 葛一龍
K'o Shih-huang .. .. 柯士璜
Ku Chên-i .. .. 顧振儀
Ku Chêng-i .. .. 顧正誼
Ku Ch'i-fang .. .. 顧啓芳
Ku-chia .. .. 古甲

Ku Fu	顧復
Ku I-tê	顧懿德
Ku Ning-yüan	顧凝遠
Ku Ping	顧炳
Ku Shan-yu	顧善有
Ku Shih-ch'i	顧時啓
Ku Ta-tien	顧大典
Kuan Ssŭ	關思
Kuei Ch'ang-shih	歸昌世
Kuei Chuang	歸莊
Kuei Ming-yung	眭明永
Kuo Hsü	郭詡
Kuo Tien	郭甸
Lan Ying	藍瑛
Li Ao	李璈
Li Chu	李著
Li Hang-chih	李杭之
Li I-ho	李一和
Li I-po	李一白
Li Jih-hua	李日華
Li K'ung-hsiu	李孔修
Li Lin	李麟
Li Liu-fang	李流芳
Li Pin	李彬
Li Shao-ch'i	李紹箕
Li Shih-ta	李士達
Li Tsai	李在
Li Tsung-mo	李宗謨
Li Yü	李郁
Li Yung-ch'ang	李永昌
Liang Chih-chung	梁志中
Lin Hsüeh	林雪
Lin Liang	林良
Lin Shan	林山
Lin T'ai-hêng	林台衡
Lin Yu-ch'un	林由春
Ling Pi-chêng	凌必正
Liu Chieh	劉節
Liu Chüeh	劉珏
Liu Chün	劉俊
Liu Kuang	劉廣
Liu Shih-ju	劉世儒
Liu Ta-hsia	劉大夏
Liu Tu	劉度
Liu Yüan-ch'i	劉原起
Lu Ch'ao-yang	盧朝陽
Lu Chih	陸治
Lu Fu	陸復
Lu K'o-chêng	陸克正
Lu Shih-jên	陸士仁
Lu Shih-tao	陸師道
Lu Tê-chih	魯得之
Lü Chi	呂紀
Lü Ching-fu	呂敬甫
Lü Tuan-chün	呂端俊
Lü Wên-ying	呂文英
Ma Chün	馬俊
Ma I-ch'ing	馬一卿
Ma Shih	馬軾
Ma Shih-ta	馬世達
Ma Shou-chên	馬守貞
Mi Wan-chung	米萬鍾
Ming-ho	明河
Mo Shih-lung	莫是龍
Ni Tuan	倪端
Ni Yüan-lu	倪元璐
P'eng Nien	彭年
Pien Ch'u-shan	邊楚善
Pien Wên-chin	邊文進
Shang Hsi	商喜
Shang Tsu	商祚
Shao Kao	邵高
Shao Mi	邵彌
Shao Pao	邵寶
Shên Chên	沈貞
Shên Chou	沈周
Shên Hêng	沈恒
Shên Hsiang	沈襄
Shên Shih	沈仕
Shên Shih-ch'ung	沈士充
Shên Shih-kêng	沈士鯁
Shêng Mao-hua	盛茂燁
Shêng Shao-hsien	盛紹先
Shih Chung	史忠
Shih Jui	石銳
Shih Lin	施霖
Shu Chih	殳執
Sun Ai	孫艾
Sun Ch'êng-tsung	孫承宗
Sun Ch'i	孫啓
Sun Chih	孫枝
Sun I	孫儀

Sun Lung	孫 龍
Sun K‘o-hung	孫克弘
Sung Chüeh	宋 珏
Sung Hsü	宋 旭
Sung Mou-chin	宋懋晉
Ta-hsien	達 仙
Tai Chin	戴 進
T‘ang Chih-ch‘i	唐志契
T‘ang Chih-yin	唐志尹
T‘ang Hsien-k‘o	唐獻可
T‘ang Shih-shêng	唐時升
T‘ang Yin	唐 寅
Tao-hung	道 宏
T‘ao Ch‘êng	陶 成
T‘ao I	陶 佾
Ting Yün-p‘êng	丁雲鵬
Ts‘ai Shih-hsin	蔡世新
Ts‘ai Ting-ch‘ên	蔡鼎臣
Ts‘ao Fang	曹 方
Ts‘ao Hsi	曹 羲
Ts‘ao Li-chi	曹履吉
Ts‘ao Miao-ch‘ing	曹妙清
Ts‘ao T‘ang	曹 堂
Tsêng Ch‘ing	曾 鯨
Tsou Chih-lin	鄒之麟
Tsou Heng	鄒 衡
Tsou Shih-chin	鄒式金
Tsou Ti-kuang	鄒迪光
Ts‘ui Tzŭ-chung	崔子忠
Tu Chi-lung	杜冀龍
Tu Chin	杜 堇
Tu Ch‘iung	杜 瓊
Tu Ta-shou	杜大綬
Tung Ch‘i-ch‘ang	董其昌
Tung Hsiao-ch‘u	董孝初
Wan Kuo-chên	萬國楨
Wang Chao	汪 肇
Wang Ch‘ên	王 臣
Wang Ch‘i	王 綦
Wang Ch‘iao	王 翹
Wang Chien-chang	王建章
Wang Ch‘ien	王 謙
Wang Ch‘ien	王 乾
Wang Chih	王 贄
Wang Chung-li	王中立
Wang Chung-yü	王仲玉
Wang Ch‘ung	王 寵
Wang Ê	王 諤
Wang Fu	王 紱
Wang Hsien-chou	汪憲周
Wang Hsin-i	王心一
Wang Jên	王 仁
Wang Ku-hsiang	王穀祥
Wang Li	王 履
Wang Li	王 醴
Wang Li-pên	王立本
Wang Shang-kung	王上宮
Wang Shih-ch‘ang	王世昌
Wang Shu-chin	王述縉
Wang Ssŭ-jên	王思任
Wang To	王 鐸
Wang Wei-lieh	王維烈
Wang Wên	王 問
Wei Chih-huang	魏之璜
Wei Chih-k‘o	魏之克
Wei Chü-ching	魏居敬
Wên Chêng	文 正
Wên Chêng-ming	文徵明
Wên Chia	文 嘉
Wên Jan	文 枏
Wên P‘êng	文 彭
Wên Po-jên	文伯仁
Wên Shu	文 淑
Wên Ts‘ung-ch‘ang	文從昌
Wên Ts‘ung-chien	文從簡
Wên Yüan-shan	文元善
Wên-jên Kai	聞人蓋
Wu Ch‘ang	吳 昌
Wu Chên	吳 振
Wu-chieh	無 界
Wu Cho	吳 焯
Wu Êrh-ch‘êng	吳爾成
Wu I	吳 易
Wu I-hsien	吳亦僊
Wu K‘uan	吳 寬
Wu Ling	吳 令
Wu Pin	吳 彬
Wu Po-li	吳伯理
Wu T‘ing-yü	吳廷羽
Wu Wei	吳 偉
Wu Yün	吳 雲
Yang Chi	楊 基

Name	Characters	Name	Characters
Yang Ming-shih	楊名時	Yin Ch'i-fêng	尹奇逢
Yang Pu	楊補	Yin Hung	殷宏
Yang Wên-ts'ung	楊文驄	Yo Chêng	岳正
Yao Li-shih	姚履施	Yo Tai	岳岱
Yao Shou	姚綬	Yu Ch'iu	尤求
Yao Tê-hou	姚德厚	Yü Hsi-lien	喻希連
Yao Yün-tsai	姚允在	Yüan Hsüan	袁玄
Yeh-ch'üan	野泉	Yüan Shang-t'ung	袁尙統
Yeh Kuang	葉廣	Yüan Yüan	袁源
Yeh Yu-nien	葉有年	Yün-ch'iao	雲樵
Yen I	顏嶧	Yün Hsiang	惲向

Ch'ai Chên 柴楨, *t.* Chün-chêng 君正, *h.* Shih-an 適菴 or Shih-chai 適齋.
From Tung-p'ing, Shantung. Active in the 14th century. Landscapes. H, 4. M, p.265.

Tōsō p.222. Autumn Landscape. Signed. Poems by Wang Shih-tien, Chêng Yüan-yü (1292–1364) and Ch'ên Ju-yên (dated 1378). *Cf.* Sōraikan, II, 41.

Chan Ching-fêng 詹景鳳, *t.* Tung-t'u 東圖, *h.* Po-yo Shan-jên 白岳山人.
From Hsiu-ning, Anhui. B. *c.*1560. Bamboos in ink, landscapes and flowers. Prominent writer of grass characters. Compiler of *Hua-yüan pu-i* 畫苑補益 and other books. N, VII, 7. O, 7. M, p.560.

Yonezawa, 16b. A Branch of Bamboo. Signed and dated 1591.

Ōmura, II, 4. River-view in Mist; peaks in the background, trees on the islets below. Signed and dated 1591. *Cf.* Chūgoku, III.

Shina Meiga Senshū, 10. Bamboos and Bare Trees. Fan-painting. Signed and dated 1598.

Kokka 329. Landscape. Signed. Poem and colophon, dated 1599.

Nanking Exhib. cat. 236. A tall Stalk of Bamboo. Signed.

J. P. Dubosc, Lugano. Trees and Bamboos growing by a Rock. Signed and dated 1600. Fan-painting.

Tōsō p.346. Landscape. Fan-painting. Signed.

Chan Ho 詹和, or Chan Chung-ho 詹仲和, *t.* Hsi-ho 信和, *h.* T'ieh-kuan Tao-jên 鐵冠道人.
From Ssŭ-ming, Chekiang. Flourished *c.*1500. Ink bamboos in the style of Wu Chên; also figures. O, 7. M, p.560.

Honganji, Kyōto. A Branch of Bamboo. Signed. Colophon dated 1513.

N. Gashū, 7. Ink Bamboos. Signed. Poem.

Sōgen 194 (Andō collect., Kyōto). Bamboos by a Rock. Signed. Poem.

Chang Ch'êng-lung 張成龍, *t.* Po-yün 白雲.
From Ta-liang, Honan. Active at the end of the Ming period. Landscapes and figures in *pai-miao* style. X, add. p.157a. M, p.471.

Ku-kung collect. Landscape after Chang Sêng-yu; ink and colours.

Boston Museum. Two Crows on a Snowy Trunk; others flocking in the background. Signed.

CHANG CH'I-TSU 張啓祖.
Unrecorded. Late Ming period.

Ku-kung collect. (Nanking Exhib. cat. 243). Men enjoying themselves in Boats on the River. Large album-leaf. Signed and dated 1614.

CHANG CH'UNG 張翀, *t*. Tzŭ-yü 子羽, *h*. T'u-nan 圖南.
From Nanking. Active *c*.1570–1610. Figures, landscapes. N, IV, 26. O, 1. M, p.471.

National Museum, Stockholm. The Comic Drunkards. Signed and dated 1581.
British Museum, No.147. The Eight Immortals. Signed and dated 1584.
C. T. Loo Successors, New York. The Lan-t'ing Meeting. Wang Hsi-chih is watching the geese from the pavilion while the scholars are floating their cups. Signed and dated 1637.
K.-k. shu-hua chi, XXII. *P'êng-shan ying-nien t'u*: The Cart Arriving at the Grassy Mountain. Landscapes with figures. Signed.
K.-k. chou-kan 130, 139, 170, 228. Four fan-paintings.
S.c.t.k. hsü-pien, V. Celebrating New Year; People Gathered round a Juggler's Pole. Signed.
Metropolitan Museum. A Bird on a Branch of a Blossoming Pear-tree. Fan-painting. Signed.
Princeton University (Du Bois-Morris collect.) A Man Resting under Pine-trees by a Waterfall. Signed.

CHANG FU 張復, *t*. Fu-yang 復陽, *h*. Nan-shan 南山.
From P'ing-hu, Chekiang. B. 1410, d. 1490. Taoist. Landscapes in the style of Wu Chên. I, 58. N, VI, 16. O, 4. M, p.469.

Yūrintaikan, II. Confucius with a Disciple Looking at a Stream. Handscroll. Signed. Quotations from the Confucian *Analects* and *Mencius*. Colophons by Hsü Yu-chêng, dated 1465, and by Wang Shih-an. Another section of the same scroll in Tōsō, p.300.

CHANG FU 張復, *t*. Yüan-ch'un 元春, *h*. Ling-shih 苓石.
From T'ai-ts'ang, Kiangsu. B. 1546, d. after 1631. Pupil of Ch'ien Ku. Followed also Shên Chou and Sung and Yüan masters. N, III, 17. T, II, 1, 5. M, p.469.

Ku-kung collect. River Landscape; buildings on poles in the water, leafy trees in autumn colours. Handscroll. Signed and dated 1601.
J. P. Dubosc, Lugano. A Wide River-view; two men in a boat, a high pavilion in the foreground. Signed and dated 1613. Fan-painting.
Köln, Ostasiat. Museum. Two-storied Pavilion among Trees on an Island, a Man on the Bridge Leaning over it. Signed and dated 1624. Fan-painting. Köln Exhibit. 1955, No.36.
Commercial Press album. Views along the Fu-ch'un River and its Wooded Shores. Long handscroll. Signed and dated 1629.
Hamburg Exhibition, 1949–1950. Wooded Mountains. Ink and colour. Signed.
Vannotti collect., Lugano. Roofs of Temple Pavilions seen through Leafy Trees. Ink and colour. Signed and dated 1630. Fan-painting.

CHANG HO 張翮, *t*. Fêng-i 鳳翼.
From Suchou. Active *c*.1630. Landscapes, figures. O, 8. M, p.471.

Chicago Art Institute. A Flock of White-headed Black Birds Gathering Around an Old Tree. Handscroll. Ink only. Signed and dated 1626.

Tokasha Shina Meigashū, 12. Rainstorm over a Mountain River; a Man in a Boat Trying to Reach the Shore. Signed and dated 1634.

K.-k. chou-k'an 88. A Lake Scene with Sailboats. Fan-painting.

CHANG HSÜAN 張萱, *t.* Mêng-ch'i 孟奇, *h.* Chiu-jo 九岳 and Hsi-yüan 西園.

From Hui-chou, Kwangtung. *Chü-jên* in 1582. Known particularly as a writer. L, 25. M, p.469.

National Museum, Stockholm. Gazing at a Waterfall. Signed and dated 1586.

CHANG HUI 張翬, *t.* Wên-chu 文翥.

From T'ai-ts'ang, Kiangsu. Flourished in the Ch'êng-hua period (1465–1487). Followed Hsia Kuei and Ma Yüan. N, VI, 16. O, 3. M, p.469.

National Museum, Stockholm. A Fisherman under a Willow-tree. Signed.

Takeuchi collect., Kyōto. A Fisherman in a Boat; another Man on the Shore. Signed.

CHANG HUNG 張宏, *t.* Chün-tu 君度, *h.* Hao-chien 鶴澗.

From Suchou. B. *c.*1580, d. after 1660. Landscapes; figures, flowers and buffaloes. N, IV, 25. O, 8. Q, I, 1 . I, 2, 18. M, p.471.

K.-k. shu-hua chi, XXIV. Pu-tai. Signed. Poem by Wang Chih-têng (1535–1612).

Ibid. XL. The Shih-hsieh Mountain. Slight bluish and green colouring. Signed and dated 1613.

Private collect., Kyōto. Pure Solitude in the Wintry Mountains. Landscape with angular rocks and bare trees. Signed and dated 1614.

Vannotti collect., Lugano. Tall twisted Pine-trees in front of Rocks. Ink and colour. Signed and dated 1621. Fan-painting.

Ku-kung collect. River-valley in Moonlight. Inspired by Wang Wei's *Wang-ch'uan t'u*. Signed and dated 1625. *Cf.* Nanking Exhibition cat.238.

Nanju 7. (Kenninji, Kyōto). Summer Landscape before Rain, after Tung Yüan. Signed and dated 9th month, 1626. *Cf.* Tōyō, XI.

Ku-kung, XIII. Mountain Stream after Snow. Signed and dated 10th month, 1626.

K.-k. shu-hua chi, IX. Camellia and Narcissus, after Lu Chih. Signed and dated 12th month, 1626.

W. Hochstadter, New York. Views of the Chih Garden in Suchou. Several more leaves from the same album in the Hobart collect., Cambridge, Mass. Inscription by the painter, dated 1627. *Cf.* Cleveland Exhibition cat. 82

J. P. Dubosc, Lugano. Autumn Trees in front of High Mountains. Ink and colour. Signed and dated 1627. Fan-painting.

K.-k. shu-hua chi, XXX. Landscape with a small Pavilion. Signed and dated 1629.

Tōan 36. Landscape. Fan-painting. Signed and dated 1629.

Yu Chêng album, 1916. An album of eight landscapes after Sung and Yüan masters. Signed and dated 1632.

Ming-jên shu-hua, 23. Man Drinking under Wu-t'ung-trees. Signed and dated 1632.

J. D. Ch'ên cat., I. 39. A Man on a River-bank. Signed. Dated 1632.

Princeton University (Du Bois-Morris collect.) Misty Morning in the Mountains; large trees in the foreground. Signed and dated 1633.

K.-k. shu-hua chi, XXVII. The Ch'i-hsia Mountain. Signed and dated 1634. *Cf.* K.-k. chou-k'an 380.

Ibid. XXVI. Landscape. Signed and dated 1637.

Vannotti collect., Lugano. The Ford of a River between Steep Cliffs; Small Bridge and Buildings. Signed and dated 1635. Fan-painting.

S.c.t.k. hsü-pien, VIII. Sipping Tea among Plantains and Bamboos. Signed and dated 1639.

J. P. Dubosc, Lugano. A Small Temple among High Trees on the Bank of a River. Ink and colour. Signed and dated 1639. Fan-painting.
Chêng Tê-k'un, Cambridge. Two Boys Leading Buffaloes across a River. Ink and slight colour. Inscription by the painter, dated 1639.
Vannotti collect., Lugano. Bare Trees in front of Misty Mountains. Signed and dated 1640. Fan-painting. *Cf.* Venice Exhib. cat., No.840.
Ibid. Wooded Mountains, after Fan K'uan. Handscroll. Signed and dated 1640.
Hui-hua kuan. A Pavilion by a Mountain River in Autumn. Signed and dated 1642.
Tōsō, p.373. Landscape after Wang Mêng. Fan-painting. Signed and dated 1642.
J. Cahill, Wash., D.C. Spring Landscape; a pavilion built over the river under blossoming-trees. Fan-painting. Signed and dated 1642.
Gems, I, 46. Large Winter Landscape: Sitting by the Mountain Stream. Signed and dated 1642.
Ku-kung, XXIII. Boat-racing. Signed and dated 1648.
Cincinnati Museum. Birds on a Flowering Branch over a Mountain Brook. Signed and dated 1648.
Ku-kung collect. River Landscape with Fishermen in a Boat. Painted in colour and imitated Shên Chou's manner. Signed and dated 1648 (?).
Hamburg Exhibition, 1949–1950. In the Mountains on a Summer Day, after Wang Mêng. Signed and dated 1649.
Boston Museum. A View of the Kou-ch'ü Mountains. A deep gully between mountains which are rising into high peaks; rich growth of grass and pine-trees along the slopes. Ink and colour. Inscription by the painter, dated 1650.
King Gustaf VI Adolf collect. Pavilion by a Mountain Lake at Night when the Moon is appearing. Two lines of poetry by the painter, dated 1652.
Ming-jên shu-hua, 25. Fishermen in Boats and on Shore under a Willow. Signed and dated 1652.
K.-k. chou-k'an 124, 147. Landscapes, fan-paintings. See also Nanga Taisei IX, 111–113 (dated 1621, 1632, 1634).
Wu-mên p'ai ming-hua chi (Shên Chou album, 1924). Landscape after Wang Mêng. Signed.
Ku-kung collect. (Nanking Exhib. cat. 392). Spring Morning on the Lake. Leaf from an album of scenes of Suchou. Signed.
River-views: A Boat with a Man and a Stork. Slightly coloured. Signed.
Hui-hua kuan. Landscape with Figures and Water-buffaloes.
K.-k. shu-hua chi, XLIV. Mountain Landscape with Leafless Trees. Signed.
Tōsō, p.372. Landscape after Tung Yüan. Signed.
Sōgen 184. Pine-trees on the T'ai Shan. Signed.
Ibid. 185. Spring in Chiang-nan. Part of a handscroll.
Vannotti collect., Lugano. Mountains in Mist, with Bare Trees. Fan-painting. Signed.
H. C. Wêng, New York. The Hundred Water-buffaloes. In the manner of Tai Sung. Long handscroll. Signed.

CHANG JUI-T'U 張瑞圖, *t.* Ch'ang-kung 長公, *h.* Êrh-shui 二水, Kuo-t'ing 果亭, and other names. From Ch'üan-chou, Fukien. *Chin-shih* in 1607. Favoured by the eunuch Wei Chung-hsien. Landscapes. N, IV, 20. M, p.472. V. p.961.

T. Moriya collect., Kyōto. River-landscape, with a Man crossing a Bridge. Short handscroll. Signed; an inscription by the artist mounted after, dated 1624.
Mayuyama collect., Tōkyō. Album of landscape-paintings and poems, on gold-flecked paper. Signed and dated 1625. *Cf.* Sekai Bijutsu Zenshū XX, pls.26, 27.
Ming-jên shu-hua, 2. Kuanyin. Signed and dated 1626. Sūtra copied by the painter.
Ibid. 3. River Landscape. Handscroll. Signed and dated 1627.
Kokka 314 (Seikadō). Mountains Rising through Clouds. Two lines of poetry, dated 1631. *Cf.* Ming-hua sou-ch'i, II, 4; Nanju 1; Tōyō, XI; Tōsō, p.367.
K. Sumitomo collect., Ōiso. Album containing four landscape-paintings and several leaves of writing. Signed and dated 1633.
Hobart collect., Cambridge, Mass. Mountains and Tall Pine-trees in Mist. Poem by the painter, dated 1633. *Cf.* Chung-kuo ming-hua, vol. XII.
Shina Nanga, I, 12. Landscape. Signed. Poem dated 1633.

Nanking Exhib. cat. 208. An Island in a River. Album-leaf. Signed and dated 1633.
Ernest Ericson, New York. A Waterfall between Steep Cliffs. Signed and dated 1635. *Cf.* Pageant, 717.
Kokka 301 (Seikadō). Pines and Rocks. Signed and dated 1636.
Nanju 22. Steep Cliffs over a River. Signed and dated 1636.
Ibid. 10. Landscape. Signed and dated 1637. *Cf.* Pageant 717.
Kokka 359. Kuanyin. Signed and dated 1638.
Shimbi, XIV. Landscape. Poem by the painter, dated 1638.
Nanga Taisei, Add. IV, 31. Pine-trees on Steep Cliffs; a Lake beyond. Signed and dated 1640.
Sirén collect. A Water-bird on a Stone under a Tall Lotus-leaf. Signed and dated 1642.
Po-mei chi. A Twig of Plum-tree with Two Blossoms. Album-leaf. Signed.
Kokka 336 (Sumitomo collect.). Landscape. Handscroll. Signed. Two lines of poetry. *Cf.* Shimbi, XIV.
Ibid. 507. Landscape. Album-leaf. Signed. Two lines of poetry.
Shimbi, XVI. Landscape. Album-leaf. Signed.
Nanju 3. Two Men Looking at a Waterfall. Signed. Two lines of poetry. *Cf.* Tōyō, XI.
Hyōjirō Hatta. Two Leafless Trees by a Rock. Signed.
Ōmura, I, 6. Landscape in Moonlight. Signed. Two lines of poetry.
Tokasha Shina Meigashū, 3. Two Men in a Pavilion at the Foot of Misty Mountains. Signed.
Sōraikan, II, 61. Steep Cliffs with a Waterfall. Poem by the painter.
Nanga Taisei VII, 57–74. The Eighteen Arhats. Album of eighteen leaves. Inscription by the artist opposite each painting. *Cf.* Hsi-leng album, 1934.
Dai Tenrankai 63. Houses in the Mountains, surrounded by Gigantic Rocks; a waterfall dropping into the void. Handscroll. Long poem, signed.
Pageant 716. A River Gorge, with Houses Built over the Water. Two lines of poetry, signed.

CHANG LING 張靈, *t.* Mêng-chin 夢晉.
From Suchou. Neighbour and friend of T'ang Yin. Figures, landscapes, flowers and birds. N, II, 21. O, 1. I, 56, 12. M, p.468.

Tōsō, p.364. A Scholar in the Autumn Woods. Signed. Colophon by Wên Chêng-ming, dated 1501.
I-shu ts'ung-pien, 11. The "Weaving Maid", Standing in half Profile; her garments flutter in the wind. Signed and dated 1504. Poem by Tsou Chih-lin, dated 1644.
Shên-chou ta-kuan, vol. 16. A Scholar's Homestead by a River. Signed and dated 1531. Poem by Lu Shih-tao. *Cf.* Nanga Taisei.
Shên-chou, XI. Su Wu Tending Sheep in the Land of the Huns. Signed.
K.-k. shu-hua chi, XXIX. Fisherman's Pleasure. Signed. Poem.
Ōmura, II, 5. Portrait of T'ang Yin. Seal of the painter. Poems by Wang Ch'ung and Wên Chêng-ming. *Cf.* Chūgoku, III.
Nanga Taisei, V, 65, 66. A Blossoming Peach-tree. Short handscroll. Signed.

CHANG LU 張路, *t.* T'ien-ch'ih 天馳, *h.* P'ing-shan 平山.
From K'ai-fêng. B. *c.*1464, d. *c.*1538. Figures in the style of Wu Wei, landscapes in the style of Tai Chin; painted often in rough manner with a dry brush. N, II, 10. O, 1. I, 56, 6. M, p.468.

K.-k. shu-hua chi, XVIII. Lao-tzŭ Riding a Buffalo. Signed.
Nanking Exhib. cat. 130. A Man in a Boat under a Cliff. Signed.
Ibid. 131. A Man Gazing at a Plum-tree beginning to Blossom in Winter. Signed.
Kokka 182 (Uchida collect.) A Traveller Knocking at the Gate of a Temple.
Ibid. 375. Landscape with a Man Speaking to a Fisherman. Attributed.
Shimbi, XIII. A Snow-bound River Scene, a Man in a Boat. Signed.

Ibid. XIV. Fisherman Throwing out his Net. Signed. *Cf.* Tōyō, X; Dai Tenrankai 54.

Kyōto Museum. Tung-fang So Returning with the Peaches from Hsi-wang-mu. *Cf.* Shimbi, XV.

Shimbi, XVI. Fishing for Pleasure, Man asleep in a Boat.

Shimbi Shoin Shina Meigashū, II. A Man Seated under a Pine-tree Looking at a Waterfall. Signed.

Kyūka, I (Hashimoto collect., Takatsuki). Two Hermits Listening to a Crane.

Ibid. Chuang-tzŭ Dreaming of the Butterfly. Signed.

Ibid. The Crane of the Taoist Temple. Signed.

Bukkyō Bijutsu, 18. A Man Sleeping, Bending over a Table. Signed.

Tōsō, p.245. The Immortal Liu Hai-chan. Signed.

Miss A. O'Brien collect., St. Paul, Minn. Scholars Walking along a Mountain Path. Signed. *Cf. Later Chinese Painting*, pl.38.

J. Cahill, Wash., D.C. A Scholar Seated, Playing the *Ch'in* to a Friend. Large album-leaf. Signed.

CHANG LUNG-CHANG 張龍章, *t.* Po-yün 伯雲, *h.* Ku-t'ang 古塘.

From Suchou. Flourished *c.*1595. Landscapes; also figures and horses after Chao Mêng-fu. M, p.471.

Kokka 343. Landscape; from an album called The Eight Views of Hsiao and Hsiang. Dated 1595.

Nanju 15. A Taoist Walking under the Moon. Signed. Two lines of poetry.

K.-k. chou-k'an 94. Three Sages in the Mountains. Fan-painting.

CHANG NING 張甯, *t.* Ching-chih 靖之, *h.* Fang-chou 方洲.

From Hai-yen, Chekiang. Chin-shih in 1454. Calligraphist and poet. Landscapes, orchids and bamboos. N, I, 22. O, 3. I, 56, 3. M, p.467.

Fu-lu. Bamboos by a Rock. Signed and dated 1458.

C. T. Loo Successor, New York. A Scholar seated in a Cottage at the Foot of a huge Rock; three tall pines by the stream. Ink and colour. Poem by the painter, dated 1490. *Cf.* Toronto, 33.

Ku-kung, XVI. Bamboos and Orchids. Signed. Poem.

CHANG TSÊ-CHIH 張則之.

Unrecorded in the Ming dynasty; possibly identical with the painter Chang Hsiao-ssŭ 張孝思 who, however, was active in the Ch'ing period.

Sōgen 166. River Landscape with Five Scholars in a Boat. Handscroll. Signed. Poem by Ch'ien-lung.

CHANG YEN 張彥, *t.* Po-mei 伯美.

From Chia-ting, Kiangsu. Flourished *c.*1630. Landscapes, flowers and figures. Sometimes placed on a level with Chang Hung. M, p.471.

Kokka 392. High Mountains and Pine-trees. Signed and dated 1637. *Cf.* Pageant 721.

CHANG YU 張祐, *t.* T'ien-chi 天吉.

Native of Fêng-yang, Anhui. Active 15th century. Painted plum-blossoms, in which he followed Wang Ch'ien 王謙. N, 6. O, 7. M, p.467.

Hikkōen, 23. Branches of a Blossoming Plum-tree. Attributed.

CHANG YÜ 張宇.
Probably identical with the 43rd *T'ien-shih* of the Taoists: Chang Yü-ch'u 張宇初. I, 58, 9. M, p.465.

Tōyō, XI. A Hermit's Hut among Trees at the Foot of a Mountain. Signed and dated 1398.

CHANG YÜ-SSŬ 張宇思.
Unrecorded. Fifteenth century. Perhaps a younger brother of Chang Yü-ch'u and Yü-ch'ing.

Shên-chou album, 1936 (together with a painting by Chao Chung, Yüan Dynasty). *Ch'in-mu-tao t'u* (The Way of Parental Affection?). Handscroll, signed and dated 1427.

CHANG YÜAN-CHÜ 張元舉, *t.* Mou-hsien 懋賢, *h.* Wu-hu 五湖.
Native of Suchou. Nephew of Ch'ên Shun. Flowers and birds after Ch'ên Shun. O, 6. M, p.468.

Mrs. B. Z. Seligman, London. Men on Mules travelling through a Mountainous Landscape. Fan-painting. Signed and dated 1627.

Vannotti collect., Lugano. A Mountain Landscape with a Clump of Leafy Trees in the foreground. Fan-painting. Signed.

CHANG YÜAN-SHIH 張元士, *t.* Shu-shang 叔上, *h.* Chih-fêng 支峯.
Flourished *c.*1570. Landscapes, flowers. *Cf.* biographical note in K.-k. shu-hua chi, XXX.

K.-k. shu-hua chi, XXX. Narcissi. Signed. Colophon, dated 1572.

CH'ANG-YING 常瑩, the priest-name of Li Chao-hêng 李肇亨, *t.* Hui-chia 會嘉, *h.* K'o-hsüeh 珂雪 and Tsui-ou 醉鷗.
From Chia-hsing, Chekiang. Flourished *c.*1630–1647. Son of Li Jih-hua 李日華 (1565–1635). Became a monk. Landscapes, grape-vine. N, VI, 18. O, 5. U, II, 1, 13. M, p.200.

Hui-hua kuan. High Mountains, Pine Groves and Streams; a River beyond. Ink and colours on paper. Long handscroll. Signed and dated 1621.

Shên-chou, XVIII. Wooded Hillocks Rising over a Stream, a Man in a Straw-covered Pavilion under tall Trees. Album-leaf. Signed and dated 1632. *Cf.* Shina Nanga, II, 8.

Chung-kuo ming-hua, 29. Landscape in the manner of Huang Kung-wang. Signed and dated 1635.

J. D. Ch'ên, Hongkong. River Landscape with Fishing-boats and Buildings. Short handscroll. Signed and dated 1638.

Nanju 15. Mountain Landscape. Signed and dated 1644. Also in Sōgen 193; Shina Meiga Senshū, III.

Chung-kuo ming-hua, XXI. Two Large Leafless Trees on a River-bank. Poem and inscription by the painter, dated 1647. Poem by Ch'ien-lung.

Po-mei chi. Branches of Plum-blossoms. Album-leaf. Signed.

K.-k. chou-k'an 142. Landscape, fan-painting.

Kurokawa collect., Ashiya. Landscape after Huang Kung-wang. Album-leaf. Signed.

J. P. Dubosc, Lugano. A River Valley at the Foot of a Mountain Ridge, Spare Trees and Buildings. Signed. Fan-painting.

CHAO CHÊ 趙浙.
Unrecorded in books on painters. According to the inscription on the picture, active in the later half of the 16th century.

Kokka 567 (Baron Go collect.) *Ch'ing-ming shang-ho.* The Ch'ing-ming Festival on the River in K'aifêng. Long handscroll. Signed and dated 1577. This is a later version of the famous scroll by Chang Tsê-tuan of Sung, now in Hui-hua kuan, Peking. A later version is in the Metropolitan Museum attributed to Ch'iu Ying.

CHAO HSÜN 趙洵, *t.* Yu-mei 又嵋.
Unrecorded. Probably Ming dynasty.

K.-k. shu-hua chi, XLII. Small Temple Compound among Trees by a River. After Ts'ao Chih-po. Inscription by the painter and his seals.

Nanga Taisei, V, 11. A Pine-tree. Signed.

CHAO HSÜN 趙珣, original name Chih-pi 之璧, *t.* Shih-wu 十五.
Native of P'u-t'ien in Fukien. Landscapes, birds and flowers. O, 5 (mistakenly called Chao Pi). M, p.617.

Nanju 12. A Pair of Pigeons Perching in a Bare Tree. Signed and dated 1632 (?). Also in Tōyō, XII.

Yamaguchi collect., Ashiya. Rocks by a River; bare trees; hills beyond. Long inscription by the artist, dated in the year *hsin-ssŭ*, or probably corresponding to 1641.

Shina Kachō Gasatsu. Studies of Vegetable Plants, Flowers and Stones. Handscroll. Poem by the painter.

Mo-ch'ao pi-chi, vol. I. A Pine-tree. Signed.

CHAO JU-YIN 趙汝殷
Active in the middle of the 15th century. Not recorded in the dictionary of painters.

Ku-kung collect. Tiger Family in the Woods. Colour on silk. Handscroll. Signed and dated 1441.

CHAO PEI 趙備, *t.* Hsiang-nan 湘南 or Hsiang-lan 湘蘭.
From Ssŭ-ming, Chekiang. Beginning of the 17th century. Ink bamboos. O, 7. M, p.617.

Shina Kachō Gasatsu. A Flowering Shrub, Narcissi and Bamboos. Handscroll. Signed and dated 1613.

National Museum, Stockholm. A Bunch of Tall Bamboos. Signed. Poem, written in his 78th year.

CHAO TSO 趙左, *t.* Wên-tu 文度.
From Hua-t'ing (Sung-chiang), Kiangsu. Active *c.*1610–1630. Pupil of Sung Hsü, rival and fellow-student of Sung Mou-chin. Landscapes in the styles of Tung Yüan, Mi Fei and the Yüan masters. Founder of the Su-Sung School 蘇松派. N, IV, 5. O, 4. P, I, 5. U, I, 2, 8. M, p.616.

J. Cahill, Washington, D.C. Mountain Landscape, with Dwellings of Scholarly Recluses. Long handscroll. Signed and dated 1609–1610.

K.-k. shu-hua chi, XVII. Autumn Mountains and Red Trees, after Yang Shêng. Signed and dated 1611.

Hui-hua kuan. Mountain Range in Mist; in the Mi style. Ink only. Long handscroll. Dated 1612.

Chang Pi-han, Hongkong. Landscape of Lake Tung-t'ing; painted while accompanying Tung Ch'i-ch'ang on a trip there. Handscroll, signed and dated 1614; another inscription by Tung.

Nanga Taisei, XI, 41–48. Album of eight landscapes, all signed, the last dated 1615. *Cf.* Shên-chou album 1929.

K.-k. shu-hua chi, IX. Landscape. Signed. A line of poetry, dated 1615. *Cf.* K.-k. chou-k'an, 133.

National Museum, Stockholm. Autumn Morning. Signed and dated 1615.

Nanga Taisei, Add. IV. An Old Pine-tree and a Rock. Signed and dated 1616. *Cf.* Sung-pê.
Saido Shobō (Tōkyō) album, 1919. Album of twelve landscapes, the last dated 1619.
Kurokawa cat. 6. Landscape with Buildings among Leafy Trees. Handscroll, painted in light colours, signed and dated 1620. Colophon by Ch'ên Chi-ju.
Ku-kung collect. (Nanking Exhib. cat. 234). A House under Pine-trees. Album-leaf. Signed and dated 1620.
Kokka 372. High Mountains in Autumn. Signed. Poem by the painter, dated 1629.
K.-k. shu-hua chi, XIV. Precipitous Rocks Rising over a Bay; Trees below. Signed.
K.-k. chou-k'an 509. Two men conversing on the Shore of a Lake. Fan-painting, signed. Colophon by Tung Ch'i-ch'ang. For other fan-paintings, see K.-k. chou-k'an 149; Nanga Taisei, VIII, 107.
Ku-kung collect. Cloudy Mountain Gully with a Waterfall. Signed.
Ibid. Cloudy Mountain Gully with a Waterfall. Colour on silk. Inscription by the painter.
Sung-chiang p'ai ming-hua chi (Shên-chou album, 1924). River Landscape, after Chao Mêng-fu. Signed.
Ibid. River Landscape, after Ni Tsan. Signed.
Ibid. A Mountain Cottage. Signed.
Ibid. Farmsteads at Wu-ling. Signed.
Hui-hua kuan. High Mountain Rising above a Winding River; a man in a pavilion under a leafy tree. Ink with light colour; misty atmosphere. Inscription by the painter.
Seikadō, Tōkyō. Towering Rocks, a Temple on a Ledge; Leafless Trees and the River below. Snow and mist. Signed.
Kokka 339. Snow Scenery. Fan-painting. Signed.
Sōraikan, I, 36. The Scholar and the Monk in the Chu-yüan Pavilion. Signed. Colophon by Ch'ên Chi-ju.
Sōgen 146. High and Distant Mountains. Signed.
Ibid. 147. River Landscape. Part of a handscroll.
Ibid. 148 (Liang Hung-chih). A Beach in Mist. Part of a handscroll. Signed. Poem by the painter.
Kurokawa cat. 7. A River Valley, with a Kiosk on the Shore. Signed.
Musée Guimet. Cottages under Old Pines. Ink on gold ground. Fan-painting. Signed.
Chêng Tê-k'un, Cambridge. Mountain Landscape on a double album-leaf. Ink and colour, gold-sprinkled paper. Signed.
Hamburg Exhibition, 1949–1950. Pavilions in a Bamboo Grove among craggy Rocks; Bare Trees and Light Snow. Ink only. Inscription by the painter.
Vannotti collect., Lugano. Garden Stones and Pine-trees. Signed. Fan-painting.

CH'ÊN CHÊN-HUI 陳貞慧, *t.* Ting-shêng 定生.
From I-hsing, Kiangsu. Active at the end of the Ming period. Well-known as a poet but not as a painter.

Chung-kuo ming-hua, XXII. A Pine, Bamboos and a Dry Tree by a Rock. Seal of the painter.

CH'ÊN CHÊNG 陳正, *t.* K'ai-t'ien 楷田.
Unrecorded. (A man by this name, active in late Ming, recorded in *Ming shih*; but he was not known as a painter.)

Nanking Exhib. cat. 169. Landscape, after Wu Chên's Endless Vista of River and Mountains. Signed and dated *hsin-wei*, or 1631? *Cf.* Chūgoku 8.

CH'ÊN CHI-JU 陳繼儒, *t.* Chung-shun 仲醇, *h.* Mi-kung 麋公, Mei-kung 眉公, Hsüeh-t'ang 雪堂, Po-shih-ch'iao 白石樵, and other names.
From Hua-t'ing, Kiangsu. B. 1558, d. 1639. Writer and poet; author of numerous books such as *Ch'ên Mei-kung shih-chung ts'ang shu* 陳眉公十種藏書, *Ni-ku lu* 妮古錄, *Shu-hua shih* 書畫史 and others; editor of *Pao-yen t'ang pi-chi* 寶顏堂秘笈. Landscapes, plum-blossoms and bamboos. N, IV, 3. P, 4. U, II, 1, 1. L, 13, 5. M, p.436.

Takashima collect., Kugenuma (formerly Yamamoto Teijirō). Autumn Landscape in Chiang-nan. Handscroll, in light colours on silk. Signed and dated 1620.

Shina Meiga Senshū, III. Mountain Landscape in Clouds and Wind. One line of poetry by the painter, dated 1623.

Shên-chou album, 1920. Six Landscapes, last one dated 1637, and three pictures of Plum-blossoms; each with a colophon.

Chung-hua album, 1919. One picture of Bamboos and four of Plum-blossoms. Signed.

Sung-chiang p'ai ming-hua chi (Shên-chou album, 1924). River Landscape. Signed. Colophon.

Shên-chou ta-kuan, vol.10. River Valley in Spring; the Rain is approaching. Two lines of poetry by the painter.

Chung-hua album, 1931. Six pictures of Plum-blossoms; each with a poem. *Cf.* Nanga Taisei, III, 17–22.

Po-mei chi. A Branch of Blossoming Plum-tree and a Rock. Album-leaf. Poem. Signed.

Nanking Exhib. cat. 192. A Branch of Blossoming-plum. Signed.

Ibid. 234 (Ku-kung collect.) Landscape in the Mi Fei manner. Section of a handscroll. Signed.

Ho Kuan-wu collect., Hongkong. Landscape. Signed.

Shimbi, XIX. Landscape, after Chü-jan. *Cf.* Ming-hua sou-ch'i, II, 3; Tōyō, XI.

Shina Nanga, II, 3. Landscape. Signed.

Ibid. III, 10. Bodhidharma Crossing the Yangtse on a Reed. Signed.

Shina Meiga Senshū, 12 (Hashimoto collect.) River Landscape in the style of Mi Fei. Signed.

Suchiku, 15 (formerly Oguri collect.) Landscape after Huang Kung-wang. Poem, signed. Colophon by Tung Ch'i-ch'ang.

Seattle Art Museum (formerly Hayashi, Gojō). Early Snow. Handscroll. Ink on paper. Poem by the painter. *Cf.* Cleveland Exhibition cat. 70.

Ton Ying Co., New York (P'ang Yüan-chi collect.) A Branch of a Blossoming Plum-tree. Fan-painting. Signed.

Vannotti collect., Lugano (Venice Exhib. cat. 833). Landscape, after Chü-jan. Fan-painting.

CH'ÊN CHIA-YEN 陳嘉言, *t.* K'ung-chang 孔彰.

From Chia-hsing, Chekiang. B. 1539, d. after 1625. Flowers. O, 6. U, II, 2, 10. M, p.437.

J. P. Dubosc, Lugano. White Herons on the Banks of a Stream. Ink and slight colours. Signed and dated 1567. Fan-painting.

Mrs. B. Z. Seligman, London. Two Birds on a Rock under a Blossoming Plum-tree. Signed and dated 1579. Fan-painting.

Nanju 20. Narcissi by a Rockery. Signed. Poem, dated 1592. Also in Tōyō, X.

K.-k. shu-hua chi, XXII. A Garden Stone and some Spring Flowers. Signed and dated 1604.

Sōgen 182. Two Magpies in a Pine-tree. Signed and dated 1604.

Ibid. 183. Three Birds in a Flowering Plum-tree and Bamboos. Signed and dated 1607.

J. P. Dubosc, Lugano. A Bird on the Branch of a Blossoming Plum-tree. Signed and dated 1612. Fan-painting.

Ton Ying Co., New York (P'ang Yüan-chi collect.) Insects by the Water and a Lotus Plant. Signed and dated 1616. Fan-painting.

Hamburg Exhibition, 1949–1950. Magpies in the Plum-trees. Signed and dated 1618. Poem by the painter.

Chicago Art Institute. Magnolias, Roses, Plum-blossoms and Fruit-trees. Handscroll. Signed and dated 1625 (at the age of 87).

CH'ÊN CH'ING 陳清, *t.* Wu-yü 無欲.

Unrecorded. Probably active in the Ch'êng-hua period (1465–1487).

Kyūka, I. A Boat in a Gorge. Signed. Poem.

CH'ÊN HSIEN 陳賢, *t.* Hsi-san 希三, *h.* T'ai-hsüan 太玄 and Pi-shui 碧水.
Flourished *c.*1635–1675. Buddhist figures. Executed most of his pictures for the Huang-po 黃檗 sect.

Ying-hua Ta-shih (Soindō, Kyōto). An album representing the Eighteen Forms of Kuanyin. Signed and dated 1636 (?). A poem on each picture by Yin-yüan. 隱元 (Teacher of Mu-an, and the founder of the Huang-po sect).
Kokka 568 (Freer Gallery, 55.17). A long series of Buddhist Priests, Arhats and Bodhisattvas. Isolated figures. Handscroll. Signed and dated 1643.
Shimbi, XVII. Bodhidharma. Signed and dated 1647(?)
Soindō, Kyōto. Album of paintings of seated monks. Signed and dated 1654.
Kokka 486. Kuanyin. Signed and dated 1654 (?).
Ibid. 327. Lao-tzŭ Riding on the Buffalo. Signed.
Shimbi, IV. Kuanyin. This picture together with the following and those reproduced in Nanju 5 and 10 form part of a series of eighteen Kuanyin, most of them with inscriptions by Yin-yüan and Mu-an 木菴 (1611–1684).
Shimbi, IV. Kuanyin.
Ibid. XIX. Kuanyin.
Nanju 2. Arhats. Poem by the monk Mu-an. *Cf.* Pageant, 740.
Ibid. 2. Arhats. Poem by the monk Mu-an. *Cf.* Pageant, 741.
Ibid. 5. Kuanyin. Poem by the monk Mu-an, dated 1657.
Ibid. 10. Kuanyin. Signed.
Ibid. 13. Kuanyin. Seals of the painter. Poem by the monk Yin-yüan.
Ibid. 13. Kuanyin. Signed. Poem by Yin-yüan.
Tōyō, X. Kuanyin, standing full length. Poem by Mu-an, dated 1676.
Ibid. X. An Arhat with his Servant-boy. Signed. Poem by Mu-an.

CH'ÊN HSIEN-CHANG 陳獻章, *t.* Kung-fu 公甫, *h.* Shih-chai 石齋.
From Hsin-hui, Kwangtung. B. 1428, d. 1500. Han-lin scholar and philosopher. Plum-blossoms. L, 13, 3. M, p.433.

K.-k. shu-hua chi, XXXIV. A Spreading Branch of a Blossoming Plum-tree. Signed and dated 1437. *Cf.* K.-k. chou-k'an, vol.XX, 473.
I-shu ts'ung-pien, 12. River View in Autumn with Scattered Trees on the Rocky Shore in the foreground. Poem by the painter, dated 1489.
Hui-hua kuan. A Long Branch of a Blossoming Plum-tree. Ink on silk; dark background. Signed. Doubtful.
Nanga Taisei, III, 5. Some Far-reaching Branches of a Blossoming Plum-tree. Long handscroll. Inscription unreadable.

CH'ÊN HUAN 陳煥, *t.* Tzŭ-wên 子文, *h.* Yao-fêng 堯峯.
From Suchou. Active *c.*1600. Landscapes in Shên Chou's manner. N, IV, 16. O, 4. M, p.435.

Hamburg Exhibition, 1949–1950. Landscape in the style of Wang Mêng. Signed, dated 1605.
Wu-men p'ai ming-hua chi (Shên-chou album, 1924). A Garden with a Pond. Signed and dated 1608.
J. P. Dubosc, Lugano. View of a Broad River with a Large Pleasure Boat; men on the shore. Ink and colour. Signed. Dated 1611. Fan-painting.
Sōgen 158. Mountains in Szechuan. Handscroll. Signed and dated 1614.
Chūgoku, III. A Brook Running between Tall Pines, a Scholar Seated on the Ground on a Summer Day. Signed and dated 1615.
Ku-kung collect. Pine Woods along a River, Buildings between the Rocks. In the manner of Shên Chou. Handscroll.
K.-k. chou-k'an 84, 95, 103, 104. Four Landscapes. Fan-paintings.
Nanking Exhib. cat. 232. Landscape after Shên Chou, with Two Men on a Bridge. Poem, signed.

CH'ÊN HUI 陳惠, *t.* Mêng-ho 孟龢.
Unrecorded. Probably 17th century.

K.-k. shu-hua chi, XLII. Plum-blossoms Rising from an Old Trunk. Poem by the painter.

CH'ÊN HUNG-SHOU 陳洪綬, *t.* Chang-hou 章侯, *h.* Lao-lien 老蓮, Fu-ch'ih 弗遲, Yün-mên-sêng 雲門僧, and other names.
From Chu-chi, Chekiang. B. 1599, d. 1652. Famous figure painter; flowers, birds and landscapes. Court-painter during the last years of the Ming dynasty in Nanking. N, VII, 20. O, 2. P, I, 11. Q, I, 1. U, I, 1, 5. M, p.437.

K.-k. shu-hua chi, IX. Camellias Growing from a Rock. Signed and dated 1626.
Chang Ta-ch'ien cat., vol.IV. A Man at a Pine-tree under Projecting Rocks, accompanied by a Boy with his *Ch'in*. Dated 1633.
Chūgoku, IV. An Old Man and a Lady seated under a Tree in the Land of Immortals. Signed and dated 1638.
C. C. Wang, New York. A Gathering of Officials in a Garden. Signed and dated 1638 (in the 8th month).
Palace Museum album, 1933. Ten studies of figures, flowers and birds; some of them accompanied by inscriptions. One dated 1645. *Cf.* Nanking Exhib. cat. 258.
Shên-chou, V. Two Buddhist Figures. Signed and dated 1646. A Sūtra at the top copied by the painter.
Commercial Press album, 1934. Eight leaves representing figures, flowers, birds, insects and landscapes. Signed and dated 1646.
Chêng Tê-k'un, Cambridge. A Tall Pine-tree and Flowering Plants by a Stone. Signed and dated 1648.
I-shu ch'uan-t'ung, X, 8. The Four Joys of Po Hsiang-shan (*i.e.* Po Chü-i). Long handscroll. Signed and dated 1649. Inscriptions by the painter and by T'ang Chiu-chin. *Cf.* Liu 85.
Chung-kuo, II, 50. Three Ladies with Plum-blossoms. Signed and dated 1650.
Êrh-shih chia. Five Ladies Seated at the Foot of a Rock. Signed and dated 1650.
Honolulu Academy of Art (Chung-hua album, 1933). Illustration to T'ao Yüan-ming's poem *Kuei-ch'ü-lai*. Handscroll. Signed and dated 1650.
Palace Museum album, 1933. Sixteen Illustrations to the Life of a Hermit. Three poems and a colophon by the painter. Dated 1651.
Chung-kuo ming-hua, XI. Humorous Figures. Handscroll. Dedicated to Chou Liang-kung and dated 1651.
Nanga Taisei XVI, 44–45. A Sparrow on a Bamboo Branch; Narcissi; a Butterfly Hovering near a Rock. Handscroll, signed and dated 1651. Colophon by Kao Shih-ch'i.
Shên-chou album, 1908. Album of ten leaves, figure studies. Signed.
Ibid. 1936. Handscroll, various figure paintings. Inscriptions by the artist.
Shên-chou, V. Narcissi by a Rockery. Handscroll. Signed. *Cf.* Shina Nanga, I, 39.
Ibid. XVI. An Old Man Carrying a Wine-barrel and a Staff Decorated with Leaves in a Landscape. Signed.
Shên-chou ta-kuan, vol.6. A Buddhist Monk Followed by his Acolyte. Poem by the painter.
Ibid. vol.8. Lu T'ung with his Servant and Maid. Poem by the painter.
Êrh-shih chia. A Girl in an Old-fashioned Costume. Signed.
Ibid. Three Ladies, One Holding a Tray with Epidendrum Flowers. Signed.
Ibid. A Man Listening to the Music of Two Girls. Signed.
T'ai-shan ts'an-shih-lou ts'ang-hua, II. An Old Man with a Staff Carrying a Basket with a Bottle. Signed.
Chung-kuo, II, 47. A Man Singing by the Lake in the Mountains. Signed.
Ibid. II, 49. A Lady with her Two Maids under Wu-t'ung-trees, after a T'ang master. Colophon. Seals of the painter. *Cf.* Shina Nanga, II, 1.
Ibid. II, 51. Hsiang-yen Perfuming Clothes at a Brazier. Poems by Kao Shih-ch'i, etc.
Ku-kung, XXXIII. Two Fairies Carrying Emblems of Longevity. Signed.
Ibid. LXII. A Bird in a Blossoming Plum-tree. Signed.
Ibid. XII. Two Butterflies and a Branch of a Tree. Signed.
Ibid. XXII. An Old Man with a Staff. Signed.
Ibid. XXVI. A Plum-tree by a Rock. Signed.
Ibid. XXXII. Narcissi and Bamboos. Seals of the painter.

K.-k. chou-k'an, vol.I, 3. Plum-blossoms Growing from a Garden Rock, a Rat on the Top of it. Album-leaf. Signed.
K.-k. chou-k'an 488. A blossoming Magnolia-tree by a Rock. Signed.
Ku-kung collect. Leaning on the Staff and Singing: T'ao Yüan-ming with chrysanthemum in his hair.
Ibid. Two Butterflies fluttering over a Thorny Branch.
Ku-kung ming-jên hua-chu chi, II. A Branch of Bamboo beside a Stone. Large album-leaf. Seal of the painter.
Hui-hua kuan. A Scholar in a Pavilion on a Mountain Slope under Tall Trees. Ink and some slight colour on silk. Signed.
Ibid. A Lotus plant Rising above a Big Stone, and Two Mandarin Ducks. Colour on silk. Signed.
Ibid. An Old Man Accompanied by Two Girls Passing an Old Tree. Ink and colour on silk.
Ibid. A series of pictures representing Old Painters Working in their Gardens, with attendants and female servants. Ink and slight colour on silk. Long handscroll.
Gems, I, 49. Lotuses and a Rock. Poem, signed.
Ibid. III, 7. An album of twelve leaves: landscapes, flowers and other subjects. Seals of the artist.
Mei-chan t'ê-k'an 26. Four Fantastic Figures. Signed.
Chang Ta-ch'ien cat. I, 29. A branch of blossoming Plum, two Sprigs of Bamboo and a fantastic Rock. Signed.
J. D. Ch'ên cat. I, 41. A Lohan with Attendant. Signed.
Ōmura, II, 5. A Scholar with Three Servants. Signed. *Cf.* Chūgoku, IV.
Shinchō 25. Three Ladies. Signed.
Tōsō, p.376 (W. Hochstadter, New York). The Wu-hsieh Mountain. Signed. Colophon by Kao Shih-ch'i.
Sōgen 175. Two Ladies, one holding a Vase with a Lotus Flower and the other holding a Fan. Signed. *Cf.* Êrh-shih chia.
Yonezawa, 28 (Mizuta collect., Kyōto). Mi Fei Bowing to a Rock. Signed.
Chang Ta-ch'ien, Hongkong. T'ao Yüan-ming and Chu-ko Liang. Signed.
Ibid. 1954. A Man Playing the *Ch'in* for a Friend on a Low Table under Trees. Signed.
Ho Kuan-wu, Hongkong. Portrait of Su Tung-p'o. Signed.
Ibid. Two Scholars on the Bank of a Stream, leaning on Staffs. Signed.
C. P. Huang, Taipei. A Lotus-plant in a Garden Pond with an Egret and a Frog on the Lotus Leaf. Signature and seal of the painter, according to which the picture was executed in the Studio of the Willows.
C. C. Wang, New York. A High Military Official with Three Retainers. Signed.
H. C. Wêng, Scarsdale, N.Y. Two albums, each containing ten leaves, representing studies of figures and landscapes. Signed.
Ibid. An album with studies of figures and landscapes, attributed to the painter and his son, Ch'ên Hsiao-lien.
W. Hochstadter, New York. A Summer Pavilion under Large Trees on a River-bank; four men in conversation. Fan-painting. Signed.
J. Cahill, Wash., D.C. Two Butterflies. Album-leaf. Signed.
Musée Guimet. The God of Longevity accompanied by Two Other Figures.
Ibid. A Rock and Fungus. Large album-leaf, on gold-flecked paper. Signed.
National Museum, Stockholm. Saluting the Old Mother. She is seated under a pine-tree, a gentleman in official costume is standing in front of her. Two servant-girls below. Signed.
Hamburg Exhibition, 1949–1950. An Old Man Playing the *Ch'in* and Two Serving Girls. Signed.
Ibid. Two figures: A Painter and a Poet. Two inscriptions, one by the painter.
J. P. Dubosc, Lugano. Album of eight landscapes with figures. Colophons by Kao Shih-ch'i. Calligraphy by the artist accompanying each leaf. *Cf.* Venice Exhib. cat. 851.
Ibid. Old man and Servant. Fan-painting. Signed. *Cf.* Venice Exhib. cat. 852.

CH'ÊN I 陳沂, *t.* Tsung-lu 宗魯 and Lu-nan 魯南, *h.* Shih-t'ing 石亭 and Hsiao-p'o 小坡.
From Ning-po, lived in Nanking. B. 1469, d. 1583. Scholar, calligraphist, admirer of Su Tung-p'o, friend of Wên Chêng-ming. Landscapes. N, II, 26. O, 3. L, 13, 4. M, p.434.

Hui-hua kuan. Mountains in Snow along a River. Handscroll. Signed.

CH'ÊN JU-YEN 陳汝言, *t.* Wei-yün 惟允, *h.* Ch'iu-shui 秋水.

From Suchou. Active 1340–1380. Provincial Secretary in Chi-nan, Shantung, but executed by order of the emperor Hung-wu. Author of *Ch'iu-shui chi*. Landscapes in the style of Chao Mêng-fu; figures in that of Ma Ho-chih. N, I, 7. O, 2. M, p.430.

Ōmura, I, 3. River Landscape with Tall Trees and High Mountains. Signed and dated 1341. *Cf.* Tōsō, p.221; Chūgoku, II.

Nanga Taisei XI, 18. A Wooded Valley in Autumn with Pavilions on the Hillsides. Signed and dated 1348.

S.c.t.k. hsü-pien, IX. Mountains and Rushing Stream. Signed and dated 1348.

K.-k. shu-hua chi, VII. Landscape with a Waterfall. Signed and dated 1360. Poems by four contemporaries. A. A different version of the picture in Shên-chou ta-kuan, vol. 14.

Ku-kung collect. (Nanking Exhib. cat. 390). A Scene from a Story of Filial Piety. Album-leaf. Seal of the artist; inscription by Ni Tsan, dated 1365. A.

C. T. Loo Successor, Frank Caro, New York. Mountain Landscape called Lo-fou shan's Wood-cutter; in the style of Tung Yüan. Signed and dated 1366. *Cf.* Cleveland Exhib. cat. 35. A.

Tōan 14. Landscape. Signed. Poems by Ni Tsan (dated 1371) and others. *Cf.* Nansō Ihatsu, vol.4; Kokka 622.

K.-k. shu-hua chi, XVII. A View of the Chin River. Poems and colophons by Wang Mêng, Ni Tsan and others. A.

Ku-kung collect. A Small Homestead in the Mountains among the Trees. Slightly coloured ink-painting, but much worn. Short handscroll. Attributed to the painter by Kao Shih-ch'i.

CH'ÊN KUA 陳括, *t.* Tzŭ-chêng 子正, *h.* T'o-chiang 沱江.

From Suchou. Flourished *c.*1550–1554. Son of Ch'ên Shun. Flowers in the style of Hsü Ch'ung-ssu; landscapes after Huang Kung-wang. N, III, 4. O, 6. M, p.434.

K.-k. shu-hua chi, X. A Hai-t'ang-tree. Signed and dated 1547.

Sōgen 125. Lakes and Mountains on a Clear and Beautiful Day. Signed and dated 1549. Poem by Wang Ku-hsiang.

Ku-kung collect. Pine-trees, Bamboo and Chrysanthemum by a River. Handscroll. Signed and dated 1550.

N. Gashū 11. Landscape. Signed and dated 1550.

Ku-kung, XLII. Flowers in a Vase. Signed. Poem.

K.-k. shu-hua chi, XLIV. Birds in Snow. Signed.

Ku-kung collect. (Nanking Exhib. cat. 146). Two leaves from an album of flower paintings. Seals of the artist.

National Museum, Stockholm. Fishermen on the River. Fan-painting. Ink and colour on gold-sprinkled paper.

CH'ÊN LIEN 陳廉, *t.* Ming-ch'ing 明卿, *h.* Hsiu-shui 繡水.

From Sung-chiang, Kiangsu. Flourished *c.*1620. Pupil of Chao Tso. Landscapes. M, p.435.

Nanju 15. Landscape. Seal of the painter.

CH'ÊN LO 陳裸. Originally called Ch'ên Tsan 陳瓚 and *t.* Shu-lo 叔裸. Later used Ch'êng-chiang 誠將 as his *tzŭ* and Po-shih 白室 as his *hao*.

From Suchou. Flourished *c.*1610–1640. Landscapes in the styles of Chao Po-chü, Chao Mêng-fu and Wên Chêng-ming. N, IV, 16. O, 4. M, p.435.

K.-k. shu-hua chi, XXXIX. Landscape. Signed. Poem and colophon, dated 1614.

Chêng Ch'i, Hongkong. The Ch'iao and Hua Mountains, after Chao Mêng-fu's famous picture. Inscribed by the artist and dated 1627. Colophon by Tung Ch'i-ch'ang.

K.-k. shu-hua chi, XXIV. Landscape. Signed. Two lines of poetry, dated 1636.

K.-k. chou-k'an 151, 227, 262, 510. Landscapes, fan-paintings. See also Nanga Taisei, VIII, 88.
I-yüan chên-shang 4. A Scholar standing under Pine-trees, beside a stream. Signed.
Shina Nanga, III, 5. Landscape. Signed.
Hamburg Exhib. 1949–1950. Landscape with a Crane's Nest.

CH'ÊN LU 陳錄, *t.* Hsien-chang 憲章, *h.* Ju-yin Chü-shih 如隱居士.
From K'uai-chi, Chekiang. Flourished *c.*1440. Pine trees, bamboos, orchids, and particularly plum-blossoms. O, 7. M, p.432.

K.-k. shu-hua chi, XXXIV. Plum-blossoms. Signed and dated 1437.
Sōgen 157. A Blossoming Plum-tree. Signed. Colophon, dated 1446.
Po-mei chi. The Moon and Plum-blossoms. Signed.
Berlin Museum. Plum-trees in Blossom and the Full Moon. Long handscroll. Signed.
Nanking Exhib. cat. 136 (ex-P'ang Yüan-chi collect.). A Branch of Plum-blossom by Moonlight. Signed.

CH'ÊN SHAO-YING 陳紹英, *t.* Shêng-fu 生甫, *h.* Hu-an 瓠菴.
A native of Jên-ho. Ming Dynasty. Landscapes after Wu Chên. H, *hsü-pien*, N. 7, M, p.436.

Pageant 666. Mountain Landscape, with a Man in a House by the River. Signed and dated *kuei-ssu* (probably 1593).

CH'ÊN SHUN 陳淳, *t.* Tao-fu 道復, *h.* Po-yang 白陽. Later he took Tao-fu as his name and Fu-fu 復甫 as his *tzŭ*.
From Suchou. B. 1483, d. 1544. Pupil of Wên Chêng-ming. Famous flower-painter. N, III, 4. O, 6. I, 56, 13. M, p.433.

Chêng Tê-k'un, Cambridge. An Angler in a Boat under a Tree near a City Gate. Signed and dated 1522.
T'ai-shan ts'an-shih-lou ts'ang-hua, II. A Deep Gully in the Mountains, a Man Seated on a Terrace looking over the Gully. Signed and dated 1523.
Chang Ta-ch'ien cat., vol., IV. A Tall Cliff with Pine-trees growing on it dominates the picture; a small boat on the water below. Signed and dated 1525.
Shên-chou, XVI. A Scholar Seated on a Stone Bench under an Overhanging Cliff. Signed and dated 1528. *Cf.* Shina Nanga, II, 10.
Tōsō, p.306. Chrysanthemum. Signed. Poem by the painter, dated 1532.
Ueno collect., Kyōto. A Branch of Loquat. Signed and dated 1534. *Cf.* Nanga Taisei, IV, 19.
Shên-chou, V. Lichee. Signed and dated 1534. *Cf.* Shina Nanga, I, 10.
Freer Gallery. Landscape in the style of Mi Yu-jên. Ink and slight colour. Signed and dated 1535. Handscroll. Colophons by Wên Chêng-ming, Tung Ch'i-ch'ang, etc.
J. P. Dubosc, Lugano. Flowering Plants and Trees, in colour. Poems by the artist accompanying the painting. Dated 1537. Handscroll.
Harada Brothers, Ōsaka. River Landscape with cloudy Mountains, after Shên Chou. Handscroll. Inscription, dated 1537.
Ku-kung collect. Flowers of the Four Seasons and Bamboos. Scattered ink-paintings on a long handscroll with beautiful inscriptions. Signed and dated 1538.
Shina Nanga, II, 2. Five Kinds of Flowers. Handscroll. Signed and dated 1538. *Cf.* Nanga Taisei, IV, 21.
Chicago Art Institute. Pavilion of Eight Poems. River Landscape with a Pavilion on the Shore; two Sailing-boats on the River. Handscroll. Inscription by the painter, dated 1538. *Cf.* Cleveland Exhibition cat., No. 63.

Nelson Gallery, Kansas City. Crabs and Sea-grass. Signed and dated 1538.

Ku-kung collect. (Nanking Exhib. cat. 139). River Landscape. Leaf in an album. Inscription by the painter on another leaf, signed and dated 1540.

C. C. Wang, New York. Towering Mountains in Successive Terraces. Long inscription by the painter, dated 1540.

Nanga Taisei, IX, 136. River Landscape with Fishermen in Boats. Signed and dated 1542.

Shina Nanga, II, 6. Flower. Signed and dated 1542.

Kawai collect., Kyōto, 1954. Lotus Flowers on a Summer Morning. Long handscroll in light colour. Signed and dated 1543. Now in Chicago Art Institute.

C. C. Wang, New York. Leafy Trees on a Shore Shaken by the Wind. Long inscription by the painter, dated 1543.

Sōraikan, II, 55. River Landscape; White Clouds over green Hills. Handscroll. Inscription by the painter, dated 1544.

Ibid. II, 56. Pine-tree and Chrysanthemum. Poems by the painter and by Wên Chêng-ming. Dated 1544.

Chung-hua album, 1934. Twenty Studies of Flowers and Fruits on album-leaves. Signed and dated 1544.

Musée Guimet. Bird on a small Rock in a Bowl. Signed and dated 1544. Poem by Wên Chêng-ming, dated 1548.

J. P. Dubosc, Lugano. A Study in a Bamboo-grove by a River. Short handscroll. Long inscription by the painter, signed and dated 1544.

Private collect., Kyōto. Misty Mountain Landscape. Handscroll, painted on silk. Signed and dated 1545.

Ming-jên shu-hua, 23. Hollyhocks and Reeds by a Stream. Signed.

Li Tai, II. Flowers. Long handscroll. Signed. Poems.

S.c.t.k. hsü-pien, VII. Misty River; Fishermen in a Small Boat by the Shore.

K.-k. shu-hua chi, XXIX. Wild Duck and Lotus Leaves. Signed. *Cf.* Nanga Taisei, VI, 71.

Ku-kung ming-shan chi, 8. Fan-paintings. *Cf.* also K.-k. chou-k'an, Index, for eleven fan-paintings; also Nanga Taisei, III, 10 and 233; V, 90; VIII, 41.

Hui-hua kuan. Mu-tan Flowers by a Rock. Colour on paper. Short handscroll. Signed by the painter.

Ibid. Grass and Flowering Plants at the Foot of a Garden Stone. Ink on paper. Inscription by the painter.

Gems, I, 37. Mountain Ridges after Rain. Poem, signed.

Ibid. II, 15. Peonies. Handscroll. Signed.

Mo-ch'ao pi-chi. A Cock among Flowers. Signed.

P'ang Yüan-chi Illust. cat. II. Camellia Flowers and Narcissi. Signed.

Kokka 721. A Misty River Landscape. Handscroll. Signed.

Shina Nanga, III, 12. Landscape. Signed.

Yūrintaikan, I. Mu-tan Flowers. Handscroll. Inscription by Wên Chêng-ming; colophons by Wu K'uan and Wang Wên-chih, the last one dated 1785.

Nanga Taisei, II, 155, 156. Two album-leaves. Chrysanthemums.

Ibid. II, 216. Plum-blossom and Bamboo. Seals of the painter.

Ibid. III, 10. Plum-blossom. Fan-painting. Seals of the painter.

Ibid. III, 232–234. Plum-blossoms. Fan-painting. Signed.

Ibid. XIV, 53. A Flowering Shrub by a Garden Rockery. Signed. *Cf.* K.-k. chou-k'an 503.

N. P. Wang, Hongkong. Narcissi and a Branch of Plum-blossom. Signed. Inscription by Chou T'ien-ch'iu.

H. C. Wêng, New York. Various Garden Flowers. Short handscroll. Signed. A.

Metropolitan Museum. River Landscape with Three Boats on the River. Handscroll. Ink and slight colour. Inscription by the painter. *Cf.* Cleveland Exhibition cat. 65.

Nelson Gallery, Kansas City (ex-Lo Chên-yü). Landscape in the style of Mi. Handscroll. Ink and slight colour on paper. Three poems by the painter. *Cf.* Cleveland Exhibition cat. 64.

Ibid. A series of Lotus Plants. Colour on paper. Long handscroll. Signed. Poem by the painter and colophon by Wang Chih-têng.

Ibid. Lily Pads. Colour on paper. Signed.

Köln, Ostasiat. Museum. A Flowering Plant in a Rockery. Signed. Fan-painting. Köln Exhibition, 1955, No.6.

Vannotti collect., Lugano. Branches of a Blossoming Plum-tree. Poem by the painter. Fan-painting.

J. P. Dubosc, Lugano. Lotus. Signed. Colophons by Wang Ch'ung (1494–1533) and Wang Ku-hsiang.

Ibid. A Blossoming Tree in a Garden Rockery by a Pond in which the Lotus grow high. Richly coloured, large picture.

Ch'ên Tsun 陳遵.
From Chia-hsing, Chekiang; lived in Suchou. Flowers and birds. O, 6. M, p.436.

J. P. Dubosc, Lugano. Three Large Birds and Bamboo on a River-bank. Signed and dated 1611. Fan-painting.
Hui-hua kuan. Two Pheasants by a Blossoming Plum-tree and Red Camellia in Snow. Bright colours on silk. In the manner of Lü Chi. Signed.

Ch'ên Tzŭ-ho 陳子和, *h.* Chiu-hsien 酒仙.
From P'u-ch'êng, Fukien. Flourished *c.*1500. Originally a sculptor but devoted himself later to painting in the manner of Lin Liang and Wu Wei. O, 1. M, p.434.

National Museum, Tōkyō. Two Pheasants on a Rock. Signed.
Tōyō, X. Three Cormorants at a Waterfall. Signed.
Honde collect., Kyōto. A Man writing at his Desk in the Garden. Signed.
British Museum, Nos.129, 130. Rockeries with Chrysanthemums. Seal of the painter. Attributed.

Ch'ên Yü 陳遇, *t.* Chung-hsing 中行, *h.* Ching-ch'êng 靜誠.
From Nanking. B. 1313, d. 1384. Painted portraits of the emperor Hung-wu. Also landscapes. N, VI, 1. O, 1. M, p.430.

Nanking Exhib. cat. 84. A Mountain Gorge filled with Mists. Signed and dated 1376.
Tōsō, p.230. Fantastic Mountains, Rapids and Large Trees. Section of a handscroll in archaistic style.

Ch'ên Yüan 陳遠, *t.* Chung-fu 中復.
Younger brother of Ch'ên Yü. Portraits in the manner of his brother. O, 1. M, p.430.

M. Halphen, Paris. Portrait of the Emperor Hung-wu. *Cf.* K.-k. chou-kan, vol.VII, 139, reproducing a similar portrait in the Nan-hsün tien of the Peking palace.

Ch'en Yüan-su 陳元素, *t.* Ku-po 古白, *h.* Su-wêng 素翁.
Active *c.*1620–1650. Poet, calligrapher. Orchids. N, VII, 24. U, II, 1, 3. M, p.436.

Hui-hua kuan. Epidendrum and Bamboo by a Stone. Painted together with Liu Yüan-ch'i. Signed and dated 1620. Eight inscriptions by his friends.
Shên-chou, XI. Orchids and Rocks by a Stream. Signed. Poem. (The Rocks by Pien Wên-yü, dated 1622.)
Shên-chou ta-kuan, vol.4. A Tuft of Epidendrum. Signed and dated 1626. Poems by six contemporaries.
National Museum, Stockholm. A Large Tuft of Epidendrum Growing on a Slope. Painted on gold-sprinkled paper. Signed and dated 1630.
Nanga Taisei, I, 81. Two Bunches of Orchids. Handscroll, signed.
Shina Meiga Senshū, III. Epidendrum, Bamboo and Grass by a Garden Rock. Painted together with Chang Fu (garden rock), Liu Yüan-ch'i (grass) and Shao Mi (bamboos). Inscriptions by the painter, and by Wên Tien and Lu Kuang-ming.

Chêng Chih-yen 鄭之彥, *t.* Lan-yen 蘭岩.
From Nanking. Active probably towards the end of the 16th century. Plum-blossoms and landscapes. M, p.642.

T'ai-shan ts'an-shih-lou ts'ang-hua, III. Hill-slopes by a River, after Huang Kung-wang. Signed.

CHÊNG CHUNG 鄭重, *t.* Ch'ien-li 千里.

From Hsieh-hsien, Anhui; lived in Nanking. Active *c.*1565–1630. Buddhist figures and landscapes. N, IV, 25. M, p.642.

British Museum., No.161. Sakyamuni. Signed and dated 1568.

K.-k. shu-hua chi, XXX. Ko Hung Moving his Residence. After Wang Mêng. Signed and dated 1612.

Tōsō, p.399. Landscape, with a Man observing a Waterfall. Signed and dated 1628.

Chung-kuo, II, 53. Bodhidharma Crossing the Yangtse on a Reed.

K.-k. shu-hua chi, XXVII. An Old Man Seated on the Floor Served by a Boy. Emblems of Longevity. Attributed. *Cf.* K.-k. chou-k'an 401.

K.-k. chou-k'an 236. Landscape. Fan-painting.

CHÊNG SHIH 鄭石.

Unrecorded. Officer in the Imperial Guard in the Ming period.

K.-k. shu-hua chi, IX. Herons and Hibiscus by a Willow on the River-bank. Signed.

CHÊNG TIEN-HSIEN 鄭顚仙, *t.* (?) Wên-lin 文林.

From Fukien. Contemporary with Chang Lu and Chung Li with whom he associated as a painter. M, p.642.

Hui-hua kuan. Two Old Men under a Tree by a Waterfall. Ink on silk. In the manner of Wu Wei.

Kyūka, I. Fishermen Dancing and Making Music. Signed.

Hashimoto collect., Takatsuki. A Man giving Food to a Beggar; a third Man watching. Forms a pair with the above picture. Signed.

CHÊNG YAO-NIEN 鄭堯年.

Unrecorded; presumably Wan-li period.

Suchiku, 12 (formerly Oguri collection). Picture of Bodhidharma seated. Colophon by Hsiang Shêng, dated 1605.

CH'ÊNG CHIA-SUI 程嘉燧, *t.* Mêng-yang 孟陽, *h.* Sung-yüan Lao-jên 松園老人.

From Hsiu-ning, Anhui; lived in Chia-ting, Kiangsu. B. 1565, d. 1643. One of the "Nine Friends in Painting". Poet. Landscapes in the styles of the Yüan masters. N, IV, 18. O, 5. P, II, 3. U, I, 2, 2. M, p.534.

Shoman 24. Landscape after Ts'ao Chih-po. Signed and dated 1587.

J. P. Dubosc, Lugano. Spare Trees and a Wanderer on River-bank. Signed and dated 1608. Fan-painting.

Metropolitan Museum. A Cock by a Tree. Fan-painting. Signed and dated 1616.

S.c.t.k. hsü-pien, XI. Landscape. Signed and dated 1618.

K.-k. shu-hua chi, II. Landscape after Ts'ao Chih-po. Signed and dated 1624. Inscription by Hsü Liang.

Tōan 32. Bamboos and Plum-blossoms. Fan-painting. Signed and dated 1625.

Nanking Exhib. cat. 194. A Man on the Bank of a River under Trees. Signed and dated 1627. *Cf.* Chung-kuo, II, 43.

Po-mei chi. A Blossoming Plum-tree. Album-leaf. Signed and dated 1627.

Tōsō, p.351. The Yangtse River. Signed. Colophon and poem, dated 1630.

Chang Ta-ch'ien cat. I, 31. River Landscape in the manner of Ni Tsan. Signed and dated 1630.

Gems, I, 45. Two Pine-trees growing by a Stream. Poem, signed and dated 1631.

Shên-chou, VI. Temple on a Cloudy Mountain. Signed and dated 1634. Poem by Ch'ên Chi-ju.

Ibid. XII. A Man and a Boy Walking on a Bridge. Album-leaf. Signed and dated 1634. *Cf.* Nanga Taisei, XI, 61.

Shanghai Museum. River Landscape in the style of Ni Tsan. Signed and dated 1635. Inscription by Ch'ên Chi-ju.

National Museum, Stockholm. River-view with Pine-trees along the Shore. Handscroll. Signed and dated 1635. *Cf.* Kokka 265.

I-yüan chên-shang 10. Pine-trees and rocks. Signed and dated 1639.

Shên-chou, XIII. "Bringing Back the Ink-stones:" Three Men under scattered Trees. Album-leaf. Signed and dated 1640.

Hua-chung chiu-yu chi-ts'e (Hakubundō album, Ōsaka, 1921). Leafless Trees on a Rocky Shore by a High Cliff. Signed and dated 1640.

Shên-chou ta-kuan, vol.4. River-view, after Ni Tsan. Poem by the painter, dated 1642.

Ōmura, I, 7. Landscape after Ni Tsan. Signed and dated 1642. *Cf.* P'ang Yüan-chi Illust. cat. II.

K.-k. chou-k'an, 6. Landscape. Fan-painting.

Hua-chung chiu-yu (Yu-chêng album, 1925). Landscape. Signed. Colophon.

Hui-hua kuan. Two Men Seated in an Open Pavilion at the Foot of a Mountain. Poem by the painter.

Musée Guimet. Landscape on gold ground. Fan-painting.

Chang Ts'ung-yü cat. A Man Standing under a Pine-tree on a River-bank.

Ku-kung collect. (Nanking Exhib. cat. 193). Two leaves from an album of landscapes. Inscriptions and seals of the artist.

CH'ÊNG-I 誠意.

From Chekiang. Active in the Yung-lo period (1403–1424). Unrecorded.

Shimbi, III (Fushimi collect.) Confucius and his Disciples on the Apricot Terrace. Signed. *Cf.* Tōsō, p.257.

CHI CHÊN 紀鎭 (not to be confused with Chi Chên 眞 of the Sung Period).

Unrecorded; evidently an artist of the Ming Academy active about the middle of the 15th century.

Kurokawa cat. 2. A Bitch and Two Puppies in a Garden. Signed. *Cf.* Pageant 495.

CHIANG AI 蔣藹, *t.* Chih-ho 志和.

From Hua-t'ing, Kiangsu. Flourished *c.*1620. Followed Shên Shih-ch'ung. Landscapes. O, 4. L, 48, 6. M, p.647.

Kurokawa cat. 11. Landscape after Tung Yüan. Signed and dated 1604.

Sōgen 364. Steep Green Cliffs. Signed and dated 1614.

Shên-chou, XV. Steep Cliffs and Leafy Trees on the Rocky Shore by a River. Album-leaf. Signed and dated 1616. *Cf.* Shina Nanga, II, 9.

CHIANG CH'ÊNG-TSUNG 姜承宗.

Unrecorded. Late Ming.

Chūgoku IV. Landscape with Bare Trees. Large album-leaf, signed and dated 1635. The label erroneously attributes the picture to a Ch'ing painter, Tsung Hao.

CHIANG CH'IEN 蔣乾, *t.* Tzŭ-chien 子健, *h.* Hung-ch'iao 虹橋.

From Nanking; lived in Suchou. Son of Chiang Sung. Active *c.*1540–1560. Landscapes. N, III, 13. O, 4. M, p.646.

Vannotti collect., Lugano. Old Trees on a River-bank. Signed and dated 1541 (?). Poem by Wang Chih-têng dated 1607.

H. C. Wêng, Scarsdale, N.Y. Water and Hills. Handscroll. Signed and dated 1548.

K.-k. shu-hua chi, XXXIV. A Cottage by the Foot of a Leafy Towering Mountain, after Wang Mêng. Poem by the painter, dated 1563. *Cf.* K.-k. chou-k'an, vol.III, 66.

Nanju 13. Landscape. Fan-painting. Signed.

K.-k. chou-k'an 254. Landscape. Fan-painting. Signed.

CHIANG LI-KANG 姜立綱, *t.* T'ing-hsien 廷憲, *h.* Tung-ch'i 東谿.

From Yung-chia, Chekiang. Famous calligraphist who invented the Chiang style. Active in the T'ien-shun period (1457–1464). Landscapes in the style of Huang Kung-wang and Wang Mêng. N, II, 2. O, 3. I, 56, 3. M, p.273.

Tōsō, p.396. Landscape with two Men and a Boy standing on a Bridge. Signed.

British Museum, No.166. Flowers and Birds.

CHIANG SSŬ-CHOU 姜思周, *t.* Chou-ch'ên 周臣, *h.* Hua-chiu t'ou-t'o 花酒頭陀.

Native of Ch'ien-t'ang, Chekiang. Active *c.*1620. Pupil of Kuan Ssŭ and friend of Lan Ying. Landscapes (and flowers) after Shên Chou. M, p.274.

C. T. Loo Successor, New York. Endless Mountains along a Broad Stream; in the manner of Mi Fei. Handscroll. Inscription by the painter, dated 1621. Colophon with biographical notes. *Cf.* Toronto, 30.

CHIANG SUNG 蔣嵩, *t.* San-sung 三松.

From Nanking. Flourished *c.*1500. Landscapes and figures. Followed Wu Wei, but painted in a rough manner with a "dry brush" like Chang Lu and his friends. N, III, 6. O, 3. M, p.646.

Shimbi, III. Landscape.

Ōmura, I, 11. Landscape with a Figure. Signed.

Nanga Taisei, VIII, 79. A Man in a Boat Playing the Flute. Fan-painting. Signed.

Nanzen-ji, Kyōto. River Landscape with Fishing-boats. Signed. *Cf.* Sekai Bijutsu Zenshū, XX, text illus. 66.

Sōgen, 142. Landscape with Two Men in a Boat. Signed.

Berlin Museum. Four Views of River Valleys. Mounted as a scroll. Signed. *Cf.* Sirén, *Later*, pl.40.

Hamburg Exhibition, 1949–1950. Winter Landscape.

Formerly Arnold Genthe, New York (1938). An Angler in a Boat at the Foot of High Mountains. Signed.

CHIANG TZŬ-CH'ÊNG 蔣子成.

From I-hsing, Kiangsu. Started as a landscape-painter, but later painted mainly figures. Worked at the court during the Yung-lo period (1403–1424) together with Pien Wên-chin and the tiger-painter Chao Lien 趙廉; they were called "The Excellent Three". N, VI, 25. O, 1. I, 55, 11. M, p.646.

Kokka 27. Pu-tai. Old attribution.

CHIANG YIN 姜隱, *t.* Chou-tso 周佐.

From Huang-hsien, Shantung. 16th century. Figures, flowers and fruits. N, VI, 15. O, 1. M, p.273.

Kokka 63. The Emperor Mu-wang visiting Hsi-wang-mu. Signed.

Ch'ien Hsü 錢旭, *t.* Tung-po 東白.
Native of Hang-chou. Landscapes. H, *Hsü-pien*. M, p.680.

Nanga Taisei, XI, 62–72. Album of eleven landscapes, the last signed (but the signature defaced) and dated 1560. Seals of the artist on each leaf.

Commercial Press album, 1935. Album of twelve landscapes, the last signed and dated *hsin-ssŭ*, or 1581 (?).

Ch'ien Ku 錢穀, *t.* Shu-pao 叔寶, *h.* Ch'ing-shih 罄室.
From Suchou. B. 1508, d. after 1574. Pupil of Wên Chêng-ming. Landscapes, orchids and bamboos. N, III, 16. O, 4. I, 56, 13. M, p.680.

Hui-hua kuan. Open Pavilion with a Scholar who is admiring the newly fallen Snow which covers the Trees and the Ground. Ink and colour on paper. Inscription by the painter, dated 1541.

Köln, Ostasiat. Museum. A Lake Scene with a Man in a Boat. Fan-painting. Signed and dated 1546.

Hui-hua kuan. A Tuft of Bamboo. Ink on paper. Signed and dated 1548.

Ming-jên shu-hua, 13. Cock-fight at a Farmstead. Signed and dated 1548.

Ma Chi-tsu, Hongkong. Album of Landscape-paintings, the last dated 1555.

C. T. Loo Successors, Frank Caro, New York. River-view illustrating Su Tung-p'o's poem The Red Cliff. Signed and dated 1558.

Hui-hua kuan. A Temple Compound in the Misty Wood. Colour and ink on silk. Short handscroll. Dated 1561.

C. T. Loo Successor, New York. A Buddhist Monastery in the Gulley between Steep Mountains. Ink and colour. Painted for the monk Hui-t'ung in 1564. *Cf.* Toronto, 28.

J. P. Dubosc, Lugano. Long-tailed Bird on a Branch of a Pine-tree. According to the inscription, painted after Shên Chou. Dated 1566. Inscriptions by Chang Fêng-i and Wên Chia, the latter dated 1572. Fan-painting.

Nanga Taisei, XI, 35. View over a broad River with Islands and Sailing-boats. Section of a handscroll? Signed and dated 1567.

Takashima collect., Kugenuma. Three landscapes in a set painted by Ch'ien Ku, Wên Chia and Hou Mou-kung, representing the holy places of Taoism. Mounted as a handscroll. One dated 1567.

Liu 65. A Mountain Gorge in Winter, with a man on a donkey crossing a bridge. Signed and dated 1569.

K.-k. shu-hua chi, XXV. Apricot-blossoms and Magpie. Signed and dated 1569.

Musée Guimet. Friends Resting in the Shade. Inscription recording a gathering on a summer day, dated 1569.

J. P. Dubosc, Lugano. River Landscape with a Man in a Boat, illustrating the legend of the Peach Blossom Valley. Ink and colour. Signed and dated 1569. Fan-painting.

K.-k. shu-hua chi, XI. Preparing Tea on Hui Shan. Signed and dated 1570.

Tōsō, p.307. The Red Cliff. Signed and dated 1570.

Nanga Taisei, IX, 148, 1. Six Men and Two Servants round a Well (?) under tall Trees and Bamboo. Signed and dated 1570.

J. P. Dubosc, Lugano. A Man on a Ledge beside a Waterfall. Fan-painting. Signed and dated 1571.

K.-k. shu-hua chi, XII. Travellers on Snow-capped Mountains. A very large picture. Signed and dated 1572.

Ibid. XXXI. Chung K'uei. Signed and dated 1572.

Ku-kung, XXIII. Collecting Fungi. Signed and dated 1574.

Hamburg Exhibition, 1949–1950. Sailing by the Red Cliff. Handscroll. Signed and dated 1575.

Pao-yün, II. A Villa on the Shore and a Man in a Boat. Fan-painting. Signed and dated 1578.

Vannotti collect., Lugano. Sailing-boats on a Lake; a Temple on an Island. Fan-painting. Signed and dated 1578.

Köln, Ostasiat. Museum. Landscape with two Men passing over a Bridge to a Rocky Island. Fan-painting. Signed and dated 1579.

Shên-chou, IV. The Nine Old Men of Hsiang Shan.

K.-k. shu-hua chi, XXIII. Washing the Wu-t'ung-tree. Signed.

K.-k. chou-k'an 13, 61, 215, 240, 244, 249, 279. Landscapes. Seven fan-paintings. For others, see Nanga Taisei, VIII, 63–69.

Shina Nanga, III, 3. Looking at the Sailing Clouds. Signed.

N. Gashū, 12. Rainy Landscape. Signed.

Nanga Taisei, VIII, 63–69. A set of fan-paintings representing landscapes after various old masters, some with figures. Signed, three of them dated.

Sōgen 126–128. Three pictures forming a set under the common title The Fishermen's Pleasure.

National Museum, Stockholm. A tall Mountain Landscape. Signed.

Hamburg Exhibition, 1949–1950. Seascape.

CH'IEN KUNG 錢貢, *t.* Yü-fang 禹方, *h.* Ts'ang-chou 滄洲.

Native of Wu-hsien. Flourished in the Wan-li period (1573–1620). Landscapes and figures. N, 3. O, 4. M, p.680.

Ho Kuan-wu, Hongkong. Mountain Landscape, with Buildings and Figures. Signed and dated 1584.

Nanga Taisei, VIII, 109. Two Men seated beneath Pines, watching a Waterfall. Fan-painting. Signed and dated 1599. For other fan-paintings, see K.-k. chou-k'an 65, 201, 266, 269.

Frau Hasler, Winterthur. View of a Winding River and Steep Cliffs in front. Ink and colour. Signed and dated 1606. Fan-painting.

CHIN SHÊNG 金聲, t. Chêng-hsi 正希.

B. 1598, d. 1645. Native of Hsiu-ning in Anhui. Not recorded in the standard dictionaries of painters. V, p.613.

Nanking Exhib. cat. 226. Seated portrait of Buddha. Signed and dated 1619.

CHIN SHIH 金湜, *t.* Pên-ch'ing 本清, *h.* T'ai-shou-shêng 太瘦生 and Hsiu-mu Chü-shih 朽木居士.

From Ning-po, Chekiang. Chü-jên in 1441. Became a secretary in the Grand Council. Painted rocks and bamboos in outlines. Calligraphist. N, VI, 5. O, 7. M, p.234.

Sōgen 89. Bamboos by a Rockery. Signed. Poem. *Cf.* Nanking Exhib. cat. 132.

Sōraikan, II, 46. Two Bamboos in Outline Growing by a Rock. Inscriptions by the painter and by Chang Pang-ch'i (1484–1544). *Cf.* Chung-kuo ming-hua, XII.

CHIN WÊN-CHIN 金文進, *t.* Yen-hui 彥輝, *h.* Yün-shih 筠石.

From Suchou. Active 1400–1450. Bamboos. M, p.234.

Fogg Museum, Cambridge, Mass. Ten Thousand Bamboos. Short handscroll. Signed and dated 1438. Fourteen colophons including one by the painter. *Cf.* Cleveland Exhibition cat. 38.

CH'IU SHIH 仇氏 (Miss Ch'iu) or Ch'iu Chu 仇珠, *h.* Tu-ling Nei-shih 杜陵內史.

From Suchou. Flourished *c.*1550. Daughter of Ch'iu Ying. Figures in the style of her father. N, V, 1. O, 1. M, p.10.

Êrh-shih chia. Four album-leaves: (1) A Girl Playing the *Ch'in* under Wu-t'ung Trees. Signed. (2) A Lady at a Table with a Chess-board. Signed and dated 1567. (3) A Lady under Plum-trees with Books. Signed. (4) A Lady at her Writing-desk. Signed. *Cf.* Nanga Taisei Intr. 22; VII, 33–35; Add. IV, 24.

K.-k. shu-hua chi, XXXIX. A Lady in a Garden. Illustration to a T'ang poem. Signed.

Kokka 147. Threading Needles in the Evening of the 7th of the 7th Moon.

Tōsō, p.284. Lady Musicians.

K.-k. chou-k'an 82. Kuanyin. Full length. Signed.

CH'IU YING 仇英, *t.* Shih-fu 實父, *h.* Shih-chou 十洲.
From T'ai-ts'ang, Kiangsu; lived in Suchou. First half of the 16th century. Pupil of Chou Ch'ên. Figures, landscapes and architectural scenery. His paintings in colour have been much imitated. N, III, 7. O, 1. I, 56, 12. M, p.10.

Ku-kung collect. *Yüan-chü t'u.* The Garden of a Scholar, and two men in the pavilion. Painted in *kung-pi* manner with colour. Short handscroll. Signed and dated 1532. Colophon by Wang Ch'ung. A.

Min Shitaika, 61. A Man Seated under a Tree by a Stream. Signed. Two lines of poetry by Wang Ch'ung (d. 1533).

Tōsō, p.277. A Pavilion among Bamboos and Wu-t'ung-trees. Signed. Poems by Wang Ch'ung, Wên Chêng-ming, etc. *Cf. Later Chinese Painting*, pt.103.

Ōmura, I, 10. The Fairy Mountain. Poem by Lu Shih-tao, dated 1535.

J. D. Ch'en, Hongkong. River Landscape in Spring. Handscroll, colours on silk. Signed. Inscription by Wên Chêng-ming, dated 1539.

National Museum, Stockholm. The Journey of the Emperor Ming-huang to Shu. The road is winding between the mountains on palisades and on bridges over the streams. Long handscroll, with colour in an archaistic manner. According to inscription executed by Ch'iu Ying in 1541 after a picture by Chao Po-chü (Ch'ien-li). Studio picture.

Tōsō, p.278. Portrait of Ni Tsan. Epitaph copied by Wên P'êng, dated 1542.

Boston Museum. A Harp-player in a Pavilion. Seal of the painter. Poem by Wên P'êng; colophons by Ch'ên Tao-fu (dated 1542) and by Tung Ch'i-ch'ang. *Cf.* Chung-kuo, II, 25. A.

H. C. Wêng, Scarsdale (Venice Exhibition, No.815). Chao Mêng-fu writing a Sūtra. Handscroll, datable to the year 1543.

Tōan 27. The Eight Drunkards. Handscroll. Illustration to a poem by Tu Fu, copied by P'êng Nien, dated 1543.

Chung-kuo, II, 28. Plum-blossoms and Easter Lilies. Signed and dated 1547.

Ku-kung collect. Six album-leaves representing Landscapes after Sung and Yüan Masters. Colour on silk. Colophon by Hsiang Yüan-pien, dated 1547. Remounted by Hsiang Sheng-piao, grandson of Hsiang Yüan-pien, in 1578.

Ibid. Palace Pavilion in a Beautiful Mountain Valley. Colour on paper. Signed. Inscription by Lu Shih-tao, dated 1548.

K.-k. shu-hua chi, XXI. The Fairy Mountain. Signed. A rhymed prose by Lu Shih-tao, dated 1548.

C. T. Loo Successor, Frank Caro, New York. Gathering Lotus-seeds. Two women in a boat on a lake, a man seated in an open pavilion looks at them. Colour on paper. Fifteen old poems copied by Yü Yün-wên, dated 1567, and by later men. Attributed.

Hamburg Exhibition, 1949–1950. Crossing a River in a Boat, after Liu Sung-nien. Signed and dated 1578?

Shên-chou, IV. A Man playing the *Ch'in* under Pines by a Stream. Signed.

Ibid. XI. A Lady Seated in a Hall, her Maid in the Courtyard. Signed.

Shên-chou ta-kuan, vol.I. Lady Wên Yü standing in a Bamboo Grove. Seal of the painter.

I-shu ts'ung-pien, 11. A Scholar enjoying the Evening Calm in a Pavilion built over a River. Signed.

Chung-kuo ming-hua, vol.9 Listening to a Waterfall in an Autumn Forest. Signed.

Ibid. 17. Fishermen's Village. Painted in colour.

Ibid. 19. A Lady with her Attendant. Signed. Colophons by Wang Ch'ih-teng and Chou T'ien-ch'iu.

Ibid. 24. A Man in White, followed by his Servant, walking along the Embankment of a Lake under Willows on a Spring Day. Attributed.

Chung-kuo, II, p.22 (Ti P'ing-tzŭ). Landscape with a Scholar. Signed. Short handscroll. Painted together with T'ang Yin.

Ibid. II, 23. A Young Woman beating Clothes. Signed. Also in Sōgen 110; P'ang Yüan-chi cat. 8.

Ibid. II, 24. Peasants Wading across a Stream. Signed.

Ibid. II, 26. A Man in a Pavilion looking at the Stormy Sea.

Ibid. II, 27. An Old Man and his Boy-servant under a Pine-tree. Ink only. Signed.

Êrh-shih chia. Listening to the *Ch'in*; Ladies making Music in a Garden. After Chou Fang. Short handscroll. Signed.

Ku-kung, IV. The Eighteen Scholars on the Island of the Immortals. Signed. School picture.

Ibid. XVIII. A Man Playing the *Ch'in* for a Visitor under Plum-trees. Signed.

Ibid. XXI. A Summer Pavilion in the Mountains. Seal of the painter (?).

K.-k. shu-hua chi, VII. Playing the *Ch'in* and the *P'i-p'a* in the Shade of Banana-trees. Signed. *Cf.* Nanking Exhibition cat. 150. A.

Ibid. IX. Waiting for the Ferry-boat; a broad river-view. A.

Ibid. XIV. The Gathering of Poets at Lan-t'ing. Seals of the painter.

Ibid. XVIII. A Scholar in a Fishing-boat on the Willow-stream. Inscription by Wên Chia. Signed.

Ibid. XIX. Two Men under a Wu-t'ung Tree. Signed.

Ibid. XXXVIII. The Poetical Gathering in the Western Garden. Signed. School picture.

K.-k. chou-k'an, vol.II, 50. A Scholar seated under Bamboos listening to a Mountain Brook. Poem by Ch'ien-lung. *Cf.* Ming-hua ling-lang.

Ibid. vol.XIV, 308. A Summer Palace in a Gully between sharply cut Rocky Mountains. Signed. Long colophon by Ch'ien-lung.

Ku-kung ming-shan chi 6. Five fan-paintings. *Cf.* K.-k. chou-k'an Index for nine fan-paintings; also Nanga Taisei, VIII, 43–49.

Ku-kung collect. *Kao-shih t'u.* A version of the same motif represented in T'ang Yin's picture with the same title, but with the addition of one figure. Whereas T'ang Yin's is painted in the manner of Liang K'ai, Ch'iu Ying's picture is in the manner of Li Kung-lin. Inscription by Wên Chêng-ming. A.

Ibid. Buddha Enclosing the Son of Hariti in the Bowl. Short handscroll. Signed.

Ibid. Spring Banquet in the Peach and Plum-garden. Long handscroll. Brightly coloured school work.

Ibid. Listening to the Brook in a Bamboo-grove. Large album-leaf. Signed.

Ibid. *Han-kung ch'un-hsiao t'u*: Spring Morning in the Gardens of the Han Palace. Long brightly coloured handscroll. School work.

Ibid. The Lan-t'ing Meeting at the Foot of High Mountains. The scholars are seated on mats along the winding brook. Long handscroll. Executed in *pai-miao* manner. Signed.

Pao-yün, II. Refining Cinnabar, after Chao Po-chü. Landscape with a towering mountain; a man in a cave. Signed.

Hui-hua kuan. River Landscape. Men on a Promontory bidding Farewell to a Friend who leaves in a Boat. Green mountains rising through clouds in the background. Short handscroll. Signed.

Ibid. A Man saluting an Official seated in a Pavilion. In *Kung-pi* manner. Small handscroll. Signed.

Shanghai Museum. A Scholar resting under a Willow; a Servant approaches. In the manner of Tai Chin. Signed.

Gems, I, 34. Travellers riding through the Chien-ko Pass in Winter. School picture.

Ibid. II, 13, 14. Picking Lotus Flowers; The Feast. Two sections of a handscroll. Attributed.

I-yüan album. A Girl in her Spring Dreams. Six album-leaves.

Ibid. (Ch'u-i chai collect.) Gentlemen meeting to play the *Ch'in.* A scroll divided on four sheets. Poem by the painter.

Liu, 59. Wang Hsi-chih writing on a Fan. Other versions of the same painting in Ku-kung and P'ang Yüan-chi's collection. *Cf.* Gems, I, 35; Nanking Exhib. cat. 151.

P'ang Yüan-chi Illust. cat. I. Scholar seated under a Projecting Pine by a Mountain Stream. A boy-servant is wrapping up a bundle. Signed.

Nanking Exhib. cat. 149 (Wu Hu-fan collect.) Kuanyin with a Baby, surrounded by Attendant Figures. After Li Lung-mien. Signed.

Ibid. 152. Travellers in the Mountains in Autumn. After Liu Sung-nien. Signed.

Ibid. 153 (Chang Ta-ch'ien collect.) Two Taoist Immortals. Sections of a handscroll. Inscriptions and seals of the artist.

Chang Ta-ch'ien cat. I, 25. A Man enjoying the Cool Air in a Pavilion over a River. Signed.

Ibid., vol.IV. T'ao Yüan-ming is seated under a Tall Pine, and a Boy with his *Ch'in* is approaching. On the other side of the pond, a boy is crossing a wooden bridge. Handscroll. Signed.

Chang Ts'ung-yü cat. A Party of numerous Noble Persons with their Servants and Horses in a Garden Landscape. Long handscroll.

Shên-shou album, 1930. Six album-leaves representing Old Sages and legendary persons of Chinese history. Seals of the artist. *Cf.* Nanga Taisei, VII, 27–32.

Hikkōen, 18. Pavilions under Trees on a Garden Terrace. Album-leaf. Attributed.

Ibid. 19. Two House-boats; one with a Lady and the other with a Man and their Servants. Fan-shaped. Attributed. *Cf.* Kokka.

Kokka 193. Mountain Landscape with Figures and high Pavilions. Signed. *Cf.* Shimbi, XI.

Ibid. 237 (Chion-in, Kyōto). The Garden of Peach and Pear-blossoms. *Cf.* Shimbi, II; Tōsō, p.276; Tōyō, X. Fetc. A.

Ibid. 245. The Chin-ku Garden. *Cf.* Shimbi, II; Tōsō, p.275; Tōyō, X; Sekai Bijutsu Zenshū, XX, colour pl.1. A.

Ibid. 254. Interior with six Ladies playing Cards. Signed. The screen by Lu Chih. *Cf.* Êrh-shih chia.

Ibid. 295. The Poetical Gathering in the Western Garden. A reduced version. Handscroll. Part of it also in Nanju 25.

Ibid. 475 and 481. Seven album-leaves (out of sixteen), illustrating poems of the T'ang period.

Yamato Bunkakan, Ōsaka. Court Ladies enjoying themselves in the Garden. Handscroll. Signed. *Cf.* Dai Tenrankai 65.

Tōyō, X (Berlin Museum). A Monk receiving a Visitor on a Garden-terrace. Handscroll. Signed. *Cf.* Bijutsu, VIII.

Ibid. X. High Mountains and Pavilions; a *Ch'in* Player under the Pine-trees (?).

Ibid. X. Crossing a Mountain Stream in Autumn. Poem by P'êng Nien.

Ibid X. Pulling a Boat along a Rocky Shore in Storm. Signed.

Shimbi Shoin Shina Meigashū, II. Travellers on Mule-back among Snow-covered Mountains. Forms a pair with the above-mentioned picture: Crossing a Mountain Stream in Autumn. Both with poems by P'êng Nien.

Shoman 20. A Solitary Angler. Fan-painting. Signed.

Shina Nanga, III, 3. Reclining upon the Verandah. Signed.

Min Shitaika, 59 (Tomioka collect., Kyōto). Hsiao I trying to obtain the Lan-t'ing manuscript from the Monk Pien-ts'ai. Signed. Long inscription at the top by Lu Shih-jên (the son of Lu Shih-tao). The main group of this picture also in Shina Meiga Senshū, II.

Ibid. 60. Princess Plum-blossom. Signed.

Ibid. 62. Listening to the *Ch'in*. After Chou Fang. *Cf.* Naito Konan, *Shina Kaiga Shi*, pp.235–238.

Ibid. 63. River Scenery. Fan-painting. Signed. Poems by Chou T'ien-ch'iu, Wên Chia and P'êng Nien.

Tōsō, p.279. Landscape with Fishermen, Woodcutters, Farmers and Scholars. Handscroll. Green, blue and white colours. School work.

Ibid. 280. The Shang-lin Imperial Park. Handscroll. Green, blue, white. School work.

Ibid. 281. A Scholar and his Servant. Seal of the painter. A double album-leaf.

Ibid. 282. Wên Chi Returning Home. Signed. Green, blue and white. School work.

Ibid. 283. Five out of ten screen-paintings called: A Spring Morning in the Han Palace. Green, blue and white. School work.

Sōraikan, II, 32. The Chiu-ch'êng Palace. Signed. Handscroll. Richly coloured. School work.

Yūrintaikan, II. Sixteen Lohans in a Landscape. After a T'ang model (?). Signed.

Sōgen 109. Among the Peach-trees in the Realm of the Immortals. Signed. Blue and green. School work.

Ibid. 111. Mountain Landscape in blue and green. Signed. School work.

Ibid. 112. Friends Departing on the River-bank. Part of a handscroll. Signed.

Chūgoku, III. Landscape with a Rider. Large album-leaf. In green and blue. Signed.

Ibid. III. Six double album-leaves representing Mountain and River-views with figures in various occupations and boats in the water. Last one signed.

Ibid. III. Eight double album-leaves: Figure-studies in landscape. Signed.

Kurokawa cat. 3. A Man seated on the Bank of a River. Album-leaf, painted in colours on paper.

Ars Asiatica, IX, 43 (1). A Lady in a Pavilion by a Lake. Seal of the painter.

Lo Chia-lun, Taipei. A Small Homestead among Leafy Trees by a Brook at the Foot of High Mountains; a man is knocking at the gate. Subdued colouring.

N. P. Wang, Hongkong. The Mountain of the Immortals, rising through Circling Clouds; a Man playing the *Ch'in* by the Stream at the Entrance of a Cave. Painted in green and blue.

Boston Museum. Two Men with a Servant under a Tall Pine-tree. Signed.

Ibid. Two Ladies in a Pavilion near a Lake. Signed.

Ibid. A Tartar Soldier leading a Horse. Signed. Colophons by Wang Ku-hsiang (dated 1553) and Lu Chih.

C. T. Loo Successor, F. Caro, New York. Landscape with a Fisherman in a Boat. Illustration to the story of the Enchanted Peach-blossom Garden. Painted in blue and green. Handscroll. Colophon by Wên Chêng-ming dated 1530. A later version of this picture is in the Chicago Art Institute.

Freer Gallery. Mountain Landscape leading up to River Pavilions and Temples in the Gullies. Travellers on the roads. According to the artist's inscription, after Li T'ang. Long handscroll.

Ibid. (53.84). A Man playing the *Ch'in* beneath a Pine-tree on a rocky Ledge by a River. Slight colour. Short handscroll. Signed.

Metropolitan Museum. A Beauty in a Bamboo Grove. Signed.

Nelson Gallery, Kansas City. Saying Farewell at Hsün-yang. Gaily coloured. Handscroll. Signed.

British Museum. A Young Woman and two Children under a Tree. Fan-painting, on gilt ground. Attributed.

Ton Ying Co., New York. The Eight Lohans in Landscapes, after Li Lung-mien. Long handscroll. Signed.

C. T. Loo Successor, F. Caro, New York. Emperor Kuang-wu of the Western Han dynasty fording a River. Beyond, tall mountain peaks above circling clouds. Ink and full colour on silk. Signed. *Cf.* Toronto, cat. 17.

H. C. Wêng, Scarsdale, N.Y. *Tu-lo yüan t'u*, illustrating partly Ssŭ-ma Kuang's description of his own garden. A free version of an earlier picture. Short handscroll. The text of Ssŭ-ma Kuang copied by Wên Chêng-ming.

Ibid. The Garden of Hsü by the River-side. Handscroll in colour. Signed.

Lilly collect., Indianapolis. Two Ladies on a Terrace watching a Parakeet. Signed.

Vannotti collect., Lugano. A Young Lady standing under a Tree by a Rock. Ink and colour. Signed. Fan-painting.

J. P. Dubosc, Lugano. A Man in a Pavilion on a River-bank. Painted in colour on gold ground with incised pattern. Signed. Fan-painting.

Ibid. Lohans gathered on a Rocky Ledge. Ornamental clouds in the background. Signed. Fan-painting.

Ibid. A Lady by a Garden Stone. Inscription by the master. Signed. Ink and colour on gold ground. Fan-painting. *Cf.* Venice Exhibition cat. No.816.

CHOU CH'ÊN 周臣, *t.* Shun-ch'ing 舜卿, *h.* Tung-ts'un 東邨.

From Suchou. Active *c.*1500–1535. Pupil of Ch'ên Hsien 陳暹. Followed Li T'ang and the Ma-Hsia School. Landscapes and figures. N, II, 20. O,3. I, 56, 12. M, p.246.

W. Hochstadter, New York. A series of Monks, Beggars and Other Street Figures on double album-leaves. Signed and dated 1516. Realistically characterized.

K.-k. shu-hua chi, XXIX. Landscape, after Tai Chin: Two Men listening to a Mountain Torrent and seated under tall Pine-trees. Signed and dated 1534.

I-shu ts'ung-pien, 13. The Enchanted Peach Garden: Flowering Peach-trees and Pines in a Mountain Valley. Signed. Dated in the Chia-ching period (1522–1566).

Chung-kuo, II, 34. Landscape with Mountains and Sea.

K.-k. shu-hua chi, III. Ning Ch'i Feeding a Buffalo. Signed.

Hui-hua kuan. Illustrations to Popular Stories. Six double leaves of landscapes with figures. Ink and colour on paper. Signed.

Hsü-ching chai. Yen-tzŭ chi, the Swallow Cliff in the Yangtse River. Signed. Colophon by a later man.

Shên-chou ta-kuan, vol.9. View of the Chin-shan Rock on the Yangtse River. Handscroll. Poem by the painter. Colophon by a man called Ku Ling, dated 1651.

Nanga Taisei, XIV, 55. A Country Village under bare Trees; Men watching a Cock-fight. Signed. *Cf.* Tōsō, 272.

I-shu ch'uan-t'ung, IX. The North Sea. Short Landscape with leafy Trees on Rocks, and a Pavilion. Handscroll. Signed.

S.c.t.k. hsü-pien, IX. Celebrating the New Year.

Ibid. XI. Immortals. Signed.

Mei-chan t'ê-k'an, 22. A Man bidding Farewell, ready to step into a Boat at the Shore. *Cf.* Liu, 50.

Nanking Exhib. cat. 110. Hsia-ma and his Toad. Signed.

Ku-kung ming-shan chi, 8. Fan-paintings. *Cf.* also K.-k. chou-k'an, Index, for thirteen fan-paintings; also Nanga Taisei, VIII, 25–31.

Nanga Taisei, IX, 131. Wide River-view. Craggy Rocks between which a River flows, Fishing-boats in the distance. Signed.

Ibid. IX, 132. A River spanned by a small Bridge between Rocks at the Foot of a misty Mountain.

Shimbi, XIII. Old Trees and Rocks by the Shore. A Seascape called Pei Min. Short handscroll. Signed. *Cf.* Tōyō, X.

Ibid. XVI. Landscape. Fan-painting. Signed.

Tōyō, X. Snowy Mountain; Cottage with a Figure. Signed.

Kyūka, I (Hashimoto collect., Takatsuki). Homeward bound in Wind and Rain. Fan-painting. Signed.

Ibid. I. A Boat moored by the Shore. Fan-painting. Signed. Poem.

Ōmura, I, 1. A Mountain Cottage. Signed.

Tōsō. p.273. A Pavilion between tall Pines in a Mountain Gully. Signed.

Ibid. p.274. A Rocky Promontory with Large Trees, Pavilions and some Figures. Probably a fragment.

Sōgen 107 (Ōgawa collect., Kyōto). Wading a Stream in Autumn. After Chao Kan. Signed.

Ibid. 108 (Nelson Gallery, Kansas City). The White Pool. Signed.

Yen Kuang Co., Peking. Collotype reproduction. Storm over the River Valley. Signed.

P'ang Yüan-chi Illust. cat. III. A Mountain Village on a Summer Day. Signed. Poem by T'ang Yin.

Kawai collect., Kyōto, 1954. River-view, high Rocks along the Shore. Signed.

Boston Museum. Landscape with high Mountains and Pavilions. Signed.

Ibid. Two Men Seated under a Tree on the Bank of a Brook in a Mountain Gully. Signed.

Cincinnati Museum. A Fisherman on a Reedy Bank.

Cleveland Art Museum. Pines and towering Mountains. Album-leaf. Ink and light colour on silk. Attributed. *Cf.* Cleveland Exhibition cat. 45.

C. C. Wang, New York. A Man walking under Willow-trees followed by his Servant. Signed.

H. C. Wêng, Scarsdale. Sharply cut Rocky Mountains and tall Pine-trees. Handscroll. Signed.

National Museum, Stockholm. Han Hsin and the Old Woman. Signed.

Victoria and Albert Museum, London. A Man on Horse-back and Some Wanderers on a Mountain Road. Signed. Fan-painting.

J. P. Dubosc, Lugano. Rocky Promontories with Large Pine-trees in a Mountain Torrent; Two Men Seated in Conversation. Ink and slight colour. Signed. Fan-painting.

Vannotti collect., Lugano. A Man seated at his Desk under Trees; a Boy making Tea. Fan-painting, Signed.

CHOU CHIH-MIEN 周之冕, *t.* Fu-ch'ing 服卿, *h.* Shao-ku 少谷.

From Suchou. Flourished *c.*1580–1610. Flowers and birds. He combined the merits of Ch'ên Shun and Lu Chih. N, III, 28. O, 6. I, 57, 9. M, p.247.

Gems, III, 4. Two flower-paintings. Album-leaves. Signed and dated 1572.

Sōgen 152. A Branch of Blossoming Plum-tree. Signed. Poems, dated 1578.

Ars Asiatica, IX, pl.53 (1). Fish swimming in Water. Signed and dated 1582.

Nanga Taisei, VI, 89. Two Sparrows fighting. Fan-painting. Signed and dated 1587.

Ton Ying Co., New York. Shrimps in the Water under a Branch of a Blossoming Peach-tree. Fan-painting. Signed and dated 1592.

J. P. Dubosc, Lugano. Quail under some Bamboo and Morning-glories. Ink and colour. Signed and dated 1593. Fan-painting.

Chêng Tê-k'un, Cambridge. Swallows and other Small Birds among Blossoming Spring Trees. Hand-scroll. Inscription by the painter, dated 1600. Three colophons by later men.

Sōgen 153. Hundred Flowers. Part of a handscroll. Signed and dated 1602. Poems by Ch'ien-lung and others.

Hui-hua kuan. A Cock by a Cliff and some Bamboos.

Ink on paper. Signed and dated 1602. *Cf.* Nanking Exhib. cat. 170.

Shina Kachō 15. Two Birds in a Flowering Shrub by a Rockery. Signed and dated 1609.

Chung-kuo, II, 59. Cock Crowing at Noon.

Ming-jên shu-hua 10. Plum-blossoms, Bamboos and Narcissi by a Rock. Signed. *Cf.* Shina Nanga, III, 11.

Ibid. 11. A Hare Resting on the Grassy Ground. Signed.

Ku-kung, XXV. Mandarin Ducks and Flowers. Signed.

K.-k. shu-hua chi, XIII. Eight Minah-birds. Signed.

Ibid. XLIII. Grape-vine and Squirrels. Signed.

K.-k. chou-k'an, Index p.13. Reference to ten fan-paintings. Also Nanga Taisei, III, 15; VI, 89.

Ibid. 381–390. Album of ten paintings, landscapes with birds. The last is signed.

Ku-kung collect. Flowers painted in colours on silk. Long handscroll. Signed.

Ibid. Climbing Vine and Squirrels. Slightly coloured on silk. Signed.

Ibid. Bamboo, Quail and Large White Flowers. Signed. Inscriptions by eight men.

Hui-hua kuan. A Flowering Peach-tree on a Rock by a Pond; Two Mandarin Ducks in the Water. Colour on silk. Signed.

Shoman. Flowers and Birds. Fan-painting. Signed. *Cf.* Shina Meiga Senshū, III.

N. Gashū 13 (T. Inoue). Cock and Chicken under a Banana-tree. Signed. *Cf.* Tōsō, p.344.

Shina Kachō 74. Ducks, Magpies, Kingfishers and other Birds among Reeds. Handscroll.

Tōsō, pp.342, 343. Four pictures of Flowers and Birds, forming a set. Attributed.

Nanga Taisei, XV, 19. Various Flowers. Handscroll. Signed.

H. C. Wêng, Scarsdale. Flowers representing various Seasons; some united in Bouquets. Signed.

British Museum. Two Sparrows by a Pond. Fragment of a larger picture. Signed.

Köln, Ostasiat. Museum. "The Three Friends of Winter", a Bouquet of Pine, Blossoming Prunus and Narcissus. Signed. Fan-painting. Köln Exhibition, 1955, No.23.

J. P. Dubosc, Lugano. A White Heron Standing on the Bank of a Stream. Signed. Fan-painting.

Ibid. Mutan Flowers and a Kingfisher seated on a Slender Branch. Painted in colour. Signed. Fan-painting.

CHOU CH'ÜAN 周全.

15th century. Officer of the Imperial Guard. Painted horses. O, 5. M, p.246.

K.-k. shu-hua chi, III. A Mongol Chief on a White Horse Shooting Pheasants. Signed.

CHOU FAN 周藩, *t.* Tzŭ-kên 自根, *h.* Huang-t'ou 黃頭.

From Suchou. Active *c.*1570–1590. Flowers and birds in ink. M, p.248.

Ming-jên shu-hua, 7. Flowers and Birds. Handscroll. Signed and dated 1571.

Ku-kung, XXXIX, Hollyhock and Two Cocks. Signed and dated 1594.

CHOU-HSIEN WANG (PRINCE) 周憲王. Personal name Yu-tun 有燉.

D. 1449 (or 1439). Famed as a poet and calligrapher. Biography in *Ming shih* (with Chou-ting Wang, also in the *I-wên chih* section); also L. I, 66.

Nanking Exhibition cat. 94. Chu-ko Liang Reading. Long inscription by the artist written above the painting. Signed and dated 1416.

CHOU HSIN 周璕, *t.* K'un-lai 崑來, *h.* Sung-shan 嵩山.

From Chiang-ning. Figures, birds, dragons and horses. Q, 1, 3. M, p.252.

S.c.t.k. hsü-pien, VIII. Portrait of a Wandering Monk.

CHOU K'AI 周愷, *t.* Ch'ang-k'ang 長康, *h.* Hsüeh-hang 雪航 and Chien-ch'i-tzŭ 劍溪子.
Native of Ch'ang-shu. Landscapes after Huang Kung-wang; also figures, especially of women. Biography in *Yü-shan hua-chih* 虞山畫志. (Not to be confused with another Ming painter of the same name, M, p.248, etc.)

Nanking Exhib. cat. 179. River Landscape, with houses and rice fields on the shore. Poem, signed and dated *hsin-ssŭ*, or 1641?

CHOU KUAN 周官, *t.* Mao-fu 茂夫 or Mou-fu 懋夫.
From Suchou. Active in the second half of the 15th century. Friend of the painter Chang Ling. Figures and landscapes in *pai-miao* style. N, III, 18. O, 1. I, 56, 12. M, p.246.

Yūrintaikan, I. An Old Woman Twisting Ropes. Handscroll. Signed. Colophon by Chou T'ien-ch'iu. *Cf.* Nanga Taisei, VII, 37.

CHOU LUN 周綸, *t.* Lung-hung 龍泓.
From Ching-k'ou, Kiangsu. Active in the Wan-li period (1573–1619). Famous for his large landscapes. O, 4. M, p.248.

Kokka 370. A Rabbit by a Rockery with Flowering Plants. Signed.

CHOU LUNG 周龍, *t.* Tung-yang 東陽.
From Chiang-nan. Flourished *c.*1620–1640. Landscapes in the style of Chü-jan. Figures. O, 1. M, p.248.

National Museum, Stockholm. The Sixteen Friends of the Wine Cup. Handscroll. Signed and dated 1642.

CHOU SHIH-CH'ÊN 周時臣, *h.* Tan-ch'üan 丹泉.
From Suchou. Flourished *c.*1600. N, VII, 11. M, p.248.

Ming-jên shu-hua, 6. Portrait of the Artist (?). Signed and dated 1598.

CHOU T'IEN-CH'IU 周天球, *t.* Kung-hsia 公瑕, *h.* Huan-hai 幻海, (yu-hai 幼海) Liu-chih-shêng 六止生, and other names.
From Suchou. B. 1514, d. 1595. Followed Wên Chêng-ming in his calligraphy. Landscapes and orchids. N, VII, 7. O, 6. M, p.247.

Nanga Taisei, I, 58. Epidendrum. Fan-painting, signed and dated 1594.
Ku-kung collect. Tufts of Different Kinds of *Lan-hua*. Ink painting on paper.
Tōsō, p.324. River Landscape. Signed. Poem.
Nanga Taisei, I, 59–66. Studies of Epidendrum Plants. Eight album-leaves. Seals of the artist.
Ibid. I, 67. Epidendrum. Fan-painting. Signed.
Ibid. I, 68. Bamboo and Rocks. Fan-painting. Signed.
C. T. Loo Successors, New York. A Tuft of Epidendrum Signed.
C. C. Wang, New York. Six Studies of Epidendrum Plants; the last in *pai-miao* technique. Handscroll. Long inscription by the artist.
Vannotti collect., Lugano. A Tuft of Epidendrum. Signed. Fan-painting.

CHOU TSUNG-LIEN 周宗濂, *t.* Yu-ch'ü 友蕖.
From Ch'ien-chiang, Chekiang. Unrecorded. Probably Ming dynasty. V, p.530.

Metropolitan Museum (A. W. Bahr collect.) An Old Plum-tree in Blossom. Signed.

CHOU WEI 周位, *t.* Yüan-su 元素.
From Chên-yang, Kiangsu. Summoned to the palace at the beginning of the Hung-wu period. Landscapes. O, 2. M, p.245.

Kyūka, I (J. D. Ch'en, Hongkong). Two Fishermen in a Boat. Attributed.
Li-ch'ao hua-fu chi-ts'ê. T'ao Yüan-ming Returning Home Drunk. *Cf.* Chinese cat., London Exhib., p.104.

CHOU WÊN-CHING 周文靖, *h.* San-shan 三山.
From P'u-t'ien, Fukien. Flourished *c.*1430–1460. Court painter. Landscapes in the style of Hsia Kuei and Wu Chên. Also figures, flowers, birds and buildings. N, VI, 4. M, p.246.

Tōsō, p.239. Chou Tun i admiring Lotus-flowers. Signed and dated 1463.
K.-k. shu-hua chi, XLIII. Wang Hui-chih Visiting Tai K'uei on a Snowy Night. Signed.
Shimbi, XX. Landscape. Signed.
Tōyō, X. A Village on the River and Fishermen in a Boat. Signed.

CHOU YUNG 周用, *t.* Hsing-chih 行之, *h.* Po-ch'uan 白川.
From Wu-chiang, Kiangsu. B. 1476, d. 1548? President of the Board of Officials. Pupil of Shên Chou. Landscapes. O, 3. I, 57, 1. M, p.246.

Ku-kung collect. River-view with Pointed Rocks in Mist. Ink painting with slight colour in Shên Chou's style. Long handscroll. Signed and dated 1514.
Toledo Art Museum. Winter Mountains and Lonely Temple, after Li T'ang. Handscroll. Ink on paper. Inscription by the painter, dated 1548. Two colophons, the second by Shên Shih (of the 16th century). *Cf.* Cleveland Exhibition cat. 66; Nanga Taisei, XV, 17.

CHU CHIH-FAN 朱之蕃, *t.* Yüan-chieh 元介 or Yüan-shêng 元升, *h.* Lan-yü 蘭嵎.
A native of Chin-ling. *Chin-shih* with top honours in 1619; sent as envoy to Korea. Landscapes after Mi Fei and Wu Chên; bamboos after Su Shih and Wên T'ung. N, 4. M, p.99. V, p.248.

Ku-kung collect. (Nanking Exhib. cat. 243). Orchids and Bamboo growing beside Rocks. Large album-leaf. Signed and dated 1609.

CHU CH'ING-YÜN 朱慶雲, *t.* Wan-chung 萬重.
Chin-shih in the Ch'êng-hua period (1465–1487). Landscapes in Mi style.

Nanju 7. (Matsumoto, Ōsaka). Mountain Stream in the Summer. Signed and dated in the year of *ping-tzŭ* (1456 or 1516). *Cf.* Pageant, 494.

CHU CHU 朱竺.
From Ch'ang-chou, Kiangsu. Flourished *c.*1600. Landscapes. M, p.98.

K.-k. shu-hua chi, XXV. A Cedar-tree, Stones and Fungi. Signed and dated 1608.

CHU FEI 朱芾, *t.* Mêng-pien 孟辨, *h.* Ts'ang-chou-shêng 滄洲生.
From Sung-chiang, Kiangsu. Summoned to the palace in the Hung-wu period. Wild geese, landscapes and figures. O, 6. M, p.93.

Nanking Exhib. cat. 92. The Eighteen Arhats, after Fan-lung. Handscroll. Signed and dated 1371.

K.-k. shu-hua chi, IV. Geese flocking on the Shore among Reeds. Signed and dated 1374.

CHU HSÜN 諸勛, *t.* Shu-ming 叔銘.
Native of Chia-hsing. Ming period. Figures; landscapes in the manner of the Wên family. See biographical note in the volume cited below.

Nanking Exhib. cat. 180. Wên-shu Bodhisattva as a Monk. Signed.

CHU LANG 朱朗, *t.* Tzŭ-lang 子朗, *h.* Ch'ing-ch'i 清溪.
From Suchou. Flourished *c.*1540. Pupil and imitator of Wên Chêng-ming. Flowers and landscapes. N, III, 13. O, 6. M, p.97.

Ton Ying Co., New York. Three Birds and a Spray of Bamboo. Signed and dated 1559. Three poems by contemporaries. Fan-painting. From P'ang Yüan-chi collect.

Nanju 4. Landscape. Signed.
Kokka 557 (H. Imai, Tōkyō). An Old Temple.

CHU LING 朱陵, *t.* Tzŭ-wang 子望 or Wang-tzŭ 望子, *h.* I-ch'ao 亦巢.
From Suchou. Landscapes after Huang Kung-wang. M, pp.100, 101.

Nanga Taisei, III, 16. Section of a Scraggy Plum. Signed and dated the year *kêng-shên*.
Ibid. VIII, 130. A Mountain Landscape in Mist. Fan-shaped. Inscription by the painter.

Ibid. XI, 108. A Grassy Mountain. At the foot a mud bank with bare willows, a boat on the water. Album-leaf. Signed.

CHU LU 朱鷺. Original name Chia-tung 家棟, *t.* Po-min 白民, *h.* Hsi-k'ung Lao-jên 西空老人, and other names.
From Suchou. B. 1553, d. 1632. Student of *I-ching*. Bamboos in the style of Wên T'ung and Wu Chên. N, IV, 17. O, 7. M, p.100.

Ming-jên hsieh-chu. Bamboos. Signed and dated 1602.
Ming-jên shu-hua, 24. Bamboos by a Rock. Signed and dated 1626.
Hamburg Exhib. 1949–1950. Bamboos. Long handscroll. Signed, dated 1627.

Ming-jên hsieh-chu. Bamboos by the Water. Signed.
Nanga Taisei, I, 78. Two paintings of Bamboo, both signed.

CHU MING 朱明.
Unrecorded. Lived probably in the end of the 16th century.

Köln, Ostasiat. Museum. The Lan-t'ing Meeting. Wang Hsi-chih's pavilion is at the end of the stream in the centre; along the borders are the scholars floating their cups. Fan-painting. Signed and dated *hsin-hai* (1611?). *Cf.* Köln Exhibition, 33.

CHU NAN-YUNG 朱南雍, t. *t.* Yüeh-ching 越崢.
From Shan-yin, Chekiang. Chin-shih in 1568. Landscapes and rocks, after Shên Chou and Ni Tsan. O, 4. M, p.99.

Chêng Tê-k'un, Cambridge. River-views; hills and leafy trees. Signed (?). Colophon by Yeh Kung-cho.

CHU PANG 朱邦, *t.* Chêng-chih 正之, *h.* Chiu-lung Shan-ch'iao 九龍山樵.
From Hsin-an, Anhui. Flourished *c.*1500. Landscapes and figures. Style similar to that of Chang Lu. O, 1. M, p.96.

British Museum, No.125. Fishing Boats by the River Bank. Signed.
Ibid. No.144. View of the Imperial Palace in Peking. Provided with Chu Pang's seal but signature of Fêng-ch'i 豐溪.
Dai Tenrankai 53. Two Men crossing a Bridge near a Waterfall, on their way to join others above. Fishing-boats on the river. Poem, signed.

CHU TUAN 朱端, *t.* K'o-chêng 克正, *h.* I-ch'iao 一樵.
From Hai-yen, Chekiang. Court-painter in the Chêng-tê period (1506–1521). In landscapes, he followed Ma Yüan; in figures Shêng Mou; in flowers and birds Lü Chi; in bamboos, Hsia Ch'ang. Given by the emperor Wu-tsung (Chêng-tê) a seal on which were engraved *Ch'in-tz'ŭ I-ch'iao t'u-shu* 欽賜一樵圖書. N, I, 16. O, 3. M, p.98.

Boston Museum. A Man and a Boy in a Boat under Trees. Signed and dated 1518.
K.-k. shu-hua chi, XIX. Looking for Plum-blossoms on a snowy Day. Signed.
Shimbi, V. Winter Landscape. Signed.
Bijutsu, XIX. Autumn Landscape: Two Men seated in a small House. Signed.
Tōyō, X (Tōkyō National Museum). A solitary Angler on a Snowy River. Signed. Also in Tōsō, p.312.
Kyūka, I. Bamboos on a River-bank. Signed.
National Museum, Stockholm. A large Shore Landscape, after Kuo Hsi. Signed.
Nelson Gallery, Kansas City. Escaping the Heat of Summer. Seals of the artist.

CHU WEI 朱蔚, *t.* Wên-pao 文豹.
From Hua-t'ing, Kiangsu. Military chin-shih in 1601. Commander-in-chief in Fukien. Epidendrums in the style of Wên Chêng-ming. N, VII, 13. M, p.99.

K.-k. chou-k'an 23. Orchids and Bamboo. Fan-painting. Signed and dated 1628.

CHU YO-CHI 朱約佶, *h.* Yün-hsien 雲仙, also Lung-wan Shan-jên 弄丸山人.
15th–16th centuries. A descendant of a member of the Ming imperial family. Not recorded in the standard works on painters. V, p.256.

Gems, I, 24. Portrait of Ch'ü Yüan Seated beneath a Cliff. Poem, signed.

CHÜ CHIEH 居節, *t.* Shih-chên 士貞, *h.* Shang-ku 商谷.
From Suchou. Pupil of Wên Chêng-ming and Wên P'êng. Landscapes. N, III, 14. O, 4. M, p.220.

Ku-kung collect. Eight album-leaves representing landscapes. Colour on paper. Poems by the painter. On the last leaf, signed and dated 1523.
Ibid. The Spring of Chiang-nan. Colour on silk. Signed and dated 1531.
K.-k. chou-k'an, vol.II, 28. *P'in-ch'a t'u*. A Cottage at the Foot of a Mountain Peak by a tall Pine-tree; a Man enjoying his Tea served by a Boy. Many poems on tea-drinking copied by the painter, dated 1534. A long colophon by Ch'ien-lung. Picture and poems copied from a picture by Wên Chêng-ming. Cf. *K.-K. shu-hua chi*, XXXII.
Metropolitan Museum. Tall Mountain Landscape: Watching the Stream. Ink on paper. Inscription by the painter, dated 1559. *Cf.* Cleveland Exhibition cat. 59.
Chung-kuo ming-hua, vol. 20. Two Men seated on a rocky Shore under Trees, a high Mountain rising through the Mist. Signed and dated 1568. Composition in the manner of Wên Chêng-ming.
C. T. Loo Successor, New York. A River at the Foot of steep Mountains; a small Homestead on the Shore. Dated 1574. *Cf.* Toronto Exhibit. cat. 37.
National Museum, Stockholm. Spring Mountains after Rain. Signed and dated 1575.
Vannotti collect., Lugano. River Landscape, with Rows of Fishing-boats. Handscroll. Signed and dated 1576.
K.-k. shu-hua chi, XXIV. The Pavilion of the Old Drunkard, illustrating a famous essay by Ou-yang Hsiu. Signed and dated 1582.
Shên-chou, XVI. River Landscape with steep Banks in Snow. Poems by the painter and by Wên Chia.
S.c.t.k. hsü-pien, XI. Landscape in the manner of Li T'ang. Signed.
Chang Ta-ch'ien collect., Hongkong. Landscape illustrating the Red Cliff. Signed.

CHÜ CHIH-P'U 璩之璞, *t.* Chün-hsia 君瑕.
From Shanghai. Active *c.*1600. Landscapes, flowers, birds and bamboos. M, p.689.

Sōgen 156. Landscape in Snow. Signed. Poem dated 1607.

CHÜ MOU-SHIH 居懋時.
From Suchou. Flourished *c.*1600. Son of Chü Chieh. M, p.220.

K.-k. shu-hua chi, XII. Reading on an Autumn Day, illustrating a poem of the Sung period. Signed.

CHUNG HSING 鍾惺, *t.* Po-ching 伯敬, *h.* T'ui-ku 退谷.
From Ching-ling, Hupeh. B. 1574, d. 1624. Head of the so-called Ching-ling school of poetry. Became later a Ch'an Buddhist. Landscapes. U, II, 1, 4. V, p. 1689. M, p.694.

Shên-chou ta-kuan, vol.8. Wooded Mountains after Huang Kung-wang. Dated 1621. *Cf.* Shina Nanga, III, 8.

CHUNG LI 鍾禮, *t.* Ch'in-li 欽禮, *h.* Nan-yüeh 南越.
From Ch'ang-shu, Kiangsu. Court-painter in the Ch'êng-hua and Hung-chih periods (*c.*1480–1500). N, II, 10. O.3. M, p.694.

Kokka 318. A Man seated on a Mountain Terrace contemplating a Waterfall. After Hsia Kuei. Signed. *Cf.* Pageant 532.

FAN CHING-WÊN 范景文, *t.* Mêng-chang 夢章, *h.* Chih-kung 質公 and Ssŭ-jên 思仁.
From Suchou. B. 1587, d. 1644. Poet and high official. Unrecorded in the biographies of painters. V, p.712.

Nanju 8, Five Pine-trees. Signed and dated 1639. Also in Tōyō, XI; Pageant 715.
C. B. Hoyt collect. (formerly), Cambridge, Mass. A Man pulling a House-boat. Large trees in the foreground. After Fang Ts'ung-i. Dated 1642. Album-leaf.

FAN LI 范禮, *t.* Tsung-ssŭ 宗嗣.
From Ch'ang-shu, Kiangsu. 15th century. Followed Ma Yüan. O, 2. M, p.280.

Shên-chou, III. The Hêng-t'ang Bridge. *Cf.* Nanga Taisei, XI, 22.

FANG CHIN-SHIH 方矜式.
Unrecorded; probably late Ming period.

Chūgoku, IV. Reading the *I-ching* in the Mountains. Album-leaf. Signed.

FANG HSIAO-JU 方孝孺, *t.* Hsi-chih 希直 and Hsi-ku 希古; called Master Chêng-hsüeh 正學先生.
From Ning-hai, Chekiang. B. 1357, d. 1402. Scholar and high official. Executed by order of the emperor Yung-lo. O, 7. M, p.22.

Chung-kuo, II, 1. Two intertwining Pine-trees by a Stone. Signed. Poem. Also in Shina Nanga Taikan, 7. Long inscriptions and colophons.

FANG PI 方弼. *t.* Huan-shan 環山.
Lived in Chia-ching period (1522–1566). Unrecorded.

Kyūka, I. Three leaves from an album called: Ten Views of Ling-yang. (Note: The attribution to Fang Pi is based upon the first colophon, which actually states only that the album was owned by Fang. A later colophon attributes it to the painter Hsia Chih, *q.v.*)

FEI CH'ÊNG 費澄.
Unrecorded. End of the Ming dynasty. Mentioned as a landscapist only in a book called *T'ui-an hsin-shang lu* (see note in Pageant).

Kokka 402. River Landscape, after Hsü Pên. Signed and dated *jên-wu* (probably 1642). *Cf.* Pageant 724.

FU TAO-K'UN 傅道坤, a lady painter who was married to a scholar whose name was Fan 范.
From K'uai-chi, Chekiang. Landscapes after the T'ang and Sung masters. N, V, 6. O, 5. M, pp.512–3.

Hui-hua kuan. Two Dry Trees and Some Bamboos by a Rock. Ink on paper. Signed and dated 1621.

Ho Ch'êng 何澄, *t.* Yen-tsê 彥澤, *h.* Chu-hao Lao-jên 竹鶴老人.
From Chiang-yin, Kiangsu. Chü-jên in 1403; Governor of Yüan-chou. Active during the Hsüan-tê period (1435–1464). Landscapes in the style of Mi Fei. N, I, 18. M, p.132.

Shimbi, XV. A Mountain Village enveloped in Mist.

Ho Lung 何龍, *t.* Tzŭ-yu 子猶.
From Ch'üan-chou, Fukien. Flourished *c.*1630. Famous dragon-painter; hence his name "Dragon Ho". Also landscapes and figures. M, p.133.

Tōyō, X. Ladies Playing Music in Gardens. Two pictures; one signed and dated 1638.

Ibid. X. Mountain Landscape with a Man Wading a Stream, after Huang Hsien-jên. Signed. Poem. *Cf.* Nanju, vol.16.

Hou Mou-kung 侯懋功, *t.* Yen-shang 延賞, *h.* I-mên 夷門.
From Suchou. Active at the end of the 16th century. Pupil of Wên Chêng-ming. Landscapes. O, 4. M, p.272.

C. T. Loo Successor, New York. High Mountains. Two scholars seated under tall pines served by two boys. Ink and colour. Signed and dated 1569. Later inscriptions on the margins of the picture. *Cf.* Toronto, 37.

Takashima collect., Kugenuma. Two landscapes: one in the manner of Wang Mêng, dated 1573; the other with a colophon by Lu Shih-tao. Mounted in a handscroll with paintings by Ch'ien Ku and Wên Chia, in a series representing holy places of Taoism.

Tōsō, p.397. Cliffs and Pine-trees. Signed and dated 1580.

I-shu ts'ung-pien, 8. A tall Mountain Landscape; A Pavilion and a Fisherman in Boat in the foreground. After Wang Mêng. Signed and dated 1604.

K.-k. shu-hua chi, VIII. Mountain Landscape after a Yüan master. Signed. Colophon by Tung Ch'i-ch'ang.

Ku-kung collect. A Mountain Path. The path leading to the mountains is following a river-bed. In Yüan style.

Chêng Tê-k'un, Cambridge. A Buddhist Sanctuary under Large Trees in which a Flock of Small Birds are gathering. Signed. *Cf.* Liu, 77.

Chang Ts'ung-yü cat. (*Cf.* J. D. Ch'ên cat. II, 29). View over a River between Mountains. Signed.

Hsia Ch'ang 夏昶, *t.* Chung-chao 仲昭, *h.* Tzŭ-tsai Chü-shih 自在居士 and Yü-fêng 玉峯.
From K'un-shan, Kiangsu. B. 1388, d. 1470. Chin-shih in 1415. Like his elder brother Hsia Ping 夏昺, he was a prominent calligrapher. Followed as a bamboo-painter Wang Fu. I, 55, 8. N, I, 14. O, 7. M, p.319.

P'ang Yüan-chi Illust. cat. III. Two Stems of Bamboo and slender Twigs growing from a Rock. Signed and dated 1407. Five colophons at the top of the painting. A.

Chicago Art Institute. Bamboos, Pines and Plum-trees along a rocky Shore. Long handscroll. Signed and dated 1441. A.

Ming-jên hsieh-chu. Bamboos by a Rockery. Signed and dated 1442. *Cf.* Nanga Taisei, I, 27.

Kokka 485 (Shinozaki collect.). Bamboos and Rockery. Signed and dated 1445. *Cf.* Shina Nanga, III, 10; Tōsō, p.235.

K.-k. shu-hua chi, IV. Kuanyin seated under a few swaying Bamboos. Signed and dated 1446.

St. Louis Art Museum. *Ts'ang-yün-ku t'u.* The Old Bamboo Valley. Long handscroll. Signed and dated 1446 (7th month).

Chang Ta-ch'ien cat. I, 20. Wind and Rain on the Hsiang River. Long handscroll depicting bamboo growing on a river-bank. Signed and dated 1446.

Yūrintaikan, II. Bamboos and Rocks. Handscroll. Signed and dated 1448. A.

K.-k. shu-hua chi, XIV. Bamboos in Wind. Signed and dated 1450. A.

Berlin Museum. Spring Rain over the Bamboos along the Hsiang River. Handscroll. Signed and dated 1455.

K.-k. ming-jên hua-chu chi, II. Stems of Bamboo growing by a Rock. Signed and dated 1459.

Gems, II, 9. Bamboo growing on a River-bank, among large Rocks. Handscroll. Inscription by the artist dated 1462. The same design as the picture in the Nelson Gallery, Kansas City.

Freer Gallery (52.27). *Hsiao-Hsiang kuo-yü t'u.* Bamboos and Rocks along the River. Handscroll. Dated 1464. Several colophons. A.

Ku-kung collect. Tall Bamboos among Strange Rocks. A very large ink-painting done in a broad manner. Signed: Chung-chao.

Ibid. A Bamboo Scroll. Scattered tufts of bamboo bending freely between stones and rocks and drooping over the cliffs into the water. Signed.

Liu 47. A Pavilion in a Bamboo Grove; a Scholar and his Servant crossing a Bridge. Short handscroll. Signed. A.

Shên-chou, XIV. Bamboos. Signed.

Shên-chou ta-kuan, vol.8. Two Stems of Bamboo. Signed. Poems by three contemporaries.

S.c.t.k. hsü-pien, X. Bamboo and Rocks. Colophon signed by Li Ssŭ-ch'êng.

K.-k. shu-hua chi, VI. A Branch of Bamboo. Signed.

Ibid. XVI. Three Bamboos. Signed.

Hui-hua kuan. Bamboo in Wind. Ink on paper. Two short scrolls. Signed.

Mr. Wang Shên, Taipei. *San-hsiang yen-yü t'u.* Groups of Bamboos, Cliffs and Rushing Water. Long handscroll. Title of the picture written by the painter.

Nanjū 8 (Manju-in, Kyōto). Bamboos by a Rockery. Signed. Poem.

Bijutsu, XIV. Bamboos by a Rockery. Signed.

Shina Nanga, I, 4. A Branch of Bamboo. Signed. Poems by several contemporaries. A?

Ibid. III, 3. Bamboos in Wind. Signed. A.

N. Gashū 6. Bamboos after Rain. Signed.

Nelson Gallery, Kansas City. The Banks of the Serene Hsiang River. Bamboos and large rocks along the shore; a pine-tree and clumps of bamboo in the fissures. Long handscroll. The original signature has been interpolated with the name of Wang Fu. Six colophons, including two by Wang Ao (active *c.*1465) and one by Fu Han (active 1464–1506). *Cf.* Cleveland Exhibition cat. 39. A.

Pennsylvania Museum, Philadelphia. Bamboo and Spring Rain; Rocky Shore with Reeds and Bamboo. Long handscroll. Colophons of recent date. A.

Honolulu Academy of Arts. Sections of Bamboo bending over Rocks and Rushing Streams. Handscroll. Signed. A.

C. C. Wang, New York. Bamboo by a Rock, called "Spring Rain". Signed.

HSIA CHIH 夏芷, *t.* T'ing-fang 廷芳.

From Ch'ien-t'ang, Chekiang. 15th century. Brother of Hsia K'uei. Followed Tai Chin. N, VI, 4. M, p.319.

Gems, I, 25. A Scholar on the Bank of a River, gazing at a Waterfall. Signed.

Sōgen 113. The Fishermen's Pleasure. Part of a handscroll.

Cf. the album listed under the name of Fang Pi, which is also attributed to Hsia Chih.

HSIA K'UEI 夏葵, *t.* T'ing-hui 廷暉.

From Ch'ien-t'ang, Chekiang. Followed Tai Chin. N, VI, 4. M, p.319.

Chicago Art Institute. Two Landscapes: Summer and Winter. Signed.

HSIA PING 夏昺, *t.* Mêng-yang 孟暘.

From K'un-shan, Kiangsu. Active *c.*1450. Elder brother of Hsia Ch'ang. Famous calligraphist of his time. Landscapes in the style of Kao K'o-kung. Also bamboos and stones, but painted seldom and therefore less known than his brother. I, 55, 8. N, I, 15. M, p.319.

K.-k. shu-hua chi, XLI. Bamboos and Stones. Signed and dated 1459.

HSIANG SHÊNG-MO 項聖謨, *t.* K'ung-chang 孔彰, *h.* I-an 易菴 and Hsü-shan-ch'iao 胥山樵.
From Chia-hsing, Chekiang. B. 1597, d. 1658. Grandson of Hsiang Yüan-pien. Landscapes in the style of Wên Chêng-ming. Followed later the Sung and Yüan masters. Also flowers and bamboos. Q, I, 1. U, I, 2, 4. L, 41, 5. M, p.523.

Nanking Exhibition cat. 225. Landscape with a Small Pavilion under Trees; after Wên T'ung's picture Evening Clouds. Signed and dated 1632.

Shina Nanga, III, 3. Bare Trees and a Solitary Pavilion. Signed. Colophon, dated 1632 (first month).

Shên-chou, IV. A Scholar's Study, surrounded by a Wall, among Trees. Signed and dated 1632 (fourth month). *Cf.* Shina Nanga, II, 8.

I-shu ts'ung-pien, 15. River, Mountains and tall Trees, after Wên T'ung. Fan-painting. Signed and dated 1633.

Ming-jên shu-hua, 6. The Hsien Mountain. Signed and dated 1637.

Chung-kuo ming-hua, vol. 18. Pavilion on a rocky Shore under leafy Trees, Boats on the Water. After Wên T'ung. Colophon by the painter, dated 1639.

K.-k. shu-hua chi, XIV. Mountain Stream, lofty Peak in the background. Signed. Poem and colophon, dated 1640.

Hui-hua kuan. A Creek of a River, with Trees in Snow. Ink and slight colour. Signed and dated 1641.

Chung-hua album, 1929. The Mountain Village at Lan-t'ing, after Wang Wei. Handscroll. Signed and dated 1649.

Chūgoku, IV. Eight large album-leaves representing Mountain Landscapes, the first one with two Scholars walking on the River-bank under leafy Trees, the last ones after Chang Sêng-yu and Wang Wei. Inscriptions by the painter, two dated 1649.

Vannotti collect., Lugano. A River View. Signed and dated 1649. Fan-painting.

Liu, 73. Landscape with Pine-trees and Cranes. Signed and dated 1650. According to the inscription, this is one of an album of eight paintings in archaic styles.

S.c.t.k. hsü-pien, IV. Landscape: Wet Spring Day on a River. Signed and dated 1651.

Chūgoku, IV. Eight album-leaves: Studies of Rivers and Mountain Peaks; the first one after Mi is dated 1651. Inscriptions and poems by the painter.

Shanghai Museum. A Waterfall between two Rocks; leafy Trees growing across the Gorge. Signed and dated 1651.

Po-mei chi. Branches of Plum-blossoms. Signed and dated 1653.

Tōsō, p.332. The Painter's Journey to Fukien. Handscroll. Signed. Poem dated 1655.

Shên-chou ta-kuan, vol.6. The bright Moon shining on the Snow; River Landscape in Winter. Signed and dated 1655.

Sōgen 238. Trees by a River in Snow. Signed. Poem dated 1657.

Shên-chou, IV. Two Poppies. Album-leaf.

Ibid. X. River-landscape: a small Pavilion with a Man under some Trees. Signed. Poem.

Ibid. XII. Pine, Fungus, Orchid and Cassia by a Rockery. Signed.

Shên-chou ta-kuan, vol.1. A Man passing a large leafless Tree. Colophon by the painter.

Ming-hua sou-ch'i, I, 3. A Pine-tree. Signed.

Ku-kung, III. Bare Trees and Bamboos. Signed. Poem.

Ibid. XXII. Peaches. Signed. Poem.

K.-k. shu-hua chi, XIII. Autumn Trees in Rain. Signed. Poem.

Ibid. XV. A Branch of Peach-blossoms. Signed. Poem.

Ibid. XVI. Wild Geese on the reedy Shore. Signed. Poem.

Ibid. XLIII. Three Bamboos. Signed.

K.-k. chou-k'an 393–400. Album of eight Landscapes in old styles, the last signed. Colophons by Hsüeh-ch'êng and Hui-yüan.

K.-k. ming-jên hua-chu chi, II. Tall Bamboo growing on a Hillock. Poem, signed.

Hui-hua kuan. A Man walking under a large leafless Tree. Ink and colour on paper. Signed.

Ibid. Studies of Flowers. Six album-leaves. Colour on paper.

Ku-kung collect. A Branch of Apricot Flowers.

I-shu ch'uan-t'ung, X, 5. A Butterfly on the Calamus. Inscription by the painter.

Chang Ts'ung-yü cat. Rocks and Trees along the Banks of a River. Signed.

I-yüan chên-shang 3. A Temple in the Autumn Mountains. Album-leaf.

Ibid. 10. Houses on the Bank of a River. Signed.
Nanking Exhibition cat. 223 (Ku-kung collect.) Friends arriving in boats. Section of a handscroll.
Ibid. (Ku-kung collect.) Two leaves froman album of Landscapes. Signed.
Chou Li-yüan, 13. A Man walking with a Staff along a River-bank. Album-leaf, signed.
Ku-kung ming-shan chi 7. Nine fan-paintings. For others, see K.-k. chou-k'an 128, 219, 249, 257, 309, 323; also Nanga Taisei, VIII, 115–118.
Shina Nanga Taikan 4. Bamboo Branches and Shoots. Signed. Poem and colophon.
Tōan 35. Landscape after Rain. Signed. Poem. *Cf.* Tōsō, p.331.
Kurokawa cat. 8. Landscape. Signed.
Nanga Taisei, IX, 213. Four Men walking through a Grove of Pine-trees. Signed.
Chang Ta-ch'ien, Hongkong. Mountains and Water. Handscroll. Signed.
Hung Yu-lin, Hongkong. Landscape. Album-leaf.
Shêng P'ing-ch'ên, Hongkong. Landscape.
Chicago Art Institute. View of the Shore with Trees on the Rocks and a Man in a Boat.
National Museum, Stockholm. A Blossoming Peach-tree. Signed. Poem.
Ibid. A Flowering Epidendrum. Fan-painting. Signed.
Ibid. Chang Kuo-lao's Grotto near I-hsing. Ink and slight colour. A long colophon describing the grotto and a poem by the painter.
Musée Guimet. Chrysanthemum Flowers. Ink on gold ground. Fan-painting. Signed.
J. P. Dubosc, Lugano. *Yün-ho kao-sung t'u.* Tall Pine-trees and Mountain Range with Pointed Peaks Ending in Barren Cliffs. Signed. Handscroll. *Cf.* Venice Exhibition cat. 850.
Ibid. An album of eight leaves representing flowers.
Vannotti collect., Lugano. Bamboo and Epidendrum. Signed.
Ibid. A Branch of Flowering Begonia. Album-leaf. Signed. *Cf.* Venice Exhibition cat. 848.
Sir Harry and Lady Garner, Beckenham, Kent. Bouquet of Flowers. Ink-painting. Signed.

HSIANG TÊ-HSIN 項德新, *t.* Fu-ch'u 復初 and Yu-hsin 又新.
Son of Hsiang Yüan-pien. Landscapes, flowers and birds. O, 4. M, p.523.

Musée Guimet. Rocks and leafless Trees by a River. Colophon by the painter, dated 1601.
Köln, Ostasiat. Museum. Two Old Pine-trees among Rocks in a Stream. According to the inscription, after Wang Mêng. Signed and dated 1605. Fan-painting. Köln Exhibition 1955, 29.
Ku-kung collect. *Ch'iu-chiang yün-shu t'u.* Steep Rocks by a Stream, in the style of Ni Tsan. Signed with two seals. Colophon on the left by Ch'ên I-hsi.
Hui-hua kuan. Rocks and Bamboos along the Bank of a Mountain Stream. Signed.
Nanking Exhib. cat. 233. A Stem of Bamboo. Poem, signed.
Ku-kung ming-shan chi 7. Five fan-paintings. For others, see K.-k. chou-k'an 12, 207, 248 and 319; also Nanga Taisei, I, 69–72; II, 222; III, 240.
Chūgoku 8. A Tree and Bamboo, after Wang Fu. Signed.

HSIANG YÜAN-PIEN 項元汴, *t.* Tzŭ-ching 子京, *h.* Mo-lin 墨林.
From Chia-hsing, Chekiang. B. 1525, d. *c.*1602. Famous collector and connoisseur. Landscapes in the style of the Yüan masters. Plum-blossoms, orchids, bamboos and stones. O, 4. N, III, 21. L, 41, 5. M, p.522.

Kokka 284. Leafless Trees and Bamboos, after Ni Tsan. Signed. Poem by the painter, dated 1578.
Chang Ta-ch'ien collect., Hongkong, 1954. River View with fantastic Rocks, in broad ink-style. Handscroll. Signed and dated 1578. Long Colophon in large characters by the painter. *Cf.* Chang Ta-ch'ien cat. I, 27.
Chūgoku, III. Waiting for the Ford; towering mountain peaks in the far distance. Handscroll. Inscription by the painter, dated 1579.
Nanga Taisei, I, 47. Bamboo growing by a Rock. Signed and dated 1580. Colophon by Ch'ien-lung.
Hsü-ching chai. Mountain Valley with a Stream. Poem by the painter, dated 1589. *Cf.* Nanga Taisei, IX, 162.

Tōsō, p.330. Pine-tree, Bamboos and Stones. Signed. Colophon, dated 1591.

Shina Nanga, II, 5 and 7. Four Pictures of Stones and Trees (parts of a scroll?). One with a poem and a colophon, dated 1602. Chung-kuo ming-hua, 11. *Cf.* Nanga Taisei, IV, 32, 33.

Chung-kuo, II, 55. Bamboos, Chrysanthemums and Stones. Signed. Colophon by the painter. *Cf.* Ōmura, I, 11; Sōgen 141.

Ming-jên shu-hua, 16. Epidendrum and Bamboos. Signed. Two lines of poetry.

Po-mei chi. Plum-blossoms. Album-leaf. Signed.

K.-k. shu-hua chi, X. Bamboos, Epidendrum and Stones. Signed. Poem.

Ming-hua ling-lang. A Tuft of Epidendrum. Album-leaf. Poem by Ch'ien-lung.

Hui-hua kuan. Two Plants by a Garden Rock, one with a large Fruit. Inscription by the painter.

Ku-kung collect. Tufts of *Lan-hua* (Epidendrum). Large album-leaf. Signed.

Liu, 72. Bamboo, Epidendrum and Rock. Fan-painting.

Ōmura, II, 4. A Branch of Cassia. Signed. Colophon.

Tōsō, p.330. Lotus Plants. Signed. Two lines of poetry.

C. C. Wang, New York. A Tree, Bamboos, Epidendrum and a Stone. Signed and colophon by the painter.

Ku-kung ming-shan chi, 7. Five fan-paintings. For others, see K.-k. chou-k'an 256, 280 and 325; also Nanga Taisei, I, 48–51 (bamboo).

Köln, Ostasiat. Museum. Branches of a Flowering Shrub and Bamboo. Signed. Fan-painting. Köln Exhibition 1955, 20.

Hsiao-an 曉菴.

A monk-painter of the early Ming period. Native of Tung-wu. Painted grapes. N, 6. O, 7. M, p.667.

Hikkōen 25. A Grape Vine. Album-leaf. Attributed.

Hsiao Hai-shan 蕭海山.

Unrecorded. According to his signature he was an officer in the Imperial Guard.

British Museum, No.199. Cormorants. Signed.

Hsieh Ch'êng 謝成, *t.* Chung-mei 仲美.

Late Ming. Painted landscapes, birds and flowers. L, 55; *cf.* also Chou Liang-kung: *T'u-hua lu.*

Chou Li-yüan I. Landscape with rolling Hills. Album-leaf. Seal of the painter.

Hsieh Chin 謝晉, *h.* K'uei-ch'iu 葵丘.

From Honan. Flourished *c.*1560. Landscapes in the style of the Sung and Yüan masters. N, VI, 18. L, 55, 4. M, p.704

Shimbi, XI. A Fisherman in a Boat under a projecting Cliff. After Liang K'ai. Signed and dated 1561. Also in Tōyō, X.

Ibid. XI. Landscape in the manner of Ma Yüan. Signed and dated 1561.

Ming-jên shu-hua, 25. An Angler in a Boat, high Peaks in the background. Signed. Poem.

P'ang Yüan-chi Illustr. cat. 1940, II. Landscape with Trees in Autumn and a Fisherman. Signed. Poem by Ch'ên Chi.

HSIEH HUAN 謝環, *t.* T'ing-hsün 庭循; later adopted this as his name.
Flourished about the middle of the 15th century. Landscapes after Ching Hao and Kuan T'ung, Mi Fei, etc. N, I. O, II, 10a. M, p.704.

I-yüan chên-shang 9. Landscape: "Shining Water, Mountain Colours". Signed and dated 1452.

HSIEH SHIH-CH'ÊN 謝時臣, *t.* Ssŭ-chung 思忠, *h.* Ch'u-hsien 樗仙.
From Suchou. B. 1487, d. after 1567. Landscapes in the style of Shên Chou, influenced by Tai Chin and Wu Wei. Famous for his seascapes. N, III, 12. O, 3. M, p.704.

Ku-kung collect. (Nanking Exhibition cat. 140). Three Scholars in a Garden. Signed and dated 1529.

Dr. H. Müller, Peking, 1934. Returning Home in Mist and Rain. Handscroll. Signed and dated 1530.

L. J. Huang, Yenching, 1935. Landscape. Signed and dated 1535. *Cf.* Sirén, *Later*, pl.65.

W. Hochstadter, New York. Scenery from the Tiger Hill, Suchou Handscroll. Ink and colour on paper. Signed and dated 1536. Three colophons by later men. *Cf.* Cleveland Exhibition cat. 67.

Hui-hua kuan. Pavilion on the Rocks rising over a Mountain Stream; Wooded Peaks above the Clouds. Ink and slight colour on silk. Signed and dated 1546 (at 60). Inscriptions by Wên Chia and Ch'ien Ku.

Ibid. Wooded Mountains rising above a broad Stream; a Bridge leading over a Gully. In the manner of Shên Chou. Ink on paper. Signed and dated 1546 (at 60). Inscriptions by Wên Chia and Ch'ien Ku. *Cf.* Nanking Exhib. cat. 141.

Tōyō, XI (Berlin Museum). Two sections of a handscroll, called Endless Streams and Mountains. Signed and dated 1546.

Metropolitan Museum (52, 177, 20). A Man with a Servant walking in the Lo-fou Mountain meeting a White Deer on the Road. Ink on silk. Signed and dated 1548.

K.-k. shu-hua chi, IX. Landscape. Handscroll. Signed and dated 1551. Poem by Wên P'êng.

Ku-kung collect. Two Men listening to the Wind in the Pines. Short handscroll. Signed and dated 1551. Inscriptions by Huang Chih-shun and Ku Shih-hua.

Tōsō, pp.315–318. Four pictures illustrating Events from the Lives of four ancient Heroes who suffered from Poverty. Last one with a colophon, dated 1551. Two of them also in Kokka 307.

Sumitomo collect., Ōiso. Large Landscape; a Man ploughing a Field. Signed and dated 1551.

Ku-kung, XLI. Mountains with Waterfall in the Summer. Signed and dated 1553.

Tokasha Shina Meigashū, 2. Pavilion on a River-bank, returning Boats on the Water. Poems by the painter, dated 1553.

Gems, I, 38. Roaming in the Mountains. Signed and dated 1555.

Kokka 272. Landscape. Handscroll. Signed and dated 1555.

Chang Pi-han, Hongkong. Landscape, with a Scholar in a House. Handscroll, mounted together with T'ao Yüan-ming's *Kuei-ch'ü-lai* poem, copied by Wên Chêng-ming. Signed and dated 1555.

Mayuyama collect., Tōkyō (formerly Baron Dan). Willow-trees by a Stream; two Men in a House overlooking the Water. Signed and dated 1557. *Cf.* Sekai Bijutsu Zenshū, XX, text illus. 68.

Suchiku 10. Landscape after Wang Mêng. Signed and dated 1557.

Liu, 44. Landscape with a Scholar listening to the Waterfall. Long inscription by the painter, dated 1558.

Tōsō, p.320. Landscape after Rain. Album-leaf. Signed and dated 1559.

Ibid. 321. Landscape. Long handscroll. Signed and dated 1560 (at 74).

Nanju 14 (Hashimoto collect., Takatsuki). Landscape. Signed at the age of 74 (1560). *Cf.* Kyūka, I.

National Museum, Stockholm. The Study-pavilion. Signed. Colophon dated 1560.

K.-k. shu-hua chi, XXIV. Landscape. Signed and dated 1567.

Ming-jên shu-hua, 23. Cloudy Mountains; Two Pavilions by a Stream. Signed.

Ku-kung, XXXIV. Green Pine-trees and white Clouds. Signed. Poem.
K.-k. shu-hua chi, X. The Four Hermits of Shang Shan. Signed.
Ibid. XXXIV. A Homeward Boat on a River in Snow. Signed.
Ibid. XLI. Autumn Landscape. Signed.
K.-k. chou-k'an 483. Summer Landscape, with two Men on a Ledge gazing at a Waterfall. Signed.
Ibid. 60, 67, 318. Fan-paintings. See also Nanga Taisei, II, 220; VII, 40; VIII, 42.
S.c.t.k. hsü-pien, VII. Assembling for a Boating Party. Signed.
Hui-hua kuan. Studies of Landscapes with Figures in Boats and in a Pavilion. Four album-leaves. Ink and slight colour on paper.
Kokka 240. A rainy Landscape. Signed. *Cf.* Tōsō, p.314.
Ibid. 377. Storm over the Mountain. Signed.
Nanju 22. Spring and Autumn. Two landscapes from a series of four, representing the Four Seasons. Signed.
Tōyō, XI. River Landscape with high Mountains, Trees and Figures. Signed.
Shina Nanga, III, 8. A Hermit. Signed. Poem.
I-shu ts'ung-pien, 14. The Lu Mountain. Signed. *Cf.* Shina Nanga, III, 12.
Kyūka, I. Two Men seated in a Mountain Study. Signed.
Ibid. I. A View of Hua Shan. Signed.
Ōmura, I, 2. Valley in Spring and a Man in a Pavilion. Short inscription by the painter. *Cf.* Chūgoku, III.
Ibid. II, 5. A Donkey-rider. Album-leaf. Signed.
Tōsō, p.319. Two Pine-trees. Signed. Poem.
Sōgen 130. River between Overhanging Cliffs with Temples in Pine-groves. After Wang Mêng. Signed.
Ibid. 131. Rain Clouds gathering over Wang-ch'uan. Signed. A very large picture.
Ibid. 132 (Tōkyō National Museum). The Wang-ch'uan Mountain enveloped in Mist and Clouds. Signed.
Ibid. 133. Reading in the Shade of a Willow. Signed.
Ibid. 134. Clouds in the Wu Gorge. Signed.
Chūgoku, III. A Traveller on Horseback followed by his Servant passing along a rocky Shore. Album-leaf. Signed.
Nanga Taisei, IX, 150. A Visitor arriving at a Riverside Villa; his Host has come out to meet him. Signed.
Ibid. XV, 18. Autumn Landscape with bare Trees; two Men in a Pavilion, another crossing a Bridge. Handscroll. Signed.
Yūrinkan, Kyōto. A Scholar in a Room overlooking a River; Men in a Boat below. Signed.
National Museum, Tōkyō. Mountains in Mist, Rice-fields below. Two Men tramping at a Water-wheel. Signed.
J. D. Chên, Hongkong. T'ao Yüan-ming in his Garden Pavilion. Short handscroll. Signed. Long colophon by Wên Chêng-ming.
Metropolitan Museum. Mountains and Streams; Two Men on a Bridge. Fan-painting. Poem by the painter.
Freer Gallery (54.17). A Scholar in a Pavilion under a Pine-tree admiring a Waterfall behind the Building. Signed.
Chicago Art Institute. A Mule-transport passing a Bridge over a Stream in the Winter. Heavy snow in the valley. Handscroll. Signed.
Vannotti collect., Lugano. Bare Trees and Mountain Range in Snow; Two Men Travelling on Mules on the Road below. Signed. Fan-painting. *Cf.* Venice Exhibition cat. 820.
Hamburg Exhibition, 1949–1950. Travellers in a Mountain Pass after heavy Snowfall. Ink and slightly coloured.

HSIEN TSUNG, EMPEROR CH'ÊNG-HUA OF MING 明憲宗 (1465–1487). B. 1448, d. 1487. Figures. O, 1. L, I, 5. M, p.95.

K.-k. shu-hua chi, XXVI. Chung K'uei. Signed. Poem dated 1481.

HSING T'UNG 邢侗, *t.* Tzŭ-yüan 子愿.
From Chi-nan, Shantung. B. 1551; *Chin-shih* in 1574. Poet and calligrapher. Landscapes, bamboos in the style 60 Wên T'ung. His fame as a painter reached even Korea and the Liu-ch'iu Islands. N, IV, 10. O, 7. L, 34, 4. M, p.11.f,

Shên-chou ta-kuan, vol.5. Stones Overgrown with Grass. Signed and dated 1612. Painted for a friend called Hsü. *Cf.* Ōmura, I, 8; Sōraikan, I, 34.

Hsing Tz'ŭ-ching 邢慈靜.
Younger sister of Hsing T'ung. Flowers, also pictures of Kuanyin in the manner of Kuan Tao-shêng. N, V, 5. L, 69, 3. M, p.116.

K.-k. shu-hua chi, VIII. Kuanyin, painted in gold. Inscription by the painter.

Hsü Chên 許震, *h.* Mo-lung Tao-jên 墨龍道人 (as signed).
Ming dynasty (?) Unrecorded.

Hui-hua kuan. Chung-li, the Taoist Immortal, carrying a Basket of Flowers and a Gourd. Signed. *Cf.* Tōsō, p.224.

Hsü I 許儀, *t.* Tzŭ-shao 子韶, *h.* Hao-ying-tzŭ 鶴影子 and Hsieh-kung 歇公.
From Wu-hsi, Kiangsu. Active *c.*1640. Flowers in Hsü Hsi's style. P, IV, 2. M, p.410.

K.-k. shu-hua chi, XXVII. Lotus. Seals of the painter.
Mo-ch'ao pi-chi, vol.I. Sparrows among Bamboos.

Hsü Lin 徐霖, *t.* Tzŭ-jên 子仁, *h.* Chiu-fêng 九峯 and K'uai-yüan-sou 快園叟.
From Suchou; lived in Nanking. Active *c.*1510–1550. Favourite of the emperor Wu-tsung, who, on his travels to the South, cut off the painter's beard and used it for a duster. Hence known as Jan-wêng 髯翁, The Old Man with a Beard. Landscapes and flowers. N, II, 24. O, 6. M, p.357.

K.-k. shu-hua chi, XLI. A Branch of a Peach-tree and the Moon. Signed and dated 1514. Poems by the painter and five friends.
Shên-chou, XIX. A River with steep Banks, Man in a Boat. Signed and dated 1548.
Nanju 3. Chrysanthemums and a Hare. Signed. Poem.
Tōsō, pp.308–311. Four landscapes representing the Four Seasons; each with a poem. Two of them also in Shimbi, XIX and in Tōyō, X.

Hsü Mou-wei 徐懋緯.
Unrecorded. Active in the Ming period.

Shina Kacho Gasatsu. A Cabbage Plant. Signed. Poems by Chang Fêng-i, Wang Chih-têng and two others.

Hsü Pên or Hsü Fên 徐賁, *t.* Yu-wên 幼文, *h.* Pei-kuo-shêng 北郭生.
From Szechuan; lived in Suchou. Summoned by the emperor Hung-wu in 1374; later thrown into prison, where he died. One of the "Four Worthies of Suchou" at the beginning of Ming. Poet and calligrapher. Followed as a painter the Yüan masters, particularly Wang Mêng and Ni Tsan. N, I, 9. O, 2. M, p.357.

Yūrinkan, Kyōto. Landscape. Album-leaf, probably a fragment of a handscroll. Signed and dated 1345. The artist's inscription may have been copied from a section now missing.
Shina Kaiga Shi (Naitō Konan), p.137. A Man in a Pavilion by a River. Large album-leaf. Signed and dated 1362.
K.-k. shu-hua chi, XI. A Mountain in Szechuan. Signed. Poem and colophon. Colophon by Sung K'o, dated 1371. A.

W. Hochstadter, New York. A Winding Pass over high Mountains; a Pavilion among Trees at their Foot where a Man is approaching. Five inscriptions, one by the painter, dated 1372. A.

Boston Museum. Mountain Ranges and Water; Trees and Buildings in the Misty Gorges. Long handscroll. Signed and dated 1376. Imitation.

Freer Gallery (47.17). Endless Rivers and Mountains. Handscroll. Signed and dated 1377. Probably a later picture.

C. T. Loo's Successor, Frank Caro, N.Y. The Hidden Retreat of Shih-chien. Handscroll. Signed and dated 1393. Five colophons and two poems by Chao Mêng-fu and Chang Yüan-fu respectively. Possibly a later picture illustrating the poem by Chao Hêng-fa.

Ku-kung collect. Two Dry Trees on a River-bank. Signed and dated 1395. One seal of the painter: Yu-wên.

Sōraikan, II, 43. Spring Clouds over Mountain Terraces. Ink on paper. Signed and dated 1395. Inscription by Ch'ien-lung.

K.-k. shu-hua chi, XX. The Lu Mountain. Signed and dated 1397.

Yen Kuang album, 1928. The Shih-tzŭ-lin, or Lion Grove Garden, in Suchou. Album of twelve paintings. A.

Hui-hua kuan (ex-P'ang Yüan-chi). Clearing after Snowfall on a River. Mounted on the same scroll as Huang Kung-wang's picture with same title.

Shên-chou ta-kuan, vol.6. Wooded Hills in Autumn. Poem by the painter.

Li Tai, I. Landscape. Handscroll. Signed. Poem. Colophons and poems by Yang Chi, Kao Ch'i and later men.

K.-k. shu-hua chi, VIII. Travellers crossing a Bridge at the Foot of Grassy Mountains. Signed. Poem. Probably later.

J. D. Ch'ên cat. I, 21. Scenery from Wu-hsing. Handscroll. Signed.

Chūgoku, II. Listening to a Mountain Stream running over precipitous Cliffs; a Man walking on a Bridge. Poem and inscription by the painter. Also inscription by Ch'ien-lung.

Hsü Wei 徐渭, *t.* Wên-ch'ing 文清 and Wên-ch'ang 文長, *h.* T'ien-ch'ih 天池 and Ch'ing-t'êng 青籐. From Shan-yin, Chekiang. B. 1521, d. 1593. Literary writer, poet and calligraphist. Landscapes, figures, flowers, bamboos and stones. N, III, 8. O, 6. M, p.358.

Vannotti collect., Lugano. Four Birds on a Frozen Branch. Signed and dated 1570.

Tōsō, p.328 (Takashima collect., Kugenuma). Flowers etc. Long handscroll. Signed and dated 1575. Poems.

Commercial Press album, 1934. An album consisting of fifteen leaves, eight with figures in landscapes and seven with flowers. Signed and dated 1588.

K. Sumitomo collect., Ōiso. Flowers, Vegetables, Crabs, etc. Handscroll. Signed and dated 1591. *Cf.* Sekai Bijutsu Zenshū, XX, pl.25.

Shên-chou, V. Pine and Bamboos by a Rockery. Signed. Poem.

Shên-chou ta-kuan, vol.4. Rice Plants and a Crab. Poem by the painter.

Yu-chêng album, 1923. Studies of Flowers, Fruits, Banana and Plum-trees. Long handscroll. Signed.

Chung-kuo, II, 46. The Study of the Green Creeper, the name of the painter's studio. Signed. *Cf.* Shina Nanga, I, 11; Tōsō, p.326; Chūgoku, III. A similar picture in the Chêng Tê-k'un collect., Cambridge.

Hsü-ching chai. A Tuft of Epidendrum. Signed. Colophons by later men added on.

Mo-ch'ao pi-chi, I. Flowers in a Vase. Signed. Poem by the painter.

Hsü Wei miao-hua chi (Anon. publisher). An album of nine leaves representing Birds, Crabs, Flowers and Landscapes; one of which represents Yüan An seated in a Snow-covered Hut.

Ming-hua sou-ch'i, I, 2. A Cat under a Banana-tree. Poem by the painter.

Ming-jên shu-hua, 23. Bodhidharma seated in Meditation. Signed. Poem.

K.-k. shu-hua chi, I. A Pomegranate Fruit. Signed. Two lines of poetry.

Ibid. XL. Plum-blossoms and Banana Leaves. Signed. Two lines of poetry.

Hui-hua kuan. A Scholar riding on a trotting Donkey

under the Branches of an old Tree. Sketchy ink-painting. Inscription by Chang Hsiao-ssŭ.

Ibid. Lotus Leaves and a Crab. In *p'o-mo* manner. Inscription by the painter.

Ibid. Studies of Flowers, Bamboos, etc. Album-leaves mounted on a scroll. Ink only. Inscription by the painter.

Shanghai Museum (Gems, II, 17). Sketches of Bamboo and Flowers on Silk. A long handscroll in a free and expressionistic manner. Inscription by the painter.

Liu, 63. Landscape in Wind and Rain. Poem and signature by the painter.

Ibid. 64. Two Trees and a Rock. Poem by the painter. *Cf.* Nanking Exhib. cat. 164.

Shina Nanga, II, 11. Pine-trees and Bamboos. Signed. Poem.

Ōmura, II, 1–4. Seven pictures from an album of thirty-six leaves which was once in the possession of the painters Sung Lo and Wu Li.

Shina Kachō Gasatsu. Lotus-flowers, Tree-peonies and other Flowers.

Tokasha Shina Meigashū, 13. Two tall Pine-trees by a Rockery. Poem by the painter.

Tōsō, p.327. A Lotus Plant. Poem by the painter.

Ibid. p.329. Swallows on a Blossoming Branch. Handscroll. Signed.

Sōgen 140. A Banana-plant by a Rock. Two poems by the painter.

Sōraikan, I, 33. A Donkey-rider. Signed. Poems.

Yūrintaikan, I. Thatched Houses below a precipitous Rock; a Crane walking in the Garden. Colophon by the painter.

Suchiku 11. Narcissus and Bamboo growing beside a Rock. Signed.

Nanga Taisei, I, 55–57. Three album-leaves, studies of Bamboo and Orchids. Signed.

Chūgoku, III. Two album-leaves, one representing a Mountain Gorge, the other a Man with a *Ch'in* seated on the Ground under Pine-trees. Inscriptions by the painter.

Kawai collect., Tōkyō. Flower-studies. A series of separate pictures mounted in the form of a handscroll; some of them signed.

Shêng P'ing-ch'ên, Hongkong. Figure studies.

Metropolitan Museum (A. W. Bahr collect.) Fishes at the Bottom of a Lake. Signed.

Freer Gallery (54.8). Studies of Bamboo and Flowering Plants. Handscroll. Poems by the painter.

Chicago Art Institute. A Mynah-bird on a Branch. Fan-painting. Poem by the painter.

Honolulu Academy of Arts. A Mynah-bird on a Branch of a Flowering Shrub. Fan-painting. Poem by the painter and signed.

Musée Guimet. Banana Leaves. Signed.

Berlin Museum. Two Cockscomb Flowers. Signed. Poem.

National Museum, Stockholm. A large Banana Plant and a Plum-tree by a Rockery. Signed. Poem.

Ibid. Sketchy Landscape. Signed. Poem.

Ibid. The Four Seasons represented by various Flowers and Fruits. Handscroll. Signed. Poem.

Ibid. A Branch of Climbing Vine. Fan-painting. Ink on gold-sprinkled paper. Signed.

Hamburg Exhibition, 1949–1950. A large Crab below some Branches growing from an Overhanging Rock. Inscription by the painter.

Sirén collect. A Banana Plant and Two Small Birds in a Shrub. Poem by the painter. Signed T'ien-shui-yüeh with two seals of the painter.

Ibid. Lotus Plants and a Reed. Signed: Ch'ing-t'êng Tao-jên.

J. P. Dubosc, Lugano. A Lotus-plant. Signed.

HSÜ YÜAN 徐瀹, *t.* Tzŭ-hsü 子胥.

From Lung-ch'i, Fukien. Flourished *c.*1600. Flowers and birds in the manner of Huang Ch'üan. M, p.358.

Nanju 12. Magnolias and Birds. Signed.

HSÜAN-TSUNG, EMPEROR HSÜAN-TÊ OF MING 明宣宗 (1426–35). B. 1398, d. 1435.

Poet, calligrapher. Landscapes, figures and animals. O, 1. N, I, 1. L, I, 5. M, p.94.

K.-k. shu-hua chi, XX. Two Cats by a Rockery. Signed and dated 1426.

Ibid. VIII. Monkeys. Signed and dated 1427.

Hui-hua kuan. A Squirrel on a Stone watching Fruits hanging from a Tree. Short handscroll. Dated 1427.

Fogg Museum, Cambridge, Mass. Two Hounds. Album-leaf. Signed and dated 1427.

Nelson Gallery, Kansas City. Dog and Bamboo. Signed and dated 1427.

Palace Museum album, 1936. Two small Birds on leafless Branches and some Sprays of Bamboo. Signed and dated 1428. Nine leaves of inscriptions by the emperor, dated 1428, and three leaves of calligraphy by Huang Tao-chou, dated 1638.

Hui-hua kuan. A fat Man lying on his Back in a Bamboo Grove. Ink only. Short handscroll. Dated 1428.

Ku.-kung, XVII. A Cat under a Hanging Vase of Flowers. Colophon by a courtier, dated 1429.

Metropolitan Museum. Five Kittens in a Garden. Handscroll. Signed and dated 1429. *Cf.* Sōgen 102. Copy.

K.-k. shu-hua chi, XIX. Three Goats. Signed and dated 1432.

Tōsō, p.241. Two Dogs by a Garden Stone. Signed. B?

Sōgen 101. A Cat and Butterflies. After a picture by the emperor Hui-tsung of Sung. Signed.

HSÜEH SU-SU 薛素素 (also called WU 五) *t.* Jun-ch'ing 潤卿 or Su-ch'ing 素卿, *h.* Jun-niang 潤娘. Born in Suchou *c.*1564, lived in Nanking, and died *c.*1637. Painted bamboo, epidendrum and Buddhist figures. N, V, 4. M, p.692.

Honolulu Academy of Arts. Tufts of Epidendrum growing among Rocks along a River-bank. Long handscroll. Signed, dated 1601.

HSÜEH-YAI 雪崖.

Unrecorded. According to the signature on the following pictures, his *tzŭ* was Hung-tao 洪道. Possibly identical with Wu Hsüeh-yai 吳雪崖, from Fêng-ch'êng, Kiangsi, known as a bamboo-painter in the Ming period. M, p. 162.

Tokasha Shina Meigashū, 34, 35. A pair of pictures: Bamboos by Tall Rockeries. Poems by the painter.

HU CHÊNG-YEN 胡正言, *t.* Yüeh-ts'ung 曰從.

From Hsin-an, Anhui. B. 1584, d. after 1667. Editor of the *Shih-chu chai shu-hua p'u* 十竹齋書畫譜, for which he made some drawings of flowers and birds and executed wood-engravings.

HU CHING 胡靖, *t.* Hsien-ch'ing 獻卿.

From Nan-p'ing, Fukien. Ming dynasty. Became a monk and took the name Ch'êng-hsüeh 澄雪. Visited the Liu-ch'iu Islands where he made landscape sketches. L, 10, 3. M, p.294.

Tōsō, p.400. Pine-tree and Stones. Signed and dated *chi-yü*, possibly corresponding to 1609. *Cf.* Sung-po ming-hua chi.

J. D. Ch'ên cat., 1, 40. A Snow Scene. Poem by the painter, dated *chi-yü*.

Fu-lu. Sprays of Bamboo. Handscroll. Poem by the painter, dated *jên-tzŭ*. *Cf.* Ming-jên hsieh-chu.

HU KAO 胡臯, *t.* Kung-mai 公邁.

Native of Nanking. Active first half of the 17th century. He was sent to Korea on a mission with General Chao Yu in the T'ien-ch'i era (1621–1627). His works have been treasured by the Koreans. L, 10, 3, M, p.295.

C.T.Loo's Successor, Frank Caro, N.Y. Mountain Landscape in Autumn. A homestead at the foot of the mountain; an old man on the bridge below. Ink and colour. Signed and dated 1620. *Cf.* Toronto Exhibition cat. No. 38.

HU TSUNG-HSIN 胡宗信, *t.* K'o-fu 可復.
From Shang-yüan, Kiangsu. Brother of Hu Tsung-jên. Active in the beginning of the 17th century. M, p.294.

Shên-chou ta-kuan, vol.5. A Scholar's Study under Trees at the Foot of misty Mountains. Signed and dated 1604.

HU TSUNG-JÊN 胡宗仁, *t.* P'êng-chü 彭舉, *h.* Ch'ang-po 長白.
From Nanking. Flourished *c.*1600. Poet. Landscapes in the styles of the Yüan Masters. N, III, 28. U, I, 2, 5. P, 2, 4. O, 5. M, p.294.

Shên-chou, XVIII. River Landscape in the style of Ni Tsan. Signed and dated 1598.
Nanju 12. Landscape. Signed and dated 1601. Also in Tōyō, XI.
Vannotti collect., Lugano. Landscape. Fan-paintings. Signed and dated 1629. *Cf.* Venice Exhib. cat. 844.

HU YÜ-K'UN 胡玉昆, *t.* Yüan-jun 元潤.
Nephew of the painter Hu Tsung-jên. Landscapes in the family tradition. Flowers. O, 5. P, 2, 5. U, I, 2, 11. M, p.294.

Ming-jên shu-hua, 24. Plum-tree, Bamboos and Fungi by a Rock. Signed; poem, dated 1610. *Cf.* Po-mei chi.
Hu Yüan-jun Chin-ling ku-chi t'u-ts'ê (Commercial Press, 1934). Twelve Landscape-sketches from Nanking and Vicinity, each accompanied by a poem. The last picture dated 1613.
Hu Yüan-jun Chin-ling ming-shêng (album). Views of Nanking.

HUANG CH'I-MIN 黃起溟, took later the name Huang Jih-kuan 黃日琯 and Huang Shêng 黃生. *t.* Fu-mêng 扶孟, *h.* Hsiang-shan 向山.
From Hsi-hsien, Anhui. Author of various books. Also painted landscapes. M, p.544. V, p.1230.

S.c.t.k. hsü-pien, VIII. A Man Seated on a Mountain Terrace among some Thin, Sparse Trees. Inscription by the painter, dated *kêng-tzŭ* (1600 or 1660).

HUANG CHÜAN 黃卷, *t.* Shêng-mo 聖模.
From P'u-t'ien, Fukien. Probably 16th century. Landscapes and figures. M, p.542.

Tōsō, p.401. Ladies on a Terrace under Willow-trees. Signed.

HUANG JUI 黃瑞.
Unrecorded. Probably later Ming dynasty.

Tōsō, p.403. Travellers among Old Trees in a Mountainous Country. Seals of the painter.

Huang Shih-fu 黃石符, *t.* Ch'i-jên 圯人.
From Fukien. Lived at the end of the Ming period. Portraits of ladies in the style of Chou Fang. N, VII, 19. M, p.543.

Chūgoku, IV. A Young Lady seated and leaning on a Garden Rock. Poem and inscription by the painter, dated 1640.

Huang Tao-chou 黃道周, *t.* Yu-yüan 幼元 and Ch'ih-jo 螭若. *h.* Shih-chai 石齋.
From Chang-p'u, Fukien. B. 1585, d. 1646 .Scholar, President of the Board of Rites. Imprisoned in Nanking by the Manchus 1644 and executed 1646. Landscapes. L, 31, 3. U, II, 1, 6. M, p.544.

Sōraikan, II, 63. Cabbage and other Vegetables. Long handscroll. Signed and dated 1625. Colophon by Liang Ch'ang-chü.

Shên-chou, VI. An Old Pine-tree on the rocky Shore; Mountains in the background. Signed. Poem by the painter, dated 1635. *Cf.* Shina Nanga, I, 17.

Ōmura, I, 7 (formerly Abe collect.) A Pine-tree. Signed. Poem dated 1637.

Liu 82. River Landscape, with a small Pavilion on the Shore. In the manner of Ni Tsan. Signed and dated 1641.

Sōgen 168. Sketchy Mountains and Trees. Signed and dated 1642.

Mei-chan t'ê-k'an 21. Bamboos, Epidendrum, Fungi and Stones. Signed and dated 1642.

Chung-kuo ming-hua, 21. Two very tall Pine-trees growing on a Rocky Ledge. Signed.

Liu 81. A Pine-tree growing by a Rock. Signed.

Tōsō, p.366 (Kuan Mien-chün). River and Mountains in Mist. Signed. Poem.

Sōraikan, I, 39. Pine-trees and Rocks. Handscroll. Signed. Several colophons.

Huang Wên-li 黃文立, *t.* Chih-hsien 質先.
Unrecorded. End of Ming dynasty.

Ōmura, I, 2. A Scholar in an open Pavilion at the Foot of high Mountains teaching his Son. Signed and dated *kuei-wei* (1643?).

I Ch'ang-wu 易昌武.
Unrecorded. Probably Ming dynasty. The seal on the picture reads: *Hsin-ch'ou chin-shih*, which may correspond to 1541 or 1601.

Chung-kuo, II, 29. Two Drunkards. Signed. Two lines of poetry, dated *hsin-wei* (1571, or more probably, 1631).

Ju Wên-shu 汝文淑.
A woman painter from Wu-chiang. Lived *c.*1600. Grandmother of the painter Mao Hsi-nien 毛錫年. Landscapes, flowers and insects. L, 70, 3. M, p.78.

C. T. Loo Successor, New York. Winter Scene after Kuo Hsi. A man on muleback approaching on the bridge. Ink and colour. Signed and dated 1597. *Cf.* Toronto, Exhibition cat. 35.

JU-T'AI 如泰.
From Hua-t'ing, Kiangsu. A priest. Ming dynasty. Said to be recorded in the Shanghai local chronicle.

Nanju 25. River Landscape in blue and green. Short handscroll.

K'ANG HAI 康海, *t.* Tê-han 德涵, *h.* Tui-shan 對山.
Native of Wu-kung in Shensi. B. 1475, d. 1540. Not recorded in the standard dictionaries of painters. V, p.919.

Nanking Exhib. cat. 137. Landscape with Pine-trees and Buildings by a River. Handscroll. Signed.

KAO T'ING-LI 高廷禮. Originally named Ping 棅. *t.* Yen-hui 彥恢, *h.* Man-shih 漫士.
A native of Ch'ang-lo. B. 1350, d. 1423. A member of the Han-lin Academy in the Yung-lo period. A follower of Mi Fei in landscape-painting. Biog. in *Ming-shih*, also M. p.332.

Hikkōen 52. Mountains in Summer after Rain. Album-leaf. Signed: *Lung-mên Man-shih*, and dedicated to Po-shih. *Cf.* Shimbi, XX; Sōgen Meigashū, 13; Bijutsu Kenkyū, 13.

KAO YANG 高陽, *t.* Ch'iu-fu 秋甫.
From Ssŭ-ming, Chekiang. First half of the 17th century. Son-in-law of Chao Pei. Flowers, birds, stones; later also landscapes. N, VII, 17. L, 20, 4. M, p.332.

Köln, Ostasiat. Museum. Temple Pavilions in a Mountain Gorge; a Man on a Bridge Leading to the Temple. Signed and dated 1623. Fan-painting. Köln Exhibition 1955, No.48.
Chung-kuo, II, 30. Daffodils and Rocks, in ink. Signed and dated 1626.
J. D. Ch'ên cat. II, 41. Trees by a Rock. Album-leaf. Signed and dated 1629.
Nanju 9. Old Trees and Stones. Signed and dated 1631.
National Museum, Stockholm. A Garden Rock. Large album-leaf. Signed.
Nanking Exhib. cat. 177. Two fantastic Rocks. Signed.

KO CHÊNG-CH'I 葛徵奇, *t.* Wu-ch'i 無奇, *h.* Chieh-k'an 介龕.
From Hai-ning, Chekiang. Chin-shih in 1628. Landscapes. N, VII, 20. M, p.566.

Kokka 30 (Seikado collect.) Landscape. Signed. Poem, dated 1634. Also reproduced in Nanju 2; Tōyō, XI; Tōsō, p.363.
Ōmura, I, 12. Landscape. Album-leaf. Signed. *Cf.* Chūgoku, IV.
Bijutsu Kenkyū, 16. Landscape. Signed. A line of poetry.

KO I-LUNG 葛一龍, *t.* Chên-fu 震甫.
From Suchou. B. 1567, d.1640. Poet. Flowers, followed Ch'ên Shun. P, I, 4. M, p.566.

T'ai-shan ts'an-shih lou ts'ang-hua, II. Two Stems of Chrysanthemums by a Rockery. Poem by the painter, dated 1615.
Po-mei chi. A Branch of Plum-blossoms. Album-leaf. Signed.

K'O SHIH-HUANG 柯士璜, *t.* Wu-hsia 無瑕.
From P'u-t'ien, Fukien. Flourished *c.*1580. Flowers in colours. M, p.262.

Nanju 14. Flowers. Signed and dated 1577.
Ibid. 12. Banana-trees. Signed and dated 1580. *Cf.* Tōyō.

KU CHÊN-I 顧振儀.
Unrecorded. Ming period.

Nanga Taisei, XI, 60. Two Men in a thatched Pavilion on a rocky Ledge. In the manner of Wang Fu. Large album-leaf. Signed.

KU CHÊNG-I 顧正誼, *t.* Chung-fang 仲方, *h.* T'ing-lin 亭林.
From Hua-t'ing, Kiangsu. Flourished *c.*1580. Government Secretary in the Wan-li period. Poet; author of *Shih shih* 詩史 and *T'ing-lin chi*. Landscapes in the style of Huang Kung-wang. Friend of Sung Hsü and Sun K'o-hung. Founder of the Hua-t'ing School 華亭派. I, 5, 7, 8. N, IV, 4. M, p.738.

K.-k. shu-hua chi, V. Autumn Landscape. Signed and dated 1575.
Ibid. VII. Trees and Stones, after Ni Tsan. Signed. Poems by the painter and his contemporaries.
Ibid. XVII. The New Year's Day. Signed. Poem.
Ibid. XLIV. A Man among big Trees in the Mountains. Signed. Colophon.
Hui-hua kuan. Landscape-studies after various Old Masters. Ink and some colour on paper. Four album-leaves.
Mrs. B. Z. Seligman, London. A Steep Mountain Range and a Row of Pine-trees in front of it. Signed. Fan-painting.

KU CH'I-FANG 顧啓芳.
Unrecorded. End of Ming period and contemporary of Pien Wên-yü.

Nanju 18. Man in a Pavilion Looking at a Waterfall. Large album-leaf. Signed and dated *kuei-yu* (1633?). Also in Tōyō, XI.

KU-CHIA 古甲.
Unrecorded. A monk of the Ming period.

Sōgen 192. Waterfalls over steep Cliffs. Signed.

KU FU 顧復.
Native of Ching-chiang. Summoned to the capital in the Ch'êng-hua era (1465–1487). Not recorded in the biographies of painters. V, p.1793.

Chou Li-yüan 3. Landscape, after Ni Tsan's *An-fu chai* picture. Inscribed and dated 1488. Another version of the picture is in Chêng Tê-k'un collect., Cambridge.

KU I-TÊ 顧懿德, *t.* Yüan-chih 原之.
Nephew of Ku Chêng-i. Landscapes in the style of Wang Mêng; also pictures of Kuanyin. M, p.738.

K.-k. shu-hua chi, XXII. Landscape. Signed. Colophon, dated 1620. Also colophons by Tung Ch'i-ch'ang and Ch'ên Chi-ju.
Metropolitan Museum. A Moonlit Mountain Valley with a Pavilion. Signed and dated 1628. In a colophon, Tung Ch'i-ch'ang says that the picture is in the style of Wang Mêng.

Nanga Taisei, XI, 51. A Group of Trees on a Rocky Knoll; a Mountain rising from Mists beyond. Large album-leaf, signed and dated 1631.

Ōmura, II, 4. A broad River-view, with three tall Pine-trees standing on the near Bank. Album-leaf. Signed and dated 1633. *Cf.* Chūgoku, IV.

KU NING-YÜAN 顧凝遠, *h.* Ch'ing-hsia 青霞.

From Suchou. Flourished *c.*1636. Landscapes in the styles of Tung Yüan and Chü-jan. Author of *Hua-yin* 畫引. M, p.738.

Shên-chou, I. A Man seated in a Pavilion at the Foot of a Mountain. Signed. Poem, dated 1636.

K.-k. shu-hua chi, XXVIII. Landscape after Chao Mêng-fu. Signed. *Cf.* Nanga Taisei, IX, 235.

Sōgen 186. A Man standing under a Tree. Signed. Poem.

KU PING 顧炳, *t.* An-jan 黯然, *h.* P'ei-ch'üan 怀泉.

From Hangchou. Lived in the 16th century. Flowers and birds after Chou Chih-mien. N, III, 29. M, p.739.

Hui-hua kuan. Kingfisher on a Branch of a Mutan Shrub. Colour on paper. Signed and dated 1594.

KU SHAN-YU 顧善有.

Early 17th century. Son of Ku I-tê. Landscapes. O, 4. M, p.738.

Musée Guimet. Pointed Mountains and Bare Trees; small pavilions below. Ink and colour. Signed.

Vannotti collect., Lugano. Album of nine leaves; studies of trees and landscapes in the manner of Sung and Yüan masters. Ink and colour. Signed. Inscriptions by Ch'ên Chi-ju and Tung Ch'i-ch'ang.

KU SHIH-CH'I 顧時啓.

End of Ming.

Private collect., Japan. Buddha-fingered Oranges. Poem. Signed and dated 1626.

KU TA-TIEN 顧大典, *t.* Tao-hsing 道行, *h.* Hêng-yü 衡寓.

From Wu-chiang, Kiangsu. Chin-shih in 1568. Poet, calligraphist. Landscapes. L, 52, 4. M, p.738.

Mo-ch'ao pi-chi, I. Steep Hills. Signed and dated 1568.

Musée Guimet. Bamboos and a Garden Rock. Ink on gold ground. Fan-painting. Signed and dated 1582.

Shên-chou, VII. The Chiang-yin Study. Signed. Poems and colophon, dated 1584. *Cf.* Shina Nanga, III, 11.

Tōsō, p.341. Yen-tzŭ chi, The Swallow Cliff on the Yangtse. Signed and dated 1585. Colophon by Wang Chih-têng and poem by Chang Fêng-i.

KUAN SSŬ 關思, *t.* Ho-ssŭ 何思, *h.* Hsü-po 虛白. Used also the name Chiu-ssŭ 九思, and the *tzŭ* Chung-t'ung 仲通.

From Wu-ch'êng, Chekiang. Active *c.*1590–1630. Landscapes. Rival of Sung Hsü. I, 57, 8. M, p.721.

Shanghai Museum. High Mountains and tall Pine-trees, after Wang Mêng. Signed and dated 1590. A.

K.-k. shu-hua chi, XXVIII. Landscape. Signed and dated 1600. *Cf.* Nanga Taisei, IX, 166.

Nezu Museum, Tōkyō. Clearing after Rain, large Landscape with Buildings and Figures. Signed and dated 1600.

Kyūka, I. Trees by a River in Autumn. Signed and dated 1619.

K.-k. shu-hua chi, XXI. The Hermit and his Cranes. Signed and dated 1622.

Chūgoku, III. The Jade Pond. Water running down through a tunnel in the mountains; men on the terrace and on the bridge. Inscription by the painter, dated 1623.

K.-k. chou-k'an 504. A large River Landscape, with strolling Scholars. Inscription dated 1625.

Ku-kung collect. High Mountains forming Terraces; a Boat on the River below. After Wang Mêng. Signed and dated 1627. A.

Nanga Taisei, IV, 34. Plum-blossoms by a Rock. Signed and dated 1629. *Cf.* Po-mei chi.

Tōsō, p.340. Streams and Mountains after Rain. Signed and dated 1630. *Cf.* Sōgen 145.

Kokka 299 (Seikadō). Travellers resting at an Inn on a moonlit Night. Signed. Poem dated 1630. *Cf.* Nanju 1; Tōyō, XI; Tōsō, p.399.

Shên-chou, IX. A solitary Angler on a Mountain Stream. Signed. Poem.

K.-k. shu-hua chi, XXXIII. White Clouds and red Trees, after Chao Mêng-fu. Signed.

Ōgawa collect., Kyōto. River at the Foot of steep Mountains. A very tall view. Slightly coloured. Signed.

K. Sumitomo, Ōiso. Autumn Landscape; a Man in a Boat under a Tree, Bamboo Groves on the distant Bank. Signed. *Cf.* Kokka 755.

Yūrinkan, Kyōto. Winter Landscape, in the manner of Wang Wei. Signed.

Hamburg Exhibition, 1949–1950. River Landscape in Sung style with an Angler. Ink and slight colour on silk. Signed.

KUEI CH'ANG-SHIH 歸昌世, *t.* Hsiu-wên 休文, or Wên-hsiu, *h.* Chia-an 假庵.

From K'un-shan, Kiangsu. B. 1574, d. 1645. Landscapes and bamboo. O, 7, p.7. N, IV, p.26b. M, p.708.

Princeton University (Du Bois-Morris collect.) Wind-swept Bamboos by a Rock. Signed and dated 1613.

Nanking Exhib. cat. 196. Thin Stems of Bamboo. Signed and dated 1627.

National Museum, Stockholm. Bamboo-studies. Long handscroll. Signed and dated 1629.

Shina Meiga Senshū, III. Bamboo and Bamboo Sprouts. Poem by the painter, dated 1631.

Nanga Taisei, I, 84. Two Studies of Bamboo and Rocks, both signed.

KUEI CHUANG 歸莊, also called Kuei Tsu-ming 歸祚明, *t.* Yüan-kung 元恭, h. Hêng-hsüan 恒軒 and other names.

B. 1613, d. 1673. Son of Kuei Ch'ang-shih and intimate friend of Ku Yen-wu 顧炎武. Bamboos. U, II, 2, 3. M, pp.708, 709.

Ming-jên hsieh-chu. Bamboos and Stones. Signed and dated 1663.

KUEI MING-YUNG 眭明永, *t.*? Sung-nien 嵩年.

Unrecorded. According to a colophon attached to the picture below, a native of Tan-yang in Anhui; chü-jên in 1642, died in 1645.

Nanking Exhib. cat. 249. Trees by a River. Signed and dated 1639.

KUO HSÜ 郭詡, *t.* Jên-hung 仁宏, *h.* Ch'ing-k'uang 清狂.

From T'ai-ho, Kiangsi. B. 1456, d. after 1526. Landscapes and figures. Summoned to the palace in the Hung-chih period. Friend of Wu Wei, Shên Chou, etc. N, VII, 4. L, 60, 4. M, p.399.

K.-k. shu-hua chi, XV. Hsieh An (a high official of the Chin dynasty) with his Concubines. Signed. Poem dated 1526 (at 71).

T'ai-shan ts'an-shih lou ts'ang-hua, I. A Man on a Donkey passing under a projecting Rock. Signed.

Detroit Institute of Arts (ex-P'ang Yüan-chi collect.) Landscape with Pavilions and Water. Ink on paper. Handscroll. Signed. *Cf.* Cleveland Exhibition cat. 44.

Shina Meiga Senshū, III. Portrait of Hsieh Tung-shan. Signed. Inscription by Wên Chêng-ming.

KUO TIEN 郭甸.

Unrecorded. Signature reads: from Honan. Probably Ming period.

Ku-kung, XXVII. Crows and Wild Geese. Signed, dated *wu-shên*.

LAN YING 藍瑛, *t.* T'ien-shu 田叔, *h.* Chieh-sou 蜨叟 and Shih-t'ou-t'o 石頭陀.

From Ch'ien-t'ang, Chekiang. B. 1585, d. after 1660. Landscapes, imitated various old masters. Traditionally called the last representative of the Chê school. N, IV, 24. O, 5. Q, I, 1. U, II, 1, 16. M, p.709.

Ōmura, I, 12. Tall Pine-trees on the Po-yo Mountain. Signed and dated 1620. *Cf.* Chūgoku, IV.

Chūgoku, IV. Six Landscape Studies after Old Masters: Li T'ang, Wu Chên, Chü-jan, Wang Mêng, Li Ch'êng, Chao Ling-jang. Large album-leaves. Signed. Two of them dated 1622. *Cf.* Fu-lu.

Tōsō, p.385. Landscape. Long handscroll. Signed. Colophon dated 1624.

Ibid. 386. Landscape after Tung Yüan. Signed and dated 1624.

Seattle Art Museum (ex-Katō, Tōkyō). River Landscape in the manner of Four Yüan Masters. Handscroll. Ink and colour on gold-flecked paper. Inscription by the painter, dated 1624. *Cf.* Cleveland Exhibition cat. 75.

Shên-chou, XX. Mountain Landscape with rich Growth. After Huang Kung-wang. Dated 1625.

Boston Museum. Lofty Sung Shan. Signed. Poem by the painter, dated 1627.

Kyūka, I. Tall Pine-trees on the I-mu Mountain. Colours on silk. Signed and dated 1629.

Köln, Ostasiat. Museum. A River between Grassy Hills, a Fisherman in a Boat. Signed and dated 1629. Fan-painting. Köln Exhibition 1955, No.51.

Metropolitan Museum. Cottages in the Mountains. Fan-painting. Signed and dated 1633.

Gems, I, 48. A Bird on a Branch in Autumn. Poem, signed and dated 1634.

Commercial Press album, 1923. Winding Waters, Slopes with rich Growth, Buildings and Bridges, and Fishermen in Boats. After Wu Chên. Long handscroll. Inscription by the painter, dated 1634. *Cf.* Nanga Taisei, XV, 22–25.

W. Hochstadter, New York. A Man in a Boat by a Shore under Leafy Trees. Signed and dated 1634.

J. D. Ch'ên cat. II, 39. Landscape after Wang Mêng. Handscroll, signed and dated 1635.

Dr. Moriya, Kyōto. Views along a River Winding between Wooded Banks with buildings; fishing-boats on the water. After Huang Kung-wang. Handscroll. Signed and dated 1636.

J. P. Dubosc, Lugano. Old Trees, Fantastic Rocks and a Small Pavilion on a River-bank. Signed and dated 1636. Ink and colour. Fan-painting.

Ibid. Fantastic Cliffs, Dry Trees and a Small Pavilion on an Island. Signed and dated 1637. Ink and colour. Fan-painting.

Ton Ying Co., New York (ex-P'ang Yüan-chi collect.) A Bird on the Branch of a Maple-tree. Fan-painting. Signed and dated 1637.

Vannotti collect., Lugano. Landscape with a Man in a Boat. Fan-painting. Signed and dated 1637.

Kokka 303 (Seikadō). Landscape after Wang Mêng. Signed and dated 1638. *Cf.* Tōsō, p.384.

Philadelphia Museum. A Mountain Stream; tall Cliffs. Signed and dated 1638.

Ibid. A Scholar's Pavilion by a Stream at the Foot of high Mountains. Signed. Forming a pair with the preceding picture.

Hamburg Exhibition, 1949–1950. Snow over the Rocks by the River. Signed and dated 1639.

Nanking Exhib. cat. 178. Cloudy Landscape, in the manner of Kao K'o-kung. Signed and dated 1639.

Shên-chou, VIII. Pavilion under Trees by a River. Signed and dated 1640.

Ibid. X. Cottages and bare Trees by a River. Signed. Poem dated 1641.

Tōan 34. Eight Landscapes after Old Masters forming an album. Signed and dated 1642.

Tōyō, XI. Autumn Landscape after Chao Mêng-fu. Signed and dated 1642.

Lan T'ien-shu fang-ku shan-shui ts'ê (Bunseidō, Kyōto, 1920). An album of twelve Landscape Studies after Old Masters from Wang Wei to Wu Chên. Signed and dated 1642.

Chung-kuo, II, 36. Autumn Landscape after Chang Sêng-yu. Signed and dated 1643.

National Museum, Stockholm. A broad River at the Foot of wooded Rocks and Peaks. Pavilions on poles in the river. After Wu Chên. Signed and dated 1644.

Chung-kuo ming-hua, 3. A deep Gully between towering Mountains, Pavilions in the far Bottom of the Gully. Signed and dated 1644.

Dr. J. Lacan, Paris. Landscape. Signed and dated 1644.

Hyōjirō Hatta. Two album-leaves: (1) A Boat on the River, after Chang Sêng-yu. (2) Temples on a cloudy Mountain, after Kao K'o-kung. Signed and dated 1645.

Shimbi, XV. Landscape after Ching Hao. Signed and dated 1646.

Vannotti collect., Lugano. Landscape with a Man in a Boat. Fan-painting. Signed and dated 1647.

Ibid. Rocky Mountains and sparse Trees, after Huang Kung-wang. Handscroll. Signed and dated 1647.

Ming-hua sou-ch'i, I, 4. Mountain Landscape with a Fisherman in a Boat on the River. In the manner of Huang Kung-wang. Signed and dated 1649 (at 72).

Hui-hua kuan. Two Men under tall Pine-trees on a River-bank. After Kuan T'ung. Dated 1651.

Ku-kung collect. Studies of Flowers, Birds, Butterflies and Stones. An album of twelve leaves. Signed and dated 1561.

Shoman 33. Landscape. Fan-painting. Signed and dated 1651.

Lilly collect., Indianapolis. Two Men seated under old Trees by the Water. Ink and colour. Inscription by the painter, dated 1652. *Cf.* Cleveland Exhibition cat. 76.

Gems, I, 47. Autumn on Hua Shan, in the manner of Kuan T'ung. Signed and dated 1652.

Vanotti collect., Lugano. Large Trees in Autumn Colours. Signed and dated 1653. Fan-painting.

Nanju 17. The Towers of the Immortals on the Red Mountain, after Chang Sêng-yu. Signed and dated 1653.

Sōgen 177. Landscape after Kuo Hsi. Signed and dated 1654 (at 77) (?).

J. Cahill, Wash., D.C. Winter Landscape in the manner of Fan K'uan. Signed and dated 1655.

Wên-ming album, 1922. Album of eight landscapes in old styles. Inscriptions by the painter, several dated 1655. *Cf.* Nanga Taisei, XI, 97–105.

Yu-chêng album, 1922. Album of sixteen landscapes after old masters. Inscriptions by the painter, one dated 1656.

Nanga Taisei, IV, 211–226. Album of sixteen Studies of Stones. All signed, the last dated 1656.

Suchiku 16 (Oguri collect.) Fungus and Orchids growing by a Rock. Signed and dated 1658.

S.c.t.k. hsü-pen, X. Listening to the Waterfall. Signed and dated 1658.

Hamburg Exhibition, 1949–1950. Landscape. Signed and dated 1658.

Shên-chou, XX. A towering Mountain by a River, large Trees and a Man in a Cottage. After Chao Yung. Dated 1659.

K.-k. shu-hua chi, IX. Landscape. Signed and dated 1659.

Chūgoku, IV. A Lady washing an Ink-stone by a Garden Rock under a Banana-plant. Painted together with Hsü Chieh-p'ing. Inscription by Lan Ying, dated 1659.

Chung-kuo ming-hua, vol.12. A Mountain Landscape after Tung Yüan. Signed.

Ming-jên shu-hua, II. Epidendrum by a Stream, after Wu Chên. Signed. Colophon. *Cf.* Shina Nanga, III, 1.
Ibid. V. Mountain Landscape. Signed.
K.-k. shu-hua chi, XXIV. A Bird on a Branch of Wu-t'ung Tree. Signed.
K.-k. chou-k'an 118 and 148. Fan-paintings.
Ku-kung collect. *Ch'iu-t'ing shih-ssŭ t'u.* A man in the pavilion among old trees under a projecting rock. Colour on silk. Inscription by the painter.
T'ai-shan ts'an-shih lou ts'ang-hua, IV. River Landscape, after Wang Mêng. Handscroll. Signed.
T'ai-shan album, series II. Landscape handscroll, in the manner of Wang Mêng. Signed.
Liu, 100. A Mountain River and White Clouds, after Chang Sêng-yu. Signed.
S.c.t.k. hsü-pien, I. Admiring the Waterfall.
Kokka 232. Landscape after Mi Fei. Signed. *Cf.* Shimbi, X; Nanju 1; Tōyō, XI; N. Gashū 16; Tōsō, p.383.
Ibid. 477. Mountains in Snow.
Ibid. 509. A red Pine-tree after Wu Chên. Signed. *Cf.* Sōgen 180.
Ibid. 640. View from Fu-ch'un Mountain.
Nanju 9. A Man humming below a Cliff. After Chao Mêng-fu. Signed.
Ibid. 14. Landscape after Chao Mêng-fu. Signed.
Ibid. 25. Mountains in sharp Silhouette, after Wu Chên. Signed. *Cf.* Kyūka, I.
Bijutsu, IV. Sparse Trees by a River. Signed.
Hyōjirō Hatta. Waterfalls on a cloudy Mountain after Wu Chên. Signed. Poem.
Tōyō, XI. Farmsteads by a Stream, after Chao Ta-nien. Signed.
Tokasha Shina Meigashū, 38. A Singing Bird on a slender Branch. Signed.
Ōmura, I, 10. Two Men under high Pines, after Kuo Hsi. Signed. *Cf.* Sōraikan, I, 40.
Shinchō 33. River Landscape with tall Trees, after Chao Yung. Signed.
Dai Tenrankai 59. A Man standing on the Edge of a Cliff; an overhanging pine above. Signed.
Ibid. 61. Autumn Landscape, in the manner of Li T'ang. Signed.
Tōsō, p.387. Bamboo Shoots by a Rockery. Signed.
Sōgen 178. Landscape in Snow, after Wang Wei. Signed.
Ibid. 179. A Man seated in Contemplation in the Mountains, after Chang Sêng-yu. Signed.
Ibid. 181. River Landscape with an Angler in a Boat. Handscroll.
Voretzsch collect., Colmberg. A Red Pine-tree and Creepers on a Rock. Signed.
Boston Museum. Two Landscapes representing Spring and Winter. The former, Hearing the Oriole among the Weeping Willows, after Chao Ta-nien; the latter, beautiful Spring Snow, after Wang Wei. Signed.
Princeton University (Du Bois-Morris collect.) Autumn Morning on the Ch'u River. Signed.
Hobart collect., Cambridge, Mass. High Cliffs and Pavilions along a River. After Fan K'uan. Signed.
W. Hochstadter, New York. Pine-tree by a Rock and some Sprays of Bamboo and a Fungus. Signed.
H. C. Wêng, Scarsedale, N.Y. Studies of Epidendrum; the Flowers and the Leaves mostly separated. Handscroll. Signed.
Musée Guimet. River Landscape after Chao Mêng-fu and Shêng Mou. Album-leaf on silk. Signed.
National Museum, Stockholm. Winter Landscape. Signed.
Hamburg Exhibition, 1949–1950. Bamboo and Rocks. Painted together with Sun T'i.
Ibid. Landscape in the style of Li Ch'êng.

LI AO 李璈.
Unrecorded. Ming dynasty.

Ku-kung, XX. Dog watching a Cicada. Inscription, dated the Chêng-tê period (1506–1521).

LI CHAO-HÊNG: see Ch'ang-ying.

LI CHU 李著, *t.* Ch'ien-fu 潛夫, *h.* Mo-hu 墨湖.
From Nanking. Flourished *c.*1500. First studied landscape-painting with Shên Chou, but became later a follower of Wu Wei. N, VI, 21. O, 1. M, p.199.

Hakubundō album, Yü-lo t'u-chüan (Hashimoto collect., Takatsuki). The Fishermen's Pleasure. Handscroll. Seals of the artist.

LI HANG-CHIH 李杭之, *t.* Sêng-fa 僧筏.
Son of Li Liu-fang. M, p.200.

Shên-chou ta-kuan, vol.5. River View with sparse Trees. Signed and dated 1638.

Ming, Li Sêng-fa shan-shui ts'ê (Shên-chou kuo-kuang shê, Shanghai, 1922). An album of ten small leaves representing landscapes, dated 1643.

LI I-HO 李一和.
Unrecorded. *c.*1430(?) From Shang-hang, Fukien.

Kokka 422. Five Phoenixes. Signed.
Tōyō, X. Mandarin Ducks under Flowering Peonies.
Ibid. X. Two Pheasants and Two Magpies. Signed.

LI I-PO 李一白.
Unrecorded.

Nanju 8. Autumn Stream and a far away Temple. Fan-painting. Signed, dated *wu-wu* which probably corresponds to 1558. *Cf.* Tōyō, XI.

LI JIH-HUA 李日華, *t.* Chün-shih 君實, *h.* Chiu-i 九疑 and Chu-lan 竹嬾.
From Chia-hsing, Chekiang. B.1565, d. 1635. Connoisseur, critic. Landscapes. N, IV, 12. O, 4. P, I, 1. U, II, 1, 1. M, p.200.

Ming-jên shu-hua, 16. Orchids and Bamboos. Signed. Poem, dated 1624. *Cf.* Shina Nanga Taikan, 10.
Yonezawa, 19 (Tomioka collect., Kyōto). River Landscape. Handscroll. Signed and dated 1626.
Ming-jên shu-hua, 5. Mountain Landscape. Signed. Colophon dated 1630.
Chūgoku, IV. Mountain Landscape. Two Men in a Rowing-boat approaching a Bridge. Signed and dated 1631. Poem by Hsiang Shêng-mo.

LI K'UNG-HSIU 李孔修, *t.* Tzŭ-ch'ang 子長, called himself Pao-chên-tzŭ 抱眞子.
Native of Hsün-tê in Kuangtung; lived in Kuang-chou. Active in the 15th and early 16th centuries. Friend of the plum-blossom painter Ch'ên Hsien-chang. Landscapes and birds. M, p.198.

Nanking Exhib. cat. 174. Geese and other Birds in a Landscape. Signed and dated *wu-yin*, or 1518?

Li Lin 李麟, *t.* Tz'ŭ-kung 次公.

From Ssŭ-ming, Chekiang. Flourished *c.*1635. Buddhist figures in black and white. Pupil of Ting Yün-p'êng. He used the signature Lung-mien hou-shêng 龍眠後生, "the reborn Li Lung-mien". N, IV, 13. M, p.200.

Ōmura, II, 2. Mañjušrī and Vimalakīrti. Signed and dated 1635. *Cf.* Chūgoku, IV.

Tōsō, p.374. A Carp. Attributed.

Li Liu-fang 李流芳, *t.* Ch'ang-hêng 長蘅, *h.* T'an-yüan 檀園 and other names.

From Hsieh-hsien, Anhui; lived in Chia-ting, Kiangsu. B. 1575, d. 1629. One of the "Nine Friends in Painting". Scholar, poet. Landscapes in the style of Wu Chên. Flowers and birds. N, IV, 10. O, 5. P, I, 5. U, I, 2, 1. M, p.200.

Chung-kuo ming-hua, IX. River-view in the style of Ni Tsan. Poem by the painter, dated 1589.

S.c.t.k. hsü-pien, II. Landscape in the style of Wu Chên. Signed and dated 1589. *Cf.* Nanga Taisei, Intro. 4.

Metropolitan Museum. A Man among sparse Trees. Fan-painting. Signed and dated 1613.

Sōgen 167. Landscape after Tung Yüan. Signed and dated 1614.

Tōyō, XI. Landscape. Signed and dated 1615.

Ōmura, I, 7. Scattered Trees and a solitary Pavilion. Signed and dated 1617.

J. P. Dubosc, Lugano. Old Pine-trees and Rocks. Signed and dated 1617. Fan-painting.

Shên-chou, XVII. River Landscape with a Fisherman in a Boat. Signed and dated 1618.

Ming-jên shu-hua, 14. Lake Landscape in an Autumn Night. Signed. Colophon, dated 1618.

Boston Museum. An album of six Landscape Studies, illustrating poems of the T'ang period, copied by the painter. Dated 1618. Five colophons of the 17th and 18th centuries.

Yūrintaikan, I. Far-away Mountains; a rocky Shore seen from a Distance. Handscroll. Colophon by the painter, dated 1619.

J. P. Dubosc, Lugano. Album of eight Landscape Studies accompanied by inscriptions in seal characters. Signed and dated 1621. Inscription by the master dated 1622.

Ibid. A Man in an Open Pavilion under Some Spare Trees on a River-bank. Signed and dated 1621. Fan-painting.

Vannotti collect., Lugano. Narcissi in Bloom and Bamboo Sprouts. Signed and dated 1621. Fan-painting.

Chung-kuo, II, 44. Landscape. Signed and dated 1622. *Cf.* Nanga Taisei, IX, 190.

Nanking Exhib. cat. 199. Pine-trees growing by a Rock. Signed and dated 1622.

Hua-chung chiu-yu chi-ts'ê (Hakubundō album, Ōsaka, 1921). A Mountain Slope with sparse Trees. After Huang Kung-wang. Signed and dated 1622.

Commercial Press album. Eight Landscape Studies after various Old Masters. Colophon by the painter, dated 1622. A.

Chang Pi-han, Hongkong. River Landscape. Dated 1623.

Shên-chou ta-kuan, vol.5. Two tall Trees on the River-bank. Signed and dated 1624. *Cf.* Shina Nanga, II, 3.

Chung-kuo, II, 46. Landscape. Signed and dated 1624. *Cf.* Liu, 79; P'ang Yüan-chi cat. Add. 2.

Pao-yün, II. A Pavilion in a Grove. Fan-painting. Signed and dated 1624.

Shanghai Museum. River-view, after Ni Tsan. Signed and dated 1625.

Musée Guimet. Mountain Landscape. Fan-painting. Signed and dated 1625.

Köln, Ostasiat. Museum. A Small Pavilion with Two Men, at the Foot of High Rocks, and Pine-trees. Signed and dated 1625. Fan-painting. Köln Exhibition 1955, No.47.

Chung-kuo, II, 45. Landscape. Signed. Poem by the painter, dated 1625. *Cf.* Nanga Taisei, IX, 190.

Shên-chou, XXI. A Cottage at the Foot of a steep Hill. Signed and dated 1626. Colophon by Tung Ch'i-ch'ang.

Shina Nanga, I, 14. Landscape. Signed and dated 1626.

Ibid. III, 11. Landscape. Signed and dated 1626.

Nanju 8. Landscape after Wu Chên. Signed and dated 1626.

Chêng Tê-k'un, Cambridge. Steep deeply Folded Mountain Rising above a Stream; a scholar's pavilion built over the water. Signed and dated 1626.

Vannotti collect., Lugano. River Landscape. Fan-painting. Signed and dated 1626. *Cf.* Venice Exhibition cat. 835.
Shên-chou, XVIII. A Man seated by a Mountain Stream looking at the Waterfall. After Wu Chên. Signed and dated 1627.
Ibid. XXI. River Landscape with sparse Trees, in the manner of Ni Tsan. Signed and dated 1627.
Commercial Press album. Ten Landscape Studies. Colophon by the painter, dated 1627.
P'ang Yüan-chi Illust. cat. IV. An old Tree, Narcissi and Bamboos by a Rock. Signed and dated 1627.
N. Gashū, 14. Landscape. Signed and dated 1627.
Tōsō, p.362 (Cleveland Museum). Landscape. Signed. Poem by the painter, dated 1628.
Kurokawa collect., Ashiya. Landscape. Handscroll. Signed.
Kurokawa cat. 5. Chrysanthemums. Signed.
K.-k. chou-k'an 22. Landscape, fan-painting. See also Nanga Taisei, VIII, 106 (dated 1627).
Shên-chou album. Four pictures of Orchids. Signed. Colophon.
Hua-chung chiu-yu (Yu-chêng album). Landscape. Signed.
Gems, III, 6. Two leaves from an album of Ten Scenes from Suchou. Inscription, seals of the artist.
Hui-hua kuan. Studies of Flowering Shrubs and Plants. Six album-leaves. Ink on paper.
Ku-kung collect. (Nanking Exhib. cat. 200). Two leaves from an album of Landscapes, illustrations to T'ang poems. Signed.
Chang Ts'ung-yü cat. Mountain River with a Man in a Boat.
Ibid. Tall Trees and small House at the Foot of a Hill.
J. D. Ch'ên cat. II, 34. Landscape after Tung Yüan. Handscroll; signed.
Cleveland Museum of Art. Thin Forest and distant Mountains by a Stream. Poem by the painter. *Cf.* Cleveland Exhibition cat. 71.
Hobart collect., Cambridge, Mass. Landscape Studies after Old Masters. Two album-leaves.
Musée Guimet. Mountain Landscape. Signed.

LI PIN 李彬, *t.* Wên-chung 文中.
From Ssŭ-ming, Chekiang. Figures. M, p.198.

Chang Ta-ch'ien, Hongkong. The Moving of the Shepherds. Handscroll. Signed.

LI SHAO-CH'I 李紹箕, *t.* Mou-ch'êng 懋承.
From Hua-t'ing, Kiangsu. Son-in-law of Ku Chêng-i, whom he followed in landscapes. O, 4. M, p.199.

K.-k. shu-hua chi, III. Landscape. Signed and dated 1589.
Nanju 14. Landscape. Signed and dated 1610.
Nanga Taisei, XI, 52. Houses in a Valley between precipitous Mountains. Large album-leaf, signed.

LI SHIH-TA 李士達, *t.* Yang-huai 仰槐.
From Suchou. Active in the Wan-li period (1573–1619). Landscapes and figures. Published an essay on the five merits and five defects in landscape-painting. N, IV, 16. O, 1. M, p.199.

Frau R. Berk, Neuhemmerich bei Frechen. A Man Riding a Buffalo on a Mud-bank Crossing over a River. Signed and dated 1605. Fan-painting. Köln Exhibition 1955, No.27.
Nanju 4. Rainy Landscape. Signed. Two lines of poetry, dated 1608.
Hashimoto collect., Takatsuki. Scholars drinking in a rocky Landscape. Fan-painting, executed in fine detail. Signed and dated 1610.
Sōraikan, II, 59. Chung K'uei walking under tall Trees. Signed and dated 1611.
Ku-kung, XLIII. The Eight Drunkards. Fan-painting. Signed and dated 1613.

Tōsō, p.349. Scratching the Back in the Shade of the Pine-trees. Signed and dated 1614.

K.-k. shu-hua chi, XXXI. Chung K'uei and the Demons. Signed and dated 1614.

Kokka 309 (Seikado). Writing Poems on New Year's Day. Two lines of poetry, dated 1615.

Chūgoku, III. Two Men conversing by a tall Pine-tree in front of a Bamboo Grove. Two lines of poetry by the painter, dated 1615.

National Museum, Stockholm. A Village in the Mountains. Signed and dated 1615.

K.-k. shu-hua chi, XXVIII. Listening to the Sounds of the Pine-trees. Signed and dated 1616.

Hui-hua kuan. Three Old Humpbacks. Signed and dated 1617. Poems by four contemporaries.

Kokka 317 (Seikadō). A Mountain Pavilion enveloped in Clouds. Signed and dated 1618. *Cf.* Tōsō, p.348.

Shên-chou, II. Man seated in a Chair under Banana-trees served by Two Boys. Signed and dated 1618.

Horiuchi collect., Ōsaka. An old Man seated beside bare Trees, while Servants prepare Tea. Signed and dated 1618.

Tōyō, X (Seikadō). Storm in the Valley; Travellers on Donkeys arriving at an Inn. Signed and dated 1619. *Cf.* Nanju 13. Same composition as K.-k. shu-hua chi, XXI.

Kyūka, I. A Donkey-rider on a Bridge. Fan-painting. Signed and dated 1619.

K.-k. shu-hua chi, XXI. Rainstorm in the Valley; Men on Muleback. Some lines of poetry as on the preceding picture, dated 1620. *Cf.* Tōyō, X.

Shimbi, XII. The Peach and Plum Garden. Signed, at the age of 73.

Bijutsu, XVII. Bamboo Grove with Figures. Fan-painting. Signed.

Kyūka, I (J. Cahill, Wash., D.C.) Chung K'uei. Signed. Poem.

Ibid. I. Men Seated in a Bamboo Grove; Cloudy Mountains. Signed. Two lines of poetry.

Tōsō, p.347. River-bank with Flowering Trees. Signed. Two lines of poetry.

Chang Ting-ch'ên, Hongkong. Groups of Children celebrating New Year. Signed.

J. D. Ch'ên cat. I, 38. T'ao Yüan-ming Enjoying Chrysanthemums beneath a Pine-tree. Signed.

W. Hochstadter, New York. Meeting of nine Scholars in a Temple Garden. Short handscroll. Each of the scholars has added a colophon.

K.-k. chou-k'an 81 and 502. Fan-paintings.

LI TSAI 李在, *t.* I-chêng 以政.

From P'u-t'ien, Fukien. Lived for some time in Yünnan. Served in Jên-chih tien together with Tai Chin in the Hsüan-tê period (1426–1435). Landscapes in the style of Kuo Hsi, Ma Yüan and Hsia Kuei. L, 43, 6. N, II, 10. O, 2. M, p.198.

Gems, I, 22. Ch'in Kao Riding on a Carp. Signed.

National Museum, Tōkyō. A misty Landscape, with figures in a Boat and a distant Temple. Signed. *Cf.* Pageant 493; Sekai Bijutsu Zenshū, XX, pl.13.

Tōsō, p.20 (Ogawa collect.) High Mountains in Snow; a Traveller on the Road below. Signed.

Boston Museum. River Landscape with leafless Trees. Album-leaf. Signed.

LI TSUNG-MO 李宗謨, *h.* Hsiao-ch'iao 小樵.

From Yung-an, Fukien. Contemporary of Tung Ch'i-ch'ang (1555–1636). Figures and sometimes landscapes. M, p.199.

Ku-kung collect. The Lan-t'ing Meeting. Wang Hsi-chih is seated in a pavilion; a great number of scholars are placed along the border of the river; they are occupied in floating their cups. Possibly after Chao Mêng-fu. Long handscroll. Signed.

LI YÜ 李郁.
Military officer at Fêng-yang, Anhui; said to have died in the field in 1635. Unrecorded.

Nanju 6. Autumn Rain in the Mountains. Finger painting. Signed. Poem, dated 1618. Also reproduced in Tōyō, XI.

LI YUNG-CH'ANG 李永昌, t. Chou-shêng 周生.
Late Ming. From Hsiu-ning, Anhui. Landscape in the style of Yüan. Also a poet. N, IV, 26. M, p.200.

S.c.t.k. hsü-pien, XI. Landscape in the Yüan style. Signed and dated 1634.

LIANG CHIH-CHUNG 梁志中.
Unrecorded. Flourished *c.*1630.

K.-k. shu-hua chi, XLV. Bare Trees and Bamboos by a Stream. Signed. Poems by Wei Chih-huang (dated 1635), Chêng Chung and the painter.

LIN HSÜEH 林雪, *t.* T'ien-su 天素.
Courtesan from Fukien or Nanking. Epidendrum. N, V, 4. M, p.231.

J. P. Dubosc, Lugano. River Landscape, a Fisherman in a Boat. A small homestead at the foot of a hill. Fan-painting. Signed and dated 1620.
Ibid. A Slender Plum-tree in Bloom, Two Small Bamboos. Signed and dated 1621.

LIN LIANG 林良, *t.* I-shan 以善.
From Kwangtung. Served in the palace during the Hung-chih period (1488–1505). Flowers and birds, also trees in monochrome ink. N, II, 5. O, 6. M, p.230.

Sōgen 92. Three Doves on a Branch. One of a pair of scrolls. Signed and dated 1496(?).
K.-k. shu-hua chi, I. An Eagle and a Crow. Signed.
Ibid. XXXIII. A Pair of Eagles. Signed.
S.c.t.k. hsü-pien, VII. Pigeons on a Pine Branch. Signed.
Nanking Exhib. cat. 114. A Pair of Peacocks. Signed.
Shimbi, XVIII. A Peacock.
Ibid. XIX (Sōkoku-ji, Yamato Province). A Phoenix. Signed. *Cf.* Tōsō, p.258; Yonezawa, 6.
Shimbi Shoin Shina Meigashū, II (Baron Gō). Two White Herons on a River-bank, two Mynah birds and a Kingfisher on a Branch.
Kyūka, I. Two Ducks by a Stream. Signed.
Tōyō, X. Two Cormorants and Reeds. Signed. *Cf.* Shina Meigashū.
National Museum, Stockholm. Three Eagles, one of them white, seated in a Pine-tree by a Rock. Signed.
Collection Culty, Paris (1934). A Flock of Crows and an Eagle perched on snowy Rocks. Signed.
Honolulu Academy of Art. Two Cormorants. Signed. *Cf.* Sirén, *Later*, pl.43.
Metropolitan Museum. A Fêng-huang bird and Bamboo. Signed.
Ibid. (Bahr collect.) Wild Ducks. Signed.
Princeton University (Du Bois-Morris collect.) A White Egret Standing under a Willow Branch. Signed.
Ibid. Two Birds on the drooping Branches of a Willow by the Water. Signed.
British Museum, No.77. Wild Geese by a Mountain Stream. Signed. Doubtful.
Hamburg Exhib. 1949–1950. Two Ducks and tall Reeds. Signed.

LIN SHAN 林山.
Unrecorded.

K.-k. shu-hua chi, XLIV. Fisherman returning through the Rain in a small Boat. Signed.

LIN T'AI-HÊNG 林台衡, *t.* Chao-ch'ing 兆清.
From P'u-t'ien, Fukien. Chü-jên in 1621. Poet. Landscapes and flowers. M, p.230.

Kokka 277. Bamboos and Rocks. Signed and dated 1626.
Nanju 15. Landscape. Signed and dated 1631.

LIN YU-CH'UN 林由春, *t.* Ch'ang-ying 長英.
From Lin-chang, Fukien. Flourished *c.*1640. Landscapes. Unrecorded.

Nanju 16. Landscape, illustrating T'ao Yüan-ming's *Kuei-ch'ü-lai*. Handscroll. Signed and dated 1639.

LING PI-CHÊNG 凌必正, *t.* Chên-ch'ing 貞卿, Mêng-ch'iu 蒙求, *h.* Jo-an 約庵.
From T'ai-ts'ang, Kiangsu. Chin shih in 1631. Painted coloured landscapes; also flowers and birds. N, IV, 24. U, II, 1, 10. M, p.382.

Hui-hua kuan. Studies of Flowers and Birds in six album-leaves. Colour on paper.

LIU CHIEH 劉節.
From An-ch'êng, Honan. Son of the painter Liu Chin 劉進. Served as a court-painter in the Chia-ching perio (1522–1566). Specialized in fish painting. N, VI, 15. M, p.661.

Metropolitan Museum (Bahr collect.) Fishes in an Inlet of shallow Water. Signed.

LIU CHÜEH 劉珏, *t.* T'ing-mei 廷美, *h.* Wan-an 完菴.
From Suchou. B. 1410, d. 1472. Poet, calligraphist, and official. Landscapes in the style of Wang Mêng. N, II, 1. O, 2. I, 56, 2. M, p.660.

J. P. Dubosc, Lugano. Houses by a Lake. Fan-painting. Signed and dated 1438.
Shên-chou ta-kuan, vol.3. Cliffs by a River. Signed and dated 1441. Poem by Yang Hsün-chi. *Cf.* Liu, 46.
S.c.t.k. hsü-pien, IX. Pine-trees and Pavilions. Poems by the painter, dated 1441. *Cf.* Nanga Taisei, IX, 107; Chūgoku, II.
K.-k. shu-hua chi, IV. The Ch'ing-po Pavilion (the painter's study). Signed. Colophon dated 1458. Poems by Shên Chou dated 1474 and his father and grandfather.
Bukkyō Bijutsu, 18. A Mountain Stream spanned by a Bridge, and Pine-trees. Signed and dated 1467. *Cf.* Sōgen, p.90.
C. C. Wang, New York. Mountain Valley; on the Road to the West Lake in Hangchou. Signed and dated 1471. Poems by Shên Chou, Shih Chien, Chêng Mêng and two more.
Shên-chou ta-kuan, vol.16. River Landscape; a Man with a *Ch'in* seated on a Cliff. Poem by the painter.
Hui-hua kuan. Mountain Peaks, Clouds and Rushing Water. In the style of Chü-jan.

Liu, 45. Cloudy Mountains in Summer, after Wu Chên. Seal of the painter. Poem by Shên Chou, dated 1505.

Tōsō, p.243 (Motoyama collect.) Landscape. Signed. Poems by Shên Chou and Wên Chêng-ming.

Musée Guimet. Landscape with steep Mountains in the manner of Ni Tsan. Poems by the painter and by Shên Chou. *Cf.* Cleveland Exhibition cat. 40.

LIU CHÜN 劉俊, *t.* T'ing-wei 廷偉.

Court-painter *c.*1500. Officer of the Imperial Guard. Taoist figures and landscapes in Wu Wei's style. N, VI, 27. M, p.660.

Chung-kuo, II, 52. Drinking Wine in a Snow-covered Hall. Signed.

Kokka 278. Two Taoist Immortals. Signed. Also in Tōsō, p.394.

Ibid. 403. Two Taoist Immortals by the River.

Ibid. 432. Tung-fang So with the Peaches of Immortality.

Shimbi, III. Landscape with Figures, illustrating a poem by Wang Wei. Signed. Also in Tōyō, X.

Ibid. III. The Poet Li Shê on his Way to the House of a Friend.

Tōsō, pp.392, 393. Han-shan and Shih-tê in Landscapes.

Sōkoku-ji, Kyōto. Ch'ên Chuan Walking on the Waves. Signed.

Boston Museum. Three Taoist Immortals doing a Toad-dance. Signed.

LIU KUANG 劉廣, *t.* Yüan-po 元博.

From Suchou. Ming dynasty. Flowers. Unrecorded.

K.-k. shu-hua chi, XXV. Flowers. Signed and dated *ping-wu*.

LIU SHIH-JU 劉世儒, *t.* Chi-hsiang 繼相, *h.* Hsüeh-hu 雪湖.

From Shan-yin, Chekiang. Flourished in the first half of the 16th century. Plum-blossoms in the style of Wang Mien. Author of *Mei-p'u* 梅譜, in four volumes. N, VII, 2. O, 7. M, p.661.

Po-mei chi. Branches of Plum-blossoms. Handscroll. Signed.

Tōsō, p.231. Branches of Plum-blossoms. Signed. Poem.

Fogg Museum, Cambridge, Mass. Branches of an Old Plum-tree in Blossom.

LIU TA-HSIA 劉大夏, *t.* Shih-yung 時雍.

From Hua-jung, Hunan. B. 1436, d. 1516. President of the Board of War. Bamboos. V, p.1430.

National Museum, Stockholm. Bamboos in Snow. Signed. Inscription by Ch'ên Wu-hsi.

LIU TU 劉度, *t.* Shu-hsien 叔憲 or 叔獻.

Native of Ch'ien-t'ang. Active toward the end of Ming. Landscapes after Li Chao-tao and Chao Po-chü, and also figures. N, VII, 18. U, I, 2, 19. M, p.662.

Ku-kung collect. Rocky Landscape painted in colour in an archaistic style. Handscroll. Dated 1366.

LIU YÜAN-CH'I 劉原起. Originally called Liu Tsu 劉祚. *t.* Tzŭ-chêng 子正, *h.* Chên-chih 振之.
From Suchou. Active *c.*1620–1633. Poet. Landscapes; pupil of Ch'ien Ku. O, 4. M, p.661.

Hui-hua kuan. Epidendrum and Bamboo by a Stone. Painted together with Ch'ên Yüan-su who signed and dated 1620. Eight inscriptions by contemporaries.
Köln, Ostasiat. Museum. River Landscape in Rain. Signed and dated 1621. Fan-painting. Köln Exhibition 1955, No.34.
J. P. Dubosc, Lugano. Tall Pine-trees on Rocky Hills, Wide Waters, an Old Man Crossing the Bridge, Signed and dated 1623, Fan-painting.
Chūgoku, IV. An Old Man followed by a Servant crossing a Bridge to reach a Cottage surrounded by leafy Trees on a Mountain. Signed and dated 1631.
K.-k. shu-hua chi, XLII. New Year's Day; Landscape with Figures. Signed, dated 1632.
J. P. Dubosc, Lugano. Small Pavilions in a Dense Growth of Leafy Trees on the Border of Wide Waters. Ink and slight colours. Signed and dated 1632. Fan-painting.
Hamburg Exhibition 1949–1950. Winter Landscape. Signed and dated 1633.
K.-k. shu-hua chi, XLIV. Man seated under tall Pine-trees. Signed.
K.-k. chou-k'an 70 and 74. Two Landscapes. Fan-paintings.
J. P. Dubosc, Landscape with Figure. Fan-painting. Signed.

LU CH'AO-YANG 盧朝陽.
From Sha-hsien, Fukien. 16th century. Birds in the style of Pien Wên-chin, his fellow-townsman. M, p.677.

John Herron Art Museum, Indianapolis. A Pair of Peacocks among Mu-tan Flowers and Blossoming Fruit-tree. Signed and dated 1552.
Chung-kuo, II, 31. Eagles and Sparrows. Signed.

LU CHIH 陸治, *t.* Shu-p'ing 叔平, *h.* Pao-shan 包山.
From Suchou. B. 1496, d. 1576. Famous flower-painter in the style of Hsü Hsi and Huang Ch'üan, but painted also landscapes. Pupil of Wên Chêng-ming and Chu Yün-ming. N, III, 12. O, 6. I, 57, 2. M, p.418.

K.-k. shu-hua chi, XII. T'ao Yüan-ming. Poem. Colophon dated 1572, fifty years after the execution of the picture in 1523.
Ku-kung collect. Winter Scenery. A Scholar in a Hut reading the *I-ching*. In the manner of Huang Kung-wang. Painted for I-chai Hsüeh-shih, dated 1524.
Ibid. (Nanking Exhibition cat.) A Temple on a Peak. Leaf in an album. Signed and dated 1539.
Sōgen 135. Landscape in blue and green. Seals of the painter. Poem by Wên Chêng-ming, dated 1540.
Ibid. 137. Narcissi and Fungi; two Mynah birds. Signed and dated 1540.
Vannotti collect., Lugano. A Pavilion among Trees on a High Cliff. Ink and colour. Signed and dated 1540. Fan-painting.
K.-k. shu-hua chi, XVIII. Parrot and Swallows in a Peach-tree. Signed. Poem dated 1544.
Shên-chou, VII (VI). Steep terraced Mountains. Signed. Poem dated 1544.
T'ang Hsiao-min, Taichung. Quail among Stalks of Wheat and tall Thistles. Signed and dated 1545.
Shên-chou, III. Epidendrums in a Pot, placed on Top of a Rockery. Signed and dated 1548.
J. P. Dubosc, Lugano. A River Valley Spanned by a Bridge. Slight greenish colour. Signed and dated 1548. Fan-painting.
Mo-ch'ao pi-chi, I. High Mountains, after Wang Mêng. Long handscroll. Signed and dated 1549.
Shina Meiga Senshū, 9. Steep Mountains with Waterfalls. Pavilions at their foot. Colophon by the painter, dated 1549. Poem by Ch'ien-lung.
Nelson Gallery, Kansas City. Cavernous Cliffs with leafy Trees. Handscroll – light colours on paper. Signed and dated 1549. Poem by the painter and

colophon by Tung Ch'i-ch'ang dated 1632. *Cf.* Cleveland Exhibition cat. 60.

K.-k. shu-hua chi, XLV. *T'ien-ch'ih shih-pi.* Steep overhanging Rocks by a River. Signed. Poem, dated 1550.

Ibid. XXV. Bamboos and Quails. Signed and dated 1552.

Private collect., Shanghai. Mountain Landscape with a Man seated in Meditation in a Cave. Clouds and leafy trees. Signed and dated 1552.

K.-k. chou-k'an 503. An ornamental Rock and Grass in a square Tray. Signed and dated 1553. Long poem written by Shên Shih-tuan, dated 1560.

Tōsō, p.322. Mountains and Stream. Signed. Poem, dated 1554.

Freer Gallery (39.3). River Scenery in Autumn. Illustration to Po Chü-i's *Song of the P'i-p'a.* The poem is added to the picture in Wên P'êng's writing. Ink and light colours; handscroll. Signed and dated 1554. *Cf.* P'ang Yüan-chi cat. 4; Kokka 757.

Ton Ying Co., New York. Flowering Branches of Pear and Crabapple-trees. Fan-painting. Poem by the painter, dated 1554.

P'ang Yüan-chi Illust. cat. V. The Island of the Immortals. Poem dated 1554.

Boston Museum. A View of Shih-hu. Short handscroll. Signed and dated 1558. *Cf.* Kokka 757.

Vannotti collect., Lugano. A Garden View; Two Men in an Open Pavilion. Signed and dated 1561.

Shina Nanga, III, 2. Bats and Flowers. Signed and dated 1561.

Gems, I, 39. A Cuckoo on a Branch of Blossoming Apricot. Poem, signed and dated 1562.

Ku-kung collect. *Lung-yüan t'u*: The Dragon Spring. Short handscroll with slight colour. Signed and dated 1563. Painted as a gift to a monk called after the place Lung-yüan.

Ōmura, II, 2. Hollyhocks and Pomegranates. Signed and dated 1563. *Cf.* Chūgoku, III.

Ku-kung collect. Searching for Plum-blossoms after Snow. Large album-leaf. Signed and dated 1564. A.

Ming-hua ling-lang. View of a River with sharply-cut rocky Shores and Islands. Signed and dated 1564. Poems by the painter and by Ch'ien-lung.

J. P. Dubosc, Lugano. Wide View over Rocky Islands in a Lake. Signed and dated 1565. Slight greenish coloured. Fan-painting.

C. T. Loo's Successor Frank Caro, N.Y. A River Landscape, with sparse Trees and steep Cliffs rising from the opposite Bank. Long inscription by the artist, dated 1567. *Cf.* Toronto 21.

K.-k. shu-hua chi, XXVI. A Hermit-fisherman by the Flower Stream. Signed and dated 1568.

Nanga Taisei, I, 44. Tall Stalks of Bamboo, painted in outline. Signed and dated 1569.

Ibid. XVI. Lily and Pomegranate. Signed and dated 1570.

Ibid. VIII. Peony. Signed. Colophon dated 1571.

Ku-kung collect. Views of the Country around the T'ai-hu Lake. Travellers on horseback and in sedan-chairs and boats; green hills beyond. A remarkable handscroll. Signed and dated 1571.

J. P. Dubosc, Lugano. A River in the Mountains between Terraced Cliffs. Signed and dated 1572.

Shên-chou, XIV. A Chrysanthemum Garden in the Mountains. Signed. Poem.

Shên-chou album (1917). Six Views of an Autumn Night. Signed.

Mo-ch'ao pi-chi, II. Birds and Flowers. Signed. Poem by the painter.

Ku-kung, XIX. The Jade Cave in the Mountain of Immortals. Signed. Poem.

Ibid. XXIX. The Chih-hsin Mountain (where the painter lived in his old age). Signed. Poem.

K.-k. shu-hua chi, VII. Magnolia and Bamboo. Poem by the painter.

Ibid. XXXII. Pine-trees, Fungi, and Bamboos by a Rock. Signed.

Ibid. XXXVI. A Pair of Peacocks in a Garden. Signed.

K.-k. chou-k'an 501. A Branch of Flowering Pear. Poem, signed.

Ibid. 510. Various Flowers growing beside an Ornamental Rock. Inscribed and signed.

Ku-kung collect. *Tan-fêng ch'iu-sê t'u*: Red Leaves in Autumn. Slight colour on paper. Short handscroll. Poem by the painter.

Ibid. A small album of ten leaves representing flowers. Signed.

Ibid. Hai-t'ang and Magnolia Flowers. Painted together with Wang Ku-hsiang. Signed, and inscriptions by three friends of the painters.

Chang Pi-han, Hongkong. Two Landscapes. Fan-paintings. Signed. For other fan-paintings, see K.-k. chou-k'an Index for nine paintings; also Nanga Taisei, VIII, 70.

T. T. Ma, Hongkong. A Tuberose-plant (Yü-chan). Poem by the painter.

Palace Museum album. An Album of twelve Flower-paintings.

Hui-hua kuan. A Scholar seated in a Bamboo Grove at the Foot of sharply-cut Mountain. Coloured.

Ibid. Landscape Studies with Figures. Four of eight double album-leaves.

Gems, I, 40. Mountain Landscape: the P'an-ku Retreat. Poem, signed.

Hsü-ching chai. Tree-peonies in a Rockery. Poems by the painter, and by Wang Shih-chên, Wang Shih-mou, and Chi Yung.

Yen Kuang Co., Peking. A Hermit-fisherman on the Peach-blossom Stream. Signed.

Kokka 315 (Seikadō, Tōkyō). Lotus Plants by a Rock. Signed. Poem.

Ibid. 749. Doves in a Blossoming Plum-tree. Poem, signed.

Bijutsu, XXII. Pavilion in a Mountain Gorge. Signed.

Ōmura, II, 1. Lotus Plants. Signed. Poem by the painter, same as that in Kokka 315. Poem by Wên Po-jên. *Cf.* Chūgoku, III.

Tōsō, p.323. Flowers and Birds. Signed. Poems by the painter and by Chu Yün-ming.

Sōgen 136. The Lin-wu Mountain on the Tung-t'ing Island in T'ai-hu. Poem by the painter.

Ibid. 138. A Yü-lan Flower by a Rockery. Signed. Poem. *Cf.* P'ang Yüan-chi cat. Add. 2.

Ibid. 139. Narcissi after Chao Mêng-chien. Part of a handscroll.

Kurokawa cat. 5. Daffodils growing beside a Rock. Signed.

Metropolitan Museum. Autumn Grove; spare Trees and a Pavilion by a River. Signed.

Chicago Art Institute. View over the River; Fisherman in a Boat, and Clump of Trees on the Rocky-bank. Poem by the painter. Signed.

Hobart collect., Cambridge, Mass. Steep Mountains rising like Towers from the River. Inscriptions by the painter, and by Wên Chia, Lu Shih-tao, Huang Chi-shui.

R. W. Finlayson, Toronto. Magnolias. Ink and colour on paper. Poem by the painter. *Cf.* Toronto 22.

Howard Hollis Co., Cleveland (ex-T. Tomioka collect.) Landscape with Blossoming Trees. Fan-painting. Ink and colour on gold paper. Inscription by the painter. *Cf.* Kokka 731; Cleveland Exhibition cat. 62.

Ton Ying Co., New York. Album of twelve leaves with Landscape-studies. Inscriptions by the painter.

Vannotti collect., Lugano. Steep Rocks rising above a River. Fan-painting. Signed.

Musée Guimet. A Flowering Plant with large Leaves and Flowers like Lilies. Poem by the painter.

Ibid. A Bird on a Branch of a Fruit-tree. Fan-painting. Colours on gold ground. Signed.

Hamburg Exhibition, 1949–1950. The Waterfall at Kuang-lu. Colours on silk. Handscroll. Colophon by Wên Chêng-ming.

National Museum, Stockholm. River Landscape. Fan-painting.

J. P. Dubosc, Lugano. A View of Hu-ch'iu, the Tiger Hill. Temple Pavilions on a craggy Rock; light Mist. Short handscroll. Inscription by the painter.

Ibid. Three fan-paintings representing river-views, gardens and blossoming trees.

B. Z. Seligman, London. A Plant with Large Leaves and Flowers like Lilies. Ink and colour. Signed. Fan-painting.

LU FU 陸復, *t.* Ming-pên 明本, *h.* Mei-hua Chu-jên 梅花主人.
From Wu-chiang, Kiangsu. 15th century. Plum-blossoms. O, 7. M, p.417.

Ku-kung, XII. Plum-blossoms in Snow. Signed. Two lines of poetry.

Kokka 195. A Plum-tree. Signed.

Juncunc collect., Chicago. A Branch of a Blossoming Plum-tree. Short handscroll. Poem, Signed.

Private collect., Hongkong. Plum-blossoms. Long branches stretching over the entire scroll, covered with blossoms. Handscroll. The background is greyish blue. Several inscriptions; three of them by Shên Chou, Wên Chêng-ming and T'ang Yin.

Lu K'o-chêng 陸克正.
Unrecorded. Probably Ming period.

Metropolitan Museum. Mountains in Mist and Trees. After Tung Yüan. Fan-painting.

Lu Shih-jên 陸士仁, *t.* Wên-chin 文近, *h.* Ch'êng-hu 澄(承)湖.
Son of Lu Shih-tao. Landscapes after his father. N, II, 27. O, 4. M, p.418.

Chêng Tê-k'un, Cambridge. Fisherman in an Autumn Landscape. Album-leaf. Signed and dated 1605.

J. P. Dubosc, Lugano. Scholar's Homestead under some Trees by a Mountain Stream. Fan-painting. Ink and colour. Signed.

Lu Shih-tao 陸師道, *t.* Tzŭ-ch'uan 子傳, *h.* Yüan-chou 元洲 and Wu-hu 五湖.
From Suchou. Lived *c.*1510–1570. Chin-shih in 1538. Pupil of Wên Chêng-ming. Poet, calligraphist; landscapes in the style of Ni Tsan. O, 4. N, II, 27. M, p.418.

K.-k. shu-hua chi, III. Mist over a Mountain River. A Man reading. Signed. Poem, dated 1544.
Chūgoku, III. A broad winding Stream between hilly Banks; a small Figure on the Promontory below. Album-leaf.
I-yüan chên-shang 10. Landscape. Signed, and with colophons by several famous contemporaries of the painter.
C. T. Loo's Successor Frank Caro, N.Y. A Man by a Waterfall in an Autumn Wood. Poem by the painter. Signed. Inscription by Wu Hu-fan. *Cf.* Toronto, 24.

Lu Tê-chih 魯得之. Original name Lu Shên 魯參, *t.* Lu-shan 魯山. *t.* K'ung-sun 孔孫, *h.* Ch'ien-yen 千巖.
From Ch'ien-t'ang, Chekiang. Calligrapher. Ink-bamboos and epidendrums; pupil of Li Jih-hua. Painted with left hand when old. O, 7. Q, I, 1. U. II, 1, 10. M, p.631.

Hamburg Exhibition, 1949–1950. Bamboo Branches. Handscroll. Signed and dated 1637.
Nanga Taisei, I, 87–97. Album of Studies of Bamboo, the last signed and dated 1640.
Ibid. I, 98. Tall Bamboo and Bamboo Sprouts. Signed and dated 1654.
Ibid. IV, 210. Briers growing from behind a Rock. Seal of the painter.

Lü Chi 呂紀, *t.* T'ing-chên 廷振, *h.* Lo-yü 樂愚 or 樂漁.
From Chin-hsien, Chekiang. Active *c.*1500. Famous painter of flowers and birds in the style of Pien Wên-chin. Also landscapes and figures. Probably the head of a studio for the production of bird and flower paintings. Summoned to the palace in the Hung-chih period and appointed an officer in the Imperial Guard. I, 56, 10. N, II, 5. O, 6. M, p.124.

L. Bataille, Paris. Two Cranes under Pine-trees. Inscribed with the painter's name and the date 1493.
Chung-kuo, II, 57. Peach-blossoms, Peonies and Birds. Signed.
Li-tai, IV. Wild Geese in the Moonlight. Signed.
Ku-kung, X. Birds in Snow. Signed.
Ibid. XXVIII. Swallows and Ducks. Signed.
Ibid. XXX. A Pair of Mandarin Ducks. Signed.
K.-k. shu-hua chi, II. A Pheasant in Snow. Signed.
Ibid. VI. Herons among Lotus Plants in Autumn. Signed.
Ibid. X. Peacock and Apricot-blossoms. Signed.
Ibid. XI. Tall Reeds, Grass and Pair of Pheasants. Signed. Poems by Shên Chou and Ch'ien-lung.
Ibid. XIX. Birds in Snow. Signed.
Ibid. XXXIII. Birds, Flowers and Fish. Signed.
Ibid. XXXVI. Cranes, Pine-trees by a Waterfall. Signed.
Ku-kung collect. Three Egrets, one standing and two flying, among Hibiscus and Lotus-plants. Colour on silk. Signed. *Cf.* Nanking Exhibition cat. 118.
Ibid. A Pair of Pheasants among Reeds by the Shore.

Inscriptions by Shên Chou and Ch'ien-lung. Reproduced in colour in *Time Magazine*, May 6, 1957.

Gems, I, 36. Two Orioles in a Pomegranate-tree. Signed.

Hui-hua kuan. A Mynah and other large Birds; Rocks and Chrysanthemums. Rich colours on silk. Signed.

Ibid. An Eagle on a Cliff, a Magpie below. Ink on paper. Signed.

Nanking Exhib. cat. 119. Birds perched on a Blossoming Plum-tree; two Pheasants below. Signed.

Kokka 78. A Cat.

Ibid. 328. Birds and Ducks.

Ibid. 328. A Pheasant and Plum-blossoms in Snow. Signed.

Ibid. 335. A Pair of Mandarin Ducks, Birds and Peach-blossoms.

Ibid. 335. A Pair of Ducks, Birds and Flowers.

Ibid. 488. Flowers and Birds.

Shimbi, VII. Flowers and Birds in Snow.

Tōyō, X. Three Partridges and Magpies by a Pine-tree. Signed.

Ibid. X. Two Pheasants and small Birds among wild Tea-plants and Plum-trees. Signed.

Ibid. X. Two Pheasants and small Birds by a Blossoming Tree.

Ibid. X. A Crane standing by a Banana-plant in Snow.

Ibid. X. Two Ducks and small Birds by a Willow on the Shore.

Ibid. X. Two Herons by a Waterfall under an overhanging Pine. Signed.

Yūrintaikan, I. Two Long-tailed Birds on the Branch of an old Pine-tree. Signed. *Cf.* Tōsō, p.261.

Shina Kachō Gasatsu 12. Cormorants on a Cliff by a River. Attributed.

Ibid. 13. Eagles and Magpies on snowy Cliffs and Trees by a River. Attributed.

Ibid. 14. An Eagle killing a Fox. Attributed.

Ibid. 21. Five Mynahs in a Plum-tree. Attributed.

Ibid. 25. Doves standing by a Bowl with Water, Rockery with Blossoming Tree-peonies and Peaches. Attributed.

Ibid. 29. Three Herons and Rushes on a River-bank. Attributed.

Ibid. 30. Ducks on a River-bank, Long-tailed Birds in a Plum-tree. Attributed.

Tōsō, p.259. Pheasants, Birds and Flowers. Signed.

Ibid. 260. Three white Herons and small Birds in a Willow. Signed.

Sōgen Appendix, 18–21 (Tōkyō National Museum). Flowers and Birds of the Four Seasons. Four pictures, one signed. *Cf.* Yonezawa, 5.

Private collect., Shanghai. Three white Herons and Flowering Lilies under a Willow by a winding Stream. *Cf.* Liu, 49.

J. D. Ch'ên cat. I, 28. A Pheasant on the Branch of a Plum-tree in Winter. Signed.

Freer Gallery. Nine white Herons and a Willow-tree. Attributed. An earlier version of the same picture in the Boston Museum.

Philadelphia University Museum. An Eagle on the bare Trunk of a Tree over a Stream; two Sparrows on a Branch of a Blossoming Plum-tree under the Moon. Signed. *Cf.* P'ang Yüan-chi cat. 8.

Honolulu Academy of Arts. A pair of White Swans and Hibiscus Flowers. Signed.

Hamburg Exhibition, 1949–1950. Mandarin Ducks and Hibiscus Flowers. Signed. (Studio work.)

LÜ CHING-FU 呂敬甫.

From Wu-chin, Kiangsu. 14th century. Grass and insects in the style of the Monk Chü-ning of the Sung dynasty. O, 6. M, p.123.

Kokka 424 (Nezu Museum, Tōkyō). Melons and Insects. Seal of the painter.

LÜ TUAN-CHÜN 呂端俊.

From Yao-chiang. Ming dynasty. Bamboos. M, p.123.

K.-k. shu-hua chi, XX. Bamboos in Wind by a Garden Rock. Signed.

J. Cahill, Wash., D.C. Bamboo growing beside a Rock. Seals of the artist.

Lü Wên-ying 呂文英.
From Kuo-ts'ang, Chekiang. Figures. In the Hung-chih period (1488–1505), summoned to the palace together with Lü Chi. Called the Little Lü. O, 1. I, 56, 10. M, p.124.

Kokka 47. An old Toy-pedlar.
Ibid. 505. An old Toy-pedlar.

Ma Chün 馬俊, *t.* Wei-hsiu 惟秀, *h.* Na-kan 訥斧.
From Chia-ting, Kiangsu. 15th century. Landscapes, imitated the T'ang and Sung masters; painted also Buddhist subjects. N, VII, 6. O, 1. M, p.339.

Kyūka, I. Winter Landscape with a Man on Horseback, followed by a Servant.

Ma I-ch'ing 馬一卿, *t.* Ch'ing-ch'iu 青丘.
From Nanking. Flourished *c.*1600. Landscapes. N, VII, 3. O, 5. M, p.340.

Nanju 14. Landscape. Signed and dated 1604. Also in Tōyō, XI.

Ma Shih 馬軾, *t.* Ching-chan 景瞻.
From Chia-ting, Kiangsu. Served in the Imperial Observatory in the Hsüan-tê period (1426–1435). Landscapes, followed Kuo Hsi. Equally famous with Tai Chin and Hsieh Huan. I, 55, 17. O, 3. M, p.339.

Shina Meiga Senshū, 4 (Naitō collect.) A Man riding on a Donkey across a misty Field. Album-leaf. Signed.

Ma Shih-ta 馬世達, *t.* Fang-chih 方知.
From Yen-shan, Hopei. Unrecorded. Probably Ming period.

Metropolitan Museum (Bahr collect.) A Cabbage Plant. Signed.

Ma Shou-chên 馬守貞, *h.* Hsiang-lan 湘蘭 and Yüeh-chiao 月嬌.
Lady-painter from Nanking. Active *c.*1592–1628. Orchids in the style of Chao Mêng-chien; bamboos in that of Kuan Tao-shêng. Poetess. Great friend of the author Wang Chih-têng (1535–1612). N, V, 3. O, 6. M, p.340.

Kurokawa collect., Ashiya. Two Tufts of Epidendrum. Signed and dated 1592.
Chung-kuo, II, 60. Epidendrum and Bamboos. Signed. Poem dated 1594.
Shên-chou, XI. Epidendrum, Bamboos and Fungi in a Bouquet. Signed and dated 1598.
Ming-jên shu-hua, 10. Epidendrum and Bamboos by a Rockery. Signed and dated 1604. *Cf.* Shina Nanga Taikan, 6.
Fu-lu, 3. Epidendrum Plants. Handscroll. Signed and dated 1604.
Lilly collect., Indianapolis. Epidendrum, Bamboo and Rocks. Handscroll. Signed and dated 1604.
Shên-chou ta-kuan, vol.9. Tufts of Epidendrum and Bamboo. After Chao Mêng-chien. Signed and dated 1605.
Ōmura, II, 5. Epidendrum and Bamboos. Part of a handscroll. Signed and dated 1612. *Cf.* Chūgoku, IV.

Ibid. I, 2, 4, 5, 6, 7 and 8. Twelve pictures from one album: six Landscapes in ink, three Epidendrum pictures in light colours, and three in ink. Last one dated 1613.
Ibid. I, 3. Bamboos and Epidendrum by a Rockery. Signed and dated 1627. *Cf.* Chūgoku, IV.
Ku-kung collect. (Nanking Exhib. cat. 181). Two leaves from an album of Flower-paintings. Signed.
Ibid. Epidendrums among Stones. Inscription by Wang Chih-têng. Signed.
Shên-chou, XVIII. A Tuft of Epidendrum, after Chao Mêng-chien. Poem by the painter and by Ch'ên Yüan-su. *Cf.* Shina Nanga, III, 3.
T. T. Ma, Hongkong. A Tuft of Epidendrum between Rocks. Signed. Colophon of later date.
Shina Meiga Senshū, II, 14 (Hashimoto collect.) Kuanyin seated under slender Bamboo. Signed.
Tōsō, p.329. Narcissi. Part of a handscroll.
Yūrintaikan, II. Epidendrum and Rocks, after Kuan Tao-shêng. Handscroll. Signed. Poems and colophons.
National Museum, Stockholm. Lotus in late Summer. Signed. Poem and colophon.
C. C. Wang, New York. A tall Stone, Bamboo and Epidendrum. Signed.
Chang Ting-chien, Hongkong. Epidendrum and Bamboo. Signed.
K.-k. chou-k'an 506. Flowers and Butterfly. Fan-painting.

MI WAN-CHUNG 米萬鍾, *t.* Chung-chao 仲詔, *h.* Yu-shih 友石.
From Shensi; lived in Peking. Chin-shih in 1595; d. 1628. Famous calligrapher. Landscapes in the style of Ni Tsan; flowers in that of Ch'ên Shun. Like his ancestor, Mi Fei, he kept stones of strange shapes; hence his *hao*: Friend of Stones. N, IV, 13. O, 4. U, II, 2. M, p.82.

S.c.t.k. hsü-pien, VI. A strange Rock, a leafless Tree and a Bird. Signed and dated 1630.
Nanju 19. River Landscape in early Sung style. Handscroll. Poem dated 1619.
Shên-chou ta-kuan. Overhanging Cliffs and Trees by a River; two Men fishing. Signed and dated 1620.
Chicago Art Institute. River-view with Buildings and Trees between Rocks. Slightly coloured. Signed and dated 1621.
Hamburg Exhibition, 1949–1950. The enchanting View at Yang-so (in Kuangsi). Huge peaks rising over a stream. Ink and slight colours on paper. Exceptional size: 3·45×1·00 m. Inscription by the painter, dated 1625.
Hui-hua kuan. A deeply hollowed Garden Stone. Ink-painting on gold-sprinkled paper. Signed.
Kokka 437. Chrysanthemums and Bamboos by a Rock. Signed. Poem.
Nanju 24. Mountain Stream and Trees in Autumn. Signed. *Cf.* Tōyō, XI.
Kyūka, I. Snow-bound Travellers in the Mountains. Signed. Poem.
Tōsō, p.361 (National Museum, Tokyo). Misty Mountain Gorge and Large Pine-trees. Signed.
Vannotti collect., Lugano. Landscape. Fan-painting.
K.-k. chou-k'an 298. Bird and flowers. Fan-painting.

MING-HO 明河, *t.* T'ai-ju 太如, *h.* Kao-sung 高松.
*c.*1630. Monk and Poet. Unrecorded.

Nanju 17. Landscape. Signed and dated 1632. Also in Tōyō, XI.

MO SHIH-LUNG 莫是龍, *t.* Yün-ch'ing 雲卿. Took this *tzŭ* as his name and adopted another *tzŭ*: T'ing-han 廷韓. h. Ch'iu-shui 秋水, Chên-i Tao-jên 貞一道人, and other names.
From Hua-t'ing, Kiangsu; lived in Shanghai. Active *c.*1567–1600. Famous critic of painting. Author of *Hua-shuo* 畫說. Poet and calligraphist. Landscapes. N, III, 14. O, 4. M, p.380.

Princeton University (Du Bois-Morris collect.) High Mountains and a winding Brook. Signed and dated 1567.

Ōmura, I, 10. Landscape in the style of Ni Tsan. Signed and dated 1576. *Cf.* Sōraikan, II, 58.

Nanga Taisei, IX, 164. A River Landscape, with Houses on the Bank. Signed and dated 1586.

C. T. Loo's Successor Frank Caro, N.Y. Landscape in the style of Ni Tsan. Signed and dated 1601.

K.-k. shu-hua chi, VII. A Straw-covered Hut on the Eastern Hill. Signed. Poem.

Nanking Exhib. cat. 210. Houses in a Ravine among bare Trees. Inscription, signed.

Gems, II, 19. River Landscape; Buildings in a deep Ravine. After Huang Kung-wang. Handscroll. Signed.

Sōgen 159. Deeply folded grassy Mountains. Signed. Poems.

Musée Guimet, Paris. Landscape on Gold Ground. Fan-painting.

Hamburg Exhibition 1949–1950. Mountain Landscape in Yüan style. At the top of the picture is a letter by the painter in which he expresses his wish to do his picture when in the right mood.

C. T. Loo's Successor Frank Caro, N.Y. Houses at the foot of a Mountain. Poem, signed; inscription by three contemporaries.

NI TUAN 倪端, *t.* Chung-chêng 仲正.
From Hangchou, Chekiang. Summoned to service in the palace in the Hsüan-tê period (1426–1435). Buddhist and Taoist figures. Landscapes in Ma Yüan's style. N, VI, 15. O, 1. M, p.315.

K.-k. shu-hua chi, XLIV. Fisherman Drawing his Net. Signed.

NI YÜAN-LU 倪元璐, *t.* Yü-ju 玉汝 or 玉如, *h.* Hung-pao 鴻寶; posthumous name, Wên-chên 文貞.
From Shang-yü, Chekiang. B. 1593, d. 1644. High official; hanged himself when the Ming dynasty fell. Poet, calligrapher. Landscapes, bamboos and orchids. N, IV, 27. U, II, 1, 6. M, p.315.

Chêng Tê-k'un, Cambridge. River-view in the manner of Ni Tsan. Signed and dated 1622.

Sōgen 169. The cloudy Valley with a Hermit's Cottage, after Tung Yüan. Signed. Colophon dated 1627.

Shina Nanga, III, 10. A Man Seated under tall Pine-trees. Signed and dated 1632. *Cf.* I-yüan chên-shang 8.

Liu, 84. A fantastic Landscape, with Rocks, Trees and Bamboo. Handscroll. Signed and dated 1633.

I-shu ts'ung-pien, 15. Slender Branches of Bamboo by a Rockery. Signed and dated 1634. *Cf.* Nanking Exhib. cat. 215.

Chêng Tê-k'un, Cambridge. Fruits and Flowers of various Seasons. Handscroll. Signed and dated 1634.

Shên-chou album, 1918. An album consisting of two pictures of Rocks, one Landscape, and several Letters. Signed and dated 1635.

P'ang Yüan-chi Illust. cat. I. Cloudy Mountains. Signed and dated 1636.

Shina Nanga, III, 6. Bamboos. Signed and dated 1636.

Sōraikan, I, 41. A Garden Rock. Signed. Poem by the painter, dated 1636.

Nanking Exhib. cat. 217. Trees by a River. Signed and dated 1640.

Ibid. 219. River Landscape, with a Pavilion and Houses. Handscroll. Signed and dated 1642. Mounted with a poem written by Huang Tao-chou.

Shên-chou, V. Winter Landscape; an Angler in a Boat on the River. Signed.

Shên-chou album, 1918. One Landscape and two pictures of rocks. Signed.

Shên-chou ta-kuan, vol.2. A Gnarled Pine and Stones. Sketchy picture. Poem by the painter. *Cf.* Liu, 83; Nanking Exhib. cat. 218.

Nanju 13 (Seikadō). Steep Rocks by a River and tall Pines; Boats in the Distance. *Cf.* Tōsō, p.368; Kokka 391; Tōyō, XI.

Tōsō, p.369. Leafless Trees on the Bank of a Misty River. Signed.

S. Shimada, Kyōto. River Landscape; a House in the foreground. Signed.

Freer Gallery. Six kinds of Flowers. Accompanied by poems by the painter. Handscroll. Signed.

P'ÊNG NIEN 彭年, *t.* K'ung-chia 孔嘉, *h.* Lung-ch'ih Shan-ch'iao 隆池山樵.

Native of Ch'ang-chou. B. 1505, d. 1566. In his youth, a friend of Wên Chêng-ming. Famous as a writer; his collected works known as *Lung-ch'ih shan-ch'iao chi*. Biog. in *Ming-shih*; also V, p.1150.

Ku-kung collect. (Nanking Exhib. cat. 160). A Man in a House at his Desk; a Boy and Chickens in the Garden outside. Handscroll. Colophon by Ch'ien Ku.

National Museum, Stockholm. Landscape in the blue-and-green manner, with two Scholars watching a Waterfall, two others on a Bridge. Poem, signed.

PIEN CH'U-SHAN 邊楚善.

Second son of Pien Wên-chin. Flowers, fruits and birds. O, 6. M, p.721.

Kokka 155. Birds in Summer. Signed. Also reproduced in Tōsō, p.237.

PIEN WÊN-CHIN 邊文進, *t.* Ching-chao 景昭.

From Sha-hsien, Fukien. Summoned to the palace and appointed tai-chao in the Yung-lo period. He served all through the Hsüan-tê period (1426–1435) in Wu-ying tien. Celebrated flower and bird painter. N, II, 5. O, 6. M, p.720.

K.-k. shu-hua chi, XXXIX. Hundred Birds, Bamboos, Pines and Plum-trees. Signed and dated 1413.

Tōsō, p.236. Quails and Cranes. Signed and dated 1428. *Cf.* Bukkyō Bijutsu, 18.

Chung-kuo, I, 119. Peony and Crane. Signed. A?

K.-k. shu-hua chi, XXIII. Magpie and Chestnut Tree. Signed. A.

Ibid. XXIX. Cock and Chickens. Signed.

Ibid. XLII. Cranes and Bamboos. Signed. The Bamboos by Wang Fu. A.

Ku-kung, VII. Three Magpies fighting; Bamboos and white Flowers.

K.-k. chou-k'an, 476. A Pair of Cranes; Plum-blossoms and Bamboos.

Tōyō, X. Two pictures representing Flowers and Birds. One signed.

Ars Asiatica, I, 23. A Pair of Cormorants. Signed. B?

K. Sumitomo collect., Ōiso. Three Turtle Doves on a Branch of a Blossoming-tree. Part of a handscroll. Colour on silk, now darkened. Signed. *Cf.* Kokka 742; Yonezawa 2. A.

Hashimoto collect., Takatsuki. A Hawk on the Branch of a Tree; a Pheasant and a Dog(?) below. Signed.

Boston Museum. A Falcon striking a flying white Swan. Signed: Ching-chao, and seal of the painter. B?

Heeramaneck Galleries, New York. Landscape with Wild Horses. Album-leaf. Ink and colour on silk. Signed. *Cf.* Cleveland Exhibition cat. 37.

British Museum (Add. 128). Geese among Reeds. Signed.

SHANG HSI 商喜, *t.* Wei-chi 惟吉.

From P'u-yang, Honan. Court-painter *c.*1430–1440. Officer of the Imperial Guard. Tigers, landscapes, figures, flowers and birds after Sung masters. N, VI, 3. O, 2. M, p.376.

K.-k. chou-k'an 504. A Man seated beside a River. Fan-painting. Signed and dated 1427.

Ku-kung, III. The Emperor Hsüan-tsung's Hunting Party. In colour. 6 ft. 6 in. × 11 ft.

K.-k. shu-hua chi, XV. Flowers. Signed and dated 1441. Colophon by Wang Ku-hsiang.

Ibid. XXIII. Dog, Cat and Birds on a Garden Terrace.

Chūgoku, II. The Abode of Immortals on the Ying-chou Island. Large album-leaf. Seal of Ch'ien-lung.

Hakone Museum. Lao-tzŭ passing the Barrier. Short handscroll. Signed. *Cf.* Yonezawa 3.

SHANG TSU 商祚, *t.* T'ien-chüeh 天爵.
Grandson of Shang Hsi. Tigers and flowers. O, 2. M, p.376.

K.-k. shu-hua chi, XXXVIII. Autumn Hollyhocks. Signed.

SHAO KAO 邵高, *t.* Mi-kao 彌高.
From Suchou. Flourished *c.*1627. Landscapes. N, VII, 18. M, p.227.

Tōsō, p.368. Landscape, with a Man in a Pavilion over the River. Signed and dated 1627.

SHAO MI 邵彌, *t.* Sêng-mi 僧彌, *h.* Kua-ch'ou 瓜疇, Kuan-yüan-sou 灌園叟, and other names.
From Suchou. Active *c.*1620–1660. One of the "Nine Friends of Painting". Landscapes; followed Ni Tsan and Chao Mêng-fu. O, 5. P, I, 15. Q, II, 1. U, I, 2, 2. M, p.226.

Ku-kung, XIII. Kuanyin. Signed and dated 1626.
Nanga Taisei, XIV, 82. A misty River Gorge, with steep Cliffs; a Man in a Pavilion over the Water. Signed and dated 1627.
Hua-chung chiu-yu (Yu chêng album). Landscape. Signed and dated 1630.
Shanghai Museum. A Goose, in a free *mo-ku* style. Inscription by the painter, dated 1630.
Chung-kuo, II, 35. A Branch of a blossoming Plum-tree. Signed and dated 1631.
Vannotti collect., Lugano. Two Dry Trees on a Rocky Shore, Mountains in the background. Signed and dated 1631. Fan-painting.
King Gustaf VI Adolf collect. A Man in a Mountain Pavilion waiting for his Friend who is approaching below. According to the inscription, painted for Wei-ch'i 1633.
Shên-chou, XVII. A Civil Official with a Staff standing under two Palm-trees. Signed and dated 1633.
Hua-chung chiu-yu chi-ts'ê (Hakubundō, Ōsaka, 1921). Old Trees by a Mountain Stream. Signed and dated 1634.
Chūgoku IV (J. P. Dubosc, Lugano). A Man on a rocky Ledge observing a Waterfall. Signed and dated 1634.
Chung-kuo, II, 42. Ink Bamboos after Ni Tsan. Signed and dated 1634.
Shên-chou album, 1926. An Album containing eight Studies of Plum-blossoms. Signed and dated 1635.
Shên-chou album, 1916. Album of eight landscapes, the last signed and dated 1636.
Shên-chou, XXI. Pavilions at a Waterfall. Signed. Poem and colophon by the painter, dated 1637.
K.-k. chou-k'an 509. Two Men entering a Lakeside Pavilion. Signed and dated 1638. Fan-painting.
J. P. Dubosc, Lugano. Album of Mountain-landscapes and a Homestead with figures. Signed and dated 1638.
Ibid. A Lonely Man sitting on a High Terrace under an Old Pine-tree. Signed and dated 1639. Fan-painting.
Metropolitan Museum. Weeping Willows on a small Island. Fan-painting. Signed and dated 1640.
Sōraikan, I, 42. Clouds and distant Mountains in the style of the Yüan masters. Handscroll. Signed and dated 1640. *Cf.* Kokka 593. Sirén, *Later*, pl.142.
Shên-chou ta-kuan. *Ch'iu-shêng*: The Dirge of Autumn, v7. River Landscape. Handscroll. Signed and dated 1642.
British Museum. Spare Trees and pointed Hills. Album-leaf. Signed and dated 1643.
K.-k. shu-hua chi, XXXII. Plum-blossoms in ink. Signed and dated 1662. *Cf.* Po mei-chi, vol.I.
Ku-kung collect. A small album of ten leaves representing landscapes, some of them after T'ang Yin. Painted in colour.
Ibid. (Nanking Exhib. cat. 102). Two leaves from an Album of Landscapes. Signed.
Hui-hua kuan. A Pavilion with a Man, built over a Stream at the Foot of a high Mountain, shaded by old Trees. Ink and colour on silk. According to the inscription by the painter, after T'ang Yin.
Ibid. Twelve album-leaves of Landscape Studies. Ink and slight colour on paper.

Commercial Press album, 1939 (Wu Hu-fan collect.) An Album of Landscape Studies. Colophon by Tung Ch'i-ch'ang.

Wu-mên p'ai ming-hua chi (Shên-chou album, 1924). A Boat on a River, after Kuo Hsi. Colophon.

Ibid. A Man on a River-bank, after Chao Mêng-fu. Seal of the painter.

Nanga Taisei, IX, 214–218. Album of five Landscapes, painted on coarse silk. Seals of the painter.

Shina Kachō Gasatsu 73. Studies of Branches of Trees and Bamboos.

Ōmura, I, 5. A Bamboo Grove, after Ni Tsan. Signed.

Ho Lok, Hongkong. Pine-tree, Bamboo and Plum-tree. Signed.

H. C. Wêng, Scarsedale, N.Y. Mountains in Mist; a Scholar in his Study. Handscroll. Signature uncertain.

D. Westman, Stockholm. A Man Standing on a Mountain Path by an old Tree looking at a Waterfall. Poem by the painter.

SHAO PAO 邵寶.

Unrecorded in biographies of painters. According to the Chronicle of Wu-hsi: *t.* Kuo-hsien 國賢, *h.* Ch'üan-chai 泉齋 and Êrh-ch'üan 二泉. B. 1460, d. 1527. President of the Board of Rites. Flowers. V, p.606.

Ku-kung, XXVIII. Plum-blossoms and Wild Tea Flowers. Signed and dated 1518. *Cf.* K.-k. chou-k'an 404.

SHÊN CHÊN 沈貞, *t.* Chên-chi 貞吉, h. Nan-chai 南齋 and T'ao-jan Tao-jên 陶然道人.

From Suchou. B. 1400, d. after 1480. Uncle of Shên Chou. Landscapes, followed Tung Yüan. N, II, 12. O, 3. I, 56, 2. M, p.145.

Tokasha Shina Meigashū, I. Scholar in his Study under a Wu-t'ung Tree. Signed and dated 1441.

Private collect., Peking. Two Men meeting in a Pavilion in a Bamboo Grove; another pavilion built over a stream. Inscription by the painter, dated 1471. Poem by Ch'ien-lung. *Cf.* Chūgoku, IV.

Liu, 67. A Man seated on the Shore of a Lake; Hills in the distance. Seals of the painter.

Chūgoku, IV. A Cottage under tall leafy Trees by the Foot of Grassy Mountains, after Wu Chên. Two lines of poetry by the painter. No signature, but seals of the painter.

SHÊN CHOU 沈周, *t.* Ch'i-nan 啓南, *h.* Shih-t'ien 石田, Po-shih wêng 白石翁, and Yü-t'ien wêng 玉田翁.

From Suchou. B. 1427, d. 1509. Poet, calligraphist and painter. Followed Tung Yüan, Chü-jan and the Four Yüan masters. Landscapes, flowers and birds. I, 56, 7. N, II, 12. O, 3. M, p.145.

Min Shitaika, p.3. Spring Morning with Mist around a Homestead at the Foot of high Mountains. Poem signed and dated 1464; also poems by his uncle, brothers, etc. *Cf.* Sōraikan, I, 27. A.

Ibid. p.1 (Ueno collect.) Gathering Water Chestnuts. Poem dated 1466.

Pao-yün, II. Handscroll, consisting of six small landscapes with figures. Inscriptions by the painter, one dated 1466 and another 1490.

Ōsaki collect., Tōkyō. Album of twelve landscapes in early style, the last signed and dated 1466. (Photographs in Bunkazai Kenkyūjo, Tōkyō). A?

Chicago Art Institute. River-view. A bit of the rising Shore and a Boat on the Water. Handscroll. Poem by the painter, dated 1466.

Shên P'ing-ch'ên, Hongkong. Landscape. Signed and dated 1466.

K.-k. shu-hua chi, I. The Lofty Lu Mountain. In the manner of Wang Mêng. Signed. A long rhymed prose inscription dated 1467. *Cf.* Chūgoku, II. A different version in I-yüan chên-shang 10.

J. P. Dubosc, Lugano. Blossoming Tree on a Rock with Birds and Flowers. According to the inscription, in the manner of Wang Yüan. Signed and dated 1468. A.

Chung-kuo ming-hua, XVI. Four Men and a Servant in an open Pavilion by a River at the Foot of a terraced Mountain. Six inscriptions; one dated 1469.

Min Shitaika, p.4 (G. Harada). A Man seated under Large Trees on the Bank of a Rushy Stream in the Mountains. Signed. Colophon dated 1470.

Wên-ming album (Ling-yin shan t'u-chüan). Views of the Ling-yin Mountains; Temples and River below. A handscroll reproduced in fourteen leaves. Poem by the painter, dated 1471. A.

Min Shitaika, pp.8–13 (ex-Hayashi collect.) *Chiu tuan ching hua-ts'ê.* Album containing Landscapes in the manner of various Sung and Yüan masters. One with a poem by Tu Ch'iung, dated 1471. *Cf.* Kokka 495, 498; Sōgen, 95 (partly); Shina Meiga Senshū, III. A.

Sōraikan, II, 50. Six album-leaves representing famous Views in Wu. The last one with descriptive text by the painter, dated 1471. A?

Ibid. II, 47. Temple Pavilions and Figures on high Mountain Terraces. Painted as a record of the painter's and his friends' stay at the Ling-yin Temple in 1472. *Cf.* Tōsō, p.249.

Ibid. I, 28. The Ta-shih Mountain. Handscroll. Signed. Poem by Wu K'uan, dated 1472. A?

Shên-chou, X. A Man lying on a Couch in a snow-covered Cottage among Trees. Poem dated 1474.

C. C. Wang, New York. Yüeh Ch'uang Walking in Autumn Wood. Trees, Rocks and running Water. Dated 1474. In his inscription the painter quotes Yüeh Ch'uang's words that the picture has the flavour of Tung Yüan and Chü-jan. Another version of the same picture in Hui-hua kuan, Peking.

Yen-kuang Co., Peking. Collotype. Rainy Landscape. Album-leaf. Two poems dated 1475.

Tōsō, p.250. Landscape after Ni Tsan. Poems by Ch'ên Mêng, etc. and by the painter from which it becomes evident that the picture is a copy made about 1505, after a picture which was probably painted *c.*1475.

Nanking Exhib. cat. 105. Viewing Plum-blossoms at the Chu-t'ang Temple. Long inscription by the artist, signed and dated 1475. A.

Nelson Gallery, Kansas City. Hollyhocks. Signed. Poem by the painter, dated 1475. *Cf.* Min Shitaika, p.21; Ōmura, I, 6; Tōsō, p.254. A.

Chang Ta-ch'ien cat., IV, 28. A Scholar seated on a River-bank in Autumn. Inscription by the painter, dated 1475.

Ibid. I, 22. Mooring a Boat at T'ing-tzŭ Beach. Inscription dated 1477. Colophon by Wu K'uan mounted above.

C. C. Wang, New York. Two Fishermen on the Maple River. Poem dated 1477, but the painting was executed six years earlier. *Cf.* Shên-chou ta-kuan, vol.9. A.

C. T. Loo's Successor Frank Caro, N.Y. Landscape Panorama. Streams running between low mountains with rich growth of trees; a fishing-boat on the water. Handscroll. Ink and colour. Poem by the painter, dated 1477. Colophons by Wu K'uan, Wên P'êng, Wang Ku-hsiang, P'êng Nien and Wu Yin-chi. *Cf.* Toronto, Exhibit. cat. 15.

Sōgen 97. Mountains in Snow. Signed. Poem by the painter, dated 1478.

Chung-kuo, II, 2. Landscape. Poems by the painter, by Liu Chüeh and Wei Ch'ang, the last one dated 1479. C.

Kokka 545 (Hakubundō collect., Ōsaka). Wooded Mountains; Pavilions and Homesteads among the Trees. Slightly coloured long handscroll. Painted for Wu K'uan in 1479 when he left for Peking.

H. C. Wêng, Scarsedale, N.Y. Hsieh An on the East Mountain. Ink and colours on silk. According to the inscription, in the manner of Tai Chin. Signed and dated 1480. A.

Piacentini collect., Tōkyō (1951). The White Cloud Spring. A long handscroll, painted on silk, signed and dated 1481. Colophon by Wang Shih-chên. A.

Yu-chêng album, 1922. Long landscape scroll in the manner of Wu Chên. Inscription by the painter dated 1481.

Palace Museum album, 1932. Ten leaves of Landscape sketches with Figures. Poems. The last one dated 1482. *Cf.* K.-k. chou-k'an, vols.I–II, 19–46.

Tōsō, p.246. A Man reading in the Shade of a large Banana-plant. Poem, dated 1482.

Chūgoku, III (Takashima collect., Kugenuma). Scenes from Wu-chiang. Two sections of a long handscroll. Pavilions along the river shore, people working in thatched cottages. One colophon and two poems by the painter, dated 1483.

Ibid. II. Three old Scholars standing and conversing under tall Pine-trees by a Brook. Poem and inscription by the painter, dated 1484.

Tōsō, p.255 (Tung Ch'êng-ju collect.). Young Geese and a Peach-tree. Two lines of poetry, dated 1484.

Nelson Gallery, Kansas City. Landscape in the manner of Ni Tsan. Signed and dated 1484. *Cf.* Ōmura, I, 9; Cleveland Exhibition cat. 52. A.

Piacentini collect., Tōkyō. The top Parts of four old Juniper Trees, from the seven called "Seven Stars", with spreading branches. Handscroll. Colophon by the painter, dated 1484. A.

Chung-kuo ming-hua, IV. The Study among Apricot-trees in the Mountains. Signed and dated 1486. A.

J. D. Ch'ên cat. II, 24. Shifting Views along a River bordered by rolling Hills and low Shores with Fishermen's Cottages. A few fishermen in boats, other men meeting on the shore. Handscroll. Colophon by the painter, dated 1486, and by eight other men. A?

Ming-jên shu-hua, vol.23. Two Swallows on a Willow Branch. Signed and dated 1488.

H. C. Wêng, Scarsdale. A Farewell Party at Tiger Hill in Suchou; some Friends meeting under the Trees. Painted for Wu Tun-an. Ink and colour. Long inscription dated 1489. A?

Ibid. Rose Mallows and a Pine-tree. Ink and colour on paper. Signed and dated 1489. Several colophons, one of them by Yao Shou. A.

S.c.t.k. hsü-pien, XI. Cabbage and Persimmons. Signed and dated 1490. *Cf.* Nanga Taisei, V, 193.

Freer Gallery (34.1). A Man seated in his Study by the River-side; two Men in a Boat, and a Visitor approaching on a Bridge. Slightly coloured handscroll. Dedication to a friend, dated 1491. Colophon by the painter. Three poems by Ch'ien-lung. A.

C. C. Wang, New York. Album of Landscape-studies with Mountains, Trees, Temple Compounds, etc. Signed and dated 1491. Four leaves from the same album are in the Indianapolis Art Institute. A.

Freer Gallery (56, 28). Mountain Landscape with rushing Streams and Pavilions; a Man walking over a Bridge at the bottom. In the style of Wang Mêng. Signed and dated 1491. *Cf.* Chūgoku, II. A.

K.-k. shu-hua chi, XLIII. A Scholar's Hermitage at the Foot of Pointed Mountains. Inscription by the painter dated 1492. *Cf.* *Time Magazine*, May 6, 1957. A.

Yen-kuang Co., Peking; photographs. Album of eight Landscapes after Old Masters. Signed. Colophon by the painter, dated 1492.

Min Shitaika, p.30. Landscape. Fan-painting. Signed and dated 1492. A.

Ku-kung collect. Large album of sixteen leaves. Paintings of flowers, vegetables, birds, fishes, and animals, such as a cat and a donkey. Ink paintings. Signed and dated 1494. Two reproduced in Nanking Exhibition cat., pl.103.

Nanking Exhib. cat. 106. Chrysanthemums growing by a Rock. Poem, signed and dated 1494. A.

Nanga Taisei, XV, 15, 16. Autumn Landscape, with Buildings and Figures. Handscroll, signed and dated 1496. *Cf.* Wên-hua album, 1925.

C. C. Wang, New York. A long handscroll with Studies of Flowers and Fruits. Colophon by the painter, dated 1497. A.

J. P. Dubosc, Lugano. Recollections of the Artist's Travels in the Hsi-shan Region. Very large handscroll. Signed and dated 1497. A?

J. D. Ch'ên cat. II, 23. The Gentleman Pines. Sections of the trees with intertwined branches. Handscroll. Poem by the painter written in 1498 on the occasion of the eightieth birthday of a high official.

H. C. Wêng, Scarsedale, N.Y. *Chang-kung t'u.* A Cave with Stalactite Formations in a wooded Mountain near Wu-hsi. Descriptive colophon by the painter, dated 1499. *Cf.* Nanga Taisei, XVI, 36, 37.

C. T. Loo's Successor Frank Caro, N.Y. Autumn landscape of T'ung-kuan. Signed and dated 1499. Mounted with a painting by Chou Chih in a single handscroll.

Kao Yen-yüeh, Hongkong. Scenery along a River between rocky banks. Boats on the water. Signed and dated 1499.

Min Shitaika, p.18. A Small Branch of Cherry Apple (*Hai-t'ang*) in Blossom. Signed and dated 1500. *Cf.* Tōan 20; Shina Meiga Senshū, III. A.

Hui-hua kuan. A Temple in the Mountains. Ink and colours. Painted for Yang I-ching (at the age of 80). Signed and dated 1500.

National Museum, Stockholm. River-view in Autumn. Short handscroll. Signed and dated 1500. Colophon by Ch'ên Shun.

N. P. Wang, Hongkong. View over an Open River; a

Man taking Farewell. Handscroll. Signed and dated at 73 (1500). Colophons by Wang Chih-têng and two others.

C. T. Loo's Successor Frank Caro, N.Y. Scenery of Wu-chung. A rocky river-bank; men in boats. Handscroll. Long inscription by the painter, signed and dated 1500.

Li-tai, III. Landscape. Poem by the painter, signed and dated 1501. Poems by Liu Chüeh, Wu K'uan, Wên Lin (father of Wên Chêng-ming), etc. A.

Shên-chou, IV. A Crab among Rushes. Signed and dated 1501.

Tōsō, p.251. Landscape; a Man standing on a Terrace under Pine-trees. Signed. Poem by the painter, dated 1501.

Nelson Gallery, Kansas City. An Immortal with a Gourd. Poem by the painter, signed and dated 1501. *Cf.* Shina Meiga Senshū, 6; Sōgen 98.

Vannotti collect., Lugano. Long View of a Coast-line, extending over Bays and Promontories with leafy Trees and Pavilions; an Island with towering Hills in the open Sea. Inscription in large letters, dated 1501. A.

I-shu ts'ung-pien, 15. The T'ung-kuan Mountain on a clear Day rising over a quiet Water. Poem by the painter, dated 1502. *Cf.* Shina Nanga, III, 1.

K.-k. shu-hua chi, XXXIII. An Orange and Chrysanthemums. Signed and dated 1502.

Commercial Press album, 1934. *Shên Shih-t'ien shan-shui san-chüan.* Three scrolls of Landscapes in one album: (1) River Landscape from Chiang-nan. Seals of the painter. Colophon by Wu K'uan. (2) River in Autumn. Signed and dated 1502, at 77. Poems and colophons by the painter, by a friend and other men. (3) Officials on a Stroll in the Mountains. Signed. Poem by the painter; other poems and colophons by later men. A. The pictures also reproduced, in smaller size, in Nanga Taisei, XV, 9–12; XVI, 34, 35, 38.

Kokka 256 (Lo Chên-yü collect.) landscape. Handscroll. Signed and dated 1502.

Nanga Taisei, XVI, 34, 35. Autumn on the River: a Man in a Pavilion gazing over a wide Expanse of Water. Handscroll, signed and dated 1503.

Min Shitaika, pp.14–16 (Saitō collect.) Clouds over the River before Rain. Long handscroll. Signed and dated 1504. *Cf.* Tōan 17.

Kokka 465 (ex-Yamamoto collect.) Autumn Landscape. River-view, in the manner of Ni Tsan. Signed and dated 1504, at 78. *Cf.* Tōsō, p.247. A?

Shina Kachō. A Wild Goose by a Rockery. Poem by the painter, dated 1504.

Sōgen 99 (Akira Ariyūshi). Landscape. Signed. Poems by the painter, by Wu K'uan, Ch'ien Fu and Yang Hsün-chi, dated 1505.

Wang Shih-chieh, Taipei. Falling Flowers. Men walking beneath blossoming trees by a river. Brightly coloured short handscroll; probably after an earlier model. Painted at 80 (1506). Poetic inscriptions by Shên Chou and Wên Chêng-ming, referring to the falling flowers. A.

C. C. Wang, New York. *Ti-tsai t'u.* A Scholar seated in his Pavilion under some Willow-trees on the River-bank. Ten colophons; the first dated 1506. Handscroll.

Sōraikan, II, 49. A Hen and two Butterflies under a tall Chrysanthemum Plant. Poem by the painter, dated 1509, the year of his death.

H. C. Wêng, Scarsdale, N.Y. Mountains and open Views over a winding River, with Fishermen's Boats. Long handscroll of about sixty feet. According to the inscription, Wên Chêng-ming did the last section after the death of Shên Chou. A.

Shên-chou, VIII. A Man entering a Grove of Trees on the Bank of a River in the Mountains. Signed. Poem.

Ibid. XV. Mountains along a River; Man with a Staff walking on the Terrace in the foreground. Illustration to a T'ang poem copied by the painter.

Shên-chou ta-kuan, vol.4. Listening to the Orioles by a Bridge. Poem by the painter. C?

Chung-kuo, II, 3. A Mountain Pavilion among Pine-trees in Snow. Long poem by the painter.

Ku-kung, XXII. A Crab. Poem by the painter. Signed.

Ibid. XXX. Floating on a Lake among Lotuses. Poem by the painter. A.

K.-k. shu-hua chi, XI. Landscape in the manner of Ni Tsan: a Man with a long Staff among the spare Trees on the Shore. Poem by the painter. A.

Ibid. XXX. Sketchy Landscape. Long inscription recording friendship with Liu Chüeh (who died 1472).

K.-k. chou-k'an, vol.III, 76. A Bird on a Branch. Poem. Signed.

Ibid. vol.VIII, 152–159. Eight Scenes from San-Wu. Album-leaves. Seals of the painter.

Hui-hua kuan. A Man standing in an Autumn Wood. Poem by the painter. A.

Ku-kung collect. Low Buildings in the Shade of Leafy Trees. Slightly coloured. Album-leaf. Signed by the painter.

Ibid. Scenery of Suchou. Colour on paper. Signed. B?

Ibid. A Magnolia-tree and Epidendrums growing in a Rock. Inscriptions by Chu Yün-ming and Wu K'uan.

Ibid. *Ch'ang-p'u* (long grass) growing by a Stone. Signed.

Gems, I, 26. Talking about the past in an Autumn Forest. Poem, signed.

Ibid. II, 10. The Three Cypresses. Handscroll in three sections. *Cf.* Chung-kuo, II, 5; Shina Nanga, I, 6. A.

Ibid. A Crow on a dry Branch. Ink on paper. Poem by the painter. A.

Ibid. Portrait of Tu Chin Seated in an open Pavilion in a Bamboo Grove on the River-bank. Handscroll. Ink and bluish colour on paper. Signed. A.

Ibid. View from Chang-chou. Trees on the Rocks; a Man in a Pavilion, others in the Boats on the River. Ink and colour. Long handscroll.

Ibid. Four Views of the West Lake in Hangchou. Ink and slight colours, partly in *p'o-mo* manner. Album-leaves with poems by the painter.

Former National Museum, Peking (1928). A Wild Pigeon on a dry Branch. Signed. Poem. A.

Peking National Museum album. Album with Landscapes by Ni Tsan, Wên Pi, Shên Chou and T'ang Yin. Poems by the painter, by Liu Chüeh, Wu K'uan and Wên Lin.

Chung-hua wên-wu chi-ch'êng, IV, 384, 385. Two double album-leaves, one representing a curled-up Cat, and the other a walking Donkey. Both with inscription by Ch'ien-lung.

Chung-kuo ming-hua, XXI. Steep and pointed Mountain Peak rising above a River. Poem by the painter. A?

Ibid. XXVII. Two Men in a Pavilion over a Stream. After a poem by Tu Fu. Signed.

Ibid. XXXVI. River Landscape. Trees in the foreground. Signed. Poem by a contemporary.

I-yüan chên-shang shê album (Hua I-chih collect.) Studies of Landscape with two Scholars meeting in open Pavilions, walking over a Bridge, fishing in a Boat and riding on Donkeys. Poems by the painter. A.

Commercial Press album, 1940 (P'an Po-shan collect.) Ten Landscapes, painted on silk. Signed; colophons by Wên Chia, Wang Shih-chên and others.

Shanghai Museum. A Branch of a Blossoming Peach-tree. Slight colour on paper. Poem by the painter, and two other inscriptions. A.

Liu, 51. A Scholar with a Flute listening to the Wind in the Pine-trees.

Nanking Exhib. cat. 103 (Ku-kung collect.) Two leaves from an album: a Donkey; a Frog on a Lotus-leaf. Seals of the painter. A.

Ibid. 104. Two Birds perched on a Branch in Winter. Poem, signed.

Lo Chia-lun, Taipei. *An-lao t'ing t'u*. Leafy trees; spotted hills. Pavilion with some men enjoying the summer. Inscriptions by the painter and by his friends Wu K'uan and Ch'ien Fu.

Mr. Huang, Taipei. Three Large Trees on a Sloping River-bank. Mountains in rain. Inscription by the painter with reference to his old age. The manner is very broad, the paper grey.

Hung Yu-lin, Hongkong, 1951. Landscape: The Ning-yün Monastery. Signed.

J. D. Ch'ên cat. I, 25. Landscape in the manner of Ni Tsan. Short handscroll; seal of the artist.

Ibid. I, 32. Reading in the Autumn Hills. Poem by the painter and Wu K'uan.

Shên collect., Hongkong. Two low Buildings on the River-bank; Mountain Slope beyond. Short handscroll. Long inscription by the painter. Signed.

Chang Ts'ung-yü Catalogue. River-views with Trees and Mountains. Short handscroll.

Nanju 1 (Okubo collect.) A solitary Wanderer in an Autumn Wood. Poem by the painter, signed. *Cf.* Tōyō, XI.

Ibid. 13 (Count Tanaka). Tall Cliffs Rising above a River; leafy Trees below. Poem by the painter.

Ibid. 18. Two Men in a Cottage by a River at the Foot of wooded Mountains. Poem by the painter; signed. *Cf.* Tōyō, XI.

Sekai Bijutsu Zenshū, XX, pl.18. Travellers passing a Village. Portion of a handscroll.

Tōyō, XI. Great Mountains and a Pavilion on the River-bank. Poem. Signed.

Shoman 14. Landscape. Fan-painting. Signed.

Ibid. 15. Landscape. Fan-painting. Signed.

Ibid. 16–18. Three of the "Ten Views of Suchou": Pao-hua shan, Kuang-fu ssŭ, Lin-yen shan. Seals of the painter.

Shina Nanga, I, 5. Boiling Tea under a Wu-t'ung-tree, after Chao Mêng-fu.

Ōmura, I, 3, 4. Views of T'ai-hu. Short handscrolls. Signed. *Cf.* Min Shitaika p.17; Chūgoku, III. A.

Ibid. I, 7. Misty Landscape. Poem. Signed.

Ibid. I, 12. Lily, Stones and Magpie. Signed. Poem. *Cf.* Min Shitaika, p.22.

Min Shitaika, p.5. Playing the *Ch'in* under the Moon by a River. Poem by the painter. *Cf.* Sōraikan, II, 48. A.

Ibid. p.2. Two Men on a River-bank. Album-leaf. Long inscription by the painter.

Ibid. p.6. Wu-t'ung-tree, Bamboos and a Rock. Signed. A.

Ibid. p.7 (Saitō). River-view after Ni Tsan. Signed. Poem. *Cf.* Tōan 19. A.

Ibid. p.19. A Pheasant. Signed. Poem.

Ibid. p.20. A Cock. Signed. Poem.

Ibid. pp.23–29. Seven album-leaves: (23) Mulberry-leaves and Silkworms. Signed. (24) An Arbutus Branch. Signed. Poem. (25) An Egg-plant. Signed. B? (26) Persimmons. Signed. *Cf.* Tōan 22. (27) Chrysanthemums. Signed. Poem. *Cf.* Tōan 21. (28) Wild Tea Flowers. Signed. Poem. (29) Narcissi. Signed. Poem. A.

Shina Kachō. Tree-peonies, Chrysanthemums and other Flowers.

Shina Meiga Senshū 5 (Seattle Art Museum). A Man seated in an open Pavilion by a Lotus Pond under a Willow. Poem by the painter. Album-leaf.

Nanga Taisei, vol.XI, 23. Watering a Ricefield. Illustration to a poem by Wang Wei. Possibly of same series as the album-leaves in the Nelson Gallery, Kansas City. A.

Kokka 750 (Kawai collect., Kyōto). Scenery of the Wu-chung Area. Long handscroll. Poem and signature of the painter. A.

Seikasha, Kyōto, album reproduction, 1935. Eight leaves of an album: seven of them Landscapes, the eighth a Rock and Banana-palm. Signed.

Tōan 18. Landscape. Fan-painting. Signed. A.

Tōsō, p.247 (Piacentini collect., Tōkyō). Listening to the Cicada's Song. A Man resting in a Garden, another Man knocking at the Gate. Poems by the painter and Ch'ien-lung. A.

Ibid. p.248 (Huang Ssŭ-ch'ing). Reading by the River in the Mountains. In Yüan style. Signed. Poem.

Ibid. p.252 (Tsang Hsi). A Man fishing seated under Some Trees on a River-bank. Large album-leaf. Signed. Poem.

Ibid. p.253 (Yamamoto collect.) "The Maple Leaves are Dropping in the Cold Wu River". Inscriptions by the painter, by Hsiang Shêng-mo and Ch'ien-lung. A.

Ibid. p.256. Deep Mountain Gully. Signed. Poem. C.

Sōgen 94. A Man in a Boat on the Ts'ang-lang River. Signed. Poem.

Ibid. 96 (Chang Hsüeh-liang). Misty Landscape in the Wu Chên manner. A.

Bijutsu Kenkyū 136 (Nakamura, Hyōgo). Large Autumn Landscape. Long inscription by the painter.

Chūgoku, II (Boston Museum). Album with eight double-leaves: Landscape Studies with grassy Mountains, Streams and Cottages. The last one with a Man seated under Bamboos by a River. Each leaf with the painter's signature and seal. A.

Ibid. II. Album of twelve leaves: Sketchy studies of Mountains, Streams, Cliffs and Buildings, in the broad manner of Wu Chên. The last one with an old Man holding a Staff and standing under a Cliff. Some with the painter's seal.

Ibid. II. Album of fourteen leaves called *Wo-yu*: Studies of Landscapes, Flowers, Fruits, Animals and Insects. All with a poem by the painter. The last album-leaf consists of a long inscription by the painter.

Ibid. II. Album of thirteen leaves called *Sui-hsing*: Landscapes from Nature, some with Figures; Branches of blossoming Trees. The first leaf with a poem by the painter, and the last one consists of the painter's inscription.

Shina Meiga Senshū, III (Hashimoto collect., Takatsuki). River-landscape with precipitous Cliffs, leafy Trees, Pavilions and Homesteads on the banks. Long handscroll. Inscription in small characters in between the landscape by Kao Fêng-han. Attributed but not in his manner.

Ogawa collect., Kyōto. The Long River (Yangtse chiang). Rocky Islands and Stones; sailing boats moored in the harbours. Ink and colour. Inscription by the painter; colophons by writers of Ming and later. A.

Boston Museum. The Painter and his Friends looking at the Autumn Moon. Short handscroll. Signed. A.

Freer Gallery (39.2). Fishing Village by a River. Several Fishermen are working in their small Boats; others are resting or eating on the shore. Slightly coloured handscroll. Poem by the painter. (P'ang Yüan-chi collect.) A.

Metropolitan Museum. A Man in a Boat; a Willow on the Shore. Fan-painting. Signed.

Nelson Gallery, Kansas City (46.90). Saying Farewell to a Friend. The river is winding between the terraced rocks; two men are standing in conversation by a bridge. Short handscroll in light colours. Poem by the painter. A.

Ibid. (46.51). Five large album-leaves: (1) Three Men working in a Garden enclosed by a Fence. Signed. (2) A Man standing on a steep Promontory rising through the Mist. Poem by the painter. (3) A Man and a Crane in a Boat, which is being paddled across a River. Poem by the painter. (4) River-view with Sailing Boats. Poem by the painter. (5) Small Huts in a leafy Grove by a Creek. Poem by the painter. (6) The last leaf which represents a Rainstorm is signed by Wên Chêng-ming. A.

Detroit Institute of Arts. A Branch of Pomegranate-tree. Long poem by Wang Ao (1450–1514). A. *Cf.* Venice Exhibition cat. 797.

Honolulu Academy of Arts. Bird, Bamboo and Banana in Snow. Inscription by the painter.

National Museum, Stockholm. Winter Landscape. Signed. Poems by the painter and his friends, Chu Ts'un-li, K'o Ch'ing, Yao Shou, etc. Uncertain.

Ibid. Two Crows. Short poem by the painter.

Ibid. The Pavilion at the Water's Edge. Signed. Poem. Uncertain.

Ibid. Autumn Landscape. Fan-painting. Signed.

Musée Guimet. Man in a Boat on a River between stony Banks. After Wu Chên. Poem by the painter. Inscription added on the top by Tung Ch'i-ch'ang.

Berlin Museum. Two Men in a Pavilion looking at Wind and Rain on the River. Long handscroll, in a rough style. Two lines of poetry. Signed. School-work.

Hamburg Exhibition, 1949–1950. A Man sitting alone in a Mountain Cottage.

W. Hochstadter, New York. Two album-leaves: River-view with Pavilion on a high Cliff, representing Summer; two Men fishing in Boats by an Overhanging Willow, representing Autumn. A.

Former Minkenhof collect. The Idle Fisherman. Album-leaf. Poem by the painter.

Lilly collect., Indianapolis. Two Men standing under three large Trees. Poem by the painter referring to a temple of the Fan family. Another inscription by Chou Ting.

B. Hobart collect., Cambridge, Mass. One leaf from an album containing Scenes from the Tiger Hill at Suchou. Seal of the painter. *Cf.* Cleveland Exhibition cat. 51. A.

British Museum. The Haven of T'ao Yüan. River landscape, bare trees on the near bank, the farther bank rising into undulating hills. According to the inscription by Wên Chêng-ming, "A genuine picture by Shên Chou". Among the colophons is a copy of Wang Wei's poem the "Haven of T'ao Yüan" written by P'u Ju, former owner of the scroll.

J. P. Dubosc, Lugano. Tall Mountains forming Terraces, as in Huang Kung-wang's pictures. A man seated below on a rocky ledge. Signed.

Ibid. Three fan-paintings, representing figures in landscape.

Ku-kung ming-shan chi 5. Three fan-paintings. For others, see K.-k. chou-k'an 36, 37 and 216; also Nanga Taisei, VIII, 32, 33.

Vannotti collect., Lugano. A Homestead on the Border of a River; a Man Walking along the Shore. Signed. Fan-painting. *Cf.* Venice Exhibition cat., 801.

SHÊN HÊNG 沈恒, *t.* Hêng-chi 恒吉, *h.* T'ung-chai 同齋.

From Suchou. B. 1409, d. 1477. Brother of Shên Chên, father of Shên Chou. Landscapes, followed Tu Ch'iung. N, II, 12. O, 3. I, 56, 2. M, p.145.

Ho Kuan-wu, Hongkong. Landscape. Signed.

SHÊN HSIANG 沈襄, *t.* Shu-ch'êng 叔成, *h.* Hsiao-hsia 小霞.
From Shan-yin, Chekiang. Plum-blossoms. O,7. M, p.146.

Po-mei chi. Plum-blossoms. Signed. Poem.

SHÊN SHIH 沈仕, *t.* Mou-hsüeh 懋學 and Tzŭ-têng 子登, *h.* Ch'ing-mên shan-jên 青門山人.
From Hangchou. 16th century. Collector of paintings and writings. Landscapes, flowers and birds. N, III, 14. M, p.146.

Hui-hua kuan. View of the Nine Dragon Mountain which rises above a River. Signed. Ink only. Handscroll. Dated 1571 or 1631(?)
K.-k. chou-k'an 58 and 431. Two fan-paintings representing flowers.
Nanju 21. Peony and Rock. Signed. Poem.
Bijutsu, XVIII. Pavilion and Travellers on snowy Mountains. Signed.

SHÊN SHIH-CH'UNG 沈士充, *t.* Tzŭ-chü 子居.
From Hua-t'ing, Kiangsu. Flourished *c.*1611–1640. Pupil of Sung Mou-chin and Chao Tso. Landscapes in the style of the Yün-chien School. N, IV, 16. O, 4. U, I, 3, 5. M, p.146.

Köln, Ostasiat. Museum. Tall Trees at the River-bank, Pointed Mountain Peaks on the Further Shore. Signed and dated 1611. Fan-painting. Köln Exhibition 1955, No.45.
Hamburg Exhibition 1949–1950. River Landscape in the manner of Chao Tso. Ink and light colours. Handscroll. Signed, dated 1622.
K.-k. shu-hua chi, VIII. The Study in Fragrant Nature. Signed and dated 1623.
Sōgen 150. Two pictures from a series of ten representing the Peach Garden Streams. Signed and dated 1624.
Ku-kung collect. (Nanking Exhib. cat. 234). A Cottage by the River. Short handscroll. Signed and dated 1625.
Shên-chou, XVIII. Hillocks by the River, Pavilion under Pine-trees. Album-leaf. Signed and dated 1626.
Nanga Taisei, XI, 50. The Peach-blossom Studio, after Wang Mêng. Signed and dated 1631.
Private collect., Tōkyō. Landscape with rocky Hills and Groups of twisted Trees. Long handscroll. Signed and dated 1632.
Kurokawa cat. 10. Landscape in the manner of Wang Mêng. Album-leaf. Signed and dated 1632.
Nanga Taisei, XIV, 78, 79. The T'ien-ch'ih Rock by the River. After Huang Kung-wang. Dated 1633.
Sōgen 151. Bare Trees by a River in Mist. Signed and dated 1633.
Ming, Shên Tzŭ-chü fang-ku shan-shui shih chên (Shên-chou kuo-kuang shê, 1922). An album of ten landscapes after old masters. Last one dated 1641.
Sung-chiang p'ai ming-hua chi (Shên-chou album, 1924). Trees and Cloudy Peaks. Signed.
Hui-hua kuan. Landscape Studies after Old Masters. Six exhibited. On gold-sprinkled paper.
Ming-jên shu-hua, 20. Two album-leaves: A Man walking in the Mountains; A Temple in the wooded Mountains. Signed.
Sōgen 149. Mountain Landscape. Part of a handscroll. *Cf.* Nanga Taisei.
K.-k. chou-k'an 25. Landscape in the manner of Wang Mêng. Fan-painting, signed.

SHÊN SHIH-KÊNG 沈士鯁.
Flourished *c.*1620–1640. Landscapes and figures in T'ang Yin's style. M, p.147.

Nanju 17. Landscape. Signed.

SHÊNG MAO-HUA 盛茂燁 or Shêng Mao-yeh 茂曄, *h.* Yen-an 研菴.
From Suchou. Active *c.*1625–1640. Landscapes and flowers. N, IV, 17. O, 8. M, pp.389, 390.

Horiuchi collect., Ōsaka. Crows on a bare Branch. Fan-painting. Signed and dated 1615.

I-yüan chên-shang 9. Landscape. Signed and dated 1619.

J. P. Dubosc, Lugano. A Temple Pagoda on the Bank of a River and Sailing Boats on the Water. Ink and colour. Inscription dated 1625. Fan-painting.

Nanju 22 (Seikadō collect.) Some Old Men Celebrating New Year's Day. Signed. Poem dated 1626. *Cf.* Tōyō, XI.

Ōmura, I, 6 (Piacentini collect., Tōkyō). Landscape with Figures. Two lines of poetry. Signed and dated 1630 (in the spring). *Cf.* Tōsō, p.371.

Tōsō, p.370. Landscape after Huang Kung-wang. Signed and dated 1630 (in the 7th month).

W. Hochstadter, New York. Lonely Retreat beneath tall Trees. Ink and slight colour on silk. Inscription by the painter, dated 1630. *Cf.* Cleveland Exhibition cat. 72.

Private collect., Kyōto. A Villa at the Foot of a Mountain; a Fisherman's House in the foreground. Signed and dated 1632.

Kyūka I (Hashimoto collect., Takatsuki). Scholars gathered in a Hut enjoying the first Plum-blossoms. Two lines of poetry. Signed and dated 1633.

Ibid. I. Scholars viewing a Waterfall. Signed. Two lines of poetry dated 1633.

Tōan 33. Landscape after Huang Kung-wang. Fan-painting. Signed and dated 1634.

Monumenta Serica, III, 2 (1938). Scholars Gathered in a Bamboo Grove. Signed; dated 1634.

Ōmura, I, 12. A Scholar's Cottage at the Foot of high Mountains. Two lines of poetry. Dated 1636. *Cf.* Chūgoku, IV.

K. Sumitomo collect., Ōiso. Landscape. Fan-painting. Signed and dated 1636.

Kokka 543. A Cottage in the Mountains and a Man approaching. Signed. Two lines of poetry dated 1637.

Nanju 24. Landscape with Figures. Two lines of poetry. Signed and dated 1637. *Cf.* Tōyō, XI.

Vannotti collect., Lugano. Two Men Occupied in a Small Cottage between Trees, another Approaching on a Road. Signed and dated 1637. Fan-painting.

Shimbi, XV. Scholars viewing a Waterfall. Signed and dated 1638.

Nanju 10. Rainstorm over City Wall and Willows. Dated 1639.

National Museum, Stockholm. Landscape with Waterfall, after Ma Yüan. Signed and dated 1640.

Kokka 258 and 283. Three landscapes from an album. Each with two lines of poetry. Signed. *Cf.* Pageant 680, 681.

Ku-kung collect. (Nanking Exhib. cat. 392). Lake Scene, with two figures crossing a bridge. Leaf from an album of scenes at Suchou. Signed.

Nanju 11. Landscape. Signed.

Tōyō, XI. A Fisherman on a Mountain River. Signed.

N. Gashū, 15. Wu-t'ung Trees. Signed. Two lines of poetry. *Cf.* Nanga Taisei, IV, 39.

Kyūka, I. A Man seated sleeping in a Boat at the Foot of misty Mountains.

W. Hochstadter, New York. Misty Mountains, Cottages built in the Water at their Foot. Handscroll. Two lines of poetry. Signed.

SHÊNG SHAO-HSIEN 盛紹先, *t.* K'o-chên 克振.
From Yang-chou, Kiangsu. Flourished *c.*1600. Landscapes. O, 8. M, p.390.

Nanju 7. Landscape after Kao K'o-kung. Signed. Poem. Also in Tōyō, XI; Pageant 711.

Hyōjirō Hatta. Snow Landscape after Li Ch'eng. Signed. Poem.

SHIH CHUNG 史忠. Originally called Hsü Tuan-pên 徐端本, *t.* T'ing-chih 廷直, *h.* Ch'ih-wêng 癡翁.
From Nanking. B. 1437, d. *c.*1517. Landscapes in the Yüan tradition. Friend of Shên Chou. N, II, 7. M, p.77.

K.-k. shu-hua chi, XXXVIII. Landscape after Huang Kung-wang. Signed. Poem and colophon by the painter. Signed, dated 1504.

Boston Museum. Mountain-ridges, Pine-trees and Travellers in Mist and Snow. Handscroll. Ink on paper. Poem by the painter, dated 1504. *Cf.* Cleveland Exhibition cat. 43.

Museum of Ostasiat. Kunst, Cologne. Winter Landscape. Poem and colophon by the painter, dated 1506. *Cf.* P'ang Yüan-chi cat. Add. 2. Sirén, *Later*, pl. 63.

Ming-jên shu-hua, 15. Portrait of a High Official. Poem and Seal of the painter.

I-yüan chên-shang 6–10. An Album of Figure Sketches and Writing. Signed.

SHIH JUI 石銳, *t.* I-ming 以明.

From Ch'ien-t'ang, Chekiang. Summoned to the palace in the Hsüan-tê period (1426–1435). Landscapes, palaces and figures in Shêng Mou's style. N, VI, 10. O, 1. M, p.75.

Chang Ta-ch'ien cat. I, 26. Tartar Horsemen preparing for a Hunt. Signed and dated 1444.

Kokka 230 (Marquis Inoue). A Mountain Pass; Travellers on the Winding Road. Picture in the "green and gold" manner traditionally ascribed to the painter.

Ibid. 283. Ning Ch'i Riding the Ox. Seal of the painter. Poems by contemporaries. Ni K'uan Ploughing his Field. Seal of the painter. Poems by four contemporaries. The two pictures form a pair.

Shimbi, IX. Chu Mai-ch'ên, the poor Scholar carrying dry Wood. Seals of the painter. Also in Tōyō, X.

Kyūka, I. River and Mountain View. Handscroll. Signed.

Private collect., Kyōto. 'Searching for Flowers.' Landscape in the blue-green style. Handscroll. Colophon by Wu K'uan, dated 1469.

Nezu Museum, Tōkyō. A Landscape with Palace Buildings. Signed.

SHIH LIN 施霖, *t.* Yü-hsien 雨咸.

From Nanking. Flourished *c.*1520. Landscapes in the styles of the Yüan masters. P, 4, 10. U, I, 2, 21. M, p.276.

Shên-chou, X. Mountain Landscape with Precipices. Colophon by Cha Shih-piao, dated 1664.

SHU CHIH 殳執.

Unrecorded. Perhaps identical with the Ming painter Shu Yin-chih 殳胤執; *cf.* M, p.9.

Chūgoku 4. A Scholar in a House at the Mouth of a Valley. Album-leaf. Signed and dated *kuei-yu*.

SUN AI 孫艾, *t.* Shih-chieh 世節, *h.* Hsi-ch'uan-wêng 西川翁.

From Ch'ang-shu, Kiangsu. Pupil of Shên Chou and once painted a portrait of Shên Chou. Landscapes after Huang Kung-wang and Wang Mêng. M, p.347.

Hui-hua kuan. A Branch of Flowering Shrub. Colour on paper. Inscription by Shên Chou.

SUN CH'ÊNG-TSUNG 孫承宗.

Unrecorded in the biographies of painters. t. Chih-shêng 稚繩. From Kao-yang (Pao-ting), Hopei. B. 1563, d. 1638. President of the Board of War. Hanged himself when the Manchus captured the city of Kao-yang. V, p.755.

Tōsō, p.406. Landscape. Poem.

SUN CH'I 孫啓.

Unrecorded. According to the note in *Ku-kung*, of the Ming period. Seals read: (*t.*) Shih-lun 士倫, (*h.*) Hsüeh-hsien 雪軒. Plum-blossoms.

Ku-kung, XXXIX. Plum-blossoms. Signed.

SUN CHIH 孫枝, *t.* Shu-ta 叔達, *h.* Hua-lin Chü-shih 華林居士.
From Suchou. Flourished *c.*1550–1580. Landscapes in the style of Wên Chêng-ming. Also figures and flowers. N, III, 13. M, p.348.

K.-k. shu-hua chi, VII. Plum-blossoms and Narcissi. Signed and dated 1559.

Freer Gallery (45, 37). River-view in Autumn with Flocks of rising Waterbirds. Handscroll. Signed and dated 1579.

K.-k. shu-hua chi, XII. Landscape, illustrating two lines of a poem by Tu Fu. Signed.

Ibid. XVII. The Jade Cave and the Peach-tree Forest. Signed.

K.-k. chou-k'an 154, 459. Landscapes. Fan-paintings. Also Nanga Taisei, VIII, 86 (dated 1576).

SUN I 孫儀.
Unrecorded. Probably end of Ming period.

Nanju 24. Mountains and Autumn Clouds. Signed.

SUN K'O-HUNG 孫克弘, *t.* Yün-chih 允執, *h.* Hsüeh-chü 雪居.
From Hua-t'ing, Kiangsu. B. 1532, d. 1610. Flowers; landscapes in the style of Ma Yüan and Mi Fei; also Buddhist and Taoist figures. N, III, 25. O, 6. I, 57, 8. L, 16, 5. U, II, 1, 8. M, pp.347–8.

Tōyō, XII (Count Tanaka). Plum-blossoms. Signed and dated 1607. *Cf.* Sirén, *Later*, pl.122.

Tōsō, p.333. Han-shan and Shih-tê. Signed and dated 1609(?)

Shina Nanga, I, 22. Kuanyin with the Fish-basket. Signed and dated 1609.

Shên-chou album. Ten pictures of Rocks. Signed. Colophon dated 1609. Other colophons by Ch'ên Chi-ju and Hsiang Shêng-mo.

Hui-hua kuan. A Blossoming Magnolia-tree; minor Flowers below at the Foot of a Stone. Colour on paper. Signed and dated 1609.

Shên-chou, IX. A Tree-peony. Signed. Two lines of poetry.

Ming-jên shu-hua, 12. Amarantus Gangetica at a Rock. Signed. Poem.

K.-k. shu-hua chi, XXI. Flowers of the Fifth Month. Signed.

K.-k. chou-k'an, vols.V, VI, 107–126. *Hsiao-hsia ch'ing-k'uo t'u.* Twenty Landscape Studies with Pines, leafy Trees and open Pavilions where Scholarly Men are resting and enjoying Life. Album-leaves.

Ku-kung collect. Plum-blossoms and Narcissi. Long handscroll. Painted in ink (in the manner of Wang Ku-hsiang). Signed.

Nanga Taisei, II, IV, VIII. Four fan-shaped paintings of Bamboos and Plum-blossoms.

Kyūka, I. Bodhidharma Crossing the Yangtse on a Reed. Seals of the painter. Poem by Ch'en Chi-ju. A similar picture in the Ōgawa collect., Kyōto.

Ku-kung ming-shan-chi, 8. Landscape. Fan-painting. For others, see K.-k. chou-k'an 8, 218, 224, 273, 276; also Nanga Taisei, VIII, 85.

Nanga Taisei, II, 221. Two Paintings of Flowering Plum and Bamboo. Fan-paintings, one dated 1600. See also ibid. IV, 37 (Gardenia); VII, 85 (Landscape).

Ogawa collect., Kyōto. Album; twelve Views of Water. Free rendering of Ma Yüan's version of this subject. Signed.

C. T. Loo's Successor, Frank Caro, N.Y. Monastery in a Mountain Gully in Mist. Inscription by the painter. Colophon by Ch'ên Chi-ju. *Cf.* Toronto 29.

Ton Ying Co., New York (P'ang Yüan-chi collect.) Branches of a Blossoming Peach-tree. Fan-painting. Poem by the painter.

Köln, Ostasiat. Museum. A Bird on a Branch of a Wu-t'ung-tree. Signed. Fan-painting. *Cf.* Venice Exhibition cat., 829; Köln Exhibition 1955, No.24.

J. P. Dubosc, Lugano. Chrysanthemum and Bamboo. Signed. Fan-painting.

Ibid. Daruma Crossing over the Yangtse River standing on a Reed. Ink and colour. Signed.

SUN LUNG 孫龍, *t.* Ts'ung-chi 從吉, *h.* Tu-ch'ih 都癡.
Native of P'i-ling (Wu-chin), Kiangsu. Early Ming period; said to be contemporary with Lin Liang. M, p.347.

Gems, III, 2. An album of twelve leaves: Vegetables, Flowers, Birds and Insects. Attributed.

SUNG CHÜEH 宋珏 or Sung Ku 宋穀, *t.* Pi-yü 比玉, *h.* Li-chih-hsien 荔枝仙.
From P'u-t'ien, Fukien; lived in Nanking. B. 1576, d. 1632. Poet and calligraphist. Landscapes in the styles of Mi Fei and the Yüan masters. N, VII, 21. Q, II, 1. U, I, 3, 1. M, p.128.

K.-k. shu-hua chi, XXXVI. Landscape. Signed. Poem and colophon, dated 1608. Another poem and colophon (also by the painter), dated 1617.
Shina Nanga, II, 4. Landscape. Fan-painting. Signed. Poem and colophon, dated 1616.
Sung Pi-yü chiang-t'ing ch'iu-mu chüan (Shên-chou kuo-kuang shê, Shanghai, 1909). Autumn Twilight; Bare Trees along a River-bank. Handscroll. Colophon by the painter.
Hui-hua kuan. A Mountain Slope by a River. A low Pavilion on the Bank. Ink on paper. Inscription by Ch'ên Chia-yen.

SUNG HSÜ 宋旭, *t.* Ch'u-yang 初暘 and Shih-mên 石門.
From Chia-hsing, Chekiang. B. 1523, d. *c.*1605. Became a monk, called Tsu-hsüan 祖玄. Influenced by Shên Chou. Teacher of Chao Tso and Sung Mou-chin. N, III, 27. O, 4. M, p.127.

Hamburg Exhibition, 1949–1950. Free version of Wang Wei's *Wang-ch'uan t'u*. Light colours and ink. Handscroll. Signed and dated 1574.
Hui-hua kuan. High Mountain rising over a Stream; scattered Trees with red Leaves. Ink and colour on paper. Dated 1580. *Cf.* P'ang Yüan-chi cat. 8.
K.-k. shu-hua chi, XVIII. Cloudy Peaks and Waterfall in Autumn. Signed and dated 1583.
Metropolitan Museum. River Landscape. Fan-painting. Signed and dated 1587.
J. P. Dubosc, Lugano. Two fan-paintings, one dated 1587, another, 1592.
Tōsō, p.338. The Rainbow over the T'ien-mu Mountain. Signed and dated 1589.
I-shu ts'ung-pien, 13. View from Annam: Mountain Landscape with coloured Trees and a long high Bridge. Signed and dated 1596. *Cf.* Shina Nanga, III, 12.
Tōsō, pp.334–337. Eight Landscapes called "The Eight Views of Hsiao and Hsiang". Signed, at the age of 76 (1598).
S.c.t.k. hsü-pien, vol.IV. Landscape. Signed and dated 1600.
Kokka 619 (Yōmei Bunko, Kyōto). Landscape. Handscroll. Dated 1600.
Sōgen 143. Landscape, painted in blue and green. Signed and dated 1603, at the age of 81.
Hui-hua kuan. A Fisherman on a River in Winter; Snow-covered Mountain in the background. Dated 1604. *Cf.* Liu, 62.
Sōgen 144. Geese descending over a River. Signed and dated 1605.
National Museum, Stockholm. Far away Sails and returning Boats on a misty River. Signed and dated at 83 (1605).
Ming-jên shu-hua, 18. The Rainbow over the T'ien-mu Mountain. Signed.
K.-k. chou-k'an 72. Landscape. Fan-painting.
Ku-kung collect. Celebrating the New Year. Signed.
Köln, Ostasiat. Museum. The Lung-ch'iu Waterfall in Yen-tang Mountains. Signed. Fan-painting. Köln Exhibition 1955, No.19.

SUNG MOU-CHIN 宋懋晉, *t.* Ming-chih 明之.
From Sung-chiang, Kiangsu. End of 16th century. Pupil of Sung Hsü. N, IV, 15. O, 4. M, p.128.

Sung-chiang p'ai ming-hua chi (Shên-chou album). A Garden with Magnolia-trees and High Rockeries. Signed.

Ibid. Cottages and overhanging Cliffs. Signed.

Shên-chou album, 1918. An album of paintings of rocks. Signed.

T'ai-shan ts'an-shih lou ts'ang-hua, II. Hills and leafy Trees rising through the Mist. After Tung Yüan. Signed.

Hamburg Exhib., 1949–1950. A Temple in a Cave and Monastery on the Cliff.

TAI CHIN 戴進, *t.* Wên-chin 文進, *h.* Ching-an 靜菴.

From Ch'ien-t'ang, Chekiang. Summoned to Court in the Hsüan-teh period, but left soon again for his home province. Landscapes in the styles of Ma Yüan and Hsia Kuei. Figures, flowers and birds. Principal master of the Chê School. I, 55, 16. N, I, 20. O, 2. K, 54, 1. M, p.715.

Chang Ta-ch'ien cat., vol.IV. Bamboo and Blossoming Plum-tree. Painted together with Wang Ch'ien who did the plum-tree. Inscription by Wang Ch'ien, dated 1439.

Tōyō, X. Autumn and Winter, from a series of the four Seasons. One signed and dated 1444.

Shanghai Museum. Old Pine-trees on a Slope; a Scholar followed by his Servant is approaching. Signed and dated 1445.

Berlin Museum. Scholars in a Pavilion under Pine-trees by a Stream. Handscroll. Signed and dated 1446.

Shimbi, XX (Kuwana collect.) View over a Bay; an open Pavilion on the Shore. Handscroll. Signed and dated 1446.

K.-k. shu-hua chi, XX. Snow Scene. Signed and dated in the Ching-t'ai reign (1450–1456). B?

Li-tai, II. Wang Hui-chih Visiting Tai K'uei. In Sung style. Signed. Poem.

Ku-kung, XIII. Rainstorm over a River; two Men in a Boat, Others passing over a Bridge. Signed. *Cf.* Chinese cat., London Exhibition, p.188.

K.-k. shu-hua chi, XVIII. An Arhat with a Tiger Seated in Front of a Cave. Signed.

Ibid. XIX. Man with a Silky Yak under a Pine-tree. Signed.

Ibid. XXII. Four Men in a Pavilion built over a Mountain Stream. Signed.

Ibid. XXV. Five Deer in a Pine Forest. An unusual picture, possibly by the master. Poem by Wên Chêng-ming.

Ibid. XXX. Travellers in Spring.

Ibid. XXXIII. Wên-wang of the Chou Dynasty visiting T'ai-kung Wang on the River-bank.

Ibid. XXXV. Returning Home on a Spring Evening. Signed.

Ku-kung collect. A River Landscape; a man on donkey crossing a bridge. Ink on silk and slightly coloured. Signed with one seal.

Hui-hua kuan. Landscape with three Heroes coming to the Gate of Chu-ko Liang. Ink and colour on silk. Signed.

Ibid. Traveller's Inn at the Foot of high Mountains. In the style of the Yüan masters. Ink and colour on paper. Signed.

Ibid. Butterflies and Hollyhock. Signed. Poems by four contemporaries. *Cf.* P'ang Yüan-chi cat. Add. 2 and Illust. cat. IV.

Ibid. Trunks and Branches of large Pine-trees. Painted in a broad manner. Long handscroll. Signed.

Nanking Exhibition cat. 97 (C. T. Loo's Successor, Frank Caro, N.Y.) A Man in a Boat on the River. Signed. *Cf.* Toronto 19.

Ibid. 98. Peasants happily returning on a Mountain Path. After Ma Yüan. Signed. *Cf.* J. D. Ch'ên cat. I, 30.

Kokka 171. Fisherman asleep in a Boat among Reeds.

Ibid. 265. Landscape with Summer Pavilions. Signed.

Shimbi, XIII (Kuwana collect.) Mountain Landscape with Pines and Figures in a Pavilion. Inscribed with the painter's name.

Ibid. XVIII. Two pictures of Quails among Flowering Plants.

Shimbi Shoin Shina Meigashū, II. A Scholar's Homestead at the Foot of high Mountains. A man is sweeping the ground, while a visitor approaches on the bridge. Signed.

Bijutsu, I. Summer Landscape in a Storm. Signed. *Cf.* Ku-kung, XIII.

Tōyō, X. Two Mountain Landscapes representing Spring and Winter. One of them signed.

Ibid. X. Three Men in a Pine Grove playing Chess. Part of a handscroll.

Sōraikan, II, 45. Steep Mountains, Temple Pavilions in the Crevices; high Pines on the Terraces. Signed. *Cf.* Tōsō, p.238.

Sōgen 88 (Lo Chên-yü collect.) A Cat and a Butterfly under a Banana-tree. Signed.

I-yüan chên-shang 7. Chung K'uei. Signed.

Nanga Taisei, VII, 19. A Man on a Donkey, followed by his Servant, passing under a Willow-tree. Section of a handscroll? No signature or seal.

John Herron Art Institute, Indianapolis. Large landscape. Signed.

Freer Gallery (24.3). Breaking Waves and Autumn Winds. Ink only, Handscroll. Signed. A.

Ibid. (30.90). Fishermen in Boats on a broad River. Ink and slight colours on paper. Handscroll of 26 ft. long. Signed. Colophon. A.

Cleveland Art Museum. Ten Thousand Li of the Yangtse. Wide Bays bordered by Mountains, Fishermen's Harbours, Bridges and Pavilions among Trees and Bamboo Groves. Long handscroll. Signed. A long colophon by Wang Wên-chih, dated 1794, and another of recent date. *Cf.* Cleveland Exhibition cat. 41. Possibly schoolwork.

National Museum, Stockholm. A Poet on a Terrace; Monkeys playing in a Tree. Signed.

Chêng Tê-k'un, Cambridge. *Chiang-shan ta-kuan*: Views along a broad River; Fishing Boats in the distance and Travellers on Horseback and on Foot. Long handscroll. Signed. A.

P'ang Yüan-chi Illust. cat. II. A Homestead among Trees at the Foot of cloudy Mountains. Said to be in the style of Yen Wên-kuei. Signed. Inscription by Tung Ch'i-ch'ang.

Monumenta Serica, III, 2 (1938), pl.XXV. A Spring Landscape with Travellers. Signed. A.

T'ANG CHIH-CH'I 唐志契, *t.* Hsüan-shêng 玄生 and Fu-wu 敷五.

From Hai-ling, Kiangsu. Flourished *c.*1560–1570. Author of *Hui-shih wei-yên* 繪事微言. Landscapes. N, VII, 17. O, 8. M, p.326.

Shoman, 23. Landscape after Mi Fei. Fan-painting. Signed.

T'ANG CHIH-YIN 唐志尹, *t.* P'ing-san 聘三.

Younger brother of T'ang Chih-ch'i; they were called the "Two T'angs". Flowers and birds. Followed Lü Chi. N, VII, 17. M, p.326.

Ton Ying Co., New York. A Bird and Stalks of Millet. Signed and dated 1579. Fan painting. From P'ang Yüan-chi collect.

K.-k. shu-hua chi, XXXV. Birds Pecking Grain. Signed.

T'ANG HSIEN-K'O 唐獻可, *t.* Chün-yü 君俞.

From Ch'ang-chou. Calligraphist, following Mi Fei; paintings after Sung and Yüan styles. Late Ming. N, IV, 23. M, p.327.

I-yüan chên-shang 5. Landscape of Mt. Hsi-hsia. Signed.

Nanking Exhib. cat. 208. Mountain Peaks. Fan-painting. Inscription, signed.

T'ANG SHIH-SHÊNG 唐時升, *t.* Shu-ta 叔達.
Native of Chia-ting. Poet and antiquarian. Not mentioned in the standard dictionaries of painters. V, p.737.

Nanga Taisei, III, 14. A Branch of Blossoming Plum, in the manner of Wang Mien. Long inscription by the artist, dated 1608.

T'ANG YIN 唐寅, *t.* Po-hu 伯虎 and Tzŭ-wei 子畏, *h.* Liu-ju chü-shih 六如居士, T'ao-hua an-chu 桃花庵主, and other names.
From Suchou. B. 1470, d. 1523. Landscapes, figures, flowers, etc. N, II, 20. O, 3. I, 30, 3. L, 56, 11. M, p.326.

Ku-kung collect. Summer Houses of Scholars among Rocks along a Stream. Colour on silk. Long handscroll. Signed and dated 1504. Inscription by Wên Chêng-ming.

Ōmura, II, 4 (Hayashi collect.) The Hua Mountain. Signed. Poem, dated 1506. *Cf.* Min Shitaika, 40; Tōsō, p.267; P'ang Yüan-chi cat. 8: Chūgoku, III.

Yen Kuang Co., Peking (photo). A View of the P'ei-t'ai Garden. Signed. Colophon and poem, dated 1506. *Cf.* Nanga Taisei, XI, 24.

Min Shitaika, 39. A Samli (fish). Signed. Poem by Shên Chou, dated 1508.

Ibid. 42 (Ueno collect.) Storm over Mountains and River. Signed. Poem, dated 1508. *Cf.* Yonezawa, 9.

Ibid. 31. A Branch of Plum-blossoms. Signed. Poem, dated 1509. *Cf.* Sōraikan, II, 51.

Shên-chou, III. T'ang Yin's Cottage, T'ao-hua an. Signed. Poem, dated in his fortieth year (1509).

Chicago Art Institute. Drinking Tea under Wu-t'ung Trees. A Scholar receiving a Visitor. Short handscroll. Signed and dated 1509. Poem by Chu Yün-ming.

Shêng P'ing-ch'ê, Hongkong. Spring on the Lake. Signed and dated 1509.

Juncunc collect., Chicago. A Young Lady adorning herself with Flowers in her Hair. Colour on silk. Poem dated 1509. Possibly school-work.

Shên-chou, VIII. A Scholar's Study by a Stream. Signed and dated 1510.

Chung-kuo, II, 20. A Man seated on the Bank of a Stream; spare Trees. Handscroll. Signed and dated 1513.

National Museum, Stockholm. Bamboo Branches in Rain and Wind. Signed and dated 1513. *Cf.* Tōsō 269 Sirén, *Later*, pl.92. Possibly school-work.

Ming-jên shu-hua, 34. A Branch of a Plum-tree. Signed. Poem dated 1515. *Cf.* Shina Nanga Taikan, 10.

Sōraikan, II, 52. Mountain Torrent at the Foot of high Peaks; an old Man walking over the Bridge. Poem by the painter, dated 1517.

I-yüan chên-shang 3. A Fisherman in a Boat; Pine-trees on the Shore. Fan-painting, signed and dated 1517.

Chung-kuo ming-hua, 12. A Pea Vine hanging from a Tree. Signed and dated 1517. A.

Pao-yün, II. A Scholar at his Desk in a House by a Stream; a guest arriving by boat. Handscroll. Signed and dated 1519. A.

Chung-kuo, II, 19. A Branch of Plum-blossoms. Signed. Poem, dated 1520.

Li-tai, V. Gathering Lotus Seeds. Handscroll. Signed and dated 1520. *Cf.* Nanking Exhib. cat. 122. A.

Gems, I, 33. A Lady playing a Flute. Signed and dated 1520. A.

Mrs. B. Z. Seligman, London. The Straw-covered Cottage at the Western Mountain. View over a wide Bay. Handscroll. Poem by the painter and eight more colophons, the first dated 1520. A.

Ōmura, I, 11. An Arhat. Signed and dated 1521. *Cf.* Min Shitaika 35; Tōsō, p.271; Chūgoku, III.

K.-k. shu-hua chi, XVIII. Landscape. Signed. Poem, dated 1521. Imitation.

Shên-chou album, 1911. The T'ung-an (T'ung-tree Retreat). Handscroll. Long inscription by the painter, dated 1521.

I-shu ts'ung-pien, 24. View over a wide River. Leafless trees in the foreground, a man in a boat, and rocky shore in the distance. Poem by the painter, dated 1521.

National Museum, Stockholm. Preparing Tea. Short handscroll. Signed and dated 1521. *Cf.* Sirén, *Later*, pl.95. A.

P'ang Yüan-chi Illust. cat. II. Fine grassy Plants in a Pot and a small Rock. Poem by the painter, dated 1521. Colophons by Wên Chêng-ming and two later men.

Hui-hua kuan. Two Palace Ladies in T'ang Costume taking Refreshments, served by two Servants. Colour on silk. Inscription by the painter, dated 1523.

Shên-chou, II. A Straw-roofed open Pavilion by a Stream. Signed. Poem.

Ibid. VII. Two Men seated on the Bank of a Stream in the Mountains. Signed. Poem.

Ibid. XII. A Lady in a Garden, Resting from her Sewing Work. After Chou Wên-chü. Signed. Poem.

Ibid. XIII. Chang Shêng asking the Maid-servant to take a Letter to her Mistress. Illustration to the *Hsi-hsiang* novel. Seals of the painter. *Cf.* Nanga Taisei, VII.

Ibid. XIV. A Branch of a Plum-tree. Signed. Poem.

Shên-chou ta-kuan, vol.8. Two small Birds on Sprays of Bamboo. Poem by the painter and dedication to a friend called Yen Chu-sha. A.

S.c.t.k. hsü-pien, I. Chrysanthemums, Rocks and Bamboo. Poem by the painter.

Chung-kuo, II, 11. The Nan-chou Lodge at the Foot of high Mountains. Signed. Poem. *Cf.* J. D. Ch'ên cat. I, 34.

Ibid. II, 12. Studying in the Autumn. Signed. Poem(?)

Ibid. II, 13. Misty Landscape. Signed. Poem(?)

Ibid. II, 14. Bamboos and leafless Trees. Signed. Two lines of poetry. *Cf.* Shina Nanga, I, 7.

Ibid. II, 15. A Young Lady and Two Maids by a Garden Rock. Signed. Poem.

Ibid. II, 16. Straw-covered Huts and two Men on a River-bank at the Foot of a Mountain. Signed. Poem. *Cf.* Chung-kuo ming-hua, 8; Shina Nanga, II, 3.

Ibid. II, 17. Feeding Cranes. Landscape with deeply creviced Rocks. Short handscroll. Signed. Colophons and poems by Shên Chou and other friends.

Ibid. II, 18. A Lady with a Fan. Signed. Poem. *Cf.* Shina Nanga, I, p.8; Sōgen 105; P'ang Yüan-chi Illustr. cat. IV, 1940.

Ibid. II, 21. Wild Geese and leafless Trees. Signed. Poem. *Cf.* Min Shitaika, 44.

Chung-kuo ming-hua, 4. A Man standing on the River-bank leaning on an old Tree under a sharply-cut curving Rock. Poem by the painter.

Ibid. 14. A small Homestead in a Bamboo Grove at the Foot of Mountains on the River-bank. Short hand-scroll. Signed.

Ibid. 16. Deeply-creviced rocky Mountain rising over a River, tall Pine-trees growing in the Crevices.

Ibid. 17. River landscape; a man is seated under a twisting tree looking at a crane. Handscroll. Colophons by Shên Chou and others.

Ibid. 17. A Man in a Pavilion on a River-bank at the foot of grassy mountain. Handscroll. Poems by the painter and by Ch'ien-lung.

Ibid. 37. A Tangled Grove of Bare Trees; two men on a path below. Poem by the painter. A.

Ibid. 38. A Man walking with a Staff beneath Bare Trees; a flock of birds. Poem by the painter. A.

I-shu ts'ung-pien, 11. A Scholar playing the *Ch'in* in his Study under leafy Trees; a Visitor is Approaching. Poem by the painter.

Ibid. 12. A Poet in a Pavilion built over the Water by a steep River-bank. Poem by the painter.

Li-tai, IV. A View of T'ai-hu. Bamboo grove on a sloping promontory. Long inscription by the master.

Ku-kung, IX. Late Spring Landscape. Signed. Poem.

K.-k. shu-hua chi, I. Listening to the Pine-trees. Signed. Poem. A.

Ibid. XIII. The Han-ku Pass in Snow. Signed. Poem.

Ibid. XV. Hibiscus Flowers at the Waterside. Signed.

Ibid. XVII. The Painter speaking of Old Times with his Friend Hsi-chou. Signed. Poem, colophon. A.

Ibid. XX. A Mountain Valley with Waterfall. Signed. Poem.

Ibid. XXIII. Farmsteads in Chiang-nan. Signed. Poem.

Ibid. XXVII. Apricot-blossoms. Signed. Poem.

Ibid. XXXII. Ch'ang-o, the Moon Fairy. Signed. Poem.

K.-k. chou-k'an, vol.III, 55. *Mu-ch'un lin-ho t'u.* Rocky Mountain and Trees in late Spring. Poem by the painter.

Ku-kung collect. *Ch'i-shan yü-yin t'u*: A Fisherman among Mountains and Streams. Colour on silk. Long handscroll. Poem by the painter and signed. Inscriptions by Ch'êng Ta-lun, Lu Chih, Ku Têh-yen, Chü Chieh and Ch'ien-lung. A.

Ibid. A Farewell Scene at the Chin-ch'ang Gate of Suchou where the painter's friend Chêng Ch'u-chih is departing. Ink on silk. Handscroll. Inscription by the painter, and colophons by Wang Chih-têng and Chou T'ien-ch'iu. A.

Ibid. *Han-kuan hsüeh-chi t'u*. Snow Landscape. Wagons passing through the narrow Kan-ku Gorge, a temple is seen in the distance. Ink and slight colour on silk. Poem by the painter.

Ibid. Homestead of a Scholar under Leafy Trees on a River-bank. Handscroll. Long colophon by Wang Chih-têng.

Ibid. An album of ten leaves of landscape-studies. Signed.

Ibid. The *Fu-yung* Flower bending over a Stone in the Water. Signed.

Ibid. Spring View in a Garden. A scholar seated on a low couch protected by large screens decorated with landscape-paintings. Two young women are standing by his side. Inscription by the painter. Reproduction in colour in *Time Magazine*, May 6, 1957.

Ibid. An Old Tree and some Young Bamboos. Poem by the painter. Part of the album *Yüan Ming shan-shui chi*.

Ibid. *Kao-shih t'u* after Liang K'ai. (K.-k. shu-hua chi, XIX). Three scholars and a servant in a garden. Ink on paper, executed in sketchy fashion. There were originally four pictures mounted on a scroll, known as *Kao-shih t'u*, executed in the manners of (1) Li Po-shih, (2) Liu Sung-nien, (3) Ma Ho-chih and (4) Liang K'ai. This scroll belonged to a man called Wu Wên-hsin, who when approaching death, ordered that it should be burned; it was, however, snatched out of the fire by a servant, and as a result, only the last picture of the four survived. For another version of it, see Ch'iu Ying's *Kao-shih t'u*, with inscription by Wên Chêng-ming.

Ibid. Lady Pan Chao of Han standing under two Palm-trees, with a moon-shaped silk fan in her hand. Signed with two seals. Inscriptions by Chu Yün-ming, Wên Chêng-ming and Wang Ku-hsiang.

Pao-yün, II. Villas on the Banks of a River. Handscroll. Signed. A.

Ni Tsan, Wên Pi, Shên Chou and T'ang Yin (National Museum album, Peking). A Cottage in a Bamboo Grove and Boats in a Bay. Poem by the painter. *Cf.* Pao-yün, I.

Yen-kuang Co., Peking. Leafless Trees and young Bamboos by a Stream. Poems by the painter and by Ch'ien-lung.

Hui-hua kuan. A weeping Man seated between two old Trees which are shaken by the Storm. According to the poem by the painter, the picture was done for a friend whose father died recently. Ink on paper. Short handscroll.

Ibid. Wang Kung Travelling in a Cart through a Mountain Landscape. Ink and slight colour. Short handscroll. Signed.

Ibid. View from Tung-shan. River at the foot of a Mountain. Ink and slight colour on paper. Short handscroll. Inscription by the painter.

Ibid. Mountain with Trees and Cottages in a Bamboo Grove in Snow. Ink on paper. Poem by the painter.

Gems, I, 31. A Pomegranate-tree. Poem, signed.

Ibid. I, 32. Old Trees and Bamboo by a Stream. Signed.

Shanghai Museum. A Lady with a Fan. Poem by the painter, in which he asks: "Why does the lady look so sad?" The face drawn in *kung-pi* style, like a work of Ch'iu Ying.

Nanking Exhib. cat. 120 (Ku-kung collect.) T'ao Ku in his Garden, listening to a Young Girl playing the P'i-p'a. Poem, signed.

Ibid. 121. Trees and Bamboo by a River. Poem, signed.

Ibid. 124. Landscape with perpendicular Cliffs; a Scholar in his House under Pine-trees. Poem, signed.

Ming-jên shu-hua, 1. A Branch of Plum-blossoms. Signed. Same poem as on the picture in Shên-chou, XIV.

Ibid. 11. A Branch of an Apricot-tree. Signed. Poem.

Liu, 58. Portrait of Tung-fang So. An old Man holding a Peach.

Ibid. 56. Thatched Houses by a River; a Man in a Boat. Poem by the painter.

Ibid. 57. A Scholar in a Pavilion by the River, beneath an overhanging Cliff. Poem by the painter, with a dedication to a Mr. Tê-fu.

Po-mei chi. A Plum-tree with a few Blossoms. Long handscroll. Signed.

Mei-chan t'ê-k'an. An old Woman speaking to a Scholar seated among Bamboos on a Terrace.

P'ang Yüan-chi Illust. cat. I. Men wandering in Mountains in Spring. Poem by the painter.

Chang Ts'ung-yü cat. Scholar's Pavilion under Willows at the Foot of a Mountain.

Kokka 133. The Fairy of the Lo-fou Mountain.

Ibid. 517. Resting in the Garden. Signed. Poem.

Nanju 11. Ch'ang-o, the Moon Fairy. Signed. Poem.

Ibid. 25. Cold Peaks and scattered Trees. Signed. Poem.

Tōyō, X. High Mountains by a River. In blue and green colours. Signed. Poem.
Bijutsu, XXII. Looking at Farmers from a Pavilion by a River. Signed.
Shoman 19. Talking of the Past in a Pavilion by the River. Fan painting. Signed.
Shina Nanga, I, p.9. Autumn Landscape. Signed. Poem.
Ibid. II, 6. Travellers on a Mountain. Signed. Poem.
Kyūka, I. The Red Cliff. Signed.
Sōgen 103. Friends departing. Short handscroll. Signed.
Ibid. 104. Summer Day in the Mountains. Signed.
Ibid. 106. A Scholar on a Bridge viewing a Waterfall. Signed. Poems.
Ōmura, I, 3. The Herb Collector. Signed. Poem. *Cf.* Min Shitaika 36; Chūgoku, III.
Ibid. I, 8. A View of T'ai-hu. Handscroll. Signed. *Cf.* Min Shitaika 45.
Ibid. I, 9. Plum-blossoms. Signed. Poem. *Cf.* Min Shitaika 32.
Ibid. I, 10. A Mountain River. Signed. Poem.
Min Shitaika 33. Plum-blossoms. Signed. Poem(?)
Ibid. 34. Plum-trees and Bamboos by a Rockery. Signed. Two lines of poetry. A.
Ibid. 37. Peonies. Signed. Poem.
Ibid. 38. A Day Lily. Signed. *Cf.* Suchiku 9.
Ibid. 41. Listening to a Waterfall. Signed. Poem. *Cf.* Tōsō, p.268. A.
Ibid. 43. Pavilion over a Stream. Signed. Poem by Wên Chêng-ming.
Ibid. 46. Figures under Pine-trees. Fan-painting. Signed. Two lines of poetry.
Tōan 26. Pine-trees by a Stream.
Shina Nanga Taikan 2. An old leafless Tree growing on the Rocks by a River. Two men conversing. Inscriptions by the painter and by Wên Chêng-ming and two others.
Tōsō, p.230. Rocks by a River. Handscroll. Signed.
Ibid. 262. Ou-yang Hsiu. Signed. His biography from the Sung History, said to be copied by Chu Yün-ming (1460–1526) but dated 1569(?)
Ibid. 263. Meditating in a Water Pavilion. Signed. Poem. A.
Ibid. 264. A Crow on a dry Branch. Signed. Two lines of poetry. *Cf.* P'ang Yüan-chi cat. Add. 2. A.
Ibid. 265. Four Court Ladies in the Shu Country. Signed. Poem and colophon.
Ibid. 266. Ladies. Signed. Poem.
Ibid. 270. Landscape after Li T'ang. Signed. Poem.
Sōraikan, I, 29. A Scholar's Retreat in the high Mountains. Handscroll. Slightly coloured. Signed. *Cf.* Nanga Taisei.
Ibid. XX. Pavilion built over the Water, shaded by Willow-trees. Signed.
Chūgoku, III. High Peaks and Rushing Cascades; Pavilions with Figures in the Gully. Poem by the painter.
Shina Meiga Senshū, III. The Sound of Autumn. A man seated in a pavilion on a promontory. Handscroll. Signed.
Private collect., Kyōto. A River Gorge, with Scholars enjoying the Scenery. Signed.
K.-k. ming-shan chi 6. Nine Landscapes. Fan-paintings. *Cf.* K.-k. chou-k'an Index for ten fan-paintings; also Nanga Taisei, VIII, 34–40.
Later Chinese Painting, pls.86–88. An album of eight double-leaves: Sketches of river landscapes with boats and gardens. Attributed.
Chang Ch'ün collect., Tapiei. The Fairy Ch'ang-o with a branch of Cassia. Poem by the painter. Numerous colophons on the edges of the painting. *Cf.* Nanking Exhibition cat. 123.
Chang Ta-ch'ien collect., Hongkong, 1954. A Boat among Reeds by the Shore on a Moonlight Night. Inscription by the painter. *Cf.* Chang Ta-ch'ien cat. I, 24.
Hung Yu-ling, Hongkong. A Scene of Parting. Signed.
Huang Pan-jo, Hongkong. The Sleeping Beauty. Signed.
Ho Kuan-wu, Hongkong. Bamboo Branches. Ink only. Short handscroll. Large inscription by the painter.
Ibid. Cliffs by the River with a Man seated on a Terrace. Colophons by nine painters of the Ming period.
Boston Museum. A Scholar seated under a Tree; a Servant is preparing Tea. Signed. Short handscroll.
Ibid. A Misty Gorge; Buildings by the Stream in the foreground. Signed.
Metropolitan Museum. Snow Landscape and two Men on a Bridge. Fan-painting. Signed.
Ibid. (Bahr collect.) A Beauty sleeping on a Banana Leaf. Short handscroll. Signed. Poems by Wên P'êng and Wang Ch'ung. Possibly school-work.
Freer Gallery (39.60) (ex-P'ang Yüan-chi). The Scholar's

Dream. Shore landscape with high mountains and knotty trees. Handscroll. Poem by the painter and six colophons. *Cf.* P'ang Yüan-chi cat. 4.

Ibid (53.78). A River Gorge. Travellers on Foot and Muleback on the Road winding along the Cliffs. Short handscroll. Signed. A.

Chicago Art Institute. Pine-trees on a Hill (*Sung-kang t'u*). Handscroll. Signed and dedicated to a friend. Several colophons.

Indianapolis Art Museum. Landscape with strange Peaks and a Scholar's hidden Retreat; a bridge over the stream below. Ink and slight colour on silk. Colophon by the painter.

Honolulu Academy of Arts. A Man meditating in a Straw-covered Pavilion under a branch of a blossoming Pear-tree. Signed.

C. T. Loo Successor, Frank Caro, New York. Rocks and a Pavilion under Pine-trees. Ink and slight colour. Short handscroll. Signed. Colophons by later men.

Ibid. A Wanderer Crossing a Stream on a Stone Bridge; strange Cliffs and twisted Trees bending over the River. Colophon by the painter. *Cf.* Cleveland Exhibition cat. 47; Toronto Exhibition cat. 18.

C. C. Wang, New York. Sharply silhouetted high Mountains. Water and Trees in the foreground. Signed.

Ibid. A Man meditating on a Cliff in a Mountain Landscape. Handscroll. Colophon by the painter. *Cf.* Cleveland Exhibition cat. 48.

Hamburg Exhibition, 1949–1950. A Mountain River spanned by a Bridge; Scholar's Pavilion built over the Stream under shady Trees. Ink on silk. Poetic inscription by the painter. Much worn.

J. P. Dubosc, Lugano. Three fan-paintings representing garden views, cottages and boats. Signed.

Vannotti collect., Lugano. Chrysanthemum and Bamboo. Signed. Fan-painting. *Cf.* Venice Exhibition cat. 813.

TAO-HUNG 道宏.

A monk painter known only through the picture mentioned below. Active at the beginning of the 15th century.

Freer Gallery (11.190). Lohans placed in the Landscape. Painted in gold outlines on deep blue ground. According to the inscription which contains the painter's name and the date 1427, it is one of two scrolls copied after originals by Wu Ssŭ-tsang which represented the 500 Lohans.

T'AO CH'ÊNG 陶成, *t.* Mêng-hsüeh 孟學 or Mou-hsüeh 懋學, *h.* Yün-hu hsien-jên 雲湖仙人.

From Pao-ying, Kiangsu. Active *c.*1480–1532. Landscapes, figures and flowers in the style of Southern Sung masters. N, III, 2. O, 3. M, p.394.

Chang Ta-ch'ien cat. IV. Farewell in Ta-t'ung. Handscroll. Poem by the painter, dated 1486. Colophons by later men.

K.-k. shu-hua chi, XXXIV. New Year's Flowers in a Vase. Signed and dated: Chia-ching *jên-shên*, a date which does not exist; the date may be *jên-ch'ên* (1532).

Formerly Hoyt collect., Cambridge, Mass. An old Plum-tree in Bloom. Signed.

W. Hochstadter, New York. Chrysanthemums and Cabbages. Handscroll. Poem, signed. *Cf.* Nanking Exhibition cat. 133.

T'AO I 佾, *h.* I-shan 一山.

Unrecorded. According to Waley, flourished *c.*1530.

British Museum, No.134. Dragons and Clouds. Signed.

TING YÜN-P'ÊNG 丁雲鵬, *t.* Nan-yü 南羽, *h.* Shêng-hua chü-shih 聖華居士.

From Hsiu-ning, Anhui. Active *c.*1584–1638. Buddhist and Taoist figures in the styles of Wu Tao-tzŭ and Li Lung-mien. Also landscapes. Friend of Tung Ch'i-ch'ang. N, IV, 13. O, 1. M, p.3.

Ku-kung collect. *Lu-shan kao.* The lofty mountain peaks of Lu-shan are surrounded by circling clouds. Signed and dated 1575. (*Wan-li i-hai*, a surprisingly early date.)

Tōsō, p.256. Landscape. Signed and dated 1584.

Shên-chou ta-kuan, vol.6. High Mountains and leafless Trees in Winter. Poem by the painter, dated 1585. *Cf.* Shina Nanga, III, 5.

Sōgen 160. A little Monk at the Foot of towering Mountains. Signed. Colophon by the painter, dated 1585. *Cf.* Nanking Exhib. cat. 166.

Metropolitan Museum. River Landscape with Boats; illustrating Po Chü-i's Song of the P'i-p'a. Signed and dated 1585. The poem is copied by Liu Jan, dated 1586. *Cf.* Cleveland Exhibition cat. 77.

F. Vannotti collect., Lugano. Pavilions among rocky Mountains. Fan-painting. Signed and dated 1591.

I-shu ch'uan-t'ung, X, 3. Waiting for an Imperial Audience. A Man in Court Dress is seated by a Rock under a tall Pine; a boy in attendance. Signed and dated 1592. Colophon by his pupil Chou Tsu, dated 1593.

Ferguson, *Chinese Painting*, p.164. Portrait of Lu Yu. Signed and dated 1594.

Shên-chou, XIV. Bodhidharma seated in Meditation and facing the Cliff. Signed and dated 1594.

Chūgoku, III. White Clouds in the midst of sharp Peaks. In the manner of Mi Yu-jên. Handscroll. A line of poetry by the painter, dated 1596.

J. P. Dubosc, Lugano. Pavilions among Spare Trees in a Misty Mountain Valley. Signed and dated 1597. Ink and colour. Fan-painting.

Kokka 477. Boats on a River. Signed and dated 1601. *Cf.* Tōsō, p.353.

Shên-chou, XIII. A Buddhist Saint (Śakyamuni?) Seated on a Mat under two Banana-trees. A boy at his side and a fantastic animal before him. Signed and dated 1604.

K.-k. shu-hua chi, XXVIII. Buddhist Figures. Signed and dated 1606.

I-shu ts'ung-pien, 14. A Buddhist Monk (Amida Buddha) seated on a Mat. Signed and dated 1606.

Chung-kuo ming-hua, 19. Bodhidharma seated in a Cave. Signed and dated 1607. *Cf.* P'ang Yüan-chi cat. Add. 2 and Illust. cat. V.

Nanking Exhib. cat. 165. Śakyamuni, three Arhats and Servants; a Dragon appearing in the foreground. Signed and dated 1607.

J. P. Dubosc, Lugano. A Pine-grove in the Mountains. Two Scholars Meeting on the Road. Signed and dated 1608. Ink and colour. Fan-painting.

I-shu ts'ung-pien, 23. An Arhat seated on a Mat under tall Pines, in front of him a Lion and a visiting Man and behind him a Servant with a Staff. Signed and dated 1609.

K.-k. shu-hua chi, XL. Kuanyin. Signed and dated 1609.

Hui-hua kuan. Yü Chuan preparing Tea. He is seated in front of a rockery under a banana plant. Ink and colour on paper. Archaistic. Signed and dated 1612.

K.-k. shu-hua chi, XXXVIII. Buddhist Figures. Signed and dated 1613.

J. P. Dubosc, Lugano (I-shu ts'ung-pien, 14). Deep Gully in the Mountains filled with Circling Clouds and rushing Water. Signed and dated 1614. *Cf.* Shina Nanga, III, 7.

Ibid. Bodhidharma seated in Meditation facing a Cliff. Signed and dated 1614. *Cf.* Shina Nanga, III, 1.

Ibid. Washing of the White Elephant. Signed and dated 1615. Colour painting. Köln Exhibition 1955, No.32.

I-shu ts'ung-pien, 15. A Grove of leafy Trees. Signed and dated 1616. Fan-painting.

Ibid. 17. The Sixth Ch'an Patriarch seated at a Table under a Tree. Three monks in conversation in front of him. Inscription by Tung Ch'i-ch'ang. *Cf.* Chung-kuo ming-hua, vol. 10.

Nanju 19 (Hashimoto collect., Takatsuki). Summer Mountains before Rain; after Kao K'o-kung. Signed and dated 1618.

Sōgen 161. A Child catching a Butterfly. Signed and dated 1618.

Ibid. 162. Sakyamuni seated under a Pine-tree. Signed.

Chūgoku, III. An old Man seated on a Stone Bench under tall Trees; a boy is preparing Tea beside him. Signed and dated 1619.

Tōsō, p.354. Buddhist Figures. Signed. A *Sūtra* copied by Wên Chung-i, dated 1621.

K.-k. shu-hua chi, XXXIV. The White Horse Carrying the first Buddhist Sūtras to China. Signed and dated 1625.

C. T. Loo's Successor, Frank Caro, N.Y. Bodhidharma crossing the Yangtse on a Reed. Signed and dated 1634. *Cf.* Toronto Exhibition cat. 32.

Liu, 76. Large Mountain Landscape with Buildings and Figures; in Wang Mêng's style. A Man enjoying potted herbs. Signed and dated 1638.

Chung-kuo, I. Inquiring about the Way to T'ien-t'ai. Signed. *Cf.* Chung-kuo ming-hua, 30.

Ibid. I. T'ao Yüan-ming making Wine.

K.-k. shu-hua chi, I. The Mother of Tsêng Sêng Biting her Finger. Signed.

Hui-hua kuan. Illustration to the Story of the Court Lady who sacrificed herself in order to save the Emperor from the wild Bear. Colour on silk. Handscroll. Signed.

I-yüan chên-shang, 4. An Arhat seated under a Cliff, with two Attendants. Signed.

Shina Nanga, I, 19. An Arhat. Signed.

Ōmura, I, 12. Epidendrum. Signed. Colophon by Tung Ch'i-ch'ang. *Cf.* Chūgoku, III.

Kokka 559 (ex-Manchu Household collect.) A Hermit's Abode in a Mountain. Ink and colour. Signed.

Boston Museum. A Buddha seated on a Rock which rises out of a whirling Stream. At the top of the picture an extract from a Sūtra. Signed.

Nelson Gallery, Kansas City. Five Forms of Kuanyin. Handscroll. Signed.

Honolulu Academy of Arts. The Eighteen Arhats; painted with ink and gold on purple silk.

British Museum. Two Fairies by a Stream. Album-leaf. Signed.

Museum for Asiatic Art, Amsterdam. Sakyamuni in the Mountains. Signed.

Chang Ts'ung-yü cat. Pine-trees and Rocks along a River-bank.

K.-k. chou-k'an, 172, 237, 255, 258. Landscapes. Fan-paintings. See also Nanga Taisei, VIII, 89, 90.

TS'AI SHIH-HSIN 蔡世新, *t.* Shao-ho 少壑.

From Ch'ien-nan, Kiangsi. Flourished *c.*1600. Portraits, bamboos and flowers. O, 1. M, p.633.

Tōsō, p.404. Bamboos, Chrysanthemums, Hen and Chickens. Signed and dated 1601.

TS'AO FANG 曹方, *t.* Tzŭ-mei 子美.

From Mo-ling, Kiangsu. Active about the middle of the 17th century. Unrecorded.

Shên-chou ta-kuan, vol.2. Huang Tao-chou (Shih-chai) Standing in front of the Imperial Palace Waiting for an Audience. Dated 1645.

TS'AO HSI 曹羲, *t.* Lo-fou 羅浮.

From Suchou. Flourished *c.*1600. Landscapes, figures. N, VII, 16. O, 5. M, p.405.

Mayuyama collect., Tōkyō. A Man asleep in a Boat among Reeds. Fan-painting. Signed and dated 1616.

Nanking Exhib. cat. 176. A River Landscape in Winter. Signed and dated 1637.

National Museum, Stockholm. Evening Calm. Signed.

K.-k. chou-k'an 9 and 16. Two Landscapes. Fan-paintings.

TS'AO LI-CHI 曹履吉, *t.* T'i-sui 提遂.

Native of Tang-t'u in Anhui. Active at the end of the Ming period. Landscapes in the manner of Ni Tsan. O, 4. M, p.404.

Nanking Exhib. cat. 230. River Landscape, with a Pavilion. Signed and dated 1621.

Lin Nan-hai, Kōbe. Mountainous Landscape. Signed and dated 1624.

Ts'ao Miao-Ch'ing 曹妙清, *t.* Pi-yü 比玉, *h.* Hsüeh-chai 雪齋.
A lady, active in the middle of the 14th century. From Ch'ien-t'ang, Chekiang. Poetess and calligraphist. M, p.405.

K.-k. chou-k'an, vol.VI, 129. Narcissus Plants and Flowers. Fan-painting. Signed and dated 1379.

Ts'ao T'ang 曹堂, *t.* Chung-shêng 仲升.
From Chi-ch'i, Anhui. Flourished *c.*1630. N, VII, 18. M, p.404.

Shina Nanga, III, 11. Landscape after Wang Mêng. Signed and dated 1629.

Tsêng Ch'ing 曾鯨, *t.* P'o-ch'ên 波臣.
From P'u-t'ien, Fukien. B. 1568, d. 1650. Celebrated portrait-painter. N, IV, 19. O, 1. M, p.514.

Ōmura, I, 11. Wang Shih-min at the age of 25. Signed and dated 1616. *Cf.* Chūgoku, IV.
Hamburg Exhibition, 1949–1950. Portrait of a Man. The Rock at his side painted by Ts'ao Hsi-chih. Signed and dated 1639.
Yonezawa, 30 (Yonoki collect.) Portrait of Su Tung-p'o. Signed and dated 1641.
Shên-chou ta-kuan, vol.1. Portrait of Ch'ên Chi-ju with a Crane. Signed.
Ibid. 10. The Painter Shao Mi seated in a Garden; two boys are gathering flowers. Poems by three other painters.
Hui-hua kuan. Portrait of Doctor Ko Ch'êng-fu. Handscroll. Several inscriptions.
Mei-chan t'ê-k'an 24. Portrait of Chou Ching-wên seated under a Pine-tree. Signed.
Ming-jên shu-hua, XIII. Portrait of Wo-tzŭ, a contemporary poet.

Tsou Chih-lin 鄒之麟, *t.* Ch'ên-hu 臣虎, *h.* Mei-an 昧庵, I-po shan-jên 衣白山人, I-lao 逸老.
From Wu-chin, Kiangsu. Chin-shih in 1610. Poet and collector. Landscapes after Huang Kung-wang. Q, I, 1. N, IV, 11. O, 5. U. I, 1, 5. M, p.568.

Nanga Taisei, V, 138. Banana Palms growing by a Rock. Signed and dated 1610.
Pageant 695. Two Men standing outside a Riverside Cottage; a boat sails by. Signed and dated 1651.
Hui-hua kuan. A Mountain Hump, spare Trees and an open Pavilion below. Signed.
Hsü-ching chai. The Golden Mountain in the Yangtse River. Signed.
Chung-kuo ming-hua, 25. River Landscape. Poem by the painter.
K.-k. chou-k'an 18. Landscape. Fan-painting. *Cf.* Nanga Taisei, VIII, 131.
Nanga Taisei, IX, 222, 223. Two Landscapes with small Houses, each with an inscription by the artist.
Ch'ên collect., New York. Landscape Studies. Twelve large album-leaves, slightly coloured. Signed.

Tsou Hêng 鄒衡.
Active at the end of the 15th century. Followed Wang Fu in his broad and forceful brush manner. Not recorded in the dictionary of painters.

Ku-kung collect. A Study-pavilion under Large Trees. Handscroll. Signed and dated 1497.

TSOU SHIH-CHIN 鄒式金, *t.* Mu-shih 木石.
From Wu-hsi, Kiangsu. Active in the Ch'ung-chên period (1628–1643). Landscapes. N, 7. M, p.568.

Ch'ing êrh-shih chia. A Branch of Plum-trees. Album-leaf. Signed.

S.c.t.k. hsü-pien, IV. View over a broad River; high rocky Shore and Mudbank. Signed.

TSOU TI-KUANG 鄒迪光, *t.* Yen-chi 彥吉, *h.* Yü-ku 愚谷.
From Wu-hsi, Kiangsu. Chin-shih in 1574. Landscapes in the styles of Mi, father and son, and of the Yüan masters. N, IV, 9. O, 4. M, p.567.

Nanju 15. Landscape after Mi Fei. Signed.

TS'UI TZŬ-CHUNG 崔子忠, *t.* Tao-mu 道母, *h.* Pei-hai 北海 and Ch'ing-yin 青蚓.
From Lai-yang, Shantung; lived in Peking. Active at the beginning of the 17th century. D. 1644. Celebrated figure painter, equally famous with Ch'ên Hung-shou. Starved to death when the Ming dynasty was overthrown. N, IV, 28. O, 1. U, II, 1, 15. M, p.388.

Gems, II, 18. Scene from the story "The Fairy Rabbit". A man with a staff; a white rabbit beside him. Handscroll. Signed and dated 1634.

Shên-chou, V. A Lady writing at a Table on a Terrace, served by two Maids. Signed and dated 1636. *Cf.* Êrh-shih chia.

K.-k. shu-hua chi, V. Su Tung-p'o and his Friends enjoying Antiques under Wu-t'ung Trees. Signed and dated 1640.

Ibid. VI. "Chickens and Dogs among the Clouds", *i.e.* Travellers in a Mountain Landscape. Signed, poem.

Ibid. XXII. Su Tung-p'o in Conversation with the Monk Fou-yin. Signed.

Ibid. XXXV. Washing the Elephant. After an old design. Signed.

Shina Meiga Senshū, III. Portrait of a Court Lady. Inscriptions by the painter and by Wang Ch'ung-chien.

TU CHI-LUNG 杜冀龍, *t.* Shih-liang 士良.
From Suchou. Landscapes in the manner of Shên Chou. M, p.122.

Hui-hua kuan. River-view; Pavilions and dry Trees on the Bank. Ink-painting on gold sprinkled paper. Signed. In the tradition of Sung-chiang School.

Vannotti collect., Lugano. Steep Rocks on the Border of a Wide Bay; Boats on the Water; Pavilions on the Shores. Ink and colour. Fan-painting.

TU CHIN 杜堇, *t.* Chü-nan 懼南, *h.* Ch'êng-chü 檉居, Ku-k'uang 古狂 and Ch'ing-hsia t'ing-chang 青霞亭長.
From Tan-t'u, Kiangsu; moved to the capital in the Ch'êng-hua period (1465–1487). Landscapes, figures, executed in the *tai-pai* manner. L, 45, 1. N, II, 25. M, pp.121, 122.

Hui-hua kuan. A Pavilion with two Men in a small Garden on a Terrace. Ink and colour on paper. Signed and dated 1509. Colophon by Wên Po-jên.

Ibid. Scholar writing on a Bamboo accompanied by a Friend and his Boy. Ink and colour on silk. In the manner of Tai Chin. Signed.

Gems, I, 27. A Scholar on a Mountain Terrace, under a Plum-tree. Signed.

Sōgen 100. Landscape. Handscroll. Signed.

Cleveland Art Museum (ex-C. C. Wang, New York). A Man passing an old Plum-tree in the Mountains in the Moonlight. Ink and slight colour on paper. Signed. *Cf.* Cleveland Exhibition cat. 42; Nanking Exhib. cat. 138.

Tu Ch'iung 杜瓊, *t.* Yung-chia 用嘉, *h.* Lu-kuan Tao-jên 鹿冠道人. Also known as Master Tung-yüan 東原. From Suchou. B. 1396, d. 1474. Scholar. Landscapes in Tung Yüan's style. N, II, 1. L, 45, 1. I, 56, 2. M, p.121.

Ku-kung collect. Landscape after Wang Mêng. Inscription by the painter, dated 1443. Two other inscriptions by his friends.

Chūgoku, II. Thatched Cottages in a Grove at the Foot of a grassy Mountain. Poem by the painter, dated 1451.

Sōgen 91 (P'ang Yüan-chi collect.) Two Men in a Garden Pavilion by a River. Signed. Poem, colophon, dated 1463. Poem by Ch'ien-lung.

Shên-chou, X. Cottages among Pine-trees; high Peaks in the background. Signed. Poem dated 1468.

Shên-chou ta-kuan, vol.16. A Study among Pine-trees; a Scholar is being served with Tea. Poem by the painter, dated 1468.

Ku-kung collect. Views of the Shih-tzŭ-lin Garden. Ink painting, similar to the views of Hsü Pên. Long inscription by the painter, dated 1468.

Ibid. *Nan-hu ts'ao-t'ang t'u*. A Mountain Landscape in the manner of Shên-chou. Colophons by Sun Ch'êng-ssŭ, Kao Shih-ch'i and a long inscription by the painter.

Honolulu Academy of Arts. Winding Streams, creviced Rocks, Pavilions, Trees and open Views. Ink on paper. Long handscroll. Signed. Colophon by Wên Chung-i.

Tu Ta-shou 杜大綬, *t.* Tzŭ-yü 子紆.
From Suchou. Active *c.*1560. Calligraphist. Landscapes and flowers. N, VII, 11. M, p.122.

Musée Guimet. Three Epidendrum Plants. Signed. A *fu* poem by the painter, dated 1558.

Hamburg Exhib., 1949–1950. Orchids. Handscroll. Signed and dated 1567.

Tung Ch'i-ch'ang 董其昌, *t.* Hsüan-tsai 玄宰, *h.* Ssŭ-po 思白.
From Hua-t'ing (Sung-chiang), Kiangsu. B. 1555, d. 1636. President of the Board of Rites. Great calligraphist and critic of painting. One of the "Nine Friends in Painting". Landscapes in the style of Tung Yüan and Chü-jan. N, IV, 1. O, 4. P, I, 3. U, I, 1, 1. I, 58, 1. M, p.572.

Ōmura, I, 4. River-view at Yang-shan. Signed. Executed in 1592. Poem and colophon dated 1622. *Cf.* Shên-chou ta-kuan, I. A.

Chung-kuo, II, 41. Landscape. Signed and dated 1597. Two inscriptions by the painter. Twenty-one poems by Ch'ien-lung. *Cf.* Chung-kuo ming-hua, 19. A.

Peking National Museum album, 1920. An album of ten Landscapes after Sung and Yüan masters, accompanied by writings dated 1598 and 1627.

H. C. Wêng, Scarsdale, N.Y. River-view: structural Cliffs and a few large Trees. Handscroll. Signed and dated 1599. A?

J. P. Dubosc, Lugano. River Landscape after Huang Kung-wang. Handscroll. Signed and dated 1601. Colophons by Ch'ên Chi-ju and Tung Ch'i-ch'ang.

Sōraikan, I, 35. Mountains in Summer before Rain, after Tung Yüan. Signed and dated 1603. School-work.

National Museum, Stockholm. View of creviced Mountains along a River, after Kuo Chung-shu. Handscroll. Two inscriptions by the painter, both signed and dated 1603.

Kokka, 703 (Tomioka collect., Kyōto). River Landscape. Signed and dated 1604. Colophon by Li Liu-fang.

J. P. Dubosc, Lugano. Album of six leaves representing Landscape Studies in fan-shape, in the manner of old masters. Signed. One of them dated 1604. Ink and colour.

Nanju 21. Landscape. Signed. Colophon, dated 1609. *Cf.* Tōyō, XI.

Shên-chou, XIV. River Landscape, after Huang Kung-wang. Signed and dated 1611.

Ibid. XVI. Mountains in Summer, after Tung Yüan. Colophon by the painter, dated 1611. Poem by Ch'ên Chi-ju. *Cf.* Nanga Taisei, IX, 170. B.

Sōgen 165. Spare Trees, after Li Ch'êng. Colophon by the painter, dated 1611. School-work.

H. C. Wêng, Scarsdale, N.Y. Mountain Ridge in Mist;

Plumy Trees. After Mi Fei. Short handscroll. Signed and dated 1611. Long colophon written in the following year, in which the painter states that it was painted after Mi's *Yün-shan t'u.*

Ibid. The Hermit's Abode by the Ching-hsi River. Many streams, trees and buildings. Ink-painting with dry brush. Handscroll. Signed and dated 1611. Colophon and poem by the painter, and also by Wu Chung. A.

Hamburg Exhibition, 1949–1950. Landscape after Mi Yu-jên. Album-leaf. Dated 1612.

K.-k. shu-hua chi, XXXVI. Landscape. Poems and colophons dated 1612 and 1625. A.

Ibid. XL. The Yü Mountain. Signed. Colophon dated 1613. School-work.

Mei-chan t'ê-k'an 28. River Landscape. Poem by Liu P'u copied by the painter, dated 1614.

Ōmura, I, 12. (Chêng Ch'i, Hongkong). Landscape after Yang Shêng, painted in colours on silk. Colophon dated 1615. *Cf.* Tōsō, p.356; Bijutsu Kenkyū, 180; P'ang Yüan-chi cat. 8; Chūgoku, III, etc.

Tōan, 30 (Saitō). Landscape. Poem dated 1616. *Cf.* Tōsō, p.359. B?

C. T. Loo's Successor, Frank Caro, N.Y. The Hsiao and Hsiang Rivers, after Mi Yu-jên. Handscroll. According to the painter's inscription, painted around 1616. *Cf.* Toronto Exhibit. cat. 34. A.

H. C. Wêng, Scarsdale, N.Y. The Ch'ing-pien Mountain. Sharply cut Rocks and Terraces with Trees rising over a Bay. Poem by the painter, dated 1617. A.

C. T. Loo's Successor, Frank Caro, N.Y. River Landscape, with a Row of foreground Trees and Houses on the further Bank. Signed and dated 1617. *Cf.* Chung-kuo ming-hua, 39. A.

P'ang Yüan-chi Illust. cat., II. River-view; topped Hill in the Distance, Pine-trees on rocky Hump. Inscription dated 1618.

I-shu ts'ung-pien, 7. River Landscape with Reeds along the Shore; Cliffs and Large Trees. After Yang Shêng. Dated 1620. *Cf.* Chung-kuo ming-hua, 38.

I shu ch'uan-t'ung, X, 4. Eight Autumn Scenes. Landscapes with Mountains, Pines and Cottages. Poems by the painter, one dated 1620. Also published in an album by Wên-ming Co., 1940.

F. Vannotti collect., Lugano. Album of eight leaves, landscape studies. Signed and dated 1621.

H. C. Wêng, Scarsdale, N.Y. Pine-trees and Pavilions in Autumn, in the manner of Ni Tsan. Ink on brownish paper. Poem by the painter, dated 1621.

Chang Ta-ch'ien cat., IV, 31. Landscape inspired by Wang Wei's poem. Inscription by the painter, dated 1621.

Hsü-ching chai. River-view after Ni Tsan. Two colophons by the painter, both dated 1623.

Ku-kung collect. (Nanking Exhib. cat. 188) Two leaves from an album of landscapes. Signed, one dated 1623.

Takashima collect., Kugenuma. River Landscape. Long inscription by the artist, dated 1623. *Cf.* Nanga Taisei Add. IV, 27; Pageant 665, Sōgen 163. A?

Chung-hua album, 1928. Ten Landscapes after Li Kung-lin, Yen Wên-Kuei, Ni Tsan, Wang Mêng, Li Ch'êng, Chao Ta-nien, Chao Mêng-fu. Dated 1621, 1623 and 1624. *Cf.* Nanga Taisei, IX, 172–180, 183. A.

Hui-hua kuan. A Mountain-view: *Hsi-shan mu-hsi.* Ink on paper. Signed and dated 1624.

Yu-chêng album. Ten Landscape Studies after Old Masters. Dated 1624.

W. Hochstadter, New York. A View of the Shang-lin Park. Dated 1624. *Cf.* P'ang Yüan-chi Illust. cat. IV.

Ibid. Steep pointed Rocks rising above a winding River; light Clouds and tall Pine-trees. Two inscriptions by the painter, one of them dated 1625. A.

Ho Kuan-wu collect., Hongkong. A River Landscape. Two inscriptions by the painter, one dated 1625.

T'ai-shan ts'an-shih lou ts'ang-hua, II. A small Pavilion among scattered Trees by a River. Dated 1626.

Chūgoku, III. A broad River-view; few Pine-trees on stony Ground. After Chu Hsi's poem which was copied by the painter, dated 1626.

Hui-hua kuan. Cliffs with Trees along a River. Painted for Chia Hsüan. Ink on paper. Dated 1626.

H. C. Wêng, Scarsdale, N.Y. Free copy of a portion of Huang Kung-wang's *Fu-ch'un shan-chü t'u.* Long colophon dated 1626. School-work.

Liu, 74. River Landscape, painted on a trip to Yü-shan. Signed and dated 1626. A?

Chung-kuo ming-hua, vol.21. A Sketchy View of sharp Cliffs and Trees along a Mountain-river. Inscriptions by the painter, dated 1626 and 1634. A.

Palace Museum scroll, 1935. White Clouds and red

Trees, after Chang Sêng-yu. Handscroll. Signed. Colophon dated 1628.
Nanking Exhib. cat. 189. Landscape with rocky Hills. Poem, signed and dated 1628.
K.-k. shu-hua chi, VI. A Straw-covered Hut on the Eastern Hill, after Ni Tsan. Signed. Poem and colophons, dated 1629. B.
Shina Nanga, II, 12. Landscape. Signed and dated 1631.
Tōan, 31 (Saitō). Leafless Trees, after Kao K'o-kung. Signed. Poem by the painter, dated 1631. Schoolwork.
K.-k. shu-hua chi, XII. Clouds over the Stream. Signed. Poem dated 1632. *Cf.* Nanga Taisei, IX, 181. B?
Commercial Press album. Ten Landscape Sketches. Colophons of later date, according to which the album was painted 1633.
S.c.t.k. hsü-pien, V. Landscape after Tung Yüan. Signed and dated 1634. B.
Chang Ta-ch'ien collect., Hongkong, 1951. River Landscape with steep Rocks, after Ni Tsan. Poem by the painter, dated 1634.
Shên-chou, IV. River Landscape with a Boat and Scattered Trees. Album-leaf. Signed.
Ibid. V. Mountain Peaks and Cottages, after Tung Yüan. Signed.
Ibid. VIII. Landscape after Tung Yüan. Signed. Colophon. *Cf.* Nanga Taisei, IX, 184. B.
Ibid. IX. River Landscape, after Tung Yüan. Signed. B.
Ibid. XIII. Mountains and Streams in Mist, after Tung Yüan. Signed. B?
Ibid. XXI. A Stream between craggy Mountains. A man approaching the homestead. Album-leaf. Signed. B?
Shên-chou ta-kuan, vol.7. Wooded Hills along a River; the Mist is rising. Inscription by the painter.
Chung-kuo, II, 38. Landscape. Illustration to a poem by Shên Chou. Signed. *Cf.* Chung-kuo ming-hua, 29.
Ibid. II, 39. Three Trees by a River. Signed. Poem. B?
Ibid. II, 40. Landscape. Signed. Two lines of poetry. *Cf.* Chung-kuo ming-hua, 1.
Ku-kung, XXIV. Peaks and Clouds. Signed. Poem.
Ibid. XXXI. Autumn Landscape. Signed. Poem. B?
K.-k. shu-hua chi, I. Pavilions for Study among Autumn Trees, after Ts'ao Chih-po. Signed. *Cf.* K.-k. chou-k'an 498. B?
Ibid. IV. Trees in Summer, after Tung Yüan. Signed. A very large picture. Colophon.
Ibid. XXI. A frosty Forest, illustrating a T'ang poem. Signed. B?
Ibid. XXIV. The Hills and Valleys of Shan-yin, after Ni Tsan. Signed. Colophons by the painter and by Ch'ên Chi-ju. A?
K.-k. ming-shan chi 3. Fans; Landscapes and Poems.
For others, see K.-k. chou-k'an 241, 247 and 259; also Nanga Taisei, VIII, 91–105.
Hui-hua kuan. Album of Landscape Studies after Old Masters. Ink only. Small size.
Gems, I, 43. A Village in the Mountains, after Tung Yüan. Signed. A.
Ibid. I, 44. A few Trees and distant Mountain, after Ni Tsan. Poem, signed.
Shu-hua ho-pi (Palace Museum album). Nine Sketches after Yüan and Sung masters, with accompanying text.
Tung Ch'i-ch'ang shih-hua t'ieh. An Album of ten Poems and ten Landscapes; two of them after old masters.
Commercial Press album, 1938. Landscape-studies in old styles. Inscriptions by the painter on separate leaves.
Sung-chiang p'ai ming-hua chi (Shên-chou album). Mountain Landscape with Cottages. Signed.
Hua-chung chiu-yu (Yu-chêng album). The Saddle Mountain. Signed. *Cf.* Nanga Taisei, I. B.
Nanking Exhib. cat. 184. Reading the *I-ching* by a Window near Pine-trees. Poem, signed. A.
Liu, 75. A Clump of Leafy Trees in front of a Mountain. Signed.
T'ien-hui ko album, 1929 (Wu Hu-fan collect.) Summer Mountains, after Tung Yüan. Handscroll, signed.
Ming-hua sou-ch'i, II, 1. Mountains in Mist, a quiet River in the foreground. Two lines of poetry by the painter. Signed. *Cf.* Nanju, I; Tōyō, XI; Nanga Taisei, IX, 186. Reproduction blurred.
Po-mei chi. Plum-blossoms. Signed.
I-yüan chên-shang, 6. River-landscape, after Chao Mêng-fu. Signed.
Chang Ts'ung-yü catalogue. Mountain Landscape, Plum-trees in the foreground. A.
Ibid. River-view with Rocks and Trees, in the manner of Ni Tsan. A.
Ibid. Two large album-leaves with Landscape Studies.
Shimbi, XVII. Bamboos and Rocks. Signed. Two lines of poetry. B?

Shina Nanga, I, 16. Landscape after Mi Yu-jên. Signed. Colophon.

Shina Meiga Senshū, 11 (Hashimoto collect.) Summer Mountains in Rain, after Chü-jan. Signed.

Shina Nanga Taikan 3. Two Cottages at the River-bank. Signed. Poem.

Sōraikan, II, 60. River Landscape. Illustration to Han Yü's essay *P'an-ku-hsü*, which is copied by the painter as a colophon to the picture. *Cf.* Tōsō, p.351. A?

Tōan 28. Landscape after Tung Yüan. Fan-painting. Signed.

Ibid. 29. Landscape after Chao Mêng-fu. Signed. B.

Hua-chung chiu-yu chi ts'ê (Hakubundō album, Ōsaka, 1921). Mountains by a River in Mist. After Tung Yüan. Signed.

Tōsō, p.355. Peaks enveloped in Clouds, after Mi Fei. Signed. Poem. School-work.

Ibid. p.357. Rainy Landscape. Signed. Poem and colophons by Ch'ên Chi-ju. B.

Ibid. p.358. Landscape. Long handscroll. Signed. Poems by the painter and by Ch'ên Chi-ju.

Ibid. p.360. Landscape after Ni Tsan. Signed.

Sōgen 164. Mountains and Trees, painted in blue and green, after Chang Sêng-yu. Signed. Poem by Ch'ên Chi-ju.

Ibid. 166. Misty River Landscape, after Mi Fei. Handscroll. Signed. Poem.

Suchiku 13. Houses at the Foot of a Mountain. Poem, signed.

Nanga Taisei, I, 80. A Tuft of Bamboo growing out from an overhanging Rock.

Ibid. VIII, 91–105. Landscape Studies after Old Masters. Fifteen fan-paintings. Signed.

Chang Ta-ch'ien cat. I, 28. Landscape. Signed. A.

Hung Yu-ling, Hongkong. Landscape Studies. Album-leaves. Signed.

Ogawa collect., Kyōto. Rain Clouds over Mountains in Spring, after Tung Yüan. Signed. Inscription by Tan Ch'ung-kuang. *Cf.* Sirén, *Later*, pl.117. School-work.

Boston Museum (39.35). A small album with twenty landscape sketches.

Tōkyō National Museum. An Imaginary Journey to the Five Peaks. Album of eight landscapes. *Cf.* Sekai Bijutsu Zenshū, vol.20, coloured pl.2. A.

H. C. Wêng, Scarsdale, N.Y. River-view in the manner of Ni Tsan. Large Rocks and scattered Trees. Ink on satin. Handscroll. Poem by the painter; eight colophons by Li Liu-fang and other contemporaries. A.

Ibid. Wooded Mountains and Hills rising from a Bay. Ink only on silk. Long colophon by Ch'ên Chi-ju (possibly attached later).

Ibid. Eight large album-leaves of Landscape Studies after old masters. Ink and colour on gold ground. Corresponding pages of calligraphy. A.

Ibid. Large album of eight leaves. All after Wu Chên. Important.

Ibid. Small album. Four Landscapes, and four leaves of calligraphy.

Hobart collect., Cambridge, Mass. River Landscape; Small Cottages under the Trees on the Rocks. Poem. Signed.

Hamburg Exhibition, 1949–1950. Large Mountain Landscape. Ink and touch of brown and green colours. *Cf.* Cleveland Exhibition cat. 69. A.

King Gustaf VI Adolf collect. Five double album-leaves with landscape sketches. According to the painter's inscriptions, in the manner of the following masters: 1. Huang Kung-wang, 2. Ching Hao and Kuan T'ung, 3. Chao Ta-nien, 4. Tung Pei-yüan and 5. Mei tao-jên. All signed by the painter. A.

B. Z. Seligman, London. Landscape in the manner of Chang Sêng-yu. Inscription by the painter.

Ibid. A small album of landscape-studies accompanied by inscriptions by the painter. Signed.

J. P. Dubosc, Lugano. Four leaves of an album of landscape studies accompanied by inscriptions by the painter. Ink and slight colours on gold ground.

TUNG HSIAO-CH'U 董孝初, *t.* Jên-ch'ang 仁常.

From Hua-t'ing, Kiangsu. Active at the end of the Ming period. Landscapes, followed the Yüan masters. N, VII, 16. O, 5. M, p.572.

Sung-chiang p'ai ming-hua chi (Shên-chou album). Temple in Mountains, after Tung Yüan. Signed.

Chūgoku, IV. Mountain Peaks by a Stream; a Man in a Pavilion under leafy Trees on the Bank. Album-leaf. Signed and dedicated to Fêng-wêng.

WAN KUO-CHÊN 萬國楨, *t.* Po-wên 伯文.
From Nan-hai, Kwangtung. Flourished *c.*1600–1620. Bamboos, flowers and birds. O, 6. M, p.564.

Shimbi, V. Seagulls. Signed.

Tōyō, X. A Seagull standing on a Cliff and Bamboos. Signed.

WANG CHAO 汪肇, *t.* Te-ch'u 德初, *h.* Hai-yün 海雲.
From Hsiu-ning, Anhui. Flourished *c.*1500. Landscapes and figures in the styles of Tai Chin and Wu Wei. N, II, 11. O, 3. M, p.135.

Shimbi, XVI. Pine-tree and Cranes. Signed.

Tōyō, X. Two Wild Geese and Rushes. Signed.

Tōsō, p.223. T'ao Yüan-ming enjoying Chrysanthemums. Signed.

Chūgoku, II. A Hermit seated on a Cliff below a Waterfall. The attribution to the Yüan priest known as Hai-yün, is probably misleading.

Yamaguchi collect., Ashiya. A Man in a Pavilion beside a Stream, among Groves of Bamboo. Handscroll. Signed. *Cf.* Nanga Taisei, XVI, 32, 33.

Ton Ying Co., New York. Rabbits by a Tree. Fan-painting. Signed. From P'ang Yüan-chi collect.

Princeton University (Du Bois-Morris collect.) Two Men seated by some Pine-trees on a Terrace. Signed: Hai-yün.

WANG CH'ÊN 王臣.
Unrecorded; probably early 16th century.

Hui-hua kuan. A slender Bamboo. Painted in outline. Poem by the painter. *Cf.* Nanga Taisei, I, 102.

WANG CH'I 王綦, *t.* Li-jo 履若.
From Suchou. Active *c.*1600–1637. Flowers and Landscapes. Grandson of Wang Chih-têng, the author of *Wu-chün tan-ch'ing chih*. O, 4.M, p.42.

Chūgoku, IV. Two Men in an open Pavilion under tall Trees and Pines. Wild geese flying above. Signed and dated 1600.

K.-k. shu-hua chi, V. Autumn Trees by a Bridge. Signed and dated 1606.

J. D. Ch'ên cat. I, 36. A River Landscape in Winter. Signed and dated 1616.

Ming-jên shu-hua, 26. A Garden of Cassia-trees in Mist. Signed and dated 1619.

Hui-hua kuan. Landscape Studies. Six album-leaves. Ink on paper. Signed and dated 1620.

K.-k. shu-hua chi, XVI. Chrysanthemums by a Garden Stone. Signed and dated 1626.

Ho Kuan-wu, Hongkong. Flower and Stone. Signed and dated 1637.

Ming-jên shu-hua, 25. The Trunk of a Pine-tree. Signed.

Po-mei chi. Plum-blossoms. Signed.

WANG CH'IAO 王翹, *t.* Shu-ch'u 叔楚 and Shih-yü 時羽, *h.* Hsiao-chu 小竹.
Native of Chia-ting. Painted flowers and plants, insects and fish. M, p.41.

Nanga Taisei, XV, 20, 21. Dragon-flies, Fish, a Crab, etc. Handscroll. Seals of the artist(?) See colophons (Add. V, 71) for further biographical data.

WANG CHIEN-CHANG 王建章, *t.* Chung-ch'u 仲初, *h.* Yen-t'ien 硯田.
Active *c.*1625–1650. Landscapes in the style of Tung Yüan; Buddhist figures after Li Kung-lin. M, p.43.

Princeton University (Du Bois-Morris collect.) Branches of an Old Plum-tree in Blossom. Signed and dated 1628.

Shoman, 26. Viewing the Waterfall on the Lu Mountain. Signed and dated 1630. *Cf.* Pageant 718.

Nanju 11. Arhats. Handscroll. Signed and dated 1631.

Tōsō, p.381. A Fairy Island. Signed and dated 1633.

Hakubundō album (with colophon by Lo Chên-yü, dated 1917). Twenty-four small Landscape Studies in the manner of Sung and Yüan masters. The last picture dated 1633.

Nanju 22 (Seikadō). Twisted Pine-trees and fantastic Rocks. Signed and dated 1635. Also in Tōyō, XI.

Ibid. 17. River Landscape with steep Cliffs and sparse Trees in the foreground. Signed and dated 1637. Also in Tōyō, XI; Nanga Taisei, IX, 221.

Kyūka, I (Seattle Museum). The Island of the Immortals on a Spring Morning. Handscroll. Signed and dated 1638.

Kokka, 746 (Harada, Ōsaka). Various Flowers. Handscroll, signed and dated 1638. *Cf.* Yonezawa, 21.

Ibid. 294. Playing Chess. Fan-painting, Signed and dated 1638.

Shoman 27. Fishermen's Pleasure. Fan-painting. Signed and dated 1640.

Kokka 294. Landscape. Fan-painting. Signed and dated 1641. Also in Shoman 28.

Shoman 29. The Seven Worthies of the Bamboo Grove. Fan-painting. Signed and dated 1641.

Ibid. 30. A Temple on a Mountain. Fan-painting. Signed and dated 1642.

Ibid. 31. Man in a Pavilion listening to a Waterfall. Fan-painting. Signed and dated 1649.

Kokka 291. Seventeen Horses, after Chao Mêng-fu. Signed. Colophon.

Ibid. 304 (Seikadō). The River and the Rising Sun. Signed. Also in Nanju 3; Tōsō, p.380.

Ibid. 351. Two Landscapes from an album. Signed.

Nanju 7. The Yü-hua Mountain. Signed. Also in Tōyō, XI.

Ibid. 12. Landscape after Rain. Poem. Seals of the painter.

Tōyō, XI. A Grove of Wu-t'ung-trees. Album-leaf. Signed. Poem.

Shoman 32. A Boat on the River in Spring. Colophon by Mei Ch'ing.

Sōraikan, II, 62. Hills rising through the Mist; Water falling down into the River. Poem by the painter. *Cf.* Kokka 552.

Sōken-an Kanshō, III, 34–39 (Matsumoto collect.) Twelve album-leaves representing Landscapes, with inscriptions by the painter.

K. Sumitomo collect., Ōiso. The Yen-t'ien Villa. Landscape in the manner of Chao Po-chü. Fan-painting, signed. For other fans by the artist, see Nanga Taisei, VIII, 119–128; also Add. IV, 173–182.

WANG CH'IEN 王謙, *t.* Mu-chih 牧之, *h.* Ping-hu Tao-jên 冰壺道人.
From Ch'ien-t'ang, Chekiang. Flourished *c.*1500. Keeper of the imperial ancestral temple. Plum blossoms. Invited by Chang Yu, Duke of Lung-p'ing (*c.*1500–1530), as his tutor in plum-blossom painting. N, I, 23. O, 7. M, p.38.

Chang Ta-ch'ien cat., vol.IV. Bamboo and Blossoming Plum-tree. Painted together with Tai Chin who did the bamboo. Inscription by the painter, dated 1439.

K.-k. shu-hua chi, XXVII. Plum-blossoms. Signed.

WANG CH'IEN 王乾, *t.* I-ch'ing 一清, *h.* Ts'ang-ch'un 藏春 and T'ien-fêng 天峯.
From Lin-hai, Chekiang. First half of the 16th century. Birds. N, VI, 20. O, 6. M, p.39.

Ku-kung, XX. Birds in Snow. Signed.

Nanju 4. Birds on a River-bank. Signed. Also in Tōyō, X.

Shina Kachō Gasatsu 11. Two long-tailed Birds under a Tree and Lotus Flowers in a Basket. Attributed.

WANG CHIH 王贄, *t.* Tzŭ-mei 子美.
Unrecorded. End of Ming Dynasty.

Nanking Exhib. cat. 209. Two Birds in a flowering Bush beside a Rock. Signed and dated 1624.

WANG CHUNG-LI 王中立, *t.* Chên-chih 振之.
From Suchou. Flourished *c.*1620. Flowers and birds. O, 6. M, p.42.

Chung-kuo ming-hua, XII. A Cat under a Mu-tan Tree. Signed and dated 1618.
K.-k. shu-hua chi, XLV. Swallow and Roses by a Rockery. Signed and dated 1622.
J. P. Dubosc, Lugano. Banana Plants and Leafy Trees by a Garden Stone on the Bank of a River. Signed and dated 1622. Ink and colour. Fan-painting.

WANG CHUNG-YÜ 王仲玉.
Active in the Hung-wu period (1368–1398). O, 8. M, p.37.

Hui-hua kuan. Portrait of T'ao Yüan-ming. Long inscription at the top of the picture.

WANG CH'UNG 王寵, *t.* Li-jên 履仁 or Li-chi 履吉, *h.* Ya-i shan-jên 雅宜山人.
From Suchou. B. 1494, d. 1533. Poet and calligraphist, pupil of Wên Chêng-ming. Landscapes. N, II, 23. I, 56, 13. M, p.39.

Liu, 70. A Deep Gorge between Pointed Rocks. Inscription by the painter.

WANG Ê 王諤, *t.* T'ing-chih 廷直.
From Fêng-hua, Chekiang. Court painter in the Hung-chih period (1488–1505); called by the emperor "Ma Yüan of our day". Appointed officer of the imperial guard in the Chêng-tê period (1506–1521). Landscapes and figures. N, VI, 7. O, 3. M, p.39.

K.-k. shu-hua chi, XI. Landscape. Signed.
Hui-hua kuan. Scholars travelling in the Snow looking for Plum-blossoms. Ink on silk. Signed.
Shimbi Shoin Shina Meigashū, II. An Angler in a Boat by a rocky Shore. Album-leaf.
Bijutsu, VII. Shore Landscape with Figures: Sakugen leaving for Home. Signed.
Tōyō, X (Marquis Maeda). Mountain Paths in Snow with Travellers. Signed. *Cf.* Tōsō, p.391.
University Museum, Philadelphia. Two Men seated on a Terrace Looking at a Waterfall. Signed.

WANG FU 王紱, *t.* Mêng-tuan 孟端, *h.* Yu-shih 友石, Chiu-lung shan-jên 九龍山人, Ch'ing-ch'êng shan-jên 青城山人, and other names.
From Wu-hsi, Kiangsu. B. 1362, d. 1416. Landscapes in the styles of Wang Mêng and Ni Tsan, also bamboos. L, 28, 3. N, I, 12. O, 7. M, p.37.

Ōmura, I, 2. Terraced Mountains with rich Growth of Trees. Signed and dated 1393. *Cf.* Chūgoku, IIA.
Nanking Exhib. cat. 90 (ex-P'ang Yüan-chi collect.) A Temple in the Mountains; pine-trees on a knoll in the foreground. Signed and dated 1396. A.
National Museum, Stockholm. A narrow Gorge. Inscription by Wang Ta (dated 1396) and by a man called Ao-sou. The same design, but executed on silk, in the collection of J. D. Ch'ên in Hongkong. Signed. *Cf.* Catalogue I, 25.
Yūrinkan, Kyōto. A Scholar viewing Plum-blossoms in the Snow. Large album-leaf. Signed and dated 1397.
Kokka 466. Landscape after Ni Tsan. Signed. Poem dated 1401. Poems by three contemporaries. *Cf.* N. Gashū 5; Ōmura, I, 4; Tōsō, p.234. A.
Li-tai, VI. A Fisherman's Boat on an Autumn River. Signed and dated 1403. Poems by later men. B?
Ku-kung collect. Three Young Bamboos. Ink on paper. Signed and dated 1403. *Cf.* Ku-kung ming-jên hua-chu chi, II. A.

K.-k. shu-hua chi, XVII. A Literary Meeting in a Mountain Pavilion. Signed and dated 1404. A.
Ibid. XX. A solitary Tree. Signed and dated 1404. A.
Sōraikan, II, 44. A broad River-view; Friends taking Farewell on the Bank. Painted for Mi Chai in 1404. Short handscroll. A.
C. T. Loo's Successor, Frank Caro, N.Y. (ex-Chang Ts'ung-yü collect.) A tall Wu-t'ung-tree and a low Straw-covered Pavilion. In the style of Ni Tsan. Long inscription by the painter dated 1408. A. *Cf.* I-yüan chên-shang 7; Nanga Taisei, IX, 102.
Sōgen 87. Thin Bamboos and a tall Tree. Signed. Poem dated 1409. *Cf.* Yūrintaikan, I.
Chūgoku, II. Spring Clouds over the T'ai Mountain. Long inscription by the painter, dated 1410. B.
Freer Gallery (53.7). Ten thousand Bamboos along the River in Autumn. Signed and dated 1410. Long handscroll. Eight colophons. A.
Ku-kung, VIII. A Farewell Meeting at Fêng-ch'êng. Signed. Poem by the painter, and twelve poems by the friends who were present at the meeting. A.
K.-k. shu-hua chi, X. Seated with a Friend in a Pavilion at the Foot of steep Mountains. Signed. A.
Ibid. XVIII. Reading in a Hut. Signed. Poems by two contemporaries. A.
Ibid. XXXI. The Cliff of Hidden Jade. Signed. Colophon. *Cf.* Nanga Taisei, XI, 21. A.
Ibid. XLII. Man Seated in a Bamboo Grove. Signed. Pien Wên-chin. A.
Ibid. XLII. Man seated by a Bamboo Grove. Signed.
Ibid. XLV. Man Seated in a Straw-covered Pavilion by a River. Signed. Poem by the painter. A.
Ku-kung collect. A Branch of Bamboo. Seal of the painter.
Hui-hua kuan. The Lu-ko Bridge. Wooded landscape in Moonlight. Large handscroll.
Ibid. Three Bamboos in Rain. Signed. A.
Ibid. River Landscape with Cliffs and Mountains. Long handscroll. Ink on paper. Part of the picture by Ch'ên Shu-chi.
Yen-kuang Co., Peking. A small Dwelling at the Foot of the Nine Dragon Mountains. Large album-leaf. Seal of the painter. *Cf.* Liu, 43; Pageant 462. A.
Shên-chou ta-kuan, vol.6. Bamboos growing in a Rockery. Five poems by contemporaries. C?
Mei-chan t'ê-k'an, 17. Four Men under Trees reciting Poems. Seal of the painter. Poems by three contemporaries.
Gems, I, 20. Branches of Bamboo. Signed.
Ōmura, II, 5. Old Tree and Bamboos. Poems by the painter and by several contemporaries. *Cf.* Chūgoku, II. A.
Tōan, 15. A solitary Pavilion. Album-leaf. Signed. *Cf.* Kokka 569. A.
Kokka 583 (S. Komura, Tōkyō). A Mountain Stream with towering Peaks in the background. Two long inscriptions, one by Wang Ta, the brother of the painter.
Kawai collect., Kyōto, 1954. Bamboos growing by a Rock. Ink only. Signed.
Chang Ta-ch'ien, Hongkong, 1951. River-bank with high pointed Cliffs. Signed. Two colophons, one by Ch'ien Chung-i. A.
Fogg Museum, Cambridge, Mass. Bamboo Spray. Album-leaf. Signed.
C. C. Wang, New York. River Valley with small Homestead on the stony Bank; Rocks in the background. Handscroll. A.
W. Hochstadter, New York. View along a broad River with Fishing-boats in the Bays; Rocky mountains on the further bank. Handscroll. A.

WANG HSIEN-CHOU 汪憲周.
Unrecorded. Possibly Ming period.

Shina Kachō Gasatsu, 23. A Cat Catching a Butterfly by a Rockery.

WANG HSIN-I 王心一, *t.* Ch'un-fu 純甫, *h.* Yüan-chu 元珠.
From Suchou. Chin-shih in 1613. Pupil of Ch'ên Huan. N, VII, 17. U, II, 1, 4. M, p.41.

Wu-mên p'ai ming-hua chi (Shên-chou album). River Landscape. Signed and dated 1643.

S.c.t.k. hsü-pien, VI. Landscape after Tung Yüan. Signed and dated 1648? *Cf.* Nanga Taisei, IX, 233.

WANG JÊN 王仁, *t.* Tê-jên 得仁.
Unrecorded. B. 1404, d. after 1465.

Shimbi, XVIII. River Landscape. Handscroll. Signed and dated 1465 (at 62).

WANG KU-HSIANG 王穀祥, *t.* Lu-chih 祿之, *h.* Yu-shih 酉室.
From Suchou. B. 1501, d. 1568. Chin-shih in 1529. Flowers and birds. N, III, 1. O, 6. M, p.40.

Sōgen 129. Flowers by a Rock. Fan-painting. Signed and dated 1528.
Ōmori (Kyōto), album pub., 1915. Album of Landscapes after Hsia Shên (son of Hsia Kuei). Signed and dated 1541. Colophon by Kao Shih-ch'i. *Cf.* Nanking Exhib. cat. 154 (Ku-kung collect.)
Chung-kuo, II, 58. Bamboos and Chrysanthemums. Signed and dated 1542.
L. Bataille, Paris. Two Men in a Pavilion in a Ravine. Album-leaf. Signed and dated 1549.
Vannotti collect., Lugano. View of a River with Mandarin-Ducks. Flowering Plants in the foreground. Signed and dated 1559. Fan-painting.
C. T. Loo's Successor, Frank Caro, N.Y. Narcissi, Handscroll. Signed and dated 1561. Poem written by Wên Chêng-ming. *Cf.* Toronto, 25.
K.-k. shu-hua chi, XXIX. Plum-tree and Narcissi. Signed.
K.-k. chou-k'an 56, 63, 66, 189, 217, 220, 284. Seven fan-paintings of various flowers.
Ku-kung collect. *Hai-t'ang* and Magnolia Flowers. Painted together with Lu Chih. Signed, and inscriptions by three friends of the painters.
Gems, I, 41. Chrysanthemums growing by a Rock. Poem, signed.
Tōsō, p.313. Bamboos and Sparrows. Poems by the painter, by Wên Chia, Wên P'êng and Chou T'ien-ch'iu.
Ton Ying Co., New York. Narcissus Plants. Fan-painting. Signed. From P'ang Yüan-chi collect.
Köln, Ostasiat. Museum. Hanging Branches of a Blossoming Peach-tree. Signed. Fan-painting. Köln Exhibition 1955, No.13.
J. P. Dubosc, Lugano. Three fan-paintings with flowers and bamboos. *Cf.* Venice Exhibition cat. No.822,823.

WANG LI 王履, *t.* An-tao 安道, *h.* Ch'i-wêng 奇翁 and Chi-sou 畸叟.
A native of K'un-shan in Kiangsu. B. 1332, active at the beginning of Ming. Landscapes, followed the Ma-Hsia school. Painted forty scenes of Hua-shan. Biog. in *Ming shih*; also O, 2. M, p.37.

Gems, III, 1. Four album-leaves: Landscapes of Hua-shan. Inscriptions by the artist. This album which consists of eleven (?) leaves was published by the Shên-chou kuo-kuang shê in 1929 under the misleading attribution to Fan K'uan.

WANG LI 王醴, *t.* San-ch'üan 三泉.
From Chia-hsing, Chekiang. Early 17th century. Flowers and birds, imitated Chou Chih-mien. M, p.43.

J. P. Dubosc, Lugano. A Large Flower on a Thin Stem Growing from the Water; a Small Bird hunting a Dragon-fly. Signed and dated 1634. Ink and colour. Fan-painting.
Sōgen 172. Flowers of the four Seasons. Part of a handscroll.

WANG LI-PÊN 王立本.

Native of Chia-shan (Ning-po). Born in the Yüan period; active later. Landscapes; flowers; figures after Liang K'ai. O, II, 6b. M, p.37.

Kawasaki cat. 28. A pair of large Flower Pictures: one representing two Pheasants and Peony Flowers; the other, two Doves and Peony Flowers. The first also in Kokka 314. A?

WANG SHANG-KUNG 王上宮.
From Suchou. Flourished *c.*1590. Figures. M, p.41.

Tōsō, p.352. Filial Sons and loyal Subjects, after a T'ang master. Long handscroll. Signed and dated 1593.

WANG SHIH-CH'ANG 王世昌, *h.* Li-shan 歷山.
Native of Shantung. 15th century (?) Landscapes and figures. N, 7. O, 3. M, p.40.

Freer Gallery (16.95). Mountain Landscapes; a scholar's abode by the river. Signed Shih-ch'ang; seal reading Li-shan. Formerly attributed to Hsü Shih-ch'ang of the Sung period.

WANG SHU-CHIN 王述縉, *h.* Shih-ch'üan 石泉 (?)
Unrecorded. Ming period.

Sōgen 196 (K. Takeuchi). River Landscape with two Boats. Signed.

WANG SSŬ-JÊN 王思任, *t.* Chi-chung 季重, *h.* Sui-tung 遂東.
From Shan-yin, Chekiang. Chin-shih in 1595. As a calligraphist and poet he was compared to Tung Ch'i-ch'ang and Ch'ên Chi-ju. Landscapes in the styles of Mi Fei and Ni Tsan. N, IV, 27. U, II, 1, 2. M, p.42.

Nanju 3 (Seikadō). River-landscape in Ni style. Poem dated 1629. *Cf.* Ming-hua sou-ch'i, II, 2; Tōyō, XI; Pageant 722.

WANG TO 王鐸, *t.* Chio-ssŭ 覺斯, *h.* Hsüeh-shan Tao-jên 雪山道人, Yün-yen man-shih 雲巖漫士 and other names.
From Mêng-chin, Honan. B. 1592, d. 1652. President of the Board of Rites. Calligrapher. Landscapes in the styles of Ching Hao and Kuan T'ung. Q, I, 21. U, I, 2, 3. M, p.44.

Yūrintaikan, II. Landscape with precipitous Rocks. Colophon by the painter, dated 1637.

J. P. Dubosc, Lugano. Studies of Garden Rocks, Trees and Plants in Bloom. Signed and dated 1647. Ink on paper. Handscroll.

Nanga Taisei, III, 24. A Blossoming Plum-tree growing from an overhanging Rock. Signed and dated 1649.

Sōgen 234. River Landscape. Fan-painting. Signed. Colophon by the painter, dated 1649.

Ibid. 233. Mountains in Snow, after Wang Wei. Fan-painting, executed 1649. Colophon dated 1650.

Tōsō, p.379. Landscape in Snow. Signed and dated 1650.

Sekai Bijutsu Zenshū, XX, pl.51. Orchids growing by Rocks. Handscroll. Signed and dated 1651.

Ernest Erickson, New York. Mountain Landscape. Signed. Colophon by the painter, dated 1651. *Cf.* Nanga Taisei, XIV, 80; Tōsō, p.378.

Ōmura, I, 9. Listening to the Stream. Large album-leaf. Signed and dated 1651. *Cf.* Nanga Taisei, XI, 87.

Shên-chou, IV. A Pavilion among scattered Trees, after Ni Tsan. Signed. Colophon.

Shên-chou ta-kuan, vol.3. Steep Hills along the River-bank. Poem by the painter; signed.

Kokka 496. Landscape. Seal of the painter.

Bijutsu, XXII. River Scene with a Boat pulled by Ropes. Signed.

Shina Nanga, II, 10. High Mountains in Mist. Signed. Poem.

Tōsō, p.377. River flowing through a Grove, after Tung Yüan. Signed.

Sōraikan, I, 48. Mountains in Mist. Accompanied by specimens of writing also by the painter.

Seikadō. Mountains rising through Layers of Mist; Buildings below in a Grove of leafy Trees. Splashy ink-painting. Signed.

Ogawa collect., Kyōto. Bamboo and Orchids. Hand-scroll, painted on silk. Signed.

Wang Wei-lieh 王維烈, *t.* Wu-ching 無競.

From Suchou. Active *c.*1590–1620. Pupil of Chou Chih-mien. Flowers and birds. O, 6. M, p.41.

Ton Ying Co., New York (ex-P'ang Yüan-chi). Willow-trees and white Birds. Fan-painting. Signed and dated 1614.

K.-k shu-hua chi, XVI. A Pair of Magpies. Signed.

K.-k. chou-k'an 14, 79. Two fan-paintings.

Hui-hua kuan. Cypress, Bamboo, Camellia and Narcissi. Colour on silk. Signed.

Kokka 330 (Iwasaki collect.) The three Friends of Winter: an Old Pine-tree, Bamboo and a Blossoming Plum-tree, growing by a Garden Stone. Signed.

Tōsō, p.300. Flowers and Birds. Handscroll.

Wang Wên 王問, *t.* Tzŭ-yü 子裕, *h.* Chung-shan 仲山.

From Wu-hsi, Kiangsu. B. 1497, d. 1576. Landscapes in the Yüan tradition. N, III, 4. O, 6. I, 57, 1. M, p.40.

Nanga Taisei, XI, 36, 37. Landscape with a Temple, Horses and a Riverside Pavilion. Short handscroll, signed and dated 1539.

K.-k. shu-hua chi, XXXVII. A tall Mountain and Stream. Poem. Signed and dated 1552.

Ku-kung collect. Two Men seated on the Ground; one of them is boiling tea-water, the other writing on a scroll. Inscription by the painter, dated 1558. *Cf.* Nanking Exhibition cat. 147.

Chicago Art Institute. A Man angling among the Reeds by a River. Handscroll. Signed and dated 1574.

Ku-kung, XV. The Painter's Home at the Red Pool Mountain. Poem. Signed.

Kokka 310 (Seikadō). Lake Shore and Mountains in Mist. Poem. Signed.

Shên-chou album, 1930. Album of landscapes and figures, painted on silk. Signed.

J. Cahill, Wash., D.C. The sixteen Arhats. Handscroll. Signed.

Wei Chih-huang 魏之璜, *t.* K'ao-shu 考叔.

From Nanking. B. 1568, d. after 1645. Poet, calligraphist. Landscapes, flowers; also pictures of Kuanyin. N, IV, 18. O, 5. P, I, 8. U, I, 2, 11. M, pp.712, 713.

Shina Nanga, II, 4. Landscape. Fan-painting. Signed and dated 1602.

W. Hochstadter, New York. Studies of Flowers. Part of a handscroll. Signed and dated 1604.

Musée Guimet, Paris. Landscape in Sung style. Fan-painting. Signed and dated 1611.

J. D. Ch'ên cat. II, 41. Landscape. Album-leaf; signed and dated 1628.

Kyūka, I. Cloudy Mountains. Signed. Poem dated 1645 (at 78).

Tōsō, p.350. Flowers of the Fifth Month.

WEI CHIH-K'O 魏之克, later on changed into Wei K'o 魏克, *t.* Shu-ho 叔和.
From Ho-pei, and moved to Nanking. Active *c.*1620. Younger brother of Wei Chih-huang. Poet. Landscapes, flowers; also pictures of Kuan-yin. N, IV, 18. O, 5. U. II, 1, 17. M, p.713.

Lilly collect., Indianapolis. The twenty-four Flowers of the four Seasons. Handscroll. Signed and dated 1604.
Toledo Art Museum. "Thousand Hills Rivalling in Beauty and ten Thousand Streams Competing in Speed." Handscroll. Colour on paper. Inscription by the painter, dated 1624. *Cf.* Cleveland Exhibition cat. 80.
R. Chait Gallery, New York. Views along the Grand Canal. Long handscroll. Signed and dated 1635.

WEI CHÜ-CHING 魏居敬.
Ming period. Landscapes. M, p.712.

J. P. Dubosc, Lugano. Literary Meeting in the Western Garden. Fan-painting. Ink and colour. Signed.

WÊN CHÊNG 文正, *t.* Ch'üan-shih 泉石.
Early Ming period. Cranes. M, p.17.

Shimbi, X (Kyōto Museum). Two pictures: A flying Crane; A Crane standing under the Moon. Signed. Also in Tōsō, pp.232, 233; Tōyō, X.

WÊN CHÊNG-MING 文徵明. Original name Pi 璧 and *t.* Chêng-ming. Later on he adopted Chêng-ming as his name and took the *tzŭ* Chêng-chung 徵仲 and the *hao* Hêng-shan 衡山.
From Suchou. B. 1470, d. 1559. Scholar, poet, calligraphist and painter. Followed Shên Chou and the Yüan masters. Landscapes and flowers. N, II, 16. O, 3. I, 56, 12. M, p.16.

Ku-kung collect. *Yü-yü ch'un-shu t'u*: Trees after Spring Rain. River landscape; pine-trees along a neatly cut river-bank. Pale greenish and reddish colours. Inscription by the painter, signed Wên Pi, and dated 1507. A.
Chung-kuo, II, 10. Misty Landscape. Poems by the painter, dated 1508. Inscriptions by Chu K'ai and Wu I. *Cf.* Ōmura, I, 11; Min Shitaika, 47; Tōsō, p.292; Sōraikan, II, 52.
Chung-kuo ming-hua, 18. Wooded Mountains, after Huang Kung-wang. Poems by the painter, dated 1508, and by Ch'ien-lung.
Gems, I, 29. A View of T'ien-p'ing shan. Four poems by the artist. Signed and dated 1508. *Cf.* early copy in the Musée Guimet (formerly in the Piacentini collect.)
Ikeda collect., Tōkyō. Two Figures beside a Bridge, at the Foot of a Waterfall. Long inscription by the artist, dated 1530, in which he states that the painting was executed twenty years earlier (*i.e.* in 1510).
Shên collect., Hongkong. A View of the Wu Mountains along a River and some Pavilions. Ink and slight colour, partly damaged by water. Signed and dated 1510.
Min Shitaika, 55. Chrysanthemums by a Stone. Signed. Poem by the painter, dated 1512. *Cf.* Sōraikan, I, 30.
Nelson Gallery, Kansas City. Storm over a Lake, illustrating two lines of a T'ang poem. Album-leaf. Inscription by the painter, dated 1516. This is the last section of the scroll which contains five pictures by Shên Chou. *Cf.* Cleveland Exhibition cat. 53a.
Hui-hua kuan. The Goddess of the Hsiang River with her Attendant. Dated 1517. Illustrating a passage from the Nine Songs by Ch'ü Yüan, which is copied by the painter. Colophons by Wên Chia and Wang Chih-têng. *Cf.* Sōgen 114; Chūgoku, III.
K-k. shu-hua chi, XXVII. A Man seated on a Terrace listening to a Waterfall; another Scholar approaching. Signed and dated 1519. *Cf.* Nanga Taisei, XI, 26. A.

Sōraikan, II, 54. Bamboos and Epidendrum among Rocks. Handscroll. Inscription by the painter, dated 1519.

Musée Guimet. A Gully in the Mountains; Two Men on the Road by the Torrent. Signed and dated 1520.

I-yüan chên-shang, 3. Two Men in a House among Leafy Trees. Long inscription by the painter, dated 1521.

K.-k. shu-hua chi, XLV. Pine Forest and Waterfall. Signed. According to the colophon by the painter the picture was begun in 1527 and finished in 1531.

J. D. Ch'ên, Hongkong. Epidendrum growing among Rocks. Handscroll. Poem by the artist, dated 1527.

Tōsō, p.295. View of the Wu-sung River. Poem by the painter, and by Wang Ku-hsiang, dated 1558, but indicating that the picture was executed in 1528.

Ibid. p.297. A Place of Pure Delight. Handscroll. Signed. Poem by the painter, dated 1528.

J. P. Dubosc, Lugano. Two Gentlemen Meeting in a Garden; Two Boys Preparing Tea. Signed and dated 1528. Fan-painting.

Hui-hua kuan. A Scholar's Garden with Straw-covered Pavilions among the leafy Trees; Visitors approaching. Slight colour and ink on silk. Short handscroll. Dated 1529. A.

Mrs. B. Z. Seligman, London. An Open Pavilion and Two Large Trees on a Ledge in the foreground; River-view and Mountains behind. Signed and dated 1529. Fan-painting.

Gems, I, 30. Landscape with old Trees, in the manner of Ni Tsan. Signed and dated 1530.

K.-k. shu-hua chi, XXXVII. Drinking Tea. Signed. Poem by the painter, dated 1531.

Ku-kung collect. Five Men in a Pine-wood; high mountains beyond. Slightly coloured. Signed and dated 1531.

Sōgen 115. Leafless Trees and Bamboos by a Rock. Signed. Poem by the painter, dated 1531 (in the sixth month).

Ibid. 121. Trees and Stones by a Stream. Signed. Poem by the painter, dated 1531 (in the sixth month).

Los Angeles County Museum. Landscape with a Waterfall. Two Men standing and talking on the Shore in the foreground. Colophon by the painter, dated 1531. *Cf.* Cleveland Exhibition cat. 54.

Vannotti collect., Lugano. A Farewell Visit. The Men are Seated under Old Trees. Signed and dated 1531.

Ku-kung collect. Snow over the Mountains along a River. Painted in subdued colours according to Wang Wei's style. Long handscroll. Long inscription by the painter, according to which it was started in 1528 and finished in 1532.

Tōsō, p.298. Peony. Signed. Poem by the painter, dated 1532.

Honolulu Academy of Arts. Seven Juniper Trees, after Chao Mêng-fu. Long handscroll. Signed and dated 1532. Long colophon by Ch'ên Shun (Tao-fu), dated 1538. *Cf.* Cleveland Exhibition cat. 55. A.

P'ang Yüan-chi Illust. cat. V. A Garden in the Moonlight. Long poem by the painter, dated 1532.

Vannotti collect., Lugano. Two Men on a Ledge watching a Waterfall. Fan-painting, signed and dated 1532.

J. P. Dubosc, Lugano. The Eighteen Sages on Lu-shan, after Li Lung-mien. Fan-painting. Signed and dated 1532.

Chang Pi-han, Hongkong. Travellers in the Snow. Handscroll. Seals of the artist; inscription by him mounted after the painting, dated 1532.

K.-k. chou-k'an 507–510. Album of eight Bird and Flower Paintings. Inscription by the artist on the ninth leaf, dated 1533.

Chung-hua album (1929). The Cho-chêng Garden in Suchou. Thirty-one garden views with poems and a long colophon by the painter. Signed and dated 1533. Also including some copies and inscriptions by later men.

National Museum, Stockholm. A slender Bamboo and two bare Trees growing by a Garden Rock. Poem by the painter, dated 1533, 4th month.

Chung-hua wên-wu chi-ch'êng, vol.IV, 387. Chung Kuei in a cold Forest. Signed and dated 1534. *Cf.* K.-k. chou-k'an 509.

Takashima collect., Kugenuma (formerly Lo Chên-yü). Landscape. Handscroll, signed and dated 1534.

Liu, 53. A Recluse seated in his Mountain Retreat. Long inscription by the artist, dated 1534.

Ōmura, II, 2. Two Pavilions for Study; four Men in one of the Pavilions. Poem. Colophon. Painted probably in 1528, but poem copied 1534. *Cf.* Shina Nanga Taikan 9; Chūgoku, II.

Tōsō, p.289. Looking at a Waterfall. Signed and dated 1534.

Ibid. 293. Talking of the Past in Candle-light. Signed. Poem, dated 1534.

K.-k. shu-hua chi, XIII. Red Bamboos. Illustration to a poem by Kao Ch'i, Signed and dated 1534.

Ibid. XV. Tall Mountain Landscape after Wang Mêng. Signed and dated 1535.

Li-tai, VI. Two Men Seated under Pine-trees by a Mountain River. Signed and dated 1535.

Hsü-ching chai. Two Men drinking Tea under leafless Trees on the Mid-autumn Night. Three poems by the painter, dated 1535.

J. P. Dubosc, Lugano. The Twin Cedars. Short handscroll. Poem by the painter dated 1535.

Freer Gallery (39,51). Mist over the River. Water cascades over the Rocks, large leafy Trees, and Scholars in pavilions built on poles over the Water. Handscroll. Signed and dated 1536.

J. P. Dubosc, Lugano. Four Fishermen in Small Boats and Broad Waters divided by low wooded Promontories. Signed and dated 1536. Fan-painting.

Liu, 54, 55. Illustration to Su Tung-p'o's *fu*-poem The Red Cliff. Dated 1537.

Palace Museum album, 1936. Ten Studies of Bamboos and Stones. Colophon by the painter, dated 1538. Poems by Kao Shih-ch'i on another leaf.

Kawai collect., Kyōto, (1954). Landscape in Sung style. Slightly coloured. Signed and dated 1538.

Yen-kuang Co., Peking. Two Men seated in Conversation in a Garden Pavilion under tall Trees. Poems by the painter, dated at 70 (1539), and by Ch'ien-lung.

Ku-kung collect. Spare Trees and Shallow Water, in the manner of Ni Tsan. Short handscroll. Signed and dated 1540. Seventeen poems were copied by the painter.

N. P. Wang, Hongkong. View along a Mountain Stream bordered by Trees, Rocks, small Homesteads and Pavilions. Boats and Bridges. Long handscroll. Long inscription by the painter, dated 1540, and six colophons by later men.

T. T. Ma, Hongkong. View of the Chün-shan Island in the Tung-t'ing Lake. Poetic inscription by the painter dated 1540. Colophon by Wang Ku-hsiang who accompanied the painter to this place.

British Museum. Views along a River Valley with two small Homesteads on the Borders. Mountains and leafy trees. Long handscroll. Signed and dated 1540. According to the inscription, this was painted by Wên Chêng-ming after a picture by Shên Chou who had made his picture after a painting by Wu Chên. Colophons by Ch'êng Chêng-k'uei and Ko Chêng-ch'i.

Sōgen 118. Landscape after Wang Mêng. Signed and dated 1541 (in the autumn).

Freer Gallery. Chrysanthemums and Pine-trees. Signed and dated 1541. Short handscroll. Colophon by the painter consisting of a copy of the poem *Kuei-ch'ü-lai*. *Cf.* P'ang Yüan-chi cat. Add. 2.

K.-k. shu-hua chi, XXXVI. Luxuriant Pines by a clear Stream. A *Ch'in* Player seated on the Ground. Signed and dated 1542. *Cf.* K.-k. chou-kan, vol.I.

Yamaguchi collect., Ashiya. Album of four paintings of Bamboo and Epidendrum; *fu* poem written by the artist, dated 1542.

J. P. Dubosc, Lugano. The Fisherman at the Entrance to the Peach Blossom Valley. Painted in green and blue. The legend, written by the artist, is dated 1542. Fan-painting.

K.-k. chou-k'an 480. The Mountains West of Lake Tung-t'ing. Signed and dated 1543.

J. P. Dubosc. A Lake Scene with small Islands and Sailing Boats. Fan-painting, signed and dated 1543. Venice Exhib. cat. 804.

Ku-kung collect. *Sung-yin hsieh-chang t'u*: Two Men walking through a Pine-grove. Signed and dated 1544. A.

Tōsō, p.294. T'ao Yüan-ming's Garden. Signed and dated 1544.

Ibid. 291. Listening to the Autumn Rain. Signed. Poem, dated 1544.

Chūgoku, III. A Man seated in an open Pavilion on the Shore of Shih-hu (Stone Lake); high Mountain Peaks rising beyond. Long inscription by the painter, dated 1544.

Ku-kung, XXXVII. A Poet in the still Forest. Signed and dated 1545.

Tōsō, p.285. A Man lying in a Boat listening to the Rain. Signed. Colophon, dated 1545.

Kokka 516. Landscape after Wang Mêng's "Mountain Dwellers". Signed and dated 1545. *Cf.* Ōmura, I, 10; Min Shitaika, 48.

Ibid. 464. Landscape. Signed and dated 1545.

Sōgen 119. Landscape. Illustration to a poem by T'ang Tzŭ-hsi. Colophon, dated 1545(?)

Ku-kung collect. A View of the Imperial Summer Palace Garden Hsi-yüan. Colour on silk. Signed and dated 1546.

Min Shitaika, 49 (Ueno collect.) Two Men in a Pavilion, the Third on a Bridge. Signed. Poem by the painter, dated 1546. Another version in the Nagatani collect. dated 1534. *Cf.* also K.-k. shu-hua chi, XXXVII, dated 1531.

K.-k. shu-hua chi, IV. Spring in Chiang-nan. Signed. Poem, dated 1547.

Ibid. XXXIX. The Tung-t'ing Island in T'ai-hu. Signed. Poem and colophon, dated 1548.

Ibid. II. Waterfall and old Trees. Signed and dated 1549. *Cf.* Nanga Taisei, IX, 143.

Gems, II, 12. The Chên-shang Studio. Handscroll. Signed and dated 1549. A.

Sōgen 120. Landscape in Rain. Signed and dated 1549 (in the 10th month).

Nanga Taisei, XIV, 51. A Man seated in a Lakeside House; a Visitor approaching on a Bridge. Signed and dated 1549.

Yamaguchi collect., Ashiya. Old Junipers Growing among Rocks by a Waterfall. Signed and dated 1549. A.

Chang Ta-ch'ien cat. I, 23. Portrait of Confucius. Long inscription written by the painter mounted above, signed and dated 1550, "at the age of 81". A.

Ni Tsan, Wên Pi, Shên Chou and T'ang Yin (National Museum album, Peking). A Man Seated by a Mountain Stream in Autumn. Signed and dated 1550.

Nelson Gallery, Kansas City. An Old Juniper bending over a Garden Rock. Short handscroll. Poem by the painter and several colophons by his friends, one of them written in 1550. A.

Min Shitaika, 50. Old Trees and cold Springs. Signed and dated 1551. *Cf.* Sirén, *Later*, pl.78. A.

Tōan 24. Eight Garden Scenes. Album-leaves. Signed. Poem by the painter, dated 1551.

Gems, II, 11. A thatched Pavilion by the T'iao River. Handscroll. Signed and dated 1551.

Musée Guimet. A Magnolia-tree by a Rockery. Signed. Poem by the painter, dated 1551.

Freer Gallery (39.1). Illustration to Su Tung-p'o's *The Red Cliff*, which is copied by the painter. Dated 1552. Handscroll. *Cf.* P'ang Yüan-chi cat. 3.

Suchiku 7 (former Oguri collect.) Bamboo and an Old Tree growing by a Rock. Signed and dated 1552.

J. P. Dubosc, Lugano. Four Men Paddling in a Boat across the River. The artist has copied Su Shih's *fu*-poem *The Red Cliff*. Dated 1552. Ink and colour. Fan-painting.

Shên-chou, VIII. A Man with a Boy seated in a Ravine. Signed and dated 1553.

Musée Guimet. High Mountains, winding Streams, Buildings in the Groves. Short handscroll. Signed and dated 1553.

Commercial Press album, 1925. Landscape. Handscroll. Long inscription by the painter, dated 1554.

Ming-jên shu-hua, 8. Chung K'uei among leafless Trees. Signed and dated 1554.

Ku-kung collect. *Lin-ch'üan ya-shih t'u*. River and rocks. Ink and colour on silk. Poem by the painter, dated 1554.

Sōgen 116. The Verdant Peaks of the Lung-ch'ih Mountain. Signed. Colophon by the painter, dated 1554 (at 85).

Ibid. 122. A Solitary Boat on a Snow-covered River. From an album of landscapes in blue and green, painted in the *kung-pi* style. Signed and dated 1554 (in the 3rd month).

Ernest Erickson, New York. A Solitary Wanderer in the late Autumn Woods. Leafless Trees along a winding Brook; Blackbirds soaring above. Signed and dated 1554 (on a winter day). Inscription on the margin by Ts'ai Chih-ting. A.

K.-k. shu-hua chi, XVI. Red Bamboos. Illustration to a poem by Kao Ch'i. Signed and dated 1555.

Shanghai Museum (Gems, I, 28). A Mountain River between large Pine-trees in Snow. Ink and light colour. Signed and dated 1555 (at 86).

Ku-kung collect. *Ch'i-shan kao-i t'u*: Famous Scholars in a Pavilion by a River. Short handscroll. Long colophon by the painter dated 1555.

Ernest Erickson, New York. An old Juniper by a Mountain Brook; two Men in Conversation listening to the Water Cascade, while a Boy is approaching with a *Ch'in*. Signed and dated 1556 (in the fifth month).

Yen-kuang Co., Peking. Rain and Mist over the River, a Man reading in the Pavilion. Signed and dated 1556. *Cf.* Nanga Taisei, XIV, 52. *Cf.* Chung-kuo ming-hua, vol.38.

J. D. Ch'ên, Hongkong. Happy Land of Chiang-nan. Handscroll. Signed and dated 1556. Several poems copied by the painter as colophons.

Ku-kung collect. (Nanking Exhib. cat. 125). The Garden of Solitary Pleasure. Handscroll. Signed and dated 1558. Poem by Ch'ien-lung. A.

Shên-chou, XIV. High Peaks and winding Streams after Rain. Signed. Poem by the painter, dated 1558.

Tōsō. p.287. Landscape. Signed and dated 1558.

Chūgoku, III. Tower-like Mountain rising through Mist; an open Pavilion by a winding Stream at its Foot. Poem by the painter, dated 1558.

Sōgen 117. Spring in Chiang-nan, after Ni Tsan. Signed. Poems by the painter and by Ni Tsan, copied by Wên Chia (dated 1558) and Wên P'êng. A.

Fei-tun lu hua-hui. Moonlit Night and Wu-t'ung-trees. Handscroll. Signed. Poem dated 10th day of the 10th month (no year).

Shên-chou, V. Two Men standing on a Bridge among high Peaks and tall Pines. Poem by the painter.

Ibid. X. A Man and a Boy with a *Ch'in* in the Deep Valley. Signed. Poem.

Shên-chou ta-kuan, vol.8. A small River winding between the tall Trees at the Foot of high Mountains. Poems by the painter, by his three pupils and by Ch'ien-lung. *Cf.* P'ang Yüan-chi cat. 8.

Chung-kuo, II, 6. A solitary Donkey-rider in Snow. Signed. Poem.

Ibid. II, 7. Crossing a Stream. Signed. Poem.

Ibid. II, 8. Plum-blossoms and Bamboos. Signed.

Chung-kuo ming-hua, 17. A Scholar in a Pavilion built over a Mountain Stream under leafy Trees at the Foot of a Precipice. Poem by the painter.

Ibid. 14. Three Men Seated on the Bank of a River; others standing near them. Short handscroll. Signed.

Ibid. 21. Village in Snow, some Men approaching a Homestead. Short handscroll. Seals of the painter.

Ibid. 19. Landscape; a man walking with a staff. Signed.

Ibid. 22. A Tall Landscape with Pines, Firs and Other Trees. Poem by the painter.

Ibid. 25. A Man in a Boat; a Lady in a House on the Shore. Poem by the painter.

Ming-jên shu-hua, 1. Man seated in a Pavilion among Bamboos and Pines. Signed. Poem.

Ku-kung, II. Three Friends under Pine-trees. Signed. Poem.

Ibid. III. Snow Landscape. A Man on a Donkey passing over a Bridge. Signed. Poem.

Ibid. VIII. Landscape. An ink-play after Wu Chên. Signed.

Ibid. XXXVI. Spring Clouds over a Valley. Signed. Poem.

Ibid. XLII. Cloudy Mountains. Fan-painting. Signed.

K.-k. shu-hua chi, XI. Epidendrum and Bamboos. Signed. Poem.

Ibid. XXIII. Two Men Talking in a Pavilion by the Stream. Signed. Poem.

Ibid. XXIX. The Study in the Green Shade. Signed. Poem.

Ibid. XLI. Listening to the Sounds of the Pine-trees. Signed. Poem. A.

K.-k. chou-k'an, vol.II, 37. Bamboos and Tufts of Epidendrum. Poems by the painter and by Ts'ai Yü and Ch'ien-lung. *Cf.* Ming-hua lin-lang. A.

Ibid. 501. Two Men in a House conversing; outside is a Crane and a Boy bringing a *Ch'in*. Poem, signed.

Ibid. 504. Landscape after Rain; a Man seated by a Stream, listening to the Water. Poem, signed.

Ku-kung collect. *I-ch'uan t'u*. A Summer Resort near Suchou. Short handscroll. Colophons by Wang Ku-hsiang and Fêng Tao-shêng. A.

Ibid. Bamboo, a Dry Tree and a Stone. A small ink-painting. Poem by the painter.

Ibid. Tufts of *Lan-hua* and Bamboo. Ink painting on silk. Part of a large album called *Ming-hua lin-lang*. Inscription by Ts'ai Yü. A.

K.-k. ming-shan chi 5. Two Landscapes. Fan-paintings. *Cf.* also K.-k. chou-k'an, Index, for twenty fan-paintings; also Nanga Taisei, VIII, 52–62.

Pao-yün, I and II. Two Landscapes, from an album of twelve leaves. Seals of the painter. Colophons by contemporaries on the opposite leaves.

Hui-hua kuan. A Brook winding between Trees at the Foot of a high Mountain. Ink on paper. Inscription by the painter and by three of his friends.

Ibid. A Wanderer is standing on a Bridge looking at the Mountain Scenery. Large leafy trees. Ink on paper. Poem by the painter.

Ibid. Cloudy Mountain Range along a River, after Mi Yu-jên. Large handscroll. Ink only.

Mo-ch'ao pi-chi, II. River Landscape with Pavilions on the Bank. Signed. Poem.

Wên-ming album, 1930. Five Views of Suchou. Album-leaves. Poems by the painter after each painting.

Fu-lu. Chrysanthemums by a Rockery. Poem by the painter.

Shanghai Museum. Distant Mountains and a Rocky Hump. Pine-trees and Pavilions built over the Water; Bridges and Islands. Colours on paper, in a style reminiscent of Shên Chou. Handscroll. A long colophon by T'ang Yin. A.

Gems, III, 3. An album of ten leaves: Landscapes, Trees, Bamboo, etc. Seals of the artist.

P'ang Yüan-chi Illust. cat. I. Landscape. Poems by the painter and by Ch'ien-lung.

Chang Ts'ung-yü catalogue. Two Scholars meeting in a Mountain Valley.

Ibid. Leafy Trees and Bamboo Sprouts at a low River-bank.

Liu 52. Two Men seated beside a Stream. Poems by the painter and by Ch'ien-lung.

Nanking Exhib. cat. 126 (Ku-kung collect.) A Broad-leafed Plant Growing from a Rock. Album-leaf. Inscription, seals of the artist.

Ibid. 128. Discussing Tea. Long inscription. Signed.

Ibid. 129. Trees and Rocks by a River. Poem, signed.

Kokka 254. A Spray of Bamboo. Signed.

Nanju 8. Landscape. Fan-painting. Signed.

Tōyō, XI. A small Bamboo Garden on a Promontory. Fan-painting. Signed.

Shina Nanga, II, 9. Rain over a Bamboo Grove. Signed. Poem.

Ōmura, I, 4. T'ai-hu (The Great Lake). Signed. *Cf.* Min Shitaika, 56.

Ibid. I, 8. Leafless Trees, Bamboos and Stones. Signed. Poem. *Cf.* Sōraikan, I, 31.

Shina Meiga Senshū, 7. Pavilions Built over a Stream, Trees on the Shore, a Hill Range in the background. Fan-painting. Signed.

Min Shitaika, 51. Straw-covered Pavilions by a River. Signed. Poem. *Cf.* Tōan 25; Tōsō, p.286.

Ibid. 52 (Nelson Gallery, Kansas City). Old Cedars by a Stream and Crows. Seal of the painter. A.

Ibid. 53. A Pavilion at the Foot of Steep Cliffs by the Shore after Rain. Poems by the painter and by Wang Ku-hsiang.

Ibid. 54. A Sleeping Cat. Signed. Poem.

Ibid. 57. Landscape. Fan-painting. Signed.

Ibid. 58. Orchids by a Stone. Fan-painting. Signed.

Tōan 23. Landscape. Signed. Poem.

Tōsō, p.288. Traveller on the River returning Home. Poems by P'êng Nien, Lu Shih-tao, Wang Ku-hsiang and the painter.

Ibid. p.290. Landscape after Wu Chên. Signed.

Ibid. p.296. Landscape. Signed. Poem.

Sōgen 113. Landscape. Part of a handscroll.

Ibid. 123. Bamboos and Epidendrum. Short handscroll. Seal of the painter.

Kokka 736 (Kawai collect., Kyōto). Landscape handscroll: the Wang-ch'uan Villa, after Wang Wei, Inscription by the painter. *Cf.* Sekai Bijutsu Zenshū. XX, pl.19.

Nanga Taisei, I, 37, 38. Four Studies of Bamboo and Epidendrum, with poetic inscriptions by the painter.

Ibid. I, 39–42. Four fan-paintings of Bamboos and Epidendrums. Signed. Three similar paintings with birds in Nanga Taisei, VI, 74, 75. Signed.

Kawai collect., Kyōto, 1954. Two Men Drinking Tea in a Pavilion. Signed.

Suchiku 8 (former Oguri collect.) Bamboo and Orchids. Poem, signed.

Ogawa collect., Kyōto. A Branch of Blossoming Plum, and a Spray of Bamboo. Poem by the artist, signed.

Lo Chia-lun, Taipei. *Yün-shan yen-shên t'u.* River Landscape in Mi Fei's style. Short handscroll. Colophons by the painter and Wang Ku-hsiang.

N. P. Wang, Hongkong (ex-Ti P'ing-tzŭ collect.) River View with a Boat, two-storey Pavilion and tall Pine-trees. Poem by the painter. *Cf.* Chung-kuo, II, 9.

Ibid. A High Pavilion under tall Trees on the Shore, overlooking the Water where a Boat is moving. Inscription by the painter.

Ho Kuan-wu, Hongkong. Landscape. Signed.

Hung Yu-ling, Hongkong. Riders in Snow. Signed.

Kao Yen-ju, Hongkong. Landscape.

J. D. Ch'ên cat. I, 33. Washing the Feet in a Mountain Stream. Poem by the painter.

Ibid. II, 26. Orchids. Handscroll. Signed.

Ibid. II, 27. Landscape in Chiang-nan. Handscroll. Signed.

Boston Museum. Small Homesteads on the Bank of a Mountain River. Poem by the painter.

Metropolitan Museum. River Scenery in Rain. Fan-painting. Poem by the painter.

Chicago Art Institute. Autumn Landscape in the style of Ni Tsan. Handscroll. Signed. *Cf.* Venice Exhibition cat. 808.

Princeton University (Du Bois-Morris collect.) River Landscape; two Men walking over a Bridge. Album-leaf. Signed.

Musée Guimet. A Mountain Stream between steep Banks; large Trees in the foreground. Signed.

Ibid. Epidendrum and Stones. Poem by the painter.

Hamburg Exhibition, 1949–1950. Green Mountains by a Cold Stream.

Ibid. Epidendrum. Album-leaf.

National Museum, Stockholm. Illustration to Su Tung-p'o's *The Red Cliff*. Handscroll. Same motif has been represented with some variations in two other pictures by the painter. The *fu*-poem is copied by Wên P'êng.

Ibid. River Landscape. Short handscroll. Signed.

C. T. Loo's Successor, Frank Caro, New York. Plum-blossoms and Bamboo. Short handscroll. According to the painter's inscription, painted for Yu-mei. Long colophon by the painter. *Cf.* Toronto, 23.

H. C. Wêng, Scarsdale, N.Y. The Red Cliff. Short handscroll. Signed. The composition is different from that of the picture with the same motif in the Freer Gallery.

C. C. Wang, New York. Two Scholars drinking Tea under the Pine-trees. Poetic inscription by the painter.

Lilly collect., Indianapolis. A Winter Landscape, with rocky Crags and a Temple among bare Trees. Seal of the artist. B.

Chêng Tê-k'un, Cambridge. Narcissus, Pine and Rock. Poem by the painter. Seals of Liang Ch'ing-piao and Ch'ien-lung.

Dr. J. Lucan, Paris. Snow Landscape. A poem by the painter above the picture.

J. P. Dubosc, Lugano. Discourse in the Green Shade. Poem by the painter.

Ibid. Pine-tree and a Rock. Poem by Wên Chia.

Ibid. A Scholar Seated in the Porch of his House under High Trees; a servant is occupied in the room behind. Short handscroll. Painted for Tzŭ-ch'ung. Signed.

Ibid. A Branch of an Old Juniper-tree. A short handscroll. Signed. Venice Exhibition cat., 811.

Ibid. Album of twelve leaves. Landscape Studies, partly in the blue and green manner, and partly in ink; on gold sprinkled paper. Each leaf accompanied by an inscription.

Ibid. Twelve fan-paintings representing landscapes, garden-views, bamboos, blossoming trees and flowering plants. All signed but not dated.

WÊN CHIA 文嘉, *t.* Hsiu-ch'êng 休承, *h.* Wên-shui 文水.

B. 1501, d. 1583. Second son of Wên Chêng-ming. Landscapes in the style of his father, influenced by Ni Tsan and Wang Mêng. N, II, 18. O, 3. M, p.17.

C. T. Loo's Successor, Frank Caro, N.Y. Chung-k'uei in a wintry Forest. Long inscription by the artist, signed and dated 1548.

Kokka 759. Landscape after a Tu Fu poem. Signed and dated 1548.

Ming-jên shu-hua, 23. Cloudy Peaks and Cottages by a River. Signed. Poem dated 1558.

Musée Guimet. A Lakeside Pavilion; Willow-trees. Fan-painting. Signed and dated 1558. Venice Exhib. cat. 227.

Mei-chan t'ê-k'an, 27. River-view with Large Pine-trees in the foreground. Poem by the painter, dated 1559.

Hamburg Exhibition, 1949–1950. Landscape. Signed and dated 1561.

Pao-yün, II. Two Men Seated on the Bank of a River. Signed and dated 1562.

Köln, Ostasiat. Museum. A River with Rocky Islands. Signed and dated 1562. Fan-painting. Köln Exhibition 1955, No.10.

Bijutsu, XXII. River Landscape in Spring. Signed and dated 1563.

Po-mei chi. A Blossoming Plum-tree. Album-leaf. Signed and dated 1563.

Vannotti collect., Lugano. A River-view with Sailing Boat. Fan-painting. Signed and dated 1564.

Gems, II, 16. Long Days in the quiet Mountains. Handscroll. Poem, signed and dated 1567.

Kokka 442. Landscape, illustrating Po Chü-i's poem *The P'i-p'a Song*, which is copied by the painter on the picture. Signed and dated 1569. *Cf.* N. Gashū, 10; Sōraikan, II, 57.

Takashima collect., Kugenuma. Five Landscape-paintings, depicting Holy Places of Taoism. Signed; two dated 1573. Mounted in a scroll with paintings of related subjects by Ch'ien Ku and Hou Mou-kung.

Hui-hua kuan. Pavilion and Bridge at the Foot of a Mountain. Winding Steps leading up through the Gully towards the Clouds. Ink on paper. Signed and dated 1574.

K.-k. shu-hua chi, XXXI. Landscape. Large album-leaf. Signed. Two lines of poetry, dated 1576.

Yen-kuang Co., Peking. Waterfall and strange Peaks rising through the Mist. Poem by the painter, dated 1576. Also poem by Ch'ien-lung. *Cf.* Chung-kuo ming-hua, 39.

Nanking Exhib. cat. 155. River Landscape. Signed and dated 1578. Painted for Hsiang Yüan-pien, who has added a long colophon.

Tōsō, p.299. Landscape. Signed. Colophon dated 1578.

K.-k. shu-hua chi, XII. Listening to the Waterfall. Signed. Poem dated 1579.

Ming-jên shu-hua, 6. River View with Snow-covered Shores. Signed and dated 1579.

S.c.t.k. hsü-pien, II. A Branch of Plum-tree. Poem by the painter, dated 1579. *Cf.* Nanga Taisei, III, 11.

K.-k. shu-hua chi, XVII. The Island of Immortals. Signed. Poem.

Ibid. XXI. Waterfall, Peaks and Pine-trees. Signed. Poem.

Ibid. XXIV. A Lotus Plant. Signed. Poem.

K.-k. chou-k'an, vol.II, 45. The Shih-hu Lake. A steep Mountain rising on the Shore. Poems by the painter and by Wên P'êng and Ch'ien-lung.

Nanking Exhib. cat. 156 (formerly P'ang Yüan-chi). Landscape of Tiger Hill in Suchou. Poem, signed.

Ibid. 157 (Ku-kung collect.) An album of landscapes, illustrations to poems. Signed. Two reproduced.

Ku-kung collect. A Mountain by the T'ai-hu Lake in Autumn. Large album-leaf. Inscription by Wên P'êng.

Ku-kung ming-shan chi 4. Four Landscapes. Fan-paintings. For other fan-paintings see K.-k. chou-k'an, Index, for fifteen fan-paintings; also Nanga Taisei, VIII, 71–73; also ibid. I, 46 (Bamboo and Rocks, dated 1579).

Shoman 21. Plum-blossoms. Fan-painting. Signed. Poem written originally by Wang Ch'ung on one of Wang Mien's pictures, copied by Wên Chia.

Tōsō, p.300. The Chin-shan and the Chiao-shan in the Yangtse River.

Chūgoku, III. River-view with a low Pavilion on a Promontory. Album-leaf. Two lines of poetry by the painter.

Metropolitan Museum. Pavilions by the Water-edge. Fan-painting. Signed.

C. T. Loo Successor, Frank Caro, New York. A House beside the River; a Man on a Donkey crossing a Bridge. Signed. Inscription above by Wang Ch'ih-têng.

H. C. Wêng, Scarsdale, N.Y. Album with landscape studies and corresponding leaves of writing. Painted by Wên Chia and Wên P'êng, with their signatures.

Musée Guimet. Pavilion by the Water's Edge. Fan-painting.

Chêng Tê-k'un, Cambridge. A View of a Mountain River; two men on a rocky ledge under some trees; called the Lu-yin Pavilion. Poem and signature by the painter, and by his brother, Wên P'êng.

J. P. Dubosc, Lugano. Scene of Parting by a River-bank. Handscroll, slightly coloured.

Chang Ts'ung-yü cat. River Landscape with a Pavilion and some Men on the Shore. Colophons.

WÊN JAN 文枬, *t.* Ch'ü-yüan 曲轅, *h.* K'ai-an 慨菴.

B. 1596, d. 1667. Son of Wên Ts'ung-chien and descendant of Wên Chêng-ming. After the fall of Ming dynasty, retired with his parents to the mountains. Landscapes in the family tradition. L, 15. Q, II, 1 (under Wên Ts'ung-chien). R, II, 15. M, p.18.

Liu, 89. Autumn Landscape. Scholars seated beneath the Pine-trees. Signed and dated 1654.

Wu-mên p'ai ming-hua chi (Shên-chou album, 1924). Trees. Signed. The mountains and cottages by Shao Mi.

WÊN P'ÊNG 文彭, *t.* Shou-ch'êng 壽承, *h.* San-ch'iao 三橋.

B. 1498, d. 1573. Eldest son of Wên Chêng-ming. Calligraphist; painted bamboo in ink, also landscapes and flowers. Biography in *Ming-shih* (*I-wên-chih*); also N, II, 18. O, 7. M, p.17.

K.-k. chou-k'an 164. A Man reading in a House at the Foot of Cliffs. Inscription by the artist above the painting.

Nanga Taisei, V, 197. Bunches of Cabbage and Radishes. Two album-leaves, one signed.

K.-k. ming-shan chi IV. Bamboo. Fan-painting, signed. For other fans, see K.-k. chou-k'an 222; Nanga Taisei, I, 45.

J. P. Dubosc, Lugano. A River Bay at the Foot of High Mountains, Pavilions over the Water, a Fisherman in a Boat. Ink and colour. Signed. Fan-painting.

WÊN PO-JÊN 文伯仁, *t.* Tê-ch'êng 德承, *h.* Wu-fêng 五峯, Pao-shêng 葆生 and Shê-shan lao-nung 攝山老農.

B. 1502, d. 1575(?) Nephew of Wên Chêng-ming. Landscapes. Continued the family tradition, influenced by Wang Mêng. N, II, 18. O, 3. M, p.17.

Ku-kung collect. (Nanking Exhib. cat. 158). Yang Chi-ching playing the *Ch'in*. Album-leaf. Inscription by the artist on another leaf, signed and dated 1526.

Metropolitan Museum. River Landscape. Short handscroll. Signed and dated 1528.

Cleveland Museum of Art. The Mountain of the Immortals; after Wang Mêng. Ink and light colours. Signed and dated 1531.

K.-k. shu-hua chi, XXII. Tall River-view, creviced Rocks and leafless Trees. Signed and dated 1547.

Shên-chou album, 1919. An album of eight Landscape Studies. Signed and dated 1548.

Musée Guimet. Mountain Landscape with a Pavilion built over a Stream. Fan-painting. Poem by the painter, dated 1548.

National Museum, Stockholm. Mountain Landscape. Signed and dated 1548.

Kokka 467. Four Landscapes forming a series, called the *Ssŭ-wan* (Four Myriads). One of them is signed and dated 1551. Colophons by Tung Ch'i-ch'ang. *Cf.* Tōsō, pp.302–305; two of them in N. Gashū, 8 and 9; one in Shina Meiga Senshū, 8.

Chêng Tê-k'un, Cambridge. Scholars Meeting in a Pavilion on a River-bank under a tall Pine. Inscription by the painter, dated 1557.

K.-k. shu-hua chi, XXXV. The Western Tung-t'ing Island in T'ai-hu. Poems by the painter, and by Wang Ku-hsiang, Wên Chia, Hsieh Shih-ch'ên, Wên P'êng, Lu An-tao and one more. Hsieh Shih-ch'ên's poem dated 1559.

Musée Guimet. Mountain Landscape with Men riding along a River. Fan-painting. Signed and dated 1559.

Ibid. Leaves and Branches. Fan-painting. Signed and dated 1559.

Shên-chou ta-kuan, vol.8. Mountain Pavilion with old Friends in Conversation. Colophon dated 1560. *Cf.* Shina Nanga, III, 5.

Tōsō, p.301. Temples on a Fairy Mountain. Signed and dated 1561.

Seattle Art Museum (ex-Yamamoto collect.) River Landscape with towering Mountain Peak in the background and a Cottage under leafy Trees by a Bridge in the front. Ink and colour on paper. Signed and dated 1561. *Cf.* Cleveland Exhibition cat. 57.

I-yüan chên-shang 4. A Lake Scene, with two Men on a Bridge. Fan-painting, signed and dated 1562.

I-shu ch'uan-t'ung, X, 2. Mountain Landscape with People saying Farewell near a Gate. Painted on the occasion of Ku Hsiao-hsien's departure. Seven inscriptions by his friends, one dated 1562.

K.-k. shu-hua chi, XV. The Fang-hu Island. Signed and dated 1563.

Chūgoku, III. Illustration to Po Chü-i's *P'i-p'a hsing*. Handscroll. Signed and dated 1563.

Nanga Taisei, XI, 27–34. Eight views of T'an-tu. Album of landscapes, the last signed and dated 1563 (?)

Ku-kung collect. Bamboo Hut on Sung-kang. Tall mountains. Slightly coloured. Signed and dated 1564.

K.-k. shu-hua chi, XIV. Landscape, executed in 1564. Signed. Poem dated 1570.

Liu, 68. Mountains in Snow with Travellers. Signed and dated 1565. Poem by Ch'ien-lung. *Cf.* Nanking Exhib. cat. 159.

I-shu ts'ung-pien, 17. The T'ien-mu Mountain. Signed and dated 1567.

J. P. Dubosc, Lugano. Landscape. Signed and dated 1567. *Cf.* Wildenstein cat. (1949), p.32.

Ku-kung, XXIX. Landscape. Signed and dated 1568 (in the spring).

K.-k. shu-hua chi, V. Landscape. Signed and dated 1568 (in the 6th month).

I-shu ts'ung-pien, 14. Tall Mountains with rushing Streams and Men on rocky Ledges in the foreground. Signed and dated 1568. *Cf.* Shina Nanga, III, 12.

Hui-hua kuan. A Temple Compound on the Rocks, Water running below. Ink and colour on paper. Short handscroll. Dated 1568.

Shên-chou, I. A View of Fu-ch'i: River Landscape with Boats. Signed and dated 1569. Poem by Wang Chih-têng.

Hui-hua kuan. A View over T'ai-hu, rocky Shore and Bridge in the foreground. Signed and dated 1569. *Cf.* P'ang Yüan-chi cat. 8.

Ming-jên shu-hua, 6. Mountain Landscape with Cottages and Temples. Signed and dated 1570. *Cf.* Shina Nanga Taikan 10.

K.-k. shu-hua chi, XLI. Landscape. Signed and dated 1570.

Palace Museum album, 1936. Twelve pictures illustrating old poems, four in colour. Last one signed and dated in the *kêng-shên* year of the Lung-ch'ing period, which did not exist, but probably refers to either 1570 or 1572.

Chūgoku, III. Water Cascades pouring through a high Mountain Wall; a Pavilion with two Men below. Signed and dated 1573.

Ming-jên shu-hua, 23. A Mountain Stream. Signed and dated 1574.

K.-k. chou-k'an 507. Landscape with Figures. Fan-painting, signed and dated 1580.

K.-k. shu-hua chi, V. The Mountain of the Immortals. Ibid. XXVI. Man Walking in the Shade of Pine-trees. Signed. *Cf.* K.-k. shu-hua chi, XL.

Ku-kung collect. *Wu-yüeh chiang-shên t'u*: River Scene in the Fifth Month. Green slopes rising over the water. Signed. Painted in T'ing-yün kuan, the study of Wên Chêng-ming.

Ibid. *Tan-t'ai ch'un-hsiao t'u*. A Taoist burning Incense of Immortality on a Mountain. Ink-painting, slightly coloured. Signed by the painter. Inscription by Hsü Wei.

Hui-hua kuan. Rocky Mountains and Rushing Water. Signed.

Shanghai Museum. Dense Groves of Pine-trees on successive Terraces of a lofty Mountain; rushing Water and Figures below. Signed.

Pao-yün, II. Windswept Pines in Numberless Valleys. Tall landscape. Signed.

Gems, I, 42. Hermits fishing in Hua-ch'i. Signed. Poem by Ch'ien-lung.

I-yüan chên-shang, 5. Houses and Temples set among Trees on a Towering Mountain. Signed. Poem by Ch'ien-lung.

Kokka 354. Landscape. Handscroll.

Sōgen 124. Hermits in a Pine Grove on a Mountain. Signed.

Metropolitan Museum. River Landscape with Figures walking over a Bridge or seated on rocky Ledges. A miniature scroll. Signed.

Cleveland Art Museum (ex-Yamamoto collect.) The *Pi-p'a Song*. Saying Farewell at Hsün-yang. A broad River Landscape with a Boat. Handscroll. Ink and slight colour. Inscription signed by the painter. Colophons, the first of which is a transcription of *P'i-p'a hsing* by Po Chü-i. *Cf.* Cleveland Exhibition cat. 58.

Ku-kung ming-shan chi 4. Four Landscapes. Fan-paintings. Signed. For others, see K.-k. chou-k'an 43, 216, 218, 219, 253, 256, 507 (dated 1580?). Also Nanga Taisei, VIII, 74–78.

J. P. Dubosc, Lugano. Bamboos by a Garden Stone. Signed. Fan-painting. Venice Exhibition cat., 824.

WÊN SHU 文淑, *t.* Tuan-jung 端容.

From Suchou. B. 1595, d. 1634. Daughter of Wên Ts'ung-chien (great-grandson of Wên Chêng-ming); married to Chao Ling-chün (1591–1640). Flowers and insects. N, V, 7. O, 6. Q, II, 2. M, p.18.

C. T. Loo's Successor, Frank Caro, N.Y. Lily, Narcissus and a Garden-rock. Ink and colour. Signed and dated 1627. *Cf.* Toronto Exhibit. cat. 36.

K.-k. chou-k'an 506. Butterfly and Flowers. Fan-painting. Signed and dated 1628. For other fan-paintings, see ibid. 245; K.-k. ming-shan chi, 4.

K.-k. shu-hua chi, XV. Butterfly and Flowers. Signed and dated 1630.

Ibid. II. Silkworms and Mulberry Leaves. Signed and dated 1630.

Nanking Exhib. cat. 256. Lilies growing by a Rock; a Butterfly above. Signed and dated 1631.

I-yüan chên-shang-shê album. Studies of Fishes, Crabs, Butterflies, Grasshopper, Dragon-flies and other Insects. Eight sections of a handscroll.

Shên-chou ta-kuan 16. Chrysanthemums by a Rockery. Signed.

S.c.t.k. hsü-pien, X. Lilies at a Rockery. Signed.

Pageant 737. Flowers growing by a Rock; a Butterfly above. Signed.

Ming-jên shu-hua, 15. A Blossoming Plum-tree. Signed.

WÊN TS'UNG-CH'ANG 文從昌, *t.* Shun-chih 順之, *h.* Nan-yüeh 南岳.

Grandson of Wên Po-jên. Landscapes in the Wên family style. N, II, 19. U, II, 1, 14. M, p.17.

C. T. Loo's Successor, Frank Caro, N.Y. A View of Hu-ch'iu Hill. Signed and dated 1615. Toronto Exhibit. cat. 26.

K.-k. chou-k'an 97. Sailing Ships on rough Water. Fan-painting, signed. For other fan-paintings, see K.-k. ming-shan chi 4; Nanga Taisei, VIII, 83 (dated 1596).

F. Vannotti collect., Lugano. Two Men Seated in Conversation on a Rocky Ledge under a Pine-tree by a River. Signed. Ink and colour. Fan-painting.

WÊN TS'UNG-CHIEN 文從簡, *t.* Yen-k'o 彥可, *h.* Chên-yen lao-jên 枕煙老人.

B. 1574, d. 1648. Eldest son of Wen Yüan-shan. In his landscapes he followed the family tradition but also Ni Tsan and Wang Mêng. Painted also figures, flowers and birds. N, II, 19. Q, II, 1. U, II, 1, 12. M, p.17.

Ōmura, I, 10. Low Hills and far-reaching Streams. Signed and dated 1614. Also reproduced in Sōraikan, I, 38.

K.-k. shu-hua chi, III. Buddhist Figures. Signed and dated 1643. *Cf.* Nanking Exhibition cat. 197.

Shên-chou, XV. A Scholar's Cottage under leafy Trees on a Terrace. Album-leaf. Signed.

K.-k. shu-hua chi, XVI. A Bird among Lotus Plants. Signed. Colophon by Chao Fan-fu, friend of the painter.

Wu-mên p'ai ming-hua chi (Shên-chou album). Five Men seated under the Moon. Signed.

Ku-kung ming-shan chi, 4. Landscape. Fan-painting, signed.

WÊN YÜAN-SHAN 文元善, *t.* Tzŭ-ch'ang 子長, *h.* Hu-ch'iu 虎丘.

B. 1554, d. 1589. Son of Wên Chia. Followed his father as a painter and calligraphist. Wang Chih-têng wrote in his epitaph: "A better painter than a writer". M, p.17.

K.-k. shu-hua chi, XXI. Pine-tree, Fungi and Bamboos. Signed and dated 1585.

WÊN-JÊN KAI 聞人蓋, *t.* Chung-chi 仲璣. Native of Yü-yao in Chekiang. O; M. p.597.

J. D. Ch'ên cat. 11, 31. Two leaves from an album with Landscapes in Old Styles. Seals of the artist. Another leaf inscribed and dated 1584.

Hui-hua kuan. An old Tree and some Bamboos by a Garden Stone. Ink on paper. Signed. Dated 1609?

WU CH'ANG 吳昌, *t.* Ch'ang-po 昌伯.

Son of Wu Chên 吳振. Landscapes. Followed his father. N, IV, 15. M, p.164.

Sung-chiang p'ai ming-hua chi (Shên-chou album). A Man seated among Pines and a Wu-t'ung-tree. Signed.

K.-k. chou-k'an 82. Landscape. Fan-painting.

Wu Chên 吳振, *t.* Chên-chih 振之, *h.* Chu-hsü 竹嶼.
From Hua-t'ing, Kiangsu. Flourished *c.*1610. Landscapes. Yün-chien school. N, IV, 15. M, p.164.

Sung-chiang p'ai ming-hua chi (Shên-chou album). Misty Mountains. Signed and dated 1615.
Private collect., Kyōto. Misty Mountain Landscape. Signed and dated 1629.
Kawai collect., Kyōto. Long River Landscape. Hand-scroll, painted in various styles. Signed and dated 1632. *Cf.* Kokka 759.
Kokka 370 (Seikadō). Autumn Mountains in Mist; after Hsia Kuei. Signed.

Wu Cho 吳焯, *t.* Ch'i-ming 啓明.
From Hua-t'ing, Kiangsu. Flourished at the end of the Ming dynasty. Landscapes. M, p.165.

Nanju 17. Looking at a Waterfall. Signed, dated *kêng-wu* year (1630?) Also in Tōyō, XI.
Sirén collect. A White Goose among Reeds on the Shore. Large album-leaf. Poem by the painter, signed.

Wu Êrh-ch'êng 吳爾成, *t.* Hsüan-shui 玄水, *h.* Kuang-yu 光祐.
Unrecorded; presumably 16th–17th century.

Liu 71. A large, rocky Landscape, in the manner of Wang Mêng. Inscribed and signed by the artist; a colophon by Tung Ch'i-ch'ang, dated 1626. *Cf.* Nanking Exhib. cat. 190.

Wu I 吳易, *t.* Su-yu 素友.
From Shanghai. Flourished *c.*1638. Pupil of Tung Ch'i-ch'ang. M, p.164.

K.-k. shu-hua chi, XXVI. Landscape. Signed. Poem, dated 1638.

Wu I-hsien 吳亦僊 (possibly I-ts'an 亦傪), *t.* Hsien-chou 僊周.
Unrecorded. Probably first half of 16th century.

Berlin Museum. Rainstorm, Boat seeking Shelter by the rocky Shore. Signed. *Cf.* Sirén, *Later*, pl.36.

Wu K'uan 吳寬, *t.* Yüan-po 原博, *h.* P'ao-an 匏菴.
From Suchou. B. 1435, d. 1504. *Han-lin* scholar. President of the Board of Rites. Great friend of Shên Chou. V, p.328.

Nanju 25. Landscape. Signed and dated 1470.
Ku-kung ming-shan chi, 8. Fan-paintings.

Wu Ling 吳令, *t.* Hsin-chih 信之, *h.* Hsüan-yüan 宣遠.
From Suchou. Flourished at the end of the Ming period. Flowers and birds. M, p.164.

Ton Ying Co., New York. A Branch with white Flowers and a Bird. Fan-painting. Signed and dated 1640. From P'ang Yüan-chi collect.
K.-k. shu-hua chi, X. Pine-tree, Flowers and Birds. Signed, dated 1649.
K.-k. chou-k'an, XV, 214. Two landscapes. Fan-paintings.

WU PIN 吳彬, *t.* Wên-chung 文中, *h.* Chih-hsien 質先.
From P'u-t'ien, Fukien; lived in Nanking. Court painter in the Wan-li period (1573–1620). Landscapes and figures. N, IV, 14. O, 1. M, p.163.

Ku-kung collect. The Eighteen Arhats, after Li Lung-mien. Long handscroll. Signed and dated 1583(?)

J. D. Ch'ên, cat. II, 32. The Sixteen Arhats. Handscroll, signed and dated 1591. Title written by Mi Wan-chung.

Liu, 66. River Landscape. Handscroll. Signed and dated 1598.

W. Hochstadter, N.Y. Greeting the Spring. Landscape with Villages, Temples and Figures. Handscroll. Signed and dated 1600.

Hamburg Exhibition, 1949–1950. A Range of Mountain Peaks and Clouds. Light colours on paper. Signed and dated 1601.

Metropolitan Museum. Wooded Mountain Slope by a River. Fan-painting. Poem by the painter, dated 1603.

J. A. Jones collect., London. Illustration to a Buddhist legend (?), containing humorously characterized Lohans in strange situations and a meditating youthful figure on a lotus flower (Śakyamuni?) Short handscroll. Signed and dated 1607.

K.-k. shu-hua chi, XXXIV. Sharp Mountain-peaks and Deep Gullies, forming a tall landscape. Signed and dated 1609.

Sōgen 171. Landscape in Snow. Signed. Two lines of poetry, dated 1610.

Nanju 23 (Hashimoto collect., Takatsuki). Mountains and Streams far from the World. Poem by the painter, dated 1615. *Cf.* Kyūka, I.

Frederick Mote, Princeton. Chung K'uei and Demon Attendant. Signed and dated 1615. Colophon by Wang Wên-chih.

Nanking Exhib. cat. 227. Washing the Elephant. Signed and dated 1621.

K.-k. shu-hua chi, XXXIX. Buddhist Figures. Signed.

K.-k. chou-k'an, vol.I, 9. Two Birds on a Branch of a Blossoming Apricot-tree. Poem by Ch'ien-lung.

Ibid. vols.II, III, 50–74. Twenty-five Studies of Buddhist Figures. Album-leaves.

S.c.t.k. hsü-pien, X. Reading beneath the Pines. Signed.

WU PO-LI 吳伯理, *h.* Ch'ao-yün tzŭ 巢雲子.
From Kuang-hsing, Kiangsi. Taoist monk. Active in the Yung-lo period (1403–1424). Trees and bamboos. M, p.161.

Shina Meiga Senshū, 3. A tall Pine-tree. Poem by the painter. *Cf.* J. D. Ch'ên cat. II, 13.

WU T'ING-YÜ 吳廷羽, *t.* Tso-ch'ien. 左千.
Native of Hsiu-ning in Anhui. Figures; landscapes. Followed Ting Yün-p'êng. N, IV, 14. O; M, p.163.

J. D. Ch'ên cat. I, 37. Landscape; a Lady Embroidering in a House. Inscription signed and dated 1612.

WU WEI 吳偉, *t.* Shih-ying 士英, *h.* Lu-fu 魯夫. Later *t.* Tz'ŭ-wêng 次翁, *h.* Hsiao-hsien 小仙.
From Chiang-hsia, Hupeh. B. 1459, d. 1508. Celebrated figure painter, favourite of the emperors Hsien-tsung and Hsiao-tsung. Founder of the Chiang-hsia school. N, II, 8. O, 1. I, 56, 6. M, p.161.

Ku-kung, XV. An Immortal with his Servant-boy and a Crane. Signed.

K.-k. shu-hua chi, XXVIII. An Immortal with a Fungus. Signed.

Nanking Exhibition cat. 116. A Scholar seated under a Projecting Pine-branch growing from a Cliff, playing the *Ch'in*. Signed.

T'ai-shan ts'an-shih lou ts'ang-hua, II. Two Men playing Chess, a Third looking on. Album-leaf. Signed.

Mei-chan t'ê-k'an 29. A Man carrying Bundles of Firewood on a Shoulder-pole.

Hui-hua kuan. A Man seated on the Ground reading, leaning against a Buffalo. Ink on silk. Signed.

Gems, I, 23. A Man leaning on the Trunk of a Blossoming Plum-tree. Signed.

Liu, 48. A Scholar seated at his Desk under a Pine-tree. Handscroll. Colophon by Wu Hu-fan.

Chung-hua wên-wu chi-ch'êng, IV, 381. A Taoist

Immortal riding on a Tortoise. Signed. Colophon by Shên Chou. *Cf.* Nanking Exhib. cat. 115.

Shimbi Shoin Shina Meigashū, II. River-views with a Fisherman and other Figures. A pair of pictures. One of them also in Tōyō, X. B?

Ibid. II (Myōshin-ji, Kyōto). Li T'ieh-kuai standing in Profile to the Left. *Cf.* Shimbi Taikan, X.

Bukkyō Bijutsu 18. An Angler under a Pine-branch. Fan-painting. Signed.

J. D. Ch'ên cat. I, 31. A Man in a Boat beneath the Moon in Autumn. Signed.

Yūrintaikan, I. Fishing in a River in Spring. Handscroll. Signed. B?

Tōsō, p.244 (Shinozaki). Fishermen, Woodcutter, Farmers and Scholars. Handscroll. Signed.

Chūgoku, II (C. T. Loo's Successor, N.Y.) Twelve album-leaves representing legendary characters in landscapes. Seals of the painter.

Boston Museum. A Man seated in Contemplation under a Tree. Signed. *Cf.* Sirén, *Later*, pl.32.

British Museum. Lady Lao Yu with the *Luan* Phoenix. B?

National Museum, Stockholm. Fishermen Drawing their Nets. Ink and colour on paper. Handscroll. Signed. *Cf.* Sirén, *Later*, pl.33.

Ibid. Four Views of Streams and Rivers. Large album-leaves, one of which is signed. *Cf.* Sirén, *Later*, pl.34.

Hamburg Exhibition, 1949–1950. Li T'ieh-kuai. Ink and slight colour on satin. Signed.

Ibid. Studies of Buffaloes and Figures. Five album-leaves mounted on a handscroll. Ink on silk.

Chang Ta-ch'ien cat., I, 21. The Fairy Ma-ku. Signed.

Ibid. IV. The Courtesan Wu Ling-ch'un, seated by a table stone. Handscroll. Seals of the painter. Attached to the picture is a biography of the courtesan written by the painter Hsü Lin.

J. Cahill, Wash., D.C. The Pleasures of Fishermen. Handscroll. Signed; title written by Sung Chüeh.

Lilly collect., Indianapolis. A Lady holding a *P'i-p'a*. Signed. Three inscriptions.

C. T. Loo's Successor, Frank Caro, N.Y. A Man in a Boat by a Rocky Bank. Signed. *Cf.* Toronto 20.

WU YÜN 吳雲, *t.* Yu-yün 友雲.

D. 1375. Native of I-hsing. Landscapes and other subjects. See *Ming-shih*; also O, 5. M, p.161.

Nanking Exhibition cat. 85. A Tall Plantain Plant. Inscription in running style. Ink-painting in *p'o-mo* manner.

YANG CHI 楊基, *t.* Mêng-tsai 孟載, *h.* Mei-an 眉菴.

From Szechuan, lived in Suchou. One of the "Four Talents" at the beginning of the Ming period. Landscapes and bamboos. N, I, 10. O, 7. I, 55, 1. M, p.584.

P'ang Yüan-chi Illustr. cat. 1940, III. A Hermit's Cottage near the Sung River. Signed. Poems by Wang Fu and Ch'ien-lung.

YANG MING-SHIH 楊名時, *t.* Pu-ch'i 不棄.

From Hsieh-hsien, Anhui. Active *c.*1590. Connoisseur of painting and friend of Tung Ch'i-ch'ang. Landscapes and epidendrums. N, VII, 14. O, 4. M, p.499.

Hui-hua kuan (ex-Chang Ts'ung-yü collect.) A bare Tree, slender Bamboos and a Large Stone. Ink on paper. Signed and dated 1595. *Cf.* Nanking Exhib. cat. 211.

YANG PU 楊補, *t.* Wu-pu 無補, Po-pu 白補, *h.* Ku-nung 古農.

B. 1598, d. 1657. From Ch'ing-chiang, Kiangsi, and lived in Suchou. After 1644, retired to the Têng-wei Mountain. Poet. Landscapes after Ni Tsan and Huang kung-wang. O, 5. U. I, 2, 5. M, p.586.

K.-k. chou-k'an, vol.IX, 188. Mountain Landscape with tall Trees, in Yüan style. Signed and dated 1648.

I-yüan chên-shang, 10. A large Mountain Landscape. Signed and dated 1655.

YANG WÊN-TS'UNG 楊文驄, *t.* Lung-yu 龍友.

From Kueichou; lived in Nanking. B. 1597, d. 1645. Governor of Nanking; captured and killed by the Manchus. Scholar, calligraphist. One of the "Nine Friends in Painting". Landscapes, orchids and bamboo. N, VII, 20. O, 5. P, 3, 8. U, I, 1, 6. M, p.585.

Shên-chou, XVII. High Mountains and two Figures in a Ravine looking at a Waterfall. After Wang Fu. Signed and dated 1623.

Tōsō, p.375 (Takashima collect., Kugenuma). Cottages by a River. Handscroll. Signed and dated 1628.

Vannotti collect., Lugano. Mountains in Mist, a few Tall Pine-trees in the foreground. Signed and dated 1629. Fan-painting.

Sōraikan, II, 64. Autumn Trees and distant Hills. Signed and dated 1631.

Metropolitan Museum. Autumn Landscape; a Man approaching a Riverside Pavilion. Signed and dated 1635.

Hua-chung chiu-yu (Yu-chêng album). Humming in the Valley. Signed and dated 1638.

Shên-chou, I. Epidendrum and Bamboos by a Rockery. Signed and dated 1638.

Ku-kung, XII. Bamboos and Epidendrum. Signed and dated 1638.

Chung-kuo ming-hua, 8. A high Mountain with Humps and Trees. Signed. Two lines of poetry, dated 1638. *Cf.* Shina Nanga, I, 13.

Lung-yu mo-miao ts'ê (Hakubundō album) (Kawai collect., Kyōto). Twelve Landscapes after old masters. Last picture dated 1638. *Cf.* Yonezawa, 25.

Shoman 25. Landscape. Fan-painting. Signed and dated 1638.

J. D. Ch'ên, Hongkong. River Landscape: nine Peaks and three Streams. Long handscroll. Signed and dated 1640.

Nanking Exhib. cat. 222. Trees and Houses on a River-bank. Album-leaf. Signed and dated 1640.

Kokka 262. Landscape after Shên Chou. Signed. Colophon by the painter, dated 1643. *Cf.* Nanju 9; Tōyō, XI.

Chūgoku, IV. Cottage under tall Trees on the River-bank; a Mountain Peak on the yonder side. After Ni Tsan. Inscription by the painter, dated 1643.

Shên-chou ta-kuan, vol.16. River-view with sparse Trees. Poem by the painter, dated 1644.

P'ang Yüan-chi Illustr. cat. V. Epidendrums and Bamboos. Poem by the painter.

Chang Ts'ung-yü cat. Steep Mountain rising in Terraces over a River.

Shanghai Museum. Two Tufts of Epidendrum and a Bamboo. Ink on silk. Inscription by the painter.

Hua-chung chiu-yu chi-ts'ê (Hakubundō album). Misty River Landscape with a long Bridge built on Poles. Signed and dedicated to Wu Wei-yeh.

Sōgen 174. Houses on the Bank of a River. Portion of a handscroll.

Tokasha Shina Meigashū, 4. River Valley in Mist, spare Trees in the foreground. Poem by the painter.

Ibid. 5. River-view with bare Cliffs and spare Trees in Autumn. Poem by the painter.

Shina Nanga Taikan, 5. Two Men at the Foot of a Waterfall in the Mountains under leafy Trees. Inscription by the painter.

C. T. Loo's Successor, Frank Caro, New York. Two Tufts of Epidendrum, Rocks and Bamboo Sprouts. Signed.

YAO LI-SHIH 姚履施, *t.* Yün-chi 允吉.

From Nanking. Active in the end of Wan-li period (1573–1619). Calligraphist. Plum-blossoms. M, p.287.

Po-mei chi. Plum-blossoms. Album-leaf. Signed.

YAO SHOU 姚綬, *t.* Kung-shou 公綬, *h.* Ku-an 穀菴, Yün-tung i-shih 雲東逸史 and other names.
From Chia-shan, Chekiang. B. 1423, d. 1495. Poet, calligraphist. Landscapes in Wu Chên's style, also bamboos, birds and stones. N, II, 6. O, 3. I, 56, 5. M, p.287.

Nanga Taisei, V, 5. A Cypress Tree growing beside a Rock. Signed and dated 1471.
Tōsō, p.242 (J. D. Ch'ên cat. I, 26.) Bamboos and Rocks. Signed. Poem and colophon, dated 1470 and 1472.
Hui-hua kuan. A Fisherman on the River in Autumn. Poem by the painter, dated 1476. Colophon by Tung Ch'i-ch'ang. *Cf.* P'ang Yüan-chi Illust. cat. III; Nanking Exhib. cat. 99.
K.-k. shu-hua chi, XXXVII. Nine Fungi. Signed and dated 1477.
Chūgoku, II. Fishing alone on an Autumn River, after Chao Mêng-fu. Poem and inscription by the painter, dated 1479. Also a poem by Ch'ien-lung.
Chung-kuo, II, 33. Peonies and Butterflies. Signed. Poem and colophon dated 1484. *Cf.* Chung-kuo ming-hua, 35.
T'ai-shan ts'an-shih lou ts'ang-hua, I. Thin Bamboos growing on a projecting Rock. Poem and colophon by the painter, dated 1486.
C. C. Wang, N.Y. Bamboo growing from behind a Rock. Inscription, dated 1494.
Shên-chou ta-kuan, vol.5. Magpies in a leafless Tree.
Ming-jên shu-hua, I. Fungi in a Pot, placed on Top of a Rockery. Signed.
Chung-kuo ming-hua, XXI. A Man standing at the Foot of high Mountains looking at a Waterfall. Poem by the painter. Imitation.
K.-k. shu-hua chi, I. A Mynah Bird on a Dry Branch. Signed. Poem.
K.-k. chou-k'an, vol.II, 36. Bamboos and a Tree with a Spring Bird flying on their Top. Poems by the painter and by Ch'ien-lung. *Cf.* Ming-hua lin-lang. A.
Ku-kung collect. Bamboo and a Large Bird with one Wing stretched out. Slightly coloured ink-painting. Large album-leaf. Signed. A.
Gems, I, 21. Bamboo and a Tree growing beside a Rock. Poem, signed.
Mei-chan t'ê-k'an 23. River between steep Mountains; Fishermen in Boats under Trees in foreground.
Wên-ming album, 1931. An album of eight landscapes. Signed. Colophons by the painter.
Shina Nanga, III, 6. A Bird. Signed. Poem.
Shina Kachō Gasatsu 28. A Branch of a Lichee-tree. Album-leaf. Inscription by the painter.
Sōgen 103. River Landscape with a Boat. Handscroll. Signed.
Chang Ta-ch'ien, Hongkong. Parting at the Gate of the Capital. Signed.
J. D. Ch'ên cat. II, 22. A Branch of Plum-blossoms. Long inscription by the painter.
Ho Kuan-wu, Hongkong. A Village by the Water, Figures and Buildings. Short handscroll. Several colophons. Signed.
Chicago Art Institute. A River-view with three Men in a Boat, Bamboos and a Bird on a Branch. Handscroll. Inscriptions by the painter.
C. C. Wang, New York. Two Men seated under Pine-trees. Signed.
Ibid. A Temple on the top of Steep Mountains by a Stream. Signed. *Cf.* Nanking Exhibition cat. 100.

YAO TÊ-HOU 姚德厚.
Unrecorded. According to the signature, *t.* Shu-ya 叔雅. From Jung-ch'êng, Szechuan. Probably Ming period.

Ku-kung, XL. A solitary Angler. Signed. Eight poems by contemporaries.

YAO YÜN-TSAI 姚允在, *t.* Chien-shu 簡叔.
From K'uai-chi, Chekiang. Flourished *c.*1600. Landscapes in the styles of Ching Hao and Kuan T'ung; figures. N, VII, 15. U, I, 2, 4. M, p.288.

Hamburg Exhibition, 1949–1950. Winter Landscape in the Sung style. Signed and dated 1576.
Nanju 19. Landscape after a Yüan master. Signed and dated 1603.

YEH-CH'ÜAN 野泉.
Unrecorded. Chia-ching period (1522–1566).

Tōyō, X (Sugawara collect., Kamakura). Farewell to the Priest Sakugen: Shore Landscape with a departing Boat. Signed.

YEH KUANG 葉廣.
From Ch'ao-hsien, Anhui. 16th century. Landscapes. M, p.575.

K.-k. shu-hua chi, IX. A Fisherman by the River. Signed.

Hui-hua kuan. Two Fishermen in a Boat. Snow covering Trees and Cliffs. Ink only on paper. Signed.

YEH YU-NIEN 葉有年, *t.* Chün-shan 君山.
From Nan-hui or Hua-t'ing, Kiangsu. Lived at the end of Ming period. Pupil of Sun K'o-hung. Landscape-painter. U, II, I, 28. M, p.576.

Chūgoku, IV. Mountain Landscape; open Pavilions standing on Poles in the Stream. Album-leaf. Signed and dated 1633.

YEN I 顏嶧, *t.* T'ung-k'o 桐客.
Native place unknown. Active in the Ch'ung-chên period (1628–1643). Landscapes in Sung style; also birds. M, p.710.

Chung-kuo, II, 148. River Landscape. Signed and dated 1640.

Ibid. II, 147. A Flock of Crows, some flying; others perched in a Tree. Signed. Poem.

Hashimoto collect., Takatsuki. River Scene with Houses among Willow-trees, after a painting by Liu Sung-nien. Signed.

YIN CH'I-FÊNG 尹奇逢.
Ming dynasty. Unrecorded.

Nanking Exhib. cat. 237. Bamboo growing from an overhanging Ledge. Poem. Signed (?)

YIN HUNG 殷宏. Native of Ch'ên-chün in Honan. Ming Period. Figures, birds and flowers. N, VI, 21; M, p. 310.

J. D. Ch'ên cat. I, 29. Birds and Flowers. Signed.

YO CHÊNG 岳正, *t.* Chi-fang 季方, *h.* Mêng-ch'üan 蒙泉.
From Kuo-hsien (T'ung-chou), Hopei. B. 1418, d. 1472. Grapes. O, 7. M, p.219.

Tōan 16. Grapes and Squirrels, after Wên Jih-kuan. Signed and dated 1450. Poem by Chang Ning. *Cf.* Bukkyō Bijutsu, 18.

YO TAI 岳岱, *t.* Tung-po 東伯, *h.* Ch'in-yü shan-jên 秦餘山人 and Chang-yü-tzŭ 漳餘子.
From Suchou. *c.*1570. Landscapes. Travelled to all the famous mountains in the southern provinces. M, p.219.

Fogg Museum, Cambridge, Mass. Mountains in Snow; Temples, Cottages, and a Boat on the River. Signed and dated 1571. *Cf. Later Chinese Painting*, pl.79B.

Ming-jên shu-hua 24. River Landscape with high Peaks. Signed. Poems by the painter, by Chou T'ien-ch'iu, Huang-fu Ch'ung, and his three brothers. *Cf.* P'ang Yüan-chi cat. Add. 2.

YU CH'IU 尤求, *t.* Tzŭ-ch'iu 子求, *h.* Fêng-ch'iu 鳳丘.
From Suchou; lived in T'ai-ts'ang, Kiangsu. Active *c.*1570–1590. Followed Ch'iu Ying, influenced by Liu Sung-nien and Ch'ien Hsüan. N, III, 7. I, 57, 9. M, p.12.

Hui-hua kuan. The Eight Wine-bibbers, illustrating Tu Fu's poem. In *pai-miao* manner, on paper. Handscroll. Signed and dated 1571.

Ku-kung collect. Scholars Gathering in the West Garden. Signed and dated 1571. Two seals of the painter.

Hui-hua kuan. Scholars Studying old Paintings under the Trees in a Garden. Dated 1572.

Sōgen 154. Chao-chün on her Way to Mongolia, after Li Lung-mien. Part of a handscroll. Signed and dated 1572.

National Museum, Stockholm. Wang Hsi-chih at the Lan-t'ing Meeting. Landscape with numerous figures. Signed and dated 1572.

Ku-kung collect. Nine Scholars examining Antiquities under Pine-trees. Signed and dated 1579.

Vannotti collect., Lugano. River Scene with a Sailing Boat. Fan-painting, signed and dated 1580.

Sōgen 155. Threading the Needle on the seventh of the seventh Month. Signed and dated 1583.

K.-k. shu-hua chi, V. Landscape with Figures. Signed.

Ming-jên shu-hua 7. On the Way to Lan-t'ing. *Cf.* Tōsō, p.229.

Gems, III, 5. Two leaves from an Album of Landscapes and Figure-paintings. Seals of the artist.

Yūrintaikan, I. The Song of Lasting Sorrow, after the poem by Po Chü-i. Handscroll. Signed. The complete poem copied in a colophon.

Tōsō, p.345. Portrait of Hsüeh-ko shan-jên. Signed.

Chūgoku, III. A Man on Horseback followed by a Servant passing over a Bridge to reach a Pavilion built on Poles on a Mountain Lake. Signed. Poem by Ch'ien-lung.

J. D. Ch'ên cat. II, 30. Ko I-chuan moving his Residence. Handscroll. Signed.

Nelson Gallery, Kansas City. Scholars in various Occupations in a Garden. Handscroll. Signed.

National Museum, Stockholm. The Taoist Master Yüan Hsüan. Signed.

Nü-wa chai. Peasants feasting, dancing and drinking in the Forest. Handscroll. Signed.

W. Hochstadter, New York. Scholars in a Garden throwing Arrows. Signed.

J. P. Dubosc, Lugano. Landscape with Figures. Fan-painting. Bright colours on gold ground. Signed.

YÜ HSI-LIEN 喻希連, *t.* Lu-wang 魯望, *h.* Su-ch'ih 素癡.
From Yü-shan, Kiangsi. Wan-li period (1573–1620). Landscapes in the style of Shên Chou. O, 4. M, p.500.

Nanju 4. Landscape after Shên Chou. Signed. Poem. Also in Tōyō, XI.

YÜAN HSÜAN 袁玄, or Yüan Yüan 袁元, *t.* Yu-hsüan 又玄.
From Suchou. Flourished *c.*1610. Landscapes. M, p.323.

Ōmura, II, 5. Snow Landscape after Kuo Hsi. Album-leaf. Signed and dated 1613. *Cf.* Chūgoku, IV.

Chūgoku, IV. River Landscape after Chao Ling-jang. Album-leaf. Signed.

YÜAN SHANG-T'UNG 袁尚統, *t.* Shu-ming 叔明.
From Suchou. B. 1570, d. 1661. Landscapes, figures, followed the Sung masters. M, p.323.

Nanju 18. A Mountain Cottage among bare Trees. Signed, dated 1633. Also in Tōyō, XI.
Li-tai, III. In a Boat Looking at the Crows. Signed, dated 1636. *Cf.* Pao-yün, I.
Ku-kung collect. (Nanking Exhib. cat. 392). A Lake Scene. Leaf from an album of scenes of Suchou. Signed and dated 1637.
Hamburg Exhibition, 1949–1950. Large Mountain Landscape in Sung style. Signed, dated 1642.
Sōgen 195. Storm on the Tung-t'ing Lake. Signed, dated 1652.
K.-k. shu-hua chi, XLIII. Two Crows. Signed, dated 1654.
Ibid. XXV. Landscape: New Year's Day. Signed. Poem, dated 1661 (at 92).

YÜAN YÜAN 袁源, *t.* Hsiang-t'ing 湘亭.
From Wu (Suchou). End of the Ming period. Figures and bamboos. M, p.323.

Bijutsu, XV. Bamboos by a Rockery. Signed.

YÜN-CH'IAO 雲樵. Unrecorded, if not identical with Ch'ên Hsien 陳暹, *t.* Chi-chao 季昭, *h.* Yün-ch'iao.
B. *c.*1410, d. *c.*1490. Teacher of Chou Ch'ên.

Tokasha Shina Meigashū, 33. Trailing Mist around craggy Mountains; a small Building by the Water in the foreground. Signed and dated: *hsin-ssŭ* year (1461).

YÜN HSIANG 惲向, original name Tao-shêng 道生, *t.* Pên-ch'u 本初, *h.* Hsiang-shan wêng 香山翁.
From Wu-chin, Kiangsu. B. 1586, d. 1655. Landscapes. Followed Tung Yüan and Chü-jan; later on, Ni Tsan and Huang Kung-wang. P, I, 14. Q, I, 1. U, I, 2, 1. N, IV, 24. O, 5. M, p.510.

Hui-hua kuan. Mountain Peak and leafy Trees. Signed and dated 1615.
Private collect., Shanghai. Mountain Peak by a Stream, a Tree in front. Handscroll. Signed and dated 1638.
S.c.t.k. hsü-pien, I. Landscape in the style of Ni Tsan. Poem by the painter, signed 1646.
J. D. Ch'ên cat. II, 39. Album of Landscape Studies in various styles. Signed and dated 1648.
Hamburg Exhibition, 1949–1950. Landscape. Signed and dated 1652.
Ku-kung, XXV. Landscape after Ni Tsan. Signed and dated 1654. Colophon.
Nanga Taisei, IX, 237. Houses at the Foot of a high Mountain, among leafy Trees. Signed and dated 1654. *Cf.* Chung-kuo ming-hua, vol.35.
P'ang Yüan-chi Illust. cat. V. Cloudy Mountains, after Mi Fei. Colophon by the painter, dated 1655(?)
Shên-chou ta-kuan, vol.5. River Landscape in Autumn. Short handscroll. Colophon by the painter.
Chung-kuo ming-hua, 26. A House among Trees; a Man approaching. Poem, signed.
Nanking Exhib. cat. 248. Pine-trees in a River Valley. Signed.
P'ang Yüan-chi Illust. cat. II. Landscape in Spring Rain. Colophon by the painter.
Chou Li-yüan, 17. Landscape with Lakeside Buildings. Album-leaf. Signed.
Nanga Taisei, XI, 88–95. Album of eight Landscape Studies. Seals of the artist.
Nanju 25. Trees by a River, after Chü-jan. Signed. Two lines of poetry.
Tōyō, XI. Tall Pine-trees by a Waterfall, after Chêng Hsi (of the Yüan period). Signed.
Shina Meiga Senshū, 18. Small Houses under sparse Trees on the rocky Shore. Colophon by the painter.
Sōgen 239. Tall Pines by a Waterfall, after Hsü Tao-ning. Signed. Colophon.
Ibid. 240. Rain after a long Drought. Signed.
King Gustaf VI Adolf collect. View of a Rocky River-bank and some Bare Trees. According to the inscription by the painter, he has here imitated Ni Tsan in order to amuse a friend.
Howard Hollis Co., Cleveland (ex-Tomioka collect.) Landscape after Ni Tsan. Fan-painting. Inscription by the painter. *Cf.* Cleveland Exhib. cat. 81.

VI

Painters of the Ch‘ing Dynasty

A Êrh Pai	阿爾粺
Ai Ch‘i-mêng	艾啓蒙
Ch‘a Chi-tso	查繼佐
Ch‘a P‘u	查浦
Ch‘a Shih-piao	查士標
Chai Chi-ch‘ang	翟繼昌
Chai Ta-k‘un	翟大坤
Chan-fu	湛復
Chang Chao	張照
Chang Cho	張琢
Chang Fêng	張風
Chang Hao	張鎬
Chang Hsia	張洽
Chang Hsin	張莘
Chang Hsiung	張熊
Chang Hsüeh-tsêng	張學曾
Chang Hsün	張恂
Chang Jên-shan	張仁山
Chang Jo-ai	張若靄
Chang Jo-ch‘êng	張若澄
Chang Kêng	張庚
Chang Ku	章谷
Chang Mu	張穆
Chang Nai-chi	張迺耆
Chang P‘ei-tun	張培敦
Chang P‘êng-ch‘ung	張鵬翀
Chang Shao-chiu	張韶九
Chang Shêng	章聲
Chang Shih-chang	張世掌
Chang Su	章疏
Chang Tao-wu	張道渥
Chang T‘ing-chi	張廷濟
Chang T‘ing-yen	張廷彥
Chang Ts‘ai	章采
Chang Tsung-ts‘ang	張宗蒼
Chang Tung	張棟
Chang Tz‘ŭ-ning	張賜甯
Chang Wên-t‘ao	張問陶
Chang Yen-ch‘ang	張燕昌
Chang Yin	張崟
Chang Yü	章于
Chang Yü	張敔
Chang Yü-sên	張雨森
Chao Ch‘êng	趙澄
Chao Chih-ch‘ên	趙之琛
Chao Chih-ch‘ien	趙之謙
Chao I	趙懿
Chao Ming-shan	招銘山
Chao Ping-ch‘ung	趙秉冲
Chao Shih-ch‘ên	趙史臣
Ch‘ao-k‘uei	超揆
Ch‘ên Chuan	陳撰
Ch‘ên Hao	陳豪
Ch‘ên Hsien	陳銑
Ch‘ên Hsing	陳星
Ch‘ên Hung-shou	陳鴻壽
Ch‘ên K‘o	陳邁
Ch‘ên K‘un	陳坤
Ch‘ên Man	陳曼
Ch‘ên Mei	陳枚
Ch‘ên Min	陳砇
Ch‘ên Shan	陳善
Ch‘ên Shao-ying	陳紹英
Ch‘ên Shu	陳書
Ch‘ên Shu	陳舒
Ch‘ên Shun	陳舜
Ch‘ên Sung	陳崧
Ch‘ên Tan-chung	陳丹衷
Ch‘ên Ting	陳鼎
Ch‘ên Tsun	陳墫
Ch‘ên T‘ung	陳桐
Ch‘ên Tzŭ	陳字
Ch‘ên Yo	陳岳
Chêng Hsieh	鄭燮
Chêng Min	鄭旼
Chêng T‘ieh-yai	鄭鐵崖
Ch‘êng Chêng-k‘uei	程正揆
Ch‘êng Ming	程鳴
Ch‘êng Sui	程邃
Ch‘êng T‘ing-lu	程庭鷺
Ch‘êng Tsêng-huang	程曾煌
Ch‘êng Yün	程雲

Fang Shih-shu	方世庶
Fang Ta-yu	方大猷
Fang Tsung	方琮
Fang Wan-i	方畹儀
Fei Êrh-ch'i	費而奇
Fei Tan-hsü	費丹旭
Fêng Ch'i	馮箕
Fêng Hsien-shih	馮仙湜
Fêng Ning	馮甯
Fu Shan	傅山
Fu Wên	傅雯
Han Chu	韓鑄
Han Hsia	韓洽
Han Jun	韓潤
Han K'uang	韓曠
Han Yen	韓炎
Hang Shih-chün	杭世駿
Ho Ch'ing-t'ai	賀清泰
Ho I	郝頤
Ho Shao-yeh	何紹業
Ho T'êng-chiao	何騰蛟
Ho Yüan	何遠
Hou Mei	侯梅
Hou Ssŭ-ping	侯思炳
Hsi Kang	奚岡
Hsia Chin	夏今
Hsiang K'uei	項奎
Hsiao Ch'ên	蕭晨
Hsiao Yün-ts'ung	蕭雲從
Hsieh Lan-shêng	謝蘭生
Hsieh Pin	謝彬
Hsieh Sui	謝遂
Hsieh Sun	謝蓀
Hsü Ching	許敬
Hsü Fang	徐枋
Hsü Jung	徐溶
Hsü-ku	虛谷
Hsü Mei	徐玫
Hsü Mêng-ts'ai	許盟材
Hsü Pin	許濱
Hsü T'ai	徐泰
Hsü Tan	徐澹
Hsü Wang-hsiung	徐王熊
Hsü Wei-jên	徐渭仁
Hsü Yang	徐揚
Hsü Yu	許友
Hsü Yu	許佑
Hsü Yüan-wên	徐元文
Hsüeh Hsüan	薛宣
Hu Chang	胡璋
Hu Chên-k'ai	胡貞開
Hu Hsi-kuei	胡錫珪
Hu Kuei	胡桂
Hu Shih-k'un	胡士昆
Hu Ts'ao	胡慥
Hu Yüan	胡遠
Hua Kuan	華冠
Hua-lin	化林
Hua Yen	華嵒
Huang Chi	黃基
Huang Chi	黃驥
Huang Chü	黃鞠
Huang Chün	黃均
Huang Hsiang-chien	黃向堅
Huang I	黃易
Huang Lü	黃呂
Huang Nien-tsu	黃念祖
Huang Pi	黃壁
Huang Shên	黃慎
Huang Ting	黃鼎
Huang Wan-chung	黃萬鍾
Huang Wei	黃衛
Huang Yeh	黃冶
Huang Ying-shên	黃應諶
Huang Yüeh	黃鉞
Hung-jên	弘仁
Hung Wu	弘旿
I Hai	伊海
I-jan	逸髯
I Ping-shou	伊秉綬
Jao Ching	饒璟
Jên Hsiung	任熊
Jên Hsün	任薰
Jên I	任頤
Jên Shih-chung	任時中
Kai Ch'i	改琦
K'ang T'ao	康濤
Kao Ch'êng-mo	高承謨
Kao Ch'i-p'ei	高其佩
Kao Chien	高簡
Kao Fêng-han	高鳳瀚
Kao Hsiang	高翔

Kao Pin	高鑌
Kao Shih-ch'i	高士奇
Kao Shu-ch'êng	高樹程
Kao Ts'ên	高岑
Kao Ts'êng-yün	高層雲
Kao-tsung, Emperor Ch'ien-lung of Ch'ing	清高宗
Kao Yen	高儼
Kao Yü	高遇
Ku An-jen	顧安仁
Ku Ch'iao	顧樵
Ku Chien-lung	顧見龍
Ku Fang	顧昉
Ku Fu-chên	顧符稹
Ku Hao-ch'ing	顧鶴慶
Ku Lien	顧廉
Ku Lo	顧洛
Ku Mei-shêng	顧眉生
Ku Pao-wên	顧豹文
Ku Shan-yu	顧善有
Ku Shun	顧蒓
Ku Ta-ch'ang	顧大昌
Ku Ta-shên	顧大申
Ku Wên-yüan	顧文淵
Ku Yin	顧殷
Ku Ying	顧瑛
Ku Ying-t'ai	顧應泰
Ku Yüan	顧原
Ku Yün	顧澐
Kuan Hsi-ning	管希寧
Kuan Huai	關槐
K'un-ts'an	髡殘
Kung Hsien	龔賢
Kuo Ching-yen	郭璟燕
Kuo Wan	郭完
Kuo Ying-chung	郭應中
Lan Mêng	藍孟
Lan Shên	藍深
Lan T'ao	藍濤
Lang Shih-ning	郎世寧
Lao Chêng	勞澂
Lêng Mei	冷枚
Li Chien	黎簡
Li Chih	李致
Li Fan	李蕃
Li Fang-ying	李方膺
Li Hsi-t'ai	李熙泰
Li Hsiao	李孝
Li Hsiu-i	李修易
Li K'un	李崑
Li O-shêng	李蕚生
Li Ping-shou	李秉綬
Li, Prince	禮親王
Li San-wei	李三畏
Li Shan	李鱓
Li Shih-cho	李世倬
Li Yin	李因
Li Yin	李寅
Li Yü	李育
Lien Ch'i	蓮溪
Lin Ch'i	林祁
Lin Chih-fan	林之蕃
Lin Chün	林濬
Lin Ling-hsü	林令旭
Liu Pin	劉璸
Liu Tê-liu	劉德六
Liu Tu	劉度
Liu Yin	柳隱
Liu Yü	柳堉
Liu Yü	柳遇
Liu Yüan	劉源
Lo Kuang	羅光
Lo Mu	羅牧
Lo Pin	羅彬
Lo P'ing	羅聘
Lo T'ing-hsi	羅廷禧
Lu Chan	盧湛
Lu Ch'ao	盧潮
Lu Chi-pian	路嘉賓
Lu Fei	陸飛
Lu Han	陸翰
Lu I-t'ung	魯一同
Lu Tao-huai	陸道淮
Lu Wei	陸暐
Lu Yüan	陸遠
Lü Ch'ien	呂潛
Lü Hsüeh	呂學
Lü Huan-ch'êng	呂煥成
Ma Ang	馬昂
Ma Ch'üan	馬荃
Ma Kuan-wo	馬觀我
Ma Yüan-yü	馬元馭

Mao Ch'i-ling	毛奇齡
Mao Hsiang	冒襄
Mei Ch'ing	梅清
Mei Ch'ung	梅翀
Mei Kêng	梅庚
Mêng Chin-i	孟覲乙
Mêng Yung-kuang	孟永光
Min Chên	閔貞
Ming-chien	明儉
Ming-chung	明中
Mu Ta-shou	穆達受
Nan-hai	南海
Ni Yün	倪耘
Nien Ju-lin	年汝隣
Niu Shih-hui	牛石慧
Niu Shu	鈕樞
Pa Wei-tsu	巴慰祖
Pan Ta Li Sha	班達里沙
P'an Kung-shou	潘恭壽
P'an Ssŭ-mu	潘思牧
Pao K'ai	鮑楷
Pao K'un	包坤
Pao Tung	包棟
Pi Han	畢涵
Pi Lung	畢瀧
Pien Shou-min	邊壽民
Pien Wên-yü	卞文瑜
Po Êrh-tu	博爾都
P'u-ho	普荷
Shang-jui	上睿
Shang-kuan Chou	上官周
Shên Chih	沈治
Shên Cho	沈焯
Shên Ch'üan	沈銓
Shên Fêng	沈鳳
Shên Hao	沈灝
Shên Huan	沈煥
Shên Jung	沈榮
Shên T'ien-hsiang	沈天驤
Shên Tsu-yung	沈祖永
Shên Tsung-ch'ien	沈宗騫
Shên Tsung-ching	沈宗敬
Shên Ying-hui	沈映暉
Shên Yü	沈喩
Shên Yüan	沈源
Shêng Tan	盛丹
Shih Lin	施霖
Shih P'u	施溥
Shih Sê	碩塞
Shih-tsu, Emperor Shun-chih of Ch'ing	清世祖
Shih Yen-chieh	史顏節
Shih Yüan	施原
Shih Yün-yü	石韞玉
Sou-hsüeh Shan-jên	湫雪山人
Ssŭ-ma Chung	司馬鍾
Su I	蘇誼
Su T'ing-yü	蘇廷煜
Sun Hu	孫祜
Sun I	孫逸
Sun Ti	孫杕
Sung Chün-yeh	宋駿業
Sung Lin	宋霖
Sung Lo	宋犖
Sung Pao-shun	宋葆淳
Ta-p'êng	大鵬
Ta-shan	大汕
Ta-shou	達受
Tai Ch'ü-hêng	戴衢亨
Tai Hsi	戴熙
Tai I-hêng	戴以恆
Tai Ming-shuo	戴明說
Tai Pên-hsiao	戴本孝
Tai T'ien-jui	戴天瑞
Tan Chung-kuang	笪重光
T'an Hsiang-lu	談象稑
T'ang I-fên	湯貽汾
T'ang Li-hsüeh	唐履雪
T'ang Lu-ming	湯祿名
T'ang Mi	湯密
T'ang Tai	唐岱
T'ang Ying	唐英
Tao-chêng	道正
Tao-chi	道濟
T'ao Ch'i	陶淇
Tien Tao-jên	顚道人
Ting Kuan-p'êng	丁觀鵬
Ting Yüan-kung	丁元公
T'ing-wêng	聽翁
Ts'ai Chia	蔡嘉
Ts'ai Han	蔡含
Ts'ai Tsê	蔡澤

Ts‘ao Chien	曹澗
Ts‘ao K‘uei-yin	曹夔音
Ts‘ao Yin	曹隱
Ts‘ao Yu-kuang	曹有光
Tsêng Yen-tung	曾衍東
Tso Chên	左楨
Tsou Chê	鄒喆
Tsou Chih-lin	鄒之麟
Tsou Hsien-chi	鄒顯吉
Tsou I-kuei	鄒一桂
Ts‘ui Hui	崔鏏
T‘u Cho	屠卓
T‘u Hsüan	屠暶
Tung Hsün	董洵
Tung Kao	董誥
Tung Pang-ta	董邦達
Tung Yü	董俞
T‘ung-wei	通微
T‘ung Yü-hsiu	佟毓秀
Wan Ch‘i-fan	萬其藩
Wan Kang	萬岡
Wan Shang-lin	萬上遴
Wan Shou-ch‘i	萬壽祺
Wang Ai	汪靄
Wang Chao-hsiang	王兆祥
Wang Ch‘ên	王宸
Wang Chêng	王正
Wang Ch‘êng-fêng	王承楓
Wang Ch‘êng-p‘ei	汪承霈
Wang Chieh	王詰
Wang Chien	王鑑
Wang Chih-jui	汪之瑞
Wang Ching-ming	王敬銘
Wang Chiu	王玖
Wang Chung	汪中
Wang Chün	汪鋆
Wang Fang	汪昉
Wang Hsien	王巘
Wang Hsüeh-hao	王學浩
Wang Hui	王翬
Wang Kai	王概
Wang Kang	王岡
Wang K‘un	王琨
Wang Kung	汪恭
Wang Lin	王霖
Wang Lo	王犖
Wang Mei-ting	汪梅鼎
Wang Ming-shêng	王鳴盛
Wang Ping	王炳
Wang P‘u	汪樸
Wang San-hsi	王三錫
Wang Shih-i	王時翼
Wang Shih-min	王時敏
Wang Shih-shên	汪士慎
Wang Shu-ku	王樹穀
Wang Su	王素
Wang T‘ao	王韜
Wang T‘ao	王濤
Wang Tsuan	王撰
Wang Wên-chih	王文治
Wang Wu	王武
Wang Wu-t‘ien	王無忝
Wang Yeh-mei	王冶梅
Wang Ying-shou	王應綬
Wang Yü	王昱
Wang Yüan-ch‘i	王原祁
Wang Yüan-ch‘u	王元初
Wang Yün	王雲
Wang Yün-hsiang	王韻香
Wei Hao-ling	魏鶴齡
Wên Tien	文點
Wên Ting	文鼎
Wêng Lo	翁雒
Wu Chao	吳照
Wu Ch‘i	吳琦
Wu Ch‘i	吳祺
Wu Hsi-tsai	吳熙載
Wu Hsiao	吳綃
Wu Hsin-lai	吳心來
Wu Huan	吳煥
Wu Hung	吳宏
Wu I-lin	吳一麟
Wu Jung-kuang	吳榮光
Wu Kên	吳艮
Wu Kuei-ch‘ên	吳規臣
Wu Li	吳歷
Wu Li	吳履
Wu Lien	吳漣
Wu Mou	吳楙
Wu Na	吳訥
Wu Pao-shu	吳寶書
Wu Shan-t‘ao	吳山濤

Wu Shih	吳時
Wu Tan	吳丹
Wu T'ao	吳滔
Wu Ting	吳定
Wu T'ing-k'ang	吳廷康
Wu Tzŭ	吳鼒
Wu Tzŭ	吳咨
Wu Wei-yeh	吳偉業
Wu Wên-chêng	吳文徵
Wu Ying-chên	吳應貞
Wu Yüan-k'ai	吳元楷
Wu Yün	吳雲
Yang Chin	楊晉
Yang Chou	楊舟
Yang Hsüan	楊鉉
Yang Pu	楊補
Yang Ta-chang	楊大章
Yang Wei-ts'ung	楊維聰
Yang Yün-hua	楊韞華
Yao Hsieh	姚燮
Yao Jo-i	姚若翼
Yao Sung	姚宋
Yao Wên-han	姚文瀚
Yao Yüan-chih	姚元之
Yeh Hsin	葉欣
Yeh Tao-fên	葉道芬
Yeh Tao-pên	葉道本
Yeh T'ao	葉洮
Yen Hsien	嚴顯
Yen Kuan	嚴冠
Yen Shêng-sun	嚴繩孫
Yen Tsai	嚴載
Yen Yü	嚴鈺
Yin Hsi	尹錫
Yin Shu-po	殷樹柏
Yin Yeh	尹埜
Yin Yüan-liang	殷元良
Ying Pao	瑛寶
Ying Shih-liang	應時良
Yo Kao	岳皋
Yu Yin	尤蔭
Yü Chi	余集
Yü Chih-ting	禹之鼎
Yü Ching-hsing	虞景星
Yü-Fêng	與風
Yü Hsing	余省
Yü Ling	俞齡
Yü Shou-po	于壽伯
Yü Sung	余崧
Yü Tsung-li	俞宗禮
Yü Yüan	虞沅
Yüan Chiang	袁江
Yüan Hsüeh	袁雪
Yüan Nien	阮年
Yüan Yao	袁耀
Yüan Ying	袁瑛
Yüan Yüan	阮元
Yün Hsi	允禧
Yün-k'o	韻可
Yün Ping	惲冰
Yün Shou-p'ing	惲壽平
Yün Yüan-chün	惲源濬
Yung Hsing	永瑆
Yung Jung	永瑢

A Êrh Pai 阿爾稗, *h.* Hsiang-ku 香穀.

A Manchu. Court painter in the Ch'ien-lung period. Birds and animals. Influenced by Lang Shih-ning. L, 61, 5. M, p.215.

Li-tai, II. A Tiger under a Pine-tree. Signed.

Ibid. VI. A Tiger standing by a steep Cliff. Signed.

Ku-kung, XXVII. Wild Geese among Lotus-leaves. Signed.

Ai Ch'i-mêng 艾啓蒙, or Ignatius Sichelbart.

B. 1708 in Bohemia. Jesuit missionary, arrived in China 1745, served at court together with Lang Shih-ning, d. 1780. Birds and animals. S. M, p.83.

Shih-chün t'u (Palace Museum album, 1935). Five Horses by Ai Ch'i-mêng and five by Lang Shih-ning. Poems by Ch'ien-lung.

K.-k. chou-k'an, vol.VI, 17. Two Pictures of Animals in Landscapes.

CH'A CHI-TSO 查繼佐, *t.* I-huang 伊璜, *h.* Tung-shan 東山, Tiao-sou 釣叟 and other names.
From Hai-ning, Chekiang. B. 1601, d. 1677. Scholar, author of historical works. Landscapes in the style of Huang Kung-wang. R, III, 15. M, p.267.

Ming-jên shu-hua, X. Chung K'uei striking a Musical Stone. Signed. Also in Shina Nanga, III, 11.

Chêng Ch'i, Hongkong (formerly Chang Ts'ung-yü). Ten Landscapes, large album-leaves, mounted as a handscroll. Title written by the artist. Signed.

Chūgoku, 8. A River Landscape with Sailing boats. Handscroll. Signed.

CH'A P'U 查浦.
Unrecorded. 18th and 19th centuries.

Musée Guimet (Dubosc collect.) Rocky Shore in front of steep Hills. Album-leaf. Colophon by the painter dated 1821 (at 90).

CH'A SHIH-PIAO 查士標, *t.* Êrh-chan 二瞻, *h.* Mei-ho 梅壑.
From Haiyang, Anhui. B. 1615, d. 1698. Chu-shêng in the Ming dynasty; after 1644 he devoted himself to writing and painting. One of the "Four Masters of Anhui". Followed first Ni Tsan, then Wu Chên and Tung Ch'i-ch'ang. Q, I, 1. R, III, 2. U, I, 2, 7. M, p.267.

Bijutsu, XXII. Stones and sparse Trees by a River. Signed, dated 1646.

J. Cahill, Wash., D.C. Album of ten Landscapes, the last signed and dated 1654.

Nanju 3. Mist and Clouds over Hsiao and Hsiang. Signed, dated 1660. Also in Sogen 236.

Ōmura, II, 3, 5. Four album-leaves of bare Trees, Bamboos and Stones, with inscriptions by the artist on the opposite leaves. Signed, dated 1666. *Cf.* Chūgoku 7.

Shên-chou, XI. A solitary Wanderer in Autumn Mountains. Signed. Poem dated 1667.

Mei-chan t'ê-k'an. Eight tall River-landscapes with Cliffs and Trees, panels of an eight-fold screen. One dated 1667.

Shên-chou, VIII. An Angler in a Boat on the River. Signed. Poem dated 1671. Also in Shina Nanga, II, 8.

Sōgen 237. Autumn Trees in the Twilight. Signed. Colophon dated 1671.

Ku-kung collect. Two Leaves from an Album of Landscapes. Seals of the artist; one dated 1672. *Cf.* Nanking Exhib. cat. 270.

Shina Nanga, III, 6. Trees in Autumn and terraced Mountains by a River, a Man crossing the Bridge. Poem by the painter, dated 1673. Also in Nanga Taikan 11.

Nanga Taikan 11. Mountains in Autumn, a Man walking over the Bridge in the front. Signed. Poem dated 1673. *Cf.* painting in J. P. Dubosc collect.

Chung-kuo, II, 151. Lake View in the Evening, after Shên Chou. Signed. Two lines of poetry, dated 1674. *Cf.* Chung-kuo ming-hua, 21.

K. Sumitomo collect., Ōiso. An album of ten leaves: sketches of rocks and bare trees. Signed and dated 1674.

Shên-chou ta-kuan, XI. A Dwelling by the Water, in the manner of Ni Tsan. Poem signed and dated 1676.

National Museum, Stockholm. A Mountain Ridge and a solitary Wanderer. Signed. Two lines of poetry dated 1675. *Cf.* Sirén, *Later*, 180.

Musée Guimet, Paris. Landscape with a Man on a Donkey passing over a Dike. Poem by the painter dated 1678.

Gems, I, 61. A thatched Pavilion by a Stream. Poem, signed and dated 1678.

Vannotti collect., Lugano. Landscape in the style of Mi Fei. Fan-painting. Signed, dated 1679.

Chêng Tê-k'un, Cambridge. Wide Mountain Ranges rising over misty Valleys beyond a River. Handscroll. Inscription by the painter, dated 1680.

C. T. Loo Successor, Frank Caro, N.Y. Album of Landscapes in various Styles. Signed and dated 1684. *Cf.* Cleveland Exhib. cat. 107.

Chang Ta-ch'ien cat., IV, 40. A Woodcutter in the early Morning. Illustration to a poem by Shên Chou copied by the painter. Long handscroll dated 1687. Colophon in praise of the picture by Tao-chi, dated 1700.

Chung-hua album, 1929. Ten Landscapes after Mi Fei, Huang Kung-wang, Wu Chên, Shên Chou and others. Signed and dated 1688.

Nanga Taisei, VIII, 165, 166. Two Landscapes. Fan-paintings, one dated 1689.

Sōkoku-ji, Kyōto. Landscape after Tung Yüan as interpreted by Shên Chou. Signed and dated 1693.

Hsin-an p'ai ming-hua chi (Shên Chou album). An Angler on a River in Autumn. Signed and dated 1693.

Freer Gallery (55, 19). Buildings at the Foot of a lofty Mountain. After Li Ssŭ-hsün. Signed and dated 1694.

Chêng Tê-k'un, Cambridge. Album of ten landscape-paintings. Inscriptions by the painter, dated 1694.

Shên-chou, XV. Two old Pine-trees. Poem by the painter dated 1696.

Nanga Taisei, X, 33. A Boat sailing on the River on a windy Day. Signed and dated "at age 82", *i.e.* in 1696.

British Museum. Sparse Trees and Pavilion. Album-leaf. Signed and dated 1697.

Ming-jên shu-hua, XXV. River Landscape; high Cliff and small Pavilion. Signed. Poem. *Cf.* Nanga Taikan 3.

Hsü-ching chai. Mountain Landscape; a Hermit seated in a Hut on a high Ledge. Dedicated to "Tan Hsien-sheng".

S.c.t.k. hsü-pien, III. Two bare Trees at a River-bank, a Man in a Boat. Signed. *Cf.* Nanga Taisei, X, 34.

Hui-hua kuan. Grazing Horses and Buffaloes on a low River-shore.

Ibid. Mountains grown with Grass and Trees. Imitating Mi Fei. Painted together with Wang Hui.

Shanghai Museum. High Cliffs on a Shore with Trees and open Pavilions. A fisherman on the water. In the manner of Ni Tsan. Inscription by the painter.

Nanking Exhib. cat. 271. A River Valley. Poem, signed.

Shimbi, XVII. Illustration to Su Tung-p'o's poem The Red Cliff. Signed. Poem. *Cf.* Tōyō, XII.

Shina Nanga, I, 51. Looking at the Fisherman. After Wu Chên. Signed.

Ibid. II, 4. Landscape. Fan-painting. Signed.

Tokasha Shina Meigashū 27. Mountain-slopes and a winding Stream. Poems by the painter and by three contemporaries.

Ibid. 28. Sketchy River View in Autumn. Poem by the painter.

Shinchō 35. A Boat in a deep Gorge. Signed. Poem.

Piacentini collect., Tōkyō. Two Landscapes, both in the manner of Wang Mêng. Signed.

Kurokawa cat. 12. Trees growing by a Rock, after K'o Chiu-ssŭ. Signed.

Lilly collect., Indianapolis. Large Mountain Landscape, with a Man in a Grass-thatched Pavilion. Poem, signed. *Cf.* Cleveland Exhib. cat. 105.

Musée Guimet, Paris. River Landscape with high Cliffs and a Pavilion in the foreground. Poem by the painter.

Ibid. River Landscape, a Man walking at the Foot of a steep Cliff. Poem by the painter.

British Museum (Add. No. 20). Tall Trees and a Wanderer. Signed.

Berlin Museum. River Landscape with Pavilions, illustrating some lines from T'ao Yüan-ming's *Kuei-ch'ü lai*. In the manner of Huang Kung-wang. Signed.

Hamburg Exhibition, 1949–1950. A Man by an old Tree.

Kawai collect., Kyōto, 1954. River-view with Pine-trees. Signed.

J. D. Ch'ên, Hongkong. Rolling Hills, leafy Trees and Pavilions built over the Water.

Chêng Tê-k'un, Cambridge. Landscape Studies after Old Masters. Ten album-leaves.

W. Hochstadter, New York. A Mountain Gully. A small pavilion on a rocky ledge; tall trees below. Signed.

CHAI CHI-CH'ANG 翟繼昌, *t.* Nien-tsu 念祖, *h.* Ch'in-fêng 琴峯.
From Chia-hsing, Chekiang. Active *c.*1790–1817. Son and pupil of the painter Chai Ta-k'un; imitated in his later works Wu Chên and Shên Chou. Landscapes and flowers. T, V, 3. U, III, 2, 16. M, p.602.

Ming-jên shu-hua, XXI. Bamboos, Roses and Narcissi by a Rockery, after Huang Ch'üan. Signed, dated 1793.
Ming-jên hsieh-chu. Bamboos and a Garden Stone. Signed. Poem dated 1803. *Cf.* Nanga Taisei, II, 6.
Nanga Taisei, II, 7 (right). Bamboo growing beside a Rock. Signed and dated 1804.
Sōgen 347. Wên Chêng-ming, Shên Chou and T'ang Yin seated by a Rock. After Ch'iu Ying. Signed, dated 1807.
Fei-tun lu shan-shui. Misty Hills, Cottages by the Stream. Signed, dated 1811.
Ch'ing êrh-shih chia. A sleeping Beauty. Poem and colophon by the painter, dated 1811.
Ming-jên shu-hua, XV. Blossoming Plum-trees by a River, after T'ang Yin. Signed. Poem dated 1811.
Ibid. The Ch'ing-pi Pavilion, after Ts'ao Chih-po. Signed. Poem dated 1811.
Ibid. XII. Flowers and Trees. Painted together with Wang Hsüeh-hao, Chiang Hsün, Chu Ang-chih and Chou Li. Peaches by Chai Chi-ch'ang. Signed. Also in Nanga Taikan I.
Ibid. XII. Narcissi, Bamboos and Orchids, after Chao Mêng-fu. Album-leaf. Signed.
Ibid. XVIII. A Tartar Soldier leading a Horse. After a Yüan model. Signed. Poems.
Ho Kuan-wu, Hongkong. A Man asleep in a House; a Visitor arriving in the Garden Outside. Handscroll. Signed.
Nanga Taisei, II, 7 (left). Bamboo growing beside a Rock. Poem, signed.

CHAI TA-K'UN 翟大坤, *t.* Tzŭ-hou 子厚, *h.* Yün-p'ing 雲屏 and Wu-wên-tzŭ 無聞子.
From Chia-hsing, Chekiang. Active *c.*1770–1804. Landscapes after the Yüan masters and Shên Chou; flowers and birds after Ch'ên Shun. T, V, 3. U, III, 1, 23. M, p.602.

I-yüan chên-shang 5. A Temple in the Mountains among Pine-trees. Signed and dated 1767.
Kokka 355. Landscape. Fan-painting. Signed. Poem dated 1773.
Hamburg Exhibition, 1949–1950. Autumn Mountain in the Style of Wang Mêng. Ink on gold ground. Dated 1787.
Tokasha Shina Meigashū 78. A quiet Bay, Pavilions built over the Water, Mountain Peaks along the River. Signed. Poem dated 1792. *Cf.* Nanga Taisei, XII, 128.
Shên-chou album, 1909. Album of landscapes with figures. Signed, one dated 1804.
Shina Nanga, I, 124. Landscape. Signed. Poem.
Ibid. I, 125. Landscape. Signed.
Ibid. II, 3. Landscape. Signed. Two lines of poetry.
Ibid. III, 5. Landscape after Huang Kung-wang.
Ibid. III, 8. Landscape after Tung Yüan. Signed.
Sōraikan, II, 86. A Man in a Pavilion listening to the Mountain Torrent. Also in Ōmura, I, 10.
Hamburg Exhibition, 1949–1950. Landscape in the style of Wang Fu (1362–1416).

CHAN-FU 湛復.
A priest, active *c.*1640–1664. Landscapes. Unrecorded.

Sōgen 197. Mountains in Snow. Signed, dated 1664.

CHANG CHAO 張照, *t.* Tê-t'ien 得天, *h.* Ching-nan 涇南, Wu-ch'uang 梧囪 and T'ien-p'ing chü-shih 天屏居士.

From Hua-t'ing (Sung-chiang), Kiangsu. B. 1691, d. 1745. President of the Board of Justice. Plum-blossoms, and pictures of Kuan-yin. R, IX, 13. U, I, 3, 13. M, p.475.

British Museum. Pine-trees and Cliffs. Handscroll. Signed, dated 1718.

Nanga Taisei, III, 82. Branches of Flowering Plum in a Vase. Signed and dated 1724.

K.-k. shu-hua chi, XXII. A Branch of a Plum-tree, after Wang Ku-hsiang. Signed, dated 1729.

Nanking Exhib. cat. 337. A Flowering Plum-tree. Two inscriptions by the artist, dated 1730 and 1732.

Po-mei chi. Branches of Plum-blossoms. Signed. Poem and colophon dated 1734.

Nanga Taisei, III, 84. A Branch of Plum-blossoms. Signed and dated 1738.

CHANG CHO 張琢, *t.* P'u-shan 璞山.

From Ch'ü-fu, Shantung. Landscapes and flowers, which were much praised by Chang Wên-t'ao (1764–1814). T. M, p.491.

Sung-pê. Pine-trees, after Ch'ên Shou-shan. Signed, dated *jên-ch'ên* (1832?) *Cf.* Nanga Taisei, V, 35.

CHANG FÊNG 張風(飌), *t.* Ta-fêng 大風, *h.* Shêng-chou tao-shih 昇州道士.

From Nanking. Active *c.*1645–1674. Chu-shêng at the end of the Ming dynasty; after 1644, he devoted himself to Buddhism. Painted landscapes, figures, flowers. P, III, 5. Q, I, 1. U, I, 1, 7. M, p.472.

Ōmura, II, 5. A Study-pavilion built over a Stream. After a Yüan master. Signed, dated 1646. *Cf.* Sirén, *Later*, pl.196.

T'ai-shan album, Series I. Album of four landscapes and four leaves of writing. Signed, dated 1647. *Cf.* Nanga Taisei, XI, 106–107.

Shina Nanga, II, 6. A Man standing by a twisted Tree amidst Rocks. Lightly sketched. Handscroll. Signed, dated 1648. *Cf.* Shên-chou ta-kuan, XI.

Nanking Exhib. cat. 284. A Man standing beneath an overhanging Rock on the Bank of a River. Signed and dated 1648.

Chung-kuo, II, 139. A Wanderer in Autumn Woods. Signed, dated 1651.

K.-k. shu-hua chi, VI. Chu-ko Liang. Signed, dated 1654.

Chung-kuo, II, 140. The Hermitage in the wooded Valley. Signed, dated 1658. Also in Shina Nanga, I, 38.

Nanjū 17. A Man on a Cliff looking across a Precipice. Signed, dated 1660. Also in Tōyō, XI.

Chang Ta-ch'ien cat. I, 30. T'ao Yüan-ming smelling a Chrysanthemum-flower. Poem, signed and dated 1660.

S.c.t.k. hsü-pien, II. Rocks and Streams in T'ien-hua Mountain. Signed, dated 1660. *Cf.* Nanga Taisei, IX, 240.

C. T. Loo's Successor, Frank Caro, N.Y. A Man with a Staff crossing a Natural Bridge. Inscription by the painter, dated 1660. *Cf.* Toronto 59.

Breuer collect. (formerly) Berlin. Three Leaves from an Album of Landscape Sketches. Signed, dated 1673. London Exhibition Nos.2981. *Cf.* Sirén, *Later* pl.197.

T. T. Ma, Hongkong. Precipitous Cliffs and Waterfall. Inscription by the artist.

T'ai-shan ts'an-shih-lou ts'ang-hua, III. A Man writing on a Cliff. Signed.

Nanking Exhib. cat. 282. Four Leaves from an Album of Landscapes. Seals of the artist.

Ibid. 283. A Man standing under Trees, looking at a Waterfall. Signed.

Mei-chan t'ê-k'an 56. A Man writing on a Mountain Wall. Poem by the painter. *Cf.* Nanga Taisei Add. IV, 33r.

S.c.t.k. hsü-pien, III. A deep Ravine between towering Rocks. Signed. *Cf.* Nanga Taisei, IX, 241.

Yonezawa, pl.29 (Mayuyama collect., Tōkyō). Portrait of Chu-ko K'ung-ming. Inscription, seal of the artist. Another version of the picture in T'ien-ch'i shu-wu.
Shina Meiga Senshū 19. Clearing after Rain in the Valley; a man seated in a small hut. Poem.
Chicago Art Institute. Portrait of Tu Chün seated by a Rockery under a Tree. *Cf.* Shên-chou, IV; Hsü-ching chai.

CHANG HAO 張鎬, *t.* Wu-ch'ien 武遷, *h.* Ch'ing-shan 卿山.
From Ch'ien-t'ang, Chekiang. Court-painter in the Ch'ien-lung period. Figures. S.

K.-k. shu-hua chi, XV. The Lien-ch'ang Palace. Illustration to a poem by Yüan Chên, a T'ang poet.

CHANG HSIA 張洽, *t.* Yüeh-ch'uan 月川 and Yü-ch'uan 玉川, *h.* Ch'ing-jo ku-yü 青弱古漁 and other names.
B. 1718, d. *c.*1800. Nephew of Chang Tsung-ts'ang. Landscapes. U, I, 3, 16. M, p.483.

Voretzsch. Four Landscape Studies on album-leaves. Signed. Two of them dated 1755.
Fei-tun lu shan-shui. River Scenery with a Fisherman. Signed, dated 1758. Many inscriptions.
Chūgoku, 8. A Valley filled with Mist; two figures on a ledge. Signed and dated 1759.
Ming-jên shu-hua, VIII. River Landscape, after Huang Kung-wang. Signed. Poem dated 1772. Also in Shina Nanga, III, 7; Nanga Taikan 11.
British Museum (Add. No.50). Fishermen's Pleasure. Signed, dated 1780.
Sōgen 325. Trees and strange Peaks, after Wang Wei. Signed. Poem dated 1784.
Shên-chou, XX. Sharp Mountain Peaks over a deep Gully, after Tung Yüan. Signed and dated 1795 (at 78). *Cf.* Shina Nanga, III, 1.
S.c.t.k. hsü-pien, IV. Woody Landscape. Signed, dated 1798. *Cf.* Nanga Taisei, X, 201.
Shên-chou, XXI. A winding Stream in the Mountains. Signed, dated 1799 (at 82).
Nanking Exhib. cat. 364. Two Leaves from an Album of Landscapes. Signed.
Kokka 511. Landscape. Poem. Seals of the painter.
Sōgen 324. Landscape. Handscroll.
Kurokawa cat. 37. Pine-trees, Bamboo and Orchids growing by Rocks. Signed.
Mizuta collect., Kyōto. An Album of Landscapes in early styles. Signed.

CHANG HSIAO-SSŬ 張孝思, *t.* Che-chih 則之, *h.* Lan-i 懶逸.
From Tan-t'u, Kiangsu. Early Ch'ing period. Collector and connoisseur. Painted epidendrums. M, p.480.

Musée Guimet, Paris. Epidendrums by a Rockery. Signed with the painter's seal.

CHANG HSIN 張莘, *t.* Ch'iu-ku 秋穀. Original name Chang K'un 張昆 and *t.* Ch'iu-ku 秋谷, *h.* Hsi-lêng tiao-t'u 西冷釣徒.
From Hang-chou. Went to Japan *c.*1871–1888. Flowers in the style of Yün Shou-p'ing; landscapes after Ni Tsan; orchids and bamboos after Wu Chên; plum-blossoms after Wang Mien, etc. T, V, 9. M, p.486.

Kokka 224. Lotus Flowers, after Wang Yüan. Signed. Two lines of poetry. Also in Nanju 7; Tōyō, XII.
Nanju 9. Banana Leaves. Signed. Colophon.
Sōgen 336. Tree-peonies, after the emperor Hui-tsung. Signed. Poem.

CHANG HSIUNG 張熊, *t.* Shou-fu 壽甫, *h.* Tzŭ-hsiang 子祥, Yüan-hu wai-shih 鴛湖外史 and other names. From Hsiu-shui, Chekiang. B. 1803, d. 1886. Flowers and birds; followed Chou Chih-mien and Wang Wu. Painted also landscapes and figures. T, Add. I, p.3. M, p.491.

Nanga Taisei, X, 228. Landscape with a Man in a House. Poem, signed and dated 1841; other inscriptions by the artist dated 1876 and 1885.

Ming-jên shu-hua, XII. Chrysanthemums and Hai-t'ang Flowers. Signed at 69 (1871).

Ibid. XII. *Ficus Punila.* Signed, dated 1871.

Chang Tzŭ-hsiang chên-chi ch'ung-niao hua-hui ts'ê (Hui-wên t'ang, 1925). An Album of twelve Pictures of Flowers, Birds and Insects. Signed, dated 1871.

Shina Nanga, II, 4. Flowers. Fan-painting. Signed, dated 1880 (at 78).

Sōgen 359. Ink Peonies. Signed. Poem dated 1881 (at 79).

Ibid. 360. Peonies, Magnolias and Hai-t'ang Flowers. Signed. Poem dated 1882 (at 80).

Nanga Taisei, V, 56. Cypress Tree, Bamboo and Narcissi. Signed and dated 1882.

Ibid. XII, 93–104. An Album of twelve Landscapes. Signed and dated 1884.

Nanga Taikan 3. A Garden Stone. Signed. Poem dated 1885 (at 83).

Shina Nanga, I, 140. Lotuses and a Bird. Signed.

Ibid. I, 141. Flowers and a Bird, after Hua Yen. Signed.

Ibid. III, 4. Peonies, after Tsou I-kuei. Signed.

Tōan 76. Autumn Flowers. Signed. Poem.

CHANG HSÜEH-TSÊNG 張學曾, *t.* Êrh-wei 爾唯, *h.* Yo-an 約菴.
From Shan-yin, Chekiang. Active *c.*1630–1650. Governor of Suchou. One of the "Nine Friends in Painting", according to Wu Wei-yêh. Landscapes, followed Tung Yüan. P, III, 2. U, I, 1, 6. M, p.473.

Hua-chung chiu-yu (Yu-chêng album). Landscapes. Signed, dated 1633.

Sōgen 243. High Mountains by a River. Signed, dated 1650. *Cf.* Liu, 103.

Chang Tsung-yü cat. A Bridge across a Mountain Stream. Dated 1655.

Hui-hua kuan (formerly P'ang Yüan-chi). Landscape in the manner of Ni Tsan. Signed and dated 1656.

Shina Nanga, II, 5. A Temple in the Mountains in Autumn, after a Sung master of the Northern School. Seal of the painter.

Tōyō, XI. Mountains in Mist. Signed. Two lines of poetry.

Hua-chung chiu-yu chi-ts'ê (Hakubundō album, 1921). Old Trees and low Buildings at the Foot of misty Mountains. After Chao Tso. Signed.

CHANG HSÜN 張恂, *t.* Chih-kung 穉恭. *h.* Hu-shan 壺山.
From Ching-yang, Shensi. Chin-shih in 1643. Landscapes followed Tung Yüan. R, I, 1, 9. Q, I, 1. U, II, 1, 17. M, p.473.

Chang Ta-ch'ien cat., IV, 37. River-landscape. The picture was done in co-operation with Ch'êng Sui and Fang Hêng-hsien. One inscription by Ch'êng Sui is reproduced, dated 1655.

Shinchō 32. Mountain Landscape. Signed. Poem dated 1682.

Ho Kuan-wu, Hongkong. Landscape. Signed.

J. P. Dubosc, Lugano. An album of landscapes. Signed.

CHANG JÊN-SHAN 張仁山.
Unrecorded. 18th century.

Voretzsch. T'ao Yüan-ming preparing Wine; Lin Ho-ching on a Stroll. Two album-leaves. Signed and dated *kuei-ch'ou* (1733 or 1793).

CHANG JO-AI 張若靄, *t.* Ch'ing-luan 晴嵐.

From T'ung-ch'êng, Anhui. B. 1713, d. 1746. Son of the scholar and statesman Chang T'ing-yü and inheritated some of his father's high official degrees. Flowers, bamboos, birds and insects. Q, II, 1. R, XI, 6. S, I, 4. M, p.479.

Li-tai, II. Pine-trees, Bamboos and a Bird. Signed.

Ku-kung, XXIV. Narcissi. Signed.

K.-k. shu-hua chi, VIII. Pine-trees, Bamboos and a Bird. Signed. Poem by Ch'ien-lung. *Cf.* Li-tai, II.

Ibid. XXVI. Plum Blossoms, Narcissi, Camellias and a Bird. Signed.

K.-k. chou-k'an 378. The Poet Ch'ü Yüan walking with a Staff. Signed. (Other paintings by Chang Jo-ai in various issues of K.-k. chou-k'an; see Index.)

Wên-ming album, 1940. Album of eight Landscape-paintings. Signed.

J. D. Ch'ên, Hongkong. Pine-tree, Bamboo and Plum-blossoms. Handscroll, signed.

Shinchō 61. Sparrows in a Plum-tree in Snow, after Pien Wên-chin. Signed.

Ibid. 61. A Crane under Pine-trees in Snow, after Pien Wên-chin. Signed.

Sōgen 302. Garden Pavilions by a Stream. Poems by Ch'ien-lung and the painter.

CHANG JO-CH'ÊNG 張若澄, *t.* Ching-chien 鏡堅, *h.* Lien-hsüeh 鍊雪.

B. 1722, d. 1770. Second son of Chang T'ing-yü and younger brother of Chang Jo-ai. Plum-blossoms, birds and landscapes. R, XI, 6. M, p.479.

K.-k. shu-hua chi, VII. A Pavilion by a River, misty mountains in the background. Poem by Ch'ien-lung, copied by a courtier.

CHANG KÊNG 張庚, original name Chang T'ao 張燾, *t.* P'u-shan 浦山, *h.* Mi-chia 彌伽, Kua-t'ien i-shih 瓜田逸史, and Po-ch'ü-ts'un-sang-chê 白苧村桑者.

From Hsiu-shui, Chekiang. B. 1685, d. 1760. Writer on painting, author of the *Kuo-ch'ao hua-chêng lu* 國朝畫徵錄, *P'u-shan lun-hua* 浦山論畫, and other books. Landscapes; pupil of the lady painter Ch'ên Shu. R, XI, 1, 19. T, III, 1. U, I, 3, 10. M, p.481.

Nanga Taisei, Introduct. 42. Landscape with bare Trees. Signed; another inscription by the artist dated 1716.

Nanju 6. Landscape after Chiang Kuan-tao. Signed, dated 1750. *Cf.* Tōyō, XII; Pageant, 914.

Shinchō 51. A Cottage in a Bamboo-grove. Signed. Poem dated 1754 (at 70). *Cf.* Sōraikan, I, 63.

Fei-tun lu shan-shui. Landscape with Mulberry-trees. Signed, dated 1760.

Pageant, 915. Landscape with Travellers, in the manner of Chü-jan. Signed and dated 1760.

Metropolitan Museum. Mountain Landscape after Wang Mêng. Signed.

CHANG KU 章谷, *t.* Yen-tsai 言在, *h.* Ku-yü 古愚.

From Hangchou. Active *c.*1640–1660. Calligraphist. Painted landscapes and figures. L, 30, 2. P, IV, 16. M, p.386.

Ōmura, I, 4, 5, 6, 7, 9, 11 (Marquis Sho's collect.) Nine Landscapes, all of same size. Each with two lines of poetry and seals of the painter. No.7 dated 1644.

Nanju 9. Landscape. Signed, dated 1657. Also in Tōyō, XII.

Kyūka, II. Mountain Path in Szechuan, after Wang Wei. Signed.

CHANG MU 張穆, *t.* Mu-chih 穆之, *h.* T'ieh-ch'iao 鐵橋.

From Tung-k'uan, Kwangtung. Lived *c.*1620–1700. Horses, eagles, landscapes, orchids, and bamboos. Q, I, 1. R, III, 11. M, p.473.

Shên-chou, XXI. A Horse rubbing its Neck against an old Willow. Signed, dated 1656. *Cf.* Chūgoku, 8.
Hui-hua kuan. A Man leading a Horse. Colour on silk. Signed and dated 1656.
Sung-chai. Two Horses under Willows. Signed, dated 1660.
Ming Chang T'ieh-ch'iao hua-ma chüan (Shên-chou 1921). Eight Horses. Handscroll. Signed. Poem dated 1661. *Cf.* Sung-chai.
Shên-chou, XI. Two Eagles in a leafless Tree. Signed, dated 1663.
T. T. Ma, Hongkong. Four Horses on a Pasture near two Willow-trees. Signed and dated 1666.
I-yüan chên-shang, 9. A Hawk on the Branch of a Tree. Signed, dated 1666.
Sung-chai. Eight Horses. Handscroll. Poem by the painter, dated 1669.
T'ien-ch'i shu-wu. A Deer beneath Willow-trees. Signed.
Nanga Taisei, I, 106. Orchids growing on a Rock. Seal of the artist.
Ibid. II, 243. Narcissi. Seal of the artist. Album-leaf.
Ibid. V, 83. Camellia Flowers. Seals of the artist. Album-leaf.
Ibid. VII, 93, 94. A Lion; a Wolf?; a Deer; a Tiger. Four album-leaves. Seals of the artist.

CHANG NAI-CHI 張迺耆, *t.* Shou-min 壽民, *h.* Po-mei 白眉.
Nephew of Chang Yü 張敔. From T'ung-ch'êng, Anhui; lived in Nanking. Active *c.*1820. Flowers, birds and pine-trees; also orchids and bamboos. T. M, p.483.

Sung-pê. A Cypress Tree and Mynah-birds. Signed, dated *ping-shên* (1836). *Cf.* Nanga Taisei, VI, 198.

CHANG P'EI-TUN 張培敦, *t.* Yen-ch'iao 硯樵, *h.* Yen-shih shan-jên 硯石山人.
From Suchou. Pupil of Chai Ta-k'un. Calligraphist. Landscapes and portraits. T. U, III, 2, 16. M, p.489.

Hamburg Exhibition, 1949–1950. Landscape after Chai Ta-k'un, in the style of T'ang Yin. Signed, dated 1815.
Hui-hua kuan. A Scholar in a Pavilion among Bamboos. Copy of a picture by T'ang Yin.
Nanga Taisei, XII, 161, 162. Two Landscapes. Album-leaves. See also VIII, 218 (fan).

CHANG P'ÊNG-CH'UNG 張鵬翀, *t.* T'ien-fei 天飛 or 天扉 and Liu-an 柳菴, *h.* Nan-hua 南華.
From the Ch'ung-ming Island, Kiangsu. B. 1688, d. 1745. Literary writer. Landscapes, followed the four Yüan masters. Q, I, 3. R, XI, 1. T, I, 1. U, I, 3, 13. M, p.479.

Shên-chou, XI. Bare Trees and Bamboos. Signed, dated 1736. *Cf.* Nanga Taisei Add., IV, 92.
Kurokawa cat. 23. Two intertwined Trees and some Bamboo. Signed and dated 1736. *Cf.* Shinchō 51.
K.-k. shu-hua chi, IX. Blue Peaks in the clear Autumn, after Wang Mêng. Signed, dated 9th of the 9th month, 1744.
Ibid. XVI. Same title as the preceding, though different in composition. Same date; dedicated to the emperor. Poem by Ch'ien-lung dated the same day.
K.-k. chou-k'an, 389–433 (in various issues). Album of small Landscapes. Signed.
Ibid. 476–479. Album of Flower Paintings. Signed.
Voretzsch. The Hermitage; the Morning Mist. Two album-leaves. Seals of the painter.

CHANG SHAO-CHIU 張韶九.
Unrecorded. Probably active at the beginning of the 19th century.

Boston Museum. A Man angling in a Stream. Signed and dated *wu-tzŭ* (1828?)

CHANG SHÊNG 章聲, *t.* Tzŭ-hao 子鶴.
Second son of Chang Ku. Active *c.* 1690. Landscapes, flowers. P, IV, 16. M, p.386.

Ars Asiatica, I, pl. XLVI. Magnolias, Peonies and Pheasants. Signed, dated 1694.
Kokka 496. Two Pheasants. Signed. Also in Nanju 11.
Nanju 8. Summer Mountains, after Tung Yüan. Signed. Also in Tōyō, XII; Kyuka, II.
Kyūka, II. Reading in a Pavilion by a Stream, after Tung Yüan. Signed.
Field Museum, Chicago. A natural Stone Bridge in the T'ien-t'ai Mountains. After a picture by Hsia Kuei. Signed.
Nü-wa chai. Mountain River; Rocks and Trees. Ink on gold ground.

CHANG SHIH-CHANG 張世掌, *h.* K'ua-ku 瓠谷.
From Yang-chou, Kiangsu. Active *c.*1700. Landscapes, followed the Sung masters. M, p.477.

Nanju 14. Landscape. Signed.

CHANG SU 章疏.
Unrecorded. Seals read: *t.* Chung-hu 中笏. From the Ch'ing dynasty.

Nanju 16. Two Landscape Pictures, each with two lines of poetry and seals of the painter. Second one also in Tōyō, XII.

CHANG TAO-WU 張道渥, *t.* Fêng-tzŭ 封紫, *h.* Shui-wu 水屋 and Chu-kuei 竹畦; also called himself Chang Fêng-tzŭ 張風子.
Native of Fou-shan in Shansi. Eighteenth century. Landscapes. T. U, III, 1, 27; M, p.488.

Cleveland Exhib. cat. 115 (Seattle Museum of Art). Landscape Handscroll, signed and dated 1793. *Cf.* Sekai Bijutsu Zenshū XX, text illus. 118.

CHANG T'ING-CHI 張廷濟, *t.* Shu-wei 叔未, *h.* Mei-shou lao-jên 眉壽老人.
From Chia-hsing, Chekiang. B. 1768, d. 1848. Well-known collector of antiques and paintings. M, p.495.

Shina Meiga Senshū 37. A Buddhist Figure, after Chin Nung. Signed, dated 1820. Long inscriptions by the painter.

CHANG T'ING-YEN 張廷彥.
Court-painter in the Ch'ien-lung period. Figures and palaces. S, I, p.19.

Ku-kung, XLII. The Battle of Wu-shih (a place between Aksu and Kashgar) in 1765. Signed. Poem and colophon by Ch'ien-lung dated 1768.
K.-k. shu-hua chi, XXXVIII. The Mid-Autumn Festival: Palace View with Figures. Signed.
Boston Museum. A palatial Compound by a River in Snow. Signed.

CHANG TS'AI 章采, *t.* Tzŭ-chên 子真.
Eldest son of Chang Ku. Active *c.*1670. Landscapes. P, IV, 16. M, p.386.

National Museum, Stockholm. Landscape. Signed, dated 1672.
Shimbi, XVIII. Landscape. Signed, dated 1673.
Kokka 27. Pu-tai under a Pine-tree.

CHANG TSUNG-TS'ANG 張宗蒼, *t.* Mo-ts'un 默存 or Mo-ts'en 墨岑, *h.* Huang-ts'un 篁村, Lu-shan 鹿山, and other names.
From Suchou. B. 1686, d. *c.*1756. Landscapes, pupil of Huang Ting. Began service in the palace in 1751; retired in 1755. Q, II, 2. R, XII, 2. T, III, 4. U, I, 3, 15. M, p.483.

Fei-tun lu shan-shui. Mountain Landscape, after Wang Mêng. Signed and dated 1723.
I-yüan chên-shang 4. Landscape-handscroll, signed and dated 1730.
Shina Meiga Senshū, II, 36. Overgrown Hills enclosing a Stretch of narrow River. In the manner of Huang Kung-wang. Inscription by the painter dated 1732.
Shinchō 59. Forests and strange Peaks, after Tung Yüan. Signed, dated 1732.
Ming-jên shu-hua, XXVI. Landscape. Signed. Colophon dated 1740.
K.-k. shu-hua chi, XII. Mountain Landscape with Pavilions over a Stream, after Tung Yüan. Signed, dated 1743.
Nanga Taisei, XII, 85–89. Six Landscapes. Album-leaves, the last signed and dated 1743.
Shên-chou, XIII. A deep Ravine in the Mountains; men in a boat and others walking along the river-bank. After Wang Mêng. Signed, dated 1745. *Cf.* Shina Nanga, I, 94.
Ming-jên shu-hua, X. Cloudy Mountain-landscape with high Buildings. Signed. Poem dated 1747.
Ku-kung, XXVII. Landscape after Huang Kung-wang. Signed, dated 1747. Poem by Ch'ien-lung.
Tōan 56, 57. Two album-leaves: Mountains in Snow, after Fan K'uan. Signed, dated 1748. Hermits in the Mountains. Signed. Colophon.
Ho Kuan-wu, Hongkong. Album of eight Landscapes in various Styles. Signed and dated 1748.
Kurokawa cat. 26. Two Men seated, talking, on a Ledge beside a River. Signed and dated 1749.
Shina Nanga, II, 10. Mountain Landscape, after Wang Mêng. Signed. Colophon, dated 1753.
Shên-chou, XVI. High Mountains by a River, a Grove of Trees on the Rocky Shore in the foreground. Poem by the painter, dated 1781(!)
Ibid. IX. Illustration to Ou-yang Hsiu's poem The Song of Autumn. Signed. Also in Shina Nanga, I, 95.
Chang Huang-ts'un shan-shui ts'ê (Shên-chou kuo-kuang shê, 1920). An Album of ten Landscapes with poems by the painter.
Li-tai, III. A Temple in the cloudy Mountain. Signed. Poem by Ch'ien-lung.
Ibid. V. Angling Boats on a River in Autumn. Signed. Poem by Ch'ien-lung.
Ibid. V. Playing the *Ch'in* in a cloudy Valley. Hand-scroll. Signed. Poem by Ch'ien-lung.
Ibid. VI. Mountain Landscape with a Man returning Home. Signed; poem by Ch'ien-lung.
Ku-kung, XXXIV. Pavilion among Bamboos by a Waterfall. Signed. Poem by Ch'ien-lung.
K.-k. shu-hua chi, X. Landscape. Signed. Poem by Ch'ien-lung.
Ibid. XVIII. A Man seated Cross-legged in a Thatched Hut. Signed. Poem by Ch'ien-lung.
Ibid. XXIII. Cloudy Peaks and rushing Streams. Signed. Poem by Ch'ien-lung.
Ibid. XXVI. Cloudy Peaks and Pavilions in a Gorge. Signed. Poem by Ch'ien-lung.
Ibid. XXVII. Rain over the "Willow Stream". Signed. Poem by Ch'ien-lung.
Ibid. XXXVI. Cloudy Mountains and Green Pines. Signed. Poem by Ch'ien-lung.
Ibid. XXXVIII. Mountains on a clear Autumn Day. Signed. Poem by Ch'ien-lung.
Ōmura, I, 8. The T'ien-p'ing Mountain (one of the sixteen Views of Suchou). Also in Sōraikan, I, 64.
Shinchō 60 (Howard Hollis, Cleveland). Landscape. Signed. Poem by Ch'ien-lung, dated 1768. *Cf.* Cleveland Exhib. cat. 88.

Kurokawa cat. 27. Autumn Mountains, after Chao Meng-fu. Large album-leaf, signed.

Metropolitan Museum (42.74.1). Album of eight Miniature Paintings, Landscapes and Bamboo. Signed. *Cf.* Bulletin, 1942, p.123.

National Museum, Stockholm. River Landscape in Ni Tsan's Style. Album-leaf. Signed.

CHANG TUNG 張棟, *t.* Hung-hsün 鴻勛, *h.* Yü-ch'uan 玉川, K'an-yün shan-jên 看雲山人 and other names. From Wu-chiang, Kiangsu. Active *c.* 1750–1774. Landscapes, followed Wang Yüan-ch'i. Q, II, 2. R, XII, 13. U, III, 1, 11. M, p.482.

Shên-chou, IV. Leafless Trees by a Stream. Signed. Poem dated 1773. Also in Shina Nanga, I, 96.

Nanga Taikan 2. Deeply-creviced Mountains rising through Mist; bare trees below. Poem by the artist.

Princeton (Du Bois-Morris collect.) A Pavilion by a Stream in the Mountain, a Visitor approaching. Signed: Yü-ch'uan.

CHANG TZ'Ŭ-NING 張賜甯, *t.* K'un-i 坤一, *h.* Kuei-yen 桂巖.
From Ts'ang-chou, Hopei. B. 1743, d. after 1816. Flowers, birds, figures and landscapes. T, VIII, 2. U, III, 1, 15. M, p.484.

Chūgoku, 8. A Range of steep Hills. Large album-leaf? Signed and dated 1782.

Shina Nanga, III, 2. A Scholar in a Pavilion. Signed, dated 1792.

S.c.t.k. hsü-pien, I. Orchids and Bamboo growing by a Garden Stone. Signed, dated 1796.

Tokasha Shina Meigashū 89. Tall Trees and Bamboos at the Foot of a Mountain Slope, some cottages under them. Signed, dated 1800. *Cf.* Nanga Taisei, X, 205.

Pageant 945. Amarantus Plant. Signed, dated 1801.

Shên-chou, VI. Portrait of Chi Yün; half length. Inscriptions by I Ping-shou (dated 1807) and Wêng Fang-kang.

Tokasha Shina Meigashū 90. Sketchy Landscape with two Men on a Promontory and scattered Trees on the Shore. Signed, dated 1816. *Cf.* Nanga Taisei, X, 206.

S.c.t.k. hsü-pien, VI. A Stone and Climbing Wistaria. Signed.

T'ai-shan ts'an-shih-lou ts'ang-hua, I. A Mountain Valley; tall and thin Trees, a Pavilion by a Stream. Colophon by the painter.

Fei-tun lu hua-hui. Orchids and Chrysanthemums, after Hsü Ch'ung-ssu. Signed.

Pageant 946. The Swallow Cliff at the Yangtse. Signed. Poem.

Ibid. 947. Orchids in a Rockery. Signed.

Nanga Taisei, IV, 149–154; V, 86 and 119. Various Flower Paintings.

Nanking Exhib. cat. 352. Baskets of Flowers. Poem, signed.

CHANG WÊN-T'AO 張問陶, *t.* Lo-tsu 樂祖 and Chung-yeh 仲冶, *h.* Ch'uan-shan 船山 and other names. From Sui-ning, Szechuan. B. 1764, d. 1814. Landscapes, flowers, birds, figures and horses. T, VIII, 6. U, I, 3, 19. M, p.488.

Princeton (Du Bois-Morris collect.) Two Men in a Boat on a River. After Shih-t'ao. Poem by the painter dated 1796.

I-yüan chên-shang 9. Landscape. Signed and dated 1801.

Shina Nanga, II, 4. Bodhidharma seated on a Mat. Fan-painting. Signed. Poem dated 1805.

Ibid. I, 117. Chrysanthemums and Epidendrums. Signed, dated 1810.

Fei-tun lu hua-hui. A Branch of Orange-tree. Signed, dated 1810.

Po-mei chi. Branches of Plum Blossoms. Signed. Poem.

Robert Rousset, Paris. Monkey climbing a Pine-tree. Signed.

Nanga Taisei, I, 252; III, 160; IV, 159. Various Flower Paintings.

CHANG YEN-CH'ANG 張燕昌, *t.* Wên-yü 文魚, *h.* Pao-t'ang 苞堂.
A native of Hai-yen in Chekiang. B. 1738, d. after 1810. Calligraphist, painted orchids, bamboo and landscapes. R, II, 3, 9a. T. M, p.484.

Nanga Taisei, I, 246. An Orchid Plant. Signed and dated 1793.
Ibid. I, 236–45. Album of Paintings of Orchids. Signed and dated 1795.
Ibid. Add. IV, 116. Orchids. Signed and dated 1809, "at the age of 73".
Ibid. V, 229. Cabbage. Signed and dated 1810.

CHANG YIN 張崟, *t.* Pao-yen 寶巖, *h.* Hsi-an 夕庵, Ch'ieh-wêng 且翁 and other names.
From Tan-t'u, Kiangsu. B. 1761, d. 1829. In landscape-painting he followed at first Wên Chêng-ming and Shên Chou, and later on the Sung and Yüan masters. Also flowers, bamboos and Buddhist figures. T. U, III, 2, 6. M, p.485.

Ming-hua sou-ch'i, II, 11. Landscape with two Pine-trees. Poem by the painter dated 1796. *Cf.* Chung-kuo ming-hua, 27.
Shinchō 68 (Tomioka collect., Kyōto). Mountain Landscape with a Man in a Hut. After Shên Chou. Signed, dated 1822.
Tōan 63. Pine-trees enveloped by Clouds, after Shêng Mou. Signed, dated 1822.
Gems, I, 84. The South Village. Poem, signed and dated 1822.
Chung-kuo ming-hua, 18. A Man walking in the Mountains. Poem, signed and dated 1824.
Shina Nanga, I, 135. Crows in leafless Trees. Signed. Colophon, dated 1824. Also in Chung-kuo ming-hua, vol.18.
Commercial Press Album, 1929. Album of ten Landscapes, the last signed and dated 1825.
Chung-kuo, II, 156. Listening to the Rain in the Ch'ao-yin Study, after Fang Ts'ung-i. Signed. Colophon dated 1827.
Hamburg Exhibition, 1949–1950. Scholars meeting in a Garden. Signed, dated 1827.
T'ai-shan ts'an-shih-lou ts'ang-hua, II. A Birthday Gathering. Signed and dated 1830.
Hsü-ching chai. A Lady sewing by a Window, after Yü Chih-ting. Signed. Colophon by Kuo Hsün dated 1844.
Ming-jên shu-hua, XXV. Trees on cloudy Peaks, after Li Ch'êng. Signed.
Nanking Exhib. cat. 363. Mountains in Summer before Rain. Long inscription by the artist.
Tōan 62. Cloudy Peaks, after Mi Yu-jen. Signed. Poem.
Ibid. 64. A Boat on a Stream. Fan-painting. Signed.

CHANG YÜ 章于, *t.* Tzŭ-ts'un 梓邨.
From Wu-hsi, Kiangsu. Active *c.*1680. Famous for his pictures of monkeys. M, p.386.

Kokka 398. Landscape with Monkeys. Fan-painting. Signed, dated 1688.

CHANG YÜ 張敔, *t.* Chih-yüan 芷園, *h.* Hsüeh-hung 雪鴻 and other names.
From Nanking. B. 1734, d. 1803. Flowers, birds, insects, landscapes and figures. U, III, 1, 13. M, p.483.

Wên-ming album, 1929. Twelve paintings of flowers, rocks, etc., the last signed and dated 1768.
Nanga Taisei, I, 228. Bamboo and Orchids growing by a Stone. Signed and dated 1791.
Ibid. V, 39. A Pine-tree. Album-leaf. Signed and dated 1791.
Shina Nanga, I, 122. Lychnis Flowers. Album-leaf. Seals of the painter.
Robert Rousset, Paris. A Mynah-bird on the Branch of a flowering Plum-tree. Signed.

CHANG YÜ-SEN 張雨森, original name Yü 雨, *t.* Tso-lin 作霖, *h.* Ts'ang-yeh 蒼埜.
From Tang-t'u, Anhui. Court-painter in the Ch'ien-lung period. Landscapes in the style of Wên Chêng-ming. Also flowers and birds. S. R, XI, 17. M, p.480.

British Museum, No.223. Falcon killing a Bird. Signed.

CHAO CH'ÊNG 趙澄, or Chao Chêng 趙徵, *t.* Hsüeh-chiang 雪江 and Chan-chih 湛之.
From Ying-chou, Anhui. B. 1581, d. after 1654. Scholar and poet. Landscapes after Fan K'uan, Li T'ang and Tung Yüan. P. Q, I, 1. R, III, 4. U, I, 2, 9. M, p.618.

Chao Hsüeh-chiang fang-ku shan-shui ts'ê (Kobayashi, Kyōto, 1919). An Album of twelve Landscapes after early Sung Masters. Signed and dated 1654 (at 74).

CHAO CHIH-CH'ÊN 趙之琛, *t.* Tz'ŭ-hsien 次閑.
From Ch'ien-t'ang, Chekiang. Active probably towards the end of the 18th century. Landscapes, followed Ni Tsan and Huang Kung-wang; flowers and birds in the style of Hua Yen. T. U, III, 2, 14. M, p.620.

Nanga Taisei, II, 72, right. Bamboo growing by a Rock. Signed and dated *wu-tzŭ*, or 1768?
Ming-jên hsieh-chu. Bamboos and a Rock, after Lu K'ung-sun. Handscroll. Signed, dated *kuei-mao* (probably 1783).
T'ai-shan ts'an-shih-lou ts'ang-hua, I. Two Stems of Bamboo in the *pai-miao* manner. Signed.
Po-mei chi. Bamboo Leaves and Plum Blossoms. Signed.
Sung-pê. Pine-trees. Handscroll. Signed.
(For other pictures by this artist, see Nanga Taisei, II, 72, 73 and 258; III, 184–189; V, 50, 51; VII, 175 and X, 216.)

CHAO CHIH-CH'IEN 趙之謙, *t.* I-fu 益甫 and Hui-shu 撝叔, *h.* Pei-an 悲盦.
From K'uai-chi, Chekiang. B. 1829, d. 1884. Poet, writer, calligraphist, seal engraver. Flowers in the style of Ch'ên Shun and Li Shan. M, p.621.

Nanga Taikan 1. Hundred Flowers. Handscroll. Signed, dated 1859.
Fei-tun lu hua-hui. The Sun-flower and Palm Leaves. Handscroll. Signed, dated 1866.
Shinchō 78, 79. Four Pictures of Fruits representing The Four Seasons. Last one dated 1870; also in Sōraikan, I, 70.
Hui-hua kuan. Branches of a blossoming Peach-tree. Slightly coloured. Dated 1872.
Shina Nanga, I, 142. Peonies. Signed, dated 1872.
Nanga Taikan 9. Chrysanthemums in a *Chüeh*-tripod and Peaches on a Plate. Signed. Poem.
Sōgen 366. Peonies and a Plum-tree: two of a series of eight flower-pictures. Signed.
Takashima collect., Kugenuma. Banana Leaves, Flowers and a Rock. Signed. Several other works by this artist in the same collection.
(Many paintings by this artist reproduced in Nanga Taisei. See II, 193–201 and 260; III, 210–213 and 259; IV, 187–189 and 246–247; V, 52–55, 77, 123, 186–188, 238–240; VI, 221–223; VII, 225–226; VIII, 227–230; X, 227; XII, 205; XV, 81–82; Add. 3, 42–122; Add. 4, 138–143.)

CHAO I 趙懿, original name Chao Jên-tsu 趙仁祖, *t.* I-tzŭ 懿子, *h.* Ku-an 穀庵.
Nephew of Chao Chih-ch'ên. Beginning of the 18th century. Calligraphist, specially known for his seal writing. Plum blossoms and orchids. T. M, p.620.

Po-mei chi. Plum-blossoms. Signed.

Chao Ming-shan 招銘山, *t.* Tzŭ-yung 子庸.
From Kwangtung. Active during the first half of the 19th century. M, p.215.

Musée Guimet, Paris. Bamboos. Signed.

Chao Ping-ch'ung 趙秉冲, *t.* Yen-huai 硯懷, *h.* Ch'ien-shih 謙士.
From Shanghai. Active *c.*1800. Vice-president of the Board of Revenue. Poet, calligraphist. Plum blossoms, orchids, bamboos and chrysanthemums. M, p.622.

Nanga Taikan 9. Branches of blossoming Plum-trees. Signed. Poem dated 1799.

Nanga Taisei, III, 161, right. A Branch of blossoming Plum. Poem, signed and dated 1800.

Chao Shih-ch'ên 趙史臣.
Unrecorded. According to the signature on the picture, t. Yün-chên 雲貞. Probably Ch'ing period.

Tokasha Shina Meigashū 91. A winding Stream between steep Banks grown with knotted Pines. Signed.

Ch'ao-k'uei 超揆. Priest name of Wên Kuo 文果, *t.* Lun-an 輪菴.
From Suchou. b. *c.*1620, d. *c.*1700. A descendant of Wên Chêng-ming. Entered priesthood *c.*1680, but was later called to serve in the Palace. Given the posthumous title Wên-chüeh ch'an-shih 文覺禪師. Landscapes. Q, II, 2. M, p.503.

Ku-kung, XLIII. Landscape, illustrating a Poem by Tu Mu, a T'ang poet. Signed.

K.-k. shu-hua chi, VII. River Landscape with a Man on his Way to a Friend. Short handscroll. Signed. Poem.

Ch'ên Hao 陳豪, *t.* Lan-chou 藍洲, *h.* Mai-an 邁庵 and Mo-weng 墨翁.
Native of Jên-ho in Chekiang. 18th century. Landscapes, flowers. M, p.452.

Commercial Press album, 1930. Eight landscapes; another of various subjects. Signed.

Ch'ên Hsien 陳銑, *t.* Lien-t'ing 蓮汀.
From Hsiu-shui, Chekiang. End of the 18th century. Calligraphist. Painted portraits, plum-blossoms and bamboos and a pupil of Liang T'ung-shu 梁同書 who lived in the reign of Ch'ien-lung. T. M, p.449.

Po-mei chi. Branches of a Plum-tree. Signed, dated *ping-wu* (1786).

Ch'ên Hsing 陳星, *t.* Jih-shêng 日生.
From Suchou. B. 1723, d. *c.*1810. Flowers and birds. L. M, p.450.

Bijutsu Kenkyū, LXV. Fishermen eating in their Boats at the Shore. Handscroll. Signed, dated 1787.

Chung-kuo ming-hua, 18. Ducks among Reeds. Signed, dated 1807 (at 85).

CH'ÊN HUNG-SHOU 陳鴻壽, *t.* Tzŭ-kung 子恭, *h.* Man-shêng 曼生 and other names.
From Hangchou. B. 1768, d. 1822. Landscapes, flowers and bamboos. U, I, 3, 20. M, p.447.

Nanga Taisei, XV, 69–71. Orchids, Narcissi and a Tree. Handscroll. Signed and dated 1802.

Shên-chou, IX. Orchids, Fungi and Banana-trees by a Rock. Signed, dated 1814. Also in Shina Nanga, I, 120.

Shina Meiga Senshū, II, 50. Broad River View with Fishing-boats in the foreground and Hills beyond. Double album-leaf. Signed.

CH'ÊN K'O 陳邁, *t.* Hsiao-k'uan 孝寬.
Early Ch'ing period. Unrecorded; probably either identical with or a brother of Ch'ên Mai 陳邁, *t.* Hsiao-kuan 孝觀, son of Ch'ên Yüan-su (see M, p.439).

Nanking Exhib. cat. 168. Orchids, Iris and Bamboo growing on sloping Ground. Signed and dated *chi-hai*, probably 1659. Colophons by Wên Jan (d. 1657) and three other men.

CH'ÊN K'UN 陳坤, *t.* Tsai-an 載安.
From Ch'ang-shu, Kiangsu. Flowers and birds; also portraits. M, p.442.

Ch'ing êrh-shih chia. Sprays of Plum-blossoms at a Rock. Album-leaf. Signed.

CH'ÊN MAN 陳曼, *t.* Ch'ang-ch'ien 長倩, *h.* Ya-tao-jên 崖道人.
From Shanghai. Active *c.*1630–1670. Poet. Paintings followed Mi Fei. R, II, 16. M, p.438.

T'ai-shan ts'an-shih-lou ts'ang-hua, I. Misty Hills and leafless Trees. Signed, dated 1665.

CH'ÊN MEI 陳枚, *t.* Tien-lun 殿掄, *h.* Tsai-tung 載東.
From Lou-hsien, Kiangsu. Active *c.*1730–1742. Court-painter in the Yung-chêng period. Landscapes, figures and flowers. Followed the Sung masters, but was also influenced by Western paintings. Q, II, 1. R, XI, 23. S. M, p.443.

Mei-chan t'ê-k'an 51. Leafless Trees by a Stream. Signed, dated 1728.

Po-mei chi. A blossoming Plum-tree. Signed.

Shinchō 44. Mountain-landscape. Signed. Poem.

CH'ÊN MIN 陳砥, *t.* Shan-min 山民.
From Ch'ang-shu, Kiangsu. Landscapes, plum-trees. Pupil of Ch'êng Chia-sui (1565–1643). L. R, V, 17. M, p.439.

Ch'ing êrh-shih chia. A Branch of an old Plum-tree. Album-leaf. Signed. Poem.

CH'ÊN SHAN 陳善, *t.* Jo-shui 若水.
From Ta-hsing (Peking). Court-painter during the K'ang-hsi period. Q, II, 1 (under Chang Yü-ch'eng 張御乘). R, XI, 22. S. M, p.443.

Sung-chai. Two leaves from an Album of eight Landscape-paintings after eight masters of the Yüan period. One dated 1677.

CH'ÊN SHAO-YING 陳紹英, *t.* Shêng-fu 生甫, *h.* K'ua-an 瓠庵 and Wu-huai 無壞.
From Hangchou. Seventeenth century. Landscapes, followed Wu Chên. N, VII, 21.

Kokka 306. A Man in a Pavilion at the Foot of High Mountains. Signed, dated *kuei-ssŭ* (1653?) Also in Nanju 1; Tōyō, XI; Tōsō 390.

CH'ÊN SHU 陳書, *h.* Shang-yüan ti-tzŭ 上元弟子 and (later on) Nan-lou lao-jên 南樓老人.
From Hsiu-shui, Chekiang. B. 1660, d. 1736. Prominent lady painter. Flowers, birds, insects; also landscapes and figures. Q, I, 3. M, p.439.

K.-k. shu-hua chi, XXVI. Kuan-yin. Signed, dated 1713.
Metropolitan Museum. A white Cockatoo. Signed, dated 1721.
Shên-chou, XIII. Four Magpies on the Branches of a flowering Plum-tree. Signed, dated 1722. *Cf.* Shina Nanga, III, 7.
K.-k. shu-hua chi, III. Landscape after Wang Mêng. Signed at 72 (1731).
Ibid. XI. Reading the *I-ching* in a Mountain Study. Signed at 75 (1734).
Ku-kung collect. Dwelling in the Mountains in Summer, after T'ang Yin. Colour on paper. Signed and dated at 75 (1734).
Sōgen 291, Narcissi, after Ch'ên Shun. Handscroll. Signed at 75 (1734).
Ming-jên shu-hua, II. Plum Blossoms and Narcissi. Colophon by Chang Kêng written at the painter's request. Dated 1735. Also in Shina Nanga, III, 1.
Ku-kung collect. Small album of Landscapes after Old Masters. Signed. Inscriptions by the painter's husband and emperor Ch'ien Lun-kuang.
Nan-lou lao-jên hua jên-wu hua-niao ts'ê (Yu-chêng Book Co., 1919). An Album of ten Pictures of Flowers, Birds and Figures in Landscapes.
Yu-chêng album, n.d. Six pictures: flowers, trees, landscapes. Signed.
Li-tai, III. Straw Pavilion under a tall Pine-tree. Signed.
K.-k. shu-hua chi, XIV. Cottages in Summer Mountains, after Wang Meng. Signed.
K.-k. chou-k'an, vol. III, 75. A tall Pine-tree and a Cottage by the Stream. Four colophons by Ch'ien-lung.
Shina Nanga, I, 90. A Buffalo and a Herd-boy. Seals of the painter.
Ibid. II, 1. Trees and Stones. Signed.
Ibid. II, 9. A Pavilion by a Stream. Seal of the painter.
Shinchō 87. A Branch of blossoming Plum-tree over a Stream. Album-leaf. Signed.
Nanking Exhib. cat. 322. Two leaves from an Album of Flower, Bird and Animal-paintings. Seals of the artist.

CH'ÊN SHU 陳舒, *t.* Yüan-shu 原舒, *h.* Tao-shan 道山.
From Nanking. Chin-shih in 1649; still active 1687. Flowers and birds. His style is said to be "between Ch'ên Shun and Hsü Wei". P, IV, 6. Q, I, 1. U, I, 2, 22. M, p.438.

Hashimoto collect., Takatsuki. The San-shan Study. Short handscroll. Signed and dated 1651. Mounted with Chu Han-chih's picture of the same subject, painted in the same year.
Ku-kung, XXIX. Flowers. Signed.
K.-k. shu-hua chi, XXIII. Cock and Fish. Signed.
T'ai-shan ts'an-shih-lou ts'ang-hua, III. A Man seated on a sloping River-bank by a Banana-tree. Poem by the painter.
Ibid. A dry old Pine-tree by a Stream in the Mountains. Seal of the painter (?)
Ibid. Bare Trees by a high Cliff. Poem by the painter.
Shên-chou album, 1929. Flowers. Album-leaves. Signed. *Cf.* Nanga Taisei, IV, 60–63.

CH'ÊN SHUN 陳舜.
Unrecorded. Signature reads: from Hsin-ch'êng, Shantung. Probably middle of 17th century.

Nanju 5. Fisherman on a Mountain Stream in Autumn. Signed.

CH'ÊN SUNG 陳崧, *t.* Shou-shan 壽山.
From T'ien-ch'ang, Anhui. 18th century. Pine-trees, flowers and birds. M, p.449.

Tokasha Shina Meigashū 97. A Bird on a slender Willow Branch after Hua Yen. Signed.

CH'ÊN TAN-CHUNG 陳丹衷, *t.* Wên-chao 旻昭 and Shê-chiang 涉江.
From Nanking. Chin-shih in 1640; became a monk later with the name Tao-hsin 道昕. Bamboos, landscapes. N, IV, 29. P, I, 5. U, I, 2, 26. M, p.437.

Nanking Exhib. cat. 239. Two leaves from an Album of Landscapes, one of them signed and dated 1649.

Fu-lu. Seven album-leaves representing Bamboos, each with a poem by the painter. Mounted on one scroll. Colophons by later men.

CH'ÊN TING 陳鼎, *h.* Li-chai 理齋.
Native of T'ung-ch'êng in Anhui. Contemporary with Wang Hui. Landscapes. T. M, p.448.

Nanking Exhib. cat. 268. A Mountain Landscape with Trees, Waterfalls and a Temple. Signed.

CH'ÊN TSUAN 陳撰, *t.* Lêng-shan 楞山, *h.* Yü-chi shan-jên 玉几山人.
From Ning-po, Chekiang, lived in Hangchou and Yang-chou. Chü-jên in 1711. Landscapes, flowers, particularly plum-blossoms. Q, I, 3. R, XI, 16. T. U, III, 1, 3. M, p.442.

Ming-jên shu-hua, XX. Orchids and a blossoming Tree. Signed, dated 1730.
Fei-tun lu hua-hui. Snow-covered Palm-leaves and a Branch of a blossoming Plum-tree. Handscroll. Signed. Colophon dated 1741.
Ming-jên shu-hua, XVIII. A blossoming Plum-tree. Signed. Long poem dated 1744.
Commercial Press album, 1929. Album of flower-paintings. Signed, one dated 1747. *Cf.* Nanga Taisei, I, 213–216; II, 183, 249; III, 254; V, 84, 116, 117, 180, 224.
T'ai-shan ts'an-shih-lou ts'ang-hua, III. A Fish. Signed
Nanking Exhib. cat. 274. Chung K'uei leaning on a Rock. Signed and dated 1748.
Ming-jên shu-hua, XIV. Orchids in a Vase. Signed. Poem.
Kurokawa cat. 32, 33. An Album of fourteen Flower-paintings (four reproduced). Inscriptions by the artist.
Nanga Taisei, III, 113–123. An Album of Plum-blossoms.

CH'ÊN TSUN 陳墫, *t.* Chung-tsun 仲尊, *h.* Wei-t'ing 葦汀 and Po-t'i hua-yin 白堤花隱.
From Suchou. Active *c.*1780. Landscapes. Pupil of Chai Ta-k'un. M, p.445.

Ōmura, I, 12. Landscape after Wang Mêng. Signed, dated 1782. *Cf.* Chūgoku 8.
Nanga Taisei, III, 199, 1. A Branch of flowering Plum. Signed.

Ch'ên T'ung 陳桐, *t.* Shih-shêng 石生, *h.* Yün-t'ing 筠亭 and Chü-sêng 菊僧.
From Lou-hsien, Kiangsu. Active *c.*1732. Flowers and birds. Q, II, 1. R, XI, 24. M, p.443.

Mei-chan t'ê-k'an 52. Birds in a blossoming Plum-tree. Signed, dated 1732.

Ch'ên Tzŭ 陳子, *t.* Wu-ming 無名, *h.* Hsiao-lien 小蓮.
Son of Ch'ên Hung-shou and active in early Ch'ing period. Figures; also flowers and birds. O. Q, I, 1. M, p.437. R, IX, 23. U, II, 2, 9.

Chêng Ch'i, Hongkong. Portrait of a Scholar leaning on a Rock. Short handscroll. Inscription by the artist on the theory of portrait-painting, signed and dated 1682.
Hui-hua kuan. Mountains and red Trees, white Clouds above the humpy Mountains by the River. Colour on silk. Inscription by the painter dated 1691.
Hamburg Exhibition, 1949–1950. Two Figures. Imitations of his father's work.
Ku-kung collect. Two leaves from an album of flower-paintings. Seal of the artist. *Cf.* Nanking Exhib. cat. 259.
Gems, I, 56. Old Men and Children. Signed.

Ch'ên Yo 陳岳.
Unrecorded. Probably identical with Ch'ên Yo 陳嶽, *t.* Chiang-shêng 降生, from Chin-chiang, Fukien. Active at the end of the 18th century. Specialized in painting birds. M, p.444.

Robert Rousset, Paris. A Cock on a Willow-tree. Signed, dated 1795.

Chêng Hsieh 鄭燮, *t.* K'o-jou 克柔, *h.* Pan-ch'iao 板橋.
From Yangchou, Kiangsu. B. 1693, d. 1765. Poet, calligraphist; painted orchids and bamboos. Q, II, 2. R, XI, 15. U, I, 3, 13. M, p.642.

Shina Nanga Taikan 1. Orchids. Signed. Poem dated 1752.
Takashima collect., Kugenuma. A Bamboo Grove. Three panel screen. Long inscription (written from left to right), signed and dated 1753. *Cf.* Sekai Bijutsu Zenshū XX, Pl.55.
Frederick Mote, Princeton. Orchids. Inscription, signed and dated 1754.
Sōgen 316. A "Pillar Stone". Signed. Colophon dated 1755.
Gems, I, 78. Branches of Bamboo. Poem, signed and dated 1758.
Chung-kuo ming-hua, 31. Orchids and Bamboo growing among Stones. Long inscription, signed and dated 1760.
Tokasha Shina Meigashū 53. Tuft of Epidendrums. Poem by the painter dated 1761.
Hamburg Exhibition, 1949–1950. Tufts of Epidendrums and Bamboo Shoots growing from Rocks. Poem by the painter dated 1761.
Takashima collect., Kugenuma. An Album of Bamboo Paintings, the last signed and dated 1761. *Cf.* Seigadō album, 1954.
I-shu ch'uan-t'ung 12. Orchids, Bamboo and Fungus growing from a rocky Cliff. Signed and dated 1761.
Chūgoku, 8. Bamboo and Orchids. Long inscription by the artist, signed and dated 1762.
Ming-jên hsieh-chu. Bamboos and tall Garden-stones. Signed. Poem, dated 1762.
Ibid. Bamboos and Orchids. Signed. Colophon dated 1762.
Berlin Museum. Bamboos by a tall Rock. Signed. Poem. Painted at 70. (1762.)
Musée Guimet, Paris. Bamboos. Colophon by the painter dated 1765.

Frederick Mote, Princeton. Bamboo. Inscription, signed and dated 1765.
Shên-chou ta-kuan, XV. Peonies Growing by a Rock. Poem, signed.
Po-mei chi. Bamboos and Branches of Plum Blossoms. Signed. Poem.
Fu-lu. Stems of Bamboos. Poem by the painter.
Hui-hua kuan. A Bamboo Study. Long inscription.
Suchiku, 27. Two Stalks of Bamboo. Poem, signed.
Shina Meiga Senshū 32. A Spray of Bamboo. Seal of the painter.
Tokasha Shina Meigashū 51. Four Stems of Bamboo. Signed.
Ibid. 52. Bamboo, Chrysanthemum, Crab and Lotus Seed-cases. Poem by the painter. *Cf.* Nanga Taisei, Add. IV, 99.
K. Sumitomo, Ōiso. Bamboo Branches with ruffled Leaves. Lengthy inscription. Short handscroll.
Shina Nanga, I, 99. Chrysanthemums. Signed. Poem.
Kyūka, II. Two Bamboos. Signed.
Shinchō 55. Bamboos and Rocks. Signed. Poem.
Nanga Taikan 9. Orchids by a Rock. Signed. Poem.
Sōgen 315. Bamboos and Orchids by a Rock. Signed. Poem.
Ibid. 317. A Bamboo Grove. Signed. Poem.
Kurokawa cat. 29. Orchids and Bamboo growing from Fissures in a Rock. Poem, signed.
Nanga Taisei, III, 139. An old Plum-tree. Poem, signed. (See also Nanga Taisei, I, 183–200 for various bamboo pictures by this artist, some of them reproduced elsewhere.)
T. Moriya collect., Kyōto. Orchids. Handscroll. Signed.
British Museum. Bamboos, Chrysanthemum and Orchids. Inscription in *ts'ao shu*.
Berlin Museum. Bamboo and Rocks. Poem, signed.
National Museum, Stockholm. Bamboo growing by a tall Garden Rock. Signed.
Princeton (Du Bois-Morris collect.) Thin Bamboos by a Rock. Colophon by the painter.
Shên-chou album, 1914. Twelve landscapes in old styles. Signed.

CHÊNG MIN 鄭旼, *t.* Mu-ch'ien 慕倩.
From Hsieh-hsien, Anhui. Contemporary with Hsiao Yün-ts'ung (*c.*1670). Landscapes. M, p.645.

Hui-hua kuan. The Nine-dragon Pond on Huang-shan. Signed. Poem dated 1673. *Cf.* Shina Nanga, II, 10; Shên-chou ta-kuan, vol.5.
S.c.t.k. hsü-pien, I. Autumn Landscape. Signed, dated 1681.
Hsin-an p'ai ming-hua chi (Shên-chou album, 1924). A Man on a Cliff looking at the Sea, after Ch'êng Chia-sui. Signed. Colophon dated 1682.
Ibid. Tu Fu picking Acorns. Seal of the painter.
Shên-chou album, 1914. Twelve landscapes in old styles. Signed.
Shina Nanga, II, 8. Landscape after Wu Chên. Signed. Colophon.
Sōgen 187. Mountains after Rain in Spring. Signed. Poem.
Nanga Taisei, XII, 69–72. Album of eight small Landscapes. Inscriptions and seals of the artist.

CHÊNG T'IEH-YAI 鄭鐵崖.
Unrecorded. Ch'ing period.

Tokasha Shina Meigashū 79. A Grove of slender Bamboos along a Mountain Stream. Signed.

CH'ÊNG CHÊNG-K'UEI 程正揆, original name 正葵, *t.* Tuan-po 端伯, Chü-ling 鞠陵 and Ch'ing-ch'i tao-jên 青溪道人.
From Hsiao-kan, Hupeh; lived in Nanking. Chin-shih in 1631. Became a high official in the Ch'ing dynasty, retired in 1657. Calligraphist, poet and painter of landscapes. P, II, 7. Q, I, 1. R, I, 4. U, I, 2, 3. M, p.534.

Ho Kuan-wu, Hongkong. Travels on the River (the seventh of his 100 scrolls). Signed and dated 1651.

Kokka 292. An Evening View of the Blue River. Signed and dated 1654. *Cf.* Shoman 35; Sirén, *Later* pl.176B.

Chicago Art Institute. Fantastic Rock-formations and Views over wide Waters; groups of trees and buildings. Long handscroll. Signed and dated 1655. *Cf.* Cleveland Exhib. cat. 73.

Toronto cat.31 (C. C. Wang, N.Y.) Travelling among Mountains and Rivers: No.74 of his "Hundred Scrolls". Inscription dated 1659, according to which the painting was executed in 1657 or 1658. *Cf.* Nanga Taisei, Intro. 36–38.

Vannotti collect., Lugano. Rivers and Mountains. Handscroll. Number 91 of his 100 scrolls. Signed and dated 1661.

Nanga Taisei, XV, 46–49. A rocky Landscape. Handscroll. Poem, signed and dated 1662; various other inscriptions written by the artist in the same year.

National Museum, Stockholm. Overhanging Rocks and tall Pine-trees by a Mountain Stream; a scholar studying below. Ink and colour on paper. Signed and dated 1669.

W. Hochstadter, New York. Walking through a Landscape of Mountains and Water. Handscroll. Ink and colour on paper. Signed and dated 1674.

Shên-chou, X. A Pavilion in the Mountains, after Huang Kung-wang. Signed.

Ming-hua sou-ch'i, II, 5. Landscape Studies. Two album-leaves. Signed.

Chou Li-yüan, p.6. Landscape with bare Trees and a Lakeside Pavilion. Album-leaf. Seal of the artist. *Cf.* Nanking Exhib. cat. 269.

Hui-hua kuan. Rocky Mountains with Trees and winding Streams. Long handscroll. Ink and slight colour.

Ibid. (formerly P'ang Yüan-chi). A Mountain Gorge with rushing Water; trees and buildings on the terraces. Inscriptions by the painter and by Shih-ch'i; the latter dated 1671. *Cf.* Liu 80.

Gems, III, 10. Two Landscapes. Horizontal album-leaves. Seals of the artist.

Sōgen 242. The Wine Shop in the Mountains. Album-leaf. Poem by the painter.

Kurokawa cat. 9. Houses under Pine-trees. Painted in colours only (without ink). Signed.

Hamburg Exhibition, 1949–1950. A Mountain River winding between rocky Shores. Two men conversing. Handscroll. Ink only on paper. Signed.

Chang Ting-ch'ên, Hongkong. Landscape. Signed.

J. P. Dubosc, Lugano. Mountain Slopes with sparse Trees and Buildings on the Terraces. Handscroll. Signed. Number six of his 100 scrolls.

CH'ÊNG MING 程鳴, *t.* Yu-shêng 友聲, *h.* Sung-mên 松門.

From Hsieh-hsien, Anhui. Active at the beginning of the Ch'ien-lung period. Followed Tao-chi. Q, II, 1. R, VI, 15. U, II, 2, 22. M, p.535.

National Museum, Stockholm. A Cypress and two Stones. Signed, dated 1736.

Tokasha Shina Meigashū 31. Mountain Stream; a man walking along the shore. Signed, dated 1743.

Shên-chou, XIII. River Landscape; hillocks in the background, a man under sparse trees in the foreground. Poem by the painter.

CH'ÊNG SUI 程邃, *t.* Mu-ch'ien 穆倩, *h.* Chiang-tung pu-i 江東布衣 and Kou tao-jên 垢道人.

From Hsieh-hsien, Anhui; lived in Yang-chou. Active *c.*1650–1680. Landscapes in the style of Chü-jan and Huang Kung-wang. P, III, 7. Q, I, 1. R, III, 14. U, I, 2, 17. M, p.534.

Shina Meiga Senshū, II, 30 (Ōtani collect.) An overgrown Mountain Hump; a grove of pines and small buildings at the foot. Signed and dated 1657.

Hui-hua kuan. Two Men meeting under old Trees; grassy hills in the background. Signed and dated 1676. *Cf.* Fei-tun lu shan-shui.

Kurokawa cat. 18–19. Album of Landscapes (four reproduced), the last signed and dated 1682. *Cf.* Shinchō 37.

Nanga Taikan 8. A Pavilion on a projecting Terrace by a misty Gorge. Signed. Poem and colophon dated 1688.

Ming-jên shu-hua, XXIV. Mountain Landscape. Signed at 83.

Shina Nanga, II, 11. Forests in Autumn. Album-leaf. Signed at 83.

Gems, III, 12. Two Landscapes. Album-leaves. Signed at 84.

S.c.t.k hsü-pien, IV. Village at a small River; houses built on poles over the water, men are seen in one of them. Signed.

Hui-hua kuan. Lotus, Plum-blossoms and other Flowers. Handscroll. Signed.

Freer Gallery (56, 18). Two Men seated at the Foot of a high Peak. Seals of the painter. Poems by two contemporaries. *Cf.* Shinchō, 36.

Kurokawa collect., Ashiya. A misty Landscape. Signed.

Nanga Taisei, VIII, 164. Buildings at the Foot of a Mountain. Fan-painting. Inscription, signed.

W. Hochstadter, New York. Sharply-cut towering Mountains in successive Terraces. Signed.

Chang Ta-ch'ien. River-landscape, cat.IV, 37. See under Chang Hsün.

CH'ÊNG T'ING-LU 程庭鷺, *t.* Hsü-po 序伯, *h.* Hêng-hsiang 蘅鄉 and Jo-an 弱庵.

From Chia-ting, Kiangsu. B. 1797, d. 1857. Landscapes in the style of Li Liu-fang. Author of the *Hsiao-sung-yüan ko shu-hua pa* 小松園閣書畫跋 and other books on painting. U, III, 2, 24. M, p.537.

Tomioka collect., Kyōto. An Album of Landscapes, the last signed and dated 1851.

Hamburg Exhibition, 1949–1950. Landscape after Wang Chien. Broad ink manner. Signed, dated 1855.

Nanga Taisei, X, 226. A River Valley in Autumn. Poem and inscription dated 1856.

Shên-chou, IX. The *An-ch'u* Study, after Ni Tsan. Signed. Colophon. Also in Shina Nanga, II, 1.

Po-mei chi. Plum Blossoms, after Hua Kuang. Signed.

Nanga Taisei, III, 201–205. Five Paintings of blossoming Plum. Album-leaves. Signed.

CH'ÊNG TSÊNG-HUANG 程曾煌, *t.* Yen-chün 研君.

A native of Chekiang who lived in Shanghai. Flowering plum. M, p.538.

Nanga Taisei, III, 216–223. An Album of Paintings of flowering Plum. Signed and dated *kêng-tzŭ* (or) 1840?

CH'ÊNG YÜN 程雲, *t.* Yü-lin 玉林.

From Huang-chou, Hupeh. Active *c.*1630–1650. Lived in seclusion after the fall of the Ming dynasty. Landscapes. M, p.533.

Nanju 17. A quiet Pavilion by the River. Signed. Two lines of poetry. Also in Tōyō, XII.

CHI-HUI 際慧, *t.* Ching-shêng 靜生, *h.* Ching-sun 靜蓀 and Hsüeh-chou 雪舟.

A priest. Native place unknown. B. 1723, d. 1799. Landscapes. M, p.599.

Shimbi, XIX. Landscape. Signed, dated 1751.

CH'I CHAI-CHIA 祁豸佳, *t.* Chih-hsiang 止祥, *h.* Hsüeh-p'iao 雪瓢.
From Shan-yin, Chekiang. Chü-jên in 1627. Served as an official in the Ming period but retired after 1644. Active still in 1682. Prominent also as a poet and calligraphist. Followed in his landscapes the Northern Sung masters. P, I, 17. R, I, 17. U, I, 2, 10. M, p.219.

Metropolitan Museum. River in Autumn; a man in a boat. Fan-painting. Signed, dated 1643.
Kokka 499. Autumn Landscape. Signed, dated 1645.
Ming-jên shu-hua, XXIII. River Landscape. Signed. Poem dated 1648.
Sōgen 190. River Landscape with a Man angling in a Boat. Fan-painting. Signed, dated 1649.
Kyūka, I (Hashimoto collect., Takatsuki). Mountain Landscape with two Men in a Pavilion. After Wu Chên. Signed, dated 1650.
Kokka 242. Landscape after Tung Yüan. Signed, dated 1651. Also in Nanju 10; Tōyō, XI; Sekai Bijutsu Zenshū, XX, pl.33.
Nanju 5. A Hermit in the Mountains, after Tung Yüan. Signed, dated 1654. Also in Hyōjirō Hatta; Pageant 756.
Ōmura, I, 7. A Cottage with a Figure at the Foot of high wooded Mountains. Signed, dated 1657. Also in Sōraikan, II, 69; Kokka 597.
Nanju 20. A solitary Pavilion by a Mountain Stream. Signed, dated 1666. Also in Tōyō, XI.
Sōgen 189. Landscape. Signed, dated 1669.
Shoman 34. Landscape after Mi Fei. Fan-painting. Signed.
National Museum, Stockholm. Mountain Landscape in Mist. After Huang Kung-wang. Signed.

CHIA CH'ÜAN 賈全.
Court-painter in the Ch'ien-lung period. Figures. S.

Li-tai, V. The eighteen Scholars. Signed.

CHIANG CHANG 蔣璋, *t.* T'ieh-ch'in 鐵琴.
From Tan-yang, Kiangsu. Figures, rival of Huang Shên; founded the Chiang school. M, p.649.

Ti-chih t'u-ts'ê (Wên-ming co.) The twelve Animals of the Zodiac. The last picture signed and dated 1737. Sketchy *p'o-mo* paintings. Seven of these pictures are also reproduced in Shina Nanga, vols.I, II, and III.

CHIANG CHIEH 江介, original name Chiang Chien 江鑑, *t.* Shih-ju 石如.
From Hangchou. Active *c.*1800–1830. Studied first figure-painting, but later on flower-painting in which he followed Ch'ên Shun. M, p.90.

Shên-chou, XI. Chrysanthemums, after Yün Shou-p'ing. Signed, dated 1817.
Ming-jên shu-hua, XIII. Four Pictures of Flowers representing The Four Seasons. Two in the manner of Yün Shou-p'ing. Signed, dated 1831.
Ibid. XX. T'ao Yüan-ming plucking Chrysanthemums. Signed, dated 1831.
Ibid. XX. Peonies and Magnolias, after Yün Shou-p'ing. Two lines of poetry.
Po-mei chi. An old blossoming Plum-tree. Signed.

CHIANG CHING 蔣敬, *t.* Ching-chih 敬之, *h.* Chih-chou 芝舟, Yün-shêng 芸生 and Ts'ai-chih-shêng 采芝生.
From Ch'ien-t'ang, Chekiang. Active *c.*1800. Landscapes after Li Liu-fang; also figures, flowers and pine-trees. T. M, p.650.

Po-mei chi. Branches of Plum-blossoms. Signed, dated 1804.

CHIANG CHU 江注, *t.* Yün-ning 允凝.
From Hsi-hsien, Anhui. Pupil of Hung-jên. Poet. M, p.89.

S.c.t.k. hsü-pien, VI. Fantastic Rocks and tortuous Pines. Signed.

CHIANG HAN 蔣瀚, *t.* Chêng-ch'uan 澂川, *h.* Lu-yün 綠筠.
Probably 17th century. Unrecorded.

G. Del Drago, New York. Girl at a Table seen through a circular Window. Poem and colophon by the painter.

CHIANG HÊNG 江衡, *t.* Wei-nan 位南 and Hui-nan 蕙南, *h.* Yen-ch'i 喦溪.
From Ch'ang-shu; lived in Yang-chou, Kiangsu. Probably Ch'ien-lung period. Landscapes, followed the Yüan masters. M, p.89.

Kyūka, II. Two Album-leaves: Five Pine-trees by a Stream; the Study among the fragrant Cassia-trees. Signed.

CHIANG HSÜN 姜壎, *t.* Hsiao-ch'üan 曉泉, *h.* Yüan-yang t'ing-chang 鴛鴦亭長 and other names.
From Sung-chiang, Kiangsu. B. 1764, d. 1821 (or 1834). Flowers and birds after Yün Shou-p'ing; also figures. U, III, 2, 17. M, p.275.

Ming-jên shu-hua, XXI. Portrait of Su Tung-p'o, after a picture by Li Lung-mien. Signed, dated 1806.
Ibid. XII. Flowers and Trees. Painted together with Wang Hsüeh-hao, Chu Ang-chih, Chai Chi-ch'ang and Chou Li. Chrysanthemums by Chiang Hsün. Also in Nanga Taikan 1.
Ibid. XVII. A Lady by a Lotus-pond. Signed. Poem.
Ibid. XVII. A Lady in the Chin-ku Garden.
Shinchō 84. Portrait of Lady Ch'iung-hsien. Signed.
Hamburg Exhibition, 1949–1950. A Lady under the Bamboos. Signed.
Ibid. A Lady under a Tree.

CHIANG PAO-HUA 蔣保華, *t.* Tzŭ-ying 子英.
From Hsiu-shui, Chekiang. Probably 18th century. Flowers and birds. M, pp.651–652.

Metropolitan Museum. A blue Phoenix in a blossoming Magnolia-tree. According to the inscription by the painter, in the style of I Yüan-chi.

CHIANG PAO-LIN 蔣寶林, *t.* Tzŭ-yen 子延, *h.* Hsia-chu 霞竹.
From Chao-wên, near Suchou. Active in Shanghai *c.*1830–1850. Landscapes, followed Wên Chêng-ming and later on Tung Yüan and Chü-jan. Author of *Mo-lin chin-hua* 墨林今話. U, III, 2, 19. M, p.650.

Chiang Tzŭ-yen Pao-lin shan-shui shih-liu chêng. (Shên-chou album, 1922). Sixteen Landscapes, each with a poem and a colophon. Last picture dated 1832.
Pageant 964. Mountain Landscape. Signed, dated 1835.

CHIANG P'U 蔣溥, *t.* Chih-fu 質甫, *h.* Hêng-hsien 恆軒.
From Ch'ang-shu, Kiangsu. B. 1708, d. 1761. Son of Chiang T'ing-hsi. Flowers, followed his father. Q, II, 2. R, XI, 7. U, III, 1, 6. M, p.648.

K.-k. shu-hua chi, XII. Magnolias (Yü-lan), after Wên Chêng-ming. Signed. Poem dated 1753.
Li-tai, II. Pine-tree, Bamboos and Plum Blossoms. Signed.
Ibid. III. Cassia Flowers and Rabbits. Signed. Poem.
Ibid. IV. Orchids and Bamboos. Handscroll. Signed.
Ibid. IV. Lotuses. Handscroll. Signed.
K.-k. shu-hua chi, V. Crickets. Signed.
Pao-yün, I. A Bamboo Thicket by a Stream. Inscription, signed.
Po-mei chi. A Plum-tree in Bloom. Signed.

CHIANG SHIH-CHIEH 姜實節, *t.* Hsüeh-tsai 學在, *h.* Hao-chien 鶴澗, Ssŭ-wei 思未 and other names.
B. 1647, d. 1709. From Lai-yang, Shantung; lived in Suchou. Called after his death Hsiao-chêng 孝正 (Filial and Upright). Landscapes in Ni Tsan's style. Q, II, 1. R, IV, 9. U, I, 3, 2. M, p.274.

Nanga Taisei, III, 97. A Branch of flowering Plum. Signed and dated 1698.
Wu-mên p'ai ming-hua chi (Shên Chou album, 1924). Man resting on a Couch. Signed, dated 1700.
Shên-chou ta-kuan, vol.3. Visiting a Friend in the Mountain. After T'ang Yin. Poem and colophon by the painter, dated 1705. *Cf.* Shina Nanga, III, 10.
Shinchō 31. River Landscape with Waterfalls. Signed. Colophon dated 1707 (at 61). *Cf.* Chung-kuo ming-hua, 38.
J. P. Dubosc, Lugano. Landscape; Mountain Peaks and Waterfalls. Handscroll. Five poems by the painter; signed, dated 1707.
Hui-hua kuan. A Pavilion in Autumn Mountains. Poems by the painter.
Chung-kuo ming-hua XXI. River Landscape in Ni Tsan's Style. Two poems, one by the painter, the other by Chu I-tsun.
Shên-chou, II. River Landscape in Autumn, after Ching Hao. Signed. Colophon.
J. P. Dubosc, Lugano. Landscape in the style of Ni Tsan. Fan-painting. Signed with three seals.

CHIANG TA-LAI 江大來, *t.* Lien-shan 連山 and Chia-p'u 稼圃.
Went to Nagasaki in 1804. Landscapes. M, p.90.

Kokka 349. Landscape. Signed. Poem.
Ibid. 766. Landscape. Poem, signed.
Nanju 11. Landscape after Shên Chou. Signed. Painted at Nagasaki. Also in Tōyō, XII.

CHIANG TING 蔣棡, *t.* Tso-mei 作梅.
Grandson of Chiang T'ing-hsi. Chin-shih in 1751. Flowers, followed the family tradition. M, p.648.

Shina Nanga, II, 4. Crows in a Willow Tree. Fan-painting. Signed.

CHIANG T'ING-HSI 蔣廷錫, *t.* Yang-sun 揚孫, *h.* Yu-chün 酉君, Hsi-ku 西谷 and Nan-sha 南沙.
From Ch'ang-shu, Kiangsu. B. 1669, d. 1732. Famous flower-painter. Also writer. After he had become a high official (*c.*1703), he painted mainly for the emperor; pictures for private people were executed by his pupil Ma I. Q, I, 3. R, III, 17. U, I, 3, 7. M, p.647.

Mayuyama collect., Tōkyō. Various Flowers. Handscroll, painted in ink only. Signed and dated 1681.
Mo-ch'ao pi-chi, vol.II. A Thrush on a Cliff, and Chrysanthemums. Long handscroll. Signed, dated 1685.
Chung-kuo ming-hua, 30. Monkeys. Inscription by Ma Yüan-yü, who painted the background scenery, dated 1695.
K.-k. shu-hua chi, XX. Wild Chrysanthemums. Signed. Poem by K'ang-hsi, dated 1705.

Shinchō 49. Bamboos by a Rock. Signed, dated 1707.

Chung-kuo ming-hua, VII. A Day Lily and *Ling-chih* by a Rock. Signed and dated 1712.

Sōgen 270. Auspicious Flowers and Butterflies. Handscroll. Signed, dated 1714.

Kawai collect., Kyōto. An Album of Bird and Flower paintings, the last signed and dated 1714.

Hamburg Exhibition, 1949–1950. Peonies. Ink on silk. Signed, dated 1716.

Nanking Exhib. cat. 325. Chrysanthemums, Bamboos and Sparrows. After Wang Yüan. Signed and dated 1722.

Shanghai Museum. Daffodils, *Ling-chih* and Bamboo by a Rock. Signed and dated 1723.

K.-k. shu-hua chi, XXVIII. Birds and Millets. Signed, dated 1723.

Shên Chou, XI. Peonies. Signed, dated 1724.

Metropolitan Museum. A blossoming Tree Peony and a White Egret. After Chao Mêng-fu. Signed, dated 1724.

K.-k. shu-hua chi, VIII. Bamboos, Stones and Narcissi, after a Yüan master. Signed, dated 1725.

Chūgoku 8. An Album of twelve Paintings of Vegetables, Flowers, etc., the last signed and dated 1725.

Chung-kuo, II, 154. Vegetables from the Imperial Garden. Signed, dated 1725. Also in Sōgen 271.

K.-k. shu-hua chi, II. Pine-trees and Flowers. Signed, dated 1730.

British Museum, No.193. Lotus, after Hsü Wei. Signed, dated 1730.

K.-k. shu-hua chi, XXI. Bird and Flowers. Signed. Poem by K'ang-hsi.

Shên-chou ta-kuan, XII. A Peach-tree in Blossom. Signed.

Ibid. XXXIX. A Ginseng Plant in a Pot. Signed. Colophon by K'ang-hsi.

Sōraikan, II, 76. A blossoming Wistaria Climbing on a Tree. Signed. Poem by K'ang-hsi.

Shên-chou, I and V. Six pictures of Birds. Album-leaves.

Ibid. VII. Pheasants and Banana-trees. Fan-painting. Signed.

Chung-kuo ming-hua 5. A Fungus and a Radish Plant.

Chung-hua album, 1932. Twelve Fan-paintings representing Flowers, Fruits and Birds after paintings by the Emperor Hui-tsung.

Nanking Exhib. cat. 324. Bamboo and a flowering Bush with Birds. Signed.

Ku-kung, XV. Peonies. Ink only. Signed.

Ibid. XXXIV. Flowers. Fan-painting. Signed.

Ibid. XXXIX. Grape-vine and a Cricket. Fan-painting. Signed.

Ibid. XLI. Flowers and Birds. Fan-painting. Signed.

K.-k. shu-hua chi, VII. Pine-tree, Plum Blossoms and Bamboos. Signed.

Ibid. XLIV. Red Peach-blossoms and white Pear Blossoms. Signed.

(See also K.-k. chou-k'an, Index, for various works of this artist.)

Mo-hua ts'ê (Palace Museum album). Twelve Flower Paintings.

Fei-tun lu hua-hui. Bamboos and a blossoming Plum-tree. Handscroll. Signed. Poem.

Shina Nanga, II, 2. Swallows and Plum-blossoms. Signed. Poem.

N. Gashū 29. A Peach-tree. Signed.

Ōmura, I, 7. Flowers.

Boston Museum. Lotus Plants and Sea-grass. Poem by the painter.

British Museum, No.192. Peonies, Magnolia, and Peach-blossoms. Signed.

Former C. B. Hoyt collect., Cambridge, Mass. An album containing ten Flower-paintings. Seal of the painter.

CHIANG YÜ 姜漁, *t.* Li-jên 笠人.

From Ch'ao-hsien, Anhui; lived in Kiangsu. Active *c.*1800–1820. Flowers and birds. Pupil of Chang Yü 張敔. Followed also Ch'ên Shun and Hsü Wei. U, III, 2, 6. M, p.274.

Tokasha Shina Meigashū 96. Epidendrums and Lilies by a Rockery. Signed, dated 1817.

Ming-jên shu-hua, XX. Plum Blossoms and Bamboos in a Vase; two birds. Signed. Colophon.

CHIANG YÜ-CHIEN 蔣予檢, *t.* Chü-t'ing 矩亭.
From Sui-chou, Honan. Chü-jên in 1822. Epidendrums. U, III, 2, 23. M, p.652.

Sung-chai. Epidendrum and Jujube, after Chao Mêng-chien. Poem by the painter.

Berlin Museum. An Album of Epidendrum Pictures.

CHIAO HSÜN 焦循.
From Ch'ing dynasty. Unrecorded.

Po-mei chi. A Branch of Plum-blossoms. Signed, dated 1822.

CHIAO PING-CHÊN 焦秉貞.
From Chi-ning, Shantung. Active *c.*1680–1720. Served in the Imperial Observatory and in the Palace as a painter. Flowers, landscapes, figures. Q, I, 2. R, VIII, 23. S. U, II, 2, 24. M, p.504.

Artibus Asiae, vol.5, No.2 (Frau O. J. Wegener collect.) Two Girls in a Garden. Signed, dated 1721.
Shinchō 43. Mountain Landscape with Houses and Figures. Handscroll. Signed.
Kokka 687 (T. Yamamoto, Tōkyō). Emperor K'ang-hsi's temporary Palace at Hu-ch'iu on his southward Tour.
Ars Asiatica, IX, pl.LIX (British Museum). The Journey of an Official. Section of a long handscroll. Signed.
National Museum, Stockholm. Lady in a Garden Pavilion. Signed. *Cf.* Sirén. *Later*, pl.168A.
Hamburg Exhibition, 1949–1950. General Su Wu as a Shepherd of the Huns. Album-leaf.

CH'IEN FÊNG 錢灃, *t.* Tung-chu 東柱, *h.* Nan-yüan 南園.
From K'un-ming, Yünnan. B. 1740, d. 1795(?) Calligraphist, painter of horses. M, p.687.

Chung-kuo, II, 121. Eleven Horses under Trees by a Stream. Signed and dated 1776. *Cf.* Ming-jên shu-hua, IX; Shên-chou, XVIII.
Ming-jên shu-hua, IX. Two Mongols tending a Group of Horses. Signed and dated 1778.
Ibid. IX. Two Horses. Signed and dated 1778.
Shên-chou ta-kuan, vol.7. Five Horses. One drinking, two running, and two by old trees. Signed and dated 1779.
Kuan Po-hêng collect., Peking. Three Horses by a Cliff. Signed and dated 1779.
Formerly Hobart collect., Cambridge, Mass. Clouds circled around Mountain Peaks and tall Pines. Three inscriptions, one by the painter dated 1782.
Honolulu Academy of Arts. A Study Pavilion at the Foot of Rocky Mountains. Inscription by the painter, dated 1784. Other inscriptions by later men.
Ming-jên shu-hua, IX. Two Horses in Autumn Wind. Signed and dated 1786.
Ibid. IX. Two Horses. Signed and dated 1786.
Chung-kuo, II, 119. Three Horses. Signed and dated 1795.
Chūgoku, 8. Chung K'uei and his Sister, with a Retinue of Demons. Signed and dated *chia-tzŭ*, or 1804?
Chung-kuo, II, 120. Two Horses.
Kuan Po-hêng collect., Peking. Piled-up strange Peaks. Signed. Poem.
Formerly Hobart collect., Cambridge, Mass. Three Horses by an old Tree. Signed.

CH'IEN SHAN-YANG 錢善揚, *t.* Shên-fu 慎夫, *h.* Fan-shan 凡山.
From Hai-yen, Chekiang. Grandson of the painter Ch'ien Tsai. Active *c.*1790–1800. Flowers, followed the family tradition. M, p.683.

Ming-jên shu-hua, XVIII. Pine-trees, Bamboos and Stones. Signed, dated 1790.

Ibid. XII. A Bird perching on a Branch of a Tree. Signed, dated 1795.

Po-mei chi. Branches of Plum Blossoms. Signed, dated 1803.

Ming-jên shu-hua, XXI. Bamboos and Orchids by a Rock. Signed, dated 1805.

CH'IEN SUNG 錢松, *t.* Shu-kai 叔蓋, *h.* Nai-ch'ing 耐清.
From Ch'ien-t'ang, Chekiang. D. *c.*1860. Landscapes. M, p.688.

Po-mei chi. Branches of blossoming Plum-tree. Signed, dated 1858.

Nanga Taikan 9. Mountain Landscape after Huang Kung-wang. Signed, dated 1858.

Nanga Taisei, X, 224, 225. Four Landscapes. Signed.

CH'IEN TSAI 錢載, *t.* K'un-i 坤一, *h.* T'o-shih 擇石, P'ao-tsun 匏尊 and Wan-sung chü-shih 萬松居士.
From Hai-yen, Chekiang. B. 1708, d. 1793. Scholar and poet. Flowers. Studied at first with his grandmother, Ch'ên Shu, and later under the painter Chiang P'u. Followed Hsü Wei and Ch'ên Shun. Q, II, 2. R, XII, 1. U, I, 3, 14. M, p.683.

Shinchō 52. A Branch of Plum-tree and Flowers. Signed. Colophon dated 1754.

Fei-tun lu hua-hui. Orchids. Handscroll. Signed, dated 1765.

Po-mei chi. Branches of Plum Blossoms. Signed, dated 1770. Several inscriptions.

Chung-kuo ming-hua, 26. Peony, Orchid and Bamboo. Signed, dated 1771.

Ming-jên shu-hua, I. Pine-tree, Orchids and Stone. Signed, dated 1780 (at 73).

Nanking Exhib. cat. 345. Bamboo and Orchids growing on a Rock. Signed and dated 1781.

Ming-jên shu-hua, XVIII. A Hai-t'ang-tree. Signed, dated 1786.

K.-k. shu-hua chi, XV. Orchids and Stones. Signed, dated 1786.

Ming-jên shu-hua, XXV. Bamboos and Orchids by a Rock. Signed, dated 1790. Also in Ming-hua sou-ch'i, I, 10; Shina Nanga, I, 100.

Fu-lu. A dense Bamboo Grove. Poem dated 1790.

Ming-jên shu-hua, VIII. Chrysanthemums and Bamboos by a Rockery. Signed, dated 1792 (at 85).

Kurokawa cat. 35. Bamboo and Orchids growing beside a Rock. Handscroll. Signed and dated 1792.

Ming-jên hsieh-chu. Bamboos. Handscroll. Signed. Colophon dated 1792.

Shên-chou, I. A Grove of young Bamboos. Signed.

Ming-jên shu-hua, V. Pavilions built over a Stream. Two lines of poetry. Seals of the painter.

Li-tai, III. Narcissi and Fungi. Signed. *Cf.* Pao-yün, I.

Sōraikan, II, 85. Bamboo Branches, after Su Tung-p'o. Signed. Colophons by P'an I-ch'üan (1740–1830), Yüan Yüan, Ch'ien Ta-hsin, Wêng Fang-kang and Liang Tung-shu (1723–1815).

CH'IEN TU 錢杜. Original name Ch'ien Yü 錢榆 and *t.* Shu-mei 叔枚. Used later on the name Ch'ien Tu, *t.* Shu-mei 叔美, *h.* Sung-hu 松壺.
From Ch'ien-t'ang, Chekiang. B. 1763, d. 1844. Landscapes in the style of Wên Chêng-ming; flowers in that of Yün Shou-p'ing. Author of *Sung-hu hua-i* 松壺畫憶 and other books on painting. T, XI, 1. U, I, 3, 19. M, p.685.

Tōan 69. Two Men meeting on a Garden Terrace. Signed. Poem, dated 1789.

Shên-chou ta-kuan, XII. A Man Seated beneath Trees; another Departing. Signed and dated 1791. The mountain painted by Ch'ien Tung.

Ming-jên shu-hua, XXI. A Garden in Nanking. Signed. Colophon dated 1808.

Sekai Bijutsu Zenshū XX, Pl.65 (Ōsaka Museum). A Pavilion among Bamboos on Yü-shan. Poem, signed and dated 1813.

Ming-jên shu-hua, XI. A Man in a Boat under snow-covered Cliffs. Signed, dated 1815.

Nanking Exhib. cat. 366. A Boat homeward bound from Lake Hao. Signed and dated 1815.

Shên-chou, XVII. View over a Mountain Valley filled with Mist. On the road in the foreground, a man walking under trees. Signed, dated 1816. *Cf.* Shina Nanga, I, 119.

Mei-chan t'ê-k'an 65. A Man approaching a Temple Gate. Signed, dated 1817.

Hsü-ching chai. Mountain Valley with a Homestead and Figures. After Chao Mêng-fu. Two colophons by the painter, one dated 1819, the other 1842.

Yu-chêng album, 1923. Album of landscapes with figures. Inscriptions by the artist, several dated 1822. *Cf.* Nanga Taisei, XII, 163–173.

H. C. Wêng, Scarsdale. Mountains in Mist. Short handscroll. Signed, dated 1823.

I-shu ts'ung-pien 14. Misty Mountain Landscape with large Trees in the foreground, a Hermit seated in Meditation in a straw-covered Hut. Colophon by the painter dated 1824.

C. T. Loo's Successor, Frank Caro, N.Y. Landscape. Handscroll. Signed and dated 1826. *Cf.* Cleveland Exhib. cat. 116.

Chung-kuo ming-hua, XIII. Fishermen on a Mountain River. Inscription by the painter, dated 1828.

Shinchō 71 (Howard Hollis, Cleveland). The Bamboo Pavilion at Huang-kang. Signed and dated 1828. *Cf.* Cleveland Exhib. cat. 117.

Hamburg Exhibition, 1949–1950. Landscape with a Man seated on the Ground watching the Clouds. Light green and reddish colours. Handscroll. Signed and dated 1829.

Nanking Exhib. cat. 365. Landscape in the manner of Wang Meng. Signed, dated 1830.

Ming-jên shu-hua, XI. Two Men in a Garden on a moonlit Night. Signed, dated 1831.

Shina Nanga, III, 6. Landscape after T'ang Yin. Signed. Colophon by the painter dated 1834. *Cf.* Nanga Taikan, II.

Sōgen 323. T'ai-i Chou teaching his Grandson. Signed and dated 1834.

Sumitomo collect., Oiso. A Buddhist Image enshrined in a Cave; a man approaching. Handscroll. Signed and dated 1841. Colophon by Hu Ching.

Kurokawa cat. 36. A Grotto from which a River issues; a man crossing a bridge; a broad expanse of river. After Wên Po-jên. Handscroll. Signed and dated 1842.

Chung-kuo ming-hua, XIII. A Scholar in his Study at the Foot of high Mountains. Signed and dated 1843.

Shên-chou, VIII. A Scholar seated by a Rockery under a tall Pine-tree. Signed and dated 1849.

Chung-kuo ming-hua, X. The Valley of the Immortals in Mist. Signed.

Hui-hua kuan. A Scholar's Garden. He is seated in an open pavilion by a river. Handscroll. *Cf.* I-shu ch'uan-t'ung, XII.

Po-mei chi. Branches of Plum-blossoms. Signed.

Shina Meiga Senshū 38. Man in a Pavilion under tall Pine-trees by a Stream. Two lines of poetry by the painter.

Ibid. 39. The Bamboo Pavilion at Huang-kang. Album-leaf. Seal of the painter.

Sōraikan, I, 69. Three Poets meeting in a Garden on a moonlit Night. Signed. Poem.

Nanga Taisei, VII, 167. Four Men standing under Trees. Inscription, signed.

Tomioka collect., Kyōto. Relaxing in the Shade on a hot Day. Two men in a pavilion beneath pine-trees. Signed.

CH'IEN TUNG 錢東, *t.* Tung-kao 東皐, *h.* Hsiu-hai 袖海 and Yü-yü-shêng 玉魚生.

From Hangchou; lived in Yang-chou, Kiangsu. Active *c.*1770–1820. Flowers in the style of Yün Shou-p'ing; landscapes after Wên Chêng-ming. U, III, 2, 4. M, p.685.

Nanga Taisei, XII, 147–152. Seven Landscapes. Album-leaves. Inscriptions by the artist dated 1794, 1802 and 1817.

Chung-kuo ming-hua. Twelve Studies of Landscapes, Flowers, Fruits and Fish. Album-leaves, dated 1802.

Yu-chêng album, 1923. Eleven leaves of landscapes, flowers, etc. Inscriptions, two dated 1808 and 1817.

Sōgen 358. Flowers of the Four Seasons, after Yün Shou-p'ing. Signed, dated 1811.

Shina Nanga, II, 5. Landscape in Snow, after Chang Sêng-yu. Signed, dated 1817.

CH'IEN WEI-CH'ÊNG 錢維城, *t.* Tsung-p'an 宗盤, *h.* Ch'a-shan 茶山, Jên-an 紉庵 and Chia-hsien 稼軒. From Wu-chin, Kiangsu. B. 1720, d. 1772. Chuang yüan in 1745. Court-painter. Studied first flower-painting with his grandmother Ch'ên Shu, but devoted himself later mainly to landscape-painting. Q, II, 2. R, XII, 1. T, III, 1. U, I, 3, 16. M, p.684.

Shên-chou, V. High Mountains with their Crevices filled with Mist, a river is winding at their foot. Signed. Poem by Ch'ien-lung dated 1750.
Fei-tun lu shan-shui. Landscape after Huang Kung-wang. Signed, dated 1768.
Yamaguchi collect., Ashiya (formerly Tomioka Tessai). Album of Landscapes, the last signed and dated 1780.
Shinchō 52. Landscape. Signed, dated *kuei mao* (1783?)
S.c.t.k. hsü-pien, VI. A Branch of Mutan. Signed, dated 1793 (?)
Shên-chou, I. River Landscape with a Boat. Signed.
Ming-jên shu-hua, II. Camellias and Plum Blossoms. Signed.
Li-tai, I. Pine, Cedar, Plum Blossoms, Narcissi and Orchids. Signed. Poem by Ch'ien-lung.
Ibid. II. A Mountain Ridge on a clear Autumn Day.
Ibid. II. Four pictures from an Album called Thirty-six Views of the Jehol Summer Palace.
Ibid. III. Flowers and Birds, after Lü Chi. Signed. Poem.
Ibid. IV. Mountains and Rivers. Short handscroll. Signed.
Ibid. IV. Clouds over the South Mountain. Signed. Poem by Ch'ien-lung, dated 1766.
Ibid. IV. Cedar and Peach Blossoms. Signed.
Ibid. V. River Landscape with Sailing-boats on the Horizon. Signed.
Ibid. VI. Country Villa among Willows in Rain. Signed. Poem by Ch'ien-lung dated 1771.
Ku-kung, XXXVI. Wistaria and Peony. Signed.
K.-k. shu-hua chi, VIII. Trees in Winter. Signed. Poem.
Ibid. XIII. Landscape. Signed.
Ibid. XIX. Flowers and Fungi in Vases, after Tung Hsiang. Signed. Poem by Ch'ien-lung dated 1777.
Ibid. XX. River View with Pavilions and Cottages on the Cliffs. Signed. Poem by Ch'ien-lung dated 1771.
Ibid. XXIII. Landscape. Signed.
Ibid. XXV. Magnolias, Peonies and Hai-t'ang Flowers. Signed.
Ibid. XXVIII. Mountain Landscape with a Man seated by a Stream. Signed.
Ibid. XXX. The lofty Lu-shan. Signed.
Ibid. XXXIX. Summer Flowers. Signed. Small sheet.
Ibid. XLI. Peony and Pear Blossoms. Signed. Small sheet.
Ibid. XLII. Mountain Landscape with Pine-trees and Cottages. Signed. Poem by Ch'ien-lung dated 1782.
Ibid. XLIII. The White-cloud Temple in Honan. Signed. Poem and colophon by Ch'ien-lung, dated 1750.
(See also K.-k. chou-k'an, Index, for various works by this artist.)
Hsü Ching Chai. Ch'iao-shan, an Island in the Yangtse River. Signed.
Shina Nanga, I, 98. White Clouds and Hills in Autumn. Signed.
Ibid. II, 8. Landscape. Signed. Poem by Ch'ien-lung dated 1750.
Nanga Taikan 6. Chrysanthemums by a Rockery. Signed.
Sōgen 320. The West Lake. Handscroll. Signed. Poems by Ch'ien-lung and the painter.
Sekai Bijutsu Zenshū XX, colour Pl.5. Various Flowers. Section of a handscroll. *Cf.* Kokka, 727.
Chūgoku, 8. A Village in the Mountains. Signed. Poem by Ch'ien-lung, copied by Yü Ching-chung.
Ibid. Album of twelve paintings, Landscapes and Flowers. Signed. Poems by Ch'ien-lung.

CH'IEN WEI-CH'IAO 錢維喬, *t.* Shu-ts'an 樹參 and Shu-ch'uan 曙川, *h.* Chu-ch'u 竹初. From Wu-chin, Kiangsu. B. 1739, d. 1806. Brother of Ch'ien Wei-ch'êng. Landscapes. U, III, 1, 14. M, p.684.

Commercial Press album, 1919. An Album of Landscapes, the last signed and dated 1783.

CH'IH T'UAN 遲煓.

From Chien-yang, Fukien. Active *c.*1700. Flowers, birds, grass and insects. Q, I, 3. R, X, 18. M, p.624.

Shên-chou, IX. Two Mynah Birds on a Spray of Bamboo. Signed.

CHIN CHÜN-MING 金俊明, original name Kun 袞 and *t.* Chiu-chang 九章, later *t.* Hsiao-chang 孝章, *h.* Kêng-an 耿庵 and Pu-mei tao-jên 不寐道人.

From Suchou. B. 1602, d. 1675. Chu-shêng in the Ming dynasty; led a hermit's life after 1644. Landscapes, bamboos and plum-blossoms. Q, I, 1. R, III, 8. U, I, 2, 6. M, p.235.

Nanga Taisei, II, 231–235; IV, 54–56. An Album of Paintings of Bamboo, Orchids, Pine and Plum Blossoms. One leaf signed and dated 1660. (The plum blossoms only by Chin; the remainder by various other artists.)

Ibid. III, 41–58. An album of eighteen paintings of plum-blossoms, one signed and dated 1662.

Po-mei chi. A blossoming Plum-tree. Album-leaf. Signed, dated 1662.

Shina Nanga, III, 9. Landscape after Kuo Hsi. Signed, dated 1666.

Gems, I, 53. A blossoming Plum-tree, Bamboo and Orchids. Signed and dated 1667.

Nanga Taisei, V, 18. Pine Branches. Album-leaf. Poem, signed and dated 1669.

J. P. Dubosc, Lugano. Album of plum-blossoms. Signed, dated 1670.

Shên-chou, XV. Branches of a blossoming Plum-tree. Album-leaf. Signed, dated 1672.

Ibid. II. Two Men on a Terrace by a Mountain Stream. After Wen Cheng-ming. Signed.

Ming-jên shu-hua, X. Birds in a blossoming Peach-tree. After a Sung model. Signed. Colophon.

Ch'ing êrh-shih chia. Branches of Plum-blossoms. Album-leaf. Signed.

Shina Nanga, I, 24. Plum-blossoms. Seals of the painter. Poem. *Cf.* Chung-kuo ming-hua, 12.

CHIN K'AN 金侃, *t.* I-t'ao 亦陶, *h.* Li-an 立庵, Li-t'ao 立陶.

From Suchou. D. 1703. Son of Chin Chün-ming. Plum-trees and bamboos after his father; also coloured landscapes. Q, I, 1. R, VII, 19. U, II, 2, 4. M, p.235.

Nanga Taisei, XI, 194. Two Men seated under Pine-trees. Album-leaf. Signed and dated 1675.

Po-mei chi. A blossoming Plum-tree. Album-leaf. Signed. Poem.

CHIN K'UN 金昆.

Court-painter in the K'ang-hsi era. Q, II, 1, 16. M, p.236.

K.-k. chou-k'an 357–368. A small album of twelve leaves, illustrating various anecdotes from Chinese history. Signed.

CHIN LI-YING 金禮嬴, *t.* Yün-mên 雲門, *h.* Wu-yün 五雲 and Chao-ming-ko nei-shih 昭明閣內史.

From Shan-yin, Chekiang; lived in Ch'ien-t'ang. Wife of Wang T'an 王曇, (*t.* Chung-ch'ü 仲瞿), b. 1772, d. 1807. Landscapes, flowers, figures, plum blossoms and Buddhist figures. T. M, p.238.

Po-mei chi. Plum-blossoms in a Vase, a Teapot and a Bowl of green Sprouts. After a Sung painting. Signed.

CHIN NUNG 金農, *t.* Shou-mên 壽門, *h.* Tung-hsin 冬心, Ku-ch'üan 古泉, Lao-ting 老丁, Ssŭ-nung 司農 and several other names.

From Hangchou; lived in Yangchou, Kiangsu. B. 1687, d. after 1764. Began to learn painting at 50. Painted first mainly bamboos, then successively plum-blossoms, horses and Buddhist figures. Also landscapes. Author of *Tung-hsin t'i-hua* 冬心題畫 and other books. J, II, 1. Q, II, 2. R, XI. U, I, 3, 11. M, pp.236–267.

T'ai-shan album, series III. Album of four paintings and several leaves of calligraphy. Painted, according to inscription, "at age 26", *i.e.* in 1712.

Musée Guimet, Paris. A Branch of blossoming Plum-tree. Album-leaf. Poem by the painter dated 1733.

S.c.t.k. hsü-pien, IX. Bamboo. Signed, dated 1746.

L. Sickman, Kansas City. A Blossoming Plum-tree. Poem by the painter dated 1746.

Sōraikan, II, 82. A Buddhist Monk. Signed. Poem by the painter dated 1747.

Vannotti collect., Lugano. A Prunus Branch. Fan-painting. Poem. Signed, dated 1750. *Cf.* Wildenstein cat.

Kokka 734 (Moriya collect., Kyōto). A Bamboo Branch. Long inscription, signed and dated 1750.

Shina Meiga Senshū, 30 (Takashima collect., Kuginuma). Branches of Bamboos. Signed, dated 1750. *Cf.* Sekai Bijutsu Zenshū, XX, Pl.57; Kokka 734.

Shina Nanga, III, 9. A Tortoise. Signed. Colophon dated 1752. *Cf.* Shên-chou ta-kuan, 15.

Shên-chou ta-kuan, II. Bamboo. Long inscription signed and dated 1752.

Shên-chou, XVII. An old Tree and a Row of blossoming Lilies by a low Building. Signed, dated 1755. *Cf.* Nanga Taisei, XII, 95.

Nanga Taisei, I, 181, 182; II, 180; IV, 112–115, 238; V, 69, 226–228. An Album of Paintings of Flowers and Bamboo. Inscriptions, signed, one dated 1755.

Hui-hua kuan. The Top of a blossoming Plum-tree after Wang Mien. Painted at the age of 70 (1756).

Nanga Taisei, I, 179. Orchids. Fan-painting. Signed and dated 1757.

Ho Kuan-wu, Hongkong. Plum Blossoms. Signed and dated 1758 (at 72).

Chung-kuo ming-hua, 39. Landscape: two Men gazing at a Waterfall. Long inscription, signed and dated 1759.

Fei-tun lu hua-hui. A blossoming Plum-tree. Handscroll. Signed and dated 1759 (at 73).

Honolulu Academy of Arts. Album with Figures and Landscapes. Inscriptions by the painter dated 1759. Cleveland Exhibition cat. 112. Earlier version of same pictures in the album published by Shên-chou kuo-kuang-shê, 1913.

I-yüan chên-shang 4. Šakyamuni seated under Banana-palms. Signed "at age 73", *i.e.* in 1759.

J. D. Ch'ên, Hongkong. Album of Landscape and Figure-paintings, the last signed and dated 1759.

Nanga Taisei, VII, 137. A Man walking with a Staff. Long inscription, signed and dated 1759.

Ibid. VII, 138, right. A Monk standing under a leafy Tree (Wu-liang-shou fou, or Amida Buddha). Signed and dated 1759. *Cf.* Nanking Exhib. cat. 334.

Ibid. III, 137, right. A blossoming Plum-tree. Signed and dated 1759.

Ibid. III, 138, right. Branches of blossoming Plum. Signed and dated 1760 (at 74).

Ibid. III, 138, left. Branches of blossoming Plum. Signed and dated 1760.

Nanking Exhib. cat. 335. A Boat homeward bound in Rain and Wind. After Ma Ho-chih. Signed and dated 1760.

Harada Brothers, Ōsaka. A Horse rolling on the Ground; a man standing nearby. Handscroll. Long inscription by the artist signed and dated 1760. Mounted with it is a long piece of writing by Chin Nung, signed and dated 1745.

Shina Nanga, I, 93. Bamboos, after Wang Wei. Signed. Colophon dated 1760. *Cf.* Shên-chou, XVIII.

Sōraikan, II, 83. A saddled Horse. Signed. Long colophon dated 1760.

Chin Tung-hsin hua-jên-wu ts'ê (Yu-chêng Book Co., 1922). An Album of eight Landscapes; some with figures. Dated 1761 (at 75). One also in Shina Nanga, III, 4. *Cf.* Nanga Taisei, Add. II, 84–90; Add. IV, 84–86.

Shên-chou ta-kuan, XIII. A Blossoming Plum-tree. Long inscription signed "at 75", *i.e.* in 1761.

Shina Nanga, II, 2. Chung K'uei. Signed. Colophon dated 1761.

Chūgoku, 8. A Woman at a Spinning Wheel in the

Garden; an old woman holding the spindle. Signed and dated 1761 (at 75).

Yamaguchi collect., Ashiya. Bodhidharma seated on a Rope-mat beside a Palm-tree. Signed, "at age 76", *i.e.* in 1762. *Cf.* Sekai Bijutsu Zenshū, XX, colour pl.6.

Sōgen 319. A Monk sweeping fallen Leaves. Signed. Colophon dated 1762 (at 76).

I-shu ts'ung-pien 7. A sketchy Figure standing in Profile holding a Staff. Colophon by the painter written at the age of 77 (1763).

Nanju 12. Bodhidharma. Signed, dated 1774.

Shên-chou ta-kuan, vol.7. A Man standing in Meditation under a Tree. Signed.

Shên-chou, XVIII. A blossoming Plum-tree. Long poem by the painter.

Ibid. II. A Lohan seated in Meditation beneath a Banana-tree. Inscription by the painter.

Ibid. XIX. Three Friends visiting the Painter in a Pavilion on the River. Short album-leaf. Colophon by the painter.

Ibid. XX. A Buddhist Figure in the Guise of a bearded Monk. The whole background of the picture around the figure is filled with inscriptions by the painter.

I-shu ch'uan-t'ung 12. A flowering Plum-tree overhanging a Wall. Album-leaf. Signed.

Mo-ch'ao pi-chi, vol.II. A Monk standing under a Bo-tree. Long handscroll. Signed.

Hui-hua kuan. Plum blossoms. Four album-leaves.

Po-mei chi. An old Plum-tree. Signed.

Shina Nanga, I, 92. Plum-blossoms. After a Sung model. Signed. Poem.

Ibid. II, 6. A Wanderer in the Woods. Signed. Two lines of poetry.

Ōmura, I, 1. A Man worshipping a Buddha Statuette. Signed. *Cf.* Chūgoku, 8.

Shina Meiga Senshū, 31. An Arhat seated in Meditation. Colophon by the painter.

Shinchō 55. Orchids. Signed. Poem.

Shina Nanga Taikan, 4. A Man standing on a covered Bridge by a Lotus Pond. Album-leaf. Poem. Seals of the painter.

Sōgen 318. A Taoist T'ien-shih. Seal of the painter.

Jūrakusha album, 1956. Album of eight leaves, painted on gold paper. Inscription, signed. *Cf.* Kokka 728; Sekai Bijutsu Zenshū, 20, Pl.58.

Ibid. XX, Pl.56 (Kitano collect., Kyōto). An Arhat seated on a Mat of Leaves under a Cliff. Inscription, signed.

Nanga Taisei, VII, 139. Šakyamuni supported by three Demons. Signed.

Ibid. VI, 176; VII, 140–144. Album of paintings of various subjects: Figures, Animals, etc. Signed.

Chūgoku, 8. A Horse. Long inscription, signed.

Yūrintaikan, I. A young Monk seated under Plaintains. Signed.

Voretzsch. Fading Lotus Leaves; Blossoms in Wisps of Clouds. Two album-leaves. Signed.

Kuan Po-hêng collect., Peking. Bamboo Shoots. Poem.

Chang Ting-ch'ien, Hongkong. Landscapes, illustrating snow poems. Album-leaves.

H. C. Wêng, Scarsdale, N.Y. Bodhidharma seated in Meditation. Long inscription by the painter at the top.

Ibid. Figures and Buildings; Flowers and Fruits. An album partly in colour.

Ibid. Garden Scenes and Buddhist Figures. An album of eight leaves; ink only. Colophon by the painter.

Ibid. Branches of Plum Blossoms. Ink only. Long inscription by the painter.

Baron Ozaki, Tōkyō. The Eighteen Arhats. A small album, partly in colour.

Hashimoto collect., Kyōto. A Stem of slender Bamboo. Inscription by the painter.

Mr. Suma, Tōkyō. Self-portrait. Signed and dated. Ink only. Doubtful.

CHIN SHIH 金史, *t.* Ku-liang 古良.

From Shan-yin, Chekiang. Latter part of the 17th century. Figures, followed Ch'ên Hung-shou. M, p.235.

British Museum, No.156. The Accomplishments. Signed.

CHIN T'ING-PIAO 金廷標, *t.* Shih-k'uei 士揆.

From Wu-ch'êng, Chekiang. Active *c.*1720–1760. Court-painter in the Ch'ien-lung period. Figures, landscapes and flowers. S, II, p.1. M, p.237.

Li-tai, I. Kuan-yin. Signed, dated 1761.
Ibid. IV. Worshipping an Immortal. Signed.
Ku-kung, XXXIII. A Scholar and a Farmer. Signed.
K.-k. shu-hua chi, IV. Lilies by a Rock. Signed.
Ibid. X. Autumn Flowers. Signed.
Ibid XIII. Planting a Peach-tree. Signed.
Ibid. XIX. Mencius' Mother removing her Residence. Signed.
Ibid. XXII. A Man seated among Maple-trees in the Evening. Signed.
Ibid. XXXI. Transporting Cranes in a Boat. Round fan-painting. Signed.
Ibid. XXXII. Two Immortals playing Flute. Round fan-painting. Signed.
Ibid. XXXV. Collecting Fungi in Snow. Signed.
Ibid. XXXVI. Saluting a Stone. Signed.
Ibid. XXXVII. Dredging Mud. Signed.
Ibid. XXXIX. Collecting Orchids. Signed.
Ibid. XL. Chieh-yü warding off the Bear. Signed.
Ibid. XLI. A blossoming Peach-tree. Signed.
K.-k. chou-k'an, vol.II, 35. A Mountain Stream; an old man with a staff and a boy standing on a bridge looking at the clouds.
Ibid. vol.IV, 77. Travellers on Donkeyback proceeding on a Mountain-path in Autumn. Signed.
Ibid. vol.IV, 78. View of a small Garden; two persons talking at a gate. Signed. (See also K.-k. chou-k'an, Index, for other works of this artist.)
Pao-yün, I. A Scholar seated in a Cave gazing out at a Plum-tree. Signed. Poem and seals of Ch'ien-lung.
Chung-kuo ming-hua, 33. Golden Pheasants under Pine-trees. Signed.
Sōraikan, I, 61. An old Man calling to a Monkey in a Plum-tree. Signed.
Sōgen 350. Illustration to the first Chapter of the Book of Filial Piety.
Sirén, *Later*, 235. An Angler on a snowy River. Signed.

CHIN TSUN-NIEN 金尊年, *t.* Ku-ch'ên 谷臣
From Shang-yüan, Kiangsu. Active about the middle of the 18th century. Unrecorded.

Metropolitan Museum. A yellow Parrot on a Branch of a blossoming Tree. Signed, dated 1732.

CHIN YÜEH 金玥, *t.* Hsiao-chu 曉珠, *h.* Yüan-yü 圓玉.
From K'un-shan, Kiangsu. Lady painter; became in 1667 the concubine of the famous poet Mao Hsiang, better known under the name of Mao P'i-chiang 冒辟疆 (1611–1693). Flowers and landscapes. Q, II, 2 (under Ts'ai Han). M, p.235.

J. P. Dubosc, Lugano. Landscape in the Style of Mi Fei: wooded Mountains and leafy Trees. Handscroll. Seals of the painter. One colophon by Mao Hsiang, dated 1675.
Gems, I, 55. Autumn Flowers and Butterflies. Painted together with Ts'ai Han. Inscription, signed.

CH'IN I 秦儀, *t.* Wu-yüan 梧園, *h.* Fêng-kang 鳳岡.
From Wu-hsi, Kiangsu; lived in Suchou. D. *c.*1795. Landscapes, imitated Wang Hui. Famous for his willow paintings. U, III, 1, 21. M, p.313.

Shên-chou, IX. Cottages and Willows; a Fishing-boat on the River. Signed. Poem dated 1788. Also in Shina Nanga, III, 3.

CH'IN LANG 秦朗 or Wang Lang 王朗, *t.* Chung-ying 仲英.
From Chên-chiang, Kiangsu. Ch'ien-lung period. Daughter of the poet Wang Yen-hung 王彥泓, married to Ch'in Tê-ch'êng 秦德澄. Flowers and birds. M, p.313.

Li-tai, II. A Monk explaining Ch'an Buddhism to an Official. Signed.

CH'IN PING-WÊN 秦炳文, original name Ch'in I 秦繹, *t.* Yen-yün 硯雲, *h.* I-t'ing 誼亭.
From Wu-hsi, Kiangsu. B. 1803, d. 1873. Landscapes, followed Wang Shih-min. T, Add. I, 2. U, III, 2, 25. M, p.314.

Hamburg Exhibition, 1949–1950. Landscape after Li Ch'êng: Mountains in Snow. Handscroll. Signed, dated 1840.
Nanga Taisei Add. II, 163–168. Album of twelve Landscapes. Signed, one dated 1848.
Tokasha Shina Meigashū 92. A Mountain Stream, two men walking over a bridge; bamboo-groves, trees and buildings on the shore. Poem by the painter, dated 1865.
Hamburg Exhibition, 1949–1950. Evening Bell from a Temple in Mist. In the style of Shên Chou. Signed, dated 1867.
Nanga Taisei Add. II, 169–176. Album of sixteen Landscapes. Signed.

CH'IN TSU-YUNG 秦祖永, *t.* I-fên 逸芬, *h.* Lêng-yen wai-shih 楞煙外史 and other names.
From Wu-hsi, Kiangsu. B. 1825, d. 1884. Landscapes, followed Wang Shih-min. Author of *T'ung-yin lun-hua* 桐蔭論畫 and *Hua-chüeh* 畫訣; edited *Hua-hsüeh hsin-yin* 畫學心印. M, p.314.

Shincho 77. Landscape. Signed. Poem dated 1866. *Cf.* Tōan 74.
Tōan 75. Landscape. Signed. Poem dated 1867.
Nanking Exhib. cat. 380. A Villa in the Mountains. Poem. Signed and dated 1875.
Shina Nanga, III, 1. Landscape, copy of a picture by Wang Shih-min after Huang Kung-wang. Signed. Colophon dated 1881. *Cf.* Nanga Taikan 12.
Ibid. I, 139. The Blue T'ien-p'ing Mountain. Seal of the painter.
Ibid. II, 7. Rain and Mist over the Stone Lake near Suchou. Seal of the painter.
Ibid. III, 6. Mountain Cottages among Bamboos. Seals of the painter.
Hamburg Exhibition, 1949–1950. Landscape after a painting which Wang Shih-min which he had copied from T'ang Yin's work.

CHOU CHI-JU 周吉如, *t.* Shih-chên 士珍.
From Hupei. Probably 17th century. Unrecorded.

G. Del Drago, New York. Two old Men, possibly Kuan Yü and Chou Ts'ang. Signed, dated *ping tzŭ*.

CHOU CHIH-K'UEI 周之夔, *t.* Chang-fu 章甫.
Chin-shih in 1631. Landscapes. Unrecorded.

Kokka 276. High Mountains by a River. Signed, dated 1646. Also in Nanju 6; Tōyō, XI.

CHOU CH'ÜAN 周荃, *t.* Ching-hsiang 靜香, *h.* Hua-ch'i lao-jên 花溪老人.
Native of Ch'ang-chou in Kiangsu. Active in the early Ch'ing period. Landscapes, followed Tung Yüan and Ni Tsan. Q, II, 1, 4. U, I, 2, 17. M, p.250.

Chou Li-yüan 14. A Mountain Pass. Album-leaf. Seals of the artist.

CHOU CH'ÜAN 周銓, *t.* Chü-hêng 巨衡.
From Hsiu-shui, Chekiang. Active *c.*1700. Flowers and birds, particularly lotuses and herons, hence called Chou Ho (Lotus Chou). Q, I, 2. M, p.252.

British Museum, No.179. Duck and Lotus. Signed, dated *ping-tzŭ* (1696).
Metropolitan Museum· A Pair of Mandarin Ducks and flowering Lotus Plants. Signed, dated 1701.
L. Bataille, Paris. Two Ducks under a Camellia-tree in bloom. Signed.

CHOU HAO 周顥 or 周灝, *t.* Chin-chan 晉瞻, *h.* Chih-yen 芷巖 and Jan-ch'ih 髯癡.
From Chia-ting, Kiangsu. B. 1675, d. 1763. Pupil of Wang Hui. Landscapes and bamboos. M, p.252.

Nanju 25. Landscape. Signed. Poem dated 1706.
Private collect., Kyōto. Branch of Bamboo. Signed and dated 1734.
T'ai-shan ts'an-shih-lou ts'ang-hua, I. Homestead in a Gully between wild Mountains, men on mule-back on the road. Poem by the painter, dated 1743.
Chung-kuo ming-hua, 38. Landscape with Pines and other Trees; two men watching a waterfall. Signed, dated 1757.
Freer Gallery (45.38). Endless Valleys and Mountains. Long handscroll. Signed, dated 1766 (at 81).
Hosokawa collect., Tōkyō. A Lake Scene in Storm; wild Waves, Buildings on the Shore, a Dragon appearing.
J. Cahill, Wash., D.C. Bamboo growing from Rocks above a Stream. Inscription, seals of the artist.

CHOU HSI 周禧.
Daughter of Chou Jung-ch'i 周㷇起 (V, p.542). According to the biographical note in Ku-kung chou-k'an 486, recorded in *Chiang-nan t'ung-chih* 江南通志.

K.-k. chou-k'an 486–490. Album of ten paintings of Arhats. Inscriptions by Li Chi-hsiang dated 1670.

CHOU HSIEN 周閑, *t.* Ts'un-po 存伯, *h.* Fan-hu chü-shih 范湖居士.
From Hsiu-shui, Chekiang. Active *c.*1850–1870. Flowers. M, p.257.

Nanga Taikan 8. A Branch of a blossoming Plum-tree in a Vase, Narcissi and Fruits on a Plate. Signed, dated 1874.

CHOU HSÜN 周璕, *t.* K'un-lai 崑來, *h.* Sung-shan 嵩山.
From Chiang-ning, Kiangsu. 17th century. Figures, animals, particularly dragons. Q, I, 3. R, XII, 8. M, p.252

S.c.t.k. hsü-pien, VIII. Portrait of a wandering Monk.

Princeton (Du Bois-Morris collect.) A Man and a Horse under a Pine-tree. Signed.

National Museum, Stockholm. Dragon in Clouds. Signed.

CHOU KU 周穀.
Unrecorded. Probably Ch'ing dynasty.

Sōgen 252. Wild Ducks and old Lotus-plants. Signed.

CHOU LI 周笠, *t.* Mu-shan 牧山.
From Chia-ting, Kiangsu. Active *c.*1740. Nephew of the painter Chou Hao. Landscapes in the style of Wang Hui and Yün Shou-p'ing. M, p.252.

Chou Mu-shan chün shan-shui chên-chi (Yu-chêng Book co., 1925). An Album of twelve Landscapes in the Style of Yün Shou-p'ing. Signed, dated 1743. *Cf.* Nanga Taisei, Add. II, 91–102.

Nanga Taisei, XII, 90–94; Add. IV, 87. Six Landscapes. Album-leaves. Inscription signed and dated 1743.

CHOU LI 周笠, *t.* Yüan-tsan 元贊, *h.* Yün-yen 雲巖 and Yün-lan wai-shih 韵蘭外史.
From Suchou, *c.* 1800. Started as a figure-painter but later painted flowers and landscapes in the manner of Yün Shou-p'ing. U, III, 2, 17. M, p.252.

Ming-jên shu-hua, XII. Flowers and Trees. Painted together with Wang Hsüeh-hao, Chiang Hsün, Chu Ang-chih and Chai Chi-ch'ang. Pine-tree by Chou Li. Signed. Also in Nanga Taikan 1.

Sung-chai. Two leaves from an Album of Paintings representing Flowers and Birds, after Yün Shou-p'ing.

CHOU LIANG-KUNG 周亮工, *t.* Yüan-liang 元亮, *h.* Li-yüan 櫟園.
From K'ai-fêng, Honan; lived in Nanking. B. 1612, d. 1672. Served as a Censor in the Ming dynasty and became Vice-president of the Board of Revenue in the Ch'ing period. Scholar, collector and connoisseur. Author of *Li-yüan tu-hua lu* 櫟園讀畫錄, which contains records of seventy-seven painters who were his personal friends. Landscapes. U, II, 1, 15. M, p.249. V, p.532.

Shên-chou, XIX. A misty Mountain Gully with Pavilions. Signed. *Cf.* Shina Nanga, III, 3.

CHOU NAI 周鼐, *t.* Kung-t'iao 公調.
Native of Chiang-ning, Kiangsu. Landscapes after Li Ch'êng and Tung Yüan; also orchids and bamboo. Q, I, 2, 10. M, p.250.

Nanking Exhib. cat. 246. A Hibiscus Flower. Signed and dated *hsin-mao* (or) 1651?

CHOU PA 周拔, *t.* Ch'ing-han 清漢, *h.* T'ing-shêng 挺生.
From T'ung-chou, Kiangsu. Orchids, plum blossoms and chrysanthemums; bamboos after Su Tung-p'o. M, p.254.

Ming-jên hsieh-chu. Bamboos and Rocks, after Su Tung-p'o. Signed, dated *ting-mao*, or 1747(?)

CHOU SHANG-WÊN 周尙文, *t.* Su-chien 素堅, *h.* Shih-hu 石湖.
From Suchou. Made some pictures of the emperor Ch'ien-lung's journey to the south in 1762. Landscapes, followed Wang Hui and Wang Yüan-ch'i. M, p.253.

Shên-chou, XIV. Clearing after Snowfall on the Mountains. After Wang Wei. Signed, dated 1768.
Bijutsu, XXV. Mountain Landscape in Spring. Signed.
N. Gashū 33. A Path along a Precipice, after Kuo Hsi. Signed. Poem.
Kawai collect., Kyōto. Landscape after Shên Chou. Signed.

CHOU SHAO-YÜAN 周紹元.
Unrecorded. Probably 18th century.

Tokasha Shina Meigashū 99. An Eagle on a Pine Branch watching a small Bird. Signed.

CHOU TSUNG-LIEN 周宗濂, *t.* Chien-an 簡庵, *h.* Chien-t'ang 漸堂.
From Hua-t'ing, Kiangsu. Active as a writer and a school teacher at the beginning of the 18th century. V, p.530.

G. Del Drago, New York. A Branch of a blossoming Plum-tree. Signed.

CHOU WÊN-CHING 周文經.
Unrecorded. Active middle of the 18th century.

Princeton (Du Bois-Morris collect.) Kuan Yü and Chou Ts'ang. Signed, dated 1755.

CHU ANG-CHIH 朱昂之, *t.* Ch'ing-li 青立, *h.* Ching-li 津里.
From Wu-chin, Kiangsu; lived in Suchou. Lived *c.*1760–1840. Landscapes, followed Wang Hui and Yün Shou-p'ing. U, I, 3, 21. M, p.106.

Fei-tun lu hua-hui. An old Pine-tree. Rocks and Orchids. Signed, dated 1782.
Hamburg Exhibition, 1949–1950. Landscape in the style of Tung Yüan and Chü-jan. Signed, dated 1813.
Fei-tun lu shan-shui. Autumn Landscape after an old master. Signed and dated 1818.
Chung-kuo ming-hua, XXIII. River Landscape, steep cliff rising above the river. After Huang Kung-wang Signed, dated 1824.
Shên-chou, XVIII. A Temple in a misty Mountain Gully, after Wang Mêng. Signed, dated 1826.
Nanju 4. Landscape after Mi Fei. Signed. Colophon dated 1839.
Shên-chou, XVI. A River winding between rocky Shores, groves of trees in the foreground. Colophon by the painter.
Ming-jên shu-hua, XII. Flowers and Trees. Painted together with Wang Hsüeh-hao, Chiang Hsün, Chai Chi-ch'ang and Chou Li. Rock by Chu Ang-chih. Signed. Also in Nanga Taikan 1.
Fu-lu. A Spray of Bamboos. Poem by the painter.
Shinchō 73. A Cottage among Pines. After Wang Mêng. Signed.
Kyōto Museum, Takeuchi collect. Lotus-flowers on high Stalks. In the manner of Hsü Wei.

CHU CH'ANG 祝昌, *t.* Shan-ch'ao 山嘲.
From Shu-ch'êng, Anhui. Early Ch'ing period. Landscapes, followed at first the monk Hung-jên and later the Yüan masters. Q, I, 3. M, p.309.

S.c.t k. hsü-pien, X. A rocky Slope. Signed.

Kyuka, II. A Stream in Rain. Signed. Poem.

CHU CHÊ 祝喆 or CHU CHIA 祝嘉, *t.* Ming-fu 明甫.
From Chia-hsing, Chekiang. Hsiao lien in 1760. Poet. Plum blossoms. T. M, p.309.

Po-mei chi. Blossoming Plum-trees. Handscroll. Signed. *Cf.* Nanga Taisei, III, 158.

CHU CH'ÊN 朱琛, *t.* Yün-pi 雲壁.
From Sung-chiang, Kiangsu. Kang-hsi period. Landscapes. M, p.102. V, p.260.

Kokka 634 (R. Hosomi, Ōsaka). Landscape. Signed.

CHU CHÜN 朱陵, *t.* Tzŭ-wang 子望, *h.* I-ch'ao 亦巢.
From Suchou. Lived in the beginning of the Ch'ing dynasty. Landscapes. L. M, p.100.

Nanga Taisei, II, 73. Orchids. Signed and dated *chi-hai*, (1659?)

Po-mei chi. A blossoming Plum-tree. Album-leaf. Signed, dated *keng-shên* (probably 1680).

Ch'ing êrh-shih chia. A blossoming Plum-tree. Album-leaf. Signed.

CHU HAN-CHIH 朱翰之, *t.* Jui-wu 睿瞀, *h.* (his name as a monk) Ch'i-ch'u ho-shang 七處和尚.
From Nanking. 17th century. P, I, 10. R, XIV, 17. U, II, 1, 7. M.p.1.

Chêng Ch'i, Hongkong. A Rock, after Mi Fei. Handscroll. Many colophons by contemporaries, some dated 1641.

Chou Li-yüan, 13. Horses on the Shore of a Lake. Album leaf. Signed and dated 1646.

Shina Meiga Senshū 17 (Hashimoto collect., Takatsuki). The San-shan study: extensive River View. Handscroll. Signed, dated 1651.

Nanking Exhib. cat. 275. River Landscape with perpendicular Cliffs. Signed and dated 1652.

Chou Li-yüan, 9. A Temple among sparsely-set Trees. Album-leaf. Seal of the artist.

J. P. Dubosc, Lugano. A Man in a House overlooking a Plain. Signed. A leaf in an album formerly in Chou Liang-kung's collect.

CHU HANG 朱沆, *t.* Ta-fu 達夫, *h.* Huan-yo 浣岳.
From Peking. Active at the close of the 18th century. Figures, landscapes and bamboos. M, p.107.

Robert Rousset, Paris. A Philosopher resting on the Ground looking at a Waterfall. Finger-painting. Signed.

CHU HAO-NIEN 朱鶴年, *t.* Yeh-yün 野雲 and Fu-an 復庵.
From T'ai-chou, Kiangsu; lived in Peking. B. 1760, d. after 1833. Landscapes in the style of Tao-chi; also figures and flowers. U, III, 1, 25. M, p.107.

Ming-jên shu-hua, XXI. The Ts'ang-lang Pavilion in Summer. Signed. Poem dated 1808.

Tōan 66. Landscape. Fan-painting. Signed, dated 1830 (at 71).

Nanga Taisei Add. IV, 114. An old Man and his Servant. Signed and dated 1830.

Ibid. Add. IV, 115; X, 213. Two Landscapes, dated 1832 and 1833.

Po-mei chi. A blossoming Plum-tree and a Rock. Signed. dated 1833.

Chūgoku, 8. A Man walking and a Servant pulling a Donkey along a Path, a lady awaiting them. Large album-leaf, signed.

CHU HSIEN 朱軒, *t.* Shao-chiu 韶九, *h.* Hsueh-t'ien 雪田.

From Sung-chiang, Kiangsu. B. *c.*1620, d. *c.*1690. Pupil of Tung Ch'i-ch'ang and Chao Tso. Landscapes. R, IV, 25. M, p.101.

Nanju 17. Landscape. Signed, dated 1683. Also in Tōyō, XII.

CHU HSÜAN 朱烜, *t.* Ping-nan 丙南.

From Hangchou. Landscapes, flowers, plum blossoms. M, p.108.

Po-mei chi. Branches of Plum-blossoms. Signed. Poem.

CHU I-SHIH 朱一是, *t.* Chin-hsiu 近修.

Native of Hai-ning. Chü-jen in 1642; retired after the fall of Ming. Famous as a poet. L, 9, 7, V, p.247. Also in Chou Liang-kung's *Tu-hua lu.*

Chung-kuo ming-hua, V, 35. A Lady teaching Children in a Garden. Poem by the artist.

CHU LUN-HAN 朱倫瀚, *t.* Han-chai 涵齋 and I-hsien 亦軒, *h.* I-san 一三.

From Li-ch'eng, Shantung. B. 1680, d. 1760. Descendant of the Ming imperial family. Passed the military chin shih degree in 1712. Finger painter, followed his uncle Kao Ch'i-p'ei. Q, II, 1. R, XI, 21. M, p.103.

Ōmura, I, 3. A Pine Forest. Finger-painting. Signed, dated 1741. *Cf.* Chūgoku, VIII.

British Museum (Add. No. 26). Landscape. Finger-painting. Signed, dated 1751.

Nanking Exhib. cat. 330. A Man in a House at the Foot of steep Cliffs. Finger-painting. Signed and dated 1751.

Tokasha Shina Meigashū 72. Twisting old Trees on Cliffs in Snow, and a Pavilion. Poem by the painter dated 1752.

Ming-jên shu-hua, IV. A Tiger on a Mountain Path. Finger-painting. Signed, dated 1758.

K.-k. chou-k'an 81. A Village by the River. Signed.

Li-tai, III. Pine-trees and Cranes. Signed.

Tokasha Shina Meigashū 70. An old Monk holding an Incense-burner. Signed.

Ibid. 71. Two Horses under bare Trees by a Stream. Finger-painting. Colophon by the painter.

Kunst und Künstler, 1930 (E. Preetorius collect.) A Heron under a Willow-tree. Fan-painting. Signed.

CHU PO 朱白, *t.* T'ien-tsao 天藻. L. M, p.108.

Ch'ing êrh-shih chia. Bamboos and Plum Blossoms. Album-leaf. Signed, dated *chi-wei.*

Nanga Taisei, II, 51. A Bamboo Grove; two men walking below. Signed and dated *chia-yin.*

Also in Tōyō, XII.

N. Gashū 34. Bamboos by a Stream. Signed, dated 1686.

Shina Nanga, I, 20. Bamboos. Signed, dated 1687. *Cf.* I-yüan chên-shang 5.

Princeton (Du Bois-Morris collect.) Bamboos by a Rockery under full Moon. Signed, dated 1689.

Ibid. Bamboos in Snow. Signed, dated 1689.

Voretzsch. Bamboos by a Rock. Signed, dated 1689.

Ibid. Two handscrolls representing (1) Bodhidharma crossing the Yangtse; (2) Taoist Immortal conversing with a Dragon. Signed, dated 1734.

Ming-jên hsieh-chu. Bamboos and Rocks. Screen of six panels. Signed.

British Museum, No. 222. Bamboos. Signed.

J. Fontein, Amsterdam (formerly Kuwana collect.) A Branch of Bamboo. Inscription, signed.

CHU TA 朱耷, *t.* Jên-wu 人屋, *h.* Pa-ta shan-jên 八大山人, Hsüeh-ko 雪個, Jên-wu 人屋, Shu-nien 書年, Ko-shan 個山, Shan-lü 山驢 and other names.

A descendant of the imperial Ming family, who became a monk. B. 1625, d. 1705 (the dates are not firmly established). Landscapes, flowers and birds. Q, I, 1. U, II, 1, 9. M, p.1.

Hui-hua kuan. Loquat, Ling-chih and Pines. Long handscroll, with writing by the painter dated 1666.

T'ai-shan ts'an-shih-lou ts'ang-hua, VIII. An Album of twelve tall leaves, mainly Landscape-studies and sketches of birds, trees and plants. Three leaves with writings. Five of the leaves are dated respectively 1681, 1690, 1696, 1699, 1701.

Hui-hua kuan. Studies of Birds, a Cat and Fruits. Four album-leaves. Signed and dated 1684.

J. P. Dubosc, Lugano. A sleeping Dog. Signed, dated 1684.

Nanga Taisei, V, 14. Branches of Pine, Plum and Bamboo. Long inscription, signed and dated 1689.

Ibid. VI, 102, left. A Bird on a Rock. Signed and dated 1690.

S.c.t.k. hsü-pien, III. A Ruffled Bird on the Tip of a Branch. Signed and dated 1690.

Yamaguchi collect., Ashiya. Six Mynah-birds below a projecting Cliff. Ink on silk. Signed and dated 1690.

Cincinnati Art Museum. Birds on Rocks among Lotus-plants. Handscroll. Signed and dated 1690. A similar design in Chang Ta-ch'ien cat., III, 8.

Chang Ta-ch'ien cat. III, 10–13. Small album of eight leaves of flowers, fruits, birds and bees. All leaves signed, the second and last dated 1692.

Ibid. III, 1. Bamboos, Rock and two small Birds. Signed and dated 1692. Inscription by Chang Ta-ch'ien.

Kokka 724. Album of eight paintings and two leaves of calligraphy, one dated 1692.

T'ai-shan album, series III. Album of ten leaves: landscapes, birds. Inscriptions, one dated 1693.

Ibid. Series IV. Album of fourteen leaves: seven paintings, birds, flowers, bamboo, rocks; the other seven with calligraphy, one dated 1693.

S.c.t.k. hsü-pien, IX. A Fish Swimming. Signed, dated 1694.

Chang Ta-ch'ien cat., III, 2. Two small Birds on a Stone under Lotus-flowers. Signed and dated 1694.

Ibid. IV, 36. Landscape in ink; three tall trees in the foreground. Poem by the painter dated 1694.

Private collect., Kyōto (formerly Yamamoto Teijirō). Fish swimming beneath a Rock. Signed and dated 1694.

Sōgen 208. Landscape. Signed, dated 1694. *Cf.* Gems, I, 64.

Ibid. 209. Two small Birds. Signed. Poem dated 1694.

Gems, I, 65. Lotus and Chrysanthemums. Signed and dated 1694.

Ibid. III, 8. An Album of eight Paintings of Birds, Flowers and Landscapes. Inscriptions by the artist, one dated 1694.

K. Sumitomo, Ōiso. Pa-ta shan-jên hua-ts'ê miao-p'in. An Album (published by Hakubundō) of Landscapes, Flowers, Birds and Fishes. According to the preface, fifteen pictures were painted in 1694; one of the other pictures is dated 1702. *Cf.* K. Sumitomo: I, IV, V. The picture with the Quails also in Sōgen, 211; the Kingfisher also in Kyuka, I. Five leaves in Sekai Bijutsu Zenshū 20, Pl.42–46.

Nanga Taisei, IV, 49. Branches of Lichee in a Vase. Inscription, signed and dated 1695.

Ibid. VI, 103, right. A Bird on a Rock. Signed and dated 1696.

Gems, I, 66. Two Birds and a Peach-tree. Signed and dated 1696.

Chang Ta-ch'ien cat., III, 9. A Narcissus Plant. Two inscriptions by Shih-t'ao dated 1697 when Shih-t'ao was 57 years old and Pa-ta shan-jên 73.

Chang Ta-ch'ien cat., III, 5. Lotus-blossoms, Reed and four wild Geese. Signed and dated 1698.

Noda collect., Kyōto. Album of sixteen leaves: Six Landscapes, the rest Bird and Flower Subjects. Signed, one dated 1698.

Chang Ta-ch'ien cat., III, 6. A small Tiger on a Rock under a Mugwort plant. Signed and dated 1699.

Chang Ta-ch'ien collect., Hongkong. Album of twelve leaves: Studies of Plants, Flowers and Birds. Painted at the age of 75 (1699).

Boston Museum (55.390). Hibiscus on a Cliff and two Birds on a Stone; the plant hanging down over the birds. Signed and dated 1699.

Ibid. Lotus, after Hsü Wei. Signed, dated 1699.

Chang Ta-ch'ien cat., III, 24–28. Small album of ten leaves: 1. Bird under Lotus-leaf, dated 1700. 2. Orchid by a Rock, dated 1700. 3. Lotus Flowers, signed. 4. A Quail under a Reed, signed. 5. Mountain in Rain, in the style of Mi Fei. Signed. 6. A Hut under old Pine-trees by a Mountain, signed. 7. A lonely open Pavilion on the River, signed. 8. A Study under Wu-tung-trees; signed. 9 and 10. Two examples of the painter's calligraphical work, the first Lan-t'ing essay and the second, Su T'ung-p'o essay. Dated 1700.

Nanga Taisei, V, 15. Two paintings of Pine-trees. Signed, dated 1701 and 1702. 16: another, undated.

T'ai-shan album, series I. Twelve leaves, landscapes and calligraphy. Signed, one dated 1702.

Shên Chou, IX. A swimming Fish. Signed. Poem, dated 1702.

C. C. Wang, New York. Two large Eagles. Signed, dated 1702.

Chung-kuo, II, 111. A Crow perching on a Willow Trunk. Signed, dated 1703. *Cf.* Chung-kuo ming-hua, 36.

Kyōto Museum (Sōkoku-ji). Strange Cliffs and stumpy Trees forming a tall winding design. Signed at the age of 80 (1704).

Yu-chêng album, n.d. Lohans crossing the Sea. Handscroll. Inscription mounted after the painting, dated 1705. The painting is attributed, probably wrongly, to Pa-ta shan-jên. *Cf.* Nanga Taisei, Add IV, 40, 41.

Shên-chou, XV. Two Mandarin Ducks resting on a Stone by the Water. Signed, dated 1705.

Nanga Taisei, V, 154. Lotuses. Signed and dated 1705.

Shên-chou, III. A Pine-tree. Signed.

Ibid. VII. A Bird perching on a Branch of a Tree. Signed.

Ibid. XV. Two Magpies in a blossoming Plum-tree. Signed.

Shên-chou ta-kuan, vol.6. Two Papaya Fruits. Poem by the painter.

S.c.t.k. hsü-pien, IV. Cliffs by a River. Album-leaf. Signed.

Pa-ta shan-jên (and) Shih-t'ao hua ho-ts'ê (Yu-chêng Book co., 1924). An Album of three Paintings and several Specimens of Writing by Pa-ta shan-jên, and twelve Paintings by Tao-chi.

Shên-chou album, 1923. An album of eight Landscape Sketches and three leaves of writing.

Commercial Press album, 1934. Nine small Landscapes after old Masters. Some with inscriptions by the painter.

Hsi-lêng yin-shê album. Eight Flower Sketches and eight leaves of Writing.

Chung-kuo, II, 110. Bare Trees and Rocks. Album-leaf. Signed.

Ibid. II, 112. Mandarin Ducks and Lotuses. Signed.

Ibid. II, 113. Trees on rocky Shores. Signed.

Ibid. II, 114. An Eagle on a leafless Branch. Signed.

I-shu t-s'ung pien, 14. Lotus Plants by a Rockery. Signed

Chung-kuo ming-hua, 24. Two Mandarin Ducks and a [illegible] …ore; small lotus plants rising out [illegible]

… with Pine-trees. Poem, signed.

…-lou ts'ang-hua, I. Bamboos by a … the Epidendrum Plants. Signed. The …-chi.

…m of sixteen leaves; Studies of Plants and Birds. Four leaves containing only inscriptions.

Ibid. IX. An album of ten leaves. Landscape studies, some after Sung and Yüan masters. The first leaf with a poem by the painter.

Ibid. X. An album of twelve leaves: eight Studies of Cliffs and Trees (in a very broad manner); three with inscriptions by the painter, the last with inscription by a later writer.

Ibid. Series II. Album of eight leaves, birds and flowers. Signed.

Ibid. Series III. Lotuses. Handscroll. Signed.

Hui-hua kuan. Hills rising in successive Steps, scattered trees and a few buildings. Signed.

Ibid. A Lotus Plant growing on two high Stalks; a small bird on a rock. Signed. A very tall picture.

Ibid. A long Branch of a Pine-tree; scattered needles. Signed.

Shanghai Museum. A tall painting of winding and twisted Cliffs; low buildings and pines on the terraces. Slight reddish tone. Broad brushwork, Signed.

Nanking Exhib. cat. 303. An Egret on a Rock. Poem, signed.

Ibid. 304. A large Fish. Seal of the artist.

Ibid. 306. Lotuses, after Hsü Wei. Poem, signed.

Chung-kuo ming-hua, XIII. A River in the Mountains; leafy trees and a rock. Signed.

Mei-chan t'ê-k'an 37. River-view with leafless Trees, in the manner of Ni Tsan. Signed.

Ibid. 36. Trees growing on Boulders; houses above in the cleft of a mountain. Album-leaf. Signed.

Fu-lu. A Mynah-bird on a bare Rock. Poem by the painter.

Liu 92. Three wild Geese perched on Rocks; another alighting. Signed.

Chang Ta-ch'ien cat., I, 36. A Plant on a Cliff and a Bird on a Stone. Inscription by the painter. Similar in design to the picture in the Boston Museum (55.390 dated 1699).

Ibid. III, 3. The Joy of Fishes swimming between Rocks. Signed.

Ibid. III, 4. Two Ducks; one standing on a stone under tall lotus-plants, the other one on a big rockery. Signed. Inscription by Wu Ch'ang-shih of the 20th century.

Ibid. III, 7. A Branch of Tree-peony. Inscription by the painter.

Ibid. III, 8. Birds playing in a Lotus-pond. Handscroll. Signed.

Chang Ta-ch'ien cat., III, 14–19. Album of six leaves with landscapes in style of Tung Ch'i-ch'ang. The first after Tung Yüan, the fifth after Huang Kung-wang, and the last after Ni Tsan. The inscriptions are also in style of Tung Ch'i-ch'ang. Seals of the painter. Colophon by Chang Ta-ch'ien on the last leaf.

Ibid. III, 20–23. Small album of eight leaves; four landscapes and four leaves of writing. The second painting after Mi Fei, the third coloured and the last after Tung Yüan. All signed.

Ibid. III, 29–36. *Lan-t'ing shih-hua ts'ê*: album of six landscapes after old masters. Additional leaves with writing. Signed.

Ibid. III, 37–40. *Shu-hua ho-pi ts'ê*. Small album of eight leaves; four paintings, and four writings. The four paintings are 1. Magnolia flower, signed. 2. Lotus, signed. 3. Grey Starling on a Branch of a bare Tree, signed. 4. Plum-trees, signed.

Wang Shih-chieh, Taipei. A Deer standing under the Branch of a Pine-tree. Signed.

Lo Chia-lun, Taipei. A tall Mountain Landscape; buildings on the terraces and bare trees. Signed, three seals of the painter.

Nanju 15. Lotuses and Rocks. Signed. *Cf.* Tōyō, XII.

Hyōjirō Hatta. Landscape. Signed.

Bijutsu, III. Mountains and bare Trees. Album-leaf. Signed.

Shina Nanga, I, 18. Two Melons. Signed. Poem.

Ibid. II, 9. Two Magpies in a Plum-tree. Signed.

Ibid. III, 4. Lotuses and Rocks. Signed. *Cf.* Nanju 15.

Ibid. III, 9. Two album-leaves: a Cow. Signed. A Group of bare Trees. Seal of the painter.

Pa-ta shan-jên hua-ts'ê shên-p'in (Hakubundō Album). Eight Landscapes.

Ōmura, I, 4. Cottages on a Promontory under leafless Trees. Album-leaf. Signed.

Shinchō 30. Cloudy Peaks. Album-leaf. Signed.
Tōkasha Shina Meigashū, 40. Two Vases, one with Flowers. Signed.
Tōan 40. A Fish below a Cliff. Album-leaf. Signed.
Sōgen 210. Terraced Mountains. Signed.
Ibid. 212. A Crow resting on a Rock. Signed.
Ibid. 213. A Heron perching on a leafless Willow-trunk. Album-leaf. Signed poem.
Chūgoku V. Three Quails on a Rock; bamboo and chrysanthemum. Signed.
Yamaguchi collect., Ashiya. Album of twelve leaves of flowers, fruits, birds, etc. Signed.
Ibid. A Deer with long Antlers seen in front view, standing under a projecting rock. Signed.
Horiuchi collect., Ōsaka (formerly Hashimoto Kansetsu). A large Mountain Landscape. Signed.
T. Moriya collect., Kyōto. Two Fish swimming below a Rock. Signed.
Nanga Taisei. XV, 30, 31. Lotuses. Handscroll, signed.
Ibid. See also I, 107, 108 (Bamboo); 109 (Orchids); II, 158, 159, 224 (Chrysanthemum); III, 59, 60 (Plum); III, 244 (Narcissus); IV, 43–48, 50, 51 (various Flowers); 227, 228 (Rocks); V, 98 (Peony); 139, 140 (Banana-palm); 153, 155, 156 (Lotus); 205, 206 (Fruits); VI, 102–122 (Birds and Fish); VII, 95–97 (Animals); X, 40, 41; XI, 193; Add. I, 110–126; Add. IV, 38, 39 (Landscapes).
J. P. Dubosc, Lugano. Album of seven leaves; pictures of flowers and fruits. Signed.
Vannotti collect., Lugano. River View with a rocky Island. Handscroll. Signed. Title written by Ch'a Shih-piao; colophons by Chiang Shih-chieh and Huang Ch'ang.
British Museum (Add. Nos. 55 and 56). Two album-leaves: Chrysanthemums and Narcissi. Signed.
Shên-chou ta-kuan, vol.16 (Musée Guimet, Paris). Steep Cliffs rising above a Stream. After Tung Yüan. Inscription by the painter. Colophon by P'êng Wang-hsün.
National Museum, Stockholm. Large Mountain Landscape after Tung Yüan.
C. C. Wang, New York. Lotus Plant growing through the Water. Long handscroll. Signed.
W. Hochstadter, New York. River Landscape in the style of Ni Tsan. Large album-leaf. Signed.
C. T. Loo's Successor, Frank Caro, N.Y. A Branch with two Quince. Inscription by the painter. *Cf.* Toronto, 39.
Ibid. Lotus Plants in the style of Hsü Wei. Poem by the painter. *Cf.* Toronto, 40.
Hamburg Exhibit. 1949, cat. 88. View over a Broad Stream; a rocky island with houses and open pavilions in the middle, and a tall leafless tree in the foreground. Ink and colour on paper. Signed. *Cf.* Cleveland Exhib. cat. 99.
Ibid. cat. 89–40. Birds and Rocks.
Cincinnatti Museum. A Duck and other Birds among Lotus-leaves. Handscroll. Signed.
Cleveland Museum. Landscape after Kuo Chung-shu. *Cf.* Cleveland Exhib. cat. 98.
Ibid. Fish swimming among Rocks. Handscroll. Signed.
Freer Gallery (55.21). An album of ten leaves: Flowers, Birds, Insects and Fish. Signature on all the leaves, except one. Eleven inscriptions.
Hung Yu-ling, Hongkong. An Album of Landscape Studies. Signed.
K. Sumitomo, Ōiso. A handscroll with a painting of two Birds on a Branch and another of a Landscape. Inscriptions by the artist. *Cf.* K. Sumitomo, I.
K. Harada (Hakubundō). Two Mynah Birds on the slender Branches of a leafless Willow. Long inscription by the painter.
Hachidai Sanjin Gafu (Jūrakusha, Tōkyō, 1938).

1. A large Mynah Bird on the Top of a Rock by some Bamboos.
2. Six Crows and Mynah Birds on a rocky Shore.
3. Birds, Fish and Fruits. Four leaves from an album. (Mr. Gono Kenzo.)
4. Chrysanthemum Plants by a Rockery and a small Bird. Signed, dated 1692.
5. A tall Banana Plant and a small Plum-tree by a Rockery. Signed. Dated 1694 (Nagao collect.)
6. Sixteen leaves forming an Album of Flowers, Birds and a few Landscapes. Also published by the Hakubundo under the title: Pa-ta shan-jên hua-ts'ê miao-p'in. (K. Sumitomo collect.)
7. Twelve leaves forming a small Album, representing Flowers, Trees, Bamboos, Fishes and Stones. Signed.
8. A Falcon on the old Trunk of Plum-tree. Signed.

9. Two Birds on the Trunk of an old Plum-tree. Album-leaf. Signed. (Yasuda collect.)
10. A Stag standing under a Cliff Crown with Fungi. Signed and dated 1699. (Yamaguchi collect.)
11. Misty River Landscape in Autumn. Signed.
12. A tall Cliff by a River; dry Trees on the rocky Shore. Signed. (J. Kurosawa collect.)
13. Two Mynah-birds. One descending from the air, the other seated on an old trunk.
14. Two Ducks under Lotus Plants. Signed.
15. Wooded Mountain Ridge deeply cut by a winding Stream. In the manner of Huang Kung-wang. Signed. (Abe collect.) *Cf.* Ōmura, I, 10; Sōraikan, I, 44.
16. Twelve leaves with Flowers, Fruits, Birds and Fishes, forming an album. Signed. Seals of the painter. (Yamaguchi collect., Ashiya.)
17. Landscape-studies. Eight leaves forming an album. Signed. (H. Hayashi collect.) Also published by the Hakubundō Co.
18. A Herd of Stags by a Rock. Short handscroll. Signed. (Yamaguchi collect., Ashiya.)
19. Spare Trees and Hills by the Water. Short handscroll. Signed.
20. Steep Cliffs and leafless Trees by a Stream. Signed. (Shōkoku-ji, Kyōto.)
21. A small Egret under tall Lotus Plants. Signed.
22. Rocky Shore of a Lake in Autumn. Signed.
23. Five leaves forming an album; two of them Landscape Studies and three writings. Seals of the painter. (H. Hayashi collect., Nara.)

Additional Chu Ta paintings will be found in the following works: *Pa-ta shan-jên shu-hua chi* (T'ai-shan ts'an-shih-lou album, series IV): 1. Two pheasants, dated 1690. 2. Pine, Bamboo and Plum, dated 1689. *Cf.* Nanga Taisei, V, 14. 3. Birds on Rocks beneath Lotus. Date illegible. 4. Four large landscapes. 5. Landscape, dated 1699. 6. A Deer on a Rock, dated 1700. 7. Pine-tree and Rock, date 1702.

Pa-ta shan-jên shu-hua chi. Tōkyō, 1956. Ch'êng Ch'i collection. 1. Seven examples of calligraphy. 2. A Stone. Fan-painting, signed. 3. Seven horizontal leaves: Birds, Flowers, Fish, Landscape. 4. Four leaves, Landscapes. 5. Five leaves, Fish, Ducks, Spiders, Birds, Flowers. Signed, one dated 1671.

Hachidai Sanjin Gasatsu. Tōkyō, Jūrakusha, 1956. 2 vol. 1. Four horizontal landscapes. Inscribed, signed. 2. Six Landscapes. Inscriptions by the artist on opposite leaves, one dated 1699. 3. Four Landscapes Signed. 4. Eight leaves: Flowers, Fruit, Bird. Signed, dated 1692. 5. Four leaves: Crow, Flowers, Lotus, Plum Branch. Signed. 6. Four leaves, Flowers and Birds. Signed, dated 1700.

CHU WEI-PI 朱爲弼, *t.* Yu-fu 右甫, *h.* Chiao-t'ang 椒堂.

From P'ing-hu, Chekiang. B. 1771, d. 1840. High official. Flowers, followed Hsü Wei and Ch'ên Shun. Also figures. M, p.109.

Shên-chou, VII. A Lady under a blossoming Plum-tree. Signed, dated 1822.

Po-mei chi. A blossoming Plum-tree. Signed. Poem dated 1822.

Fu-lu. A Peony Flower. Signed, dated 1828.

CH'Ü YING-SHAO 瞿應紹, *t.* Pi-ch'un 陛春, *h.* Tzŭ-yeh 子冶, Yüeh-hu 月壺, Ch'ü-fu 瞿甫 and Lao-yeh 老冶.

From Shanghai. 18th century. Followed Yün Shou-p'ing. M, p.712.

N. Gashū 35. Bamboos by a Stone. Signed. Two lines of poetry.

Shina Meiga Senshū 42. Bamboos by a tall Rockery. Poems by the painter.

Nanga Taisei, II, 19–48. Various paintings of Orchids and Bamboo.

CH'UAN-CH'I 傳綮, *t.* Tun-han 鈍漢, *h.* K'u-fou-ch'ao 枯佛巢, Ching-t'u-jên 淨土人 and many other names. A priest of the early Ch'ing period.

Ku-kung collect. Small album of fifteen leaves of fruits, flowers, vegetables, and pine-trees. Inscription and poems by the painter dated *chi-hai* (1659 or 1719).

CHUANG CHIUNG-SHÊNG 莊冏生, *t.* Yü-ts'ung 玉驄, *h.* Tan-an 淡庵.
From Wu-chin, Kiangsu. B. 1626. Chin-shih in 1647. Poet, calligraphist. Favourite of the emperor Shun-chih. Landscapes, orchids. Q, I, 1. R, II, 1. U, I, 2, 12. M, p.378.

Nanga Taisei, XI, 175. River Scene with a Man in a Boat. Album-leaf. Signed and dated 1666.
Ch'ing êrh-shih chia. A blossoming Plum-tree. Album-leaf. Signed.
Po-mei chi. A Branch of Plum-blossoms. Album-leaf. Signed.
Nanju 16. A Scholar in the Woods. Signed. Poem and colophon. Also in Tōyō, XI.
Metropolitan Museum. River View, rocky Shores. Inscription by the painter. Fan-painting. Signed.
J. P. Dubosc, Lugano. Thickly-wooded Mountains and precipitous Streams. Handscroll. Signed.
Sirén, *Later*, pl.166b. A Scholar's Pavilion by a Mountain Stream. Inscription signed.

CHÜN-MING 俊明, *t.* Chih-ch'in 智勤, *h.* Chi-ku 几谷.
From Tan-t'u, Kiangsu. Priest, poet and calligraphist; friend of Mu Ta-shou, active *c.*1850. Landscapes, followed Ching Hao, Kuan T'ung, Ma Yüan and Hsia Kuei. Unrecorded.

Nanga Taikan 10. A Temple Garden. Signed. Poem.

FA JO-CHÊN 法若眞, *t.* Han-ju 漢儒, *h.* Huang-shih 黃石.
From Chiao-chou, Shantung. B. 1613, d. 1696. Landscapes. Q, I, 1. R, II, 3. U, I, 2, 12. M, p.218.

Shên-chou ta-kuan, XV. A View of Huang-shan. Inscription, signed.

S.c.t.k. hsü-pien, V. Rocky Slope with Streams and Trees. Signed, dated 1643.
Tokasha Shina Meigashū 9. A Stream winding at the Foot of creviced Hills; scattered trees along the shore. Signed, dated 1643 (?)
Ibid. 10. Bulging Cliffs and Hills rising over a quiet Water. Signed, dated 1673.
Hashimoto collect., Takatsuki. Landscape in the manner of Tung Yüan. Signed and dated 1673.
Sōgen 241. A rocky Mountain. Signed, dated 1692 (at 80).
Kurokawa cat. 20, 21. Album of eight Landscapes (four reproduced), each with an inscription by the artist on the opposite page.
Yūrinkan, Kyōto. Large Landscape. Signed.
Fei-tun lu shan-shui. Overhanging sharply-cut Mountains. Poem. Seal of the painter.
National Museum, Stockholm. Clouds and Mist in the Mountains. *Cf.* Sirén. *Later*, pl.184.
Chang Ting-ch'en, Hongkong. Landscape. Signed.

FAN CH'I 樊圻, *t.* Hui-kung 會公 and Hsia-kung 洽公.
From Nanking. B. 1616. One of the "Eight Masters of Nanking". Landscapes, figures and flowers. Imitated Chao Mêng-fu and Chao Ta-nien. P, III, 15. Q, I, 1. R, IV, 19. U, II, 1, 17. M, p.630.

C. C. Wang, New York. Winter landscape. Ink and light colours on paper. Leaf of a collective album painted in or about 1654. *Cf.* Catalogue of the Chinese Art Society, New York, March 1955, No. 11.

Chin-ling p'ai ming-hua chi (Shên Chou album, 1924). Landscape in Snow. Signed, dated 1657.
Ostasiat. Museum, Cologne. A Scholar leaning against a Tree overhanging above a Stream. Fan-shaped. Signed and dated 1659.
Shina Nanga, I, 82. Mountain Landscape. Small sheet. Signed, dated 1663. *Cf.* Chung-kuo ming-hua, XII.
Ibid. II, 4. Donkey Riders. Fan-painting. Signed, dated 1665.
Chung-kuo ming-hua, 22. Towering Mountain Peaks, a dry tree at the rushing water below. Signed and dated 1668.
Hui-hua kuan. A Fishing Village, Men on the Shore and in Boats. Handscroll. Dated 1669.
Chūgoku 7. Landscape with flowering Trees by a River. Leaf in an album containing works of the eight Nanking masters. Signed and dated 1679.
Chêng Tê-k'un, Cambridge. Flower Studies in *kung-pi* style. An album of twelve leaves. Signed, dated 1682.
Shên Chou, XV. Narcissus, Camellia Flowers and Plum Blossoms. Signed, dated 1683. Poem by Kung Hsien.
Chang Pi-han, Hongkong. Landscape of the Four Seasons. Handscroll. Painted in colours on silk. Signed and dated 1692, "at the age of 77".
Gems, I, 59. Strolling in the Mountains in Spring. Signed and dated 1694, "at the age of 79".
Chūgoku 7. Camellia Flowers. Signed. Another leaf from the collected album of the eight Nanking masters. *Cf.* Nanga Taisei, V, 99(?)
Êrh-fan kao-tsou (Shên-chou album, 1930). Landscapes. Album-leaves. Signed.
Nanga Taisei, XI, 210–213. Four Landscapes. Album-leaves; the last signed.
Berlin Museum. A View of the Yangtse. Handscroll. Seals of the painter. *Cf.* Sirén. *Later*, pl. 185.
Venice Exhib. cat. 234 (Vannotti collect.) Scholars drinking Tea at a Table. Fan-painting. Signed.
W. Hochstadter, New York. Four album-leaves, ink and light colours on paper. *Cf.* Catalogue of the Chinese Art Society, New York, March 1955, No.10.

FANG HÊNG-HSIEN 方亨咸 (painted together with Chang Hsün).

FAN HSÜEH-I 范雪儀.
Lady painter. 18th century. Flowers, followed Yün Shou-p'ing. Also figures. M, p.281.

Chung-kuo, II, 61–64. Four Figure Paintings; illustrations to four old stories.

FAN YÜN 樊雲, *t.* Ch'ing-jo 青若.
Son of Fan Ch'i. Q, I, 1. M, p.630.

Chung-kuo ming-hua, XII. Study of a Mountain Landscape. A double album-leaf. Inscription by the painter, dated 1708.

FANG CHI 方濟, *t.* Chü-ch'uan 巨川, *h.* Hsi-yüan 西園.
Went to Japan in 1772 (according to Waley's *Index*). M, p.24.

Bijutsu, IV. A Pine-tree and a Crane. Signed.
British Museum, No.258. Two Magpies in a Plum-tree. Signed.
Berlin Museum. Album of Landscape Sketches.

FANG CH'IEN 方乾, *t.* Yu-ch'ien 又乾 and Hsi-hsien 希仙.
From Hsieh-hsien, Anhui. Early Ch'ing dynasty. Landscapes, flowers. M, p.24.

Sōgen 361. Men and Women on Horseback. Part of a handscroll.

FANG HÊNG-HSIEN 方亨咸 (or Fang Hsien-hêng), *t.* Chi-ou 吉偶, *h.* Shao-ts'un 邵村.
From T'ung-ch'êng, Anhui. Chin-shih in 1647. Landscapes in the style of Huang Kung-wang. Also flowers and birds P, II, 13. U, I, 1, 7. M, p.23.

Shina Nanga, III, 9. Two Sparrows perching in a Plum-tree. Signed. Poem dated 1669.

Chūgoku, 8. A Pine-tree growing by a Stone; a bird perched on a smaller Tree below. Signed and dated 1674.

FANG HSÜN 方薰, *t*, Lan-ti 蘭坻, *h.* Lan-shih 蘭士, Ch'ang-ch'ing 長青 and other names.
From Shih-mên, Chekiang. B. 1736, d. 1801. Landscapes, flowers and birds. Author of *Shan-ching-chü lun-hua* 山靜居論畫. T, V, 1. U, I, 3, 17. M, p.25.

Hamburg Exhibition, 1949–1950. Landscape in the style of Ni Tsan. Signed, dated 1778.

Liu 124. "An Autumnal Forest on the Empty Mountain": Landscape after Chao Mêng-fu. Inscription, signed and dated 1791.

Ming-jên shu-hua, XIV. Bare Trees by a Stream. Signed. Long poem. According to the colophon by the painter's son, the picture was executed in 1793. Also in Nanga Taikan 8.

Nanga Taisei, X, 204. Landscape after Lu Kuang. Signed and dated 1795.

Fei-tun lu hua-hui. A Pine-tree. After an old master. Long handscroll. Signed, dated 1798.

Hui-hua kuan. A Scholar's Garden on a River Shore. Dated 1801.

Ch'ing êrh-shih chia. A Lady putting Flowers in her Hair, after T'ang Yin. Signed. *Cf.* Nanga Taisei, VII, 155.

Ming-jên shu-hua, VII. A Garden View, after a Sung painting.

Ibid. XV. Bamboos, Chrysanthemums and Fungi. Signed. Poem.

Ibid. XVIII. A Bamboo Garden with a Study. Signed. Colophon.

FANG I-CHIH 方以智, *t.* Ch'ang-kung 昌公, *h.* Lu-ch'i 鹿起, Chih-k'o 智可, Mi-chih 密之, and other names.
From T'ung-ch'êng, Anhui. Chin-shih in 1640. After the fall of the Ming dynasty he became a monk, called Hung-chih 弘智, *t.* Wu-k'o 無可, *h.* Yao-ti 藥地. Landscapes, followed the Yüan masters. P, II, 8. R, XIV, 6. U, I, 2, 9. M, p.68.

Horiuchi collect., Ōsaka. A small Landscape, painted in the dry-brush manner. Inscription, dated 1642.

Tōsō 405. Sketchy Mountains. Signed. Poem dated 1652.

Chung-kuo, II, 48. Tall Trees and a Pavilion by a River. Signed. Poem.

Nanju 9. Looking at the River from a Cliff. Signed with his personal name before he became a monk. *Cf.* Pageant 755.

Hui-hua kuan. A Man on a Donkeyback passing by a Wu-t'ung-tree. Ink on paper. Signed with his monk name: Hung-chih.

Yu-chêng album, 1922. The Four Pleasures: four small album-leaves. Signed.

Chūgoku, V. The Wu-i Mountain. Album-leaf.

Ibid. Leafless Trees standing by a Rock. Poem by the painter. Signed.

Nanking Exhib. cat. 302. Withered Trees. Poem, signed.

Chêng Tê-k'un, Cambridge. An album of landscapes. Signed. Colophon by Ta-han.

FANG KUO-CH'I 方國祈, *t.* Nan-kung 南公.
From K'un-shan, Kiangsu. Bamboos after Hsia Ch'ang. R, IX, 19. M, p.24.

Ming-jên hsieh-chu. Bamboos by a River. After Hsia Ch'ang. Handscroll. Signed and dated *ting wei*.

FANG NAN-YÜN 方南雲.
Unrecorded. Active probably towards the end of the 17th century.

I-shu ts'ung-pien 15. A Man in a Grove by a River. Fan-painting. Signed, dated 1697.

FANG SHIH-SHU 方世庶, *t*. Tun-yüan 遁遠, *h*. Huan-shan 環山 and Hsiao-shih tao-jên 小獅道人.
From Hsieh-hsien, Anhui. B. 1692, d. 1751. Pupil of Huang Ting. Landscapes. Q, II, 2. U, I, 3, 12. M, p.24.

Shên-chou, X. The Cho-chêng Garden in Suchou. Signed. Colophon dated 1732.
Berlin Museum collect. Album of twelve Landscapes after old masters. Signed, dated 1733.
Nanga Taisei, X, 149. Houses on a Lakeshore in Spring. Signed and dated 1735.
Private collect., New York. Landscape; wooded mountain peaks with a building near their top. Handscroll. Signed, dated 1735. An accompanying poem inscribed by Shen Fêng, dated 1743.
Mei-chan t'ê-k'an 59. Misty River Landscape, in the Mi style. Poem by the painter, dated 1736.
Chūgoku 8. Landscape after Wu Chên. Long inscription by the artist, signed and dated 1738.
Nelson Gallery, Kansas City. Mountains in Summer before Rain, after Mi Yü-jên. Signed. Poem dated 1738. *Cf.* Sōgen 331.
Hamburg Exhibition, 1949–1950. A River Landscape. Ink on paper. Signed, dated 1741.
Shên-chou, XX. View over a wide River, bamboos and trees on the rocky shore in the foreground. Signed, dated 1743.
Nanking Exhib. cat. 340. River Landscape. Inscription (written from left to right), signed and dated 1743.
Hsü-ching chai. Mountain and Water after Chü-jan. Colophon by the painter dated 1743.
Chung-kuo, II, 142. Village by a Lake on a Spring Morning. Signed. Poem dated 1745.
Ibid. II, 144. Looking at Clouds under Pine-trees, after Wang Mêng. Signed. Poem dated 1746.
Ōmura, I, 1. A Hut among evergreen Pine-trees and Cedars, after Lu Kuang. Signed, dated 1746.
S.c.t.k. hsü-pien, VII. Hills by River, in the manner of Mi Yu-jên. Signed, dated 1746.
Ming-jên shu-hua, X. Mountain Landscape. Signed. Colophon dated 1748.
Nanking Exhib. cat. 339. Landscape in the manner of Kuo Hsi. Signed and dated 1748.
Fei-tun lu shan-shui. Landscape after Chü-jan. Signed. Poem dated 1748.
Chūgoku 8. Landscape in the manner of Wang Mêng. Signed and dated 1748.
Ibid. A Man in a House among leafy Trees; a crane outside. In the manner of Lu Kuang. Signed and dated 1749.
Chung-kuo ming-hua, 38. Summer Mountains, after Tung Yüan. Signed, dated 1749.
Nanga Taisei, X, 150. A House surrounded by Trees; a man at his desk inside. Signed and dated 1749.
Hui-hua kuan. Portrait of Chêng Hsieh seated on a Stone in a Bamboo Grove.
Ku-kung collect. Two Leaves from an Album of Landscapes after Yüan Masters. Signed. *Cf.* Nanking Exhib. cat. 338.
Chūgoku 8. Landscape after Hsieh Hsüeh-ts'un (Shih-ch'en?) Poem, signed.
Nanga Taisei, XII, 61–68. Album of eight Landscapes. Signed.

FANG TA-YU 方大猷, *t*. Ou-yü 歐餘, *h*. Yen-lan 崦藍 and Yün-shêng 允升.
From Wu-ch'êng, Chekiang. B. 1596, d. 1677. Governor of Shantung in the Ch'ing period. Landscapes, followed Tung Yüan. Q, I, 1. R, I, 7. M, p.23.

Fei-tun lu shan-shui. Two Men under Pine-trees by a Stream in the Mountains. Signed. Poem dated *i mao* (1675).
Nanju 22. Pine-trees by a Stream after Rain. Signed. Poem dated 1677. Also in Tōyō, XI.

Shina Nanga, I, 21. Crows in Bare Trees. Seal of the painter.
N. Gashū 26. Rainstorm over a River. Signed.
Kokka 573 (M. Suzuki, Tōkyō). Sailing before the Gale.
Chūgoku 8. Landscape with two Figures approaching a Riverside Kiosk. Poem, seals of the artist.

FANG TSUNG 方琮, *t.* Huang-shan 黃山, *h.* Shih-tien 石顛 and Yu-huang 有璜.
Court painter in the Ch'ien-lung period. Pupil of Chang Tsung-ts'ang. S, II, 18. M, p.24.

Li-tai, V. Spring Landscape. Signed. Poem by Ch'ien-lung, dated 1765.
K.-k. shu-hua chi, XL. Landscape. Signed. Poem by Ch'ien-lung dated 1768.
J. P. Dubosc, Lugano. Album of landscapes. Signed, dated 1770.
Li-tai, V. Travellers in the Autumn Mountains. Signed. Poem by Ch'ien-lung dated 1772.
K.-k. shu-hua chi, XVII. Listening to the Stream in a Pavilion. Signed. Poem by Ch'ien-lung, dated 1795.
Li-tai, I. Travellers in the Autumn Mountains. Signed.
Ibid. I. A Farmstead in Spring. Signed.
Ibid. II. Barren Mountains and winding Streams. Signed.
Ibid. VI. Waterfall on the cloudy Mountains. Signed.
K.-k. shu-hua chi, XXI. Autumn Trees on a Cliff. Signed.

FANG WAN-I 方畹儀, *h.* Po-lien chü-shih 白蓮居士.
From Hsieh-hsien, Anhui. B. 1732, d. after 1784. Wife of the painter Lo P'ing. Literary writer and poetess. Plum blossoms, orchids, bamboos, stones and landscapes. M, p.25.

Chung-kuo, II, 160. Azalea in a Pot. Dated 1768. Seals of the painter. Poems by some friends of the artist.
Shên-chou ta-kuan, vol.9. Bamboos and Rocks. Short handscroll. Accompanied by Wên T'ung's discussion of bamboo-painting, copied by Lo P'ing in 1778.
Shên-chou, VIII. Epidendrum and Bamboos by a Rockery, after a Yüan painter. Signed.

FEI ÊRH-CH'I 費而奇, *t.* Ko-p'o 葛坡.
From Hangchou. Active *c.*1700. Flowers and birds in the style of Hsü Hsi. Also landscapes. R, VIII, 4. M, p.508.

Tōsō 398. Landscape after Huang Kung-wang. Signed, dated 1675.
K.-k. shu-hua chi, XXIX. Plum-tree in a Pot. Signed.

FEI TAN-HSÜ 費丹旭, *t.* Yü-t'iao 子苕, *h.* Hsiao-lou 曉樓 and Huan-ch'i 環溪.
From Wu-ch'êng, Chekiang. B. 1802, d. 1850. Famous painter of "scholars and ladies". Also landscapes. T. Add. I, 3. U, I, 3, 22. M, p.509.

Ming-jên shu-hua, VIII. Men and Ladies playing Music in the Ê-yüan Garden. Signed, dated 1831.
Shên-chou, VIII. Two Ladies in a Pavilion by a Stream. Fan-painting. Signed, dated 1834.
Shinchō 85. A Lady in a Garden. Signed, dated 1837. *Cf.* Sekai Bijutsu Zenshū, XX, Pl.69.
Chung-kuo, II, 129–132. A series of four Portraits of Ladies, each with a poem. The last one dated 1843. Also in Chung-kuo ming hua 24, 36.
Shên-chou, XX. The Fairy Ma-ku standing by a Mountain Stream. Signed, dated 1846.
Ming-hua sou-ch'i, I, 12. A Man and a Woman and five Children under Cassia-trees in a Garden. Signed, dated 1848.
Shina Nanga, I, 135. Collecting Herbs on the T'ien-t'ai Mountain. Signed. Colophon dated 1848.
Gems, I, 85. A Lady with a Fan. Signed.
Shên-chou, XX. A Woman in a red Gown on a Bridge under Snow-covered Trees.

Ch'ing êrh-shih chia. A Lady mending an embroidered Coat. Poem by the painter.

Nanga Taikan 5. A Woman playing a Flute in a Boat. Signed.

Ibid. 8. An old Man with his Family in a Garden. Signed. Colophon.

Ibid. 8. Han Ch'i and his Friends admiring rare Peonies. Signed. Colophon.

Kokka 701. A beautiful Woman.

Nanga Taisei, VII, 176–200 Various Paintings of beautiful Women.

FÊNG CH'I 馮箕, *t.* Tzŭ-yang 子揚, *h.* Ch'i-hsia 棲霞.
From Ch'ien-t'ang, Chekiang; lived in Suchou, *c.*1820(?) Figures, landscapes. U, III, 2, 18. M, p.531.

Ming-jên shu-hua, XVII. A Girl gathering Water Chestnuts in a Boat. Signed, dated 1827(?)

FÊNG HSIEN-SHIH 馮仙湜 or Fêng Shih 馮湜, *t.* Chih-lan 沚灠.
From Shan-yin, Chekiang. Active *c.*1700. Landscapes. Author of *T'u-hui pao-chien hsü-ts'uan* 圖繪寶鑑續纂. Q, I, 2. M, p.530.

Nanju 13. Landscape after Ni Tsan. Signed, dated 1727. Also in Tōyō, XII.

FÊNG NING 馮甯.
Court-painter in the Ch'ien-lung period. Figures. S. M, p.531.

Li-tai, II. Catching Fish. Signed.

Ibid. V. A Scholar and a Fisherman. Signed.

FU SHAN 傅山, *t.* Ch'ing-chu 青主, *h.* Sê-lu 嗇廬, Kung-chih-t'o 公之它, Jên-chung 仁仲, Liu-ch'ih 六持, Sui-li 隨厲, and many other names.
From T'ai-yüan, Shansi. B. 1602, d. 1683. A student of Taoism. Author of *Shuang-hung k'an chi* 霜紅龕集. Landscapes. Q, I, 1. R, II, 13. U, I, 2, 6. M, p.513.

Hui-hua kuan. Bridges and a Pavilion built on Poles in a Stream at the Foot of a Mountain. Inscription dated 1666.

Tōsō 382. A Straw Hut in the Mountains. Signed. Colophon by a friend dated 1675.

Nanju 19 (Hashimoto collect., Takatsuki). A solitary Pavilion by a Mountain Stream. Signed at 80 (1681).

Shên-chou, II. Four handscrolls representing Flowers of the Four Seasons. Finger-paintings.

Ibid. XXII. Lotuses. Signed. Also in Shina Nanga, II, 8.

Ming-jên shu-hua, X. Temples on Snow-covered Mountains. Signed. Poem.

Ho Kuan-wu, Hongkong. A Monk seated, with a Sceptre and Begging-bowl before him. Long inscription, signed.

Shina Nanga, II, 10. Mountain Tops and winding Streams. Album-leaf. Signed. Poem. *Cf.* Shên-chou ta-kuan, vol.10.

Shoman 36. Trees in Winter. Fan-painting. Signed.

Ōmura, I, 6. A steep Cliff and far-off Fishing-boats. Signed. Also in Kokka 587; Sōraikan, II, 67; Sekai Bijutsu Zenshū, XX, pl. 47.

Sōraikan, I, 50. A Cedar-tree. Signed.

Yūrintaikan, I. Mountains and Woods in Rain; two people with umbrellas on a bridge. Signed.

Hamburg Exhibition, 1949–1950. A misty Mountain Gorge with Buildings, Cascades and leafy Trees. Signed.

Ibid. Tall splintered Rocks and Bamboo. Impressionistic ink-painting on satin.

Private collect., Stockholm. A long hanging-scroll. An Old Monk Seated on the Ground holding a staff. Probably the Buddhist teacher of the painter. The upper part of the picture is entirely covered by an inscription in very free running style.

FU WÊN 傅雯, *t.* Tzŭ-lai 紫來, *h.* K'ai-t'ing 凱亭.
From Kuang-ning, Manchuria. 18th century. Finger-painter, imitated Kao Ch'i-p'ei. M, p.513.

Ars Asiatica, I, pl.XLVII. Li T'ieh-kuai and Lan Ts'ai-ho. Finger-painting. Signed.
Museum für Ostasiatische Kunst, Cologne. An old Man looking at a Waterfall. Finger-painting. Signed.
Musée Guimet, Paris. An old Man seated by a Table playing on a Sounding Stone, behind him a boy. Finger-painting. Signed.

HAN CHU 韓鑄, *t.* Yeh-jen 冶人.
From Hui-chou, Anhui. Active probably in the Ch'ien-lung period. Landscapes in Mi Fei's style. Q, I, 2 (under Wang P'u). M, p.698.

Ming-jên shu-hua, XXIV. The Ling-hsü Mountain. Signed.
Tokasha Shina Meigashū 88. Misty Mountain Valley, sketchy trees. Poem by the painter, written at 79.

HAN HSIA 韓洽, *t.* Chün-wang 君望.
From Ch'ang-chou, Kiangsu. Unrecorded in the books, but according to the colophon by Ch'ên Hsien-hai, dated 1877, on the present picture, the painter was known as a poet at the end of the Ming dynasty, though active also later.

Shên-chou ta-kuan, vol.9. Winding Stems of Vine. Short handscroll. Poem, signed by the painter.

HAN JUN 韓潤, *t.* Yü-ts'un 愚村.
From Kuei-chou. Finger-painter. M, p.698.

Po-mei chi. Branches of a Plum-tree. Finger-painting. Signed.

HAN K'UANG 韓曠, *t.* Yeh-chu 野株.
From Sung-chiang, Kiangsu. Active *c.*1680. Landscapes. M, p.697.

Ōmura, I, 5. Landscape. Signed, dated 1678.

HAN YEN 韓炎, *t.* I-shan 奕山.
From Shang-yüan, Kiangsu. Active probably 17th century. Flowers and rockeries. M, p.698.

Formerly C. B. Hoyt collect., Cambridge, Mass. Bamboo Studies. Two album-leaves. Seals only.

HANG SHIH-CHÜN 杭世駿, *t.* Ta-tsung 大宗, *h.* Chin-p'u 堇浦, Chih-kuang Chü-shih 智光居士 and Ch'in-t'ing Lao-min 秦庭老民.
From Hangchou. B. 1696, d. 1773. Chü-jên at 1724. Calligraphist. Plum blossoms and bamboos; also flowers in ink. M, p.215.

Po-mei chi. Branches of Plum Blossoms. Signed. Poem dated 1733.

Fei-tun lu hua-hui. Bamboos and Rocks, after Wang Fu. Long handscroll. Signed. Colophon dated 1740.

Ho Ch'ing-t'ai 賀清泰 or Louis de Poirot.

B. 1735, d. 1814. A French Jesuit missionary who served in the imperial observatory and also as a court-painter. Birds and animals. S. M, p.505.

K.-k. shu-hua chi, XXXVIII. A White Eagle. Signed, dated 1785.

Ibid. XXVI. A Deer. Signed, dated 1790.

Ho I 赫頤 or 赫奕, *h.* Tan-shih 澹士.

A Manchu. Active *c.*1700. High official. Pupil of Wang Yüan-ch'i. Q, I, 1. R, VII, 7. U, II, 2, 22. M, p.593.

K.-k. shu-hua chi, XXXIV. A Garden by a River on a clear Autumn Day. Signed. Poem by K'ang-hsi dated 1702.

Ibid. XIII. Landscape. Illustration to The Song of the Fishermen by Wu Chên. Signed, dated 1711.

Ku-kung, XXXI. Landscape. Signed. Poem by a T'ang poet, copied by K'ang-hsi.

Ibid. XL. Landscape. Signed. Writing by Mi Fei, copied by K'ang-hsi.

K.-k. shu-hua chi, VI. Autumn Landscape. Signed.

Ibid. XVII. River Landscape in Wind and Rain. Signed. Poem by Chu Hsi, copied by K'ang-hsi.

Ibid. XVIII. Landscape in the style of Ni Tsan and Huang Kung-wang. Signed. Poem by Wang Wei, copied by K'ang-hsi.

Ho Shao-yeh 何紹業, *t.* Tzŭ-i 子毅.

From Tao-chou, Hunan. B. 1799, d. 1839. Brother of the calligraphist Ho Shao-chi. Flowers, birds and figures. Horses, imitated Ch'ien Fêng. T, Add. I, 1. M, p.134.

Ming-jên shu-hua, I. Six Horses. Copy after a picture by Ch'ien Fêng.

Ho T'êng-chiao 何騰蛟, *t.* Yü-shêng 雨生, *h.* Yün-ts'ung 雲從.

From Hui-an, Fukien. Active during the first half of the 17th century, executed by the Manchus. Landscapes. M, p.133.

Ōmura, I, 10. A Man contemplating a Stream in the Mountains. Signed, dated 1641. Also in Sōraikan, II, 65.

Ho Yüan 何遠, *t.* Li-fang 履方.

From Hua-t'ing, Kiangsu. 17th century. Landscapes and figures. R, II, 24.

Kokka 386. Landscape. Fan-painting. Signed, dated 1655.

Hou Mei 侯梅, *t.* Lai-ying 來英, *h.* Ch'u-hua pu-i 鋤花布衣.

From Lou-hsien, Kiangsu. Active *c.*1770. Landscapes, figures. M, p.272.

Kyūka, II. Listening to the Stream in a Pavilion. Signed, dated 1778.

HOU SSŬ-PING 侯思炳, *t.* Ssŭ-tsung 嗣宗, *h.* Yü-ts'un hsiao-yin 漁邨小隱.
From Lo-ch'ing, Chekiang. Active *c.*1664. R, V, 7. M, p.272.

Tokasha Shina Meigashū 24. Mountain Landscape in Snow. Signed, dated *chia-ch'ên* (probably 1664).

HSI KANG 奚岡, *t.* Ch'un-chang 純章, *h.* T'ieh-shêng 鐵生, Mêng-ch'üan wai-shih 蒙泉外史 and other names.
From Ch'ien-t'ang, Chekiang. B. 1746, d. *c.*1816. Poet, calligraphist. Painted landscapes, flowers. T, V, 1. U, I, 3, 18. M, p.304.

Nanju 18 (Sumitomo collect., Ōiso). Bamboo Groves and distant Hills, after Wang Mêng. Signed, dated 1774. Also in Tōyō, XII; Sekai Bijutsu Zenshū, XX, Pl.66.

Hsi T'ieh-shêng shan-shui ts'ê (Shên-chou, 1922). An album of eight Landscape Sketches. Signed, dated 1776.

Ōmura, I, 4, 5, 6, 7, 8, 10, 11. An album of twelve Landscapes after Old Masters; one dated 1776.

Sōgen 333. A Pavilion under Pine-trees in Rain. Signed. Poem dated 1776.

Berlin Museum. River Landscape with a Boat, after Shên Chou. Signed. Two poems and a colophon, dated 1777.

Nanking Exhib. cat. 359. Landscape after Wu Chên. Signed and dated 1779.

Shên-chou, XX. River Landscape with Pavilion under five Willows: the Homestead of T'ao Yüan-ming. Signed, dated 1785.

Kyūka, II. River in Spring. Signed. Colophon dated 1786.

Chung-hua album, 1919. Boats on a River in Rain. Handscroll. Signed. Colophon dated 1787.

Ōmura, I, 1. Streams and Mountains in Autumn. Signed, dated 1787. *Cf.* Chūgoku 8.

Shên-chou album, 1922. Eight Landscapes after Li Liu-fang. Last one signed, dated 1788.

Nanga Taisei, XVI, 82, 83. A River Landscape. Handscroll. Signed and dated 1788.

T. T. Ma, Hongkong. A blossoming Plum-tree and Narcissi by a Garden-stone. Short inscription by the painter dated 1788.

Pageant 938. Cloudy Mountains after Mi Fei. Signed. Poem dated 1789.

Shên-chou, X. Cottages by a winding Stream, after Huang Kung-wang. Signed. Poem dated 1791.

Horiuchi collect., Ōsaka. Landscape with a River flowing into the Distance; trees and figures in the foreground. Signed and dated 1791.

Kurokawa cat. 41. Album of Landscapes in old styles (two reproduced). Signed and dated 1794.

Chūgoku 8. A Grove of leafless Trees. Signed and dated 1794.

Tōan 65. Mountains in Autumn, after Huang Kung-wang. Fan-painting. Signed, dated 1795.

Gems, I, 83. Bamboo and Banana Palm. Signed and dated 1795.

Fei-tun lu shan-shui. Landscape after Hsü Pên. Signed, dated 1795.

P'ang Yüan-chi illus. cat. 1940, IV. Mountains in Autumn, after Huang Kung-wang. Signed and dated 1796.

Hui-hua kuan. Mountain Landscape in the style of Wang Yüan-ch'i. Ink and slight colour on paper. Signed and dated 1796.

Nanking Exhib. cat. 360. River Landscape, in the manner of Yüan masters. Signed and dated 1796.

Shên-chou, XVIII. Mountain Gully with a River spanned by Bridges. After Huang Kung-wang. Signed, dated 1797. *Cf.* Shina Nanga, II, 10.

Commercial Press album (1922). An Album of twenty-four leaves, thirteen of which are pictures partly after old Masters; the other leaves with poems by the painter. Dated 1797.

Shina Meiga Senshū 35. River View. Fan-painting. Signed, dated 1797.

Shên-chou, X. River Landscape with a Pavilion and leafless Trees, after Ni Tsan. Signed. Poem dated 1798.

Ōmura, I, 9. Mountains in Autumn, after Huang Kung-wang. Signed. Colophon dated 1798. Also in Shinchō 71; Soraikan, I, 67.

Ming-jên shu-hua, XVI. Four pictures of Flowers representing the Four Seasons. Dated 1798.

Ibid. II. Bamboos. Signed. Colophon dated 1798. The Stones in the same picture by Huang I, the leafless Trees by Kao Shu-ch'êng. Also in Shina Nanga, III, 1.

Po-mei chi. Branches of Plum Blossoms. Signed, dated 1798.

Ōmura, I, 12. A Flock of Birds gathering in a bare Tree, after Li Ch'êng. Signed. Colophon dated 1799. *Cf.* Chūgoku 8.

Tokasha Shina Meigashū 80. Winding Stream at the Foot of steep rocky Hills. Colophon by the painter, dated 1799.

Ibid. 81 (Takashima collect., Kugenuma). Mountain Ridge in Autumn Mist, after Tung Yüan. Signed, dated 1800.

Kyūka, II. Two Album-leaves: Playing the *Ch'in* in a Bamboo Grove, illustration to a T'ang poem; Wooded Mountain, illustration to a T'ang poem. Signed, dated 1801.

Ming-jên shu-hua, III. Mountains in Mist. Signed. Poem dated 1816.

Ibid. XIV. Mountain Landscape with Cottages, after Tung Yüan. Signed. Colophon.

Ibid. XV. Chrysanthemums and Bamboos. Signed.

Ibid. XXI. Lilacs and Orchids by a Rock. Signed.

Mei-chan t'ê-k'an 67. Kuan-yin in a Bamboo Grove. Signed.

Fu-lu. A Grove of bare Trees by a winding Stream; gathering crows. Poem by the painter.

Ibid. River Landscape, after Huang Kung-wang. Signed.

Shina Nanga, II, 4. Narcissi, after Chou Chih-mien. Fan-painting. Signed.

Tokasha Shina Meigashū 82. A high Mountain rising through Mist. In the manner of Kao K'o-kung. Signed.

Nanga Taikan 7. Mountain Landscape, after Wang Shih-min. Signed. Colophon.

Mayuyama collect., Tōkyō (formerly Kuwana). Album of Landscapes. Signed.

Ibid. An old Tree, a Rock and Birds, after Wang Hui, in the manner of Li Ch'êng. Signed.

Ogawa collect., Kyōto. An Album of Landscape Studies, partly after Yüan masters. Ink and slight colour. Signed.

Chūgoku 8. Two Landscapes, one of them after Wu Chên. Album-leaves. Signed.

Suchiku 28. White-robed Kuanyin standing on the Bank of a Stream. Signed.

Nanga Taisei, XII, 141–143. Three Landscapes. Album-leaves. Signed.

Ibid. Add. II, 145–154. Album of Landscapes. Inscriptions signed.

British Museum, No. 251. Lady Hsi Shih. Signed. Poem.

Ibid. Low River Shore with bare Trees. Album-leaf. Signed.

Hsia Chin 夏今.

Unrecorded. Ch'ing dynasty (?)

Ming-jên shu-hua, VII. A Ravine. Signed.

Hsiang K'uei 項奎, *t.* Tzŭ-chü 子聚, *h.* Tung-ching 東井 and Ch'iang-tung chü-shih 牆東居士.

From Chia-hsing, Chekiang. 17th century. Nephew of Hsiang Shêng-mo. Landscapes, orchids and bamboos, imitated the Yüan masters. Q, I, 1. R, V, 11. U, I, 3, 15. M, p.523.

Fei-tun lu hua-hui. A Pine-tree on an overhanging Rock, after Su Tung-p'o. Handscroll. Signed. Poem dated *hsin yu* (1681).

Po-mei chi. Branches with Plum Blossoms. Album-leaf. Signed. Poem. Colophon dated *jen-shen* (1692).

Nanga Taisei, II, 240, 241; III, 126–135. An Album of Plum-blossoms. Signed, one leaf dated 1692.

Shên-chou, XVI. Open View over a wide Field with Water-courses, bridges and boats. Album-leaf. Poem by the painter.

Shinchō, 34. River Landscape with cloudy Peaks. Handscroll. Seals of the painter.

HSIAO CH'ÊN 蕭晨, *t.* Ling-hsi 靈曦, *h.* Chung-su 中素.

From Yang-chou, Kiangsu. Active *c.*1680–1710. Landscapes, figures, imitated the T'ang and Sung masters. Noted for his snow-scapes. R, VI, 17. U, III, 1, 8. M, p.701.

Shên-chou, IV. A Man seated on the Shore under a projecting Cliff, attended by a boy. Signed.

Chung-kuo ming-hua 10. Education of the Children. Woman bringing children to an old man who is seated in a chair. Colophon by the painter.

K.-k. shu-hua chi, IV. Landscape in Snow. Signed.

C. C. Wang, New York. Snowy Mountains rising over dark Waters. Signed.

Former Hobart collect., Cambridge, Mass. Winter Landscape with a River at the Foot of a Mountain. Painted on dark ground.

Hui-hua kuan. A Pavilion under large Trees by a River. A long bridge in the foreground. Painted, according to inscription, for Liang Chiao-ling.

HSIAO YÜN-TS'UNG 蕭雲從, *t.* Ch'ih-mu 尺木, *h.* Wu-mên tao-jên 無悶道人 and Chung-shan lao-jên 鍾山老人.

From Wu-hu, Anhui. B. 1596, d. 1673. Poet and prominent landscape-painter. Q, I, 1. R, III, 1. U, I, 2, 7. M, p.701.

Takeuchi collect., Kyōto. Landscape, ending in Rocks and Waves. Handscroll. Inscription dated 1635.

Hui-hua kuan. Sharply-cut terraced Rocks; dry trees below. Archaistic design in blue and brownish colours. Signed and dated 1644.

Chêng Tê-k'un, Cambridge. The long Road to Szechuan, passing through a country of fantastic mountains, streams and gullies. Inscription by the painter, referring to the political upheavals, dated 1649.

S.c.t.k. hsü-pien, II. Gorge in the Nan-shan between squarely-cut towering Rocks. Signed and dated 1652.

Seligman collect., London. Small landscape handscroll, signed and dated 1652.

Shimbi, XVIII. Mountains by a winding River. Short handscroll. Signed. Colophon by the painter dated 1655.

Nanga Taisei, XV, 40–45. Long Landscape-handscroll, with various Scenes of Activity. Several inscriptions by the artist, one dated 1655.

Musée Guimet, Paris. Mountains. Ink on gold ground. Fan-shaped. Signed and dated 1655.

Shên-chou album, 1930 (2 vols.) *Kuei-yü i-yüan t'u.* Long landscape handscroll. Inscription, dated 1656.

Gems, II, 20. Cloud-surrounded Mountains and Trees. Handscroll. Inscription by the artist. Signed and dated 1656.

Hsin-an p'ai ming-hua chi (Shên-chou album, 1924). Boys planting a Tree. Signed. Colophon by the painter, dated 1656. *Cf.* Nanga Taisei, XI, 146.

Sekai Bijutsu Zenshū, 20, pl.30 (National Museum, Tokyo). Travelling in the Autumn Mountains. Handscroll. Signed and dated 1657.

J. P. Dubosc, Lugano. Mountainous Landscape in archaistic style. Handscroll. Signed and dated 1559–63.

S.c.t.k. hsü-pien, V. Plum-blossoms. Signed and dated 1663.

Cleveland Museum of Art. Clear Sounds among Hills and Waters. Ink and colour on paper. Handscroll. Signed and dated 1664. *Cf.* Shên Chou album, 1921.

Mo-yüan t'ang album, 1936. Ten Landscapes in old styles. Signed, "at age 73", *i.e.* in 1668.

Shên-chou album, 1921. Terraced Mountains; large pine-trees, buildings in the crevices, and boats by the shore. Handscroll. Signed and dated 1669.

Los Angeles County Museum. Large Pine-trees shading the Buildings and the Bridges between split Rocks along the Streams. Long handscroll. Signed. Inscription by the artist dated 1669. *Cf.* Oriental Art, Autumn 1955.

Po-mei chi. A blossoming Plum-tree. Album-leaf. Signed and dated 1669.

Shinchō, 26 (Seattle Art Museum). River Landscape, illustrating the Story of the Fisherman and the enchanted Garden. Fan-painting. Signed and dated 1672. *Cf.* Kokka 735.

Shên-chou ta-kuan, vol.6. Steep Cliffs and a few Trees in the foreground. Poem by the painter. *Cf.* Ming-jên shu-hua, XX.

Shên-chou album, 1910. Landscape, handscroll. Long inscription by the artist.

Shên-chou album, 1916. Album of eight landscapes. Inscriptions by the artist.

Hsin-an p'ai ming-hua chi (Shên-chou album, 1924). Cottages by a River, after Huang Kung-wang. Signed.

Hui-hua kuan. Open River-view with sharp Cliffs and small Islands. Ink and colour on paper. Large handscroll.

Ibid. A Man reading in a Pavilion surrounded by Trees and deeply creviced Cliffs covered by Snow. Ink on paper. Inscription by the painter.

Sōgen 290. Travellers on a Mountain-path in Autumn. Handscroll. Poem by Ch'ien-lung.

J. P. Dubosc, Lugano. Pavilions in a Garden Landscape in Autumn. Handscroll. Signed.

Hamburg Exhibition, 1949–1950. Landscape with rocky Mountains and Pine-trees. Ink and colours on silk. Poem by the painter.

J. D. Ch'ên, Hongkong. Mountain Landscape. Long handscroll.

HSIEH LAN-SHÊNG 謝蘭生, *t.* P'ei-shih 佩士, *h.* Li-p'u 理浦, or 圃.
From Nan-hai, Kuangtung. Chin shih in 1802. Poet and calligraphist. M, p.706.

Po-mei chi. Branches of Plum-blossoms, Signed, dated 1807.

Chêng Tê-k'un, Cambridge. Album of landscapes. Signed, one dated 1826.

Chung-kuo ming-hua, 23. A River Valley, leafy trees along the low shores. Poem by the painter.

HSIEH PIN 謝彬, *t.* Wên-hou 文侯.
From Ch'ang-shu, Kiangsu. Active *c.*1650. Figures. Pupil of the famous portrait-painter Tsêng Ch'ing. O, I. P, III, 12. Q, I, 1. R, XIII. M, p.705.

Chung-hua album, 1929. Twelve Pictures of Arhats. Signed.

Nanju 19. A Donkey Rider. Signed.

National Museum, Stockholm. The Fishermen's Pleasure. Signed.

HSIEH SUI 謝遂.
Court-painter *c.*1770. Figures. S, II, p.22. M. p.706.

K.-k. shu-hua chi, XXXVIII. The Great Yü controlling the Flood. Signed, dated 1776.

Ibid. XLI. Palace Buildings in Snow. Signed, dated 1777.

HSIEH SUN 謝蓀.
Native of Chiang-ning in Kiangsu. One of the Eight Masters of Nanking. Landscapes. Q, I, 1, 11. M, p.705.

Chūgoku 7. A Lotus Blossom and Leaves. Leaf in an album containing works by the eight Nanking masters. Signed and dated 1679.

HSÜ CHING 許敬, *t.* Hsüeh-hsiang 雪香.
From Hangchou. Plum-blossom. M, p.413.

Po-mei chi. Branches of Plum-trees in Bloom, after a Yüan master. Signed. *Cf.* Nanga Taisei, III, 174.

HSÜ FANG 徐枋, *t.* Chao-fa 昭法, *h.* Ssŭ-chai 俟齋 and Ch'in-yü shan-jên 秦餘山人.
From Suchou. B. 1622, d. 1694. Lived in retirement and great poverty after 1644. Followed Tung Yüan, Chü-jan and the Yüan masters. Also poet. Q, I, 1. R, III, 13. U, I, 3, 1. M, p.359.

Hsŭ Ssŭ-chai Wu-shan ming-shêng shih-êrh t'u (Yu-chêng Book co., 1919). An Album with twelve Views of the Hills in Wu. Each picture is accompanied by a colophon by the painter. Dated 1672. *Cf.* Nanga Taisei, XI, 179–191.
Nanking Exhib. cat. 272. River Landscape. In the manner of Kuan T'ung. Signed and dated 1685.
K.-k. shu-hua chi, V. Enjoying the cool Breeze in a Pavilion by the Shore. Signed. Poem.
Ming-jên shu-hua, XXI. Kuan-yin seated on a Mat of Leaves. Signed. Poem.
Shinchō, 30. River View with bare Trees. Album-leaf. Signed.

HSÜ JUNG 徐溶, *t.* Yü-t'ing 雨亭, *h.* Kuan-shan 觀山.
Landscapes, followed Mi Fei and Kao K'o-kung. Went to Japan *c.*1854–1859. R, VII, 13.

N. Gashū 40. Landscape after Mi Fei. Signed. Poem.

HSÜ-KU 虛谷. Family name Chu 朱.
From Yangchou, Kiangsu. Fought in the government army against the T'ai-p'ing rebels *c.*1850. Resigned and became a monk. Flowers, fruits. M, p.500.

Nanga Taikan 4. Two Goldfishes. Album-leaf. Signed, dated 1834.
Ōmura, I, 2. Loquats. Signed. *Cf.* Chūgoku, VIII.
Takeuchi collect., Kyōto. Flowers and Leaves. Fan-painting. Signed.
K. Sumitomo collect., Ōiso. Rocks and Bamboo, in the style of Tao-chi. Album-leaves, partly finger-paintings. Signed.

HSÜ MEI 徐玫, *t.* Ts'ai-jo 采若, *h.* Hua-wu 華塢.
From Suchou. Active *c.*1700. Figures, flowers and birds. Rival of Liu Yü. Q, I, 2. U, II, 2, 19. M, p.362.

Ars Asiatica, IX, pl.LVIII, 1. Fairy scattering Flowers, after Ma Ho-chih. Signed.

HSÜ MÊNG-TS'AI 許盟材, *t.* Ch'i-ch'êng 奇澄.
Unrecorded. Probably 17th century.

British Museum (Add. No.63). Lohan cleaning his Ear. Signed.

HSÜ PIN 許濱, *t.* Ku-yang 谷陽, *h.* Chiang-mên 江門.
From Tan-yang, Kiangsu. 18th century. R, XII, 12. M, p.413.

Ming-jên shu-hua, XII. Lotus. Signed.

HSÜ T'AI 徐泰, *t.* Chieh-p'ing 階平, *h.* Chih-yüan 枳園.
Figures and landscapes; followed Tai Chin. R, XIII, 10b.

Chūgoku, IV. A Lady washing the Ink-stone by a Garden Rock under a Banana Plant. Painted together with Lan Ying, who wrote an inscription, dated 1659. Also signed by the painter.

HSÜ TAN 徐澹.
Unrecorded. Probably Ch'ien-lung period. According to the signature, from Suchou.

Nanju 20. Landscape. Signed, dated *ping-shên* (1776?) Also in Tōyō, XII.

HSÜ WANG-HSIUNG 徐王熊, *t.* Wei-chan 渭占.
From Shih-mên, Chekiang. Flowers, landscapes. Offered twelve screen-paintings to the emperor Ch'ien-lung in 1757. M, p.365.

Ming-jên shu-hua, XIV. Mountain Landscape. Signed. Poem.

HSÜ WEI-JÊN 徐渭仁, *t.* Wên-t'ai 文臺, *h.* Tzŭ-shan 紫珊.
From Shanghai. Act. *c.*1810. Orchids, bamboos, landscapes. M, p.366.

Nanga Taikan 7. Mountain Landscape. Signed. Poem dated 1811.
Mei-chan t'ê-k'an 69. Landscape with a Temple and Pine-trees. Colophons by contemporaries of the artist.
Nanga Taisei, II, 50. Slender Branches of Bamboo, after Kuan Tao-shêng.

HSÜ YANG 徐揚, *t.* Yün-t'ing 雲亭.
From Suchou. Court-painter *c.*1760. Landscapes, figures, flowers and birds. S, I, p.10. M, p.362.

K.-k. shu-hua chi, XIV. Playing the *Ch'in* in a Pavilion. Signed. Poem by Ch'ien-lung, dated 1752.
Ibid. X. Wang Hsi-chih and the Geese. Signed. Poem by Ch'ien-lung dated 1758.
Ibid. XXXI. Two Swallows flying around a Pear-tree. Signed. Poem by Ch'ien-lung dated 1759.
Ibid. XXXIV. Arhats. Signed. Poem by Ch'ien-lung dated 1762.
Ku-kung, XL. A Pheasant and Flowers. Signed. Poem by Ch'ien-lung, dated 1764.
Li-tai, I. Two wild Geese among Reeds. Signed.
Ibid. III. A Lady. Signed.
Ibid. V. The Immortal's Staff changing into a Dragon. Signed.
Ibid. VI. A literary Meeting in the Western Garden. Signed.
Ku-kung, XXIV. A rainy Landscape. Signed.
Kokka 274. A River View, called the Imperial Tour to the South.
British Museum, No.243. Procession of the blue Dragon. Signed.

HSÜ YU 許友 or Hsü Yu-mei 許友眉, *t.* Yu-chieh 有介, *h.* Ou-hsiang 甌香.
From Hou-kuan, Fukien. Active *c.*1650–1670. Landscapes in the style of Mi Fei; bamboos in the style of Kuan Tao-shêng. P, III, 3. R, I, 18. U, II, 1, 22. M, p.410.

Shimbi, XVIII. Landscape. Signed, dated 1657. Also in Kyūka, I.
Nanju 5. Withered Trees. Signed. Poem dated 1662. Also in Tōyō, XII; Sōgen 330.
Ibid. 10. Pine, Bamboos, Orchids, Fungi and Stones. Signed.

HSÜ YU 許佑, *t*. P'i-ch'ên 辟塵 and Pi-ch'ên 弼臣, *h*. I-an 翼庵.
From Ch'ang-shu, Kiangsu. Court-painter *c*.1760. Flowers and birds. M, p.412.

K.-k. shu-hua chi, XVI. Hens under flowering Wistarias. Signed.

HSÜ YÜAN-WÊN 徐元文, *t*. Kung-su 公肅, *h*. Li-chai 立齋.
From K'un-shan, Kiangsu. B. 1634, d. 1691. Han-lin scholar. President of the Board of Revenue. Unrecorded in dictionaries of painters. V, 777.

Shên-chou, XX. River View with Cliffs and leafless Trees, after Ni Tsan. Signed.

HSÜEH HSÜAN 薛宣, *t*. Ch'ên-ling 辰令, *h*. Shui-t'ien chü-shih 水田居士.
From Chia-shan, Chekiang. Active 1700–1732. Pupil of Wang Chien. Landscapes, followed the Four Wang. Q, I, 2. R, X, 6. M, p.692.

Gems, I, 75. Mountain Landscape with Pines. Signed and dated 1704.

Hamburg Exhibition, 1949–1950. Tall Mountain-peaks rising through Mist; spare trees along the stream below. Signed.

HU CHANG 胡璋, *t*. T'ieh-mei 鐵梅.
From T'ung-ch'êng, Anhui; lived in Shanghai. Son of the painter Hu Yin 胡寅. Active *c*.1870. Went to Japan. M, p.299.

Shinchō 81. A Temple in the Pine Forests. Signed, dated 1875.

Kawai collect., Kyōto, 1954. Rocks by the Water. Signed.

Nanga Taisei Add. IV, 237–40. An Album of six Flower Paintings. Signed.

HU CHÊN-K'AI 胡貞開, *t*. Hsün-fei 循蜚, *h*. Sê-an 瑟菴 and Êrh-k'ung chü-shih 耳空居士.
From Wu-ch'êng, Chekiang. Chü-jên in 1639. Specialized in painting stones, followed by Mi Fei, and also landscapes. Q, I, 2. R, I, 8. M, p.295.

Shina Nanga, I, 91. Landscape, after Huang Kung-wang. Signed, dated 1655.

HU HSI-KUEI 胡錫珪, *t*. San-ch'iao 三橋, *h*. Hung-yin kuan-chu 紅茵館主.
Native of Ch'ang-chou in Kiangsu. Figures in *pai-miao* manner after Yen Li-pên and Li Kung-lin. M, p.299.

I-yüan chên-shang 10. Chung-k'uei Drinking. Signed and dated *kuei-wei* (or) 1823?

HU KUEI 胡桂, *t*. Yüeh-hsiang 月香.
From Suchou. Court-painter *c*. 1785. Landscapes, flowers in Yün Shou-p'ing's style. S. M, p.297.

Li-tai, V. On the Way to Shan-yin, after Wu Pin. Long handscroll. Signed, dated 1785.

Ibid. VI. Mountain Cottages. Signed.

HU SHIH-K'UN 胡士昆, *t.* Yüan-ch'ing 元清 or Yüan-jun 元潤.
Active in the late Ming and early Ch'ing periods. Landscapes and orchids. O, 5. M, p.294.

Nanking Exhib. cat. 280. An Album of Landscapes. Signed, two of them dated 1648.

Nanga Taisei, XV, 38, 39. Orchids and Rocks. Handscroll. Signed and dated 1664.

Ibid. I, 138. Orchids growing by a Rock. Poem. Signed.

HU TS'AO 胡慥, *t.* Shih-kung 石公.
From Chiang-ning, Kiangsu. One of the "Eight Scholars of Chin-ling". Landscapes, figures and chrysanthemums. Q, I, 1. U, II, 1, 18. M, p.295.

Hamburg Exhibition, 1949–1950. Grassy Hills and plumy Trees. Blotty ink manner. Signed, dated 1681. *Cf.* Liu 98.

Nanga Taisei, V, 81. Camellia Flowers. Album-leaf. Seal of the artist.

HU YÜAN 胡遠, *t.* Kung-shou 公壽, *h.* Shou-hao 瘦鶴 and Hêng-hsüeh shan-min 橫雪山民.
From Hua-t'ing, Kiangsu; moved to Shanghai 1861. B. 1823, d. 1886. Calligraphist. Landscapes, plum-blossoms. M, p.298.

Ōmura, I, 8. Two leaves from an Album of Plum-blossom Pictures. Poems by the painter, dated 1849, and by his contemporaries.

Nanga Taikan 8. Two Men on the Terrace under Trees at the Foot of cloudy Mountains. After Tung Yüan. Illustration to a poem by Wang Wei. Signed, dated 1876.

Shina Meiga Senshū 44, 45. A pair of pictures: a Pine-tree by a Waterfall; a Garden Rockery. Signed, dated 1878.

Chêng Tê-k'un, Cambridge. An album of scenes of Wu-hsing. Signed.

HUA KUAN 華冠, original name Hua Ch'ing-kuan 慶冠 or Tien 點, *t.* Ch'ing-chi 慶吉, *h.* Chi-yai 吉崖.

Native of Wu-hsi, Kiangsu. Prominent portrait painter, but he did also figures in *pai-miao* technique and landscapes, trees and flowers. R, II, 9. 6a. T. M, p.519.

I-yüan chên-shang 9. Landscape, on the theme "If you buy wine, guests will come" – *i.e.* without being invited. Signed and dated 1766(?)

HUA-LIN 化林. A Buddhist priest whose surname was Ying 偀.
From San-shan, Fukien. B. 1597, d. 1667. Went to Japan in 1660 and became an abbot. Many of his pictures are to be found in Japan. Landscapes, flowers, epidendrum and bamboo. See article by Kitanaka in *Bijutsu Kenkyū*, 127, 1942.

Bijutsu Kenkyū, 127 (E. Yamamoto, Aichi). Four Bamboos. Signed and dated 1666. Two lines of poetry.

Ibid. Chrysanthemums by a Rock. Signed. Two lines of poetry.

Ibid. A winding Stream with Mountain Peaks, Pavilions on Poles and leafy Trees on the Shores. Handscroll. Signed. Inscription by another monk, dated *chi yu* (1669).

HUA YEN 華嵒, *t.* Ch'iu-yo 秋岳, *h.* Hsin-lo shan-jên 新羅山人.
From Fukien; lived in Yang-chou and Hangchou. B. 1682, d. 1765. Poet, calligraphist. Flowers, birds, figures and landscapes. Q, II, 2. R, XI, 22. T, II, 1. U, I, 3, 11. M, p.519.

Hui-hua kuan. A singing Bird on a Bamboo. Dated 1721.
Ibid. Six Squirrels on an old Tree. Inscription by the painter dated 1721.
Nanga Taisei, VII, 125. A Boy on a Water-buffalo. Album-leaf. Signed and dated 1722.
Nanga Taikan 7. River Landscapes; a man in a boat. Poem by the painter dated 1724.
Shina Nanga, III, 4. Chêng Hsüan, a Scholar of the Han Period, teaching his Son. Inscription by the painter, dated 1724.
Hui-hua kuan. Self-portrait seated in a rocky Landscape by a Stream. Ink and slight colour. Dated 1727.
Chung-kuo, II, 116. Gathering Water Chestnuts. Signed. Poem, dated 1728.
Commercial Press album, 1939. Eight paintings of landscapes and flowers. Inscriptions, one dated 1728.
Nanga Taisei, XII, 48–59. An Album of Landscape-paintings. Inscriptions by the artist, the last dated 1729. *Cf.* Wên Ming album 1933.
Freer Gallery (55.20). An album of landscape-paintings, fifteen in colour and ink and one in ink. Inscriptions by the painter, the last dated 1729.
Nanga Taisei, XVI, 80, 81. Houses on the Shore of a River. Handscroll. Signed and dated 1730.
Boston Museum (14.79). Illustration to Ou-yang Hsiu's poem "The Dirge of the Autumn". After T'ang Yin. Fan-shaped. Inscription by the painter dated 1730.
Yu-chêng album, 1926. Two landscape handscrolls, dated 1730 and 1731.
Nanga Taisei, XV, 68. Buildings by a River under Pine-trees. Handscroll. Signed and dated 1731.
Wên-ming album, 1936. Album of twelve leaves, mostly Landscapes with Figures. Signed, one dated 1731.
Cleveland Museum of Art. Two Men in a House by a Stream, after Yüan masters. Signed, dated 1732. *Cf.* Cleveland Exhibition cat. 110; Shên-chou ta-kuan, Vol.I; Hsü-ching chai; Shina Nanga, III, 6.
C. T. Loo's Successor, Frank Caro, N.Y. Pine-trees in Mist. Poem by the painter, dated 1732. *Cf.* Toronto, 54.
Sōgen 307. Pavilion among Pine-trees and white Clouds. Signed. Poem dated 1734.
Ibid. 306. Mountain Landscape. Signed. Poem dated 1734. *Cf.* Mei-chan t'ê-k'an 54.
Ho Kuan-wu, Hongkong. Yang Kuei-fei. Signed, dated 1735. *Cf.* T'ien-ch'i shu-wu.
Chung-hua album, 1934 (J. P. Dubosc collect.) Twelve Landscapes with Figures. Signed, dated 1745.
Sōgen 312. A Herd-boy on a Buffalo, from an album of twelve pictures. Signed, dated 1746.
Ōmura, I, 9. A Squirrel on a Branch. Signed. Poem, dated 1746.
Mei-chan t'ê-k'an 53. A Man resting under Trees attended by a Boy-servant. Poem by the painter dated 1746. *Cf.* Gems, I, 77.
Tokasha Shina Meigashū 47. A misty Mountain Valley with winding Water and leafless Trees. Poem by the painter dated 1746.
Hamburg Exhibition, 1949–1950. Lofty Peaks, Mountain Brooks and Clouds. Signed, dated 1746.
Sekai Bijutsu Zenshū, 20, text illus. 105. Two Birds on a Branch. Poem. Signed and dated 1746.
Chang Ts'ung-yü cat. Lotus Plants and white Heron. Signed and dated 1746. *Cf.* Liu 120.
Ho Kuan-wu, Hongkong. Flower and a Bird. Signed, dated 1747.
Gems, I, 76. Two Mandarin Ducks under a flowering Peach-tree. Poem. Signed and dated 1748.
Chūgoku 8. The Seven Sages of the Bamboo Grove. Signed and dated 1748.
Shên-chou, X. A Cat watching a Butterfly. Signed, dated 1748.
Chung-kuo, II, 115. Crows in a bare Tree. Signed dated 1748. *Cf.* Shina Nanga, I, 81.
Ming-hua sou-ch'i, II, 7. A Bird on a Bamboo Branch. Poem by the painter dated 1748.
S.c.t.k. hsü-pien, IV. A Branch of Mutan. Signed, dated 1748.
Shina Nanga, II, 12. A Pekingese. Signed, dated 1748.
Shên-chou, XVI. An old Man in an Armchair under a Tree on a Hillock, speaking to some peasants who sit on a low bench before him. Signed, dated 1749.

Cf. Shina Nanga, II, 2.

Shên-chou ta-kuan, vol.8. Pavilions in a small Garden by a River. Signed. Poem by the painter dated 1749.

Fu-lu. A Heron standing in the Water. Signed, dated 1749. *Cf.* Chūgoku 8.

Sōgen 305. River Landscape in the *mo-ku* manner. Signed. Poem dated 1749.

Ming-jên shu-hua, X. Two Fishes. Signed, dated 1750. *Cf.* Nanga Taikan 3.

Tokasha Shina Meigashū 45. Two Cranes under a Pine-tree. Signed, dated 1750.

Shina Nanga, III, 10. Landscape in Snow. Signed. Poem dated 1751.

Wên-ming album, 1936. An album of twelve landscape-paintings. Inscriptions by the artist, one dated 1751. Nanga Taisei Add. IV, 207–216 (ten leaves).

Sōgen 311. Swallows in a Willow-tree. Signed, dated 1752.

Ibid. 310. Chrysanthemums, Cockscomb and two Birds. Signed. Poem dated 1752.

Metropolitan Museum. White Peonies by a Rockery. Signed, dated 1752.

St. Louis Museum of Art. A Scholar's Garden at a River Shore; the scholar seated in a pavilion under leafy trees, bamboo and other pavilions further away. Handscroll. Signed, dated 1753. *Cf.* Cleveland Exhib. cat. 111.

Chung-kuo, II, 117. Two Rabbits and two Bamboo Stems. Signed, dated 1754. *Cf.* Nanga Taikan 9.

Hamburg Exhibition, 1949–1950. Cranes under Pine-trees. Long handscroll. Signed, dated 1754.

Nanking Exhib. cat. 331. Cranes in a Pine-tree. Signed and dated 1754.

I-shu ch'uan-t'ung 12. Planting Chrysanthemums, after a poem by T'ao Yüan-ming. Signed and dated 1755.

Sōraikan, I, 62. Illustration to Ou-yang Hsiu's "A Dirge of Autumn". Signed, dated 1755.

National Museum, Stockholm. Two Mynah Birds by a Plum-tree and some Narcissi. Signed, dated 1758.

Shên-chou, III. Portrait of the Poet Wu Yün-chia seated under Pine-trees by a Stream. Signed. Poem.

Ibid. XI. High Peaks in Mist. Signed. Poem.

Ibid. XII. The Fairy Ma-ku. Signed. Poem. Also in Shina Nanga, I, 79.

Ibid. XVII. A Girl standing on a Slope by a blossoming Tree. Signed.

Shên-chou ta-kuan, vol.10. A Lady seated by a Table. Signed.

T'ai-shan Ts'an-shih-lou ts'ang-hua, I. A Lady (Kuan-yin?) seated on a flat Stone surrounded by Water. Seal of the painter(?)

Chung-kuo, II, 118. A Squirrel on a Branch of a Chestnut Tree. Signed. Poem. *Cf.* Shina Nanga, II, 10 and Chung-kuo ming-hua, 21.

Ming-jên shu-hua, XIV. Four album-leaves mounted on two scrolls:

1. A Man standing on a high Cliff. Two lines of poetry.
2. Two Men in a Bamboo Grove. Poem.
3. A Man carried in a Chair through a Pine Forest.
4. Cottages by a Lotus Pond.

K.-k. shu-hua chi, XXXIII. Chung K'uei attended by Demons. Signed. Poem.

Hui-hua kuan. Studies of Insects, Animals and Flowers. Eight album-leaves. Signed.

Ibid. A Bird on the Branch of a Rose-bush.

Shanghai Museum. Mountain Village in Mist; a pointed peak beyond. Signed.

Liu 119. Pine-trees after Rain. Poem,. Signed.

Ibid. 121. Two Birds on the Branch of a Pine-tree. Signed.

Yu-chêng album. Eight leaves representing Birds, River-views and wild Mountains. Poem by the painter.

T'ien-ch'i shu-wu. Five album-leaves: a Crane; "Buddha's Hand" Fruit; Horses; a Beetle; a Herd-boy on an Ox. Inscriptions, seals of the artist.

Chung-hua album, 1936. Twelve paintings of birds in landscape settings. Inscriptions by the artist.

Ch'ing êrh-shih chia. A Lady on a Couch speaking to her Maid. Signed.

Mei-chan t'ê-k'an 55. A Man on a Terrace looking over a misty Valley; after a Sung master. *Cf.* Chūgoku 8.

Fei-tun lu hua-hui. Plants and a Plum-tree behind a Rock. Handscroll. Poem.

Mo-ch'ao pi-chi, vol.II. Bamboos. Handscroll. Signed. Poem.

T. T. Ma, Hongkong. A broad Stream. Three tall trees in the foreground. Poem by the painter, and a later colophon.

Tokasha Shina Meigashū 46. White Herons under a Willow. Signed.

Ibid. 48. Pavilions built over a Mountain Stream under Pine-trees. After Li T'ang. Signed.

Nanju 19. Frosty Autumn Trees by a River. Poem. Seals of the painter.

Shina Nanga, I, 80. A Man playing the *Ch'in* in a Bamboo Grove. Album-leaf. Seals of the painter.

Ibid. II, 8. A Lady with a Cherry-flower. Two lines of poetry. Seals of the painter.

Kokka 604 (Abe collect.) Landscape.

Ōmura, I, 3. A Horse in the Autumn Wind. Signed. Two lines of poetry. *Cf.* Yūrintaikan, I.

Ibid. II, 2–5. Six figure-paintings from an album of twelve. *Cf.* Sōraikan, II, 81; Kokka, 604. One lead also in Shincho 57.

Sōgen 308. Green Mountains and white Clouds, painted with blue and green colours in *mo ku* manner. Signed. Poem.

Ibid. 309 (Sumitomo collect., Ōiso). A Roc soaring above the Clouds. Signed. Poem. *Cf.* Sekai Bijutsu Zenshū, XX, Pl.62.

Ibid. 313. A Bird perching on a leafless Tree. Signed. Poem.

Ibid. 314. Man with Staff on a Cliff by a River. Signed.

Takashima collect., Kugenuma. An Album of Landscape- and Figure-paintings, the first with a long inscription by the artist.

Ibid. Flowers, Birds, Animals and Insects. Handscroll. Signed.

Hashimoto collect., Takatsuki. Album of Landscapes and Flower-paintings, on green-tinted paper. Signed.

Dai Tenrankai 70. Three Scholars drinking beside a Stream. Inscription and seal of the artist.

Sekai Bijutsu Zenshū, 20, Pl.63. Landscape with twisted Trees and distant Crags. Poem; seal of the artist. Leaf from an album.

Chūgoku 8. Wên-chi riding a Camel, led by a Tartar. Poem by Ch'iu Shih (daughter of Ch'iu Ying) copied by the painter. Signed.

Ibid. A Man on a Horse gazing off at a Mountain. Two lines of poetry. Signed.

Ibid. An album of six leaves: Landscapes and Figures. Inscriptions; seals of the artist.

Nanga Taisei, VI, 174, 175. Four Paintings of Birds in Landscape Settings. Large horizontal album-leaves? Signed.

Ibid. VII, 131. A Village Doctor and his Patients. Poem. Signed.

Ibid. XIV, 113–120. An album of large leaves; Figures, Animals and Birds. Inscription; seals of the artist.

Boston Museum. Green Hills rising through Mist. Signed. One of a series of ten fan-paintings.

Ibid. A Cottage under Pine-trees, enclosed by a Wall; two boys and a man. Signed. One of a series of ten fan-paintings.

Musée Guimet, Paris. An album of paintings of Flowers, Landscapes, etc. Inscriptions, signed.

National Museum, Stockholm. Two Birds on a bare Branch. Signed. Poem.

Metropolitan Museum. Peony and Rocks. Signed.

H. C. Wêng, Scarsdale, N.Y. Small album of ten (?) leaves representing Children's Games.

Huang Pan-jo, Hongkong. Bird and Tree. Signed.

Chên Yung, Shanghai (1934). Single Animals and Birds represented on twelve album-leaves.

J. D. Ch'ên, Hongkong. Studies of Birds and Flowers in colour. Ten album-leaves.

T. Y. King, Hongkong. A white Monkey hanging from a Tree-branch.

Kawai collect., Kyōto. A Rose-bush at a Garden Rock; two brightly coloured ducks higher up in the picture.

HUANG CHI 黄基, *t.* Lien-ch'i 蓮溪.

From Wu-ch'êng, Chekiang. Painted peonies. Probably 18th century. Possibly identical with Huang Chi-shan 黄基善 (t. Tuan-k'uei 端揆, h. Lien-ch'i), who, however, is said to come from T'ung-hsiang, Chekiang .M, p.552.

British Museum, No.250. A Medley of Boats at the Customs' Barrier. Signed, dated *jên shên* (1752?)

HUANG CHI 黄驥.

From Nanking. An official in the Chia-ch'ing period (1798–1820). Unrecorded.

Nanju 2. Landscape, dated 1820. Also in Tōyō, XII.

HUANG CHÜ 黃鞠, *t.* Ch'iu-shih 秋士.

From Sung-chiang, Kiangsu; lived in Suchou. B. *c.*1800, d. 1860. Landscapes, flowers, followed Yün Shou-p'ing and Wang Hui. Also figures. U, III, 2, 22. M, p.552.

Ming-jên shu-hua, XIV. An Interior where some Men are playing Chess in front of a Screen. After Chou Wên-chü. Signed, dated 1854. Also in Nanga Taikan 7.

HUANG CHÜN 黃均, *t.* Ku-yüan 穀原, *h.* Hsiang-ch'ou 香疇.

From Suchou. B. 1775, d. 1850. Landscapes. Followed first Huang Ting, later Wang Shih-min. U, I, 3, 20. M, p.551.

Ming-jên shu-hua, VIII. Two album-leaves: Landscape after Wu Chên. Signed, dated 1810. Landscape after Huang Kung-wang. Signed.

Hamburg Exhibition, 1949–1950. Landscape in the style of Wu Chên. Signed, dated 1811.

Nanga Taisei, X, 215. River Landscape. Signed and dated 1828.

Hobart collect., Cambridge, Mass. Landscapes after Chao Mêng-fu. Two album-leaves. Inscriptions by the painter, dated 1829.

Nanga Taisei, XII, 177. Winter Landscape. Signed and dated 1832.

Shinchō 74. The Mo-miao Pavilion. Handscroll. Signed. Poem dated 1836.

Fei-tun lu shan-shui. Man seated on the Bank of a Stream. Signed, dated 1848.

Nanking Exhib. cat. 362. River Landscape in the manner of Tung Yüan. Signed and dated 1848.

T'ien-hui ko album, 1929. An Album of Landscapes. Signed.

Shên-chou, XII. The verdant South Mountain, after Chao Mêng-fu. Signed.

Ming-jên shu-hua, V. A Spring Morning in Chiang-nan, after Chao Mêng-fu. Signed.

Po-mei chi. Plum-blossoms. Signed.

HUANG HSIANG-CHIEN 黃向堅, *t.* Tuan-mu 端木.

From Ch'ang-shu, Kiangsu. B. 1609, d. 1673. Well-known for his filial piety. Landscapes after Wang Mêng. Q, II, 1. R, VI, 10. U, II, 2, 1. M, p.545.

Nanking Exhib. cat. 267. Listening to the Water in Autumn. Signed and dated 1655.

J. P. Dubosc, Lugano. A Deep Gully in the Mountains, cottages on the banks below. Poem by the painter, dated 1656. The painter's biography on the top of the picture is written by Ku K'ai.

Chang Ts'ung-yü cat. Steep Cliffs, Terraces and Peaks. Dated 1657.

C. T. Loo's Successor, Frank Caro, N.Y. Scenery of the San-tu Pass in Kueichow. Long inscription by the painter, dated 1667. *Cf.* Toronto 57.

Shên-chou ta-kuan, vol.3. Mountain River; motif from Yünnan. Signed.

Hui-hua kuan (ex-P'ang Yüan-chi). The Chü-yung Pass. Poem by the painter.

Ho Kuan-wu, Hongkong. An Album of Landscape-studies illustrating his Journey to Yünnan. Reproduced in an album by the Commercial Press. *Cf.* Nanga Taisei, XI, 136–145.

Hobart collect., Cambridge, Mass. Studies of Mist, Mountains and Rivers. Two album-leaves. Inscription by the painter.

HUANG I 黃易, *t.* Ta-i 大易, *h.* Hsiao-sung 小松.

From Hangchou. B. 1744, d. 1801. Prominent archaeologist and seal-engraver. Landscapes, flowers. U, I, 3, 18. M, p.551.

Shinchō 70. A Boat on a Stream. Signed, dated 1780.

Ming jên shu hua, XIV. Orchids in a Vase, after Ch'ên Tsuan. Signed, dated 1786.

Commercial Press Album, 1923. An Album of ten Leaves representing Landscapes. The last dated 1787.

Hsü-ching chai. A Crowd on a Cliff observing the rising Tide in Moonlight. Illustration to a poem by Su Shih, which is copied by the painter. Dated 1787.
Shên-chou, VII. Two Branches of a blossoming Plum-tree. Signed. Poem dated 1790. *Cf.* Shina Nanga, II, 2.
Yūrintaikan, I. Trees and Rushes at a misty Stream. Signed, dated 1790.
Kurokawa cat. 40. River Landscape in the Ni Tsan manner. Signed and dated 1790.
Chūgoku 8. Four album-leaves: a Landscape, blossoming Plum and Pear(?), a Pine Branch. Signed, one dated 1793.
Shên-chou ta-kuan, vol.10. Two Men in a Pavilion on an Inlet of Water in front of Cliffs. Poem by the painter dated 1793. *Cf.* Shina Nanga, III, 5.
Shina Meiga Senshū, II, 44. Projecting Cliffs and steep Cataracts. Signed and dated 1795.
Ming-jên shu-hua, II. Stones, Bamboos and bare Trees. Painted together with Hsi Kang and Kao Shu-ch'êng. Signed, dated 1796. *Cf.* Shina Nanga, III, 1.
Fei-tun lu hua-hui. An old Ash-tree. Handscroll. Signed, dated 1796.
Tokasha Shina Meigashū 32. River in a Mountain Gully bridged by Pavilions. Colophon by the painter, dated 1797.
Shên-chou, XIII. Large Cliffs by a River. Album-leaf. Signed. *Cf.* Nanga Taisei, XII, 140.
Ming-jên shu-hua, XV. Two Landscapes, after Tung Yüan and Ma Wen-pi.
Ibid. XXVI. Plum-blossoms and Narcissi. Signed. Two lines of poetry.
Po-mei chi. Sprays of Plum-blossoms in a Vase. Signed. Poem.
Nanking Exhib. cat. 358. Two Pine-trees. Signed. *Cf.* Nanga Taisei, V, 41.
Kawai collect., Kyōto. An old Tree, Bamboo and Rock. Signed. *Cf.* Sekai Bijutsu Zenshū, 20, text illus. 113.
Omura, I, 6. Leafless Trees, Bamboos and Stones. After K'o Chiu-ssŭ. Signed. Poem.
Shinchō 70. Collecting Lotus-seeds, after Shên Chou. Album-leaf. Signed.
Nanga Taikan 5. A Hillock with Trees on a rocky Ledge below. Signed. A long inscription above.
Ibid. 5. A Man in a Cottage by a Lake; distant mountains. Signed. A long inscription above.
Boston Museum (55.386). A Bay enclosed by Mountains on three sides; leafy trees and houses at their foot. Short handscroll. Seal of the painter.

HUANG LÜ 黃呂, *t.* Tz'u-huang 次黃, *h.* Fêng-liu shan-jên 鳳六山人.
From Hsieh-hsien, Anhui. *c.*1700. Son of the painter Huang Sheng 黃生. Landscapes, flowers, birds, etc. V, p.1232. M, p.544.

Hsin-an p'ai ming-hua chi (Shên-chou album, 1924). A Study among Bamboos, Banana and Wu-t'ung-trees. Signed. Poem.
Ming-hua sou-ch'i, I, 8. A Homestead at the Foot of high Mountains in Autumn, after Tung Ch'i-ch'ang. Signed at 86. *Cf.* Nanga Taisei, X, 180; S.c.t.k. Hsü-pien, II.

HUANG NIEN-TSU 黃念祖. Unrecorded. Probably identical with Huang Chi-tsu 黃繼祖, *t.* Kung-liang 弓良, *h.* Ch'iu-shan 秋山.
From Hsin-an, Anhui; lived in Wu-hsing, Chekiang. Active probably at the end of the 18th century. Flowers and birds in the manner of Hsü Wei and Ch'ên Shun. M, p.549.

Ming-hua sou-ch'i, I, 11. Two Magpies in an old Tree. Signed, dated 1791.

HUANG PI 黃壁, *t.* Hsiao-ch'ih 小癡.
From Ch'ao-chou, Kuangtung. *c.*1720. Followed Wu Chên in landscape-painting and calligraphy. Q, II, 2. R, XII, 15. M, p.546.

Nanju 4. Landscape in Mist. Signed. Poem dated 1720. Also in Tōyō, XII.

N. Gashū 31. Landscape in Snow. Signed. *Cf.* Nanga Taisei, X, 179.

HUANG SHÊN 黃愼, *t.* Kung-mou 恭懋, *h.* Ying-p'iao 癭瓢.

From Fukien; lived in Yangchou, Kiangsu. B. 1687, d. after 1768. Landscapes in imitation of the Yüan masters; also humorous figure-paintings. R, XI, 15. U, III, 1, 4. M, p.547.

Kokka 216. A Hermit. Signed, dated 1722.

Tōyō, XII. The God of Longevity. Signed. Colophon dated 1724.

Chung-kuo ming-hua, XII. Imaginary Portrait of Su Tung-p'o buying an Ink-stone from a Man. Inscription by the painter, dated 1726.

Fei-tun lu hua-hui. Chrysanthemums. Handscroll. Poem dated 1728.

Kokka 625 (K. Minami, Ōsaka). Album of eight figure-paintings. Signed, dated 1728.

Huang Shên hua-t'ieh (Shimbi Shoin, Tōkyō, 1914). An album of twelve double-leaves: mostly Studies of Figures, Flowers and Birds; also Landscape-compositions and a Horse. Last picture dated 1729.

Tokasha Shina Meigashū 61. The Eight Immortals. Signed, dated 1730.

Sumitomo collect., Ōiso. An Album of twelve Paintings: Landscapes with Figures, Trees, Rocks, etc. The last signed and dated 1738.

Tokasha Shina Meigashū 59. An old Man writing on a Mountain Wall, a boy holding his ink-stone. Signed, dated 1740.

Kokka 270. Snow Scenery, with a Man on a Donkey crossing a Bridge. Signed. Two lines of poetry, dated 1744. *Cf.* Pageant, 919.

Ars Asiatica, IX, pl.LVII. Ning Ch'i feeding the Ox. Signed. Colophon dated 1744.

Tokasha Shina Meigashū 62. Kśitigarbha Bodhisattva in Guise of a Monk seated on a Lion. Inscription by the painter, dated 1745.

Hamburg Exhibition, 1949–1950. The Friend of Flowers. Signed, dated 1748.

Hobart collect., Cambridge, Mass. Taoist Figures. Two album-leaves with length inscriptions. Signed, dated 1750.

Ibid. River-views with Boats and Cottages on Poles along the Shore. Two album-leaves. Signed, dated 1750.

Nanking Exhib. cat. 332. An Eagle perched on a Tree Stump. Signed and dated 1755.

T. Moriya collect., Kyōto. An Album of twelve Flower-paintings, the last signed "at age 70", *i.e.* 1756.

Nanju 24. An old Man riding on a Donkey. Signed, dated 1756.

Pageant, 920. The Fairy Ma-ku with a Lion. Signed and dated 1760.

Chung-hua album, 1933. Landscapes and Figure-paintings. Inscriptions by the artist.

Wên-ming album, 1925. An album of ten figure-paintings. Inscriptions, signed. *Cf.* Nanga Taisei, VII, 114–123.

Ibid. Album of Landscapes, Figure and Flower-paintings. Inscriptions by the artist.

Gems, III, 17. Grasshoppers and Flowers. Two album-leaves. Signed.

Mo-ch'ao pi-chi, vol.I. Magnolia Flowers in a Vase Signed. Poem.

Po-mei chi. A Plum-tree, Bamboos and Birds. Signed Poem.

Ibid. Plum Blossoms in a Vase. Signed. Poem. *Cf.* Nanga Taisei, III, 93.

Chung-kuo ming-hua, 11. Two old Scholars with Attendants seated under a blossoming Tree in a Garden.

Bijutsu, XIV. Li T'ieh-kuai. Signed.

Ibid. XXIV. Old Men examining Pictures. Signed.

Nanju 10. A Fisherman and a Woodcutter. Signed. Poem.

Ibid. 13. A Heron among Lotuses. Signed.

Ibid. 25. Palaces on the Mountain of the Immortals. Signed. Two lines of poetry. *Cf.* Tōyō, XII.

Shina Nanga, I, 101–106; II, 1, 6, 11; III, 1, 5, 8. Twelve figure-paintings from an album.

Hui-hua kuan. Portrait of his Brother who carries an Ink-stone.

Ibid. Studies of Fruits and Landscapes. Six album-leaves.

Sumitomo collect., Ōiso. (*a*) A Lakeside Inn; people arriving in a boat. (*b*) A Scholar writing in a House; a tall rock and banana-palm in his garden. Two large album-leaves, each with an inscription by the artist. The latter in Sekai Bijutsu Zenshū, 20, Pl.64.

Kawai collect., Kyōto (1954). Two Crows in a Pine-tree. Signed.

Nanga Taisei, VI, 145. A singing Bird on a Branch of a Tree. Signed.

Ibid. Add. IV, 100. Two Fishermen in Boats; bamboo on the shore. Poem, signed.

Kyuka, II. Two album-leaves representing two River-views with poems.

Ōmura, I, 4. A Crow on a Willow Branch. Signed. Two lines of poetry.

Tokasha Shina Meigashū 60. Young Sparrows on Branches of an old Plum-tree. Poem by the painter.

Shinchō 67. Two Men saluting each other. Album-leaf. Seals of the painter.

Tōan 58. Listening to the Autumn Sounds. Album-leaf. Signed. Poem.

Ibid. 58. Autumn Scenery. Album-leaf. Signed. Poem.

Sōraikan, I, 65. An old Fisherman. Signed. Poem.

Hamburg Exhibition, 1949–1950. Figures. An album.

National Museum, Stockholm. Album of twelve leaves; plants, flowers and landscapes. Ink and colours. Signed.

Princeton (Du Bois-Morris collect.) Chang Chih-ho and his Servants. Signed. Long inscription referring to the motif.

HUANG TING 黃鼎, *t.* Tsun-ku 尊古, *h.* K'uang-t'ing 曠亭, Tu-wang-k'o 獨往客, etc.

From Ch'ang-shu, Kiangsu. B. 1660, d. 1730. Landscapes in the style of Wang Mêng. Used to sketch from nature while travelling. Rival of Wang Hui. Q, I, 3. R, VIII, 14. U, I, 3, 4. M, p.546.

Honolulu Academy of Arts. Mountain Landscape after Wang Mêng. Signed and dated 1697. Colophons. *Cf.* Cleveland Exhib. cat. 87.

Shên-chou, VIII. River-view with a Fisherman in a Boat. Signed, dated 1698. Illustration to an essay by Liu Tsung-yüan of the T'ang dynasty. *Cf.* Shina Nanga, III, 3.

I-yüan chên-shang 4. Landscape, "in the manner of Sung and Yüan artists". Signed and dated 1699.

Hsü-ching chai. Wooded Mountains with Streams and Waterfalls. Colophon by the painter dated 1707. *Cf.* Nanga Taisei, X, 106.

Shên-chou ta-kuan, vol.6. A Man resting on a Cliff, admiring the Clouds. Signed, dated 1710.

K.-k. shu-hua Chi, XX. Travellers in Mountains, after Tung Yü-an. Signed, dated 1711.

Chung-kuo, II, 141. River Landscape in Autumn. Signed. Poem dated 1712. *Cf.* Chung-kuo ming-hua, 33.

K.-k. shu-hua chi, XV. Trees by a Bridge. Signed, dated 1713.

Mei-chan t'ê-k'an 57. River Landscape, after Tung Ch'i-ch'ang. Signed, dated 1714.

Pao-yün, II. Landscape in the manner of Ni Tsan. Short handscroll. Signed, dated 1714. Poem and seals of Ch'ien-lung.

Shina Nanga, I, 73. A River Gorge. Signed, dated 1714. *Cf.* Chung-kuo ming-hua.

K.-k. shu-hua chi, XIII. River-view in Ni Tsan's style. Signed, dated 1715.

Commercial Press album, 1934. A River winding beween high Mountains. On the shore is the residence of Ch'êng Su-an 程肅庵. Handscroll. Signed, dated 1715. Forty-seven poems and colophons by contemporaries and later men.

Hashimoto collect., Takatsuki. Fishermen on the River, after Wu Chên's picture. Handscroll. Signed and dated 1715.

Nanga Taisei, XII, 18–29. An Album of Landscapes, the last signed and dated 1717.

Shên-chou album. River-view, Mountains and Buildings. After Huang Kung-wang. Small handscroll. Signed, dated 1717.

Chung-kuo ming-hua, 12. Mountain Landscape after Wang Mêng. Signed and dated 1717.

Ku-kung collect. Two Leaves from an Album of Landscapes. Signed and dated 1718. *Cf.* Nanking Exhib. cat. 323.

Hamburg Museum. Mountains in Summer, after Tung Yüan. Signed. Colophon dated 1722. *Cf.* Sirén, *Later*, pl.230.

Fogg Museum, Cambridge (C. B. Hoyt collect.) Four Trees and steep Cliffs. After Ni Tsan. Handscroll. Signed, dated 1723. Colophons of recent dates.

Hamburg Exhibition, 1949–1950. River Landscape with

Willows and cloudy Peaks beyond. In the style of Kao K'o-kung. Signed, dated 1724.
Sōgen 281. Steep Mountains and Hills covered with Woods; mansions at the mountain stream. After Tung Yüan and Chü-jan. Signed. Poem by the painter, dated 1727. *Cf.* Yurintaikan, I.
C. C. Wang, New York. River Valley between high Mountains. Signed, dated 1727.
Ōmura, II, 1. The Chiu-chin Mountain, after Huang Kung-wang. Signed, dated 1728 (at 69). *Cf.* Chūgoku 7.
Nanga Taisei, XIII, 81–92. An Album of River Scenes with Fishermen. Poems, the last signed and dated 1728.
K.-k. shu-hua chi, XXXIII. Snow-covered Peaks. Signed, dated 1729.
Ibid. IV. Homestead at the Foot of steep Mountains in Autumn, after Wang Mêng. Signed.
Wên-ming album, 1923. Six landscapes. Titles, seals of the artist.
Wên-ming album, Eight landscapes after old masters. Inscriptions, Signed.
Shina Nanga, I, 74. Landscape after Fan K'uan. Album-leaf.
Ibid. II, 1. Landscape after Huang Kung-wang. Album-leaf.
Ibid. III, 9. Landscape. Album-leaf. Two lines of poetry. Seals of the painter.
Shinchō 46. Two album-leaves: 1. The Wu-i Mountain; seals of the painter. *Cf.* Pageant, 850. 2. Red Maples on the Chien-ko Mountain; seals of the painter.
Chūgoku 7. An Album of Twelve Landscapes. Inscribed. One signed.

HUANG WAN-CHUNG 黃萬鍾.
Unrecorded. Probably Ch'ien-lung period.

Tokasha Shina Meigashū 49, 50. Four Mynah Birds in a Tree; two Pheasants and Rockery. Forming a pair. Signed.

HUANG WEI 黃衛, *t.* K'uei-yüan 葵園.
From Wu-chin, Kiangsu, *c.*1800(?) Flowers. M, p.549.

K.-k. shu-hua chi, XXX. A Branch of blossoming Plum-tree. Signed, dated 1816(?)

HUANG YEH 黃冶.
Active *c.*1775. No other records are available. Figures. M, p.549.

Princeton (Du Bois-Morris collect.) Two Horses and a Groom. Signed, dated 1775.

HUANG YING-SHÊN 黃應諶, *t.* Ching-i 敬一, *h.* Chien-an 劍菴.
From Peking. Court-painter in the Shun-chih period (1644–1661). Figures. S. M, p.545.

British Museum, No.196. Chung K'uei. Signed, dated 1676.
Li-tai, IV. A Reception of Guests in a beautiful Pavilion under large leafy Trees at the Foot of a Mountain. According to inscription, illustrating a poem by the T'ang poet Liu Yü-hsi.

HUANG YÜEH 黃鉞, *t.* Tso-T'ien 左田 and Tso-chün 左君.
From Tang-t'u, Anhui. B. 1751, d. 1841. High official and scholar. Landscapes, flowers, followed Wang Hui and Yün Shou-p'ing. Author of *Hua-yu lu* 畫友錄 and *Hua-p'in* 畫品. U, III, 2, 2. M, p.550.

Fei-tun lu hua-hui. A Rock with blossoming Plum-trees. Handscroll. Signed, dated 1788.

Huang Ch'in-min kung shan-shui ch'ang-chüan (Wên-ta Book co.) Wooded Hills and Winding Waters. Long handscroll. Signed. Poem by the painter dated 1794.

Nanga Taisei, IV, 60. Flowering Branches. Signed and dated 1815.

Shên-chou, IX. River Landscape in Autumn. Signed. Colophon dated 1831. Also in Shina Nanga, II, 8.

Li-tai, I. Murmuring Streams in Autumn Woods. Signed.

Ibid. IV. Cockscombs, Chrysanthemums and Rocks. Signed.

Nanga Taisei, III, 257; IV, 161–167. Album of eight leaves, representing twenty-four different Flowers. Signed.

HUNG-CHIH 弘智: see Fang I-chih.

HUNG-JEN 弘仁, the priest-name of Chiang T'ao 江韜, *t.* Chien-chiang 漸江, *h.* Mei-hua ku-na 梅花古衲.
From Hsieh-hsien, Anhui. Chu-shêng in the Ch'ung-chên period; became a priest at the fall of the Ming dynasty. One of the "Four Masters of Anhui". Q, I, 3. R, XIV, 5. P, II, 9. U, I, 2, 8. M, p.68.

Sumitomo collect.. Ōiso. A River with marshy Banks, overgrown with Reeds; houses in a bamboo-grove; and sailing-boats. Handscroll. Signed and dated 1652. *Cf.* K. Sumitomo, III.

J. P. Dubosc, Lugano. Album of ten small landscapes, rocks, bamboo and plum-trees. Signed and dated 1656.

Vannotti collect., Lugano. Album of twelve Landscape-studies. Signed and dated 1656.

Nanga Taisei, XI, 124–131. Album of eight Landscapes, one signed and dated 1657.

Shên-chou ta-kuan, vol.3. The Study of The Ten Bamboos on a Mountain Slope. Poem by the painter, dated 1657. Also a poem by T'ang Yen-shêng, dated 1657.

Musée Guimet, Paris. Three leafless Trees. Signed. Colophon dated 1658.

Chang Ta-ch'ien cat., IV, 34. *Hsi-yüan tso-yü t'u*, "Sitting in the rain in the West Garden". Houses and pavilions by a stream at the foot of a high mountain. Poem by the painter. Signed and dated 1659.

Shên-chou, X. High Cliffs by a River; bare trees and a small pavilion. Signed and dated 1660. *Cf.* Chung-kuo, II, 143; Shina Nanga, I, 72.

Hui-hua kuan (*ex*-P'ang Yüan-chi collect.) Landscape after Ni Tsan. Poem by the painter, dated 1660.

Chūgoku, 7. A Pine-tree by a Stream. Signed and dated 1660.

Nanga Taisei Add. IV, 35. An old Tree and Bamboos. Inscription, signed and dated 1660.

I-yüan chên-shang, 9. The Sound of a Rivulet in a Hidden Valley: landscape with a rocky cliff. Signed, dated 1661.

Sumitomo collect., Ōiso. Rocky Landscape, with Pines and other Trees. Handscroll. Signed and dated 1661. *Cf.* K. Sumitomo, III; Nanga Taisei, XVI, 46–48.

National Museum, Stockholm. Views over Wide Hills and Streams. Long handscroll, painted in light colours. Inscription, signed and dated 1661. Colophon by Ch'êng Sui, written in the same year. *Cf.* Nanking Exhib. cat. 286.

Shên-chou, VIII. A leafless Tree and young Bamboos. Poem by the painter, dated 1663.

Ōmura, I, 9. A leafless Tree and some Bamboos by a Rock. Signed. Poem by T'ang Yen-shêng dated 1663. *Cf.* Sōraikan, II, 66.

Chêng Tê-k'un, Cambridge. Sketches of Rocks and Trees. Eight album-leaves. Signed and dated 1663.

Boston Museum (55.87). View of the Ch'ih-yang and Tung-hu lakes. Temple in the middle. Slightly coloured short handscroll. Signed and dated 1663.

Sirén, *Later*, pl.179. (Private collect., China.) Dwellings in the Mountains. Poem signed and dated 1669.

Nanga Taisei, XIII, 1–28. An Album of fifty Landscapes. Inscriptions and seals of the artist. Colophon by Hsiao Yün-ts'ung, written at age 80 (*i.e.* in 1675); another by Ch'êng Sui.

Ōmura, I, 2. Plum-tree and Bamboos by a Scholar's Cottage. Poem; colophon dated 1692. *Cf.* Chūgoku 7.

Hsin-an p'ai ming-hua chi (Shên-chou album, 1924). 1. A Valley; seal. 2. Young Bamboos; seal. 3. Two Pine-trees by a Stream; seals.

I-shu ts'ung-pien 15. A Pine-tree by a Rockery. Signed.

T'ai-shan ts'an-shih-lou ts'ang-hua, vol.I. Tall and thin Trees on a Slope by a River. Signed.

Po-mei chi. Branches of Plum Blossoms. Signed. Poem.

Shên-chou album, 1920. Eight Landscape Studies. Seals of the artist.

Chung-kuo ming-hua, 33. Buildings at the Foot of rocky Cliffs. Seal of the painter.

Shên-chou album, 1931. Seven Landscapes. Signed.

Shên-chou album 1932. Landscape. Handscroll. Signed.

Yen-kuang shih, Peking. Photographs of Eight Landscapes. Seals of the artist. *Cf.* Nanga Taisei Add.I, 54–61.

Nanga Taisei, I, 104. A Bamboo Grove. Album-leaf. Seal of the artist.

Ibid. Trees and a large Rock. Signed.

Shinchō 24. Plum-tree and Bamboos by a Rock. Fan-painting. Signed.

Tōsō 418. Steep Cliffs with bare Trees and Waterfall. Signed. Poem.

National Museum, Stockholm. A Homestead at the Foot of rocky Mountains. According to the inscription, painted for his friend Shih An. The same composition (larger size) in private possession in Hongkong.

Hamburg Exhibition 1949–1950. Landscape with spare Trees and a faintly visible Figure. Poem by the painter; executed after the death of the painter's mother.

Vanotti collect., Lugano. Two fan-paintings; one in the style of Ni Tsan, signed; the other a steep mountain wall, signed.

J. P. Dubosc, Lugano. Studies of steep Rocks. Three album-leaves with poems by the painter.

W. Hochstadter, New York. Terraced Mountains and sparse Trees. Signed.

Ibid. High terraced Rocks (mainly in outline). Poem by the painter. *Cf.* Cleveland Exhibition cat. 104.

Private collect., Peking. The Scholars' Cottages in the Mountains.

Chang Ta-ch'ien cat. I, 33. A Pine-tree bending down from a high Rock. Poem, signed.

Chang Ta-ch'ien collect., Hongkong (1954). A long, open River-view; boats on the water, sharply-cut rocks in the distance; scattered trees. Ink only.

Kao Yen-ju, Hongkong. Terraced Mountains and thin Trees. A very large composition in ink. Signed.

Shêng P'ing-ch'ên, Hongkong. A miniature Landscape. Signed.

Chang Ts'ung-yü cat. A Garden Pool enclosed by large Stones. *Cf.* Liu, 102.

HUNG WU 弘旿, or Ku-shan pei-tzŭ 固山貝子, *t.* Shu-chai 恕齋 and Tsui-yü 醉迂, *h.* Yao-hua tao-jên 瑤華道人, I-ju chü-shih 一如居士.

Ch'ien-lung period. Grandson of the emperor K'ang-hsi. Landscapes and flowers. M, p.68.

Sōraikan, II, 80. A Scholar's Pavilion by a River at the Foot of high Mountains, after T'ang Yin. Signed, dated 1751.

Sōgen 342. Landscape with a Man in a Boat. Signed, dated 1770.

Li-tai, III. A Boat on the Maple Stream. Signed. Poem by Ch'ien-lung dated 1776.

Ibid. III. A Pavilion over the Bamboo Stream. Signed. Poem by Ch'ien-lung, dated 1776.

Ibid. I. Pine-tree, Plum-tree and Bamboos. Signed.

Ibid. I. Pine-trees and a Stream in the Mountains. Signed.

Ibid. I. Pine-trees on cloudy Mountains.

Ibid. II. Mountain Landscape with Pine-trees.

Ibid. II. Trees and Streams in Autumn.

Ibid. II. Mountain Ridge by a Lake. Signed.

Ibid. IV. Mountains with Waterfall in Summer. Signed.

Ibid. IV. Mountains, Pine-trees, and Sailing-boats on a River. Signed.

Ibid. V. The Mountain of the Immortals. Signed.

Ibid. V. Green Mountains and richly coloured Trees. Signed.
Ibid. V. Misty Peaks and luxuriant Trees. Signed.
Ibid. VI. Pine-trees on a Mountain. Signed.
Ibid. VI. Mountains by a River. Signed.
Ku-kung, XVIII. Autumn Landscape; bamboos by a stream. Signed.
K.-k. shu-hua chi, X. Maples by a Stream with a Boat, after Kuan T'ung. Signed.
Ibid. XXIV. Men enjoying Chrysanthemums by a Stream. Signed.
Ibid. XXX. Clouds over the Peaks. Signed.
Ibid. XXXIII. Cloudy Mountains, after Fan K'uan. Signed.
Ibid. XLV. Green Peaks in Autumn, after Yang Shêng. Signed.
Pao-yün, II. A Temple on a Mountainside among Trees. Signed.
Yūrinkan, Kyōto. A Winter Landscape. Signed.
(See also K.-k. chou-k'an, Index, for other works by this artist.)

I HAI 伊海, *t.* Fu-chiu 孚九, *h.* Hsin-yeh 莘野, Hui-ch'uan 滙川, and other names.
From Suchou. Went to Japan in 1720. Landscapes. M, p.84. X.

Sekai Bijutsu Zenshū, XX, text illus. 116. The Peach-blossom Spring. Signed, dated 1742.
Tōyō, XII. High Cliffs by a River. Signed, dated 1745.
Kokka 174. Landscape. Signed. Poem.
Ibid. 278. Landscape. Signed. Poem.
Hyōjirō Hatta. River Landscape with two Boats. Signed. Poem.
N. Gashū 39. River Landscape with an Angling-boat. Signed.
Bijutsu Kenkyū 97 (Hasegawa, Mie). Mountains and Streams on a three-folded screen. Two poems by the painter.
Ibid. 137 (I. Murai, Mie). Landscape. Signed.

I-JAN 逸髯, *h.* of an unidentified painter, who according to the seal was also called Ch'ien-ch'iu yü-fu 千秋漁父. Probably beginning of the Ch'ing period.

Formerly C. B. Hoyt collect., Cambridge, Mass. Hills in Mist, a Man in a Boat. Study with fluent ink. Album-leaf.

I PING-SHOU 伊秉綬, *t.* Tsu-ssŭ 組似, *h.* Mo-ch'ing 墨卿.
From Ning-hua, Fukien. B. 1754, d. 1815. Governor of Yangchou. Famous calligraphist and writer. Landscapes, plum blossoms. U, III, 2, 1. M, p.83.

Mei-chan t'ê-k'an 62. Waterfall; Pines on a Terrace. Signed, dated 1805.
T. T. Ma, Hongkong. A Road winding along the Edge of a River-bank; tall rocks behind. Painted for Wu-mên. Signed and dated 1805. Colophon.
Ōmura, I, 8. A lonely Crane. Signed. Poem dated 1815. Also in Sōraikan, II, 88.
Mo-ch'ao pi-chi, vol.II. River Landscape after a master. Finger-painting. Signed. Poem.
Ibid. vol.II. River Landscape, after Tung ch'i-ch'ang. Signed.

JAO CHING 饒璟, *t.* Ching-yü 景玉, *h.* Shih-yao 石曜 and Lu-t'ai 麓臺.
From Hsi-hsien, Anhui. Landscapes after Wu Chên. M, p.734.

S.c.t.k. hsü-pien, III. Tall Trees growing on the Rocks by a River, after Wu Chên. Signed, dated 1716.

JÊN HSIUNG 任熊, *t.* Wei-ch'ang 渭長.
From Hsiao-shan, Chekiang. B. 1820, d. after 1860. The four painters of this family are known as "The Four Jên". Landscapes, figures, flowers and birds. M, p.87.

Ming-jên shu-hua, XX. Old Vessels of Clay and Bronze. Signed. Poem dated 1848. Also in Nanga Taikan 4.
Ibid. XVI. A Scholar with a Staff followed by a Servant-boy. Signed, dated 1856.
Ibid. XXI. A Cock on a Rock. Signed. Poem.
(See also Nanga Taisei, IV, 185; V, 76 (Flowers); VI, 218–220 (Birds, Insects); VII, 202–205 (Figures); XII, 202, 203; Add. IV, 132 (Landscapes).)

JÊN HSÜN 任薰, *t.* Fu-ch'ang 阜長.
From Hsiao-shan, Chekiang. B. 1835, d. 1893. Younger brother of Jên Hsiung. Flowers. M, p.87.

Ming-jên shu-hua, XIX. Twelve Handscrolls of Flower-paintings. The 11th dated 1875, last one dated 1873.
Nanga Taikan 11. Two pictures: Plum-blossoms; Narcissi and Orchids. Signed. Poems by the painter, by Li Chia-fu (dated 1879),

JÊN I 任頤, *t.* Po-nien 伯年.
From Shan-yin, Chekiang. B. 1840, d. 1896. Flowers, birds, imitated the Sung masters and Ch'ên Hung-shou. M, p.87.

Hui-hua kuan. Old Scholars enjoying Plum-blossoms. In the manner of Ch'ên Hung-shou. Dated 1868.
Shina Meiga Senshū 46. A black Cat seated on a Rock under a Banana-tree. Signed, dated 1879.
Sōgen 367. Two Cocks on a Rock. Signed, dated 1881.
Hamburg Exhibition, 1949–1950. Nü Wa smelting the Rocks to mend Heaven. Ink and slight colours. Signed, dated 1888.
Tōan 77. Hai-t'ang Blossoms and a Bird. Round fan-painting. Signed.
Ibid. 78. A Turkey in Snow. Signed.
Hui-hua kuan. A white Hen under a Banana-tree. Coloured.
(See also Nanga Taisei, IV, 190; V, 185 (Flowers); VI, 224–239 (Birds); VII, 227–240 (Figures); X, 246–247; Add. IV, 152 (Landscapes).)

JÊN SHIH-CHUNG 任時中, *t.* Hsüeh-k'o 學可.
Unrecorded. Probably Ch'ing dynasty.

Nanju 14. A Cock. Signed. Colophon. *Cf.* Dai Tenrankai 67.

KAI CH'I 改琦, *t.* Po-yün 伯蘊, *h.* Hsiang-po 香白, Ch'i-hsiang 七薌, Yü-hu wai-shih 玉壺外史 and other names.
His ancestors came from Sinkiang, settled in Sung-chiang, Kiangsu. B. 1774, d. 1829. Poet. Imitated Li Lung-mien, Chao Mêng-fu, T'ang Yin and Ch'ên Hung-shou. Figures, landscapes, flowers and bamboos. U, I, 3, 22. M, p.113.

Hamburg Exhibition, 1949–1950. Figures standing by a Grape Vine. The figures after Ch'ên Hung-shou. Signed, dated 1800.
Nanga Taisei, XV, 72–79. Ladies in a Palace. Handscroll. Signed and dated 1802.
Chung-kuo ming-hua, 39. A Copy of the Self-portrait of the Lady Painter Chao Wên-shu. Signed, dated 1819.
I-shu ch'uan-t'ung 12. Portrait of the Lady Lu-chu. Signed and dated 1823.
Sōgen 355. Lady with a Fan. Signed, dated 1823.
Shina Meiga Senshū 40 (Tomioka collect., Kyōto). A Taoist Fairy holding Flowers in both Hands. Seals of the painter. Long colophon by Kuo Lin, dated 1824. *Cf.* Sōgen 354.

Shên-chou, XXI. A Girl seated by a Rockery; a boy on the opposite side. Signed. Colophon dated 1825.
Compagnie de la Chine, Paris. A Lady standing by a Screen, after T'ang Yin. Signed, dated 1833.
Chung-kuo, II, 153. Two Ladies seated near a Bamboo Grove, after T'ang Yin. Signed. *Cf.* Chung-kuo ming-hua, 27.
Po-mei chi. A Branch of Plum-blossoms. Signed.
Shina Nanga, I, 134. Lady playing the Flute. Signed.
Ōmura, I, 5. Pine-tree, Bamboos and Fungi by a Rock. A leaf from an album of twelve pictures of flowers and birds. Signed.
Shinchō 85. Lady with a Fan. Signed. Poem.
Nanga Taikan 11. A *Lu* Fish. Album-leaf. Signed.
Shina Meiga Senshū 41. Branches of Plum-blossoms in a tall Vase. Poem by the painter.
Sōgen 353. Kuan-yin with a white Hood. Signed.
Bijutsu Kenkyū 5. Loquat Fruits. Signed.
(See also Nanga Taisei, II, 9 and 255 (Flowers); V, 44 (Pine); VII, 162–166 (Figures); VIII, 214–217 (Landscapes).)

K'ANG T'AO 康濤, *t.* Shih-chou 石舟, *h.* T'ien-tu lao-jên 天篤老人, Mao-hsin lao-jên 茅心老人 and other names.
From Ch'ien-t'ang, Chekiang. Active *c.*1740. Landscapes, flowers, figures and birds. U, III, 1, 9. M, p.382.

Ming-jên shu-hua, XVII. Wang Chao-chün. Signed. Colophon dated 1733.
Ch'ing êrh-shih chia. A Lady seated by a Rock. Poem by the painter, dated 1746.
Shên-chou, IX. Ladies by a Stream. Also in Shina Nanga, I, 110.
Ch'ing êrh-shih chia. A Lady standing by a Rock, after T'ang Yin. Signed.
Shinchō 68. Man standing by a Waterfall among Trees. Signed.
Hamburg Exhibition, 1949–1950. A Woman in a Fur-coat. Colour on paper. Signed.

KAO CH'ÊNG-MO 高承謨.
Unrecorded. Probably end of the 18th century.

Boston Museum. A Cat watching a Butterfly. Signed and dated *kêng-yin* (probably 1770).

KAO CH'I-P'EI 高其佩, *t.* Wei-chih 韋之, *h.* Ch'ieh-yüan 且園, Nan-ts'un 南村, Ch'ang-po shan-jên 長白山人 and other names.
From Liao-yang, Manchuria. B. 1672(?), d. 1734 (these dates not firmly established). Famous particularly as finger painter. Landscapes, figures, flowers and birds. Q, I, 3. R, IX, 2. U, II, 2, 24. M, p.334.

Nanking Exhib. cat. 326. A Bridge and old Trees. Signed and dated 1684.
K. Sumitomo, Ōiso. An Album of twelve Paintings of Birds, Insects, Flowers, etc. Signed and dated 1686. *Cf.* Sekai Bijutsu Zenshū, XX, Pl.53; Kokka 723.
Commercial Press album, 1935. Ten fan-paintings, various subjects. Signed, one dated 1698.
Princeton University. A Man and a Boy walking at the Foot of a Mountain. Signed, dated 1698.
Sōgen 274. The Three Friends of cold Winter. Album-leaves; finger-paintings. Signed, dated 1708.
Ōmura, I, 10. The Chiu-ju Mountain. Finger-painting. Signed, dated 1708. *Cf.* Sōraikan, I, 57.
Nanking Exhib. cat. 327. Three leaves from an album: Pine, Bamboo and flowering Plum. Signed and dated 1709.
Shina Nanga, I, 75. A Man seated under a bare Tree by a Stream. Finger painting. Dated 1711. Seals of the painter. *Cf.* Chung-kuo ming-hua, 13.
C. T. Loo's Successor, Frank Caro, N.Y. Li T'ieh-kuai and a Bat. Ink and colour on paper. Inscription by the painter in which he says that he painted this after Wu Wei. Dated 1711. *Cf.* Toronto 50.

Tokasha Shina Meigashū 65. A standing Horse. Finger-painting. Signed, dated 1713.

Chung-kuo ming-hua, 11. Studies of Flowers, Fishes, Fowls, Horses and Dogs. Handscroll. Signed and dated 1718.

Shina Nanga, III, 6. Figures and Flowers (mounted on one scroll). Signed. Poem dated 1718.

Chung-kuo, II, 157. Chung K'uei followed by Demons. Signed, dated 1719. Also in Shina Nanga, II, 5.

Sōgen 276. Chung K'uei. Finger-painting. Signed. Poem. Colophon, dated 1728.

Shên-chou, XIII. A white Eagle on a curving Pine Trunk. Signed. *Cf.* Sōgen, 272.

T'ai-shan ts'an-shih-lou ts'ang-hua, vol.II. Chung K'uei and a Bat. Finger-painting. Signed.

Li-tai, II. Looking at the rising Sun.

Ibid. III. Towers and Terraces on the Island of the Immortals. Signed.

Ibid. V. Magpies, Swallows and Ducks.

K.-k. shu-hua chi, V. Waterfall on Lu-shan. Finger-painting. Signed.

Ibid. XIX. River View: Homeward bound in Wind and Rain. Short handscroll. Painter's seal.

Ibid. XX. A Mountain River and large Pine-trees.

Fu-lu. Two leaves from an album of Bamboo-paintings.

S.c.t.k. hsü-pien, I. Young Woman seated under a Banana-tree. Signed.

Nanking Exhib. cat. 328. A Tiger gazing up at a Bird. Signed.

Gems, III, 15. A Bird on a flowering Branch. An old Man. Two album-leaves. Seals of the artist. Colophon by Ch'ien Tu dated 1842.

Fei-tun lu shan-shui. Man on a Cliff looking at a Waterfall. Finger-painting. Signed. Colophon.

Nanju 6. Pine-trees by a Stream. Finger-painting. Poem by Shên Chou, copied by the painter. Signed. Also in Tōyō, XII.

Shina Nanga, II, 3. Chrysanthemums and Fish. Finger-painting. Poems.

Ibid. II, 11. A Pine-tree.

Tokasha Shina Meigashū 66. A Plum-tree in Snow. Signed.

Kokka 570 (Y. Yamamoto, Tōkyō). Lotus Flowers and Waterfalls.

Ibid. 737. Four Fish. Signed.

Kyūka, II. Peonies. Finger-painting. Signed. Colophon.

Ibid. II (Mayuyama collect., Tōkyō). Five Eagles in a Pine-tree. Signed.

Ibid. II. The Nine Old Men. Finger-painting. Signed.

Shinchō 39. A Herd-boy sleeping under a Tree with a Buffalo. Album-leaf. Seals of the painter.

Tōan 55. A solitary Pine-tree on a Cliff and flying Geese. Illustration to a T'ang poem. Finger-painting. Signed.

Sōgen 273. Man with a Staff standing on a Stone Bridge. Finger-painting. Signed.

Ibid. 275. Bamboo Grove in Rain, after Chao Mêng-fu. Signed.

T. Moriya, Kyōto. A standing Figure of Kuan-yin, holding a Lotus Blossom. Signed.

Ibid. Landscape with a Man in a House; a servant brings a jug of wine from a moored boat. Finger-painting.

Ibid. Towering Mountains, dry Trees and a Hut below: a man passing through the gateway into the court-yard. Signed.

Takeuchi collect., Kyōto. A Scholar and his Servant observing a Waterfall. Large landscape, signed.

Yamaguchi collect., Ashiya. Landscape with bare Trees, after Li Ch'êng. Signed.

Rijksmuseum, Amsterdam. Album of ten Landscape studies, each inscribed and signed. Finger-paintings. *Cf.* Kokka, 743.

Kawai collect., Kyōto. Heron among Lotus Plants. Signed.

Nanga Taisei, III, 80. A flowering Plum-tree. Hand-scroll. Inscription signed.

T'ang Hsiao-min, Taichung. A Man seated by a Rock, writing. Seal of the artist. Finger-painting.

British Museum, No.238. Man with an Umbrella. Signed.

Ibid. Studies of Figures, Animals and Insects. Ten album-leaves. Seals of the painter.

Berlin Museum. Chung K'uei and a Bat. Finger-painting. Signed.

Ibid. A Lady with a Branch of Cassia in her Hand. Finger-painting. Signed.

Seattle Art Museum. A Man with a Horse by a Tree. Poem by the painter.

Formerly C. B. Hoyt collect., Cambridge, Mass. Clouds circling between grassy Hills. Signed.

Ibid. A Pheasant standing on a Terrace by a stormy Sea. Signed.

J. Cahill, Wash, D.C. A Crab among Reeds. Large horizontal album-leaf. Finger-painting. Signed.
G. Del Drago, New York. Bamboos by a Rockery under the full Moon. Poem by the painter.
W. Hochstadter, New York. Houses standing on Poles at the Foot of leafy Mountain-peaks. Buffaloes on the bridge and two men in a small boat. Signed.
Despois collect., Paris (Buhot: *Arts de la Chine*, p.139). Fishes swimming among Plants in the Water. Signed.
Hamburg Exhibition, 1949–1950. A Lady under a Willow-tree.
Chêng Tê-k'un, Cambridge. A long-tailed Bird on a Branch. Signed.
Ibid. Four album-leaves with landscapes and figures. Inscriptions and seals of the artist.

KAO CHIEN 高簡, *t.* Tan-yu 澹游, *h.* Lü-yün shan-jên 旅雲山人.
From Suchou. B. 1634, d. *c.*1708. Landscapes. Q, I, 2. R, IV, 25. U, I, 2, 18. M, p.334.

Tokasha Shina Meigashū 22. A Man in a Boat by the Shore, bare trees and rocky mountains. Signed, dated 1671.
Nanga Taisei, XV, 54–58. Landscape after Chiang Kuan-tao. Handscroll. Signed and dated 1678.
Mei-chan t'ê-k'an 58. A quiet Bay; men in a pavilion on the shore. Signed, dated 1681.
I-yüan chên-shang 3. A Lake Scene in Winter, with a Man and a Boy in a Boat. Handscroll. Signed and dated 1687.
K.-k. shu-hua chi, XXVII. Landscape. Signed. Poem dated 1692.
British Museum, No.185. Landscape in Autumn Rain. Signed, dated 1694.
Fei-tun lu shan-shui. High Mountains and bare Trees. Signed, dated 1697.
Po-mei chi. Bamboos and Plum Blossoms. Album-leaf. Signed, dated 1704.
Ibid. A Homestead among Bamboos and Plum-trees in Snow. Handscroll. Signed, dated 1705.
Wên-ming album, 1935. Six Landscapes after Yüan masters, the last signed and dated 1707.
Ming-jên shu-hua, XXIII. Man looking at a Waterfall. After Chü-jan. Signed, dated 1708.
Ibid. XXI. A Branch of Plum-tree. Seals of the painter.
Wên-ming album, 1924. Eight Landscapes. Signed.
Hui-hua kuan. River Landscape with Hills and Trees. Coloured, after Chao Ta-nien.
Ch'ing êrh-shih chia. Branches of Plum-blossoms, after Yang Pu-chih. Album-leaf. Signed.
Shina Nanga, II, 5. A Hermit on the K'ung-t'ung Mountain, after Chao Mêng-fu. Signed.
Sōgen 188. River Landscape in early Summer, after Chao Ta-nien. Signed.
Nanga Taisei, III, 69–76. An Album of Plum-blossoms. Seals of the artist.

KAO FÊNG-HAN 高鳳瀚, *t.* Hsi-yüan 西園, *h.* Nan-ts'un 南邨 and in later age, Nan-fu lao-jên 南阜老人, Kuei-yün lao-jên 歸雲老人 and several other names.
From Chiao-chou, Shantung. B. 1683, d. after 1747. Calligraphist. Landscapes, flowers. When unable to work with his right hand he used the left and called himself Hou Shang-tso-shêng 後尚左生. (Shang-tso-shêng being the *hao* of Chêng Yüan-yu, a scholar, 1292–1364, who also lost the use of his right arm.) Q, II, 1. R, XI, 12. T, I, 3. U, III, 1, 1. M, p.335.

Shên Chou album, 1926. Six Landscape studies with poems, together with six pictures representing Animals by Yo Kao, dated 1715.
Ōmura, I, 11. Landscape and Flowers. Two pictures mounted on one handscroll. Signed, dated 1720. *Cf.* Chūgoku, 8.
Shina Nanga, II, 7. Landscape with two Men seated under Pine-trees. Signed. Poem dated 1721.
British Museum. Studies of Landscapes, Stones, Pine-trees and Flowers. Twelve fan-paintings. Some of them with inscriptions by the painter and dates ranging between 1722 and 1725.
Kyūka, II. Garden Rockery in Snow. Signed. Colophon dated 1723.
Tokasha Shina Meigashū 56. Lilies on the Banks of a Mountain Stream. Signed, dated 1724. Poem by the painter.

Kyūka, II. Plum-trees in Bloom by a River. Signed, dated 1727.

Ming-jên shu-hua, X. A Man cultivating Chrysanthemums in front of his Cottage. Signed. Four poems dated 1727. *Cf.* Chung-kuo ming-hua, vol.18; Sōraikan, II, 77.

Bijutsu, III. River-view with leafless Trees. Signed, dated 1727.

Hui-hua kuan. Rocky Ledges rising from the Mountain River; a man seated on the ground looking into the water. Ink on silk. Dated 1727.

C. T. Loo's Successor, Frank Caro, N.Y. Landscape with Clouds and Mists; a thatched house in the foreground. Ink and colour on paper. Inscription by the painter, dated 1727. *Cf.* Toronto 51.

Nanju 18. Spring Mist over the Stream. Signed and dated 1734. *Cf.* Kyūka, II.

Sōraikan, II, 78. Two old Pine-trees and Clouds above. Signed. Poem by the painter, dated 1734.

Ibid. II, 79. Four leaves from an album of ten pictures on Flowers and Landscapes. Some with poems by the painter, dated 1734.

Hashimoto collect., Takatsuki. Mountains and Pine-trees. Short handscroll. Signed and dated 1734.

Sōgen 296. Cockscomb and Lily by a Rock. Signed. Poem dated 1735.

Ibid. 293. Portrait of the Painter at 54, by Li Hung-jên, dated 1736. Rocks and Lotuses by Kao Fêng-han.

Chūgoku 8. Two Landscapes. Album-leaves, one after Tai Pên-hsiao. Signed, one dated 1736. Colophons by the artist mounted above.

Berlin Museum Collect. An Album of six Landscapes. Signed, dated 1736.

Nanju 9. An Arhat in a Mountain Cave. Signed, dated 1736. *Cf.* Pageant, 886; Sirén, *Later*, 236.

Ibid. 15. Tree-peonies by a Rock. Signed, dated 1736. Also in Kyūka, II.

Ming-jên shu-hua, V. Peonies by a Rockery. Signed. Poem dated 1737.

Po-mei chi. Plum-trees in Bloom. Signed. Poem dated 1737.

Tokasha Shina Meigashū 54. Two Branches of a Tree-peony. Signed, dated 1738. Poems by the painter.

Anonymous publisher, n.d. Album of eight paintings of various subjects, each inscribed with the date, 1738. Seals of the artist.

Commercial Press album, 1935. Flowers and other Subjects, painted with the left hand. Signed and dated 1740.

Tokasha Shina Meigashū 55. A Branch of a Tree-peony. Signed, dated 1741. Colophon by the painter.

Hui-hua kuan. Lotus and Mu-tan Flowers in Vases. Broadly painted in ink. Dated 1741.

Sōgen 294. Bare Trees by a Rock. Signed. Colophon dated 1742.

Tokasha Shina Meigashū 57. Peonies and Stones. Signed, dated 1744.

Ibid. 58. Birds gathering on a broken Tree by a Mountain Homestead. Colophon by the painter, dated 1744.

Kurokawa cat. 28. A Flock of Magpies coming to roost in a bare Tree. Signed and dated 1745.

T'ai-shan album, series I. Album of twelve leaves: rocks, flowers etc. Inscriptions, one dated 1746.

Fei-tun lu hua-hui. Crows on bare Trees. Signed. Colophon, dated 1746. *Cf.* Sōgen 295; Sōraikan, I, 59.

Shên-chou, XIV. A Rock representing the Five Sacred Mountains. Signed, dated 1747 (at 65). *Cf.* Ōmura, I, 4.

Hui-hua kuan. Studies of Stones, old Trees and Bamboo. Ink and colour. Six album-leaves.

T'ai-shan ts'an-shih-lou ts'ang-hua, III. Old Tree and Banana Palms by a Rock. Signed.

Shanghai Museum. Album of Landscape-studies, painted with the left hand. Inscriptions by Chêng Hsieh. *Cf.* Nanga Taisei, XII, 39–46; Gems, III, 16.

T. Moriya collect., Kyōto. An old Tree and alighting Birds; rocks and flowers. Two album-leaves, signed.

Kokka 293. Lotus Flowers. Signed.

Shinchō 55. Lilies and Banana-leaves. Album-leaf. Seal of the painter.

Chêng Ch'i, Hongkong. Chrysanthemums. Large album-leaf. Inscription by the artist mounted above.

British Museum. Large horizontal album of ten leaves: Flowers, Fruits, Vegetables. Ink and colours on silk.

British Museum (No.225). Roses and Jasmine, after Yün Shou-p'ing. Signed.

National Museum, Stockholm. Crows gathering in dry Trees. Signed.

(See also Nanga Taisei, II, 185, 186; IV, 106; V, 111–113, 141, 179 (Flowers); III, 94–98 (flowering Plum); IV, 235–237; Add. IV, 79–81 (Rocks and Trees).)

KAO HSIANG 高翔, *t.* Fêng-kang 鳳岡, *h.* Hsi-t'ang 西唐, Shan-lin wai-ch'ên 山林外臣 and other names. From Yangchou, Kiangsu. A friend of Tao-chi. Poet; one of the "Eight Strange Masters of Yang-chou". Active 1700–1730. Plum-blossoms. Q, II, 1. R, VII, 5. U, III, 1, 4. M, p.335.

Hui-hua kuan. Soft Hills rising above a misty River. After a Yüan master. Dated 1724.
Shanghai Museum: A small album of Landscape-studies. Poem, signed. *Cf.* Gems, III, 14.
Po-mei chi. Branches of Plum-blossoms. Signed. Poem.
Pageant 892. A Branch of a Plum-tree and Bamboos. Signed. Two lines of poetry.
Hamburg Exhibition, 1949–1950. Landscape Sketches. Three album-leaves mounted on one handscroll.
Chang Ting-chien, Hongkong. Landscape. Painted on Sung paper.
Nanga Taisei, III, 111. Flowering Plum-trees. Screen in four panels. Painted with Wang Shih-shên. Inscription, signed.
Ibid. XII, 47. Landscape after a Yüan painter. Signed.
Chêng Tê-k'un, Cambridge. An album of ten landscape-paintings. Signed.

KAO PIN 高鑌.
Unrecorded. According to the signature on the following picture, from T'ieh-ling, Fêng-t'ien. Probably a relative to Kao Ch'i-p'ei.

Tokasha Shina Meigashū 67. Five swimming Fishes. Finger-painting. Signed, dated 1739.

KAO SHIH-CH'I 高士奇, *t.* Tan-jen 澹人, *h.* Chiang-ts'un 江村.
From Ch'ien-t'ang, Chekiang. B. 1645, d. 1704. Vice-president of the Board of Rites. Connoisseur, collector. Author of *Chiang-ts'un hsiao-hsia lu* 江村消夏錄 and *Keng-tzu hsiao-hsia lu* 庚子消夏錄. M, p.333.

Shinchō 42. A wooded Path leading to a Cottage. After Hsü Pen. Signed, dated 1690.

KAO SHU-CH'ÊNG 高樹程, *t.* Chin-yü 靳玉, *h.* Mai-an 邁菴.
From Ch'ien-t'ang, Chekiang. Chü-jên in 1777. Landscapes, followed the Yüan masters. U, III, 1, 20. M, p.336.

Ming-jên shu-hua, II. Bare Trees. Painted together with Hsi Kang and Huang I. Also in Shina Nanga, III, 1.
Nanga Taisei, X, 183, 184. Three Landscapes.

KAO TS'ÊN 高岑, *t.* Wei-shêng 蔚生, *h.* Shan-ch'ang 善長.
From Hangchou; lived in Nanking. Active *c.*1670. One of the "Eight Masters of Nanking". Landscapes, flowers. P, III, 14. Q, I, 1. R, IV, 20. U, II, 1, 22. M, p.333.

Chin-ling p'ai ming-hua chi (Shên-chou album, 1924). A Straw-covered Pavilion. Signed, dated 1668.
Berlin Museum Collect. Two Landscape-paintings from an album of twelve, after Sung and Yüan masters. Dated 1672. *Cf.* Tōyō, XII and Sirén, *Later*, 187.
Êrh-fan kao-tsou (Shên-chou album, 1930). Landscapes. Album-leaves. Signed. *Cf.* Pageant, 765.
Gems, I, 58. Landscape, after Fan K'uan's "Autumn Mountains and Dense Grove". Signed.
Nanga Taisei, XI, 207–209. Three Landscapes, Album-leaves. Signed.
Nanju 4. Landscape after Tung Yüan. Signed.
Chūgoku 7. Houses under tall Pines by a Stream. Two lines of poetry, signed. Leaf in an album containing works by the eight Nanking masters.
K.-k. chou-k'an 145. Landscapes with a Temple. Fan-painting. Signed.

J. P. Dubosc, Lugano. Thin Bamboos growing by a Rock. A leaf from an album formerly in Chou Liang-kung's Collection.

Ibid. Steep Cliffs and Pine-trees. A leaf from the same album as the preceding picture.

Hamburg Exhibition, 1949–1950. Autumn Trees and green Cliffs.

KAO TS'ÊNG-YÜN 高層雲, *t.* Êrh-pao 二鮑, *h.* Su-yüan 謏園.

From Hua-t'ing, Kiangsu. B. 1634, d. 1690. Scholar, connoisseur, calligraphist. Landscapes followed Tung Ch'i-ch'ang. Q, I, 1. R, V, 3. U, II, 2, 5. M, p.334.

K.-k. shu-hua chi, XVII. River-view in Yüan style; pavilions under tall trees in the foreground. Signed, dated 1683.

Nanga Taisei, XI, 236. Two Landscapes, Album-leaves. Signed; one dated 1686.

KAO-TSUNG, EMPEROR CH'IEN-LUNG OF CH'ING 清高宗.

B. 1711, d. 1799. Landscapes. Q, I.

Sōgen 303. The P'u-t'ung Study in the Imperial Garden. Signed. Colophon, poem, dated 1744. Twenty more poems by the emperor.

Ku-kung, XV. Fishing Boat on a misty River. Signed, dated 1744.

K.-k. shu-hua chi, XIV. A Cedar-tree on Sung-shan in Honan. Signed, dated 1750.

Ibid. XI. The Study of Bamboos and Incense-burners. Signed, dated 1753.

Ibid. XIX. Landscape in Rain. Signed, dated 1762.

Ibid. I. Three Sheep. Signed, dated 1772.

Chung-kuo ming-hua 24. Two Men seated on a rocky Ledge under bare Trees by a River. Signed.

Kokka 445. Three fan-paintings: 1 and 2, Landscapes. 3. Flowers.

Sōgen 304. Scattered Trees and Hillocks, after Tung Ch'i-ch'ang. Handscroll. Signed. Poem.

KAO YEN 高儼, *t.* Wang-kung 望公.

Native of Hsin-hui in Kuangtung. Skilled at poetry, calligraphy and painting; especially active as a painter in his late years, often painted by moonlight. R, III, 12. M, p.333.

Nanking Exhib. cat. 175. Buildings on a Cliff overhanging the River. Signed and dated *ping-wu* (1666?)

KAO YÜ 高遇, *t.* Yü-chi 雨吉.

Nephew of Kao Ts'ên. Landscapes, in which he followed his uncle. R, VI, 17. L, XX, 5.

Chūgoku 7. Landscape with Mists circling a central Mountain. Signed. Leaf in an album of works of the eight Nanking masters (although Kao was not himself one of them).

KU AN-JÊN 顧安仁, *t.* Tzŭ-yün 子雲.

Ch'ing dynasty. Figures, landscapes. M, p.747.

National Museum, Stockholm. A poetical Gathering in the Western Garden, after Chao Mêng-fu (and Li Kung-lin). Signed.

KU CH'IAO 顧樵, *t.* Ch'iao-shui 樵水, *h.* Jo-hsieh 若邪.
From Wu-chiang, Kiangsu. Active middle of the 17th century. Landscapes, followed Shên Chou. Q, I, 1. R, IV, 8. U, II, 2, 13. M, p.739.

Shên-chou, XVI. Tu Tzŭ-mei reading in a Study in the Garden by a Stream. Album-leaf. Colophon by the painter.

KU CHIEN-LUNG 顧見龍, *t.* Yün-ch'êng 雲程 or Yün-ch'ên 雲臣.
From Wu-chiang, Kiangsu; lived on the Tiger Hill in Suchou. B. 1606, d. after 1686. Portraits and historical motifs; influenced by Ch'iu Ying. court-painter in the K'ang-hsi period. Q, I, 2. R, XIII, 8. U, II, 1, 8. M, p.741.

British Museum. Eighteen Lohans. Album of sixteen leaves, the last signed and dated 1634.
Shina Meiga Senshū 24. Chung K'uei under a Willow. Signed, dated 1691.
Chung-kuo, II, 56. A young Woman leaning over a Table, seen through a Moon door.
National Museum, Stockholm. The Seven Sages of the Bamboo Grove. Signed.
Nelson Gallery, Kansas City. Court Ladies in a Palace Garden. Handscroll. Signed.
Boston Museum. The Girl Drummer from Fêng-yang. *Cf.* Sirén, *Later*, 167.
Formerly Hobart collect., Cambridge, Mass. A Gentleman seated on the Terrace in a Garden and five Servant-girls.
Chung-kuo ming-hua 13. A Lady on a Verandah pausing after playing on the *Ch'in.*
I-yüan album (Mi-yün-lou collect.) "A Girl embracing the Spring". Ten album-leaves.

KU FANG 顧昉, *t.* Jo-chou 若周, *h.* Jih-fang 日方, Kêng-yün 耕雲 and Wan-kao 晚皐.
From Hua-t'ing, Kiangsu. *c.*1700. Pupil of Wang Hui. Imitated Tung Yüan, Chü-jan, and the four masters of the Yüan period. Q, I, 2. R, VII, 15. U, I, 3, 6. M, p.740.

Chūgoku, 8. A Temple in the Autumn Mountains. Signed and dated 1692. Colophon by Wang Hui.
Ming-jên shu-hua, XVI. Mountain Landscape, after Wang Mêng. Signed. Poem.
Shina Meiga Senshū, II, 34. Terraced Mountains and Pine-trees by a River. Large album-leaf. Signed.
Tomioka collect., Kyōto. A Study in the autumnal Mountains. Signed.

KU FU-CHÊN 顧符稹, *t.* Sê-ju 瑟如, *h.* Hsiao-ch'ih 小癡 and Sung-ch'ao 松巢 (or Yün-ch'ao 雲巢).
From Hsing-hua (Yang-chou), Kiangsu. B. 1634, still alive at 1716. Landscapes, figures, imitated the Little General Li. Q, I, 2. R, VI, 18. M, p.740.

Shên-chou, VIII. A Man standing under an old Cedar-tree by a River. Signed, dated 1684.
Nanking Exhib. cat. 313. Landscape after Ni Tsan. Inscription, signed and dated 1688.
Fei-tun lu shan-shui. River Scenery. Signed, dated 1700.
Hamburg Exhibition, 1949–1950. An Inlet of a Mountain-river; a homestead under leafy trees. Whirling clouds, and mountains in blue and green. Inscription by the painter, dated 1708.
National Museum, Stockholm. The Chien-ko Pass in Szechuan with Travellers on the palisaded Roads and in the Rest-houses. In the coloured manner of the Little General Li. Signed. *Cf.* Tōsō, p.402.

KU HAO-CH'ING 顧鶴慶, *t.* Tzŭ-yü 子餘, *h.* T'ao-an 弢庵 and Ku-i-liu 顧驛柳.
From Tan-t'u, Kiangsu. B. 1766, still active 1830. Poet, calligraphist and landscape-painter. T. M, p.743.

Commercial Press Album, 1928. Album of Landscapes in various styles, one signed and dated 1797. *Cf.* Nanga Taisei, XII, 129–139.
Po-mei chi. Plum-blossoms. Signed, dated 1807.
Nanga Taisei, III, 166–173. An Album of Paintings of blossoming Plum. Signed and dated 1807.
Ibid. X, 212. Spring in Fu-yang. Signed and dated 1825.
Ibid. II, 257. Bamboo growing by a Stream. Signed and dated 1830.
Hamburg Exhibition, 1949–1950. Clouds in the Dawn in Spring. After Kao K'o-kung.

KU LIEN 顧廉, *t.* Yu-chien 又簡, *h.* Wan-fu 頑夫.
From Chü-hsien, Shantung. *c.*1770. Landscapes. M, p.743.

Ming-jên shu-hua, XXVI. Waterfall in Autumn, after a Sung master. Signed. Poem dated 1776.

KU LO 顧洛, *t.* Yü-men 禹門, *h.* Hsi-mei 西梅.
From Hangchou. Lived *c.*1762–1835. Figures, landscapes. U, III, 2, 9. M, p.746.

Ming-jên shu-hua, VIII. Peonies, after a Yüan master. Signed. Four poems by Huang Fu, copied by the painter, dated 1800. Also in Shina Nanga, III, 7.
Ibid. VI. Ladies in a Garden; four pictures forming a series, dated 1810.
Shinchō 83. A Lady in a Garden Pavilion by a Pond, after Ch'ien Hsüan. Signed, dated 1819.
Shên Chou, VIII. Portrait of the Girl Lü-chu. Signed, dated 1822. Also in Shina Nanga, I, 128.
Ming-jên shu-hua, XVIII. A Lady standing by a moonlit Stream. Signed, dated 1825.
Tokasha Shina Meigashū 93. An old Man and a Boy under a blossoming Plum-tree watching a flying Crane. Signed, dated 1833.
Shên Chou, XI. Man playing the *Ch'in* under Autumn Trees. Signed. Also in Shina Nanga, I, 129.
Hui-hua kuan. Portrait of a Man seated in a Boat. Signed.
Ōmura, I, 8. Mountain Landscape with a Boat on the Stream. Signed. Poem.
Nanga Taikan 3. A Fisherman in a Boat playing the Flute, after T'ang Yin. Signed.
Nanga Taisei, VII, 168–174; XII, 156–160. An album of landscapes with figures. Signed.

KU MEI-SHÊNG 顧眉生.
Lady-painter of the 17th century. Q, I, 3. M, p.742.

Shinchō 87. Orchids. Album-leaf. Signed.

KU PAO-WÊN 顧豹文, *t.* Chi-wei 季蔚, *h.* Ch'ieh-an 且菴.
From Hangchou. Chin shih in 1655. High official and author. Landscapes. V, p.1792.

Tōyō, XII. High Mountains in Rain. Signed.

KU SHAN-YU 顧善有.
From Hua-t'ing, Kiangsu. Son of the painter Ku I-tê. Active about the middle of the 17th century. Landscapes. M, p.738.

Vannotti collect., Lugano. An album of nine Landscapes in Old Styles. Colophons by Ch'ên Chi-ju, Tung Ch'i-ch'ang and others; one dated 1630.
Musée Guimet. High Mountains and a Pavilion on the River-bank. After Shêng Mou. Signed. Probably a leaf from the album in the Vannotti collection.

KU SHUN 顧蒓, *t.* Wu-kêng 吳羹, *h.* Nan-ya 南雅, Hsi-lu 息廬 and Hsi-han 希翰.
From Suchou. B. 1765, d. 1832. Chin-shih in 1802. Poet and calligraphist. Orchids and plum-blossoms. T. U, III, 2, 8. M, p.745.

Po-mei chi. Branches of Plum-blossoms. Signed, dated 1818.

Ming-jên hsieh-chu. Bamboos. Handscroll. Signed. Poem.

KU TA-CH'ANG 顧大昌, *t.* Tzŭ-ch'ang 子長, *h.* Lêng-chia shan-min 楞伽山民.
From Suchou. Active *c.*1780. Landscapes. M, p.747.

Ming-jên shu-hua, XIV. Li Tê-yü (of T'ang) receiving Guests. After the emperor Hui-tsung. Colophon, signed, dated 1783.

KU TA-SHÊN 顧大申, original name Ku Yung 顧鏞, *t.* Chên-chih 震雉, *h.* Chien-shan 見山.
From Hua-t'ing, Kiangsu. Chin shih in 1652. Landscapes, followed Tung Yüan, Chü-jan and Tung Ch'i-ch'ang. Q, I, 2. R, II. 3. U, I, 2, 15. M, p.739.

Nanju 17. Old Pine-trees by a Waterfall. Signed, dated 1651.

K.-k. shu-hua chi, III. Mountains with Cottages in Autumn. Signed, dated 1652.

Shina Meiga Senshū, III. Towered Mountain-peaks and Cascades; a man crossing a bridge below. After a Sung master. Signed and dated 1662.

Kurokawa cat. 14. A River Landscape with Sailing-boats. Handscroll, painted in colours. Inscription by the artist dated 1664. *Cf.* Shinchō 34.

Ōmura, I, 5. Old Pine-trees by a Waterfall, after Ts'ao Chih-po. Inscription by the painter, dated 1664. *Cf.* Kokka 598; Sōraikan, II, 70.

Shên-chou, XII. Landscape, Album-leaf. Signed and dated 1668.

Kyūka, II. High Mountains by a River. Signed and dated 1669.

Shina Meiga Senshū, II, 31. A River winding between rocky Promontories; leafless trees. Inscription by the painter, dated 1673.

Nanju 7 (Sumitomo collect., Ōiso). An Angler in a Boat by a rocky Shore with Pine-trees. After Tung Yüan. Signed. *Cf.* Tōyō, XII; Pageant, 822.

KU WÊN-YÜAN 顧文淵, *t.* Hsiang-yüan 湘源 or Wên-ning 文寧, *h.* Hsüeh-p'o 雪坡 and other names.
Native of Ch'ang-shu, Kiangsu. Friend of Wang Hui, and travelled about with him. Specialized in bamboo because he despaired of rivalling Wang in landscapes. Q, II, 1. U, II, 2, 1. M, p.740.

Eda collect., Tōkyō. The Villa of Li Yen-chai. Li is seen in his house; two servants outside by a boat. Handscroll. Many colophons.

J. Cahill, Wash., D.C. A Branch of flowering Plum by Moonlight. Poem, signed.

KU YIN 顧殷, *t.* Yü-kung 禹功.
From Suchou. Active *c.*1680. Landscapes. M, p.742.

Tōyō, XII. A Taoist's Hut by a Stream in the Mountains. Signed, dated 1682.

Wu-mên p'ai ming-hua chi (Shên-chou Album, 1924). The Fu-ch'un Mountain, after Huang Kung-wang. Signed.

Ch'ing êrh-shih chia. A Branch of Snow-covered Plum -blossoms. Album-leaf. Signed.
Shinchō 29. Misty Mountains. Album-leaf. Signed.
Shên-chou album, 1914. Album of eight Landscapes. Signed. Inscriptions by Wan Shou-ch'i. *Cf.* Nanga Taisei. XII, 2–9.
Ibid. XII, 10, 11. Two Landscapes, one after Huang Kung-wang. Album-leaves. Signed.

KU YING 顧瑛, *h.* Yü-shan tao-jên 玉山道人.
From Hsiu-shui, Chekiang. Latter half of the 17th century. Landscapes after Tung Yüan, flowers and birds after Huang Ch'üan and Hsü Hsi. M, p.739.

K.-k. shu-hua chi, XXXIII. Two Mandarin Ducks. Signed. Poem.

KU YING-T'AI 顧應泰, *t.* Yün-hao 雲鶴.
From Wu-hsi, Kiangsu. Active *c.*1810. Figures, imitated Li Kung-lin. U, III, 2, 11. M, p.748.

Ming-jên shu-hua, XVII. A Lady with a Looking-glass. Signed. Two lines of poetry dated 1814.

KU YÜAN 顧原, *t.* Fêng-yüan 逢源 and Hu-ch'êng 虎承.
From K'uai-chi, Chekiang. Active *c.*1720. Landscapes, flowers. R, XII, 18. M, p.741.

British Museum, No.263. The Poetry Competition at Lan-ting. Long handscroll. Signed, dated 1719.
Tokasha Shina Meigashū 26. A Man in a Pavilion under Trees after Rain. Poem by the painter.
National Museum, Stockholm. Mountain Landscape in Snow with Travellers. Ink and colours. Signed.

KU YÜN 顧澐, *t.* Jo-p'o 若波.
From Suchou. B. 1835, d. 1896. Went as an envoy to Japan *c.*1887. Landscapes, followed the Four Wang. M, p.747.

Shinchō 81. Landscape after Tung Yüan. Signed. Painted in Japan.
Nanga Taisei Add. IV, 241–248. Album of eight Landscapes, the last signed and dated 1890.
Tōan 79. Landscape after Wang Shih-min. Signed, dated 1895.
Ku Jo-p'o shan-shui chi-ts'ê (Yu-chêng Book co., 1926). An Album of fourteen Landscapes, mainly after the Four Wang.
Shina Meiga Senshū 47. A pair of pictures: Mountain Valley in Spring; Mountain Valley in Autumn. Poems by the painter.
Sōgen 368. Landscape after Hsi Kang. Album-leaf. Signed.
(See also Nanga Taisei, II, 101, 102 (Bamboo); XII, 219–230 (Album of twelve Landscapes); IV, 192 (Trees); X, 230–235; Add. IV, 151 (Landscapes).)

KUAN HSI-NING 管希寧, *t.* Yu-fu 幼孚, *h.* P'ing-yüan 平原 and Chin-niu shan-jên 金牛山人.
From Yang-chou, Kiangsu. Active *c.*1775. Scholar, seal-engraver and calligraphist. Figures, landscapes and flowers. M, p.604.

Ch'ing êrh-shih chia. Listening to the *Ch'in*, after Chou Fang. Handscroll. Signed, dated 1775.
Formerly C. B. Hoyt collect., Cambridge, Mass. An album of twelve small Landscape Sketches; two of them after Yüan masters, three of them with poems. Signed, dated 1785.
Fei-tun lu shan-shui, River Scenery with a Pavilion, after a Yüan master. Signed, dated 1785.

KUAN HUAI 關槐, *t.* Chin-hsien 晉軒.

From Hangchou. Chin-shih in 1789. Became a Han-lin member. Studied landscape-painting with Tung Kao. U, III, 1, 21. M, p.721.

Li-tai, VI. Bamboos and Plum-trees. Signed.

K.-k. shu-hua chi, XXVIII. Pine-trees, Bamboos and Plum-blossoms. Signed.

Ibid. XXIX. Snow-covered Mountains. Signed.

K'UN-TS'AN 髡殘, family name Liu 劉, *t.* Shih-ch'i 石谿, Chieh-ch'iu 介邱, *h.* Pai-t'u 白禿, Ts'an-tao-jên 殘道人 and other names.

From Wu-ling, Hunan. Active during main part of second half of seventeenth century. Entered in early age a Buddhist order of the Ch'an school; served later as abbot of the Niu-shou Monastery near Nanking. Painted landscapes. P, II, 8. Q, I, 3. R, XIV, 1, 3. U, I, 1, 8. M, p.496.

Chūgoku 7. A River Valley with Houses on the Shore; waterfalls descending from the surrounding hills. Signed and dated 1657.

Sōgen 228 (Yüan Shun-ch'u collect.) Terraced Mountains rising through the Clouds. Signed. Poem dated 1660.

Private collect., Peking (Photo). Cavernous Mountains and rushing Streams. Signed. Colophon dated 1660. *Cf.* Sirén, *Later*, pl.198.

Chung-kuo, II, 105. An Angler on a Mountain Stream. Poem, signed and dated 1660. Poem by Ch'êng Chêng-k'uei dated 1661. *Cf.* Shina Nanga, II, 2.

Sumitomo collect., Ōiso (formerly Oguri and Baron Fujita collections). Landscape with a Man in a House; a Crane flying Above. Long inscription by the artist, dated 1660. *Cf.* K. Sumitomo, V.

Chang Ta-ch'ien cat. I, 34. On the Way to the Summit of Huang-shan. Poem and inscription by the artist, dated 1660.

Gems, I, 62. A Temple in a misty Valley; a man in an open pavilion. Poem, signed and dated 1660.

Nanga Taisei, XI, 150. Two Men in a House by the River. Large album-leaf. Poem, signed and dated 1660.

Chūgoku, 7. A steeply-rising Ridge, with Waterfalls; buildings at its foot, others further up. Long inscription, signed and dated 1660.

Vannotti collect., Lugano. Houses in the Mountains. Fan-painting. Signed and dated 1660. *Cf.* Venice Exhib. cat. 246.

Liu 93. A River Valley with Mists drifting down from the Mountains; buildings on the shore; a man in a boat. Two inscriptions by the artist, one dated 1661.

National Museum, Stockholm. View of a Mountain River. Wisps of mist are driving down along the mountain towards the stream below where pavilions are built over the water; a sailing-boat on the river. Inscription, dated 1661. (In his manner.)

W. Hochstadter, N.Y., a Temple on a Mountain Ledge; a river below, with a fisherman. Inscription, signed and dated 1661. *Cf.* T'ien-ch'i shu-wu.

Shih-ch'i tao-jên mo-miao (Hakubundō album). Ten Landscape-studies, two of them with a meditating monk under the trees. Dated 1661.

I-shu ts'ung-pien, 13. Mist in the Mountain Crevices; a fisherman in a boat on the river below. Poem by the painter, dated 1662.

Chang Ta-ch'ien cat., IV, 33. Mountain Landscape, with an old man angling in a stream in the foreground. Long inscription by the painter dated 1662.

Shina Meiga Senshū 13 (Hashimoto collect.) High terraced Mountain, Buildings and scattered Trees; a monk in meditation in a pavilion. Poem by the painter, dated 1662.

Fei-tun lu shan-shui. Endless Mountains and Streams, rich Growth of Trees and Moss; a fisherman in a boat, wanderers on the road. Signed. Colophon dated 1662.

Private collect., Peking. Buddhist Monk seated in a Tree. Signed. Colophon dated 1662. *Cf.* Sirén, *Later*, pl.201.

Shên-chou ta-kuan, vol.8. River winding between Hills; misty atmosphere, old trees and cottages. Poem by the painter, dated 1663.

Shên-chou, X. High Mountains rising over a River; pavilion built over a stream. Inscription by the painter, dated 1663. *Cf.* Shina Nanga, II, 9; Shincho 23.

Chung-kuo ming-hua, 20. A tall, narrow landscape. Waterfalls within a cavern; a path leads to the foreground, following the stream. Inscription, dated 1663.

C. P. Huang, Taipei. Mountain Landscape. Colour on paper. Signed Shih-tao-jên and dated 1663 (winter).

Shanghai Museum. A narrow Path winding between the crevassed Rocks. The mist is sliding down the slope, enveloping the buildings; a crane is walking across a bridge over the stream. Long inscription by the painter, dated 1663. *Cf.* Gems, I, 63.

Liu 94. A Stream descending a Mountainside, with Houses built over it; a wood-gatherer crosses a bridge in the foreground. Long inscription by the artist, dated 1663.

Sekai Bijutsu Zenshū, 20, Pl.48. Landscape after Rain; a man in a house above the river. Inscription by the artist, dated 1663.

Sōraikan, II, 68. Mountain River between high Rocks; spare trees and pavilions along the shores. Two men in conversation, while a boat is approaching, another moored in a bay. Inscription by the painter, dated 1663. *Cf.* Ōmura, I, 7.

Shina Nanga, II, 12. A Man in a Cottage under leafless Trees. Indistinct reproduction. Doubtful Poem by the painter, dated 1663. *Cf.* Chung-kuo ming-hua 12.

Ibid. III, 12. Mountain Path in Mist and View over distant River. Poem by the painter, dated 1663. Indistinct reproduction.

Inoue collect., Tōkyō. Mountain landscape. A tall composition of a high wooded hump and circulating mist about leafy trees below. Partly in reddish colour. Inscription by the painter dated 1663.

Hui-hua kuan. A deeply crevassed Ravine with circling Mist and rushing Water. Slightly reddish tone. Inscription by the painter, dated 1664.

Sōgen 227 (K. Sumitomo). The Pao-ên Temple on a high Mountain Terrace above a wide River. Long descriptive colophon, dated 1664. *Cf.* K. Sumitomo, III. Another version in the possession of J. D. Ch'ên, Hongkong.

I-shu ts'ung-pien, 14. Tall Landscape, River winding through a mountainous Valley. Signed, dated 1665. *Cf.* Shina Nanga, III, 8.

Private collect., Peking. Mountain Landscapes in Snow. Two album-leaves painted for the Abbott of the T'ien-lung Monastery in 1665.

Chung-ku chai collect., Hongkong. Mountain Landscape with a Man playing the *Ch'in*. Signed, dated 1667.

Chūgoku 7. A River winding between steep Hills; a man in the foreground fishing. Poem, signed and dated 1667.

Ostasiat. Museum, Cologne. A Winding Mountain stream; leafy trees on the bare rocks. Inscription by the painter dated 1667.

Yamamoto collect., Tōkyō (formerly). Summer Pavilions at the Foot of misty Mountains. Signed, dated 1669. Poems by Ch'a Shih-piao, Hung-jên. Colophon by Tao-chi. *Cf.* Sirén, *Later*, pl.200.

Shên-chou, XII. Landscape. Signed. Poem, colophon dated 1670.

I-yüan chên-shang, 10. River Landscape; a man in a house built over the water. Long inscription, signed and dated 1670.

Nanga Taisei, XI, 151–160. An Album of ten leaves: Landscape Studies, Mountain Views, possibly from Huang-shan. Dated 1670.

Ōmura, I, 9. White Clouds and clear Streams. Signed, dated 1674.

Nanga Taisei, XI, 161. Landscape with a Pavilion. Large album-leaf. Signed, dated 1674.

Fogg Museum, Cambridge, Mass. Mountains with Buildings and rich Growth of Pines; a man in the open pavilion under a thatched roof. Signed. Poem dated 1674. *Cf.* Ming-hua sou-ch'i, I, 5; Nanga Taisei, vol.XI. (In his manner.)

Shên-chou album, 1923. Eight small Landscape-studies.

Chung-kuo, II, 104. A Row of straw-covered Pavilions along a Mountain Stream; a man fishing with a rod. Long colophon by the painter. *Cf.* Chung-kuo ming-hua, 25.

Shên-chou ta-kuan, vol.3. A Man meditating on a Mountain Terrace above a Waterfall; wisps of floating mist. Poem by the painter.

Ibid. 10. Seated Alone in a Pavilion by the Water. Poem, signed.

S.c.t.k. hsü-pien, III. Pavilion with two Men at the Foot of a rocky Hill where the Water is streaming down. Inscription by the painter.

I-shu ts'ung-pien, 23. High Hillocks grown with Shrubs; a man on a winding path which leads to a small temple. Signed.

Chung-kuo ming-hua 3. Wild Mountains enveloped in Mist and rich Growth of Pines. Poem by the painter.

Ibid. 27. A thickly wooded Mountain, in the manner of Huang Kung-wang. Inscription, signed.

Ming-jên shu-hua, IV. Mountain Landscape. Signed. Colophon.

Ibid. XXV. A Man reading in a Cottage in the Woods. Signed.

Ku-kung Handscroll (1935). Luxuriant Groves of Autumn-coloured Trees along a Mountain Path and around a Pavilion with three Men. Roughly dotted. Signed. Colophon by Ch'ien-lung. Doubtful.

Mo-ch'ao pi-chi, vol.II. Two Men on a Cliff by a Waterfall. Signed. Painted for his friend Ping. *Cf.* Nanga Taisei, vol.XI.

T'ai-shan ts'an-shih-lou ts'ang-hua, IV. Houses on the Shore at the Foot of Hills. Inscription, signed.

Fei-tun lu collect., Shanghai. Endless Streams and Mountains. Handscroll, signed. *Cf.* Sirén, *Later*, pl.202.

P'ang Yüan-chi illust. cat., II. Two Men seated on a Terrace, looking down into Mountain Stream; high pines and mists creeping along the valley.

Commercial Press Album, 1934. Landscape. Handscroll. Signed.

Liu 95. Houses in a Mountain Valley; pines in the foreground. Long inscription by the artist.

Nanking Exhib. cat. 281. Two Men seated on a Terrace watching a Waterfall. Inscription, signed.

Chou Li-yüan, 10. Willow beside a Lake; a fisherman in a boat. Album-leaf, signed.

Ibid. 12. Landscape after Wang Mêng. Signed.

Chang Ch'ün, Taipei. *Shan-kao shui-ch'ang*. Rugged Mountains and a winding misty Stream. Two men in a pavilion built over the water. According to the painter's inscription inspired by studies of Huang Shan. Poem and inscription by the painter.

Sumitomo collect., Ōiso. An Inlet of a Lake, with thatched Houses on its Shore. A fisherman in a boat; two other men at a window overlooking the water. Poem, signed. *Cf.* K. Sumitomo, III.

Ibid. Bodhidharma seated in Meditation, facing a Cliff. Short handscroll. Seal of the artist. Title and colophon by him mounted with the painting. *Cf.* Sōgen 229; K. Sumitomo III.

Ibid. Two Landscapes with Waterfalls. Leaves from an album. Inscriptions, signed. *Cf.* K. Sumitomo, V.

Chūgoku 7. A Mountain Gorge, spanned by a natural Stone Bridge; a man crossing it. Poem, signed.

Nanga Taikan 5. Man seated in a low Cottage under an overhanging Rock between spare Trees. Large album-leaf. Inscription by the painter.

Shina Nanga, I, 71. Mountains in Rain. Signed. Poem.

Tokasha Shina Meigashū 14. High Mountains in Snow. A man reading in a pavilion under pines by the river. Poem by the painter.

Tōan 37. A Man on a rocky Ledge looking at a Waterfall. Small album-leaf with poetic inscription by the painter.

Yūrintaikan, II. Rambling in the Mountains along a River. Hand-scroll. Signed. Imitation. Lo Chia-lun, Taipei. A Pair of large Landscapes, both inscribed.

Nanga Taisei, IV, Add. 45–48. Four Views of Rivers and Mountains. Horizontal compositions forming a series, painted, according to inscriptions, at the T'ien-kan shan-fang. *Cf.* Large hand-scroll with same motif in Stockholm.

National Museum, Stockholm. The Straits of a River between rocky Mountains spanned by a Stone Bridge. Poetic inscription by the painter. Large, short hand-scroll.

Ibid. A Hill rising out of a marshy Flatland. Buildings and boats; a lake above, with sailing ships. A small hand-scroll. Title and poem written by the artist, signed.

Chêng Tê-k'un, Cambridge. Mountain landscape with a man over a bridge. Inscription by the painter. Colophon by Ch'êng Chêng-k'uei.

T'ieh-mei hua-kuan collect., Hongkong. Landscape: T'ien-tu Mountain. Signed.

Museum of Eastern Art, Oxford. Richly wooded Mountain-landscape with abundant streams, hidden Temples, and mysterious Caverns. A man is crossing the river on a stone-bridge below. Inscription by the painter, dated *ping-tzŭ* (1696, a date that seems too late for K'un-ts'an).

KUNG HSIEN 龔賢, *t.* Pan-ch'ien 半千, *h.* Yeh-i 野遺.

From K'un-shan, Kiangsu; lived in Nanking. Active *c.*1660–1700. One of the "Eight Masters of Nanking". Landscapes, followed Wu Chên. P, II, 15. Q, I, 1. R, III, 5. U, I, 2, 10. M, p.749.

Nanking Exhib. cat. 264. A fantastic Mountain-landscape, with perpendicular Crags. Inscription, signed and dated 1655.

Chou Li-yüan, 7. Landscape with a Row of Trees in the foreground. Album-leaf. Seal of the artist, who on the opposite page wrote a long theoretical discussion of painting classification, dated 1669. *Cf.* Nanking Exhib. cat. 269.

Liu 97. The green Willow Village. Poem, signed and dated 1671.

Kung Pan-ch'ien shan-shui (Kyōto, 1919). Eleven double album-leaves representing Landscapes. Some after Sung masters (Mi Fei and others); some after Yüan masters (Ni Tsan and others). Colophon by the painter dated 1671. *Cf.* Shincho 27; Nanga Taisei Add. I, 62–71.

Kung Pan-ch'ien hsi-pi hua-ts'ê (Yu-chêng album, 1924). Ten Album-leaves with Landscape Studies, partly after old masters. Signed, dated 1671.

Ming-jên shu-hua, IV. River Landscape with Cliffs, Trees and Pavilions. Signed. Poem dated 1672.

Yūrintaikan, I. Landscape in gold and green, after Li Chao-tao. Colophon by the painter, dated 1672.

Pageant, 763. A Pavilion raised on Poles over a Stream, in a Forest of leafy Trees; misty mountains above. Poem, signed and dated 1673.

Commercial Press album, 1939. Album of twenty-four Landscapes, the last dated 1676.

C. T. Loo's Successor, Frank Caro, N.Y. An Album of Landscapes. Signed and dated 1678. *Cf.* Cleveland Exhib. cat. 101; Toronto 53.

Yamaguchi collect., Ashiya. River Landscape, with Pavilions and a Stone Bridge. Inscription by the artist; also title written by him, dated 1679.

J. P. Dubosc, Lugano. A Mountain Retreat surrounded by tall leafy Trees. Handscroll. Inscription by the painter. Signed, dated 1679.

Album published by Kobayashi, Kyōto, 1919. Eight landscapes; the last signed and dated 1681. Colophon by Ch'a Shih-piao.

Sōraikan, I, 45. A leaf from an album of nine Landscapes. Signed. Colophon dated 1683.

Ming-jên shu-hua, III. A misty Valley. Signed, dated 1684. *Cf.* Nanga Taikan 1.

Kokka 379. Landscape. Signed. Poem dated 1686.

Ibid. 636. Landscape with bare Trees. Poem, signed and dated 1686.

Yen-kuang co., Photos. Sixteen Landscape-studies with poems and colophons by the painter, dated 1688. *Cf.* Nanga Taisei, XIV, 85–100.

Honolulu Academy of Art. Landscape with Buildings on the slope of a Mountain, in the manner of Chü-jan. Long inscription by the artist (on painting theory), dated 1689.

Shên-chou, II. Mountain Cottage by a Stream spanned by a Bridge. Signed. Poem.

Ibid. XI. Pavilions at the Foot of a Mountain enveloped in Mist. Signed. Two lines of poetry.

Ibid. XVII. A Stream in a deep Gully, an open Pavilion on a Terrace in the foreground. Signed.

Shên-chou ta-kuan, vol.5. River View after Ni Tsan. Colophon by the painter.

S.c.t.k. hsü-pien, IV. A Thicket of bare Plum-trees on a frosty Day.

Ibid. VII. Bare Trees on a Stone by the River-shore. Album-leaf.

Chin-ling p'ai ming-hua chi (Shên-chou album, 1924). Landscapes. Two lines of poetry. Seal of the painter.

Ming-jên shu-hua, XXVI. Streams and Wooded Hills. Signed. Poem.

Commercial Press album, 1935. Book of Sketches for Students of Painting. Twenty leaves with explanatory notes. (Also published in Japan by Ōmura, and in Nanga Taisei, Add. III, 244–263. A similar instructional album published as part of the T'ai-shan ts'an-shih-lou series; *cf.* Nanga Taisei, Add. III, 234–243.)

Mei-chan t'ê-k'an 38. A Grove of bare Trees. Poem by the painter.

I-shu ts'ung-pien 13. Mountain Landscape; cottage in the ravine, large trees in the foreground. Poem by the painter.

Ibid. 15. Sparse Trees on a River Shore and low Huts. Poem by the painter. Fan-painting.

T'ai-shan ts'an-shih lou ts'ang-hua, vol.II. A low Pavilion and three tall Trees at the Foot of terraced Mountains. Signed.
Wên-ming album, 1909. Twelve Landscapes. Signed; colophon, in which the artist states that he painted them at an early age.
Chang Ts'ung-yü cat. An Album of Landscape-studies.
Hui-hua kuan. Massed Mountains, sweeping Mist and Clumps of Trees. Long handscroll. Signed.
Ibid. Misty Rocks by a River, a Temple on the Peak. Ink and bluish colour. Handscroll.
Ibid. Massed Hills along a River; pavilion between dry shrubs. Ink and bluish colour. Handscroll. Signed.
Liu 96. The Yo-yang Tower. A broad vista of open water. Inscription by the artist.
Gems, I, 57. Mountain Ranges and Trees in Mist. Signed.
I-shu ch'uan-t'ung 11. A River Landscape with bare Trees. Album-leaf.
C. P. Huang, Taipei. A fantastic design: Entrance to a Cave, and in front of it, a bare shrub. Inscriptions by the painter, and by eight of his friends, Tao-chi, Ch'a Shih-piao, Sung Ts'ao, Hsiao Ch'ên, Kao Ts'ai, Cho Êrh-k'an, Huang Ku'ei and Min Ling-ssŭ.
Sumitomo collect., Ōiso. A cloudy Landscape. Long handscroll. Inscription by the artist mounted after the painting.
Ibid. Album of eight Landscapes, the last with touches of reddish colour. Poem and signature of the artist on a ninth leaf. *Cf.* Sekai Bijutsu Zenshū, XX, Pl.52 and Kokka 732.
Kurokawa cat. 13. Lao-tzŭ riding an Ox. Inscription, signed.
T. Moriya collect., Kyōto. A large Landscape, with Pine-trees around a House. Painted on silk. Poem, signed.
Ibid. Rocks and Water on gold ground. Fan-shaped.
Yamaguchi collect., Ashiya. Promontory with Building and Trees. Short handscroll. Poetic inscription by the painter.
Private collect., Kyōto. A Winter Landscape, with bare Trees. Album-leaf. Poem, signed. Other leaves from the same album in various Kyōto collections.
Chūgoku 7. Buildings and Trees by a River. Sketchily-drawn landscape. Poem, signed. In an album containing works of the eight Nanking masters.
Nanga Taisei, VIII, 133–135. Landscapes. Fan-paintings.
Ibid. XI, 163, 164. Two Landscapes. Album-leaves. Signed.
Shimbi, XVIII. Landscape. Signed. Poem.
Nanju 5. Mountains in Summer after Rain. Signed. Poem. *Cf.* Pageant 764.
Ibid. 5. Mountains with Pavilions in Autumn. Signed. Poem. *Cf.* Pageant 764.
Ibid. 18. A Study at the Foot of a Cliff. Signed. Poem.
Ibid. 24 (Horiuchi collect., Ōsaka). Two Cottages in a misty Gorge. Signed. Poem. Also in Kyuka, II.
Ibid. 25. Straw-covered Pavilions on Wooded Mountains enveloped in Clouds. Signed. Poem.
Kokka 571 (Z. Fujii, Kyōto). Landscape.
Ibid. 636 (T. Ogura, Tōkyō). Landscape.
Bijutsu, XVIII. Mountains and Winding Streams. Signed.
Tōyō, XII. Bare Trees. Signed. Colophon.
Shina Nanga, I, 83. Mountain Landscape with a Pavilion. Signed.
Ibid. III, 1. Cottages in the Mountains. Poem by the painter. Signed. *Cf.* Shên-chou, XIII; Tōan 42.
Ibid. III, 6. Rugged cloudy Mountains. Signed. Also in Tōsō 419.
Kyūka, II. Bare Willows by a River, after Li Liu-fang. Signed.
Ibid. II. Bare Trees by a Stream. Album-leaf. Seal of the painter.
Shina Meiga Senshū 20. Two tall Pine-trees by a Cliff. Signed.
Ibid. 21. Houses among bare Shrubs by a Mountain Stream in Moonlight. Poem by the painter.
Sōgen 322. Wooded Hills. Signed. Album-leaf.
National Museum, Tōkyō. Mountains rising through Clouds; buildings on a terrace amidst leafy trees. Large design. Long inscriptions.
Nelson Gallery, Kansas City. Mountains and Trees along a River. Long handscroll. Colophon by Lo Chên-yü.
Toronto cat., 52 (R. W. Finlayson, Toronto). Scenery of Mt. Chü-ch'ü. Inscription, signed.
Los Angeles County Museum. Pointed Hills rising through the Clouds; tall trees below. Signed.
Chicago Art Institute. River and Mountains. Handscroll. Signed.
C. T. Loo's Successor, Frank Caro, N.Y. Houses on the Shore of a River. Inscription, signed. *Cf.* Venice Exhib. cat. 248.

National Museum, Stockholm. Thatched Cottages on Wooded Mountains. Inscription by the painter.

Ibid. Four Album-leaves. River landscapes with driving mist, cottages and tall trees. Seals of the painter.

Hamburg Exhibition, 1949–1950. Landscape: View of Ch'i-hsia shan near Nanking.

Musée Guimet, Paris. Album of Eight Landscapes. Inscriptions, signed. A similar album, but with ten leaves, published by Shên-chou Kuo-Kuang shê, 1909.

T. T. Ma, Hongkong. Large Mountain Landscape; a man reading in a cottage under the trees.

Shêng P'ing-ch'ên, Hongkong. Landscape. Signed.

Lo Chia-lun, Taipei. A large Mountain Landscape with Buildings. Inscription, signed.

Hashimoto collect., Kyōto. Tall Pine-trees and Rocks. Signed.

W. Hochstadter, New York. A Homestead in the Mountains. Straw-covered cottages along the winding stream. Poem by the painter.

Ibid. Fantastic Mountain View under heavy Clouds. A short scroll. Signed Yeh-i-shêng Kung Hsien.

H. C. Wêng, Scarsdale, N.Y. River Landscape, ink on paper. Album-leaf. Inscription by the painter. *Cf.* Cat. Exhibition of the Chinese Art Society, New York, March 1955, No. 1.

R. B. Hobart collect., Cambridge, Mass. Album with six landscape-paintings. Ink on paper. *Cf.* Cat. Exhibition of the Chinese Art Society, New York, March 1955, No. 8.

Ibid. Marshy Landscape. Album leaf. *Cf.* Cat. of the Chinese Art Society, New York, March 1955, No. 9, pl. 4.

J. P. Dubosc, Lugano. Landscape. Fan-painting. Signed with the painter's seal.

Vannotti, collect. Lugano. Shrubs and Trees bending over a thatched Pavilion. Fan-painting; poem by the painter.

KUO CHING-YEN 郭璟燕, *t.* Tzŭ-ch'ao 紫超.

From Ch'üan-chiao, Anhui. Lived at the end of the 18th century. Calligraphist. Landscapes and plum-blossoms. M, p.400.

Sung-pê. Two Pine-trees. Signed, dated 1798. *Cf.* Nanga Taisei, V, 40.

KUO WAN 郭完.

Unrecorded. Probably early Ch'ing period. Seal reads *t.* Chü-hsiung 巨雄.

Nanju 16. Two Landscapes, one after Mi Fei, the other after Wu Chên. Both signed and dated *chia-wu* (1654?) Also in Tōyō, XII.

KUO YING-CHUNG 郭應中, *t.* Ho-t'ien 荷田, *h.* I-hsiao tao-jên 一笑道人. Unrecorded.

C. B. Hoyt collect., Cambridge, Mass. An Egg-plant and two Radishes. Album-leaf. Signed.

LAN MÊNG 藍孟, *t.* Tz'ŭ-kung 次公 and I-yü 亦輿.

Son of Lan Ying. Active *c.*1680. Landscapes. R, VI, 24. M, p.709.

N. Gashū 17. Landscape with a Pavilion and a Pagoda. Signed. Poem dated 1686.

Nanju 20. A Fisherman's Hermit, after Ma Yüan. Signed.

Ibid. 20. A Fisherman's Hermit, after Chao Mêng-fu. Signed. Also in Tōyō, XI.

Bijutsu, IX. Mountains in Snow. Signed.

Tōsō 388. Poet in the Mountains in Autumn, after Han Huang. Signed.

LAN SHÊN 藍深, *t.* Hsieh-ch'ing 謝青.
Son of Lan Mêng. R, VI, 23. M, p.709.

Shinchō 33. Mountain Landscape with blossoming Trees and white Clouds. After Chang Sêng-yu. Signed. Colophon.

Private collect., Kyōto. A Lotus Pond in Summer, after Chao Ling-jang. Signed.

LAN T'AO 藍濤.
Son of Lan Mêng. Flowers and trees. R, VI, 24. M, p.709.

Bijutsu, XXIV (Hashimoto collect., Takatsuki). Magnolias and Tree-peonies by a Rockery. Signed, dated 1739. Also in Kyūka, I.

LANG SHIH-NING 郎世寧 or Giuseppe Castiglione.
An Italian. B. 1688, d. 1768 in Peking. Came to China in 1715, served as a painter in the Palace, chiefly in the Ch'ien-lung period. Famous particularly for his pictures of horses. Q, II, 1. M, p.306. Notes in *Lang Shih-ning hua.*

Ku-kung, XXXII. Pine-trees, Bamboos and Plum-blossoms. Fan-painting. Signed. Inscription by the emperor Yung-chêng, dated 1724.
Sōgen 326. Auspicious Plants in a Vase. Signed, dated 1726.
Chung-kuo, II. An Antelope. Signed, dated 1726. Also in Sōgen 327.
Lang shih-ning hua, vol.IV, published 1936. Fifteen sections of the scroll known as The Hundred Horses. Dated 1728. Also published by the Yen Kuang Co., Peking.
Lin Nan-hai, Kōbe. A Lioness and her Cubs on a Mountain Ledge. Signed and dated 1738.
Tōsō 422. The Emperor Ch'ien-lung inspecting Horses in a Field in Spring. Handscroll. Signed, dated 1744. Inscription by Ch'ien-lung. Also in Yūrintaikan, II; partly in Bijutsu Kenkyū 10 and Sekai Bijutsu Zenshū, XX, coloured pl.4.
Ku-kung, XXXI. Three Sheep. Signed, dated 1746.
British Museum (Add. No.7). An Imperial Prince and Tartar Huntsmen. Signed, dated 1763.
Hui-hua kuan. Flowers in bright Colours. Album-leaves.
I-shu ts'ung-pien 8. A young Woman with a Child in her Arms. Another running in front of her.
Ibid. 10. Market by the River outside Canton.
Ibid. 10. Tiger seated under a Tree.
Chung-kuo, II, 122. A Tiger.
Ibid. II, 123. White Eagle on a Cliff. Also in Li-tai, II, and in Lang Shih-ning hua, vol.I.
Ibid. II, 124. Flowers by a Rockery.
Ku-kung, II. The Emperor Ch'ien-lung examining Antiquities. Signed.
Ibid. II. Landscape in Mist. Signed. Also in Lang Shih-ning hua.
Ibid. XIV. Eight Horses on the River-shore. Signed. Poem by Ch'ien-lung. Also in Lang Shih-ning hua, vol.I.
Lang Shih-ning hua, vols.I, II, published by the Palace Museum, 1931. Forty-seven pictures of Flowers, Birds and Animals.
Ibid. vol.III, published 1936. Sixteen pictures of Flowers and Birds.
Ibid. vol.V, published 1935. Four pictures of Flowers and Birds and seven Portraits of the Emperor Ch'ien-lung.
Shih-chün t'u, published by the Palace Museum, 1935. Ten Pictures of Horses; only five executed by Lang Shih-ning.
Kokka 260. Two Monkeys. Signed.
Ibid. 357. Flowers and Birds, painted together with T'ang Tai.
Ibid. 615 (S. Sakai, Tōkyō). A Pair of Steeds by a Willow.
Shinchō 45. Huntsmen in the Woods. Handscroll. Signed.

Tōsō 420. A Hsi-ling Dog in the Shade of Bamboos.
Ibid. 421. Two Cranes by an old Pine.
Ibid. 423. Tending Horses in a Meadow. Handscroll.
Sōraikan, I, 60. A Tiger.
Sōgen 328. Hundred Birds saluting the Fêng-bird.
Yūrintaikan, I. A Sage seated under Pines.
Bijutsu Kenkyū 10. Hundred Horses on Pasture. Two sections of the scroll in the Palace Museum.
Musée Guimet, Paris. Emperor Ch'ien-lung examining the Qazaq Horses.
Ibid. Illustrations to the Travels of the Emperor Ch'ien-lung. Four long handscrolls, painted by the painter together with Chin K'un, Ting Kuan-p'êng, Ch'êng Chih-tao, and Li Hui-lin.
Robert Rousset, Paris. A She-dog under Bamboos and winding Cucumber-plants. Signed.
Ho Kuan-wu, Hongkong. Portrait of the Emperor Kao-tsung. Signed.

LAO CHÊNG 勞澂, *t.* Tsai-tzŭ 在玆, *h.* Lin-wu shan-jên 林屋山人.
Native of Ch'ang-chou in Kiangsu; spent his last years in the mountains near Lake Tung-t'ing. Landscapes. U, II, 1, 14. M, p.499.

Liu 125. Landscape after Tung Yüan. Signed.

LÊNG MEI 冷枚, *t.* Chi-ch'ên 吉臣, *h.* Chin-mên hua-shih 金門畫史.
From Chiao-chou, Shantung. Active during the first half of the 18th century. Pupil of Chiao Ping-chên. In 1713, he took part in making the pictures of the ceremonies on the occasion of the emperor's 60th birthday. Q, I, 2. R, X, 7. S. U, III, I, 9. M, p.114.

Li-tai, I. Two Hares under a Wu-t'ung Tree. Signed. *Cf.* K-k. chou-k'an, vol.III, 70. *Cf.* Chung-kuo ming-hua, 40.
K-k. chou-k'an 407–426. Album of twenty pictures of Arhats, the last signed.
Ars Asiatica, IX, pl.LXIII, 2. A Lady at a Door looking out on the Garden. Long handscroll. Signed. Poem.
British Museum. Portrait of a Lady. Seals of the painter. Formerly attributed to Hsü Fang. *Cf.* Ars Asiatica, IX, pl.LV.
Ibid. (Add. No. 21). An Official in his Garden Study. Signed.
Boston Museum. A Lady with her four Children and two Attendants.
Ibid. A Lady walking on a Garden Terrace. Signed. *Cf.* Kokka 383.
Ibid. A Girl playing the Flute to a Lady. *Cf.* Sirén, *Later*, pl.169.
Private collect., Peking. Li T'ieh-kuai at a Mountain Stream. Signed. *Cf.* Sirén, *Later*, pl.168b.

LI CHIEN 黎簡, *t.* Chien-min 簡民 and Wei-ts'ai 未裁, *h.* Êrh-ch'iao 二樵.
From Shun-tê, Kuangtung. Chü-jên in 1789. Landscapes. T, VII, 6. U, III, 2, 3. M, p.630.

Chūgoku 8. Landscape, with a solitary Figure gazing over the Water. Long inscription, signed and dated 1778.
Chung-kuo, II, 126. A Pavilion among Trees by a Stream. Signed, dated 1781. *Cf.* Chung-kuo ming-hua, 34.
Shên-chou, XVII. River Scenery with two Sailing-boats in the Distance. Signed, dated 1781. Also in Shina Nanga, I, 118.
Kyūka, II. A Poet on Donkey-back. Album-leaf. Signed, dated 1784.
Chung-kuo ming-hua, 23. A Man seated on a Rock on a Terrace. After a Sung Master. Signed and dated 1785.
Shên-chou ta-kuan, vol.5. Two Men seated in a Pavilion under large Trees by a Stream. Colophon dated 1786.
Shên-chou, VIII. Mountains in Summer before Rain, after Huang Kung-wang. Signed, dated 1790. Also in Mo-ch'ao pi-chi, vol.I.
I-yüan chên-shang 4. A Monk seated on a Cliff, under sparse Bamboo. After Wang Mêng. Signed and dated 1792.

Li Chih 李致.
Unrecorded. Probably a court-painter in the Ch'ien-lung period.

Li-tai, III. Winter Flowers. Signed.
Ibid. VI. Flowers and Birds. Signed.

Li Fan 李蕃, *t.* Su-fu 素夫 and Chieh-jên 介人.
From Hua-t'ing, Kiangsu. Active *c.*1720. Landscapes. M, p.201.

Shên-chou, XIV. Two Men under a Tree on the River Shore. Signed, dated 1724.
Kokka 383. A Man in a Boat in the Mountains. Signed. Also in N. Gashū 20.

Li Fang-ying 李方膺, *t.* Ch'iu-chung 虬仲, *h.* Ch'ing-chiang 晴江 and Ch'iu-ch'ih 秋池.
From T'ung-chou, Kiangsu. B. 1695, d. 1754. Famous for his pictures of pine-trees, bamboos, epidendrums and chrysanthemums in the *hsieh-i* manner. Q, II, 1. R, XI, 10. U, III, I, 1, M, p.205.

Robert Rousset, Paris. A Stag. Signed, dated 1742.
Gems, II, 21. Flowering Plum-trees. Handscroll. Signed and dated 1743.
T'ai-shan ts'an-shih-lou ts'ang-hua, vol.II. Chung K'uei holding an Umbrella. Poem by the painter, dated 1745. *Cf.* Nanga Taisei, VII, 134.
Ibid. vol.II. Fishes in Water. Poem by the painter, dated 1746. *Cf.* Nanga Taisei, VI, 170.
Yamaguchi collect., Ashiya. A Branch of flowering Plum. Two lines of poetry, signed and dated 1746. *Cf.* Suchiku 25.
T. Moriya collect., Tōkyō. Pine growing from a Rock. Signed and dated 1746.
Tokasha Shina Meigashū 95. Branches of a Pine-tree. Signed, dated 1747. *Cf.* Nanga Taisei, V, 33.
Yamaguchi collect., Ashiya. Flowers growing beside a Rock. Signed and dated 1749.
Yu-chêng album, n.d. Six Flower-paintings, hanging scrolls. Inscriptions, two dated 1752.
Nanga Taisei, I, 164, 1. Orchids growing from Rocks. Poem, signed and dated 1752. See also Ibid. V, 181, r; Lotus, also dated 1752.
Ibid. I, 165–176. An album of paintings of Orchids. Signed and dated 1754.
Hamburg Exhibition, 1949–1950. Branches of an old Plum-tree in Bloom. Poem by the painter, dated 1754.
Po-mei chi. Blossoming Plum-trees. Handscroll. Signed and dated 1755. *Cf.* Nanga Taisei, III, 136.
Hui-hua kuan. Bamboo Studies. Long inscription.
Ibid. Bamboo Studies. Six album-leaves.
Private collect., Tōkyō. Album of Bamboo-paintings. Signed. Colophon by Cheng Hsieh.
Nanga Taisei, IV, 110–111; V, 34. Five Paintings of flowering Bushes, Trees and Rocks.
Hobart collect., Cambridge, Mass. Branches of old Plum-trees. Two album-leaves. Poems by the painter.
T. T. Ma, Hongkong. Cabbage Plants and tall flowering Reeds. Inscription by the painter.

Li Hsi-t'ai 李熙泰.
Unrecorded. A seal on the picture reads *t.* Hsiao-tung 曉東. Probably Ch'ing period.

Tōyō, XII. Mountain Landscape, after Wang Mêng. Signed.
K. Sumitomo collect., Ōiso. Landscape of steep Mountain. Slightly coloured. Signed.

Li Hsiao 李孝.
From Wu-wei-chou, Anhui. Early Ch'ing period. Birds. M, p.204.

Nanju 12. Cock and Hen under a Wu-t'ung Tree.

LI HSIU-I 李修易, *t.* Tzû-chien 子健, *h.* Ch'ien-chai 乾齋.
From Hai-yen, Chekiang. 18th century. Landscapes, flowers. T, Add. I, 9. M, p.209.

Ming-jên shu-hua, XII. Narcissi and Bamboos by a Rockery. Signed. Poem.

Nanga Taisei, XII, 195. Landscape after Wu Chên. Album-leaf. Signed.

LI K'UN 李崑, *t.* Liang-yeh 梁野, *h.* Po-lung shan-jên 白龍山人.
From Hua-t'ing, Kiangsu. Landscapes, figures. Active *c.*1784(?) M, p.210.

British Museum (Add. No.70). Album of Flower Studies, done with hot stylus. Signed. Poem dated 1784(?)

LI O-SHÊNG 李萼生.
From Chiang-tu, Kiangsu. Birds and flowers.

S.c.t.k. hsü-pien, XI. Camellias. Signed.

LI PING-SHOU 李秉綬, *t.* Yün-fu 芸甫, *h.* P'ei-chih 佩之, Chu-p'ing 竹坪.
From Ling-ch'uan, Kiangsi; lived in Kuei-lin, Kwangsi. Calligraphist. Plum blossoms, bamboos and flowers. T. M, p.208.

Sung-pê. Pine-trees. Signed, dated *hsin-mao*. *Cf.* Nanga Taisei, V, 46.

LI, PRINCE 禮親王. A member of the imperial family at the time of K'ang-hsi.

Ming-jên shu-hua, XIII. A Boat sailing Homeward. Signed, dated 1730. Poem dated 1732.

LI SAN-WEI 李三畏, *t.* Chi-liu 吉六, *h.* Po-fu 柏阜.
From Ch'ung-ming, Kiangsu. 18th century. Bamboos, landscapes and flowers. M, p.205.

Ming-jên shu-hua, XII. Chrysanthemums in a Vase. Signed. Poem.

LI SHAN 李鱓, *t.* Tsung-yang 宗揚, *h.* Fu-t'ang 復堂 and other names.
From Yang-chou, Kiangsu. Chü-jên in 1711, d. after 1754. Flowers and birds; influenced by Lin Liang and Kao Ch'i-p'ei. Q, I, 3. R, X, 9. T, I, 2. U, I, 3, 12. M, p.204.

Hui-hua kuan. An old Pine-tree and Climbing Plants. Dated 1730.

Tokasha Shina Meigashū 76. A Pine-tree and T'ien-chu Shrubs by a Rock. Poem by the painter, dated 1731.

Chung-hua album, 1934. Eight Pictures of Birds, Flowers and Insects. Signed, dated 1736. *Cf.* Nanga Taisei, Add. IV, 195–206.

Yamaguchi collect., Ashiya. Album of Paintings of Flowers and other Subjects. Signed, one dated 1736.

T'ai-shan album, series I. Eight paintings: Landscapes, Flowers, etc. Signed, several dated 1740.

Kurokawa cat. 30, 31. Album of twelve Flower-paintings (four reproduced), all with inscriptions, several dated 1740. One leaf in Shinchō, 57.

Sekai Bijutsu Zenshū, XX, colour Pl.7. Peonies growing beside Rocks. Poem, signed and dated 1741.

Shên-chou, XVI. A blossoming Plum-tree, Bamboos and Epidendrums by Rocks. Signed, dated 1744.

Fei-tun lu hua-hui. Plum Blossoms, Orchids, Bamboos and Rocks. Handscroll. Signed, dated 1744.
Sirén collect. A climbing Plant of Gourds and hanging Cucumbers. Signed and dated 1744.
Kurokawa cat. 29. Bamboo growing beside a Rock. Poem, signed and dated 1745.
Private collect., Kyōto. Album of Paintings of Flowers, Bamboo, etc. Signed, the last dated 1746.
Pageant 912. A Peony Flower in a Vase; two Fishes. Signed. Poem dated 1748.
Yamaguchi collect., Ashiya. Two tall Plants growing from Rockery. Signed and dated 1749.
National Museum, Stockholm. Narcissus and Olea. Signed, dated 1749.
Tokasha Shina Meigashū 77. Banana-trees and a Bamboo by a Rock. The bamboo and a poem by Chêng Hsieh. Dated by Li Shan 1750.
Shên-chou, IX. Peonies and Orchids on a Rock. Signed. Poem dated 1752.
Shina Nanga, II, 11. Birds in Wu-t'ung Trees. Signed. Poem dated 1753.
Ibid. III, 6. Peonies and Orchids. Signed. Poem dated 1753.
Ming-jên shu-hua, XXVI. Two Squirrels in a Pine-tree. Signed. Poem, dated 1753.
S.c.t.k. hsü-pien, IX. Lotus. Signed, dated 1754.
Sung-pê. A Pine-tree, Mutan and Orchids. Signed. Poem, dated 1754.
Ibid. A Pine-tree and a blossoming Shrub. Signed, dated 1754.
Gems, I, 80. Spring Flowers. Poem, signed and dated 1754.
Tokasha Shina Meigashū 75. Two Magpies in a blossoming Plum-tree. Poems by the painter, dated 1755.
Li Fu-t'ang hsieh-shêng ts'ê (Yu-chêng album, 1922). An Album of ten pictures of Trees and Flowers. Inscription by the painter.
S.c.t.k. hsü-pien, II. Small Birds in a blossoming Tree. Mutan-flowers and small plant in a rockery.
Mei-chan t'ê-k'an 63. A Branch of a blossoming Plum-tree. Poem by the painter.
Chung-kuo ming-hua, 25. Sailing-boats on a misty River. Signed.
Ming-jên shu-hua, II. Chrysanthemums in a Pot. Signed. Poem. *Cf.* Shina Nanga, III, 1.
Ibid. III. Trees on flooded Ground. Signed (on a stone). *Cf.* Shina Nanga, III, 10.
Po-mei chi. A Spray of Plum Blossoms and a Teapot. Album-leaf. Signed.
Hui-hua kuan. Flower Studies. Six album-leaves.
Shina Nanga, I, 76. Crabs. Signed. Two lines of a T'ang poem.
Ibid. I, 77. A Lotus-plant. Signed.
Ibid. I, 78. Cicadas on a Branch of Willow. Signed. Two lines of poetry.
Ibid. II, 2. Hollyhocks. Signed. Poem.
Ibid. III, 8. Peonies and Orchids in Wind. Signed. Poem.
Kokka 722. Banana-palm and bamboo; orchids. Two leaves from an album. Signed. *Cf.* Sekai Bijutsu Zenshū, XX, pl.59.
Tokasha Shina Meigashū 74. Peony and Epidendrum Flowers by a Rockery. Poem by the painter.
Sōraikan, I, 58. A Lotus-plant. Signed. Poem.
T. Moriya collect., Kyōto. Bamboo and an old Tree. Poem by the artist, signed. Colophon by Chêng Hsieh, in which he states that the painting was done when Li was 60.
Musée Guimet, Paris. Section of an old blossoming Plum-tree. Signed. Poem by Lin Ho-ching, copied by the painter.
Peter C. Swann, Oxford. Album of ten leaves: Flowering Plants, Trees and Stones. Inscriptions by the painter.
National Museum, Stockholm. An old Tree Trunk. Signed. Poem.
(See also Nanga Taisei, I, 151, 152; II, 242 (Bamboo and Orchids); II, 178, 179, 243 (Chrysanthemums); III, 124, 125 (Plum); IV, 118–122; V, 105–107, 128 (Flowers); V, 29–32; Add. IV, 94, 95 (Trees); V, 142 (Banana-palm); V, 174–176 (Lotus); V, 221 (Vegetables); VI, 147–152; Add. IV, 93 (Birds and Insects); XII, 79–84 (Landscapes); XIV, 122 (Fish).)

LI SHIH-CHO 李世倬, *t.* Han-chang 漢章, *h.* Ku-chai 穀齋, Ch'ing-tsai chü-shih 清在居士 and other names. From San-han, Southern Korea. Court-painter *c.*1750. Studied landscape-painting with Wang Hui and Ma I 馬逸. In figure painting he followed Wu Tao-tzŭ, in flowers and birds his uncle Kao Ch'i-p'ei. Q, I, 3. R, XI, 20. T, I, 3. U, II, 2, 25. M, p.205.

I-shu ts'ung-pien 8. Winding River, sparse Trees and steep Cliffs; a man crossing the bridge. After Mo Shih-lung. Signed, dated 1747.

Ming-jên shu-hua, XIX. An Album of eight pictures of Animals, Birds and Flowers. Signed. Last one dated 1747.

Shên-chou, IX. Mountain Landscape, after Wu Chên. Signed, dated 1750.

Ibid. I. Two Fishermen seated under a Willow by a Bridge. Signed.

Ibid. I. A Man on a Hillock looking at a Waterfall. Signed. Two lines of poetry.

Chung-kuo ming-hua 10. Friends celebrating the New Year in a Pavilion in a Mountain Gorge. Poem by Ch'ien-lung. *Cf.* Shincho 50.

Chung-hua album, 1929. Eight Landscapes. Signed.

Ming-jên shu-hua, XXIV. Streams in a wooded Mountain. Colophon by the painter.

Ibid. XXVI. Landscape, illustrating a poem by Su Tung-p'o. Signed. *Cf.* Ming-hua sou-ch'i, II, 6.

I-yüan album. Studies of Horses. Six album-leaves. *Cf.* Nanga Taisei, Add. IV, 190–194.

K.-k. shu-hua chi, IX. The Tui-sung Mountain (a part of T'ai-shan). Signed. Poem by Ch'ien-lung.

Ibid. XXVIII. The Kao-t'u Temple on the Western Hills, Peking. Signed. Poem by Ch'ien-lung.
(See also K.-k. chou-k'an, Index, for various works by this artist.)

Fei-tun lu shan-shui. Mountain Landscape; waterfall and figures below. After Ching Hao. Signed.

Pao-yün, II. A River Landscape, Buildings on the Shore. Poem, signed.

Po-mei chi. A blossoming Plum-tree. Album-leaf. Signed. Poem.

Ku-kung collect. Landscape in the manner of Ni Tsan. Leaf from an album. Inscription, signed. *Cf.* Nanking Exhib. cat. 370.

Shên-chou album, 1908. Landscapes, the last signed.

I-yüan chên-shang 9. A Winter Landscape. Signed.

Sumitomo collect., Ōiso. Album of Landscapes, some in colour, others in ink only. Signed.

Shina Nanga, II, 4. The four hoary old Men of Shang-shan. Fan-painting. Signed.

Ibid. II, 6. A Donkey-rider. Signed.

Tokasha Shina Meigashū 68. A Cock and Chrysanthemum-flowers. Finger-painting. Signed.

Ibid. 69. Winter Landscape, a Man herding two Water-buffaloes. Signed.

Ōmura, I, 7. Pavilion and Pine-trees, after Ni Tsan. Signed.

Sōgen, p.277. Steep Hills and three old Pine-trees. A man on the bridge leading over the broad river. Poem. Signed.

J. D. Ch'ên, Hongkong. An Album of Paintings of Landscapes, Animals, Shrimps, etc. Signed.

Field Museum, Chicago. The Red Cliff. Illustration to Su Tung-p'o's poem.

Cleveland Museum of Art. A Waterfall over steep Cliffs; figures below. Inscription by the painter. *Cf.* I-yüan chên-shang 3.

Hobart collection, Cambridge, Mass. Tall Pines at the Foot of a grassy Slope and some Rocks. Inscription by the painter.

LI YIN 李因, *t.* Chin-shêng 今生, *h.* Shih-an 是菴 and K'an-shan nü-shih 龕山女史.
From K'uai-chi, Chekiang. B. *c.*1610, d. 1685. Wife of the painter Ko Chêng-ch'i. Flowers and birds in the style of Ch'ên Shun. Q, I, 3. N, V, 8. M, p.201.

Nanju 18. Wild Geese among Reeds. Signed, dated 1633.

LI YIN 李寅, *t.* Po-yeh 白也.
From Yang-chou, Kiangsu. Active *c.*1700. Landscapes in the styles of the T'ang and Sung masters. Rival of Hsiao Ch'ên. U, III, 1, 8. M, p.207.

S.c.t.k. hsü-pien, VIII. Landscape. Signed and dated 1695.

C. T. Loo's Successor, Frank Caro, N.Y. An imaginative Landscape, executed in a painstaking manner with fine detail. Ink and colour on silk. Poem and inscription by the painter, dated 1698. *Cf.* Toronto, 58.

Kokka 319. Landscape. Signed. Poem, colophon, dated 1705.

Sōgen 334. River Landscape in Snow with Travellers, after Kuo Hsi. Signed. Colophon.

LI YÜ 李育, *t.* Mei-shêng 梅生, *h.* Chu-hsi 竹西.
From Yangchou, Kiangsu. Active *c.*1820. Flowers, trees and stones. M, p.208.

Shên-chou, IX. A Taoist seated in a Cave, after a Yüan master. Signed, dated 1820.
Ming-jên shu-hua, XV. Chung K'uei. Signed. Poem dated 1828.
Ming-jên hsieh-chu. Four Studies of Bamboo. Four hanging scrolls. Signed, dated 1830. *Cf.* Nanga Taisei, II, 15.
Chêng Tê-k'un, Cambridge. Album of bird and flower-paintings, in the style of Hua Yen. Signed and dated 1833.
Ming-jên shu-hua, XVII. A Lady with a Duster. Signed. Poem.
Nanju 11. Two Pine-trees and Orchids. Signed.
Nanga Taisei, Add. IV, 225–228. An Album of eight Landscapes. Inscriptions, signed.
Robert Rousset, Paris. A Boy and a Buffalo resting under a Willow-tree. Signed.

LIEN-CH'I 蓮溪.
From Yang-chou; lived in Shanghai. A priest. Active *c.*1862(?) Bamboos, stones, birds and animals. M, p.624.

Ming-jên shu-hua, XVII. A Lady spinning at the Window, after Lo P'ing. Signed, dated 1862(?)

LIN CH'I 林祁.
Unrecorded. Beginning of Ch'ing period.

Tōyō, XI. Flowers and Bamboos by a Rockery. Signed, dated 1652.

LIN CHIH-FAN 林之蕃, *t.* K'ung-shih 孔碩, *h.* Han-chai 涵齋.
From Fukien. Chin-shih in 1643. Magistrate of Chia-hsing, Chekiang. Landscapes, flowers. N, IV, 31. R, I, 13. M, p.230.

Kokka 474. "The Four Gentlemen": Plum-blossoms, Bamboos, Orchids and Chrysanthemums. Signed, dated 1644. Also in N. Gashū 19.

LIN CHÜN 林濬.
Unrecorded. One seal on the picture reads *t.* I-shan 一山. Probably the 17th century.

Nanju 4. Trees by a Stream. Signed, dated 1640(?) Also in Tōyō, XII.

LIN LING-HSÜ 林令旭, *t.* Yü-chung 豫仲, *h.* Ch'ing-chiang 晴江.
From Lou-hsien, Kiangsu. Chin-shih in 1730. Flowers, birds and ink plum-blossoms. R, XI, 7. M, p.231.

Nanga Taisei, III, 100–107. An Album of eight Paintings of flowering Plum, the last signed and dated 1741.

LIU PIN 劉璸.
From Ch'u-chiang, Hunan. Active *c.*1750. Landscapes. M, p.666.

National Museum, Stockholm. An Eagle perched on a Cliff. Signed, dated 1749.

LIU TÊ-LIU 劉德六, *t.* Tzŭ-ho 子和.
From Wu-chiang, Kiangsu. B. 1806, d. 1875. Flowers and birds. Pupil of Hsia Chih-ting. M, p.664.

Shina Nanga, I, 137. Birds bathing in Water. Seal of the painter.

LIU TU 劉度, *t.* Shu-hsien 叔憲.
From Hangchou. Active *c.*1650. Landscapes. Pupil of Lan Ying. R, VI, 23. U, I, 2, 19. M, p.662.

Shina Meiga Senshū, III. Mountain Peak and Waterfall, after Li Ch'êng. Album-leaf. Signed and dated 1633.
Ku-kung collect. Rocky Landscape, painted in archaistic style with green, brown and blue colours. Poem by the painter, dated 1636.
Hamburg Exhibition, 1949–1950. Landscape in the style of Li Ch'êng. Signed, dated 1636.
Ibid. Autum Forest, after Li Ch'êng. Signed, dated 1642.
Ku-kung, XXIV. Landscape after Chao Mêng-fu. Signed, dated 1652.
Kokka 572 (Y. Horiuchi). Landscape.

LIU YIN 柳隱, *t.* Ju-shih 如是.
From Wu-chiang, Kiangsu. D. 1664. Wife of the poet Ch'ien Ch'ien-i. Flowers and birds. Landscapes in the Yüan style. M, p.266.

Shên-chou, V. A Bird on a Branch of a blossoming Magnolia-tree. Album-leaf. Signed.
Sōgen 356. Ladies on a Terrace, after Li Kung-lin. Signed.

LIU YÜ 柳堉, *t.* Kung-han 公韓, *h.* Yü-ku 愚谷.
From Nanking. Active in the latter half of the 17th century. Poet and calligraphist. Landscapes, followed Tung Yüan and Chü-jan. R, VI, 11. U, I, 2, 22. M, p.266.

Chūgoku 7. A Pavilion by the River, under a Cliff. Leaf in an album containing works of the eight Nanking masters (although Liu was not one of the eight). Signed and dated 1679.
T'ai-shan ts'an-shih-lou ts'ang-hua, III. A Temple on a River-bank; a man on the road. Poem by the painter.
Ibid. III. Sparse Trees and Rocks. Signed.
Shên-chou album, 1930. Landscape-paintings. Signed. *Cf.* Nanga Taisei, XI, 195–206.

LIU YÜ 柳遇, *t.* Hsien-ch'i 仙期.
From Suchou. Active *c.*1700. Figures after Ch'iu Ying; also flowers. Q, I, 2. R. IX, 4. M, p.266.

K.-k. shu-hua chi, VIII. Opium Flowers. Signed.

LIU YÜAN 劉源, *t.* Pan-yüan 伴阮.
From K'ai-fêng, Honan. Active *c.*1660. Figures, flowers, landscapes and dragons. Q, I, 2. R, II, 11. M, p.663.

Nanju 11. Bamboos in Mist and Rain. Album-leaf. Signed.

Lo Kuang 羅光, *t.* Ming-yüan 明遠.
From Yü-hang, Chekiang. Active in early 19th century. Landscapes. M, p.724.

Boston Museum. The Goddess of the Lo River. After Ting Yün-p'êng. Signed, dated 1829.

Lo Mu 羅牧, *t.* Fan-niu 飯牛, *h.* Yün-an 雲菴.
From Ning-tu; lived in Nan-ch'ang, Kiangsi. B. 1622, d. after 1706. Poet, calligraphist. Pupil of Wei Shih-ch'uang 魏石牀. Imitated Tung Yüan and Huang Kung-wang. Founder of the "Kiangsi School". Q, I, 2. R, V, 5. U, II, 2, 11. M, p.723.

Metropolitan Museum (51–13). An Autumn Landscape. Handscroll. Signed and dated 1661.
Ōmura, I, 8. River-view. The inscription copied from Wang Hsi-chih's Lan-t'ing essay. Signed, dated 1672.
Shinchō 38. River-view with Mountains. Part of a scroll. Signed, dated 1681.
Kyūka, II. Two handscrolls of Landscapes from a series of eight. One signed, with a poem dated 1681.
Horiuchi collect., Ōsaka (formerly Kuwana). Two large Landscapes, forming a pair, signed and dated 1681.
Nanju 20. High Mountains by a River. Signed, dated 1687.
Hamburg Exhibition, 1949–1950. River Landscape with steep Rocks and Trees. Ink on satin. Signed, dated 1689.
Tōan 39. Pavilion at the Foot of dry old Cedars. Signed, dated 1693.
Nanju 3. Leafy Trees by a River. Signed, dated 1696. *Cf.* Pageant 821.
Tōyō, XII. An Angler on the River-bank in Autumn. Signed, dated 1698.
Nanga Taisei, Add. IV, 50. River Landscape. Signed and dated 1700.
S.c.t.k. hsü-pien, III. Lofty Hills and Trees at a River. Signed, dated 1701.
Kyūka, II. A Man seated by a Stream. Signed. Poem dated 1701.
Ku-kung collect. *Lin-ho hsiao-su t'u.* Desolate Forest and Mountains. Ink on paper. Signed with two seals and dated at 83 (1704). Poem.
N. Gashū 32. River Landscape. Signed, dated 1706 (at 85).
Bijutsu, XXII. Sparse Trees and a Boat on the River.
Nanju 5. Bare Trees and high Mountains in Autumn. Two seals of the painter. *Cf.* Pageant 820.
Ibid. 13. A River winding between Cliffs. Signed. Poem.
Tokasha Shina Meigashū 8. Huang-shan in Autumn: craggy Peaks rising through the Mist. Inscription by the painter.
Chūgoku 7. Houses under Pines and other Trees; a misty valley beyond. Inscription, signed.
National Museum, Stockholm. High Cliffs by a River. Signed. *Cf.* Sirén, *Later*, pl.183.

Lo Pin 羅彬, *t.* Wên-i 文宜.
From Ning-hua, Fukien. Unrecorded. Ch'ing period.

Kyūka, II. Mountains and Streams on a Spring Morning. Signed, dated 1767(?)

Lo P'ing 羅聘, *t.* Tan-fu 遯夫, *h.* Liang-fêng 兩峯 and Hua-chih-ssŭ sêng 花之寺僧.
From Hsieh-hsien, Anhui; lived in Yang-chou, Kiangsu. B. 1733, d. 1799. Student of Ch'an Buddhism. Plum-blossoms, orchids, bamboos, Buddhist and Taoist figures. Pupil of Chin Nung T, IV, 6. U, I, 3, 17. M, p.724.

Ming-jên shu-hua, XVIII. A blossoming Plum-tree. Signed, dated 1759.
Shina Nanga, II, 12. A Lady. Signed. Poem dated 1762.
Mayuyama collect., Tōkyō. Album of Studies of flowering Plum, Bamboo, etc. The last signed and dated 1767.

National Museum, Stockholm. Creeping Stems of Vine, after Wên Jih-kuan. Signed. Colophon dated 1771.

Shên-chou ta-kuan, vol.9. T'ai-shan in Mist and Rain. Short handscroll. Colophon by Chu Yün, dated 1773.

Metropolitan Museum. A Homestead in a Garden on the Day of the Lantern Festival. Signed, dated 1773. *Cf.* Chung-kuo ming-hua, 10.

Shina Nanga, III, 5. The Yin-ti Garden in Winter. Signed, dated 1773. *Cf.* Chung-kuo ming hua 10.

Kawabata collect., Kamakura. Album of twelve Paintings of Landscapes and other Subjects, the last signed and dated 1774. *Cf.* Kokka 748.

C. T. Loo's Successor, Frank Caro, N.Y. *Yün-t'ien sung-li t'u*: Picture of the God of Wealth. Poem by the painter, dated 1774. *Cf.* Toronto 56.

Metropolitan Museum. Spring-celebrating when the young Bamboo is sprouting in a Homestead. Signed, dated 1775.

National Museum, Stockholm. Bamboos. Signed, dated 1775.

Fei-tun lu shan-shui. A Ferryboat and two Geese, after Tao-chi. Finger-painting. Signed. Colophon dated 1776.

Chêng Tê-k'un, Cambridge. Epidendrum-plants. Finger-paintings. Album of ten leaves. Dated 1777.

Mei-chan t'ê-k'an, 66 (Chang Pi-han, Hongkong). The Patron of Medicine; a boy grinding with a stone-mill. Signed, dated 1778. *Cf.* I-shu ch'uan-t'ung 12.

Fei-tun lu hua-hui. A blossoming Plum-tree. Long handscroll. Signed. Poem dated 1779.

Shina Nanga, II, 5. A Town in the Moonlight, after Ch'ên Ju-yen. Signed, dated 1779. *Cf.* Shên-chou, XVIII.

Yamaguchi collect., Ashiya. An Album of paintings of Flowers, Birds and Animals. Signed, one dated 1781.

Chūgoku 8. Swallows flying among drooping Willow Branches. Poem. Signed and dated 1781.

Sumitomo collect., Ōiso. Chung K'uei crossing a Bridge on a Donkey; a bare Tree above. Signed and dated 1787.

Hsü-ching chai. Kuan-yin on the Clouds. Signed, dated 1787.

Chūgoku 8. Three Men viewing Plum-blossoms at the Chu-t'ang Temple. After Shên Chou. Signed and dated 1789.

Private collect., Kyōto. An Album of small paintings of Orchids, painted on silk. The last signed and dated 1790.

C. C. Wang, New York. A Monk seated in Meditation in a Pavilion under tall Bamboos. Signed, dated 1791.

Chung-kuo ming-hua 5. Two Pictures forming a pair: one representing a Tuft of Epidendrum by a Rockery; the other, an old Plum-tree in Bloom. Poem by the painter, dated 1794. *Cf.* Shina Nanga, I, 115.

J. Cahill, Wash., D.C. An old Scholar standing beside a Rock, holding a Branch of a blossoming Plum-tree. Poem dated 1798.

Shên-chou, I. Han-shan and Shih-tê. Signed. Poem. Colophon.

Ibid. I. Wu-liang-shou-fou (Amida Buddha). Represented as a man seated under wu-t'ung trees.

Ibid. II. The Scholar Chu I-tsun as a Farmer. Signed.

Ibid. VI. Chêng Hsüan teaching his Sons.

Ibid., XVI. Two large Branches of a blossoming Plum-tree. Signed.

Ibid. XIX. A Poet seated in front of his Cottage under a Willow. Album-leaf. Poem by the painter.

Ibid. XX. A Buddhist Monk (Šakyamuni?) seated on a Cliff surrounded by Clouds. Signed.

Shên-chou ta-kuan, vol.7. A Buddhist Saint in Meditation under Bamboos. Signed.

Chung-kuo, II, 159. An Arhat, after Kuan-hsiu. Signed. *Cf.* Chung-kuo ming-hua, 29.

I-shu ts'ung-pien 14. portrait of Ting Lung-hung seated in Profile on a Stone resting his Hands on a Staff.

Hui-hua kuan. A Mountain Gorge spanned by a Bridge. Inscriptions.

Ibid. Bamboos, Pines, Plum-blossoms, etc. Album-leaves.

Yu-chêng album. Ten Landscapes in colour.

Chung-hua album, 1923. Twelve leaves representing the Eighteen Arhats.

Commercial Press album, 1924. Ten leaves of Epidendrum and Bamboo studies. Colophon by the painter. *Cf.* Nanga Taisei, I, 219–223.

Ming-jên shu-hua, II. Yao Wang seated under two Palm-trees. Signed. Colophon. *Cf.* Nanga Taikan 10.

Ibid. VII. A Farewell Meeting at the River. Signed. Poems by those present.

Ibid. XI. Portraits of Tu Fu and Han Yü (on one scroll). Signed.

Ibid. XX. Two album-leaves: 1. Bamboos by a Rock, after Chang Hsüan. Signed. Poem. 2. Orchids at Rock. Signed. Poem.

Ch'ing êrh-shih chia. A Lady standing under Wu-t'ung Trees. Signed.

Ming-jên hsieh-chu. Bamboos after a T'ang Master. Signed. Poem.

Ibid. Bamboos. Signed. Colophon.

Po-mei chi. A Branch of a blossoming Plum-tree. Signed. Poem and colophon.

P'ang Yüan-chi Illust. cat. II. A Mountain Gorge with a Waterfall and a Bridge. Said to represent the road to Shu. Surrounded by ten long inscriptions.

Nanking Exhib. cat. 351. Śakyamuni kneeling in Prayer under leafy Trees. Unsigned?

Gems, I, 79. Bamboo growing beside Rocks. Poem, signed.

T. Moriya collect., Kyōto. A Branch of flowering Plum. Signed. *Cf.* Sekai Bijutsu Zenshū, XX, text illus. 104 (detail).

Yamaguchi collect., Ashiya. An old Man seated in a Chair under Bamboo, after Yen Li-pên. *Cf.* Sekai Bijutsu Zenshū, XX, Pl.61.

Ibid. Album of ten leaves of flower-studies in ink.

S. Shimada, Kyōto. Portrait of the Poet Yüan Mei. Long inscription by the artist, signed.

Nanga Taikan 2. A Man in a long Coat admiring a Plum-tree growing from a Rock. Signed.

Shina Nanga, I, 114. The Monk Hui-ch'ih in Meditation. *Cf.* Shen-chou ta-kuan, 12.

Ibid. II, 9. An Arhat.

Ōmura, I, 5. Ni Tsan, a portrait.

Shinchō 69. Two Ghosts. Fan-painting. Signed. Colophon.

Berlin Museum collect. Orchids (on two scrolls). Signed.

H. C. Wêng, Scarsdale, N.Y. A Scholar's Abode under the Trees. Signed.

Ho Kuan-wu, Hongkong. Preparing Tea. Signed.

Huang Pan-jo, Hongkong. Studies of Flowers and Trees. An album. Signed.

University Museum, Princeton, N.J. An Album of ten leaves: Landscapes and other Subjects. Signed.

Chang Ta-ch'ien collect., Hongkong. An old Man seated in a Chair made of twisted Roots, under a banana-palm. Inscription by the artist, signed.

(See also Nanga Taisei, I, 224, 225 (Bamboo); III, 155 (Plum); IV, 145 (Rock and Grass); VI, 192–196 (Birds, Insects, Frogs); VII, 152–154, Add. IV, 109–111 (Figures).)

Chêng Tê-k'un, Cambridge. Orchids, after Chao Mêng-chien. Painted in *pai-miao*. Signed.

LO T'ING-HSI 羅廷禧.
Unrecorded. According to the signature, from Nanking. Ch'ing period.

K.-k. shu-hua chi, XLII. A Cedar by a Rockery. Signed.

LU CHAN 盧湛.
Unrecorded. Probably a court-painter in the Ch'ien-lung period.

Sōgen 363. The Hermitage of T'ao Yüan-ming. Signed.

LU CH'AO 盧潮, *t.* Fang-po 芳伯, *h.* Hai-mên 海門.
From Ch'ang-shu, Kiangsu. Active *c.*1760. Flowers, particularly peonies. M, p.678.

Shina Nanga, I, 97. Peonies, after a Sung model. Signed. Poem, dated 1764.

LU CHIA-PIN 路嘉賓.
Unrecorded.

British Museum. An Eagle and a Bear. Signed with name and the words: Pai-t'a.

LU FEI 陸飛, *t.* Ch'i-ch'ien 起潛, *h.* Hsiao-yin 筱飲.
From Hangchou. Chü-jen in 1765. Poet and calligraphist. Landscapes, figures and flowers; also ink-bamboos, after Wu Chên. T. M, p.421, 422.

Po-mei chi. Branches of Plum-trees and Bamboos. Signed. Poem dated 1778. *Cf.* Nanga Taisei, II, 245.

LU HAN 陸翰, *t.* Shao-chêng 少徵.
Native of Hangchou. 17th century. Figures. M, p.419.

Chung-kuo ming-hua, 38. Su Tung-p'o Talking with a Lady in the Garden. Signed.

LU I-T'UNG 魯一同, *t.* T'ung-fu 通甫, *h.* Lan-ch'ên 蘭岑.
From Shan-yang, Kiangsu. Chü-jên in 1847. Poet. Plum blossoms. M, p.632.

Po-mei chi. Branches of blossoming Plum-tree. Signed. Poem. *Cf.* Nanga Taisei, III, 206.

LU TAO-HUAI 陸道淮, *t.* Shang-yu 上遊.
From Chia-ting, Kiangsu. Active *c.*1700. Pupil of Wu Li. Landscapes. R, VII, 17. M, p.419.

Shina Nanga, II, 6. Mountains in Autumn, after Huang Kung-wang. Signed. Colophon. Also in Fei-tun lu shan-shui.

Ho Kuan-wu, Hongkong. A Pine-tree and Cranes. Signed.

LU WEI 陸暐, *t.* Jih-wei 日爲, *h.* Sui-shan ch'iao 遂山樵. Known also by the name Lu Ch'ih 陸癡 (Lu the Fool).
From Sung-chiang, Kiangsu. Active *c.*1700. Landscapes, followed the two Mi and Kao K'o-kung. Q, I, 2. R, VII, 8. U, III, 1, 2. M, p.419.

Shina Meiga Senshū 33. A Man walking over a Bridge at the Foot of high Mountains. Signed, dated 1685.
Shinchō 66 (Hashimoto collect., Takatsuki). Mountain Landscape. Handscroll. Signed, dated 1697. Also in Kyūka, II.
Sekai Bijutsu Zenshū, 20, text illus. 115. Houses by a River; a man in a boat. Handscroll. Signed and dated 1717.
K.-k. shu-hua chi, XV. A tall Pine-tree. Signed.
Kokka 318. A Forest in Winter. Signed.
Shimbi, XVI. Willows and Plum-trees by a Stream. Signed. Also in Tōyō, XII; Kyūka, II; Sirén, *Later*, 182b.
Nanju 10. River Landscape. Signed. Also in Kyūka, II; Pageant, 828.
Kyūka, II. A Waterfall. Signed. Also in Sōgen 292.
Piacentini collect., Tōkyō. Landscape with Figures in a Boat, a distant Building. Signed.

LU YÜAN 陸遠, *t.* Ching-chih 靜致.
From Suchou. 18th century. Landscapes after Mi Fei. M, p.424.

Nanga Taisei Add., IV, 107. Trees by a River. Album-leaf. Signed and dated *i-mao* or 1795?

Nanju 6. A Cottage among Plum-trees with Figures. Seals of the painter. Also in Tōyō, XI.

Hamburg Exhibition, 1949–1950. An album of eight Landscape-studies in colour.

J. Cahill, Washington D.C. Small landscape. Seal of the artist.

LÜ CH'IEN 呂潛, *t.* K'ung-chao 孔昭, *h.* Pan-yin 半隱 and Shih-shan-nung 石山農.

From Sui-ning, Szechuan; lived in T'ai-chou, Kiangsu. Chin-shih in 1643. Landscapes, flowers. Q, II, 1. R, I, 11. M, p.124.

Shinchō 28. Landscape. Handscroll. Signed, dated 1667.

S. c. t. k. hsü-pien, IV. Spare Trees and red Rocks. Signed.

Wên-ming album, 1940. Twelve Landscapes. Signed. Poem by the artist opposite each leaf.

LÜ HSÜEH 呂學, *t.* Shih-min 時敏, *h.* Hai-shan 海山.

From Wu-ch'êng, Chekiang. Active *c.*1670. Figures, animals and landscapes. Q, I, 2. R, XIII, 11. M, p.124.

Nanju 7. Travellers on a Mountain Path. Signed. Also in Tōyō, XII; Pageant 825.

British Museum, No.220. Chung K'uei. Signed.

Ibid. No.221. Winter Scene. Signed.

Princeton (Du Bois-Morris collect.) Travellers in the Mountains. Two seals of the painter.

LÜ HUAN-CH'ÊNG 呂煥成, *t.* Chi-wên 吉文.

From Yü-yao, Chekiang. 18th century. Figures, flowers. Landscapes in the style of Lo Mu. M, p.124.

Takeuchi collect., Kyōto. A seated Figure (an Emperor?) listening to disputing Scholars. Signed and dated 1732.

Nanju 16. A solitary Pavilion by a River. Signed, dated 1751. Also in Tōyō, XII.

Piacentini collect., Tōkyō. River Landscape at Dawn with Travellers. Signed, dated 1758. *Cf.* Tōsō, 389.

Chung-kuo, II, 145. Mountain Landscape after Wu Chên. Signed. *Cf.* Chung-kuo ming-hua, 29.

MA ANG 馬昂, *t.* Yün-shang 雲上, *h.* T'ui-shan 退山.

From Suchou. Active probably in the early 18th century. Landscape. Q, I, 3 (under Li Shih-cho). R, VIII, 6. M, p.341.

Boston Museum. A Water-buffalo on the Bank of a Stream; a man walking under the trees. Signed, dated *kêng-hsü* (1730?)

MA CH'ÜAN 馬荃, *t.* Chiang-hsiang 江香.

From Ch'ang-shu, Kiangsu. Lived *c.*1768–1848, died at 81. Grand-daughter of Ma Yüan-yü. Flowers. Q, II, 2. R, XVI. M, p.341.

Shinchō 88. Flowers, after a Yüan painter. Signed, dated 1791.

Kokka 276. Flowers, Fruits and a Squirrel. Signed, dated 1796.

Shên-chou, VI. A Pine Forest. Signed, dated 1822.

Ibid. XII. Chrysanthemums in a Vase. Signed, dated 1831.

Ōmura, I, 2. Lotuses. Signed, dated 1846. *Cf.* Chūgoku 8.

Ming-jên shu-hua, IV. An Eagle in a Pine-tree. Signed. Poem.

Compagnie de la Chine, Paris. A Cat catching a Butterfly by a Rockery with blossoming Plants. Signed.

Hamburg Exhibition, 1949–1950. The three Beauties of the sixth Month: Lotus, Gardenia and Cymbidium.

O. Kamiki, Japan. Hundred Cranes along the Shore with blossoming Trees. Long handscroll. Signed.

Metropolitan Museum. Butterflies. Handscroll, signed. *Cf.* Bulletin, Feb. 1952.

MA KUAN-WO 馬觀我.
Unrecorded. 17th century.

Fei-tun lu hua-hui. Bamboos behind a Rock. Handscroll. Signed, dated 1662.

MA YÜAN-YÜ 馬元馭, *t.* Fu-hsi 扶羲, *h.* Ch'i-hsia 棲霞 and T'ien-yü shan-jên 天虞山人.
From Ch'ang-shu, Kiangsu. Active *c.*1680–1710. Pupil of Yün Shou-p'ing. Q, I, 2. R, VII, 11. U, I, 3, 5. M, p.340.

Kawai collect., Kyōto. Album of paintings of Flowers, Birds and Fish. The last signed and dated 1690.
Chung-kuo, II, 155. Monkeys beneath a flowering Tree (the monkeys by Chiang T'ing-hsi). Signed, dated 1695. *Cf.* Chung-kuo ming-hua, 30.
Preetorius collect., Munich. Peonies, after Hsü Ch'ung-ssŭ. Signed and dated 1695.
Shina Nanga, II, 4. Flowers. Fan-painting. Signed, dated 1696.
Shincho 47. Chrysanthemums on a Rock. Signed, dated 1696.
Gems, I, 74. A Hawk on a Chestnut-tree. Signed and dated 1701.
Shên-chou, IV. A Heron and two Lotus Flowers. Signed, dated 1705.
Kurokawa cat. 24. Various Flowers. Handscroll. Signed and dated 1705.
Fei-tun lu hua-hui. A blossoming Pear-tree, after Kao Ch'i-p'ei. Long handscroll. Colophon dated 1733.
Shanghai Museum. Chrysanthemums in Colour, painted in fine *kung-pi* technique. Inscription by the painter.
Shina Nanga, III, 2. A Heron. Signed. Poem.
Nanga Taisei, VI, 126–132. Album of Paintings of Flowers and Insects. Signed.
Boston Museum. Peonies in a Rockery. Signed.
British Museum, No.215. Lotus.
Musée Guimet. Two Fishes suspended on a Withe. Colophon by the painter. Poems by Yang Chin and two other men.
Formerly Hobart collect., Cambridge, Mass. Narcissi and Chrysanthemums. Two album-leaves; one signed.

MAO CH'I-LING 毛奇齡, *t.* Ta-k'o 大可, *h.* Hsi-ho 西河, Ch'u-ch'ing 初晴 and other names.
From Hsiao-shan, Chekiang. B. 1623, d. 1716. Scholar. Plum-blossoms. Q, II, 1. R, VI, 1. U, I, 2, 14. M, p.21.

Chūgoku V. Two Ladies standing opposite each other. Large album-leaf. Signed and dated 1677.
Shên-chou, XX. Looking at the Bamboos. Signed. Poem dated 1682. *Cf.* Sōraikan, I, 51.
Nanking Exhib. cat. 273. A Man leaning on a Tree beside a River. Signed and dated 1684.
Yabumoto collect., Ōsaka. Orchids. Signed and dated 1692.
Mo-ch'ao pi-chi, vol.II. Bamboos on a Rock and Narcissi. Handscroll. Signed.
Nanga Taisei, I, 148. Bamboo and Orchids. Poem, signed.

MAO HSIANG 冒襄, *t.* P'i-chiang 辟疆, *h.* Ch'ao-min 巢民.
From Ju-kao, Kiangsu. B. 1611, d. 1693. Landscapes, flowers. M, p.260.

Po-mei chi. A blossoming Plum-tree. Album-leaf. Signed, dated 1631.
Shên-chou, XXI. A straw-covered Hut by the River between steep Mountains. Signed. Poem, colophon dated 1638.
Tokasha Shina Meigashū 11. Thin Willows by a River, and a Pavilion built over the Water. Long poem by the painter, dated 1648.
Shên-chou ta-kuan, vol.2. Pine-tree and Fungus. Dedication in large writing to a friend on his 70th birthday. Dated 1691.
Shina Nanga, II, 8. Bamboos.
Ibid. III, 2. A Plum-tree. Signed.

MEI CH'ING 梅清, *t*. Yüan-kung 淵公 or 遠公, *h*. Ch'ü-shan 瞿山, Hsüeh-lu 雪廬, Lao-ch'ü-fan-fu 老瞿凡父 and other names.
From Hsüan-ch'êng, Anhui. B. 1623, d. 1697. Poet. Landscapes, pine-trees. Q, I, 2. R, V, 6. U, II, 1, 25. M, p.379.

J. D. Ch'ên, Hongkong. Mei Ch'ü-shan Hsüan-ch'êng shêng-lan hua-ts'ê. Sixteen album-leaves representing famous places, the last dated 1679.
Ho Kuan-wu, Hongkong. Landscape, dated 1679.
Shina Nanga, I, 50. A tall Pine by a Rock. Signed, dated 1685. *Cf*. Shên-chou, XVIII.
Hamburg Exhibition, 1949–1950. Landscape with Waterfall. Dated 1686.
Shên-chou, XIV. A Mountain Study, after Wu Chên. Signed, dated 1687.
Sōgen 254. A tall Pine-tree by a Rockery. Signed and dated 1689.
Piacentini collect., Tōkyō. Mountain Stream, large Pines and projecting Cliffs. Signed and dated 1691. *Cf*. Sōgen 253.
Commercial Press album. Landscape-studies of twelve leaves. Dated 1692.
Honolulu Academy of Arts. A blossoming Tree by a Rock. Short handscroll. Signed and dated 1692.
Musée Guimet, Paris. The Study of an old Philosopher on a rocky Shore under some old Pine-trees. Signed and dated 1692.
Nanga Taisei Add. I, 242–249. Album of nine Landscapes, painted "at the age of 70", *i.e.* in 1692.
Vannotti collect., Lugano. An album of twelve leaves with Studies of Trees and Rocks after old masters. Inscriptions by the painter, one dated 1693. *Cf*. Nanga Taisei, Add. I, 250–261.
Commercial Press album, 1934. Nineteen Sketches from Huang-shan, Anhui. Some with poems or colophons by the painter. According to the inscription on the last picture, painted when the painter was 71, *i.e.* 1693. Also published by the Wên-ming co. under the title: Huang-shan sheng-chi t'u-ts'e.
Fei-tun lu shan-shui. A Mountain Gorge, after Shên Chou. Signed, dated 1694.
Chêng Tê-k'un, Cambridge. Studies of fantastic Rocks and Peaks on Huang-shan. Ten album-leaves. Much worn. Inscription by the painter, one dated 1694.
Commercial Press album, 1934. Twelve Sketches of Trees, Rocks and Water, accompanied by poems and colophons by the painter. Dated 1695. *Cf*. Nanga Taisei Add. I, 220–229.
S.c.t.k. hsü-pien, X. Pine-tree at a Stone. Signed and dated 1695. *Cf*. Liu 101.
Shina Nanga, III, 12. Pine-trees on a Mountain Ridge. Signed. Colophon dated 1695.
C. T. Loo's Successor, Frank Caro, N.Y. An Album of Landscape studies from Huang-shan. Signed and dated 1695. *Cf*. Cleveland Exhib.cat. 108.
Chung-kuo ming-hua, XII. Rocks lined with Rows of Pines; misty atmosphere. Album-leaf. Poem by the painter, dated 1695.
Shên-chou, XVIII. A high Waterfall on wooded Mountains and a Pavilion among Trees at its Foot. Poem by the painter.
Hsin-an p'ai ming-hua chi (Shên-chou album, 1924). Two Men seated in a Cave; a boy is preparing tea. After Ching Hao. Seals of the painter.
T'ai-shan ts'an-shih-lou ts'ang-hua, vol.I. A Mountain Peak deeply creviced with small Roads winding to the Top. Poem by the painter.
Mei-chan t'ê-k'an 33. Mountain River and Pine Groves, after Chao Mêng-fu. Poem by the painter.
S.c.t.k. hsü-pien, VI. Misty River Valley. Signed.
Sung-pê. A Pine-tree by a Rockery. Signed.
Shên-chou album, 1909. Landscapes by Mei Ch'ing and his nephew Mei Ch'ung. Signed.
Shên-chou album, 1929. Landscapes in early styles. Inscriptions by the artist.
Chung-hua album, 1931. Twelve Views of Huang-shan. Signed.
Nanking Exhib. cat. 276. Landscape of Ching-t'ing shan. Inscription, signed.
Yamaguchi collect., Ashiya. Album of twelve Landscapes, painted in ink only. Signed. Title written by Wu Ch'ang-shih.
Sekai Bijutsu Zenshū, 20, pl.49. A Boat on the River; misty pine forests on the shore. Poem, signed. A leaf from an album.
Kokka 420. Pine-trees at the Foot of a Waterfall. Signed. Poem.
Bijutsu, XXII. Rocks and Pines. Signed.

Ōmura, I, 2. A Pine Grove. A leaf from an album of eight pictures.

Ibid. I, 12. Angling on the River in Autumn. A leaf from the same album as the preceding picture. *Cf.* Chūgoku 7.

Ibid. I, 1. The Peach Blossom Stream. Illustration to a poem by Li Po. Signed. *Cf.* Chūgoku 7.

Ibid. I, 3. The West Gorge. Signed. *Cf.* Chūgoku 7.

Sōgen 255. A Man in a Boat under an overhanging Cliff. After Liu Sung-nien. Signed. Also in Shina Meiga Senshū, 22. *Cf.* Sirén, *Later*, pl.181b.

Ibid. 256. Two Scholars viewing a Waterfall. Signed. Poem.

Hashimoto collect., Kyōto. Large album with eight leaves of Landscape Studies. Partly coloured. Painted together with Mei Ch'ung.

Hobart collect., Cambridge, Mass. Album of Landscape-studies. Signed. *Cf.* Cleveland Exhibition cat. 109.

National Museum, Stockholm. A Waterfall from an overhanging Rock; trees below. Poem by the artist. Four colophons.

Vannotti collect., Lugano. Landscape. A rocky Island with Pine-trees. According to inscription, after a picture by Li Ch'êng called *Han-yün shan-ssŭ t'u*.

J. P. Dubosc, Lugano. A large Album of twelve leaves. Landscape-studies after Sung, Yüan and Ming masters. Signed.

MEI CH'UNG 梅翀, *t.* P'ei-i 培翌.
From Hsüan-ch'êng, Anhui. Active *c.*1690. Nephew of Mei Ch'ing. Pines and stones. M, p.379.

Shên-chou album, 1919. Ten Views of Huang-shan. Poems by the painter and by Mei Ch'ing.

Cf. Mei Ch'ing album, Hashimoto collect., Kyōto, and Shên-chou album, 1909.

MEI KÊNG 梅庚, *t.* Ou-ch'ang 耦長 and Tzŭ-ch'ang 子長, *h.* Hsüeh-p'ing 雪坪 and T'ing-shan-wêng 聽山翁
From Hsüan-ch'eng, Anhui. Chü-jên in 1681. Brother of Mei Ch'ing. Landscapes, flowers. Q, I, 2. R, VI, 13. U, I, 3, 3. M, p.379.

Hamburg Exhibition, 1949–1950. Landscape: sailing down the Stream in a Boat. Handscroll. Signed, dated 1686.

Hsin-an p'ai ming-hua chi (Shên-chou album, 1924). A Temple in the Mountains. Signed, dated 1693.

MÊNG CHIN-I 孟覲乙, *t.* Li-t'ang 麗堂, *h.* Yün-ch'i wai-shih 雲溪外史.
From Yang-hu; lived in Kuei-lin, Kuangsi. Landscapes in early years, flowers and birds when old. Began to go blind, but went on painting to his death. M, p.225,

S.c.t.k. hsü-pien, II. Cats and flowering Plants. Signed.

MÊNG YUNG-KUANG 孟永光, *t.* Yüeh-hsin 月心. *h.* Lo-ch'ih-shêng.
From Shan-yin, Chekiang. Active *c.*1600–1650. Figures and portraits. Pupil of Sun K'o-hung. Served for a while as a chih-hou in the palace in the Shun-chih period, but passed most of his life in Liao-tung and also as a court-painter in Korea. Q, I, 1. R, XIII. M, p.225.

Kokka 275. A Gust of Wind: Autumn Landscape. Signed: Lo-ch'ih-shêng.

MIN CHÊN 閔貞, *t.* Chêng-chai 正齋.
From Kiangsi; lived in Hankow. 1730– after 1788. Landscapes, figures. U, III, 1, 3. M, p.507.

Ming-jên shu-hua, XVII. A Lady with a Fan. Signed, dated 1776.

Tokasha Shina Meigashū 98. Four wild Geese and Reeds. Signed.

Nanga Taisei, IV, 142. Two pictures of Flowers in Vases. Signed.
Boston Museum. Six broadly executed Figure-sketches. Album-leaves. Signed.
G. Del Drago, New York. An old Man standing in Profile holding a Goblet. Signed.
Hui-hua kuan. Chung K'uei standing full-length.
T. T. Ma, Hongkong. Bamboo and Epidendrum growing out from a steep Rock. Signed.
Chêng Ch'i, Hongkong. Bamboo, Orchids and a Rock. Signed.

MING-CHIEN 明儉. Family name Wang 王, *t.* Chih-ch'in 智勤, *h.* Chi-ku 几谷.
A priest, *c.*1820. From Tan-t'u, Kiangsu. Landscapes, followed Ching Hao, Kuan T'ung, Ma and Hsia. M, p.224.

Tōan, 70. A cloudy Peak, after Mi Fei. Signed. Poem.
Ibid. 71. Man in a Boat under a Cliff, after Ni Tsan. Signed. Colophon.

MING-CHUNG 明中, *t.* Ta-hêng 大恆, *h.* Yin-hsü 烎虛 and other names.
From T'ung-hsiang, Chekiang. A priest. Active *c.*1750–1780. Q, II, 2. R, XIV, 24. M, p.224.

Shina Meiga Senshū, 29. River Landscape after Ni Tsan. Poem by the painter, dated *kuei-ch'ou* (1733?)
Nanga Taisei, X, 181. Cliffs rising from a River; a waterfall. Signed and dated 1765.
Ming-jên shu-hua, XIV. Bare Trees, Bamboos and Stones, after Su Tung-p'o. Also in Nanga Taikan 7.
Musée Guimet, Paris. A Cottage, Bamboos and tall leafless Trees by a River. Signed. Two lines of poetry.
Suchiku 29. Houses on the Shore of a River; tall cliffs behind. Poem, signed.

MU TA-SHOU 穆達受, *t.* Liu-chou 六舟, *h.* Hsin-nan 莘南.
From Hai-ning, Chekiang. Active *c.*1850. A priest and connoisseur. Flowers. U, III, 2, 13.

Nanga Taikan 9. Narcissi by a Rockery. Signed. Poem dated 1848.

NAN-HAI 南海. A Buddhist monk whose original name was Yüan Yü 阮瑜(?)
B. 1676, d. 1751. Writer and painter of bamboos. See article by K. Tanaka in *Bijutsu Kenkyū*, No.127, 1942.

Bijutsu Kenkyū, 127. Branches of an old Plum-tree in Bloom. Poem by the painter.
Ibid. A leafless Tree and Bamboo by a Rock. Poem by the painter.
Ibid. Section of a Bamboo Stem. Poem by the painter.

NI YÜN 倪耘, *t.* Chieh-sun 芥孫, *h.* Hsiao-p'u 小圃.
From Shih-mên, Chekiang. Active *c.*1800. Portraits, flowers. M, p.317.

Ming-jên shu-hua, XX. A Banana-tree and Chrysanthemums by a Rock, after Wang Wu. Signed.

NIEN JU-LIN 年汝隣.
Unrecorded. 18th century.

Ming-jên shu-hua, XV. Mountain Landscape with a Man on a Bridge, after Ch'a Shih-piao. Signed. Also in Nanga Taikan 7.

NIU SHIH-HUI 牛石慧.
Unrecorded in the standard biographical works. Active at the end of the Ming period and at the beginning of Ch'ing. For biographical researches and speculations, *cf.* K. Sumitomo, IV, notes.

Mei-chan t'ê-k'an 32. A young Cormorant under a leafless Willow-tree. Signed.

K. Sumitomo IV. A Hen and two Chicks. Signed.

Pageant, 796. A Stag under a Pine-tree. Signed.

NIU SHU 鈕樞, *t.* Han-fan 漢藩.
From Suchou. Active probably at the beginning of the Ch'ing period. Follower of Ch'iu Ying. M, p.504.

Tokasha Shina Meigashū 21. A Man visiting a Monk in the Mountains. After a Yüan master. Signed.

PA WEI-TSU 巴慰祖, *t.* Yü-chi 予籍 and Tzŭ-an 子安, *h.* Chin-t'ang 晉堂 or Chien-t'ang 雋堂.
From Hsieh-hsien, Anhui. B. 1744, d. 1793. Collector. Landscapes, flowers. M, p.9.

Shên-chou, XI. Mountain Landscape with Pines and a Pavilion, after Fang Ts'ung-i. Signed. Poem dated 1784. Also in Shina Nanga, II, 7.

PAN TA LI SHA 班達里沙.
Unrecorded. Probably a Manchu. K'ang-hsi period.

Ku-kung, XX. Ginseng Flowers in a Pot. Poem, colophon by K'ang-hsi.

P'AN KUNG-SHOU 潘恭壽, *t.* Shên-fu 愼夫, *h.* Lien-ch'ao 蓮巢.
From Tan-t'u, Kiangsu. B. 1741, d. 1794. Landscapes, flowers. U, III, 1, 12. M, p.636.

T'ai-shan album, Series I. Twelve Landscapes. Inscription by Wang Wên-chih dated 1781. *Cf.* Nanga Taisei, Add.II, 103–114.

Shina Nanga, III, 9. Enjoying the Moon in the Mountains. Signed. Poem, colophon dated 1782.

Chang Pi-han, Hongkong. An Album of twelve Landscapes in various styles, several of them dated 1783.

Ibid. Landscape, painted in ink only on paper. Signed. Inscription by Wang Wên-chih, dated 1786.

Hamburg Exhibition, 1949–1950. Landscape, in the style of Wên Chia. Signed, dated 1788.

Gems, II, 22. Mountains before Rain, after Tung Ch'i-ch'ang. Inscription by Wang Wên-chih, dated 1791.

Nanking Exhib. cat. 356. Houses under an overhanging Mountain; a man in a boat. After Wang Mêng. Signed and dated 1792.

Shina Nanga, III, 1. High Mountains and Streams, after Wên Chêng-ming. Signed, dated 1792.

J. D. Ch'ên, Hongkong. A Villa by the River, surrounded by Bamboo. Handscroll. Seals of the artist; colophon by Wang Wên-chih, dated 1793.

Hsü-ching chai. Blossoming Trees and Four Birds by a Rockery. After Chou Chih-mien. Colophon by Wang Wên-chih.

Hui-hua kuan. Illustrations to the Story about the Musician Tai Kuei.

Ibid. Views from a Scholar's Garden.

Shên-chou, IX. A Man crossing a Mountain Stream. Poems by the painter and by Wang Wên-chih. *Cf.* Shina Nanga, I, 111.

Ibid. IX. Two Fishing-boats on a Stream between high Cliffs. Poem by the painter. Colophon by Wang Wên-chih.

T'ien-hui ko album, 1929. Landscapes and Flower-paintings. Signed.

Commercial Press album, 1933. Landscapes. Inscriptions by Wang Wên-chih. *Cf.* Nanga Taisei, Add.II, 115–128.

I-yüan chên-shang 6. Šakyamuni holding a Vajra, with two Attendants. After Ting Yün-p'êng. Signed.

Po-mei chi. A blossoming Plum-tree with a Bird. Signed. Colophon.

Shina Nanga, II, 7. An Arhat.

Nanga Taikan 5. A Mountain River between steep Rocks. Colophon by the painter.

Ōmura, I, 6. Landscape in Snow. Signed. Poem by Lu Chih, copied by Wang Wên-chih. *Cf.* Sōraikan, I, 66.

Shinchō 52. A Man on a Bridge looking at the cloudy Peaks, after Tung Ch'i-ch'ang. A seal of the painter.

Ibid. 52. Waterfall on a Hill, after Wên Chêng-ming. Seals of the painter.

Yamaguchi collect., Ashiya. Tall Rocks with Pine-trees in front and two figures in coloured Garments. Signed.

Kurokawa cat. 38. A Stream issuing from a Lake; a pavilion at its mouth. Signed.

Ibid. 39. A tall Landscape, with a Man on a Bridge. After Tung Ch'i-ch'ang. Inscription by Wang Wên-chih.

P'AN SSŬ-MU 潘思牧, *t.* Ch'iao-lü 樵侶.

B. 1756, d. after 1839. Brother of P'an Kung-shou. Landscapes, followed Huang Kung-wang and Tung Ch'i-ch'ang. M, p.637.

Shina Meiga Senshū 36. Mountains enveloped in Rain-clouds, a Stream at their Foot. After Tung Ch'i-ch'ang. Signed, dated 1827.

Sōgen 329. Landscape after Wên Chêng-ming. Signed, dated 1830 (at 75).

Hamburg Exhibition, 1949–1950. Mist and Rain in the Summer Mountains. After Kao K'o-kung. Hand-scroll. Signed, dated, 1839.

PAO K'AI 鮑楷, *t.* Tuan-jên 端人, *h.* T'ang-ts'un 棠邨.

From Hsieh-hsien, Anhui; lived in Yang-chou, Kiangsu. Active *c.*1750. Landscapes, flowers, followed Yün Shou-p'ing. Q, II, 2. R, XI, 18. M, p.675.

Ming-jên shu-hua, XVIII. Mountain Landscape, after Huang Kung-wang. Signed, dated 1753.

Po-mei chi. An old Plum-tree. Signed. Colophon.

PAO K'UN 包坤.

Unrecorded. Probably Ch'ing period.

Ars Asiatica, IX, pl.LX. A Stag resting under a Tree. Ink-painting. Signed.

PAO TUNG 包棟, *t.* Tzŭ-liang 子梁, *h.* Chin-san 近三.

From Shan-yin, Chekiang. Active *c.*1850. Figures. M, p.72.

Ming-jên shu-hua, XVII. A Girl in a Boat gathering Water-chestnuts, after Chao Mêng-fu. Poem.

Ibid. XVII. A Lady dressing her Hair in a Garden, after Lo P'ing. Poem.

I-yüan album. Studies of Figures and Landscapes. Ten leaves. Signed.

PI HAN 畢涵, *t.* Yu-han 有涵, *h.* Chiao-lu 焦麓, Chih-an tao-jên 止庵道人 and Lü-chu chü-shih 菉竹居士.
From Yang-hu, Kiangsu. B. 1732, d. 1807. Landscapes, followed Yün Shou-p'ing. U, III, 1, 14. M, p.384.

Fei-tun lu shan-shuo. Autumn Mountains, after Huang Kung-wang. Signed. Colophon by Chu Ch'u-kao, dated 1801.

PI LUNG 畢瀧, *t.* Chien-fei 澗飛, *h.* Chu-ch'ih 竹癡.
Native of T'ai-ts'ang in Kiangsu. Active in the Ch'ien-lung era. Poet, famous collector of calligraphy and paintings. Landscapes, followed Ts'ao Chih-po; bamboo. T. U, III, 1, 24. M, p.384.

Nanga Taisei, I, 247. Bamboo growing by a Stone. Signed.

PIEN SHOU-MIN 邊壽民 or Pien Wei-ch'i 邊維騏, *t.* I-kung 頤公, *h.* Chien-sêng 漸僧 and Wei-chien chü-shih 葦間居士.
From Huai-an, Kiangsu. Active *c.*1725–1747. Flowers and birds, particularly wild-geese in the *p'o-mo* manner. Q, II, 1. R, XI, 16. U, III, 1, 10. M, p.721.

Ming-jên shu-hua, VI. A Branch of a blossoming Plum-tree in a Vase. Signed, dated 1729.
Chung-kuo ming-hua, 14. Wild Geese among Reeds. Twelve-fold screen. Poem, signed and dated 1741.
Shina Nanga, III, 11. Wild Geese among Reeds. Hand-scroll. Signed. Poem dated 1741.
Ibid. I, 85–89; II, 1 and 3; III, 2 and 5. Nine pictures from an Album of Flowers and Wild Geese. I, 87 dated 1743.
Shên-chou, IX. Two Wild Geese among Reeds. Signed, dated 1744. Also in Shina Nanga, II, 9.
Shina Kacho Gasatsu. Wild Geese among Reeds. Signed, dated 1746.
Sekai Bijutsu Zenshū, 20, text illus. 103. Banana-palm Leaves. Album-leaf; another leaf dated 1747.
Chung-hua album, 1929. Twelve pictures of Flowers and Birds. Poems by the painter.
Ōmura, I, 3. Plum-blossoms and a Pine-tree. Two album-leaves.
Tokasha Shina Meigashū 42. Chrysanthemum Flowers. Album-leaf. Poem by the painter.
Ibid. 43. A Pair of Geese and Reeds. Album-leaf. Poem by the painter.
Ibid. 44. Four Geese and Reeds, one of them alighting from the air. Poem by the painter.
Nanga Taikan 6. Wild Geese among Reeds. Two album-leaves, each with a poem. The first one also in Shincho 56.
Sumitomo collect., Oiso. Wild Geese flying. Album-leaf. Inscription, signed.
Ars Asiatica, I, pl.XLIV. Two Wild Geese. Signed.
National Museum, Stockholm. Four Wild Ducks among Reeds. Poem by the painter.
Chêng Tê-k'un, Cambridge. An album of paintings of various subjects. Signed.
(See also Nanga Taisei, II, 170–172; III, 99; IV, 123–126, 239; V, 26, 27, 108, 109, 143, 177, 178, 222, 223 (Flowers, etc.); VI, 154, 155 (Butterflies); 156–169 Add. IV, 95 (Wild Geese); Add. IV, 217–224 (Household Implements.)

PIEN WÊN-YÜ 卞文瑜, *t.* Jun-fu 潤甫, *h.* Fu-po 浮白.
From Suchou. Active *c.*1620–1670. One of the "Nine Friends in Painting". Pupil of Tung Ch'i-ch'ang. Landscapes. U, I, 2, 2. M, p.13.

Shên-chou, XI. Orchids and Rocks by a Stream. (The orchids by Ch'ên Yüan-su.) Signed, dated 1622.

I-shu ts'ung-pien 14. River-view with Steep Banks; two men seated under pine-trees in the foreground. Signed, dated 1623. *Cf.* Shina Nanga, III, 8.

Ōmura, I, 8. A quiet Cottage. Signed, dated 1623. *Cf.* Sōraikan, I, p.37.

Chung-kuo, II, 32. Landscape. Signed, dated 1624.

Shên-chou, XXI. Misty River Landscape. Signed, dated 1630. *Cf.* Nanga Taikan 6.

Hui-hua kuan. Studies of Landscapes, Rocks, leafless Trees and Men in Boats. Six album-leaves. Ink only. Dated 1630.

Nanju 14. Cottages by a River. Signed and dated 1633.

Ibid. 18. Old Pine-trees and a flying Crane. Painted on gilt paper. Signed and dated 1633. *Cf.* Tōyō, XI.

Chang Ts'ung-yü cat. A Scholar's Homestead in a Garden with strange Stones and Trees. After Kuan Tao-shêng. Signed and dated 1637.

Hui-hua kuan. A Homestead among Trees at the Foot of a crevassed Mountain. Ink and some colour on paper. In Yüan tradition. Signed and dated 1639.

Chang Ts'ung-yü cat. A Scholar's Homestead in a River. Dated 1641.

Shên-chou, XI. A River Estuary. Signed and dated 1644.

Shina Nanga, I, 15. Landscape with Water Pavilions, after Tung Yüan. Signed and dated 1646.

Ming-jên shu-hua, XXVI. Mountain Landscape with Farmsteads. Signed and dated 1646. *Cf.* Chung-kuo ming-hua 18.

Chūgoku, IV. A Man in a Cottage on the Shore of a Mountain Stream; precipitous peaks behind. Signed and dated 1648.

Chang Pi-han, Hongkong. Landscape. Signed and dated 1648.

Sung-chiang p'ai ming-hua chi (Shên-chou album, 1924). Cottages in the Mountains. Signed and dated 1649.

Shên-chou, XVIII. Mountain Gully with a Temple and Buildings in the foreground. Signed and dated 1651.

Shanghai Museum. Mountain-slope rising from a River; low pavilions with men along the shore. After Chü-jan. Signed and dated 1652. *Cf.* P'ang Yüan-chi Illust. cat., V.

Hua-chung chiu-yu (Yu-chêng album). Landscape after Tung Yüan. Signed and dated 1653. *Cf.* Chung-kuo ming-hua, 37.

Chung-kuo ming-hua, 27. Landscape with Rocks. Signed, dated 1665.

Sōgen 170. Mountains in Autumn, after a Yüan master. Two lines of poetry, dated 1669.

Ku-kung album. Eighteen Landscapes in old styles. Signed. Colophon by Wang Shih-min. *Cf.* Nanking Exhib. cat. 202.

Shên-chou ta-kuan, vol.4. River in the Mountains and Pavilions. After Wang Mêng. Signed.

Hua-chung chiu-yu chi-ts'ê (Hakubundō, Ōsaka, 1921). Tall Pine-trees at the Foot of grassy Hills. After Wang Mêng. Signed.

PO ÊRH TU 博爾都, *t.* Wên-t'ing 問亭, *h.* Tung-kao yü-fu 東皐漁父.
A Manchu. Poet and painter; friend of Shih-t'ao. M, p.496.

Hashimoto collect., Kyōto. An Album of Landscapes. Signed.

P'U-HO 普荷, or T'ung-ho 通荷, *h.* Tan-tang 擔當 A priest whose original name was T'ang T'ai 唐泰, *t.* Ta-lai 大來.
From P'u-ning, Yünnan. B. 1593, d. 1683. Pupil of Tung Ch'i-ch'ang. Painted landscapes after Ni Tsan. Q, II, 2. R, XIV, I, I. U, II, I, II. M, p.502.

Boston Museum (54.89). An album of three landscapes. Sketchy studies in *p'o-mo* manner.

SHANG-JUI 上睿, *t.* Hsün-chün 尋濬 or Ching-jui 瀞睿, *h.* Mu-ts'un 目存 and P'u-shih-tzŭ 蒲室子.
From Suchou. A priest. Active *c.*1700–1720. Landscapes, pupil of Wang Hui. Q, II, 2. R, XIV, I, 13. U, I, 3, 7. M, p.6.

Ku-kung album, 1940. Ten Landscapes in old styles, the last signed and dated 1686. *Cf.* Nanking Exhib. cat. 367.

Shina Meiga Senshū 26. Pine-trees and a Temple in a Mountain. Fan-painting. Poem by the painter, dated 1704.

Kyūka, II. Two Album-leaves: 1. A Peak enveloped in Clouds, after Mi Fei. 2. A solitary Angler on a River in Snow. Signed, dated 1714.

I-yüan chên-shang 5. Landscape illustrating a T'ang poem. A scholar in his study, a visitor approaching on a bridge. Signed and dated 1714.

Sōraikan, II, 75. Two Cottages with Figures at the Foot of snowy Mountains. Poem and inscription by the painter, dated 1723.

Kurokawa cat. 16. A Man and his Servant ascending a Path between Boulders. Signed and dated 1729.

T'ai-shan ts'an-shih-lou ts'ang-hua, vol.I. River-view. Two men in conversation in a pavilion on the promontory in the foreground. Poem by the painter.

S.c.t.k. hsü-pien, II. Landscape. Inscription by the painter.

Ibid. IX. Mountain Landscape in the style of Tung Yüan. Signed.

Formerly C. B. Hoyt collect., Cambridge, Mass. Three Peonies growing in a Rockery. Poem by the painter. Signed: T'ung-hsin tao-jên, P'u-shih Jui.

SHANG-KUAN CHOU 上官周, *t.* Wên-tso 文佐, *h.* Chu-chuang 竹莊.

From Ch'ang-t'ing, Fukien. B. 1665, d. *c.*1750. Landscapes. Author of *Wan-hsiao-t'ang hua-chuan* 晚笑堂畫傳. Q, I, 3. R, VIII, 6. U, III, 1, 13. M, p.6.

Musée Guimet. A Man with a Sword standing by a Wine-jar. After a Yüan model. Signed, dated 1704.

Tokasha Shina Meigashū 18. Travellers in Mountains in Autumn; a ferry-boat on the river. Poem by a Yüan poet, copied by the painter, dated 1741 (at 77).

Shinchō 67 (J. Cahill, Wash., D.C.) A Boy riding on a Buffalo; a Man sleeping under a Tree. Album-leaves, one signed at 80 (1744).

Tokasha Shina Meigashū 20. Rushing Water at the Foot of sharply-cut Cliffs. Signed at 85 (1749).

Ibid. A Mountain Stream crossed by Bridges, two Men meeting in front of a House on the Shore. After Wu Wei. Signed.

Artibus Asiae, 1935 (Breur collect., formerly Berlin). Sailing-boats in Mist outside a City-gate.

British Museum. Two standing Figures. Album-leaf. Signed.

J. D. Ch'ên, Hongkong. A Man seated, reading, wearing Spectacles (!) Finger-painting. Signed.

SHÊN CHIH 沈治, *t.* Yo-an 約菴.

B. 1618(?) From Hsiu-shui in Chekiang. Landscapes. Q, I, 1. R, VIII, 22. M, p.149.

National Museum, Tōkyō. Dwellings of Immortals at P'êng-lai. Signed and dated *jên-wu* (1702?) at the age of 85.

SHÊN CHO 沈焯, *t.* Chu-pin 竹賓, *h.* Mo-hu wai-shih 墨壺外史.

From Wu-chiang, Kiangsu; lived in Suchou. Active *c.*1850. Painted first portraits and flowers, later on landscapes. His style resembles that of Hsi Kang. T. Add. 1. U, III, 2, 27. M, p.155.

Nanga Taisei, XII, 183–194. Album of twelve Landscapes, the last dated 1840.

Sōraikan, II, 90. River Landscape; a man in a boat looking at the lotus-flowers. After Wên Chêng-ming. Signed, dated 1841.

Ōmura, I, 4. Landscape after Hung-jên. Handscroll. Signed.

Nanga Taisei, X, 226. River Landscape, after Hung-jên. Signed.

Ibid. Intr., 54. Landscape in the manner of Ni Tsan. Signed.

SHÊN CH'ÜAN 沈銓, *t.* Hêng-chai 衡齋, *h.* Nan-p'in 南蘋.

From Wu-hsing, Chekiang. Active *c.*1725–1780. Animals, flowers and birds. Lived in Nagasaki, 1731–1733. R, XII, 9. M, p.149.

Ars Asiatica, IX, pl.LXII. Rabbits under a blossoming Tree. Signed, dated 1723.

Kokka 59. Deer under Pine-trees. Signed, dated 1725.

Ibid. 217. Birds and Flowers. Signed, dated 1729.

Ibid. 284. Cranes and a Pine-tree. Signed, dated 1731.

Ibid. 397. A Cat in a Garden. Signed, dated 1731. Also in Shimbi, XI; Tōyō, XII.

Shimbi Shoin, Shina Meigashū, vol.II. Two white Rabbits under a blossoming Plum-tree and two Birds in the Tree. Signed, dated 1731.

Chung-kuo, II, 133. Kittens playing with a Frog at the Foot of a Rockery. Signed, dated 1735. Also in Chung-kuo ming-hua 18.

Kokka 272. The Fêng Bird and the rising Sun. Signed, dated 1735.

Shinchō 63. Three Monkeys by a Waterfall. Signed, dated 1735.

Kokka 405. Two Deer. Signed, dated 1736.

British Museum, No.231. Peacocks by a Waterfall, after a Yüan master. Signed, dated 1736.

Tōyō, XII. Two Deer under Pine-trees. Signed, dated 1737.

Shimbi, IX. Plum-trees and Rabbits. Signed, dated 1737

Kokka 452. Two pictures, each representing a Crane. Signed, dated 1738. One of them also in Hyōjirō Hatta.

Shimbi, VII. Two Peacocks by a Stream. Signed, dated 1738.

Ibid. VII. Swallows and Willow-trees. Signed, dated 1738.

Sōgen 340. A Rabbit under a Wu-t'ung Tree. Signed, dated 1738.

Eda collect., Tōkyō. Landscape-handscroll, forming the setting for a Portrait of the Scholar Jui-t'ing, painted by Hsü Chang. Signed and dated 1739 (Hsü's portrait painted in 1738). Many colophons.

Sōgen 338. Cock, Hen and Chickens. Signed, dated 1740.

Ming-hua sou-ch'i, I, 9. Two Monkeys in a blossoming Tree. Signed, dated 1742.

Metropolitan Museum. Two Pheasants on the Branches of a Peach-tree. Signed, dated 1744.

Chung-kuo, II, 135. Birds. Signed, dated 1745.

I-yüan chên-shang, 10. Two Deer on the Bank of a River. Signed, dated 1746.

Kokka 264. Two Deer. Signed, dated 1748.

Ibid. 326. Eight scrolls of Flowers, Birds and Insects. Signed, dated 1748.

Ōmura, I, 9. Two Cranes in a Pine-tree. Signed, dated 1748.

British Museum, No.235. Dogs and Peonies. Signed, dated 1750.

Shimbi, XVII. Monkeys and a Deer. Signed, dated 1751.

Sōgen 339. Two Birds in a blossoming Peach-tree. Signed, dated 1753.

Shimbi, XIV. Swimming Ducks under blossoming Plum-trees. Signed, dated 1753.

Shina Nanga, III, 4. An Eagle chasing a Sparrow. Signed, dated 1753.

National Museum, Stockholm. A Pair of spotted Deer under a projecting Pine. Painted as a birthday present in 1753.

Chung-kuo, II, 137. Birds in Willows. Signed, dated 1757.

Hamburg Exhibition, 1949–1950. Wild Cats under Hibiscus Flowers. Signed, dated 1757.

Shên-chou, VI. Two Mandarin Ducks among Lotus Flowers. Signed, dated 1758.

Kyūka, II. Three Rabbits under a blossoming Plum-tree. Signed, dated 1776.

Nanking Exhib. cat. 369. Two Pheasants beneath a flowering Tree. Signed and dated 1778.

Shên-chou, XVI. Mynah Birds flying under a Willow and a Tree-peony in Wind. Signed.

Chung-kuo, II, 134. Four Wild Geese. Signed. Also in Shina Nanga, I, 127; Tōyō, XII.

Ibid. II, 136. Two Fêng Birds. Signed.

Ibid. II, 138. Peacocks. Signed.

I-shu ts'ung-pien 13. Nine Geese among Reeds. Signed. *Cf.* Shina Nanga, II, 12.

Kokka 334. Bamboos. Long handscroll. Signed.

Ibid. 384. A Cat by a Stream. Signed.

Ibid. 479. Chrysanthemums. Signed. *Cf.* Pageant, 896.
Ibid. 632. Phoenixes. Signed.
Shimbi, XVI. Horses and leafless Trees. Signed.
Ibid. XX. Two Deer. Signed.
Shina Nanga, I, 126. Sparrows in Willow-trees. Signed.
Kyūka, II. Two Cranes in a Pine-tree, after a Northern Sung master. Signed.
Tōsō 425. A Unicorn. Signed, at 78 years of age.
British Museum, No.234. Flowers and Birds. Small handscroll. Signed.

SHÊN FÊNG 沈鳳, *t.* Fan-min 凡民, *h.* Pu-lo 補蘿.
Native of Chiang-yin in Kiangsu. Seal-engraver, calligraphist and landscape-painter. Q, I, 3, R,XI, 17. U, III, 1, 11. T. M, p.149.

Pageant, 913. A broad River-view, with a pavilion and several trees on a small island. In the manner of Ni Tsan. Signed and dated 1751.
Nanga Taisei, X, 182. A Winter Landscape. Signed and dated 1766.

SHÊN HAO 沈灝, *t.* Lang-ch'ien 朗倩, *h.* Shih-t'ien 石天.
From Suchou. Active *c.*1630–1650. Poet; author of *Hua Chü* 畫麈. Landscapes. P, III, 12. N, IV, 17. U, I, 2, 19. M, p.147.

Hui-hua kuan. Scholar in a Study under old Trees. Inscription by the painter, dated 1633.
J. D. Ch'ên, Hongkong. River-landscape with Fishing-boats. In the manner of Shên Chou. Handscroll. Signed and dated 1648.
Shên-chou album, 1908. Ten landscapes in old styles. Signed.
Wu-mên p'ai ming-hua chi (Shên-chou album, 1924). Landscape with a Man seated in a Pavilion, after Wang Mêng. Signed.
Shina Nanga, I, 49. Landscape in Snow, after Ching Hao. Signed.
Ibid. II, 8. Landscape after Huang Kung-wang. Signed.
Ibid. III, 10. Landscape after Mi Fei. Signed.
Piacentini collect., Tōkyō. Landscape; pine-trees in the foreground, two figures appearing over a bluff. Signed.
National Museum, Stockholm. A Philosopher on a rocky Shore. Signed.
J. P. Dubosc, Lugano. A House under Pine-trees, Visitors arriving. A large landscape. Signed.

SHÊN HUAN 沈煥.
Court-painter in the Ch'ien-lung period. Figures. S. M, p.156.

Li-tai, III. A solitary Fisherman. Signed.
Ibid. VI. Landscape in Mist. Signed.

SHÊN JUNG 沈榮, *t.* Shih-hsiang 石薌, *h.* Ou-shih 甌史.
From Suchou. Active *c.*1830. Flowers. Landscapes, followed the Lou-tung school. U, III, 2, 22. M, p.153.

Ming-jên shu-hua, XX. Orchids in a Pot, Tea-kettle, and a Branch of Plum-tree. Signed. Poem.

SHÊN T'IEN-HSIANG 沈天驤.
Nephew of Shên Ch'üan. M, p.150.

Sōgen 341. A Crow under a Cedar-tree. Signed.

SHÊN TSU-YUNG 沈祖永, *h.* Lin-yen lao-jên 鄰煙老人.
Unrecorded. According to his inscription on the painting below, he was a sixteenth-generation descendant of Shên Chou.

I-yüan chên-shang 6. Landscape, after Shên Chou's *Pi-shan ch'in-shê* handscroll. Inscription, dated *chia-tzŭ*.

SHÊN TSUNG-CH'IEN 沈宗騫, *t.* Hsi-yüan 熙遠, *h.* Chieh-chou 芥舟 and other names.
From Wu-ch'êng, Chekiang. Active *c.*1770–1817. Landscapes, portraits. Author of the *Chieh-chou hsüeh-hua pien* 芥舟學畫編. M, p.151.

Vannotti collect., Lugano. The Goddess of the Lo River. Handscroll, painted in the *pai-miao* manner. Long inscription, dated 1769.
Shinchō 77. The Goddess of the Lo River. Signed, dated 1770.
Ch'ing êrh-shih chia. A Lady playing the *Ch'in* in a Garden, attended by a Maid. Poem by the painter, dated 1773.
Shên-chou, IX. A Lady with her *Ch'in* under a Wu-t'ung Tree. Signed. Poem dated 1778.
Hyōjirō Hatta. Mountains and Rivers. Long handscroll. Signed. Colophon dated 1782.
Ōmura, I, 1. Mountain Landscape with a Man reading in a Cottage. Signed. Poem dated 1782. *Cf.* Chūgoku, 8.
Ming-jên shu-hua, XVII. The Goddess of the Lo River. Signed, dated 1782.
Ōmura, I, 5. Mountain Terraces, a Pavilion and Houses; trees and rocks in the foreground. After Wang Fu. Signed, dated 1784. Also in Sōraikan, II, 87.
Tōyō, XII. The Garden of the Hsieh Family. Signed, dated 1786. Also in Kyūka, II.
Mo-ch'ao pi-chi, vol.I. River-view in Autumn. Signed. Poem and colophon, dated 1805.
Sōgen 348. Landscape. Signed. Poem, colophon dated 1817.
Pageant, 942. A River Scene in Autumn. Long inscription by the artist. Signed.
Boston Museum. River Scenery; high Mountains. Small sketchy picture. Colophon by the painter.

SHÊN TSUNG-CHING 沈宗敬, *t.* K'o-t'ing 恪庭 and Nan-chi 南季, *h.* Shih-fêng 獅峯.
From Sung-chiang, Kiangsu. B. 1669, d. 1735. Poet, high official. Landscapes in the styles of Chü-jan, Huang Kung-wang and Ni Tsan. Q, I, 3. R, VII, 1. U, I, 3, 4. M, p.149.

Nanju 5. Landscape with a Man on a Bridge. Two lines of poetry, dated 1705. Also in Tōyō, XII; Pageant, 843.
Fei-tun lu shan-shui. Waterfall on the steep Mountain, after a Yüan master. Signed and dated 1706.
K.-k. shu-hua chi, XXXI. Pine Groves in the Mountains. Signed.
Ibid. XXXVII. Pines in the Mountains in Spring. Signed.
Kokka 396. Mountain Landscape. Signed.
Shên K'o-t'ing Tsung-ching shan-shui ts'ê (Hakubundō, Ōsaka, 1921). An Album of eight leaves consisting of Landscape Studies, some inspired by Yüan masters. Signed.
Shinchō 47. River Landscape, after a Yüan master. Album-leaf. Signed.
J. P. Dubosc, Lugano. Landscape with two Trees and a Cottage in the foreground. Handscroll. Two inscriptions by the painter, both signed.
Shêng P'ing-ch'ên, Hongkong. Landscape.

SHÊN YING-HUI 沈映暉, *t.* Lang-ch'ien 朗乾, *h.* Kêng-chai 庚齋 and Ya-t'ang 雅堂.
From Sung-chiang, Kiangsu. Active *c.*1700. Nephew of Shên Tsung-ching. Landscapes. Q, II, 2. R, XII, 21. M, p.150.

Li-tai, I. Landscape in Autumn. Signed.

SHÊN YÜ 沈喻,
B. 1649. Treasurer of the Imperial Household in the K'ang-hsi period. Ordered in 1711 to make a picture of the Summer Palace in Jehol. Landscapes, followed Tung Yüan and Chü-jan. Q, I, 2. S. M, p.149.

Nanju 23. Landscape. Signed. Poem, colophon dated 1708 (at 60).

SHÊN YÜAN 沈源.
Court-painter *c.*1745. Figures. S, I, p.6. M, p.150.

K.-k. shu-hua chi, XXXII. An Imperial Skating-party at Pei-hai in Peking. Poem by Ch'ien-lung, dated 1746. Also in Sōgen 285.

Ibid. XXXV. Emperor Ch'ien-lung's Pavilion for playing the *Ch'in* in Pei-hai, Peking. Colophon by Ch'ien-lung.

SHÊNG TAN 盛丹, *t.* Po-han 伯含.
From Nanking. Active *c.*1640. Landscapes, followed Huang Kung-wang. P, IV, 8. R, IV, 14. U, I, 2, 23. M, p.390.

Chin-ling p'ai ming-hua chi (Shên-chou album, 1924). A Cottage among Bamboos and Trees, after T'ang Ti. Signed, dated 1638.

Chou Li-yuan 4. A Boat sailing past a high Cliff. Album-leaf. Seal of the artist.

Ibid. 18. Landscape with pointed Hills and many Houses. Album-leaf. Seal of the artist.

SHIH LIN 施霖, *t.* Yü-jo 雨若 or Yü-hsien 雨咸.
From Nanking. 17th century. Landscapes, followed the Yüan masters. P, IV, 10. U, I, 2, 21. M, p.276.

Chin-ling p'ai ming-hua chi (Shên-chou album, 1924). A Cottage. Seal.

SHIH P'U 施溥, *t.* Tzŭ-po 子博.
From Ch'ien-t'ang, Chekiang. Active *c.*1740. Landscapes, bamboos, rocks, followed the Yüan masters. M, p.276.

Nanju 16. Landscape after Tung Yüan. Signed, dated 1737. Also in Tōyō, XII.

Hyōjirō Hatta. Landscape with a Man and a Boy. Signed, dated 1741.

SHIH SÊ 碩塞, *h.* Ni-an 霓菴.
Prince Yü 裕. Cousin of the emperor Shun-chih. Landscapes, imitated the Yüan masters. M, p.593.

K.-k. shu-hua chi, XIV. Summer Landscape. Signed, dated 1682.

SHIH-TSU, EMPEROR SHUN-CHIH OF CH'ING 清世祖.
B. 1638, d. 1661. Figures and landscapes. Q, I.

K.-k. shu-hua chi, V. Landscape. Signed, dated 1655.

National Museum, Stockholm. Bodhidharma crossing the Yangtse on a Reed. Signed, dated 1655. Presented to the Secretary of the Grand Council, Fu I-chien.

Ku-kung, XVII. Chung K'uei. Signed. Presented to the President of the Board of War, Tai Ming-shuo.

Sōgen 235. Chrysanthemums by a Stream. Signed. Presented to Liu Kuang-yang.

SHIH YEN-CHIEH 史顏節, *t.* Jui-tzŭ 睿子.
From Shao-hsing, Chekiang. Early Ch'ing period. Bamboos in ink. M, p.77.

British Museum, No.184. Bamboos, after Wu Chên. Signed.

SHIH YÜAN 施原.
From Yangchou, Kiangsu. Active *c.*1770. Famous painter of donkeys. Nicknamed Shih Lü-êrh, The Donkey Shih. M, p. 278.

National Museum, Stockholm. Two Men on Donkeys. Signed, dated 1774. *Cf.* Sirén, *Later*, pl.242a.

SHIH YÜN-YÜ 石韞玉, *t.* Chih-ju 執如, *h.* Cho-t'ang 琢堂 and Chu-t'ang 竹堂.
From Suchou. B. 1756, d. 1837. Writer and poet. Bamboos. V, p.220.

Nanga Taikan 9. Bamboos and Rocks. Signed, dated 1807.

SOU-HSÜEH SHAN-JÊN 湫雪山人.
Unrecorded. B. 1710, d. *c.*1780.

Nanju 9. A Horse-rider and a Donkey-rider. Signed. Four poems by the painter, one dated 1769 at 60, another dated ten years later.

SSŬ-MA CHUNG 司馬鍾, *t.* Hsiu-ku 繡谷.
From Nanking. Lived *c.*1800–1860. Flowers and birds. T, Add. I. U, III, 2, 12. M, p.70.

Ars Asiatica, I, pl.XLI. Ducks among Reeds, after Huang Chü-ts'ai. Signed. Poem.

SU I 蘇誼, *t.* Chung-chan 仲瞻.
From Hangchou. Active *c.*1660. Landscapes, imitated Lan Ying. M, p.732.

Nanju 7. Landscape in Snow, after Wang Wei. Signed, dated 1663. Also in Tōyō, XI; Pageant, 762.

SU T'ING-YÜ 蘇廷煜, *t.* Hsü-ku 虛谷.
From Mêng-ch'êng, Anhui. Active *c.*1780. Plum-blossoms, epidendrums, chrysanthemums and bamboos. Finger painter. M, p.732.

Kyūka, II. Bamboos by a Waterfall. Finger-painting. Signed. Poem dated 1784.

K. Sumitomo, Ōiso. An album of twelve leaves. Studies of Bamboo, Chrysanthemum, Plum-blossoms Signed.

SUN HU 孫祜.
From Kiangsu. Court-painter *c.*1745. Landscapes in the style of Wang Shih-min. S. M, p.350.

K.-k. shu-hua chi, XXVII. Landscape. Signed, dated 1744.

Ku-kung, XIII. Travellers in the Mountains, after Wang Wei. Signed, dated 1745.

SUN I 孫逸, *t.* Wu-i 無逸, *h.* Su-lin 疏林.
From Hui-chou; lived in Wu-hu, Anhui. Active *c.*1655. Landscapes after Huang Kung-wang. One of the so-called "Four Masters" (of Anhui), the others being Hung-jên, Ch'a Shih-piao and Wang Chih-jui. Q, I, 1. U, II, 2, 3. R, III, 7. M, p.349.

S.c.t.k. hsü-pien, V. Clearing after Rain; steep Rocks. Signed, dated 1654.

National Museum, Stockholm. River-landscape with Mountains, after Ma Yüan. Signed.

SUN TI 孫杕, *t.* Tzŭ-chou 子周, *h.* Chu-ch'ih 竹癡.
From Ch'ien-t'ang, Chekiang. Active *c.*1700. Flowers, bamboos, rocks. R, IV, 26. M, p.349.

K.-k. chou-k'an, vols.VI–VIII, 129–151. Flower Studies on nine album-leaves. Collected in the same album as paintings by Ts'ao Yu-kuang. All signed, two dated 1650 and two dated 1651. One leaf also in K.-k. ming-hua chu-chi, II.

Ibid. vol.V, 111. Narcissus and blossoming Plum-tree by a Garden Rock. Signed and dated 1679.

Nanju 15. Camellias by a Rockery. Signed. Also in Tōyō XII.

Kyūka, I. Peonies by a Rockery. Signed.

Hamburg Exhibition, 1949–1950. Bamboos and Rocks. Painted together with Lan Ying.

SUNG CHÜN-YEH 宋駿業, *t.* Shêng-ch'iu 聲求, *h.* Chien-fu 堅甫.
From Ch'ang-shu, Kiangsu. Active *c.*1700. Vice-president of the Board of War. Pupil of Wang Hui. Q, I, 2. R, VII, 13. U, II, 2, 16. M, p.128.

Ku-kung, XXXV. Landscape. Fan-painting. Signed. Inscription by the emperor K'ang-hsi.

SUNG LIN 宋霖, *t.* Liu-yü 六雨.
From T'ung-chou, Kiangsu. Active *c.* 1800. Ink flowers after Hua Yen. M, p.129.

Kurokawa, 42. Peony. Ink on paper. Poem by the painter, dated 1808.

SUNG LO 宋犖, *t.* Mu-chung 牧仲, *h.* Man-t'ang 漫堂.
From Shang-ch'iu, Honan. B. 1634, d. 1713. Famous collector, scholar and poet. Landscapes, orchids, bamboos. Q, II. 1. R, V, 4. U, II, 2, 5. M, p.128.

Tōsō 424. Landscape in Summer, after Tai Shun. Signed, dated 1661.

Shina Nanga, II, 3. Landscape. Signed. Colophon dated 1694.

Shên-chou, XV. A Man seated on a projecting Cliff contemplating a Waterfall. Colophon by the painter.

SUNG PAO-SHUN 宋葆淳, *t.* Shuai-ch'u 帥初, *h.* Chih-shan 芝山.
From Sian. B. 1748, d. *c.* 1810. Archaeologist, connoisseur. Landscapes, followed the Northern Sung masters. M, p. 129.

Shên-chou, XV. River-view with an Angler by the Cliff in the foreground. Album-leaf. Signed, dated 1780.
Pageant, 941. River Landscape. Signed and dated 1787.
Ming-jên shu-hua, XXVI. Landscape. Signed, dated 1801.
Ho Kuan-wu, Hongkong. A Scholar's Retreat. Handscroll, signed. Title written by Weng Fang-kang.

TA-P'ÊNG 大鵬.
A Buddhist monk, who went to Japan in 1722. Did bamboo-paintings with the fingers. *Cf.* article by K. Tanaka in *Bijutsu Kenkyū*, No. 127, 1942.

Bijutsu Kenkyū, 127 (S. Yamamoto, Shizuoka). Two tall Bamboos in Snow. Signed and dated 1761. Inscription by the painter.

TA-SHAN 大汕, *t.* Han-wêng 厂翁, *h.* Shih-lien 石蓮 or 石濂.
A priest who lived in the Ch'ang-shou Temple in Kwangtung. Active in the K'ang-hsi era. Friend of Wu Wei-yeh and other painters. See *Ch'ing hua-chia shih-shih*; also V, p. 19.

Nanking Exhib. cat. 247. Landscape after Chü-jan and Wu Chên. Signed and dated 1692.

TA-SHOU 達受. Original name Ch'ên Chün 陳畯, *t.* Chi-jên 際仁, Ch'iu-chi 秋檝, Han-ch'üan 寒泉, Liu-chou 六舟 and many other names.
Buddhist monk. From Hai-ch'ang, Chekiang. Active during 1839–1852. Landscapes and flowers. T. U, III, 2, 13. M, p. 557.

Po-mei chi. Plum-blossoms. Signed. Poem.
Nanga Taisei, II, 65. Two Paintings of Orchids. Signed.
See also III, 258 (Narcissus); IV, 171 (Chrysanthemums).

TAI CH'Ü-HÊNG 戴衢亨, *t.* Ho-chih 荷之 and Lien-shih 蓮士.
From Ta-yü, Kiangsi. B. 1755, d. 1811. President of the Board of Works. Unrecorded in the biographies of painters. V, p. 1718.

Li-tai, V. A Temple in a Pine Forest. Signed.
K.-k. shu-hua chi, XL. Landscape. Signed.

TAI HSI 戴熙, *t.* Shun-shih 醇士, *h.* Yü-an 榆菴.
From Ch'ien-t'ang, Chekiang. B. 1801, t. 1860. Vice-president of the Board of Justice; Hanlin member. Literary writer. Landscapes in the style of Wang Hui. U, I, 3, 22. M, p. 718.

Ming-jên hsieh-chu. Bamboos and tall Garden Stones, after Chêng Hsieh. Handscroll. Signed, dated 1824.
Chung-kuo ming-hua 5. Steep Slopes and rushing Water. Colophon by the painter, dated 1835.
Kurokawa cat. 44. A Pavilion on a Ledge beneath a towering Cliff, in the manner of Shên Chou. Signed and dated 1837.

J. D. Ch'ên, Hongkong. Album of ten Landscapes, partly in colour, the last dated 1838. Inscription by the artist dated ten years later.

Hamburg Exhibition, 1949–1950. Pine-trees, in the style of Li Ch'êng. Signed, dated 1839.

Chūgoku 8. An old Juniper-tree by a Rock. Signed and dated 1840.

Sung-pê. A Pine-tree and a Rockery. Signed, dated 1840.

Chêng Tê-k'un, Cambridge. The upper Portion of large Pine-trees with intertwined Branches. Signed, dated 1840.

Tai Shun-shih chên-chi shan-shui ts'ê (Hui wên-t'ang Book Co., 1925). Ten Landscapes. Signed, dated 1842.

T'ai-shan ts'an-shih-lou ts'ang-hua, vol.II. A Bodhi-tree growing by a Rockery and some Sprays of Bamboo. Signed, dated 1842.

Shên-chou, XIII. River-view on a clear Autumn Day. Buildings on a cliff rising over a river. Signed, dated 1844.

Shina Nanga, I, 131. A Pavilion on a Promontory over a River. Signed, dated 1844.

Shên-chou ta-kuan, vol.10. River-landscape with rocky Shore. Handscroll. Dated 1846.

Shinchō 76. Landscape. Handscroll. Signed. Colophon dated 1846.

Chung-kuo ming-hua 18. High Mountains, rushing Stream and Pine-trees. Colophon by the painter, dated 1847.

Nanga Taisei, XIV, 124, 125. Buildings in the Mountains. Handscroll. Inscription, signed and dated 1847.

T'ai-shan ts'an-shih-lou ts'ang-hua, vol.I. Kuan-yin seated in a Bamboo Grove by a River. Signed, dated 1850.

Sōgen 351. Landscape after Wang Yüan-ch'i. Signed. Colophon, dated 1851.

Chūgoku, 8. A River winding between Hills. Signed and dated 1851.

P'ang Yüan-chi Illust. cat., 1940, II. Mountains in Autumn with an Inn, in the manner of Kuo Hsi and Fan K'uan. Signed and dated 1852.

Shên-chou, V. Buildings on a Cliff projecting over a River. Signed. Poem dated 1854. *Cf.* Shina Nanga, II, 5.

Wên-ming album, 1928. Ten landscapes. Signed; colophon dated 1854.

Shina Nanga, III, 7. Mountain Landscape with a Tower in Mist. Signed. Poem, colophon dated 1855.

Ibid. III, 12. Mountain Landscape. Long handscroll. Signed, dated 1855.

Shên-chou album, 1922. Eight Landscapes after old Masters. Each with a colophon. Signed. Last picture dated 1855. *Cf.* Chūgoku 8.

Fei-tun lu hua-hui. Five lucky Articles of the New Year. Long handscroll. Signed, dated 1857.

Shên-chou ta-kuan, vol.7. Cottages at the Foot of high Mountains, illustrating a poem by Su Tung-p'o. Dated 1857. *Cf.* Shina Nanga, III, 11.

Shina Nanga, II, 9. Mountain Abodes. Handscroll. Signed, dated 1858.

Shên-chou, VI. Large River-view with a Man passing a Bridge. Signed. Poem dated 1859. *Cf.* Shina Nanga, I, 130.

Shên-chou ta-kuan, vol.2. Mountain Lake in Spring; a man in a boat. Signed, dated 1859.

Shincho 67. The Chiu-fêng Grass-hut. Signed, dated 1859.

Shên-chou, XIX. Hilly Landscape with Mist in the Gully. After Ching Hao and Fan K'uan. Signed.

Ming-jên shu-hua, I. River Landscape, after Huang Kung-wang. Signed.

Ibid. VII. Bamboos and Rocks. Handscroll. Signed. Poem.

Chung-kuo ming-hua 18. Bamboos and two Wu-t'ung-trees in the Wind. In the manner of Li Ch'êng. Album-leaf. Signed.

Lu-ch'uang mo-hsi (Yu-chêng Book co., 1921). Ten Landscapes. Signed.

Yu-chêng album, 1921. Eight Landscapes.

Hsü-ching chai. A Tree and some Bamboos by a Rockery. According to the inscription, in the manner of Wen Cheng-ming, Li Liu-fang and Ma Shou-chen.

Mei-chan t'e-k'an 64. Broad Stretch of a River. Colophon by the painter.

Fei-tun lu shan-shui. River Landscape after Huang Kung-wang. Signed. Colophon.

Hui-hua kuan. Mountains in Mist, after Wang Yüan-ch'i.

Sung-pê. Pine-trees after a T'ang master. Handscroll. Signed.

Ming-jên hsieh-chu. Bamboos. Handscroll. Signed.

I-shu ch'uan-t'ung 12. Visiting a Hermit at Sung-ch'i. Handscroll, signed.

Chūgoku 8. A River passing between rocky Cliffs, on Top of which Bamboo is growing. Poem, signed.

Shina Nanga, I, 132. The Fu-ch'un Mountain, after Huang Kung-wang. Album-leaf. Seal of the painter.

Ibid. I, 133. Landscape. Album-leaf. Two lines of poetry. Seal of the painter.

Sōgen 352. The Hsiao and Hsiang Rivers, after Tung Ch'i-ch'ang. Album-leaf. Signed.

Nanga Taikan 2, 4, 6, 8, 10, 12. Six Landscapes from an album.

Ibid. 2. Two Buffaloes grazing among the Willows on a low River-bank. Signed.

(See also Nanga Taisei, II, 66–71 (Bamboo and Trees); IV, 174, 175, 242–245 (Trees and Rocks); V, 47–49 (Pines); X, 219–223; XII, 196, 197 (Landscapes); Add. II, 155–162; Add. IV, 126–129, 229–236 (Landscape Albums).)

TAI I-HÊNG 戴以恆, *t.* Yung-po 用伯.

From Ch'ien-t'ang, Chekiang. 19th century. Nephew of Tai Hsi. M, p.719.

Shina Meiga Senshū 43. A Mountain Valley with Buildings, a large pine-tree in the foreground. Colophon by the painter, dated 1863.

Nanga Taisei, XII, 204. A House by the Water; flowering trees. Signed and dated 1872.

TAI MING-SHUO 戴明說, *t.* Tao-mo 道默, *h.* Yen-lo 巖犖.

From Ts'ang-chou, Hopei. Chin-shih in 1634. President of the Board of War in the Shun-chih period. Bamboos, landscapes. Q, I, p.21. R, I, 7. U, II, 1, 11. M, p.715.

Nanking Exhib. cat. 299. Landscape in the manner of Ching Hao. Signed and dated 1647.

Ming-jên shu-hua, V. Bamboos by a Rock. Signed, dated 1656.

Tōsō 325. Landscape after a Northern Sung master. Signed. *Cf.* Sirén, *Later*, pl.166a.

TAI PÊN-HSIAO 戴本孝, *t.* Wu-chan 務旃, *h.* Ying-a 鷹阿.

From Hsiu-ning, Anhui. Active *c.*1660–1690. Landscapes, followed the Yüan masters. Q, I, 2. U, I, 3, 5. M, p.716.

Shên-chou, XIX. A Man resting in a Grove of tall Trees at the Foot of terraced Mountains. Poem by the painter, dated 1663.

Shên-chou album, 1910. Eight Landscapes. Inscription dated 1668.

Ibundo album, 1916. Sixteen Landscapes, the last inscribed and dated 1678. *Cf.* Nanga Taisei, Add. I, 170–185.

Nanking Exhib. cat. 260. Two leaves from an album of Landscape-paintings. Inscriptions by the artist, one dated 1678. Writings by Fu Shan on the opposite leaves.

Nanju 25. Leafless Trees. Signed and dated 1680.

Tōan, 41. Hermitages in the Mountains. Signed and dated 1680.

Nanga Taisei, XI, 230–235. An album of twelve Landscapes, the last signed and dated 1688.

National Museum, Stockholm. River Landscape with projecting Cliffs and Pavilions built over the Water. Handscroll. Signed and dated 1688.

Shina Meiga Senshū, II, 29 (Hashimoto collect.) Steep Cliffs by the River and slender Pines. Signed and dated 1689.

Gems, I, 82. Two Men in a House in the Mountains, beside a Waterfall. Signed and dated 1690.

S.c.t.k. hsü-pien, VI. High Mountains, rushing Torrents over the misty Gully. Long inscription by the painter, dated 1690.

I-yüan chên-shang 3. A House on a Ledge near a Waterfall. Inscription, signed and dated 1691.

Shên-chou, Add. 4. An album of ten Landscapes, each with a poem by the painter.

Shên-chou ta-kuan, vol. 3. A Scholar in a Study by a River, a Man in a Boat. Poem by the painter, and dedication to Mao Hsiang.

Ming-jên shu-hua, I. Mountain Landscapes. Signed. Poem. *Cf.* Shina Nanga, III, 2.

Liu 123. A Winter Landscape. Trees in the foreground, a building on a small island in a lake, near the distant shore. Signed.

Hui-hua kuan. A Mountain Village, dry Trees and small Dwellings between the Rocks. Misty atmosphere. Handscroll.

Shina Nanga, I, 113; II, 3, 9; III, 4. Four Landscapes from an album. Signed. Poems.

Shincho 28. River Landscape. Album-leaf. Signed. Poem.

Nanga Taikan 6. Mountain Landscape with a Boat under a Cliff. Album-leaf. Signed. Poem.

Sōgen 332. A Man angling in a Boat in Snow. Album-leaf. Poem. Seals of the painter.

Kurokawa cat. 22. Landscape with Groves of Bamboo; a man in a thatched house. Inscription, signed.

Nanga Taisei, XV, 50, 51. A River Landscape. Handscroll. Inscription, signed.

Mr. Suma, Tōkyō. A Mountain Gorge. Signed.

Hamburg Exhibition, 1949–1950. Creviced Rocks and Bare Trees in Snow. Poem by the painter.

TAI T'IEN-JUI 戴天瑞, *t.* Hsi-t'ang 西塘, *h.* Pên-yüan 賁園.
From Ch'ang-chou, Kiangsu. Landscapes. M, p.717.

K.-k. chou-k'an, vol.II, 29. River Landscape with two tall Pines in the foreground and a huge Rock at the back; a boat on the river. Finger-painting. Signed.

TAN CHUNG-KUANG 笪重光, *t.* Tsai-hsin 在辛, *h.* I-sou 逸叟, I-kuang 逸光, Sao-yeh tao-jên 掃葉道人, Chiang-shang wai-shih 江上外史 and other names.
From Tan-t'u, Kiangsu. B. 1623, d. 1692. Calligraphist. Landscapes. Author of *Hua ch'üan* 畫筌. Q, I, 2. R, II, 5. U, I, 2, 13. M, p.375.

Shên-chou, XVII. Stream in a Mountain Gully; an old scholar meeting a friend on the road under the trees. Signed, dated 1660. *Cf.* Shina Nanga, I, 48.

Shina Nanga, I, 47. Kuan-yin. Signed, dated 1668. *Cf.* Shên-chou ta-kuan, vol.7.

Shên-chou, XXI. A quiet Bay; a pavilion with a man at the foot of steep cliffs by the shore. After Shên Chou. Signed, dated 1671. Poem by Yün Shou-p'ing. *Cf.* Shina Nanga, II, 3.

Hui-hua kuan. Landscape after a Yüan Master. Signed. Colophons by Wang Hui, dated 1672, and by Yün Shou-p'ing.

Tokasha Shina Meigashū 30. Sketchy River-view in Autumn. Signed, dated 1680.

J. P. Dubosc, Lugano. A Scholar sitting under a tall Pine-tree. Poem by the painter, dated 1680.

National Museum, Stockholm. A River-view. Signed. Two lines of poetry dated 1681. *Cf.* Sirén, *Later*, pl.182a.

Chêng Tê-k'un, Cambridge. Steep mountain and misty valley. Inscription by the painter, dated 1684.

Shinchō 42. A Fishing-boat under a Willow-tree. Signed. Two lines of poetry dated 1686. *Cf.* Sōraikan, I, 52.

Tokasha Shina Meigashū 29. River-view. A small pavilion under a tall pine-tree in the foreground. Poem by the painter, dated 1687.

J. P. Dubosc, Lugano. Pine-trees and a Man carrying Firewood. In the manner of Wang Fu. Poem by the painter, dated 1687.

M. Prodan, Rome. A Branch of flowering Plum and other Flowers. Signed and dated 1687.

Kawai collect., Tōkyō. A Tuft of Epidendrum. Handscroll. Long inscription by the painter.

T'AN HSIANG-LU 談象稑.
A nobleman with the rank of marquis. The facts of his life are unknown. Landscapes after Tung Yüan. M, p.628.

Liu 104. Three Juniper-trees growing beside a Stream. Poem, signed and dated 1684. Colophon by Tan Chung-kuang.

T'ANG I-FÊN 湯貽汾, *t.* Jo-i 若儀, *h.* Yü-shêng 雨生.
From Wu-chin, Kiangsu. B. 1778, d. 1853. Poet, calligraphist, student of astronomy, geography, music, etc. Enlarged Tan Chung-kuang's *Hua ch'üan* into ten volumes, and published two collections of literary writings. Landscapes, plum-blossoms, pine-trees. U, I, 3, 21. M, p.527.

Sōraikan, II, 89. Landscape with a Woman teaching her Son in a Cottage at the Foot of the Mountains. Signed, dated 1805. Painted for Wang Wên-kao (1764–1849). Numerous colophons by contemporaries.
Fei-tun lu hua-hui. Branches of Plum-blossoms. Handscroll. Painted together with Tung Wan-chên, wife of the painter. Signed. Poem dated 1819.
Ming-jên shu-hua, VII. The Tiger Stream. Small handscroll. Signed. Colophon, dated 1820. Also in Nanga Taikan 10.
British Museum. View of a Garden. Inscription by the painter, dated 1826.
Chung-kuo ming-hua 5. A Man walking over a Stone Bridge. Signed, dated 1830.
P'ang Yüan-chi Illust. cat., 1940, III. Landscape. Signed and dated 1830.
Kurokawa cat. 43. A Scholar seated by a Rock, listening to Wind in the Pines. Handscroll. Signed and dated 1834.
Sung-pê. Pine-trees and a Rock. Signed, dated 1840. *Cf.* Nanga Taisei, Intro. 52.
Ikeda collect., Tōkyō. Album of Landscapes, Pine Branches, etc., the first signed and dated 1841.
Shên-chou, IX. A Branch of a blossoming Plum-tree. Signed. Colophon dated 1842.
Sumitomo collect., Ōiso. A Visitor arriving at a brushwood-fenced Cottage. Signed and dated 1843.
N. Gashū 36. Farmers' Pleasure. Signed. Poem dated 1843.
Sōgen 349. Landscape in Winter. Album-leaf. Signed. Poem dated 1846.
Sung-pê. A Pine-tree. Handscroll. Signed, dated 1847.
Shên-chou album, 1922. Ten Pictures of Plum Blossoms. Signed, dated 1848. *Cf.* Po-mei chi; Nanga Taisei, III, 191–197.
Shinchō 75. A Boat among Reeds. Signed. Poem dated 1849.
Shên-chou, XII. A Study among Rocks in a Garden. Signed. *Cf.* Shina Nanga, II, 11.
Hui-hua kuan. A high Cliff by a River; two men on the shore below. In imitation of a Yüan master.
Nanking Exhib. cat. 373. A Branch of blossoming Plum. Signed.
Yu-chêng album, 1924. Fifteen pictures of Landscapes, Flowers, Birds, Figures, Grass and Insects, painted by the painter, his wife and his children.
S.c.t.k. hsü-pien, VIII. A Mountain Stream between terraced Rocks. Signed.
Shina Nanga, II, 7. Landscape. Album-leaf. Signed.
Shinchō 75. Trees and cloudy Peaks. Signed.

T'ANG LI-HSÜEH 唐履雪.
Unrecorded. Probably Ch'ing period.

Shōman 37. Landscape. Fan-painting. Signed, dated *kêng-hsü*.

T'ANG LU-MING 湯祿名, *t.* Lo-min 樂民.
Son of T'ang I-fên. B. 1804, d. 1874. Figures in *pai-miao* manner. T, Add. I. U, III, 2, 27. M, p.527.

Chung-kuo ming-hua, 38. A Lady gazing from a Window. Signed, dated 1840.

Ming-jên shu-hua, XVII. A Lady looking at Plum Blossoms from a Window. Signed, dated 1859.

Ch'ing êrh-shih chia. A Lady in a Garden Pavilion behind Trees. Signed, dated 1860. *Cf.* Nanga Taisei, VII, 208.

Shinchō 86 (Tomioka collect., Kyōto). Two Fairies. Signed, dated 1871.

Shên-chou album, 1920. Miscellaneous pictures: four pictures of Ladies, one of Children, one of Fruits and Grass, one of Fish, and one Landscape. Signed.

T'ANG MI 湯密, *t.* Ju-lin 入林, *h.* Ko-chung-jên 个中人.
From T'ung-chou, Kiangsu. Beginning of Ch'ing period. Flowers. M, p.526.

Nanju 18. Orchids by a Rockery. Signed. Also in Tōyō, XII; Pageant, 924.

T'ANG TAI 唐岱, *t.* Yü-tung 毓東, *h.* Ching-yen 靜巖 and Mo-chuang 默莊.
A Manchu. Active *c.*1708–1750. Pupil of Wang Yüan-ch'i. Manager of the Imperial Household. Q, I, 3. R, VIII, 18. S. U, II, 2, 22. M, p.327.

Yen Kuang Co., photos. Album of twelve landscapes in old styles. Signed, dated 1708.

T'ang Ching-yen fang-ku hua-ts'ê (Shên-chou album, 1926). Ten Landscapes after old Masters. Signed, dated 1723.

Kokka 376. Landscape. Signed. Colophon dated 1723.

Cat. Ostasiatische Kunst und Chinoiserie, Köln, 1953 (No. 408). Landscape in the style of Kuan T'ung. Signed, dated 1726.

Shinchō 48. Mountain Landscape. Handscroll. Signed. Colophon dated 1732.

Ku-kung, XIV. Reading *I-ching* in the Woods in Autumn, after Chao Mêng-fu. Signed, dated 1736.

Ming-jên shu-hua, XXVI. River Landscape with Cliffs and Cottages. Signed. Colophon, dated 1736.

Sōgen 284. Mountain Landscape on a clear Autumn Day, after Kuan T'ung. Signed, dated 1737.

Li-tai, V. Peaks on a clear Spring Day, after Huang Kung-wang. Signed, dated 1741 (?)

K.-k. shu-hua chi, XXI. Landscape after Fan K'uan. Signed, dated 1743.

Ibid. XIX. Landscape after Wang Mêng. Signed, dated 1746.

Li-tai, IV. A Poet wandering in the Woods, after Shên Chou. Signed.

K.-k. shu-hua chi, VI. Waterfalls on the Mountains in Autumn, after Fan K'uan. Signed.

Ibid. XX. Homeward bound in Wind and Rain. Signed.

(See also K.-k. chou-k'an, Index, for various works of this artist.)

Kokka 357. Flowers and Birds. Painted together with Lang Shih-ning.

J. P. Dubosc, Lugano. Album with ten landscapes after old masters. Signed; poems to each leaf by Liang Shih-chêng.

T'ANG YING 唐英, *t.* Chün-kung 俊公 and Shu-tzŭ 叔子, *h.* Wo-chi lao-jên 蝸寄老人.
From Mukden. Ch'ien-lung period. Customs-inspector at Chiu-chiang, Kiangsi; director of the imperial kilns in Kiangsi. Landscapes, figures. M, p.328.

Chung-kuo, II, 127. Man listening to the Murmurs of the Stream. After T'ang Yin. Signed, dated 1743. *Cf.* Chung-kuo ming-hua, 34.

TAO-CHÊNG 道正.
Unrecorded. Ch'ing period.

Tokasha Shina Meigashū 73. Five swimming Fishes. Signed.

TAO-CHI 道濟, *t.* Shih-t'ao 石濤, *h.* Ta-ti-tzŭ 大滌子, Ch'ing-hsiang ch'ên-jên 清湘陳人, K'u-kua ho-shang 苦瓜和尚 and other names. From Ching-chiang near Wu-chou in Kuangsi.
B. 1630, a, *c.*1717. A descendant of the imperial Ming house, who became a monk. Landscapes, flowers, orchids and bamboos. Author of *Hua-yü lu* 畫語錄. Q, II, 2. R, XIV, 1, 7. U, I, 1, 8. M, p.562.

Sōgen 225 (K. Sumitomo). Garden Rock, Chrysanthemums, Grape-vines, a Cabbage Plant and Narcissi. Handscroll. Signed. Poems and colophons dated 1654. *Cf.* K. Sumitomo, III.

Cleveland Museum of Art. Epidendrums, Bamboo and other Plants. Long handscroll. Poem by the painter, dated 1662. *Cf.* Chung-kuo ming-hua, 24; Nanga Taisei, XV, 32–33.

C. C. Wang, New York. Mountain Landscape in the style of Chü-jan. Signed, dated 1663.

Kokka 313. Two Men conversing under leafless Trees. Signed. Poem dated 1669.

Ibid. 263. A Pagoda on Rocks. Signed, dated 1669.

Shina Nanga, III, 12. Landscape. Signed. Poem. Dedicated to Chou Liang-kung (who died in 1672).

Musée Guimet, Paris. Landscape; Mountain Retreat and Waterfall. Colophon by the painter, signed and dated 1671.

Kawai collect., Kyōto (Formerly Yamamoto Teijirō). A Man seated on a natural Bridge, under which a Waterfall passes. Signed and dated 1672. *Cf.* Chūgoku vol.7.

Takashima collect., Kugenuma. Album of eight paintings: Landscapes, Vegetables, Chrysanthemums, etc. Signed and dated 1672. Colophon by Kao Fêng-han.

Lo Chia-lun, Taipei. A handscroll of Mountain Landscape. The painter is seated on a stone, holding a hoe, ready to plant a tree which is brought to him by a small monkey and a boy. Signed and dated 1674.

Nanking Exhib. cat. 295. A Man in a House beside a Stream; a mountain rising from mist beyond. Poem, signed and dated 1681.

Sōgen 224. The five auspicious Plants in a Vase. Signed. Poem dated 1675.

Shên-chou, XVIII. River winding between rocky Banks; trees in the foreground. Two inscriptions by the painter, first dated 1676, the second 1694. Also in Nanga Taisei, X, 42.

C. T. Loo's Successor, Frank Caro, N.Y. The Conversion of the Demoness Hariti who was changed by Buddha from a Demoness to a devoted Symbol of Mother-love. Handscroll. Inscription by the painter in which he says that he painted this in the I-chih Pavilion (*c.*1680). Another inscription by Tu Ch'êng. *Cf.* Toronto, 44.

Nanking Exhib. cat. 287 (P'u Ju collect.) Landscape with leafy Trees; a man crossing a bridge. Signed and dated 1675.

Shina Nanga, III, 1. The Wu-i Mountain. Signed. Poem, colophon dated 1681. Also in Nanga Taikan 1.

Chang Ta-ch'ien cat., vol.II, 1. Spare Trees on a River-bank. A man standing by a little boat; mountain and buildings on the opposite shore. Inscription, dated 1682.

Chang Ta-ch'ien cat.II, 24–28. A small album of ten leaves: Landscape-studies. 1. A Study among the Plum-trees. 2. In search of Plum-blossoms. 3. Village among Willow-trees. 4. Cottage of the Painter. 5. Misty Mountains. 6. Walking with a Staff among Hills. 7. Dwelling by a sheer Cliff. 8. Landscape of Hsiao and Hsiang. 9. Plum-trees. 10. A Man seated in a Pavilion under Dry Trees. All with inscriptions; the fifth, sixth and the ninth dated 1682.

Freer Gallery (44, 16). Views along a River-valley with Rocks, Buildings and Dry Trees. Long handscroll. Inscription dated 1684. Possibly school work.

Shina Meiga Senshū, vol.II. Kuanyin Bodhisattva seated on a Lotus-leaf. Kung-pi painting. Long inscription, dated 1684.

Chang Ta-ch'ien cat., II, 14. A Record of the painter's search for Plum-blossoms. Handscroll. Inscription and nine poems by the painter dated 1685.

Sekito Meigafu. *Wan-tien o-mo*. Sections of Mountains with luxurious Growth and Buildings. Handscroll in *p'o-mo* manner. Poem by the painter, dated 1685.

Nanga Taisei, III, 62–65. Plum-blossoms. Sections of a handscroll(?) Signed, dated 1685.

Liu 86. Landscape of Huang-shan. Inscription by the artist dated 1686; another dated 1697.

S.c.t.k. hsü-pien, VIII. Pine-tree and Rocks. Inscription by the painter dated 1686.

Sōgen 217. Landscape with a Man angling in a Boat. Painted in green and blue colours after Chang Sêng-yu. Signed. Poem dated 1686.

Chung-kuo ming-hua, 23. A Man in a Pavilion built over a Stream, looking at a Friend who approaches on a Stone-bank across the River below; dry trees and cliffs. Poem by the painter, dated 1687.

Lo Chia-lun, Taipei. Bamboos, Banana plants and Rocks; writings between the pictures. Handscroll. Signed and dated 1689.

Nanking Exhib. cat. 291. Landscape with Junks sailing down a Ravine between Mountain Peaks. Signed and dated 1690.

Nanga Taisei, XIV, 84. Mountain-streams. Handscroll. Dated 1689.

S.c.t.k. hsü-pien, IV. High Peaks. A man walking along the stream below. Inscription by the painter dated 1690.

K.-k. shu-hua chi, VI. Bamboos and Epidendrums. Signed. Poem dated 1691. Stones by Wang Yüan-ch'i. Signed.

Sekito Meigafu. Nine Landscapes from an Album called *Ch'ing-hsiang lao-jên shan-shui ts'ê*. One dated 1691.

Boston Museum (55.387). River-landscape with rocky Banks, and Buildings among the Trees. Handscroll. Inscription dated 1691. Colophon by Wu Hu-fan.

Chung-kuo ming-hua, 20. A tall, narrow Landscape. A Man in a House beneath an overhanging Rock. Long inscription, signed and dated 1693.

Shên-chou ta-kuan, XII. Landscape with a Fisherman. Long inscription signed and dated 1693.

Chang Ta-ch'ien cat., II, 2. Resting in a Rowing-boat on the Fêng River. Painted for his friend Wu of Hui-chou. Poetic inscription, dated 1693.

Shina Meiga Senshū 15 (Hashimoto collect.) The God of Longevity. Poem by the painter, dated 1693.

Chang Ch'ün, Taipei. Rocks, Bamboos, Chrysanthemum Flowers, Banana-plants and old Pine-trees by a Stream. Long handscroll divided into twelve sections. Poetic inscription on the first section dated 1693, and another on the ninth section dated 1694. Four more inscriptions by the painter. *Cf.* the following picture.

Shih-t'ao ming-hua ts'ê (Anonymous Japanese publication). Twelve Landscape-sketches, mounted in a folder. Some with poems by the painter. Signed. Colophon dated 1694.

Chūgoku 7. C. C. Wang collection, N.Y. An Album of eight Landscapes, some from Huang shan, signed and dated 1694.

Chung-hua album, 1930 (Yamaguchi collect., Ashiya). Ten Landscapes. Signed, dated 1695.

Chang Ta-ch'ien cat., II, 29–33. An album of landscape-studies in the *p'o-mo* style, consisting of ten leaves. Inscription on the last leaf by the painter, dated 1695. Colophon by Chang Ta-ch'ien.

I-yüan chên-shang 5. The Blue Lotus Tower at Kuang-lung. Signed and dated 1696.

Ch'ing-hsiang lao-jên shu-hua k'ao (Yu-chêng album, 1934). Album of Landscapes and other Subjects; the last, representing a Man Imprisoned in a Tree(?), dated 1696.

Shanghai Museum. A high Pavilion in a Bamboo Grove. A scholar is seated in the upper storey; another man approaches from a bridge leading across the stream. Inscription by the painter, dated 1697.

Sōraikan, I, 43. Landscape after Ni Tsan. Signed. Colophon dated 1697.

Cleveland Art Museum. Min River Landscape. Ink and slight colour. Painted for Wang Mu-t'ing who was to leave for Min-hai. Colophon by the painter, dated 1697. *Cf.* Cleveland Exhib. cat. 94.

Ming-jên shu-hua, VIII. A Man under a Wu-t'ung-tree. Signed. Poem dated 1698. Also in Shina Nanga, III, 7.

Tomioka collect., Kyōto. Album of Landscapes and Flower-paintings, one dated 1698.

Liu 89. Bamboo and Orchids growing by a Rock. Five inscriptions by the artist, one dated 1698.

Sōgen 218. Bamboos and Orchids. Signed. Poem dated 1699.

Sekito Meigafu (K. Sumitomo). View of Huang-shan. Handscroll. Long poem by the painter, dated 1699. Also in K. Sumitomo, II; Sekai Bijutsu Zenshū, 20, pl.40.

Chung-hua album, 1930 (Chang collect.) Twelve Landscapes with Poems. Signed, dated 1699. The first leaf shows Chu Hao-nien's copy after Tao-chi self-portrait.

Chūgoku 7. Plum-tree and Bamboo growing beside a Stone. Long inscription. Signed and dated 1700.

I-shu ts'ung-pien 14. View of a River between hilly Banks, a man walking into the picture. Poem by the painter, dated 1701.

Ibid. 24. Wooded Mountains on an Autumn Evening. Signed. Two lines of poetry dated 1701. *Cf.* Ōmura, I, 9, and Nanga Taisei, X, 43.

Shên-chou ta-kuan, vol.5. A Scholar's Retreat among Bamboos in the Mountains. Signed. Dedicated to a man called Ch'iu Fêng in 1701.

T'ai-shan album, series I. Epidendrum and Bamboo-paintings. Inscriptions, one dated 1701.

Shih-t'ao shang-jên shan-shui ts'ê (Yu-chêng Book Co., 1924). Eight Landscape-studies. Signed, dated 1701.

Ōmura, I, 10. Shady Trees. Signed. Poem dated 1701.

Shina Nanga, III, 10. A Man with a Staff looking at Maple-trees. Signed. Poem dated 1701.

Sōgen 215. Landscape in colours. Signed. Colophon dated 1701.

C. C. Wang, New York. Peaks rising through the Mist, rushing Streams, sparse Trees. Inscription dated 1701. *Cf.* Sōgen, 214; Toronto, 43.

Chang Ta-ch'ien, Hongkong (1951). Viewing a Waterfall. Colophon by the painter, dated 1701.

P'ang Yüan-chi Illust. cat., II, 1940. Cloudy Mountains. Long inscription by the artist, signed and dated 1702.

Nanking Exhib. cat. 289. A Man in a House at the Foot of a Hill; bare trees outside. Inscription dated 1702.

Mo-ch'ao pi-chi, vol.II. A Scholar's Abode at the Foot of a Hill. Handscroll. Signed. Poem dated 1702.

Chang Ta-ch'ien cat., II, 5. An open Pavilion by the Stream; a tall pine-tree in the foreground. After Ni Tsan. Inscription by the painter dated 1702.

Yamaguchi collect., Ashiya. Landscape from a large album. Mountain-peaks rising through circling white clouds. Signed and dated 1702.

Wang Shih-chieh, Taipei. A small Temple-compound on a Mountain enclosed by a Wall. A small boy drawing water in a bucket from a stream; a man seated in an open pavilion lower down. After a picture by Huang Kung-wang brought to the artist by Mei Ching. Ink and slight colour. Inscription by the painter, dated 1703.

Boston Museum. Nine Landscapes from an Album of Twelve called *Ta-ti-tzŭ shan-shui ts'ê*. One dated 1703. *Cf.* Sekito Meigafu; Nanga Taisei, XIII, 34–45.

Ibid. (55.927). Walking toward a Mountain Retreat; high-pointed hills. Dry brushwork. Signed and dated 1703.

Sekito Meigafu. Seven Landscapes from an Album called *K u-kua miao-t'i ts'ê*. One dated 1703. The same pictures are reproduced together with five more in the Yu-chêng album called Ta-ti tzŭ shan-shui tsu.

Piacentini collect., Tōkyō. Small Album of ten landscape studies; partly in colour. The first dated 1704.

Vannotti collect., Lugano. Album of ten Landscape-studies, each with inscriptions, the last one dated 1704. *Cf.* Venice Exhib. cat., p.247. Probably later.

Shên-chou, X. Pine, Bamboos and Orchids by a Rockery. Signed, dated 1704. Poem. Also in Nanga Taisei, V, 17.

Ming-jên hsieh-chu. Bamboos and Stones. Signed, dated 1704. Also in Nanga Taisei, I, 110.

Ōmura, I, 3. A Farewell Scene. Signed, dated 1704. *Cf.* Chūgoku, 7.

T'ien-ch'i shu-wu. A House by the River; a Fisherman in his Boat. Long inscrption by the artist, dated 1705.

Chang Ta-ch'ien cat., II, 6. *San-chüeh t'u*: Combination of three Beauties (*i.e.*, painting, poetry and calligraphy), a small landscape-painting. Poem and inscription by the painter, dated 1705. An inscription to the right by the painter Chu Lun-han (1680–1760) who gave this picture its present title.

Ibid. II, 10. A Gōurd and a Fruit under a Bamboo-branch. Poem by the painter dated 1705.

Chung-kuo, II, 109. Epidendrum plants growing on a large Stone. Album-leaf painted for his friend Yu-lao. Poem dated 1706. *Cf.* Chung-kuo ming-hua, 25; Toronto, 42.

Tokasha Shina Meigashū 16. River Landscape with two Sailing Boats; pavilions built on the water under cliffs. Poem and colophon by the painter dated 1706.

Horiuchi collect., Ōsaka. Seven leaves from an Album of Landscapes, one dated 1706. Four other leaves from the same album in the Hashimoto collect., Takatsuki.

Shên-chou, II. Hollyhocks and Tufts of Grass. Signed. Poem.

Ibid. XII. Illustration to T'ao Yüan-ming's Poem *Kuei-ch'ü-lai tz'ŭ*. Poem copied by the painter.

Ibid. XIV. Two Landscape-sketches. Album-leaves, each with a poem.

Ibid. XV. A Man leaning against a large Pine-tree by a Stream. Poem by the painter.

Ibid. XIX. A grassy River Bank; a *ch'in*-player on the terrace. Album-leaf. Poem by the painter.

Shên-chou ta-kuan, vol.2. A Misty Mountain Gorge. Poem by the painter.

Ibid. vol.3. A Branch of wild Tea Flowers. Poem by the painter.

Shên-chou album, 1929. Landscapes after Sung and Yüan poems. Inscriptions, signed.

Chung-kuo, II, 106. Two small Fishing-boats on a Mountain River. Large trees in foreground. Inscription by the artist. Also in Tōsō, 416.

Ibid. II, 107. A Hut among Trees; high rocks behind. Poem by the artist. *Cf.* Chung-kuo ming-hua, 30.

Ibid. II, 108. Lotus-roots, Cherries, and a Gourd. Album-leaf. Poem by the artist. *Cf.* Chung-kuo ming-hua 28.

Chung-kuo ming-hua, 12. River View with rugged Trees along the rocky Shore. Poem by the painter.

Ibid. 22. A River winding between Rocks, leafy Trees and a Pine. A bridge in the foreground, four men in a boat. Inscription by the painter. (Reproduction blurred.)

Ibid. 24. Bamboo and Plum-blossoms. Signed: poem by the artist mounted above.

Ibid. 26. Bamboo, Epidendrum and Stone. Poem; seals of the artist.

Ibid. 38. Two Men in a Boat beneath an overhanging Cliff. Poem, signed.

Ibid. 40. A Man by a Stream. Leaf from an album of eight views of Huang-shan. Poem, signed.

Chung-hua album, 1930. Ten Landscapes with poems. Signed. Later versions of four of these views are reproduced in *Shina Meiga Senshū*, II.

Chung-hua album, 1930. Twelve Landscapes. Seals of the painter, but no signature.

Shih-t'ao shan-shui ching-p'in (Commercial Press, 1929), (formerly Lin Lang-an, now K. Sumitomo). Twelve Landscapes with poems and colophons by the painter. Colophons by later men. Also in K. Sumitomo, I and II; Nanga Taisei, Add. I, 158–169.

Shih-t'ao shan-shui t'u-yung (Commercial Press, 1929), (Lin Lang-an collect.) Twelve Landscapes from Chang-an with poems by the painter. Additional writings by Ho Shao-chi (famous calligraphist, 1799–1873).

Ta-ti-tzŭ chung-chüeh ch'i-ming t'u (Shên-chou album, 1931). Fowls and Birds with blossoming Plants and Trees, after a Sung master. Long handscroll. Inscriptions by the painter. Also in Nanga Taisei, XV, 35.

K'u-kua ho-shang hua-ts'ê (Yu-chêng album). Eight Landscapes, each is signed with a different *tzŭ* or *hao*.

Ta-ti-tzŭ lan-chu hua-ts'ê (Yu-chêng album). Twelve leaves of Orchids and Bamboo, with inscriptions by the painter.

I-yüan album (Ho Shao-chi collect.) Studies from Huang-shan, representing Cliffs, Mountain-streams, Pools and Trees. Seven leaves, each with a poem by the painter; some in the *p'o-mo* manner. According to the inscriptions, the pictures were painted at Pai-lung-t'an.

Shih-t'ao ho-shang hua-kuo ts'ê (Wên-ming co.) Ten pictures of Flowers and Fruits (Bamboo, Orchids, Narcissus, Chrysanthemum, Vegetables, Lotus-root, Peaches, Lotuses). Inscriptions by the painter.

Hui-hua kuan. The Garden of a Scholar on the rocky Coast of a River. Two servants carrying a chrysanthemum plant; the master in the house looking at other plants in his room. Ink and reddish colour. Inscription by the painter.

Ibid. A Man seated on the Ground playing the *Ch'in* to an Ox. Long inscriptions by the painter. Ink only. *Cf.* Liu 90.

Ibid. A Man in a Boat on a Mountain River between large Rocks. A very large horizontal composition. Painted for his friend Shu-wêng. Reddish colour on paper. Signed.

Ibid. Landscape-studies on (eight) leaves from Huang-shan. Inscriptions by the painter. Ink and slight colour on paper.

Ibid. Landscape-studies: Mountain-terrace, Bamboo-grove, Man in a Boat. Slight colour. Four album-leaves (of eight?)

Liu 87. Landscape of Nan-yang shan. Houses under pine-trees, a pavilion built over the water. Poem, signed.

Ibid. 88. A Pine-tree growing by a Rock. Poem, signed.

Gems, I, 67. Autumn in Wei-yang (Yangchou). Long inscription by the artist, signed. *Cf.* Fei-tun lu shan-shui.

Ibid. I, 68. Mountains and Pines. After Kuo Chung-shu. Poem, signed.

Ibid. III, 9. Five Landscapes on album-leaves. Signed. Inscriptions by the artist on the opposite leaves.

Nanking Exhib. cat. 288. A River Landscape, with two fishermen in boats. Poem, signed.

Ibid. 290 (Chang Ch'ün collect.) Rainy Trees and frosty Mountains. Poem, signed.

Ibid. 292. Epidendrums and Rocks. Handscroll, signed.

Ibid. 294 (Chang Ta-ch'ien collect.) A flowering Plum-tree and Narcissus by a Rock. Poem, signed.

Ibid. 296 (Chang Ta-ch'ien collect.) A House by the River; two men on a plateau above. Long inscription, signed.

Ibid. 297 (Chang Ta-ch'ien collect.) A Bamboo-grove. Poem, by the artist.

Ibid. 298 (Chang Ta-ch'ien collect.) Autumn Landscape after Rain. Poem and inscription, signed.

Chang Ts'ung-yü cat. A Lotus Plant. Signed.

S.c.t.k. hsü-pien, V. A Waterfall between strange Rocks. Inscription by the painter.

Ibid., VI. Bamboo and Plum-blossoms. Signed.

Ibid., VIII. Wooded Hills with two cottages. Signed.

Ibid. IX (Chang Ta-ch'ien collect.) The Gully of the Nine Dragons. Signed.

Ibid. X. Epidendrums, Plum-blossoms and Bamboo. Inscription by the painter.

Ibid. XI. Plum-tree and Banana-plant growing by a Rock. A man walking below. Signed.

Shih-t'ao hua-ts'ê (Wên-ta Book co., 1924). Ten Landscape-sketches, one picture of Bamboos and one of a Cabbage Plant.

Ch'ing-hsiang lao-jên hua-ts'ê (Wên-ta Book co., 1925). Ten Landscape Sketches.

Pa-ta shan-jên, Shih-t'ao shang-jên hua ho-ts'ê (Yu chêng Book co., 1924). An Album of three pictures and several writings by Pa-ta shan-jên and twelve pictures by Tao-chi.

Ming-jên shu-hua, IV. The Fairy Ma-ku. Signed.

Ibid. XI. A Lotus Flower with two Leaves. Signed. Poem. Also in Nanga Taikan 12.

Ibid. XIII. Bamboos and Bamboo Shoots. Signed. Colophon.

Ibid. XXIV. Lotuses and Roses. Signed. Poem.

Ibid. XXV. Two Boats on a River. Signed. Poem.

Palace Museum Album, 1935. Sixteen Lohans. Copies after Tao-chi. Signed.

Ming-hua sou-ch'i, I, 6. Two Hollyhock Plants. Poem by the painter.

Fu-lu. Epidendrum-plants. Handscroll. Signed.

Mei-chan t'ê-k'an 34. Landscape at Hua-shan: fantastically formed mountain peaks and rushing water. Poem by the painter.

Ibid. 35. A Branch of a Rose Bush. Poem by the painter.

Fei-tun lu shan shui. A wide River-view; a village on the foreground shore. Signed. Colophon.

Fei-tun lu hua-hui. Bamboos and Epidendrums, a Rock in the foreground. Handscroll. Signed. Poem.

I-shu ts'ung-pien 14. A Winding River, a Man walking along the River-bank; steel cliffs beyond. Poem by the painter.

Ibid. 14. Tall Landscape, River between steep Cliffs and Trees. Poem by the painter.

Ibid. 14. Bamboo-grove on the rocky Shore and Lotus flowers. Poem by the painter.

T'ai-shan ts'an-shih-lou ts'ang-hua, vol.I. Bamboos by a Rockery and some Epidendrum-plants. Signed. The Bamboos by Tao-chi, the Rockery by Chu Ta.

Ibid. vol.II. A Lotus-plant. Poem by the painter. Album-leaf.

Ibid. vol.IV. A Man walking among Trees. Signed.

Ibid. Epidendrums and Bamboo by a Rock. Signed.

T'ai-shan album, series I. Eight leaves with Flowers, Landscapes, etc. Inscriptions by the artist.

Ibid. Series II. An album of twelve leaves. Studies of Cliffs, Mountain Streams (one with a large Rowing-boat), and Buildings by a River. Each leaf accompanied by an inscription.

Ibid. An album of seven vertical leaves of Landscape-studies representing River-views, Mountains, Cottages on River-banks, etc., in Mist. Each leaf is accompanied by an inscription.

Chang Ta-ch'ien cat., II, 3. A Man seated in a thatched Hut at the Foot of Lu-shan. Poem by the painter.

Ibid. II, 4. Drunk in the Autumn Grove. Three inscriptions by the painter. *Cf.* Nanking Exhib. cat., 293.

Ibid. II, 7. Bamboos and Epidendrums by a Rock in the Wind. Poem by the painter.

Ibid. II, 8. Pine-grove in Wind at the Foot of a Mountain; an old man fishing in the stream. Signed.

Ibid. II, 9. Portrait of the Monk Pao-chang from India, seated by a rock under a blossoming tree. Ink painting. Inscription by the painter.

Ibid. II, 11. View of the Chang-kung Grotto near Kuei-lin. Handscroll, in colours. Title of the picture by Ho Tzŭ-chên; short inscription and poem by the painter.

Ibid. II, 12. River-landscape in ink. Several sailing-boats on the water and a pavilion under two trees to the left. Handscroll. Inscription by the painter.

Ibid. II, 13. The Ancestral Tombs of the Fei Family. Handscroll. Inscription by the painter, dated 1702.

Ibid. II, 16–23. An album of eight leaves: Studies of Flowers, Bamboo, Banana-leaves and Figures. The fifth leaf represents T'ao Yüan-ming holding a chrysanthemum flower; the sixth, two children flying a kite. Writings and inscriptions by the painter.

Ibid. II, 37–40. An album of eight leaves of landscape-studies, illustrating poems of the Sung and Yüan period. 1. Houses at the Entrance to a Valley. 2. Two Scholars under tall Pine-trees. 3. An open Pavilion by a Mountain Stream on an Autumn Day. 4. Spring Grass. 5. Village in the West. 6. Walking on a Country Path. 7. Two Fishing-boats anchored near a Village. 8. A Scholar's Retreat under leafy Trees. All the poems copied by the painter.

Ibid. IV, 35. Pine-wood in the Mountain; an old man with staff strolling on the path. Poem by the painter.

Chang Ch'ün, Taipei. *Tui-chü t'u*: A Homestead under a curving tall Pine-tree at the Foot of the Mountain; a broad stream in front. Edge of the mountain visible on the picture, and a man standing by the chrysanthemums in the courtyard. Poem by the painter.

Ibid. Water Streaming down from a Mountain Gully; leafy pine-trees on one side. Two lines of poetry. No signature, but seal of the painter reads: Ching-chiang Hou-jên.

Kokka 493 (Sumitomo collect., Ōiso). Waterfall on Lu-shan. Signed. Poem, colophon. Also in Tōyō, XI; Sōgen 216; Kyūka, II; Sekito Meigafu, V; K. Sumitomo, I and III.

Ibid. 560. Sailing Boats. Album-leaf.

K. Sumitomo collect., Oiso. Picnicking outside Yang-chou. Mountain slope with leafy trees; group of men enjoying themselves. Two inscriptions by the painter.

K. Sumitomo, I. Buildings among Pine-trees; a standing figure. Fan-painting. Inscription by the artist, signed.

Hakone Museum, Gora. Album of scenes of Lo-fou shan. Reproduced as an album by Jurakusha, Tōkyō, 1953. A similar album in the Cologne Museum.

Chūgoku 7. Four Flower-paintings, horizontal album-leaves. Poems, signed.

Shina Meiga Senshū, II, 16 (formerly Nagao collect.) Rocks and Pine-trees. Part of a handscroll.

Ibid. 21–24 (Inoue collect.) Four Album-leaves, Landscapes: one with two men in a boat, another with sailing-boat passing shore with overhanging trees. Later versions of paintings in Chung-hua album 1930.

Shina Nanga, I, 25. River Scenery. Album-leaf. Signed. Poem.

Ibid. I, 27. Bamboos. Album-leaf. Signed. Two poems.

Ibid. I, 28. Radishes. Album-leaf. Signed. Poem.

Ibid. II, 2. Lotus Roots, Pears, etc. Albuml-eaf. Signed. Two poems.

Ibid. II, 6. A Rocky Island between misty Mountains. Horizontal album-leaf. Signed. Poem.

Ibid. II, 12. Pomegranates. Horizontal album-leaf. Signed. Poem.

Ibid. III, 3. Bamboos and Lotus-flowers. Signed. Poem.

Ibid. III, 6. River between Rocky Banks. Horizontal album-leaf, probably same series as II, 6. Signed. Poem.

Ibid. III, 8. Landscape. Very tall narrow picture. Reproduction blurred. Signed. Poem.

Ōmura, I, 1. Landscape. Signed. Poem.

Ōmura, II, 2, 3. Four pictures of Flowers from an album of eight. Each with a poem.

Shina Meiga Senshū 14 (Fujii collect.) Misty River Landscape; a bridge leads over the stream to pavilions on the opposite shore. Poem by the painter.

Tokasha Shina Meigashū 15. Sprays of Bamboo and Plum-blossoms. Two lines of poetry by the painter.

Ibid. 17. Extensive River-view, Man in a Boat by the rocky Shore. Poem by the painter.

Tōan I, 38. Fantastic Studies of Rocks and Water. Two album-leaves. Signed.

Tōsō 415. Buildings on the Rocks at a Bay. Album-leaf. Signed. Poem.

Ibid. 417. The green Peaks of the South Mountain by a misty Valley. Signed. Poem.

I-yüan album (Hakubundō). Twelve pictures illustrating twelve poems by Su Tung-p'o. Also in Bijutsu Kenkyū and in Sōraikan, II, 72; nine leaves in Sekito Meigafu, one in Shina Nanga, I, 26; and in Shincho 22.

Hakubundō album (Sumitomo collect., Ōiso). Eight Views of Huang-shan; each with a poem. Same in Sekito Meigafu; also K. Sumitomo, I, II and V; Sekai Bijutsu Zenshū, 20, Pl.41 and colour Pl.3.

Sōgen 221 (Ti P'ing-tzŭ collect.) Bamboos and Plum-blossoms. Signed. Poem by the painter.

Ibid. 222. Four Landscape-studies on a handscroll. Signed. Four poems.

Ibid. 226. Lilies and Lotus Flowers. Two album-leaves. Signed. Poems.

Sōraikan, II, 71. High Mountains in Mist; a lonely stream and lingering rain. Poem by the painter.

Sekito Meigafu. Seven pictures of Flowers and climbing Plants; from an album called *Ch'ing-hsiang lao-jên hua-hui ts'ê.*

Ibid. A stone Bridge in the T'ien-t'ai Mountain, after Wang Mêng. Poem and colophon by the painter.

Ibid. The Purple Jade Peak of Huang-shan. Poem by the painter.

Yamaguchi collect., Ashiya. Small album of ten leaves. Studies of pine-trees and rocks, two with the painter standing under the tree. Ink only on soft brownish paper. Short inscription by the painter.

Ibid. Small album of eight leaves of landscape-studies. Mountain streams, sailing-boats, a boatmast shown above the tree tops, etc. Colour and ink. Signed. Colophon by Naitō.

Hashimoto collect., Kyōto. Branches of blossoming Plum-tree and the Top of a Hill. Slight bluish and reddish colours. Short handscroll. Long inscription by the painter, and seven poems by Hashimoto with reference to the picture.

Ibid. Portrait of Shao Hsing in Long Robe with Staff. Bold brushwork. Inscription by the painter.

Ibid. Album of eight leaves. Large folio Landscape-studies, mostly in ink, a few with colour-washes. Short inscription by the painter, and a long colophon by Hashimoto.

National Museum, Stockholm. A lonely Wanderer on a Mountain Path. Long inscription by the painter and his seal.

Ibid. Bamboo Shoots and a slender Stem. Poetic inscription by the painter.

Ibid. Two Studies of Rocks and Streams on large album leaves. Inscriptions and seals of the painter.

Hamburg Exhibition, 1949–1950. Melon, Lotus Seeds, Epidendrum, etc. grouped together. The symbolic meaning of these plants is explained in the inscription by the artist.

Ibid. Topped Hills and Mountains; a study among shady trees in the gully. Signed.

C. C. Wang, New York. A Scholar's Abode in the Mountains, called *Hsia-mu sui-yin.* In the style of Ch'ien Kuan-tso.

H. C. Wêng, Scarsdale, N.Y. An Album of twelve Flower-studies with inscriptions. Ascribed to the painter.

C. T. Loo's Successor, Frank Caro, N.Y. Lotus. Poem, signed. *Cf.* Toronto, 41.

J. Cahill, Wash., D.C. An old Palace; boats sailing along a canal between misty willows and roofs. Poem and seals of the artist.

Boston Museum (55.388). Bamboo and Rock. A very tall picture; bold brushwork on almost white paper. Long inscription by the painter.

Dr. Victoria Contag, Heidelberg. Small album of landscape-paintings. Ink and light colour on paper. Signed *Cf.* Cleveland Exhib. cat. 97.

Chang Ta-ch'ien collect., Hongkong (1951). A flowering Branch. Inscribed by the painter.

Ibid. A Mountain Gorge, with Figures on a Bridge. Handscroll. Long inscription by the artist, in which he states that he painted it at the age of 39, and refers to a meeting with the emperor K'ang-hsi.

Chang Ta-ch'ien cat. I, 35. An old House under tall Pines. Poem, signed.

Huang Pan-jo, Hongkong. Autumn Hills. Signed.

Vannotti collect., Lugano. An album with six large landscape-studies and six leaves with writings by the artist. Probably later.

Cologne, Museum. Album of twelve Leaves, Scenes of Lo-fou-shan. One is signed. Similar to the album in the Hakone Museum.

Ibid. Bamboo, Plum-blossoms and Epidendrum by a Rock. Fan-shaped. Poem by the painter.

Kao Yen-ju, Hongkong (1951). Landscape Studies of Lo-fou shan. An album.

J. P. Dubosc, Lugano. A Tall Bare Tree by a Stream between split Cliffs. Inscription by the painter.

Ibid. Small album with ten leaves of Landscape-studies, each accompanied by a poem written by the painter.

Shih-t'ao (Sekito). A Monograph by Hashimoto (1926), reproducing two albums, one of twelve Flower Paintings with poems, one of eight Landscape Studies (now Hashimoto collect., Kyōto). Also two plates from the Huang-shan series, a handscroll with prunus blossoms, and the *Wan tien o-mo* scroll.

(See also Nanga Taisei, I, 110–137 (Bamboo and Orchids); II, 160–162 (Chrysanthemum); II, 225–230, III, 62–65 (Flowering Plum, etc.); III, 246 (Narcissus); V, 17 (Pine); V, 157–161 (Lotus); V, 207–210 (Vegetables); VII, 98 (Figure); VIII, 137–141 (Landscape Fans); X, 42–43, Add. IV, 49–50 (Landscapes); XI, 217–227 (Album, Landscapes with Figures); Add. I, 127–169 (four Albums of Landscapes); Add. IV, 183–186 (Album of Landscapes). Many of these also reproduced elsewhere).)

T'AO CH'I 陶淇 or T'ao Shao-yüan 陶紹源, *t.* Chui-an 錐菴.

From Hsiu-shui, Chekiang. B. 1814, d. 1865. Landscapes, followed Wang Hui. T, Add. I. U, III, 2, 28.M, p. 395.

Ming-jên shu-hua, XV. A Garden in the Mountains, after Tung Yüan. Signed. Colophon dated 1863.

Shên-chou Album, 1921. Ten Landscapes after old masters.

TIEN TAO-JÊN 顚道人. Family name perhaps Hu 胡.

A native of Chiang-ning, lived in Yangchow. He painted when drunk. If asked his name, he refused to answer; hence the above sobriquet, which means "the Mad Taoist". When he began to be bothered by requests for his paintings, he disappeared and was never seen again. Landscapes and flowers. Q, I, 3. R, XV.

T'ai-shan ts'an-shih-lou album, First Series. Album of twelve paintings of Flowers and Fruit. Signed. *Cf.* Nanga Taisei, II, 174; III, 61; IV, 78–81; V, 66, 102, 170, 171, 225.

TING KUAN-P'ÊNG 丁觀鵬.

Court-painter *c.*1750–1760. Buddhist and Taoist figures in the style of Ting Yün-p'êng. S, I, p.8. M, p.4.

Palace Museum scroll. Emperor Ming-huang playing Polo, after Li Kung-lin. Signed, dated 1746.

K.-k. shu-hua chi, XXII. Fishermen in Snow, after a Sung master. Signed, dated 1747.

Ku-kung, XVI. A Night Banquet in T'ang Ming-huang's Palace. Fan-painting. Signed, dated 1748.

Ibid. XXVIII. The Literary Meeting in the Western Garden, after Ch'iu Ying. Signed, dated 1748.

K.-k. shu-hua chi, XL. The Literary Meeting in the Western Garden. Inscription by a courtier, dated 1748.

Ibid. II. Seven Poets passing the T'ung-kuan Gate. After Han Huang. Inscription by a courtier, dated 1748.

Li-tai, IV. Children at a Water-tub. Signed. Poem by Ch'ien-lung dated 1756.

Ibid. III. Kuan-yin. Signed, dated 1761.

Ibid. I. Šakyamuni. Inscription by Ch'ien-lung.

K.-k. shu-hua chi, XXVII. Mañjūšri.

Ibid. XXXVII. Court Ladies enjoying the Moonlight on a Terrace. Signed.

(See also K.-k. chou-k'an, Index, for various works of this artist.)

TING YÜAN-KUNG 丁元公, *t.* Yüan-kung 原躬 or 源躬.
Became a Buddhist monk when old; monk name Ching-i 淨伊, *h.* Yüan-an 願菴. From Chia-hsing, Chekiang. Active in the beginning of the Ch'ing period. Figures, landscapes. Q, I, 1. U, II, 1, 7. R, I, 23. M, p.3.

British Museum. A Hermit in red Cloak (Šakyamuni?) seated on a Mountain Terrace. Album-leaf. Signed.
Chêng Tê-k'un, Cambridge. River-view; a man in a boat, trees at the lower edge. Signed.

T'ING-WÊNG 聽翁.
Unrecorded. Active *c.*1690.

Sōgen 244. Mountain Landscape. Handscroll. Signed. Colophon dated 1686.

TS'AI CHIA 蔡嘉, *t.* Sung-yüan 松原.
From Tan-yang, Kiangsu. Lived *c.*1680–1760. Landscapes, figures. M, p.634.

Tōan, 68. Landscape. Signed, dated 1739.
Shina Nanga, III, 7. River Scenery. Signed, dated 1747.
Sōraikan, I, 68. Trees and Crows, after Ni Tsan. Signed, dated 1756.
Nanga Taisei, X, 194. Pine-trees in a Valley; a man ascending a path. Signed and dated 1776 (or 1716?)
Fei-tun lu shan-shui. Deep Gorge between steep Cliffs. Signed, dated 1782 (or 1722?)
Ming-jên shu-hua, XII. An old Man holding a Mirror. Signed. Poem.
Ibid. XV. Mountain Landscape with a Cottage under Trees, after Ch'ien Hsüan. Signed. Poem.
Chung-kuo ming-hua 21. Water-buffalo under a Tree. Inscription by the painter.
T. T. Ma, Hongkong. A Woman leaning against a blossoming Plum-tree. Poetic inscription by the painter.
Nanju 3. A Lady. Signed. Poem.
Sōgen 320. Landscape. Handscroll. Signed. Colophon.
Ibid. 321. Peonies, from an album of Flower Pictures. Signed. Poem.
Nanga Taisei, XII, 73–78. Album of twelve Landscapes. Inscriptions, seals of the artist.
C. C. Wang, New York. Landscape: Farmstead under Trees. Poem by the painter. *Cf.* Toronto, 55.
Hamburg Exhibition, 1949–1950. Landscape. Signed.
Ibid. The Blind.

TS'AI HAN 蔡含, *t.* Nü-lo 女蘿.
From Suchou. B. 1647, d. after 1691. Wife of the painter Mao Hsiang. Flowers, birds, landscapes and figures. Q, II, 2. M, p.633.

S.c.t.k. hsü-pien, III. A tall Rock and two Trees on the River Shore. Poem by the painter, dated 1681.
British Museum (Add No.3). Mynah-birds in a Wu-t'ung Tree. Signed, dated 1691.
Shên-chou, XVIII. Peonies and Lilies in a Rockery, with a Cat and Chickens. Poem by Mao Hsiang. *Cf.* Shina Nanga, I, 84.
Ibid. XVIII. Herons and Lotus Flowers.
Gems, I, 55. Autumn Flowers and Butterflies. Painted together with Chin Yüeh. Inscription, signed.

TS'AI TSÊ 蔡澤, *t.* Ts'ang-lin 蒼霖, *h.* Hsüeh-yen 雪巖.
From Nanking. Active *c.*1700. Figures, landscapes, flowers and birds. Q, II, 1. R, I, 26. M, p.633.

Kyūka, II. A Pine-tree. Signed, dated 1694.
Nanju 14. Listening to the Flute. Signed.

TS'AO CHIEN 曹澗, *t.* Hsiao-yai 小厓, *h.* (?) T'ing-shan 聽山.
Native of Hangchou; active in early 18th century. Flowers; landscapes after Ni Tsan. T. M, p.407.

Mei-êhan t'ê-k'an 60. Precipitous Cliffs over a River; fishermen in a boat. Signed and dated 1713. Colophon by Yang Chin.

Metropolitan Museum (13.220.38). A Set of twelve Landscapes in the styles of early Masters. Signed.

TS'AO K'UEI-YIN 曹夔音.
From Nanking. Court-painter *c.*1750. Landscapes. S. M, p.406.

K.-k. shu-hua chi, X. Landscape after Kuan T'ung. Signed. Poem by Ch'ien-lung dated 1748.

Shên-chou, V. A Boat on a winding Stream among luxuriant Trees. Signed.

TS'AO YIN 曹隱.
Unrecorded. Active *c.*1667.

Mo-ch'ao pi-chi, vol.I. A Man in a Boat at the Foot of high Mountains. Handscroll. Signed, dated 1667.

TS'AO YU-KUANG 曹有光, *t.* Tzŭ-yeh 子夜 and Hsi-ch'i 西畸.
From Suchou; lived by the West Lake, Hangchou. Chin shih in 1664. Landscapes, flowers and insects. R, V, 1. M, p.405.

K.-k. chou-k'an, 128–148. Seven Flower-studies on album-leaves which are collected in the same album as the Flower-paintings by Sun Ti. Poems by the painter; the last one dated 1651.

TSÊNG YEN-TUNG 曾衍東, *t.* Ch'i-ju 七如, *h.* Ch'i-tao-jên 七道人.
From Chia-hsiang, Shantung; lived in Yung-chia, Chekiang. Ch'ien-lung period (?) Figures, flowers and birds. M, p.515.

Voretzsch. Four Studies of humorous Figures. Album-leaves. Signed.

TSO CHÊN 左楨.
Landscapes. Q., II, 1. M, p.71.

Hamburg Exhibition, 1949–1950. Fantastically hollowed-out Rocks and Pine-trees. Ink on satin. Signed, dated 1700.

TSOU CHÊ 鄒喆, *t.* Fang-lu 方魯.
From Suchou; lived in Nanking. B. 1636, d. *c.*1708(?). One of the "Eight Masters of Nanking". Landscapes, followed his father Tsou Tien; trees and flowers, followed Wang Yüan. P, I, 9. Q, I, 1. R, IV, 21. U, II, 1, 20. M, p.568.

Shên-chou, IV. A Man playing the *Ch'in* in a Pavilion under high Trees. Signed, dated 1647? (or 1707?)

Liu 99. A House at the Foot of Hills; a stream in the foreground. Signed and dated *ting-hai* (same year as preceding picture), 1647 or 1707? *Cf.* Gems, I, 60.

Nanju 21. A Hermit among Pine-trees. Signed, dated 1668. Also in Tōyō, XII.

Hamburg Exhibition 1949–1950. Mountain Peaks rising through Clouds, tall pines in the gully. Signed, dated 1678.

Ibid. An Album of ten Landscapes. Signed, dated 1679.

Chūgoku, 7. Landscape with two Men in a Pine Grove, signed; a Winter Landscape, signed and dated 1679. Two leaves in an album containing works by the eight Nanking masters.

Chin-ling p'ai ming-hua chi (Shên-chou album, 1924). Trees in Mist. Signed.

Êrh-fan kao-tsou (Shên-chou album, 1930). Landscapes, album-leaves. Signed.

Nanga Taisei, XI, 214, 215. Two Landscapes. Album-leaves. Signed.

J. P. Dubosc, Lugano. Steep Mountain by a River; Houses at its foot. A leaf from an album formerly in Chou Liang-kung's collection.

TSOU CHIH-LIN 鄒之麟, *t.* Ch'ên-hu 臣虎, *h.* Mei-an 昧菴 and Po-i shan-jên 白衣山人.
From Wu-chin, Kiangsu. Chin shih in 1610. Devoted himself to painting after 1644. Landscapes in the style of Huang Kung-wang. P, I, 16. Q, I, 1. U, I, 1, 5. M, p.568.

Tokasha Shina Meigashū 37. A Banana-tree by a Rockery. Poem by the painter, dated 1610.

Sōgen 173. Landscape. Signed, dated 1651.

Chung-kuo, II, 54. Landscape. Signed. Colophon. *Cf.* P'ang Yüan-chi cat. Add. 2.

Shên-chou ta-kuan, vol.2. Sparse Trees on a River-bank. Signed.

Hsü-ching chai ming-hua chi. The Chin-shan Island (with a Pagoda) in the Yangtse River. Colophon by the painter.

S.c.t.k. hsü-pien, IV. Landscape. Signed.

TSOU HSIEN-CHI 鄒顯吉, *t.* Li-mei 黎眉, *h.* Ssŭ-ching 思靜.
Native of Wu-hsi, Kiangsu. B. 1636. Landscapes, figures, flowers. Known as Chrysanthemum Tsou. M. p. 568.

Chung-hua album, 1930. Plum-blossoms. Handscroll. Inscriptions, the last signed and dated 1700, "at the age of 65". Many colophons.

TSOU I-KUEI 鄒一桂, *t.* Yüan-pao 原褒, *h.* Hsiao-shan 小山.
From Wu-hsi, Kiangsu. B. 1686, d. 1772. High official, court-painter. Specialized in flowers, but painted also portraits and landscapes. Author of *Hsiao-shan hua-p'u* 小山畫譜. Q, II, 2. R, XI, 2. U, I, 3, 10. M, p.569.

Chūgoku 8. Landscape in the manner of Tung Yüan and Chü-jan. Signed and dated 1726.

Shina Nanga, III, 9. The South Mountain. Signed. Poem dated 1739.

Ku-kung, XIX. A Plum-tree. Signed. Poem by Ch'ien-lung dated 1744.

Chung-hua album, 1919. Twelve pictures of Landscapes, Flowers and Trees, accompanied by poems. Signed, dated 1749.

K.-k. shu-hua chi, XXXIII. Temples on a Mountain in Autumn. Signed, dated 1750.

Piacentini collect., Tōkyō. Album of Flower-paintings. Signed and dated 1751.

Sōgen 288. The Ts'ui-yün Temple. Signed. Poem by Ch'ien-lung dated 1752.

K.-k. shu-hua chi, I. A Branch of Plum-blossoms in a Pot. Signed. Poem by Ch'ien-lung, dated 1752. Poem by the painter.

Ibid. VI. The P'an shan Mountain. Signed, dated 1752.

Ibid. XXIII. Plum-blossoms, Camellias and a T'ien-chu Plant. Signed, dated 1753.

Ibid. XL. Spring Flowers and Autumn Fruits. Signed. Poem by Ch'ien-lung dated 1753.

Li-tai, I. Plum-blossoms, Orchids, Narcissi, Chrysanthemums and Cassia. Signed. Poems by Ch'ien-lung, the earliest dated 1760.

Shên-chou album, 1920. Twelve Pictures of Birds, Flowers and Insects.

Tsou Hsiao-shan hua-niao ts'ao-ch'ung ts'ê (Shên Chou album, 1920). Ten Pictures of Flowers, Birds and Insects.

Li-tai, III. Pine-trees, Bamboos and Plum-blossoms. Signed. Poem.

Ibid. V. A Study among Pine-trees at the Foot of a Mountain. Signed.

Ku-kung, XXXV. Plum-blossoms and Camellias. Signed. Poems by Ch'ien-lung.

K.-k. shu-hua chi, VII. Roses and Wistarias. Signed. Poems by Ch'ien-lung.

Ibid. X. Palm-tree and Bamboos in a Pot. Signed.

Ibid. XXV. A Fishing-boat on a River in Autumn. Signed. Poem by Ch'ien-lung.

Ibid. XXVII. Pink Peach-blossoms and white Pear-blossoms. Signed. Poems by Ch'ien-lung.

Ibid. XXVIII. Pavilions in the Gullies of high Mountains; entertaining guests in a pavilion. Signed.

Ibid. XXXI. Chrysanthemums. Signed. Poems by Ch'ien-lung.

Ibid. XXXVI. Wistarias and Peonies. Signed.

Ibid. XXXVIII. Swallows and Apricot-blossoms. Signed.

Ibid. XLV. Hibiscus Flowers. Signed.

K.-k. chou-k'an, vol.I, 1. Chrysanthemums by a Garden Rock. Signed.

Ibid. vol.I, 24. Branches of blossoming Plum-trees and various Fruits. Signed. Poems by Ch'ien-lung and the painter.

(Many other paintings by this artist in K.-k. chou-k'an; see Index.)

Shina Nanga, II, 1. A Mountain Slope. Album-leaf. Poem.

Shincho 61. Plum-blossoms, Lotuses, Magnolias, Chrysanthemums and other Flowers. Handscroll. Signed.

Sōgen 289. A leaf from an album of thirty-two Flower-pictures, painted by order of the Emperor.

Ars Asiatica, IX, pl.LVI, 1. Pine-tree at the Edge of a Plain.

Pageant 928. Seascape with the rising Sun. Handscroll. Signed.

Vannotti collect., Lugano. A Scholar's Pavilion under Trees. Signed.

National Museum, Stockholm. Chrysanthemums in various colours and other flowers. Large horizontal composition. Signed.

Ts'ui Hui 崔鏏, *t.* Hsiang-chiu 象九.
From Peking. Active *c.*1720. Figures, followed Chiao Ping-chên. Also plum-blossoms. Q, I, 3. R, X, 18. M, p.388.

Ch'ing êrh-shih chia. A Lady resting on a Garden Stone. Signed. *Cf.* Nanga Taisei, VII, 113.

T'u Cho 屠卓, *t.* Mêng-chao 孟昭, *h.* Ch'in-wu 琴隖 and Ch'ien-yüan 潛園.
From Ch'ien-t'ang, Chekiang. B. 1781, d. 1828. Landscapes. U, III, 2, 7. M, p.501.

Ming-jên shu-hua, XXVI. Landscape. Signed, dated 1804. Also in Ming-hua sou-ch'i, II, 9.

Pageant 950. Bamboos in Ink. Signed. Colophon dated 1812.

Po-mei chi. Branches of a Plum-tree. Signed. Poem dated 1819.

Hamburg Exhibition, 1949–1950. Landscape. Signed, dated 1826.

Ming-jên shu-hua, XX. A Garden in Winter. Signed.

T'u Hsüan 屠暶, *t.* I-chên 彝珍, *h.* Su-ts'un 疏村 and Fou-yü shan-nung 浮玉山農.
From Wu-hsing, Chekiang; lived in Suchou. Active *c.*1790. Landscapes. Pupil of Ch'iu T'ing-jung 丘廷溶, imitated also Huang Ting. M, p.501.

Shina Nanga, III, 2. Landscape in the Styles of Huang Kung-wang and Ni Tsan. Signed. Poem dated 1788.

TUNG HSÜN 董洵, *t.* Chih-ch'üan 企泉, *h.* Hsiao-ch'ih 小池 and Nien-ch'ao 念巢.
From Shan-yin, Chekiang; lived at Peking. Poet and seal-engraver. Orchids and bamboos. T, III, 1, 10. M, p.573.

Nanga Taisei, I, 234, 235. Two paintings of Orchids, dated 1808 and 1809.
Po-mei chi. Plum-blossoms. Signed.

TUNG KAO 董誥, *t.* Hsi-ching 西京, *h.* Chê-lin 蔗林.
From Fu-yang, Chekiang. B. 1740, d. 1818. Son of Tung Pang-ta. High official, poet. Landscapes, followed his father. U, III, 1, 18. M, p.573.

Ku-kung, XXX. Men cleaning away Snow in the Palace Courtyard. Signed. Poem by Ch'ien-lung, dated 1773.
Sung-pê. A Pine-tree, Plum-blossoms and Bamboos. In six parts. Signed, dated 1776. *Cf.* Nanga Taisei, V, 37.
Li-tai, III. A Pavilion in Mist and Rain. Signed. Poem. Poems by Ch'ien-lung dated 1781 and 1795.
Nanga Taisei, III, 255. Narcissus, Bamboo and Fungus. Signed and dated 1800.
Shina Nanga, II, 5. Landscape after Wên Chêng-ming. Signed, dated 1803.
I-shu ts'ung-pien 13. Two Branches of blossoming Apricot and Plum-trees. Signed. Poems by Ch'ien-lung and by some of his officials.
Ming-hua sou-ch'i, II, 8. River-view; Fisherman in a Boat. Part of a scroll. Signed.
Li-tai, I. River Landscape in Spring. Signed.
Ibid. V. A Mountain Torrent. Signed.
Ibid. VI. Landscape in Autumn. Signed.
(See also K.-k. chou-k'an, Index, for various works by this artist.)
Shinchō 62. Cottages among Willows. Fan-painting. Signed.
Chūgoku 8. Six Landscapes. Album-leaves. Signed.
Chang Ting-chien, Hongkong. Snow Scene.
Metropolitan Museum (52.177.18). Landscape. Signed.

TUNG PANG-TA 董邦達, *t.* Fu-ts'un 孚存, *h.* Tung-shan 東山.
From Fu-yang, Chekiang. B. 1699, d. 1769. President of the Board of Rites. One of the Compilers of the Ch'ien-lung Catalogue. Landscapes in the styles of Tung Yüan, Chü-jan and the Yüan masters. Tung Yüan, Tung Ch'i-ch'ang and Tung Pang-ta are sometimes called the "Three Tungs". Q, II, 2. R, XI, 4. T, I, 1. U, I, 3, 14. M, p.573.

Shên-chou, XIX. View over a Hilly Country. Album-leaf. Signed, dated 1737.
K.-k. shu-hua chi, XXI. A Poet on the *Pa* Bridge. Signed. Poem by Ch'ien-lung dated 1744.
Ibid. XXXIX. Sailing in the Moonlight along a reedy Shore. Signed. Poem by Ch'ien-lung, dated 1744.
Ibid. III. Snow-covered Streams and Mountains. Signed. Poem by Ch'ien-lung dated 1745.
Li-tai, IV. Kuan-yin in a Bamboo Grove. Signed. A Sūtra copied by Chang Jo-ai (who died 1746).
K.-k. shu-hua chi, XVII. The high and green Peaks. Signed. Poem dated 1746.
Shên-chou, XIV. Scholars meeting in a Pavilion on a snow-covered Mountain. Copy after Li T'ang. Signed. Colophon dated 1746. Poems by Ch'ien-lung.
S.c.t.k. hsü-pien, IX. Landscape in the style of the Wangs. Signed, dated 1746.
Sōgen 301. An Imperial Garden in Snow. Signed. Poem by Ch'ien-lung dated 1746.
K.-k. shu-hua chi, XL. The K'uang and Lu Mountains, after Ching Hao. Signed. Poem by Ch'ien-lung, dated 1747.
Ibid. XLII. Landscape in Snow. Signed. Poem by Ch'ien-lung dated 1749.
Ibid. II. Hermits in the quiet Forest, after Wang Mêng. Signed. Poem by Ch'ien-lung dated 1756.
Ibid. XXV. Landscape, illustration to an Essay by Wang Ch'ung called "My Wish", copied by Ch'ien-lung dated 1756.
Li-tai, V. Mountains in Autumn. Signed. Poem by Ch'ien-lung dated 1758.
Ibid. V. Landscape in Mist and Rain. Signed. Poem by Ch'ien-lung dated 1758.

Tōan, 60. A Fisherman on a River. Illustration to a T'ang poem. Fan-painting. Signed, dated 1758.

Hamburg Exhibition, 1949–1950. Pine-trees by the Rocks, in the style of Li T'ang. Signed, dated 1759.

K.-k. shu-hua chi, XVIII. Red Trees on green Cliffs, after Yang Sheng. Signed. Poem by Ch'ien-lung, dated 1766.

Musée Guimet, Paris. A Straw-covered Hut in the Autumn Mountains. After Chao Yüan. Signed, dated 1766.

Ming-jên shu-hua, III. Mountain Landscape, after Wang Mêng. Signed, dated 1767. Poems by Ch'ien Ch'ên-ch'ün and many other people. Also in Shina Nanga, III, 10.

Nanking Exhib. cat. 343. A River Landscape in Autumn. Signed and dated 1768.

Shên-chou, XIX. Leafless Trees by a Stream among Hillocks. Album-leaf. Poem by the painter.

Shên-chou ta-kuan, vol.16. Mountains and Streams. Eight-fold screen.

Shên-chou album, 1917. Album of eight landscapes. Signed. Poems by Ch'ien-lung.

Chung-hua album, 1929. Eight Landscapes. Signed. Poems by Ch'ien-lung.

Li-tai, I. Woodcutters returning Home.

Ibid. I. Hermits' Cottages on a Cliff. Signed.

Ibid. II. A Sailing-boat on the River. Signed.

Ibid. VI. Red Trees on a Mountain in Autumn. Signed.

Ku-kung, XXVI. Sailing in the Moonlight. Signed.

Ibid. XXXVIII. Landscape. Fan-painting. Signed.

K.-k. shu-hua chi, IX. The blue, cloudy Mountain Peaks, after Huang Kung-wang. Signed.

Ibid. X. A Fishing Village. Signed.

Ibid. XI. Travellers in the Mountains. Signed.

Ibid. XII. Hermits' Cottages on a clear Day, after Tung Yüan. Signed.

Ibid. XXII. Scattered Trees by a River, after Ni Tsan. Signed.

Ibid. XXIII. River-view with Autumn Trees. Signed. Poem by Ch'ien-lung.

Ibid. XXIV. Farmers' Life in Winter. Illustration to a poem by Fan Ch'êng-ta, a Sung poet. Signed.

Ibid. XXXVII. Landscape. Signed. Poem by Ch'ien-lung.

Ibid. XLI. Mountains and moored Boats by a Village. Signed. (Numerous pictures by the painter also in K.-k. chou-k'an; see Index.)

Fei-tun lu shan-shui. Landscape after a Yüan master. Signed.

Kurokawa cat. 34. A Pavilion behind a Clump of Trees. In the manner of Ni Tsan. Large album-leaf, signed.

Tomioka collect., Kyōto. A small album of Landscapes, the last signed.

Takashima collect., Kugenuma. A Spring in the Pine Valley. After Wang Mêng. Signed.

Shina Nanga, II, 10. Waterfall on a Mountain. Signed.

N. Gashū 30. A Man on Mule-back crossing a Bridge. Signed. Poem.

Kokka 581 (T. Isomura, Tōkyō). An Autumn Landscape.

Ōmura, I, 2 and 9. Five leaves from an Album of ten pictures of Landscapes and Flowers. *Cf.* Chūgoku 8.

Ōmura, I, 3–8 and 12. Twelve Landscapes from an album of twenty-four, painted by order of the Emperor Ch'ien-lung.

Shinchō 62. River Landscape with two Boats. Album-leaf. Signed.

Sōgen 300. Clouds and Mists on the evergreen Mountain. Signed.

Sōraikan, II, 84. Mountain Landscape after Wang Mêng. Signed.

Musée Guimet, Paris. River-view. Poem by the painter.

TUNG YÜ 董俞, *t.* Ch'ing-ch'i 清溪.
From Wu-chin, Kiangsu. Second half of the 17th century. Contemporary with Yün Shou-p'ing. M, p.573.

Shên-chou, XII. Misty Mountain Landscape. Signed.

T'UNG-HO 通荷, *cf.* P'u-ho.

T'UNG-WEI 通微, *t.* Hêng-ch'ê 恆澈.
From Hangchou. A monk active *c.*1770(?) Flowers, grass, birds and insects. R, XIV, 1, 22. M, p.375.

Sōgen 362. A Cock and Chrysanthemums by a Rock. Signed, dated 1768(?)

T'UNG YÜ-HSIU 佟毓秀, *t.* Chung-shan 鍾山.
From Hsiang-p'ing, Manchuria. Banner-man. Early Ch'ing period. Landscapes in a manner resembling Lan Ying's. Q, II, 1. R, VII, 22. U, III, 1, 6. M, p.114.

Berlin Museum. Three Pine-trees by a Rock. Signed.

WAN CH'I-FAN 萬其藩, *t.* Po-han 伯瀚.
From Fukien. Active *c.*1750. Bamboos and wild-geese. M, p.565.

Nanju 20. Bamboo Groves along a Stream, after Chao Mêng-fu. Signed, dated 1757. Also in Tōyō, XII.

WAN KANG 萬岡, *t.* Wang-ch'uan 輞川.
From Chiang-yu, Kiangsi. Active probably in Ch'ien-lung period. Plum flowers and landscapes. T. M, p.565.

Formerly C. B. Hoyt collect., Cambridge, Mass. Two Crabs under a bending Reed. Album-leaf. Signed. Poem.

WAN SHANG-LIN 萬上遴, *t.* Wang-kang 輞岡.
From Nan-ch'ang, Kiangsi. B. 1739, d. 1813. Landscapes. M, p.565.

Tokasha Shina Meigashū 84. Large Mountain Landscape with Men on Donkeys travelling along the winding Road under Pine-trees. Signed, dated 1808.

Ibid. 83. Misty Mountain Valley; two men in a boat on the river. Signed.

Hamburg Exhibition, 1949–1950. Landscape in the style of Tung Ch'i-ch'ang. Album-leaf.

WAN SHOU-CH'I 萬壽祺, *t.* Nien-shao 年少, *h.* Sha-mên-hui-shou 沙門慧壽.
From Hsü-chou, Kiangsu. B. 1603, d. 1652. A poet and student of many arts. Figures in the style of Chou Fang. Q, I, 1. R, I, 14. U, I, 2, 17. M, p.565.

British Museum. A young Woman seen through the Window in a Pavilion; bare trees at both sides. In *kung-pi* style. Album-leaf. Signed, dated 1631.

Shên-chou, I. A Lady with a Fan. Album-leaf. Signed, dated 1642.

Kyūka, I. A tall Pine-tree on a quiet Islet. Signed. Colophon dated 1646.

Vannotti collect., Lugano. Bare Trees on a rocky Shore. Signed. Fan-painting.

British Museum, No.182. The Lady of the fragrant Snow Garden. Signed. (Attributed.)

WANG AI 汪靄, *t.* Hsü-yüan 胥原, *h.* Ta-yai 滌崖.
From Hsieh-hsien, Anhui; lived in Yangchou, Kiangsu. B. 1678, d. after 1749. Landscapes, followed Huang Kung-wang. R, XII, 22. M, p.140.

Ming-hua sou-ch'i, vol.I, 7. Steep Mountains, a Man on the River Bank under tall Pine-trees. In the manner of Huang Kung-wang. Signed, dated 1749. *Cf.* Ming-jên shu-hua, XXV.

WANG CHAO-HSIANG 王兆祥.
Unrecorded. 18th century(?) According to the signature, from Chiang-tu (Yang-chou), Kiangsu.

British Museum, No.245. A Girl holding a Bird.
Signed.

WANG CH'ÊN 王宸, *t.* Tzŭ-ning 紫凝, *h.* P'êng-hsin 蓬心, Liu-tung chü-shih 柳東居士 and other names. From T'ai-ts'ang, Kiangsu. B. 1720, d. 1797. Great-grandson of Wang Yüan-ch'i. Landscapes in the style of the four Yüan masters. U, I, 3, 16. M, p.54.

Shina Nanga, II, 2; III, 4. Six Landscapes on album-leaves. Dated 1762. *Cf.* Chung-kuo ming-hua, II.
Wang P'êng-hsin fang-ku shan-shui ts'ê. (Shên-chou album, 1926) Twelve Landscapes after old masters. Dated 1764.
Ming-jên shu-hua, XVI. River Scenery after Wang Fu Signed, dated 1765. Also in Nanga Taikan 6.
Shina Nanga, III, 7. Landscape after Tung Yüan. Signed. Poem dated 1766.
Ming-jên shu-hua, XXIII. Mountains and Streams in Autumn. Signed, dated 1772.
Shên-chou ta-kuan, vol.I. The Homestead of Chang Chuang-hsi. Colophon by the painter, dated 1773. Poems by the contemporaries.
W. Hochstadter, New York. A River Valley between high Mountains, after Chü-jan. Signed, dated 1773(?)
Tokasha Shina Meigashū 23. Misty Mountain Valley. Pavilions under tall trees. After Wang Yüan-ch'i. Signed, dated 1775.
Shên-chou, I. Two Men in a Pavilion at the Foot of steep Mountains, after Wu Chên. Signed, dated 1778.
Nanking Exhib. cat. 349. Two Pine-trees growing by a Rock. Signed and dated 1778.
Ho Kuan-wu, Hongkong. A River between Hills, Men in Boats. Signed and dated 1778.
Fei-tun lu shan-shui. A Homestead at the Foot of cloudy Mountains. Signed. Poem, dated 1870.
Shên-chou, VIII. Mountain Landscape, after Wang Mêng. Signed, Poem, colophon dated 1782. Also in Shina Nanga, II, 6.
Nanga Taisei, I, 218. Bamboo, an old Tree and a Rock. Signed and dated 1782.
Sumitomo collect., Oiso. Landscape of Wu-ch'i. Hand-scroll. Signed and dated 1784. *Cf.* Sekai Bijutsu Zenshū, XX, text illust. 107 (detail).
Hamburg Exhibition, 1949–1950. Landscape in the style of Wu Chên. Signed, dated 1790.
Nanga Taisei Add. II, 129–134. An Album of Land-scapes, the last signed "at age 74", *i.e.* in 1793.
Shên-chou, XIV (Mizuta collect., Kyōto). Rain over Hsiao and Hsiang. Signed, dated 1794 (at 75).
Wang P'êng-hsin shan-shui ts'ê (Yu Chêng Book Co., 1926). Ten Landscapes after old Masters. Signed, dated 1794.
Shina Meiga Senshū 34. A deep Mountain Gully, after Li Ch'êng. Signed, dated 1796.
Hui-hua kuan. River Landscape after Tung Yüan. Handscroll.
Nanga Taisei, XII, 120–127. An Album of Landscapes. Signed.
Yūrinkan, Kyōto. The Tung-t'ing Lake on a moonlit Night. Signed. Poem. *Cf.* Shincho, 58.
Musée Guimet, Paris. River Landscape, after Shên Chou. Miniature scroll. Poem by the painter.

WANG CHÊNG 王正, *t.* Tuan-jên 端人 or Tuan-jung 端瑩.

Anonymous publisher, n.d. Album of Flower Paintings; the last signed and dated 1701.

WANG CH'ÊNG-FÊNG 王承楓, *t.* Pi-ch'ên 陛臣, *h.* Tan-lu 丹麓.
From Tz'ŭ-chou, Hopei. Active *c.*1860. Landscapes. M, p.63.

Tōan, 73. Landscape. Signed, dated 1859.

WANG CH'ÊNG-P'EI 汪承霈, *t.* Shou-shih 受時 and Ch'un-nung 春農, *h.* Shih-chai 時齋.
From Hsiu-ning, Anhui. B. *c.*1725, d. 1805. Vice-president of the Board of Revenue. Poet. Landscapes, figures and flowers. Also finger-paintings. M, p.138.

K.-k. shu-hua chi, XI. Pine-tree, Plum-blossoms, etc. Signed. Poem by Ch'ien-lung dated 1782.
Li-tai, I. A Banana-tree in Snow. Signed.
Ibid. II. Two Cassia-trees. Signed.
Ibid. IV. Two Cassia-trees. Signed.
Sōgen 286. Trees and Flowers. Handscroll. Signed.
Ibid. 287. Hundred Butterflies. Part of a handscroll.

WANG CHIEH 王詰, *t.* Mo-yeh 摩也, *h.* Hsin-hu 心壺, Ou-po 鷗白.
From T'ai-ts'ang, Kiangsu; lived at Wu-hsing, Chekiang. Poet and calligraphist. Landscapes. T. M, p.54.

Po-mei chi. Plum-blossoms, after Yün Shou-p'ing Signed.

WANG CHIEN 王鑑, *t.* Yüan-chao 圓照, *h.* Hsiang-pi 湘碧, Lien-chou 廉州, Jan-hsiang an-chu 染香菴主 and other names.
From T'ai-ts'ang, Kiangsu. B. 1598, d. 1677. The second of the "Four Wangs"; one of the "Nine Friends in Painting". Governor of Lien-chou, Kuangtung; sometimes called Wang Lien-chou. Q, I, 1. R, I, 2. U, I, 1, 2. M, p.44.

Chūgoku, V. Evening on the South Mountain. Large album-leaf. Signed and dated 1633.
Yūchikusai 6. Wooded Mountains, after Huang Kung-wang. Signed and dated 1638. Colophons by Ch'ên Chi-ju, Wang Shih-min and other people. *Cf.* Shên-chou ta-kuan, vol.2; Shincho 4.
Shên-chou ta-kuan, vol.7. Overgrown Mountains with pointed Peaks, after Tung Yüan. Signed and dated 1638.
Takashima collect., Kugenuma. A Clump of Trees. In the manner of Yüan masters, and in the spirit of Shên Chou. Signed and dated 1639. *Cf.* Sekai Bijutsu Zenshū 20, pl.34.
H. C. Wêng, Scarsdale, N.Y. Grand Mountains rising in Terraces; winding streams. After Tung Yüan. Signed and dated 1642. A very large picture.
Contag, pl.7 (Wu Hu-fan, Suchou). Mountain Gorge. In the manner of Huang Kung-wang. Signed and dated 1653.
Chung-kuo ming-hua, XIII. Mountain Landscape with Pine-trees on Terraces and rushing Water, after Wang Mêng. Signed and dated 1656. A long inscription by Chang Hsüeh-tsêng.
Hui-hua kuan. Long River between deeply-folded Mountain Slopes. In the manner of Tung Yüan. Long handscroll. Dated 1656.
Tōan 45. River Landscape after Ni Tsan. Poem by the painter dated 1656.
Ibid. 44. Mountains in Autumn, after Huang Kung-wang. Poem by the painter, dated 1657.
Nanga Taikan 12. Mountain Landscape with Cottages, after Huang Kung-wang. Signed. Two lines of poetry dated 1658. *Cf.* Mei-chan t'ê-k'an 40.
Ku-kung collect. Landscape. Album-leaf. Signed and dated 1658. *Cf.* Nanking Exhib. cat. 245.
Chūgoku, V. Landscape in the manner of Fan K'uan. Poem, signed and dated 1660.
Hui-hua kuan. River winding between sloping Hills, Trees and Buildings. In the manner of Huang Kung-wang. Signed and dated 1660. Inscription by Wang Shih-min. *Cf.* I-shu ch'uan-t'ung, 11.
C. C. Wang, New York. River Valley between high Mountain Slopes. Signed and dated 1660.
Yu-chêng album. Seven Landscapes after Tung Yüan, Chü-jan, Ni Tsan, Shên Chou, Tung Ch'i-ch'ang, etc. One dated 1660, another 1661.
N. Gashū 21. Wooded Hills and Winding Streams. Illustration to two lines of a poem by Wang Wei, called The Hsiang-chi Temple. Signed, dated 1661. *Cf.* Shina Nanga, III, 2; Shi-O Go Un 4; Ōmura, I, 1; Chung-kuo ming-hua, vol.10.

Sirén, *Later*, pl.174 (former Yamamoto collect.) Mountain Streams and Green Pines. Signed, dated 1661.

I-yüan chên-shang 8. Landscape after Huang Kung-wang. Signed and dated 1662.

Liu 108. River Landscape, with a figure standing on the shore. In the manner of Wu Chên. Signed and dated 1663.

Shên-chou, XXI. Mountain Landscape. Signed, dated 1663.

Mei-chan t'ê-k'an, 41. Peaks and Streams, after Tung Yüan. Signed, dated 1663.

National Museum, Stockholm. Eight small Landscapes after old masters. One of them dated 1665 and signed.

Contag, pl.11 (Yüeh-ku chai, Peking). Mountains after Wang Mêng. Album-leaf. Signed and dated 1666.

J. P. Dubosc, Lugano. Landscape in the style of Huang Kung-wang. Wooded mountains and a broad winding stream forming cascades; a man standing in contemplation on a promontory. Signed and dated 1666.

Chung-kuo, II, 68. Mountains with Pavilions by a Stream, after Wu Chên. Signed and dated 1667. Colophons by Yün Shou-p'ing and Wang Hui. *Cf.* Shina Nanga, II, 12; Contag, pl.12; Liu 107.

Hui-hua kuan. Mountain Landscape with large Pine-trees and high Peaks, in the manner of Wang Mêng. Dated 1667. *Cf.* P'ang Yüan-chi Illus. cat., I.

Shi-O Go Un 5. River Landscape, after Ni Tsan. Signed, dated 1667. Colophon by Wang Hui. *Cf.* Tōan 46.

Nanga Taisei, XVI, 49–53. Wooded Hills after Chü-jan. Handscroll. Signed and dated 1667.

Yu-chêng album, n.d. Ten Landscapes in Old Styles. Signed, the last dated 1668.

Shina Nanga, II, 2. Wooded Mountains and a River Valley, after Tung Yüan. Signed. Poem dated 1668. *Cf.* Chung-kuo ming-hua, 9.

Freer Gallery (56.27). White Clouds over Hsiao and Hsiang, after Chao Mêng-fu. Signed. Colophon dated 1668. *Cf.* Sirén, *Later*, pl.175.

Shinchō 5. Landscape after Chao Mêng-fu. Fan-painting. Signed, dated 1669.

Shina Nanga, I, 33. Landscape after Chü-jan. Signed, dated 1669.

Yūchikusai 7. River Landscape, after Chao Mêng-fu. Signed, dated 1669.

Chūgoku, V. Album of ten landscapes in old styles, the last signed and dated 1669.

Shanghai Museum. Soft Mountains, after Tung Yüan. Trees below along the water. Signed and dated 1669.

Ōmura, II, 2. Mountain Landscape, after Fan K'uan. Signed and dated 1670. *Cf.* Chūgoku, V.

Chung-kuo ming-hua, XIII. Boating on a Mountain Stream under a Willow. Signed and dated 1671.

Contag, pl.13 (Chin Kung-po, Peking). River-view with spare Trees and Pavilion, after Ni Tsan. Signed and dated 1671.

Shên-chou, XVIII. Winding Stream at the Foot of high Mountains in Snow, after Li Ch'êng. Poem by the painter, dated 1672.

Chūgoku, V. Landscape after Chiang Tsan. Poem. Signed and dated 1672.

T. T. Ma, Hongkong. Mountain Landscape in the manner of Chü-jan. Mist in the deep crevasses, rich growth on the slopes. Signed and dated 1672.

S.c.t.k. hsü-pien, I. Summer in a shady Forest. Signed and dated 1673.

Shi-O Go Un 6. River-view in Snow after Wang Wei. Poem by the painter, dated 1674. *Cf.* Shên-chou ta-kuan, vol.5.

Chung-kuo, II, 69. Landscape after Chiang Ts'an. Signed. Colophon dated 1674. *Cf.* Chung-kuo ming-hua, 27.

Gems, I, 52. The Stream among the deep Mountains, after Chü-jan. Poem. Signed and dated 1674.

K.-k. shu-hua chi, I. Misty Peaks, after Huang Kung-wang. Signed, dated 1675.

Chung-kuo ming-hua, 5. Mountain Ridge rising through the Mist. Large pine-trees along the stream. Signed, dated 1675.

Ibid. 18. Mountain Peaks overgrown with Trees and Shrubs in Summer. Poem by the painter, dated 1675.

S.c.t.k. hsü-pien, II. Sloping Hills by a River, after Chü-jan. Album-leaf. Signed, dated 1675.

Nanju 17. Mountains in Spring, after Huang Kung-wang. Signed, dated 1675.

Yu-chêng album, 1923. Six Pictures after Ni Tsan. Signed, dated 1676.

Shên-chou, VI. Mountain Landscape: rushing Water and luxuriant Trees. Signed. Poem, dated 1676.

Chung-kuo ming-hua, 9. Six album-leaves after Yüan master. Signed and dated 1676.

Chung-kuo, II, 67. Mountain Landscape, after Huang Kung-wang. Signed. Colophon dated 1676.

Shina Nanga, I, 31. Mountain Landscape, after Huang Kung-wang. Signed, dated 1676. *Cf.* Shina Nanga, II, 11.

Hua-chung chiu-yu (Yu-chêng album). Landscape after Chao Mêng-fu. Signed, dated 1676.

Ōmura, I, 8. Towering Mountains. Signed, dated 1677.

K.-k. shu-hua chi, XVI. Autumn Mountains, after Wang Mêng. Signed. Two lines of poetry.

Chung-kuo ming-hua 3. Leafy Trees by a quiet Bay; a fisherman in a boat on the water. Album-leaf.

Shên-chou ta-kuan, XV. A Man on a River-bank, after Tung Yüan. Inscription signed by the painter.

P'ang Yüan-chi Illus. cat., IV. Landscape after Ni Tsan. Poem by the painter.

Ch'ing êrh-shih chia. A Branch of Plum Blossoms. Album-leaf. Signed.

Hua-chung chiu-yu ts'ê (Hakubundō album, 1921). Mountain rising through Mist, Pavilions and Trees on the River-bank. Seal of the painter.

T. T. Ma, Hongkong. A Stream winding through a deep Gully; high mountains behind. After Chü-jan. Signed and dated 1672.

Kokka 548. A Pine Forest in a misty Valley. Signed.

Shina Nanga, I, 29, 30; II, 9. Three Landscapes from an album.

Ibid. II, 7; III, 5. Two Landscapes from an album.

Shi-O Go Un 7–10. A series of four landscapes called:
1. Clouds and Streams with an Angler.
2. Numberless Valleys with Pine-trees in Wind.
3. Red Maples and steep Cliffs.
4. Tall Pines in the cloudy Valley. Last one also in Ōmura, I, 6.

Ōmura, II, 5. River-view, after Wang Fu; from an album of eight landscapes after old masters.

Shinchō 6. Landscapes. Fan-painting. Signed. Colophon.

Sōraikan, I, 49. Two leaves from an Album of Twelve Landscapes after Sung and Yüan masters. Signed.

Chūgoku, V. Album of Ten Landscapes in various styles. Seals of the artist.

Ibid. Another Album of ten leaves. Inscriptions, seals of the artist.

Ibid. Three Landscapes on album-leaves, after Wu Chên and Wang Fu.

Sōgen 231. The Fishermen's Pleasure, after Ni Tsan. Signed. Colophon.

J. P. Dubosc, Lugano. Mountain Landscape in Sung style. Fan-painting. Signed.

Princeton University (Du Bois-Morris collect.) Landscape Sketches, after old masters. Twelve album-leaves. Signed.

C. C. Wang, New York. Mountain Landscape with Pine-groves at the Foot; open pavilions standing over the water in the foreground. After Wang Mêng. Signed.

Private collect., Peking. Mountain Landscape, after Wang Mêng. Album-leaf.

Contag, pl.9 (Wu Hu-fan, Suchou). Wooded Mountains and River-shops. In the manner of Tung Yüan. Album-leaf. Signed.

Ibid. pl.10. Mountain Gorge and circling Clouds. After Chao Mêng-fu. Album-leaf. Signed.

Shêng P'ing-ch'ên, Hongkong. An Album of Landscape Studies.

Ibid. Views along the Yangtse. Handscroll. Signed.

Chang Pi-han, Hongkong. Landscape after Huang Kung-wang. Signed.

WANG CHIH-JUI 汪之瑞, *t.* Wu-jui 無瑞.

From Hsiu-ning, Anhui. Active *c.*1650. Landscapes. One of the "Four Masters of Anhui". Q, I, 2. R, III, 3. U, I, 2, 8. M, p.136.

Hsin-an p'ai ming-hua chi (Shên-chou album, 1924). Mountain Landscape. Signed, dated 1649.

S.c.t.k. hsü-pien, V. River Landscape. Signed.

WANG CHING-MING 王敬銘, *t.* Tan-ssŭ 丹思, *h.* Wei-hsien 味閒.

From Chia-ting, Kiangsu. Chin-shih in 1713. Served in the palace before he took his degree. Followed Wang Yüan-ch'i in landscape-painting. Q, I, 3. R, VIII, 15. U, I, 3, 9. M, p.50.

K.-k. shu-hua chi, XXXV. Landscape. Signed.

WANG CHIU 王玖, *t.* Tz'ŭ-fêng 次峯, *h.* Êrh-ch'ih 二癡.
Lived in Suchou. Active *c.*1760–1780. Great-grandson of Wang Hui(?) Pupil of Huang Ting(?) Landscapes. U, III, 1, 16. M, p.53.

Shên-chou, XIII. Steep Mountains rising over an Inlet of Water, cottages at their foot. Signed. *Cf.* Shina Nanga, II, 10; Shincho 58.

Private collect., Hamburg. Album of Twelve Landscapes, after Yün Shou-p'ing. Signed.

WANG CHUNG 汪中, *t.* Wu-fang 無方.
From Hsieh-hsien, Anhui. Landscapes, flowers, birds and figures. M, p.137.

S.c.t.k. hsü-pien, XI. Landscape in the style of Huang Kung-wang. Signed.

WANG CHÜN 汪鋆, *t.* Yen-shan 硯山.
From I-chên, Kiangsu. 19th century. Poet. Plum blossoms. M, p.139.

Po-mei chi. Branches of blossoming Plum-trees. Signed, dated 1876. *Cf.* Nanga Taisei, III, 207, 1.

WANG FANG 汪昉, *t.* Shu-ming 叔明, *h.* Cho-shu lao-jên 啜菽老人.
From Yang-hu, Kiangsu. B. 1799, d. 1877. Connoisseur of paintings. Landscapes in the style of Wang Yüan-ch'i. T, Add. I. U, III, 2, 24. M, p.142.

Ming-jên shu-hua, V. Portrait of Tao-chi. Signed, dated 1856.

Tōan 72., Landscape. Signed, dated 1868. *Cf.* Chūgoku 8.

WANG HSIEN 王巘, *t.* Pu-yün 補雲.
From Wu-chiang, Kiangsu. Probably Ch'ien-lung period. Landscapes in the styles of Tung Yüan and Chü-jan. Q, I, 2. M, p.51.

Shimbi, XVI. A Mountain Villa on a Spring Night. Signed. Poem.

Berlin Museum. Pine-tree and blossoming Plum-tree. Signed.

WANG HSÜEH-HAO 王學浩, *t.* Mêng-yang 孟養, *h.* Chiao-hsi 椒畦.
From K'un-shan, Kiangsu. B. 1754, d. 1832. Landscapes, followed Wang Hui. T, VIII, 1. U, I, 3, 9. M, p.57.

Nanga Taisei, II, 12, 191; V, 45, 144, 232; XII, 153–155; Add. IV, 119. An Album of Paintings of Flowers, Landscapes and other Subjects. Signed and dated 1792.
Hamburg Exhibition, 1949–1950. The Snow Goose Cottage. Signed, dated 1801.
Nanga Taisei, XV, 80. Landscape-handscroll. Signed and dated 1804.
Shên-chou, II. The Poet Yüan Yüan standing by a Pine-tree. Signed, dated 1808.
Ōmura, I, 5. Landscape after Wu Chên. Signed. Colophon dated 1814.
Shinchō 73. Landscape after Chao Mêng-fu. Signed, dated 1819.
Ming-hua sou-ch'i, II, 10. Cottages at the Foot of a Hill by a River. Signed, dated 1820.
Nanga Taisei, Add. IV, 121. Landscape after a Yüan artist. Signed and dated 1825.

Pageant. River-view with Pavilion under Trees on a Promontory. Portion of a scroll. Signed and dated 1826.

Tōan, 67. Landscape in Chü-jan's and Wu Chên's style. Signed, dated 1827.

Wang Chiao-hsi hsien-shêng shih hua (Commercial Press, 1923). Fourteen Pictures of Landscapes and Plants, with poems by the painter.

Ming-jên shu-hua, XII. Flowers and Trees. Painted together with Chiang Hsün, Chu Ang-chih, Chai Chi-ch'ang and Chou Li. The Cedar-tree by Wang Hsüeh-hao. Signed. Also in Nanga Taikan 1.

Kokka 316. Landscape. Signed. Colophon.

Inoue collect., Tōkyō. Cottages on a Hill amidst Pine-trees. Dry brushwork. Signed.

Musée Guimet, Paris. High Mountains. Trees in the foreground. Signed.

WANG HUI 王翬, *t.* Shih-ku 石谷, *h.* Kêng-yen san-jên 耕煙散人, Ch'ing-hui chu-jên 清暉主人, Chien-mên ch'iao-k'o 僉門樵客, and other names.

From Ch'ang-shu, Kiangsu. B. 1632, d. 1717 (according to his epitaph). The third of the "Four Wangs" and the founder of the Yü-shan School. P, II, 11. Q, I, 2. R, IV, 1. U, I, 1, 2. M, p.48.

Chung-kuo ming-hua, XII. A Mountain Slope rising above a Road; large tree below at the shore of a river. Signed and dated 1654.

C. P. Huang, Taipei. Landscape in ink with an inscription by Wang Chien written in a boat and dated 1661.

Shên-chou, I, V, VI. Ten album-leaves representing Landscapes, in the manner of different old masters. Last one dated 1662.

Ibid. XI. Wind and Rain over the Mountain. Signed, dated 1662.

Chang Ta-ch'ien cat., IV, 39. *Ch'i-shan yü-chi t'u*: Mountain and Stream after Rain. After Chü-jan. Signed and dated 1662.

C. C. Wang, New York. Mountains and tall Pines, after Chü-jan. Signed, dated 1664. *Cf.* Toronto, 48.

K.-k. shu-hua chi, XXVII. Mountain Landscape, after Kuan T'ung. Signed, dated 1666.

Shi-O Go Un 11, 12. Mountains in Snow, after Li Ch'êng. Long handscroll. Signed. Colophon dated 1667.

Ibid. 13. Pine-trees in Wind and by Waterfalls, after Tung Yüan. Signed. Two lines of poetry dated 1669. Also in Yūchikusai, 8.

Shên-chou ta-kuan, vol.16. View of Yü-shan in Morning Mist. Colophon by the painter, dated 1669.

C. T. Loo's Successor, Frank Caro, N.Y. Misty Rain over Summer Mountains. Handscroll. Ink and slight colour on paper. Signed and dated 1668. Long inscription by Wang Shih-min, dated 1669. *Cf.* Toronto, 49.

K.-k. shu-hua chi, XLIII. Landscape. Signed. Colophons by Wang Shih-min and Yün Shou-p'ing, both dated 1670.

Shi-O Go Un 14. Waterfall on a Mountain in Spring, after Chao Mêng-fu. Signed, dated 1671. Colophon by Tan Chung-kuang.

Mei-chan t'ê-k'an 47. A Spring Morning in the Mountains; departing friends on the shore. Signed, dated 1671.

S.c.t.k. hsü-pien, VIII. Landscape after Hsü Tao-ning. Signed, dated 1671.

Wang Shih-ku fang-ku shan-shui ts'ê (Wên-ming album, 1925). Ten Landscapes after old Masters. Signed, dated 1671, 1672 and 1673.

K.-k. shu-hua chi, XLI. Mountain Dwellings on a Summer Day, after a Yüan master. Signed, dated 1672.

Yen-kuang album. Twelve Landscape-studies, some inspired by old masters. Signed, dated 1672. *Cf.* Chūgoku 6.

Shina Nanga, III, 9. The Hsiao and Hsiang Rivers, after Mi Yu-jên. Signed. Colophon dated 1672.

Shi-O Go Un 15. Floating Mist and distant Mountains, after Chü-jan. Signed, dated 1673. Colophons by Wang Shih-min, Wang Chien and the painter. *Cf.* Tōan, 47.

Contag, pls.23–25. Three large album-leaves (formerly Fêng Kung-tu, Peking): (1) Pavilion and Towers on a Hill, after Kuo Chung-shu; (2) Driving Mist in a Mountain Valley, after Tung Yüan; (3) Crows gathering in leafless Trees, after Li Ch'êng. Signed, dated 1673. Entire album of ten leaves published by Wên-hua shu-wu, 1922.

Ibid. pl.26 (Ts'ao Yu-ch'ing collect.) Mist over the Mountain Stream in Spring. Inscriptions by Wang Shih-min and three other friends of the painter who, in his own inscription, says that the Ch'ing River is like a bed of mist. Dated 1673.

Hui-hua kuan. A Mountain Gorge with rushing Water and Bridge; after Wang Mêng. Ink and some colour on paper. Dated 1673.

I-shu ch'uan-tung 11. The Chung-sung Study. Signed and dated 1673. Colophons by Wang Shih-min and others.

J. P. Dubosc, Lugano. An Album of twelve Landscapes, dedicated to Wang Shih-min. Signed and dated 1673. *Cf.* Venice Exhib. cat. 241.

K.-k. shu-hua chi, VI. The Study by the solitary Wu-t'ung-tree, after Wang Mêng. Signed, dated 1673.

Musée Guimet, Paris. A Straw-covered Hut in the Autumn Mountains, after Wang Mêng. Small picture. Signed, dated 1674.

Wang Shih-ku fang-ku shan-shui ts'ê (Yu-chêng album, 1923). Twelve Landscapes after old masters. Signed, dated 1675.

Kokka 503. Landscape in Spring. Signed. Poem dated 1675.

Yang Yin-pei, Peking. An Album of Eight Landscape-sketches after Yüan Masters. Signed, dated 1677. Colophons by Yün Shou-p'ing, dated 1683, and by Wang Chien. *Cf.* Chūgoku, 6; Sirén, *Later*, pl.214–216.

Musée Guimet, Paris. River Landscape in Autumn Colours, after Wang Mêng. Signed, dated 1677. *Cf.* Venice Exhib. cat. 239.

Shi-O Go Un 16. Walking along the Blue River, after T'ang Yin. Signed, dated 1678.

K.-k. shu-hua chi, XI. A high Peak, after Fang Ts'ung-i. Signed, dated 1678.

Ming-jên shu-hua, XXIV. A Boat moored under frosty Trees, after T'ang Yin. Signed, dated 1678.

K.-k. shu-hua chi, XXXI. Landscape after Chü-jan. Signed. Two lines of poetry dated 1680. *Cf.* Shi-O Go Un 13; dated 1669.

Shina Meiga Senshū 25. Mountain Ridges and Stretches of Water in Autumn, after Wang Mêng. Handscroll. Signed, dated 1680.

Contag, pl.29 (P'an Kung-fu collect.) Fishing Village after Rain. Coloured in Sung style. Signed, dated 1680.

K.-k. chou-k'an 14. Overgrown Hills, after Chü-jan. Signed and dated 1680.

Chung-hua album (first ed. 1919, seventh ed. 1935). Ten Landscapes after Wang Wei, Kuo Hsi, Tung Yüan, Chü-jan, Fan K'uan, Li Ch'êng, Chao Po-chü, Chao Mêng-fu, Kao K'o-kung and Huang Kung-wang. Partly coloured, on silk. Signed, dated 1682.

Wang Hui shan-shui ts'ê (Peking National Museum album). Sixteen Landscapes after old masters. Last one dated 1682.

Shi-O Go Un 17. Dawn over the Mountains in Hunan. Signed, dated 1682. Also in Ōmura, I, 9.

Kokka 250. The Kang-yen Cottage: the Study of the Painter. Signed. Colophon dated 1682. Also in Yūchikusai 9.

K.-k. shu-hua chi, VII. Cottages in the Mountains in Summer, after Wang Mêng. Signed, dated 1684. *Cf.* K.-k. shu-hua chi, XLI.

Shên-chou, XIII. River Landscape in the manner of Ni Tsan. Signed, dated 1684.

Kokka 430. Two sections of a long scroll, called The Endless River and Mountains, after Chao Mêng-fu. Signed, dated 1684.

Otsuka Kogeisha scroll reproduction. Winding River and layered Peaks. A long handscroll, signed and dated 1684. Inscription by Ch'ien-lung.

Chūgoku 6. Four Landscapes on album-leaves; two dated 1685 and 1686. Mounted together with four flower-paintings by Yün Shou-p'ing.

Chung-kuo, II, 94. Mountains at Ling-an, after Chiang Kuan-tao. Signed. Poem dated 1687.

Shên-chou, VII. Recluses' Cottages on the South Mountain. Signed, dated 1687.

Shi-O Go Un 18. Straw-covered Huts on the Sung Mountain, after Lu Hung-i. Signed, dated 1688. Also in Ōmura, I, 2; Chūgoku 6.

National Museum, Stockholm. Old Trees and Bamboos. Signed, dated 1688 (possible).

Ming-jên shu-hua, III. Peaks in Autumn, after Wang Mêng. Signed, dated 1689.

Shinchō 7. Mountain Cottages in Spring, after Chao Ta-nien. Fan-painting. Signed, dated 1689.

Shina Nanga, II, 8. Bamboos in Mist and Rain, after Ni Tsan. Signed. Colophon dated 1689.

Nanju 19 (Baron Sumitomo). Waterfall on the Mountain of the Immortals, after Chao Mêng-fu. Signed, dated 1689. Also in Tōyō, XII; Sirén, *Later*, pl.213.

Boston Museum. Homestead under bare Trees; early spring. One of a series of ten fan-paintings. Signed, dated 1689.

Shên-chou, XVII. Sparse Trees by a Rockery, after K'o Chiu-ssŭ. Signed, dated 1690.

Shi-O Go Un 19. The happy Fisherman on the Stream, after Chü-jan. Signed, dated 1690. Also in Tōan 48.

Nanju 1. The beautiful Mountains and Streams, after T'ang Yin. Signed. Two lines of poetry dated 1690.

Mei-chan t'ê-k'an 45. A House on the Shore of a River; a man inside, a crane in the garden. Three inscriptions by the artist, one dated 1690.

K.-k. shu-hua chi, XX. Clouds over Mountains in Summer, after Kuan T'ung. Signed, dated 1691.

Shên-chou ta-kuan, vol.8. An Inn among the Hills with Travellers. Dated 1691. Dedicated to Hsü Chê (*hao* Yang-ku).

Ōmura, I, 6. Birds returning to the Woods, after Li Ch'êng. Signed. Poem, colophon dated 1691.

Chung-kuo, II, 82. Pine-trees on T'ai-shan, after Chü-jan. Signed, dated 1692.

Ibid. II, 88. Reading in the Mountain in Autumn, after Wang Mêng. Signed. Colophons dated 1692. Also in K.-k. shu-hua chi, VIII; Chūgoku 6; Chung-kuo ming-hua, 31.

Shên-chou, XV. A Mountain Gully and a small Homestead on a rocky Ledge by the Water in the foreground. After Chü-jan. Signed, dated 1692.

Shanghai Museum. *T'ai-shan sung-fêng t'u.* A huge Mountain Scene, with Travellers along the Road below. Signed and dated 1692.

Tōkyō National Museum. Watching a Waterfall, after Li T'ang. Signed and dated 1692.

Chūgoku 6. Speaking of former Times in the Shade of the Pines, after Wang Mêng. Signed and dated 1692.

Ostasiat. Museum, Cologne. An old Temple surrounded by leafy Trees between two Steep Cliffs. A scholar on horseback followed by a boy in the foreground. After Shên Chou's copy of a picture by Chü-jan. Two lines of poetry. Signed and dated 1692.

J. P. Dubosc, Lugano. Steep Mountains with a winding Path, and lofty Pavilions in the midst of Pine Groves. After Kuan T'ung. Signed, dated 1692. *Cf.* Chūgoku 6.

Chung-kuo, II, 84. Peaks and Valleys, illustration to a T'ang poem. Signed, dated 1693. Also in K.-k. shu-hua chi, III; Chung-kuo ming-hua, 33.

Contag, pl.30 (P'ang Lai-ch'ên collect.) A Bouquet of early Spring Flowers. Signed by Wang Hui and four of his pupils. Dated 1693.

Chung-kuo, II, 83. Straw-covered Huts, after Lu Hung-i. Signed. Colophon dated 1694. *Cf.* Shi-O Go Un 18.

Chung-kuo ming-hua, 37. Large Landscape, after Wang Mêng. Signed, dated 1694.

Shina Nanga, III, 12. The Three Friends in the cold Winter. Signed, dated 1694. Painted together with Wang Yün and Yang Chin.

Shên-chou ta-kuan, vol.10. Rushing Streams and a distant View over winding Waters. Poem by the painter, dated 1694.

J. P. Dubosc, Lugano. Steep Mountains around a Homestead; a man passing a bridge on a donkey; another in a lonely fishing-boat in the foreground. Handscroll. Signed, dated 1694.

Ernest Erickson, New York. A River-view with Mountain in the foreground. Poem by the painter, dated 1694.

Cleveland Museum of Art. Tall Bamboo and distant Mountains, after Wang Mêng. Wang Mêng's inscription copied by Wang Hui and dated 1694. *Cf.* P'ang Yüan-chi Illus. cat., 1940, III; Cleveland Exhib. cat. 84.

Hui-hua kuan. A Scholar's Home by a River; a Visitor approaching on the Bridge. Groves of bamboo and banana and tall pine-trees. Ink on paper. Dated 1694.

Chang Ts'ung-yü cat. Large Mountain Landscape in Sung style. Signed and dated 1695.

Yen-kuang co., Peking. The endless Rivers and Mountains, after Chiang Kuan-tao. Long handscroll. Signed, dated 1695. Also in Contag, pl.56.

K.-k. shu-hua chi, XV. Drinking Tea, after Tung Ch'i-ch'ang. Signed. Poem dated 1696.

Hsi-lêng yin-shê album. Twelve Landscapes after old Masters. Signed. One dated 1696. *Cf.* Nanga Taisei, XIII, 69–80.

Chung-hua album, 1929 (First ed. 1921, third 1929). The Mountains at Ling-an (by Hangchou), after Chü-jan. Handscroll. Signed, dated 1696.

Kawai collect., Kyōto. The Pleasures of Fishermen. Handscroll. Signed and dated 1696.

P'ang Yüan-chi Illus. cat., 1940, IV. Landscape after Fan K'uan. Signed and dated 1696.

Chung-kuo ming-hua, 14. Mountains and Trees in Snow, after Hsü Tao-ning. Section of a handscroll. Signed and dated 1697.

K.-k. shu-hua chi, XXX. Plum-blossoms. Signed, dated 1697.

Hui-hua kuan. River-landscape divided in sections by small Islands and Promontories. A peak rising at the background. After Chao Ta-nien. Ink and colour on paper. Dated 1697.

Shên-chou album, 1916. Ten Landscapes. Signed, dated 1697. Preceded by a portrait of the artist.

Shên-chou ta-kuan, VII. A Homestead at the Foot of steep Mountains. Signed and dated 1697.

Ibid. XV. A Study on Mount K'uang-lu, in the manner of Wang Mêng. Signed and dated 1697.

Chung-kuo, II, 81. Clouds over a Mountain, after Chiang Kuan-tao. Signed. Poem dated 1697. *Cf.* Chung-kuo ming-hua, 4.

I-shu ts'ung-pien, 16. The Chih-ch'üan Study on the rocky Shore by a River. Painted together with Yang Chin and several others. Signed, dated 1697.

Tokasha Shina Meigashū 6. A Man in a Boat angling among Lotuses, after Hui-ch'ung. Poem by the painter, dated 1697.

Chung-kuo, II, 89. Poets' Cottages by a Stream, after Ts'ao Chih-po. Signed, dated 1698. Also in Shina Nanga, II, 5.

Ibid. II, 91. Mountains in Snow, after Fan K'uan. Signed, dated 1698. Also in Ku-kung, XII; Chūgoku, 6.

Ibid. II, 92. The South Mountain. Signed, dated 1698. *Cf.* Chung-kuo ming-hua, 36.

Shên-chou ta-kuan, vol.I. River Scenery. Dedicated to Hsü Kao-yang, dated 1698. *Cf.* Chūgoku 6.

Commercial Press album, 1934 (Private collect., Hongkong). River-view with a Boat loaded with Bamboos. Handscroll. Signed, dated 1698. *Cf.* Sōgen 250(?)

Shi-O Go Un 20. Mountain Cottages among white Clouds. Signed, dated 1698.

Sōgen 247. Bamboo Groves by a Mountain Stream. Signed, dated 1698. *Cf.* Chūgoku 6(?)

J. P. Dubosc, Lugano. An Album of Twelve Leaves, some in colour. Landscape-studies after old masters. Signed and dated 1698.

Sōgen 251. A Man washing his Feet in a River. Signed, dated 1698. The figure by Yü Chih-ting.

Liu 109. View over a Mountain-lake; a homestead among trees in the foreground where a man is fishing. Signed and dated 1698.

Kurokawa cat. 15. A misty River Valley; a pavilion on a knoll through which a stream flows. Two large album-leaves. Signed, one dated 1698.

Chung-kuo ming-hua 18. Friends meeting in front of a Pavilion in a Bamboo Grove. Signed, dated 1699.

H. C. Wêng, Scarsdale, N.Y. *Wan-li shên-ch'uan t'u*: Ten Thousand Miles of the Yangtse. Colours and ink on paper; 80 feet long. Signed, dated 1699.

Ku-kung, XIX. Peach-blossoms and a Mandarin Duck by Wang Yün, after Lu Chih. Bamboos on the picture by Wang Hui, dated 1700.

Chung-kuo ming-hua, XXII. A Scholar in a Pavilion at the Foot of misty Mountains speaking about the *I-ching* to a Friend. Signed and dated 1700.

K.-k. shu-hua chi, XII. Trees in Summer, after Chao Mêng-fu. Signed, dated 1700. Poems by contemporaries.

Shina Nanga, II, 10. Sandy Shores, after Tung Yüan. Signed, dated 1700.

Ibid. III, 7. Bamboo Groves. Signed, dated 1700.

Sōgen 250. A Man seated in a Pine-grove. Handscroll. Signed, dated 1700. The figure by Yang Chin.

Chūgoku 6. Landscape with Pines and a Temple, after Wang Mêng. Poem, signed and dated 1700.

Chung-kuo ming-hua, 24. Dry Trees and Bamboos among Rocks, after K'o Chiu-ssŭ. Signed, dated 1701.

Hsü-ching chai. A Man on Muleback in a Snowy Valley searching for Plum-blossoms. After Li T'ang. Colophon by the painter, dated 1701. *Cf.* Chūgoku 6.

Chung-hua album, 1920. Eleven pictures by Wang Hui and his friends, recording their Journey to Yü-shan in 1701.

Tōan, 49. Clearing after Snow on the Mountain Pass, after Li Ch'êng. Signed, dated 1701.

Shinchō 8. Village by a Lake, after T'ang Yin. Fan-painting. Signed, dated 1701.

Chung-kuo, II, 87. Lu-shan, after Wang Mêng. Signed, dated 1702. Also in K.-k. shu-hua chi, XIV; Chugokū 6.

Shên-chou ta-kuan, vol.2. Cloudy Mountains by a River. After Mi Fei. Colophon by the painter, dated 1702.

Mei-chan t'e-k'an 47. A Gully with rushing Water and a Temple in the background. Poem by the painter, dated 1702.

Metropolitan Museum. A Lodge by the Lake. Signed, dated 1702.

Chūgoku 6. Landscape after Chiang Ts'an: Travellers being ferried across a River to a Village. Signed and dated 1702.

Chang Ts'ung-yü cat. Overgrown Mountains rising above a River; mist in the crevices. Signed and dated 1702.

P'ang Yüan-chi Illus. cat., 1940, I. The Hua Mountain, after Wang Mêng. Signed and dated 1703.

Chung-hua album (folio size; first ed. 1918, fourth ed. 1932). Twelve Landscapes after Ching Hao, Kuan T'ung, Li Ch'êng, the monk Hui-ch'ung, Chao Mêng-fu, Ts'ao Chih-po, Kao K'o-kung, Huang Kung-wang, Wu Chên, Wang Mêng, and T'ang Yin. Signed, dated 1703.

Shên-chou ta-kuan, vol.9. The Red Cliff, according to Su Shih's poem which is partly copied by the painter. Signed, dated 1703.

H. C. Wêng, Scarsdale, N.Y. The Homestead in a Pine Grove; sloping mountains and clumps of bamboo. Signed at 72 (1703).

Hamburg Exhibition, 1949–1950. Summer Mountains, after Chü-jan. Handscroll. Signed, dated 1703.

J. P. Dubosc, Lugano. Picking Fungus, after Wang Mêng. Signed; seal of the artist reading "age 72", *i.e.* in 1703.

Chung-kuo, II, 93. Fishing Boat in a Valley, after Wang Mêng. Signed, dated 1704.

Shên-chou, XX. Large Mountain Landscape, after Huang Kung-wang. Signed, dated 1704.

S.c.t.k. hsü-pien, I. Landscape inspired by a Poem. Signed, dated 1704.

Chung-hua album, 1922. Bare Trees and Hills in Winter, after Li Ch'êng. Handscroll. Poem dated 1705.

Mei-chan t'ê-k'an 46. Mountain Valley with leafless Trees among a Stream in Winter. Poem by the painter, dated 1705.

Ku-kung, XXV. Village by a River in Summer, after Chao Mêng-fu. Signed. Poem, colophon dated 1706.

Chung-kuo ming-hua, XVI. A Mountain River between bulging Cliffs shown on two Levels, bare trees and buildings below. Signed and dated 1706.

Yu-chêng album. Twelve Landscapes after old Masters. First one dated 1706.

Shên-chou album. Twelve Landscapes, illustrations to poems by Wang Wei. Last one dated 1706. *Cf.* Chūgoku 6.

Contag, pl.57 (Sun Po-shêng collect.) A Bamboo Grove. Short handscroll. Signed, dated 1706.

Sung-pê. Pine-trees and Bamboos, after Shên Chou. Signed, dated 1708.

Gems, I, 69. A Literary Meeting in a Mountain Abode. Signed and dated 1708.

Nanking Exhib. cat. 279. Landscape with a villa: The Su Pavilion. Handscroll. Signed and dated 1708.

Ōmura, II, 5. Old Pine-trees and Bamboos in Wind, after Shên Chou. Signed. Poem dated 1708 (at 77). *Cf.* Chūgoku 6.

N. Gashū 25. Landscape after Chü-jan. Signed. Poem dated 1708.

Palace Museum Scroll, 1937. Snow on the River; Pavilions and Temples among Trees. Figures on the roads and boats moored by the shore. Illustration to a poem by Tu Fu. Signed, dated 1709. Poems by Ch'ien-lung and by many of his officials.

Shên-chou, VI. Two Men seated under tall Pine-trees by a Stream, after Chao Mêng-fu. Signed. Poem dated 1709.

Ibid. XXI. Village by a River. Signed. Two lines of poetry, dated 1710.

K.-k. chou-k'an 4. River Landscape after Wên T'ung. Signed, dated 1710 (or 1700?)

Ōmura, I, 11. Mountains in Summer with a Ferry-boat, after Tung Yüan. Signed. Colophon dated 1710.

H. C. Wêng, Scarsdale, N.Y. Bamboos and leafless Trees on the Hills, and some Houses. Short handscroll. Signed at 79 (1710).

Chung-kuo ming-hua, XXIII. A View over a Bay, many small Buildings in the Groves on the Shore, called "Spring in Chiang-nan". Signed, dated 1711.

Shên-chou, V. Cottages in the Woods at the Foot of a Mountain, after Tung Yüan. Signed. Colophon, dated 1711. *Cf.* Chūgoku 6.

Shên-chou ta-kuan, vol.3. Illustration to a Poem by Chiang K'uei (of the Southern Sung period) describing the Gathering of Lotus-seeds. Signed, dated 1711.

Hui-hua kuan. Pavilions with the Scholar, bare Trees, Flocks of Crows and Bamboos growing on the Shore.

Ink and slight colour. Painted at age of 80 (1711).

Shên-chou ta-kuan, XIII. A Cottage in a Bamboo Grove, in the manner of Ts'ao Chih-po. Signed; a second inscription dated 1711.

Ernest Erickson collect., New York. Innumerable Peaks in the Mist along the River, after Yen Wên-kuei. Long handscroll. Signed, dated 1711.

Shên-chou, V. River Landscape, after Li Ch'êng. Signed. Poem dated 1712.

Shi-O Go Un 21. Mountains on a clear Autumn Day, after Yen Wên-kuei. Signed. Colophon dated 1712.

Yūchikusai 10. Cottages by a River, after Chao Ta-nien. Signed, dated 1712. Also in Shinchō 9.

Contag, pl.31 (Sun Po-yüan collect.) River Landscape after Ni Tsan (freely transposed). A long inscription by Ni Tsan was copied by the painter. Dated 1712.

Ku-kung collect. Two Landscape-studies in colour, after Sung Masters. Album-leaves. Signed, dated 1712. *Cf.* Contag. pls. 32, 33.

Chūgoku 6. Album of eight Landscapes after old masters, the last signed and dated 1712.

Liu 110. River Landscape with bare Trees and a Traveller on a Donkey. Poem, signed and dated 1712.

Alice Boney, New York. The Wisteria Study, after Wang Mêng. Signed, dated 1712.

Chung-kuo, II, 86. Landscape after Tung Yüan. Signed. Colophon, poem dated 1713. Also in Shi-O Go Un 22.

Yen-kuang Photos. River Landscape in Snow, in the manner of Shên Chou. Handscroll. Inscription dated 1713.

Chung-kuo, II, 80 (Private collect., Hongkong). Landscape after Ching Hao. Signed. Two lines of poetry, dated 1714. Also in Shina Nanga, II, 11.

Shên-chou, XVIII. A misty River, Men in Boats collecting Water-chestnuts. After Wang (Shên Chin-ch'ing). Colophon by the painter, dated 1714.

Ming-jên shu-hua, X. Cottages among Pine-trees and Bamboos by a River. Signed. Two lines of poetry dated 1714.

Shina Nanga, I, 69. The Fishermen's Pleasure, after Chü-jan. Signed. Poem dated 1714.

Ibid. II, 2. Landscape after Fan K'uan, illustration to two lines of a poem by Su Tzŭ-mei. Signed, dated 1714. Also in Sōgen 245.

Chūgoku 6. A Riverside Village, after Hui-ch'ung. Signed and dated 1714. *Cf.* Chung-kuo ming-hua, XX.

Ibid. 7. Portrait of the Collector and Connoisseur An I-chou in his garden. The rocks and bamboo painted by Wang; the rest by Yang Chin. Signed and dated 1715.

Ibid. 6. A Man in a Riverside Pavilion, reading. Two lines of poetry. Signed and dated 1716.

Ibid. Landscape in the manner of Mi Fei. Two lines of poetry. Signed and dated 1716.

Chung-kuo ming-hua, 22. View between two steep Mountains over a River, a man is riding on a buffalo (painted by Yang Chin) on an embankment in the foreground. Signed and dated 1716.

Ibid. 26. A River Scene, with Willows. Poem, signed and dated 1716.

Ibid. 27. Landscape, after Tung Yüan, dated 1716.

T. T. Ma, Hongkong. Open Pavilions in the Bamboo-grove under tall Pines at the Foot of high Mountains; an old man inside. After Huang Kung-wang. Poem by the painter dated 1716.

Shi-O Go Un, 23 (Ueno collect.). Bare Trees, after Li Ch'êng. Signed, dated 1717.

Shên-chou, X. A Scholar's Summer Abode by the Rivers in the Mountains; two men seated in the front pavilion. Signed. Colophon.

Ibid. XIX. Hsiao I taking away the Lan-t'ing Manuscript; temple in a mountain valley. After Chü-jan. Signed.

Ibid. XIX. The Country Home of an Official by a misty Bay among Groves of Bamboos and Trees. Short handscroll. Colophon by Yang Chin, dated 1717.

Ibid. XX. River-view: Bamboos growing on the further Shore, two Fishermen on the Water. After Chü-jan. Album-leaf. Poem by the painter.

Ibid. XX. Clouds and Mists winding around richly grown Mountains in Summer. After Kuan T'ung. Album-leaf.

Shên-chou ta-kuan, vol.10. An old Pine-tree growing out from a Cliff. After Wu Chên. Poem by the painter.

Shên-chou album, 1922. Ten Landscapes after old Masters.

Chung-kuo, II, 85. A Fisherman's Cottage, after Hsia Kuei. Signed. Colophon. *Cf.* Chung-kuo ming-hua, 30.

Ibid. II, 90. Landscape in Snow.

Ming-jên shu-hua, VI. Bamboos, Plum-trees, etc. Painted together with his pupils Yang Chin, Hsü Jung and Yen-an.

Li-tai, I. Landscape in Spring. Two lines of poetry.

Chung-kuo ming-hua, 3. Mountains at Ling-an, after Chü-jan. A number of small buildings on the terraced cliffs. Album-leaf. Colophon by the painter.

Ibid. 5. Huge Mountains rising over a River, leafy Trees and Bamboo-groves covered by Snow. After a Sung master. Attributed.

Ibid. 10. An old Pine-tree, a Plum-tree and Bamboos by a River. Painted together with Yang Chin and Wang Yün.

Ibid. 24. Wide View over a Water between low Shores; leafless trees, and a boat on the water. After T'ang Yin. Poem by the painter.

Shih-ku shêng-p'ing ti-i ching-p'in lin Sung Yüan shih-êrh ching (Yu-chêng album, 1923). Twelve Landscapes after Sung and Yüan masters. Large horizontal compositions. Partly in colour.

Yün Wang shan-shui ho-ts'ê (Yu-chêng album, 1922). Twelve Landscapes after old Masters, painted together with Yün Shou-p'ing.

Palace Museum album. *Ku tsai chu t'u*. Handscroll.

K.-k. shu-hua chi, I. Landscape after Tung Yüan. Signed. Poem, colophon.

Ibid. XXIV. A Village in the Mountains after Rain. Signed.

Ibid. XLIV. Pine-trees in a Valley, after Wang Mêng. Signed.

Ch'ing êrh-shih chia. An old Plum-tree, after Chao Chih-ku. Album-leaf. Signed.

Gems, I, 70. A Dwelling in a Bamboo-grove. Copy of a painting done by Wang Mêng and Huang Kung-wang in collaboration. Seals of the artist.

Chang Ts'ung-yü cat. Small River-view with rocky Shore in the foreground. Signed.

Chou Li-yüan, 2. A Mountain Peak with Temples, after Li Ch'êng. Signed.

Hui-hua kuan. Landscape Studies after old Masters. Ink and some colour. Eight album-leaves.

Pao-yün, II. Landscape after Hsü Tao-ning. One leaf of an album. Signed.

Lo Chia-lun, Taipei. Enjoying Summer in a Pavilion by a Lake, after Chao Ta-nien. Colours on silk.

Chūgoku 6. An Album of twelve Landscapes in the styles of early Masters. Inscription by the artist.

Nanju 9. Looking at the Waterfall. Signed. Two lines of poetry.

Bijutsu, XVIII. Old Trees by a River. Fan-painting. Signed.

Ibid. XXII. The T'ai-hang Mountain. Part of a long scroll.

Shina Nanga, I, 61–68; II, 1, 3, 9. 12. Twelve Landscapes from an album, after Chao Mêng-fu, Hui-ch'ung, Yen Wên-kuei, Wang Mêng, Huang Kung-wang, Chü-jan, Kuo Pi, Hsiao Chao, Kuan T'ung and Hsü Tao-ning.

Ibid. I, 70. Woods in Autumn. Album-leaf. Poem by Yün Shou-p'ing.

Ibid. II, 7. Cottages in Bamboo Groves, after Liu Sung-nien. Signed.

Ibid. III, 2. Bamboo-groves by a Stream. Signed.

Ibid. III, 3. The Fishermen's Pleasure. Signed.

Shi-O Go Un 24. Cloudy Mountains. Handscroll. Signed. Poems.

Ibid. 25. Blossoming Plum-trees in the "Jade Cave". Landscape after Chao Po-chü. Signed. Also in Yūchikusai 11.

Ōmura, I, 5. Bare Trees, after Ni Tsan. Signed. Colophon.

Shinchō 10. River Landscape, after Huang Kung-wang. Handscroll. Signed. Colophon.

Tokasha Shina Meigashū 7. Pine Grove in a Valley in Wind, after Chao Mêng-fu. Illustrating two lines of a poem by Wang Wei. Signed.

Nanga Taikan 6. Two Landscapes after Ni Tsan and Huang Kung-wang. Album-leaves. Signed.

Sekai Bijutsu Zenshū, 20, pl.35. Travellers on a Mountain Road, after Kuan T'ung. Album-leaf. Signed.

Sōraikan, I, 54. Two Landscapes after Chü-jan and Wang Mêng. Small sheets. Signed.

Ibid. II, 74. Mountains along the River after Snow, after Li Ch'eng. Handscroll. Colophon, signed.

Sōgen 246. River Landscape. Part of a scroll.

Ibid. 248. The Yangtse River: View over a City. Part of a scroll.

Ibid. 249. River Landscape in Snow, after Shên Chou. Part of a scroll.

Yūrintaikan, I. A Boat-trip on the Lake in the Moonlight. After T'ang Yin. Signed. Colophon by the painter.

Musée Guimet, Paris. River Scenery in Winter, Birds in leafless Willows. Seals of the painter.

Chêng Tê-k'un, Cambridge. *Hsing-lu t'u*. Travellers in a Landscape. Long handscroll. Seal of the artist.

Vannotti collect., Lugano. Trees and lofty Buildings by a Waterfall; a high peak in the background. After Chiang Ts'an (of the Sung period). Signed. Poem by the painter.

Ostasiat. Museum, Cologne. Landscape after Chü-jan, as copied by Shên Chou. Inscription, signed. *Cf.* Venice Exhib. cat. 240.

H. C. Wêng, Scarsdale, N.Y. Large Album-leaves containing twelve Landscapes in the manner of old Masters. Ten of them were painted by Wang Hui, and two were by Wang Shih-min.

Kao Yen-ju, Hongkong. Landscape after Wang Mêng. Signed.

Shêng P'ing-ch'en, Hongkong. Landscape.

Huang Pan-jo, Hongkong. Views along a River. Handscroll. Signed.

(For various landscapes by Wang Hui, many of them also reproduced elsewhere. *Cf.* Nanga Taisei, X, 98–102; XII, 15–17; XIII, 105–115; XIV, 105–110; XV, 59–67; XVI, 66–75; Add. II, 56–83; Add. IV, 65–74; 187–189.)

WANG KAI 王槪. Original name Kai 丐, *t.* An-chieh 安節.

From Hsiu-shui, Chekiang; lived in Nanking. Active *c.*1680–1700. Landscapes, imitated Kung Hsien. Compiled *Chieh-tzŭ yüan hua-chuan* 芥子園畫傳. Q, I, 2. R, VI, 12. U, II, 2, 11. M, p.47.

Shên-chou album, 1913. Eight Landscapes. Inscriptions, one dated 1677.

Sōraikan, I, 46. A Man in a Pavilion listening to a Waterfall, after Chü-jan. Signed, dated 1683. *Cf.* Kokka 596.

Chūgoku 7. A Section of a twisted Pine-tree. Signed and dated 1692.

National Museum, Tōkyō. Mountains and Pines; on gold ground. Dated 1694.

Chin-ling p'ai ming-hua chi (Shên-chou album, 1924). Pavilion over a Stream, after Wang Mêng. Signed. *Cf.* Nanga Taisei, Add. IV, 58.

Kawai collect., Kyōto. Album of nine leaves: Landscapes, some in colour. Signed. *Cf.* Kokka 725; Sekai Bijutsu Zenshū, XX, text illus. 91.

Chūgoku 7. Landscape with bare Trees. A leaf in an album containing works of the eight Nanking masters. Long inscription, signed.

Shina Nanga, II, 1, 5; III, 8, 12. Four Landscapes. Album-leaves.

Kyūka, II. River View with a Woman spinning in a Cottage. Album leaf. Colophon.

Hamburg Exhibition, 1949–1950. Mountains and bare Trees. An old man in a straw-covered pavilion. Inscription by the painter.

(See also Nanga Taisei, III, 248 (Plum and Narcissus); V, 24 (Pine); V, 220 (Peaches); VII, 100 (Deer); VIII, 169–170 and XI, 237–239 (Landscapes).)

WANG KANG 王岡, *t.* Nan-shih 南石, *h.* Lü-yün shan-jên 旅雲山人.

From Nan-hui, Kiangsu. Active about the end of the 17th century. Employed by Tung Pang-ta while visiting the Capital. Flowers and figures. M, p.52.

Compagnie de la Chine, Paris. Four Magpies in a Cedar-tree by a Rockery and Shrubs. Signed, dated 1691.

WANG K'UN 王琨, *t.* Shan-hui 山輝.

From Kao-yu, Kiangsu. B. 1736, d. 1806. Son of the painter Wang Shih 王石. M, p.50.

Ars Asiatica, I, pl.XL. Lotus Flowers. Signed.

WANG KUNG 汪恭, *t.* Kung-shou 恭壽, *h.* Chu-p'ing 竹坪.
From Hsiu-ning, Anhui; lived in Wu-chin, Kiangsu. 18th century. Landscapes, figures, flowers and birds; followed Wên Chêng-ming. U, III, 2, 6. M, p.139.

Ch'ing êrh-shih chia. A Lady with a Fan seated under Wu-t'ung-trees. Signed.
(See also Nanga Taisei, II, 16 (Orchids); IV, 143 (Flowers); VI, 199–209 (Birds and Insects); VII, 161 (Dog).)

WANG LIN 王霖, *t.* Ch'un-p'o 春波.
From Nanking. 18th century. Landscapes, figures, flowers. M, p.59.

Shinchō 72. A Lady with Bow and Arrow.

WANG LO 王犖, *t.* Kêng-nan 耕南, *h.* Chia-t'ing 稼亭 and Mei-chiao 梅嶠.
From Suchou. Active in 1712. Landscapes. Q, I, 2. U, II, 2, 14. M, p.49.

Boston Museum. River with high Banks. Signed. One of a series of ten fan-paintings.

WANG MEI-TING 汪梅鼎, *t.* Ying-hsüeh 映雪, *h.* Han-yün 澣雲 and Liao-t'ang 蓼塘.
From Hsiu-ning, Anhui. Chin-shih in 1793 (or 1790). Poet and calligraphist. Landscapes, first in the contemporary style and then after the Sung and Yüan masters. Also flowers, epidendrums and stones. T. M, p.141.

S.c.t.k. hsü-pien, IV. Dry Tree and Bamboo at a Stone. Signed.

WANG MING-SHÊNG 王鳴盛, *t.* Fêng-chieh 鳳喈, *h.* Hsi-chuang 西莊.
From Chia-ting, Kiangsu. B. 1722, d. 1797. Flowers. V, p.143.

Ming-jên shu-hua, XV. Chrysanthemums. Signed, dated 1796.

WANG PING 王炳.
Court-painter *c.*1750. Landscapes. Pupil of Chang Tsung-ts'ang. M, p.52.

K.-k. shu-hua chi, XXXI. The T'ien-p'ing Mountain (at Suchou). Signed. Poem by Ch'ien-lung, copied by a courtier, dated 1751.

Ibid. XLIII. River Scenery. Signed.

WANG P'U 汪樸, *t.* Su-kung 素公.
From Hsiu-ning, Anhui. Early Ch'ing period. Landscapes, followed the Yüan masters. Q, I, 2. R, IX, 16. M, pp.136, 137.

Ming-jên shu-hua, XXIV. Pavilion and bare Trees on a River-bank, after Ni Tsan. Signed.

WANG SAN-HSI 王三錫, *t.* Pang-huai 邦懷, *h.* Chu-ling 竹嶺.
B. 1720, d. after 1798. Nephew of Wang Yü. Landscapes. M, p.52.

Hamburg Exhibition, 1949–1950. Landscape. Signed, dated 1777.
Shên-chou, XII. A Village on a wooded Mountain. Signed, at 75 (1794).
Ming-jên shu-hua, XXVI. Cloudy Mountains, after Huang Kung-wang. Signed. Colophon dated at 78 (1797).

WANG SHIH-I 王時翼, *t.* Yu-min 又溟.
From T'ai-ts'ang, Kiangsu. Cousin of Wang Shih-min. Painted landscapes after Li T'ang, figures after Sung Hsü. M, p.45.

K.-k. shu-hua chi, XLV. The Tung-t'ing Lake. Signed.

WANG SHIH-MIN 王時敏, *t.* Hsün-chih 遜之, *h.* Yen-k'o 煙客, Hsi-lu lao-jên 西廬老人, Hsi-t'ien chu-jên 西田主人 and other names.
From T'ai-ts'ang, Kiangsu. B. 1592, d. 1680. The first of the "Four Wangs"; one of the "Nine Friends in Painting." Q, I, 1. R, I, 1. U, I, 1, 1. M, pp.43, 44.

Tōyō, XI. Mountain Peaks rising above the Mist by a River. Signed, dated 1616.
Contag, pl.1 (Sun Po-yüan, Suchou). River-view with low Pavilion and spare Trees, after Ni Tsan. Signed, dated 1627.
Shên-chou, I. Mountains and Streams in Autumn, after Wang Mêng. Signed, dated 1629.
Yūchikusai 1–4. Four Landscapes forming a Series. First one also in Shincho 3, dated 1630.
Contag, pl.3 (Wu Hu-fan, Suchou). River-view; steep rock, a bridge and a few pine-trees. Signed, dated 1632.
Mei-chan t'ê-k'an 39. Misty Mountains. Signed, dated 1635.
Shina Meiga Senshū, II, 32 (formerly Hayashi collect.) Mountains and spare Trees along a winding River. Landscape in Yüan style. Inscription dated 1635.
Boston Museum. River Scenery. Signed, dated 1636. One of a series of ten fan-paintings.
Chūgoku, V. Old Trees and Bamboos growing by a Rock, after Wang Mêng. Signed and dated 1637.
Chang Ts'ung-yü cat. Steep Mountain Slope; cottages under the trees on a stony shore. Dated 1637.
Shina Nanga, II, 7. Landscape. Signed. Colophon dated 1642. *Cf.* Chung-kuo ming-hua 6; P'ang Yüan-chi cat. Add. 3.
Vannotti collect., Lugano. Wooded Mountains with a Cottage and Willow-trees in the foreground. After Huang Kung-wang. Signed, dated 1647.
S.c.t.k. hsü-pien, High Mountains, tall Pines, a Hut below. Dated 1648.
Shên-chou ta-kuan, II. Wooded Hills by a River, after Huang Kung-wang. Signed, dated 1649.
Hui-hua kuan. Autumn Mountains rising through Clouds. Two inscriptions by the painter, one dated 1649, the other 1661.
Ming-jên shu-hua, XXII. Mountain Landscape, after Wu Chên. Signed, dated 1650.
Shinchō 1. Landscape. Fan-painting. Signed, dated 1654.
J. P. Dubosc, Lugano. Wooded Mountains with a Waterfall, and a Bridge over the Stream below. Signed, dated 1654.
Chung-kuo, II, 65. Landscape after Huang Kung-wang. Signed, dated 1657. *Cf.* Shina Nanga, III, 6.
Chūgoku, V. Mountain Landscape. Signed and dated 1657. Dedicated to Keng-an.
National Museum, Stockholm. A Bunch of Flowers. Signed, dated 1657. *Cf.* Chung-kuo, II, 66; Shina Nanga, I, 32 and Shina Nanga Taisei.
Ōmura, II, 4. Flowers in a Vase. Signed, dated 1657. *Cf.* Chūgoku, V.
Yu-chêng album. Ten Landscapes after old Masters. Seven painted in 1657; three in 1667.

Liu 106. Landscape in the manner of Huang Kung-wang. Signed and dated 1660. Colophon by Wang Chien, dated 1663. *Cf.* Nanking Exhib. cat. 252.

P'ang Yüan-chi Illust. cat., 1940, I. A Scholar's Study under Pine-trees at the Foot of a Mountain. Signed and dated 1661.

T'ien-ch'i shu-wu. Landscape; a Man in his House. Signed, dated 1661.

Chung-kuo ming-hua, 4. The South Mountain with Pine-trees. Long inscription by the painter dated 1661.

Shina Nanga, II, 5. Landscape. Signed, dated 1661. *Cf.* Chūgoku, V.

Shên-chou, XI. High Peaks enveloped in Clouds, after Huang Kung-wang. Signed, dated 1663.

Kokka 285. Landscape after Huang Kung-wang. Signed, dated 1664. *Cf.* Chung-kuo ming-hua, 8.

Hakubundō album (Lo Chên-yü collect.) Five leaves (originally six?) of Landscape sketches. Signed, dated 1664.

Hua-chung chiu-yu (Yu-chêng Album). Summer Landscape, after Wang Mêng. Signed, dated 1664.

N. Gashū, 22. Landscape after Tung Yüan. Signed, dated 1665. *Cf.* Shi-O Go Un 1; Ōmura, I, 7.

J. P. Dubosc, Lugano. Landscape in the style of Huang Kung-wang. Fan-painting. Signed, dated 1665.

Shanghai Museum. Large Pine-trees below the Rocks, rising from the River Shore. The composition is a combination of Wang Mêng and Ni Tsan. Inscription by the painter, dated 1665.

Ku-kung collect. Landscape. Leaf from an album of illustrations to poems by Tu Fu. Signed and dated 1665. *Cf.* Nanking Exhib. cat. 250.

Chang Ta-ch'ien cat., I, 32. River Landscape. A section of a handscroll? Signed and dated 1666. Colophon by Wu Wei-yeh.

Gems, I, 51. A Waterfall in Summer Mountains. Signed and dated 1666.

Chūgoku, V. Homestead in Ya-i Mountain, after Ni Tsan. Signed and dated 1666.

Ibid. V. Album of ten Landscapes in the manners of early masters. Signed, one dated 1666.

Ibid. V. Landscape with rocky Hills. Signed and dated 1666.

I-shu ch'uan-t'ung, 11. Landscape painted for Wang Hui. Signed and dated 1666. Colophon by Wang Chien.

Tōan, 43. Mountain Landscape. Signed, dated 1666.

Ōmura, I, 1. Straw-covered Huts in the Mountains. Signed, dated 1666. *Cf.* Sōraikan, I, 47.

Shina Nanga, III, 11. Landscape after Huang Kung-wang. Signed, dated 1666.

Hamburg Exhibition, 1949–1950. Mountain and Trees in the manner of Huang Kung-wang. Ink on gold ground. Dedicated to a friend on his 80th birthday. Signed, dated 1666.

K.-k. shu-hua chi, XX. Landscape after Wang Mêng. Signed, dated 1667.

Yūchikusai 5. Snowy Landscape, after Fan K'uan. Signed, dated 1667.

Sōgen 230. Landscape after Huang Kung-wang. Signed, dated 1667. Colophons by the painter and by Wang Chien. Also in Contag, pl.6.

Nanking Exhib. cat. 253. Landscape in the manner of Huang Kung-wang. Signed and dated 1667.

Liu 105. Landscape in the manner of Huang Kung-wang. Signed and dated 1668.

K.-k. shu-hua chi, XVIII. Clearing after Snowfall on the Mountains, after Wang Wei. Signed, dated 1668.

Yen Kuang Co., Peking (photographs). Wang Shih-min ch'ing-luan nan-ts'ui t'u-chüan (Heian Seikasha, Kyōto). Verdant Mountains on a warm Spring Day. A handscroll reproduced on eighteen leaves. Signed, dated 1668. *Cf.* Chūgoku, V.

Nanking Exhib. cat. 251. Landscape in the manner of Huang Kung-wang. Signed and dated 1669.

Shinchō 2. Dawn over the Yao River, after Huang Kung-wang. Fan-painting. Signed, dated 1669.

K.-k. shu-hua chi, IV. Landscape after Huang Kung-wang. Signed. Colophon dated 1670. Possibly by Wang Hui.

Ibid. IX. Mountain Landscape in Spring, after Huang Kung-wang. Signed, dated 1670.

Shên-chou, X. Deeply-fissured Mountains with Trees and Cottages, after Huang Kung-wang. Signed, dated 1670.

Shi-O Go Un 2. Landscape after Huang Kung-wang. Signed, dated 1670.

Chung-kuo ming-hua 24. A quiet Bay; pines on the rocky shore, buildings on the terraces and peaks in further distance. Colophon by the painter, at 80 (1671).

Ibid. 26. Large landscape, after Huang Kung-wang. Inscription, dated 1671.

Shên-chou, VIII. The Island of Immortals. Painted on green paper with gold in the manner of Huang Kung-wang. Signed. Poem dated 1672.

Shina Nanga, III, 9. Landscape after Wu Chên. Signed, dated 1672. *Cf.* Chung-kuo ming-hua, 7.

I-yüan chên-shang 3. Landscape. Inscription dated 1675.

J. P. Dubosc, Lugano. Landscape in the manner of Wang Mêng. Handscroll. Signed, dated 1675.

Shina Nanga, III, 10. A Bunch of Flowers. Signed, dated 1676.

Shi-O Go Un 3. Snowy Mountains, after Li Ch'êng. Signed. Colophon dated 1679.

Shên-chou ta-kuan, 10. Landscape with pines, after Tung Yüan. Handscroll. Signed.

Ibid. 13. Two landscapes on album-leaves, after Huang Kung-wang and Chao Mêng-fu. Signed.

Shên-chou, XVI. Four Landscape-sketches. Album-leaves. Signed.

Chung-kuo ming-hua, 13. Two album-leaves. Landscape studies, one after Wang Mêng, the other after Hui-ch'ung. Signed. Two more in vol.16 after Huang Kung-wang and Ni Tsan.

Ibid. 14. Two sections of a long View of steep Mountains, spare Trees and winding Waters, after Huang Kung-wang. Handscroll.

Chang Ts'ung-yü cat. Twelve Album-leaves. Landscape-studies after Sung and Yüan masters.

Nanking Exhib. cat. 254. A River Valley with Houses. Signed. Colophon by Wu Hu-fan.

Wang Fêng-ch'ang fang-ku shan-shui ts'ê (Yu-chêng album, 1921). Twelve Landscape Studies after old Masters.

Hua-chung chiu-yu chi-ts'ê (Hakubundō album, 1921). Clouds over the Mountains by the River, after Huang Kung-wang.

T. T. Ma, Hongkong. Wooded Mountains, after Huang Kung-wang. Short inscription by the painter.

Shina Nanga, I, 35, 36. Landscapes after Huang Kung-wang and Wang Mêng. Signed.

Ibid. I, 37; II, 12. Four album-leaves with Landscapes. Signed.

Ibid. III, 4. Landscape after the Monk Hui-ch'ung.

Nanga Taikan 3. Mountain Landscape with Cottages under Pines, after Chao Mêng-fu. Signed.

Kokka 599 (Abe collect.) Landscape.

Yūrintaikan, II. Stones. Handscroll. Signed. Various colophons, dated 1747–1803. Colophon by Wu Wei-yeh.

C. T. Loo's Successor, Frank Caro, N.Y. Mountain Landscape with tall Pines in the foreground. After Chao Mêng-fu. Ink and colour on paper. Signed. *Cf.* Toronto, 46.

H. C. Wêng, Scarsdale, N.Y. River-views and Great Mountains. Some in Chü-jan's style, others in the manner of Mi Fei. Signed.

WANG SHIH-SHÊN 汪士慎, *t.* Chin-jên 近人, *h.* Ch'ao-lin 巢林, Ch'i-tung wai-shih 溪東外史 and other names.

From Anhui; lived in Yangchou, Kiangsu. Active *c.*1730–1750. Friend of Chin Nung and Hua Yen. Narcissi and plum blossoms. Lost the use of his right hand and worked with the left. Q, II, 2. R, XII, 11. U, III, 1, 5. M, p.137.

Anonymous publisher, n.d. Album of twelve flower-paintings. Signed, dated 1733.

Chung-kuo, II, 146. Bamboos and Orchids. Signed, dated 1734. *Cf.* Chung-kuo ming-hua, 25.

Nanga Taisei, III, 108. A Branch of flowering Plum. Signed and dated 1736.

Hamburg Exhibition, 1949–1950. A Branch of Plum Blossoms. Signed, dated 1739.

Shên-chou ta-kuan 6. Small Landscape, painted for a friend who sent him some snow-water for tea. Dated 1740. Colophons by Chin Nung and other contemporaries of the artist. *Cf.* Mei-chan t'ê-k'an, 68.

Private collect., Kyōto. Album of Paintings of blossoming Plum. Signed and dated 1741. *Cf.* Sekai Bijutsu Zenshu, XX, text illus. 106.

Chung-hua album, 1929. Twelve Pictures of Plum-blossoms. Signed, dated 1741. A portrait of the artist precedes the paintings.

Pageant, 891. A Branch of flowering Plum. Long inscription by the artist. Signed and dated 1741.

Nanking Exhib. cat. 336. A Pine-tree and Bamboo growing by a Rock. Signed and dated 1741.

Gems, III, 13. A Branch of flowering Plum. Album-leaf. Poem, signed and dated 1741.
Wang Ch'ao-lin mei-hua ts'ê (Chung-hua album, 1921). Twelve leaves of Plum-blossom Studies. Signed, dated 1747.
Shên-chou album, 1930. Twelve Paintings of Flowers, Bamboo, etc. in old styles. Signed, dated 1749.
Nanga Taisei, I, 210. Bamboo growing by a Rock. Album-leaf. Signed and dated 1749.
Fei-tu lu hua-hui. A blossoming Plum-tree. Handscroll. Signed, dated 1750.
Shina Nanga, III, 11. A Branch of Plum-blossoms. Signed. Poem dated 1751.
T'ai-shan ts'an-shih-lou ts'ang-hua, IV. Plum-trees. Four panels, forming a screen (?). Poem, signed.
Po-mei chi. A blossoming Plum-tree. Signed.
Sumitomo collect., Ōiso. A Branch of flowering Plum, painted in ink, blue-grey colour, and white pigment. Long poem by the artist, signed.
Nanga Taisei, III, 109 and 253; IV, 136–141. Leaves from an Album of Flower-paintings. Signed.

WANG SHU-KU 王樹穀, *t.* Yüan-fêng 原豐, *h.* Wu-wo 無我 and Lu-kung 鹿公.
From Hangchou. B. 1647, d. *c.*1730. Figures, followed Ch'ên Hung-shou. Q, II, 1. R, IX, 3. M, p.50.

Sōgen 346. Servants bringing Books to a Scholar. Signed. Colophon dated 1728.
Hui-hua kuan. Ch'ên Chih-an playing *Ch'in* to a Man who is falling asleep, another man standing by. Slightly coloured. Inscription by the painter.

WANG SU 王素, *t.* Hsiao-mou 小某.
From Yangchou, Kiangsu. B. 1794, d. 1877. Figures. T, Add. I.

Nanga Taisei, Intro. 56. Two Ladies standing by a Rock. Signed and dated 1844.
Shina Nanga, II, 4. Drinking Wine in the Moonlight. Fan-painting. Signed. Two lines of poetry, dated 1867.
Shên-chou, IX. A Gentleman seated on a Bedstead by a Rockery, attended by two maid-servants. Signed. Also in Shina Nanga, II, 11.
Ming-jên shu-hua, XVII. Ladies and Children around a Pot of Orchids. Signed.
Ibid. XXI. Two Birds in a Willow-tree, after Ch'en Tao-shan. Signed.
Ibid. XXI. A Fisherman and his Family in a Boat, after Lo P'ing. Signed. Poem.
I-yüan album. Landscape-sketches and graceful Girls. Eight album-leaves.
Nanga Taisei, VII, 211–222. Album of twelve paintings of Figures in Landscapes. Signed.
Shina Nanga, I, 138. A Lotus Pond. Album-leaf. Signed. Two lines of poetry.
Ibid. II, 3. The Fishermen's Pleasure. Album-leaf. Signed. Poem.
Ibid. III, 6. Visiting a Friend on a rainy Day. Signed. Two lines of poetry.
Ibid. III, 8. Landscape illustrating a poem by T'ao Yüan-ming. Signed.
Shinchō 80. Farmers resting in the Evening. Signed. Poem.
Kokka 690. A Street Story-teller.
Nanga Taikan 7. A Farmer with a Buffalo. The Wood-cutters. Two album-leaves. Signed.
Ibid. 7. A Flower-vendor. Album-leaf. Signed.
National Museum, Copenhagen. The Fairy Ma-ku. Signed.

WANG T'AO 王濤, *t.* Su-hsing 素行, *h.* Hêng-shan 衡山.
Lived in Yangchou, Kiangsu. Active *c.*1800. Flowers and birds after Yüan masters. Unrecorded.

Tokasha Shina Meigashū 94. Three Buffaloes swimming in the Water under Willows, an old man seated on the shore. After Tai Sung. Signed, dated 1798.

WANG TSUAN 王撰, *t.* I-kung 異公, *h.* Sui-an 隨菴.
B. 1623, d. after 1708. Son of Wang Shih-min. Landscapes. Q, I, 1. R, II, 24. U, I, 3, 1. M, p.47.

Shên-chou, XVI. River-view with Trees and a Bridge in the foreground. After Ni Tsan. Album-leaf. Signed, dated 1703.

WANG WÊN-CHIH 王文治, *t.* Yü-ch'ing 禹卿, *h.* Mêng-lou 夢樓.
From Tan-t'u, Kiangsu. B. 1730, d. 1802. Calligraphist. Plum-blossoms. U, III, 1, 12. M, p.57.

Shên-chou, XVI. Peony Flowers. Two poems by the painter.

WANG WU 王武, *t.* Ch'in-chung 勤中, *h.* Wang-an 忘菴.
From Suchou. B. 1632, d. 1690. Collector and connoisseur. Flowers, birds, landscapes. Q, I, 1. R, II, 21. U, I, 2, 14. M, pp.46–47.

Chūgoku 7. An Album of ten Flower-paintings, the last signed and dated 1661.

British Museum. Two Pheasants and two white Birds by a blossoming Tree. Signed, dated 1662.

Shina Nanga, I, 46. Birds and Narcissi by a Rock. Signed, dated 1667.

Ku-kung, XI. Enjoying Chrysanthemums in a Mountain Pavilion. Signed. Colophon dated 1667. Also in K.-k. shu-hua chi, VII.

Kawai collect., Kyōto. An Album of Flower-paintings, most in colour, some in ink only. Signed and dated 1676. *Cf.* Kokka; also Sekai Bijutsu Zenshū, 20, text illus. 99.

Pageant 788. Flowers growing by a Rock. Poem, signed and dated 1677.

C. T. Loo's Successor, Frank Caro, N.Y. Roses, Bees and Bulbul. Ink and colour on paper. Inscription by the painter, dated 1679. *Cf.* Toronto, 60.

Liu 122. Narcissi growing by a Garden-stone; a Willow-tree rising above. Poem, signed and dated 1682.

Chên-hsin shu-shê co., Suchou, 1926 (Wu Hu-fan collect.) Album of Paintings of Flowers, Fish, etc. Signed, dated 1683.

K.-k. shu-hua chi, XVI. Narcissi and the T'ien-chu Plant. Signed, dated 1683.

Ibid. XIV. Birds and Flowers. Signed. Poem dated 1685.

Wang Wang-an hua-hui ts'ê (Shên-chou a bum, 1923). Ten Pictures of Flowers.

Ku-kung collect. A leaf from an album of Flower-paintings. Poem, signed. *Cf.* Nanking Exhib. cat., 307.

Hui-hua kuan. Studies of Flowers, Birds and Butterflies. Eight album-leaves.

Gems, III, 11. Five leaves from an album of Flower Paintings. Seals of the artist.

Ch'ing êrh-shih chia. A Branch of a Plum-tree. Album-leaf. Signed.

Shinchō 35. Birds on a Pomegranate Tree with Lotuses and Rocks below.

Nanga Taikan 12. Peonies, after Ch'en Shun. Hand-scroll. Signed. Colophon.

Nü-wu chai. Two Birds in a blossoming Plum-tree and Narcissi by a Stone. Signed.

G. Del Drago, N.Y. A Lotus Plant with torn Leaf and Fishes. Signed.

WANG WU-T'IEN 王無忝, *t.* Su-yeh 夙夜.
From Mêng-chin, Honan. Chin-shih in 1670. Landscape. R, V, 5. M, p.49.

Musée Guimet, Paris. An album of Eight Landscapes after old Masters. Signed, dated 1721.

WANG YING-SHOU 王應綬, original name Wang Shên 王申, *t.* Tzŭ-ch'ing 子卿.
Grandson of Wang Yüan-ch'i. Landscapes, followed the family tradition. M, p.53.

Ōmura, II, 1. Landscape after Shên Chou. Handscroll. Signed, dated 1820.

WANG YÜ 王昱, *t.* Jih-ch'u 日初, *h.* Tung-chuang 東莊 and other names.
From T'ai-ts'ang, Kiangsu. Act. *c.*1680–1729. Nephew of Wang Yüan-ch'i. Author of the *Tung-chuang lun-hua* 東莊論畫. Landscapes. Q, I, 3. R, VIII, 19. U, I, 3, 8. M, p.48.

Chung-kuo, II, 152. Mountains in Mist and Rain, after Kao K'o-kung. Signed, dated 1686.
Shina Meiga Senshū 28. A Stream between two high terraced Mountains, after Huang Kung-wang. Signed, dated 1686.
Musée Guimet, Paris. River Landscape after Wang Mêng. Signed, dated 1688.
Shina Nanga, III, 11. Landscape, after Huang Kung-wang. Illustration to two lines of a poem by Wang Wei. Signed, dated 1689.
S.c.t.k. hsü-pien, VIII. Herons flying over the Marshes. Signed, dated 1689.
Shinchō 50. Cloudy Mountain Landscape after Huang Kung-wang. Signed, dated 1714.
Shên-chou ta-kuan, I. Mountain Landscape after Wu Chên. Signed and dated 1721.
Sōgen 269. Trees on the South Mountain, after Huang Kung-wang. Signed. Poem dated 1722. *Cf.* I-yüan chên-shang 3.
C. C. Wang, New York. A Mountain Landscape with many Buildings, in the manner of Huang Kung-wang. Signed and dated 1729. *Cf.* Nanking Exhib. cat. 346.
I-yüan chên-shang 10. Landscape after Ni Tsan. Signed and dated 1729.
Chung-kuo ming-hua 10. Summer Mountains and approaching Rain, after Kao K'o-kung. Signed.

WANG YÜAN-CH'I 王原祁, *t.* Mao-ching 茂京, *h.* Lu-t'ai 麓臺, Hsi-lu hou-jên 西廬後人 and other names.
From T'ai-ts'ang, Kiangsu. B. 1642, d. 1715. Grandson of Wang Shih-chên, the compiler of *Wang-shih hua-yüan* 王氏畫苑. A Han-lin scholar. Member of the Board for the compilation of *P'ei-wên chai shu-hua p'u* 佩文齋書畫譜. The fourth of the "Four Wangs". Landscapes, followed Huang Kung-wang. Q, I, 3. R, V, 2. U, I, 1, 3. M, pp.47–48.

Shinchō 12. Mountains in Autumn. Fan-painting. Signed, dated 1673.
Shi-O Go Un 26. Landscape after Huang Kung-wang. Signed, dated 1679. *Cf.* Tōan 54; Sirén, *Later*, pl.218.
Hamburg Exhibition, 1949–1950. Peaks of the Fu-ch'un Mountains, after Huang Kung-wang. Signed, dated 1679. *Cf.* Contag, p.51.
Chung-kuo ming-hua, VII. The main Peak of the Fu-ch'un Mountains after Huang Kung-wang. Signed and dated 1681.
Wang Lu-t'ai shan-shui chüan (Commercial Press). Streams and Mountains in Tung Yüan's and Chü-jan's style. Signed and dated 1684.
Shên-chou ta-kuan, vol.4. Mountain Pass between steep Hills; road leading down to an inlet of water. Inscription by the painter dated 1687. Also in Shi-O Go Un 27.
Ōmura, I, 10. Mountain Landscape with a winding Stream, after Huang Kung-wang .Signed. Colophon dated 1687.
Chung-kuo ming-hua, 12. A Mountain Ridge rising above the Mist, after Huang Kung-wang. Signed and dated 1689.
K.-k. shu-hua chi, VI. Bamboos and Stones. Bamboos by Tao-chi, dated 1691; stones by Wang Yüan-ch'i. Signed.
Chung-kuo ming-hua, 19. The Fu-ch'un Mountains. A broad valley between high mountains; clumps of trees in the foreground. After Huang Kung-wang. Signed and dated 1692.

Liu 111. River Landscape in the manner of Ching Hao and Kuan T'ung. Signed and dated 1693.

Mei-chan t'ê-k'an 49. The Fu-ch'un Mountain, after Huang Kung-wang. Dated 1693.

Ōmura, I, 1. The Hua Mountain, in Autumn. Signed. Colophon dated 1693.

Chung-kuo ming-hua, 28. Landscape in the manner of Huang Kung-wang. Inscription, signed and dated 1694.

Shi-O Go Un 28. Grassy Mountains and driving Mist. After Kao K'o-kung. Signed. Colophon, dated 1694.

C. T. Loo's Successor, Frank Caro, N.Y. The Hou Mountain, after Wang Mêng. Colophon, dated 1694. *Cf.* Chūgoku 7; Ōmura, I, 1.

Boston Museum. Misty River and Mountains. Signed, dated 1694. One of a series of ten fan-paintings.

C. T. Loo's Successor, Frank Caro, N.Y. Landscape in the manner of Wang Mêng. Signed, dated 1694. *Cf.* Toronto, 47.

K.-k. shu-hua chi, XI. Deeply-crevassed and overgrown Mountains; broad river at their foot. Long inscription dated 1695.

Wang Lu-t'ai shan-shui ts'ê (Wên-ta album, 1925). Fourteen Landscapes. Signed, dated 1695.

Shanghai Museum. Mountain-river and high Peaks, after Huang Kung-wang. Reddish and greenish colour give a coloristic touch to the design. Inscription dated 1695.

S.c.t.k. hsü-pien, VI. River Landscape; rocky shores with bamboo. Signed, dated 1696.

K.-k. shu-hua chi, XIX. Landscape after Huang Kung-wang. Signed, dated 1696.

Yu-chêng album, 1919. Ten Landscapes after Sung and Yüan Masters. Signed. Colophon dated 1696. *Cf.* Contag, pl.53.

J. P. Dubosc, Lugano. A Mountain Retreat surrounded by high Peaks; willows by a broad stream in the foreground. After Ni Tsan and Huang Kung-wang. Two inscriptions by the painter, signed and dated 1698. *Cf.* Chung-kuo ming-hua, 22.

Chung-kuo ming-hua, 20. Landscape. Topped mountains around a river-bay, after Kao K'o-kung and Mi Fei. Signed and dated 1698.

K.-k. shu-hua chi, XXII. Landscape after Li Ch'êng. Short handscroll. Signed, dated 1699.

Sōgen 257. Cloudy Mountains after Kao K'o-kung. Signed. Colophon dated 1699.

Ibid. 258. Clouds and Pine-trees on a Mountain, after Wang Mêng. Signed, dated 1699.

Contag, pl.53 (Lu Pei-yün collect.) Morning Mist in the Mountains after Huang Kung-wang. Dated 1699.

K.-k. shu-hua chi, XLV. River Landscape after Ni Tsan. Signed, dated 1700.

Chūgoku 7. Landscape after Wu Chên. Inscription, signed and dated 1700.

Hui-hua kuan. A terraced Mountain; trees and buildings. Ink with reddish and greenish colours. Strong brushwork. Dated 1701.

Yūchikusai 32. Landscape after Chü-jan. Signed, dated 1701.

Chicago Art Institute. Landscape after Huang Kung-wang. Signed, dated 1701. *Cf.* Chung-kuo, II, 97; Shina Nanga, III, 2; Cleveland Exhib. cat. 85.

Palace Museum album, 1931. Twelve Landscape Sketches after old Masters, accompanied by poems. The last picture dated 1702.

K.-k. shu-hua chi, XLIV. Pavilions and Towers on the Mountain of the Immortals, after Chao Mêng-fu. Signed, dated 1702.

Chung-hua wên-wu chi-ch'êng, vol.IV. Mountains and a broad Stream in Autumn, after Huang Kung-wang. Signed and dated 1702. Long inscription by Ch'ien-lung.

Ōmura, I, 5. Cottages in quiet Mountains. Signed. Colophon dated 1702. Also in Sōraikan, I, 56.

Sōgen 259. The Three Friends in the cold Winter. Signed. Poem dated 1702.

Vannotti collect., Lugano. Trees, Rocks and Bamboos. Handscroll. Signed, dated 1702.

Hui-hua kuan. Misty River Valley with Trees growing through the low Clouds. Illustrating a poem by Han Chang-ni. Ink and colour on paper. Dated 1702.

P'ang Yüan-chi Illus. cat., 1940, III. Landscape after Ni Tsan and Huang Kung-wang. Inscription, signed and dated 1703.

Chung-kuo ming-hua, 8. Terraced Mountains rising over a winding Stream. Signed and dated 1703.

Chung-kuo, II, 103. Landscape in the manner of Tung Yüan and Chü-jan. Signed. Colophon dated 1703.

Ibid. II, 95. River Landscape after Ni Tsan. Signed, dated 1703. Also in Shina Nanga, I, 52.

Ibid. II, 101. Village by a River, Mountain Terraces in

the background. Dedicated to Wang Hui. Colophon dated 1703. *Cf.* Chung-kuo ming-hua 5.

Ming-jên shu-hua, IV. Mountain Landscape, after Huang Kung-wang. Colophon dated 1703.

Kokka 547. The green Trees on the South Mountain, after Huang Kung-wang. Dated 1703. Also in N. Gashu 24; Ōmura, I, 4; Sōgen 260.

Musée Guimet, Paris. A small River Landscape after Ni Tsan. Dated 1703.

Shên-chou ta-kuan, vol.2. Spring Mountains in blue Mist. After Huang Kung-wang. Dated 1704. *Cf.* Chūgoku 7.

Ōmura, II, 5. Cloudy Mountains, after Kao K'o-kung. Signed. Dated 1704.

Hui-hua kuan. Mountain Landscape. A gorge between two peaks; pavilions and pine-trees. After Huang Kung-wang. Ink only. Dated 1704.

Gems, I, 73. A winding Creek and Pavilion. Poem. Signed and dated 1705.

J. P. Dubosc, Lugano. A broad River, with a Mountain Peak on one side and Trees and a Summer Pavilion in the foreground. In the style of Ni Tsan. Three inscriptions by the painter. Signed, dated 1705.

Ming-jên shu-hua, V. Landscape after Huang Kung-wang. Dated 1705.

Shi-O Go Un 29. Landscape after Wu Chên. Signed, dated 1705. Also in Ōmura, I, 8 and P'ang Yüan-chi cat. 9.

K.-k. shu-hua chi, XLIII. Landscape after Huang Kung-wang. Signed. Dated 1706.

Liu 113. A rocky Mountainside, with Waterfalls and Buildings. After Chü-jan. Long inscription, signed and dated 1706.

Cleveland Museum of Art. Landscape after Ni Tsan, painted in ink and light colours. Inscription dated 1707. *Cf.* Cleveland Exhib. cat. 86.

J. P. Dubosc, Lugano. Landscape in the style of Chao Mêng-fu. Fan-painting. Inscription, signed and dated 1707.

Chung-kuo ming-hua, 22. Landscape after Huang Kung-wang. Signed and dated 1707.

Ibid, 10. A Mountain Stream, tall Trees and Buildings on the rocky Shore. After Huang Kung-wang. Dated 1708. *Cf.* Shina Nanga, I, 54.

J. P. Dubosc, Lugano. View over a wide Bay framed by Mountains. Circling mist and tall trees. In the manner of Huang Kung-wang. Handscroll. Dated 1708.

Ibid. Landscape in the style of Ni and Huang. Dedicated to a friend. Dated 1708.

Honolulu Academy of Arts. A River spanned by a Bridge at the Foot of high Mountains; tall trees. After Huang Kung-wang. Signed and dated 1708.

P'ang Yüan-chi illust. cat., 1940, I. Landscape after Ni Tsan. Inscription, signed and dated 1708.

Shên-chou, II. The T'ung-kuan Mountain, after Huang Kung-wang. Signed. Colophon dated 1709.

Ibid. IV. River Landscape after Ni Tsan. Signed. Colophon dated 1709.

Chūgoku 7. Landscape after Wang Mêng. Inscription, signed and dated 1709.

Contag, pl.55 (Palace Museum?) Landscape in the manner of Ni Tsan. Dated 1710.

K.-k. shu-hua chi, II. Landscape after Wang Mêng. Signed, dated 1710.

Shina Nanga, I, 53. Landscape in Colours. Signed. Colophon dated 1710. *Cf.* Chung-kuo ming-hua, 9.

Vannotti collect., Lugano. Rocky Islands forming a Ridge across the River. After a picture by Tung Ch'i-ch'ang in the manner of Ni and Huang. Dated 1710.

C. C. Wang, New York. Wooded Mountain, encircled by Clouds. Dated 1710.

Shinchō 2. Mountain Landscape. Signed. Colophon dated 1711 (at 70).

H. C. Wêng, Scarsdale, N.Y. Summer Clouds in a Mountain Gorge. Dated 1711 (at 70).

Musée Guimet, Paris. Mountains in Mist. Combining the manners of Huang Kung-wang and Fang Ts'ung-i, Colophon dated 1712 (at 71). *Cf.* Shên-chou ta-kuan, vol.5.

Chung-kuo ming-hua, 8. A River between steep Mountains, after Huang Kung-wang, who imitated Tung Yüan (*Hsia-shan t'u*). Signed and dated 1712.

Wang Lu-t'ai fang-ku shan-shui ts'ê (Wên-ming album). Eight Landscapes after old Masters. Signed and dated 1712 and 1713.

Liu 112. A River Valley, after Wu Chên. Inscription, signed and dated 1713.

Chung-kuo, II, 102. Landscape after Chü-jan. Signed. Colophon dated 1713. Also in Shina Nanga, II, 12; Mei-chan t'ê-k'an, 48.

K.-k. shu-hua chi, XLI. Mountains in Autumn, after

Huang Kung-wang. Colophon dated at 72 (1713).

Shên-chou, VII. River Landscape in the manner of Ni Tsan and Huang Kung-wang. A leaf from an album of twelve pictures. Dated 1713.

Shi-O Go Un 30. Landscape after Ni Tsan and Huang Kung-wang. Colophon dated 1714.

Shina Meiga Senshū 27. River Landscape after Ni Tsan. Signed, dated 1714.

Yūrintaikan, I. A thatched Hut at the River-side. Dated 1714.

K.-k. shu-hua chi, XVIII. Landscape after a Northern Sung Master. Colophon dated 1715 (at 74).

Shên-chou, I. Landscape. Album-leaf. Signed.

Ibid. VI. Landscape after Huang Kung-wang. Album-leaf. Two lines of poetry. Seals of the painter. Also in Shina Nanga, II, 7.

Chung-kuo, II, 96. Landscape after Huang Kung-wang. Seal of the painter.

Ibid. II, 98. A Spring Morning on the Mountain of the Immortals, after Wang Mêng. Seals of the painter. *Cf.* Chung-kuo ming-hua, 3.

Ibid. II, 99. A winding Stream at the Foot of craggy Mountains, after Wu Chên. Seal of the painter. *Cf.* Chung-kuo ming-hua, 3.

Ibid. II, 100. Cloudy Mountains after Kao K'o-kung. Colophon. Seals of the painter. Also in Nanga Taikan 11.

Li-tai, VI. Landscape in Mist. From an album of twelve pictures.

Chung-kuo ming-hua 18. A craggy Mountain Ridge rising between two Arms of a Stream, buildings and bridges in the foreground.

Ku-kung, XXIII. Streams flowing out from cloudy Mountains, after Kao K'o-kung. Signed. *Cf.* Ku-kung, XLIII.

Ibid. XXXVI. Landscape. Fan-painting. Signed.

Ibid. XLII. Floating Mist on distant Mountain. Signed.

Ibid. XLIII. Streams flowing out from cloudy Mountains. Signed.

K.-k. shu-hua chi, III. Cloudy Mountain Landscape. Signed.

Ibid. XXI. Streams and Mountains on a clear Day. Signed.

Ibid. XXIII. Green Peaks and floating Mist. Signed.

Ibid. XXIV. Wooded Mountains. Signed.

Ibid. XXXII. Endless Mountains enveloped in Clouds. Signed.

K.-k. chou-k'an 79. A Stream in the wooded Mountains. Signed.

Ibid. 89–98. Twelve Landscape-studies after old Masters. Album-leaves. Signed. (Many other works by this artist in K.-k. chou-k'an; see Index.)

Nanking Exhib. cat. 314. A broad River View, in the manner of Ni Tsan. Poem, signed.

Ibid. 316. Landscape after Wu Chên. Signed.

Chang Ts'ung-yü cat. Two River Views in Ni Tsan's manner.

Ibid. Overgrown Mountains in Mist.

Ibid. Terraced Mountains in the manner of Huang Kung-wang.

Ibid. Huge Mountains with Buildings and Pine-trees.

Ku-kung collect. Two leaves from an album of Landscapes after old masters. Signed. *Cf.* Nanking Exhib. cat. 315.

Hui-hua kuan. Eight Landscape-studies after old Masters. Two after Huang Kung-wang, two after Ni Tsan, others after Kuan T'ung, Wang Mêng, etc. Ink and colour on paper.

Chung-kuo ming-hua, 7. The Island of the Immortals; mountains rising through the clouds. After Chao Mêng-fu.

Lo Chia-lun, Taipei. Endless Mountains and Rivers, and Luxurious Vegetations. Fishing-boats on the water. In Yüan style. Handscroll; about 72 feet long. Painted for emperor K'ang-hsi. Signed.

Harada Brothers, Ōsaka. Mountain Landscape: the I-yün Retreat. Handscroll. Inscription, signed.

Chūgoku 7. River Landscape, after Ni Tsan. Signed.

Ibid. Landscape after Huang Kung-wang. Inscription, signed.

Ibid. Landscape after Kao K'o-kung. Inscription, signed.

Ibid. Ten Landscapes. Fan-paintings. For other fan-paintings, see Nanga Taisei, VIII, 172–187.

Shina Nanga, I, 55. Pines and Streams in a Valley, after Wang Mêng. Album-leaf. Seal of the painter.

Ibid. II, 4. Mountains in Summer, after Huang Kung-wang. Fan-painting. Signed.

Ibid. II, 6. Misty Landscape, after Kao K'o-kung. Album-leaf. Seals of the painter.

Ibid. III, 7. Terraced Mountains. Signed.

Ibid. III, 9. Landscape in the style of Ching Hao and Kuan T'ung. Signed.

Kokka 574 (K. Ohara, Kyōto). A Landscape.

Yūchikusai, 33–36. Four Landscapes in the manners of Huang Kung-wang, Ni Tsan, Wu Chên and Wang Mêng respectively. Inscriptions by the painter.
Shinchō 13. Landscape after Chao Mêng-fu. Fan-painting. Signed.
Boston Museum. Grassy Mountains and tall Trees. Signed. One of a series of ten fan-paintings.
Ibid. (56.10). *Yen-t'an ch'un-hsiao t'u*: Spring Morning at a Mountain Stream, with homesteads, pavilions, leafy trees on both sides; bridges across the water. Long handscroll. Signed.
Musée Guimet, Paris. Landscape in the style of Huang Kung-wang and Kao K'o-kung.
C. C. Wang, New York. Rolling Hills, rich Growth of Bamboo and Fruit-trees, grazing Animals, Homestead Buildings. A free version of the *Wang-ch'uan* scroll. Long colophon by the painter.
Kao Yen-ju, Hongkong. Landscape. Signed.

WANG YÜAN-CH'U 王元初, *t.* Tzŭ-yai 紫崖.
Landscapes in the manner of Huang Kung-wang. L. *Fu-lu*

Chou Li-yüan 15. Landscape with Lakeside Buildings. Album-leaf. Signed and dated *i-wei*, or 1655?

WANG YÜN 王雲, *t.* Han-tsao 漢藻, *h.* Ch'ing-ch'ih 清癡.
From Kao-yu, Kiangsu. B. 1652, d. *c.*1735. Figures in Ch'iu Ying's style; landscapes after Sung academicians. U, II, 2, 16. M, p.50.

Shina Nanga, III, 12. The Three Friends of cold Winter. Painted together with Wang Hui and Yang Chin. Signed, dated 1694.
S.c.t.k. hsü-pien, V. Landscape after Liu Sung-nien. Signed, dated 1695.
Hamburg Exhib., 1949–1950. Fang Hu, Island of Immortals. Coloured. Archaistic. Signed, dated 1699.
Ku-kung, XIX. A Mandarin Duck and Peach-blossoms, after Lu Chih. Bamboos on the picture by Wang Hui, dated 1700. Poem by Wang Yün.
Boston Museum. Mountain Landscape; some travellers passing over a bridge. After Fan K'uan. Signed, dated 1705.
J. Cahill, Wash., D.C. A Man seated on a Mountain Ledge under Pine-trees, gazing at a Flock of Birds. Signed and dated, 1707.
Hamburg Exhib., 1949–1950. Thunderstorm in Spring. Signed, dated 1715.
British Museum, No.197. An Immortal with Peaches. Signed, dated 1732 (at 81).
S.c.t.k. hsü-pien, II. River Landscape in Sung style. Signed, dated 1733.
K.-k. shu-hua chi, V. Landscape. Seal of the painter.
I-yüan album. Eight sections of a Landscape-scroll representing Mountains, Water and Trees in South Sung style.
Hamburg Exhib. 1949–1950. Four old Men in the Shade of Willow-trees.

WANG YÜN-HSIANG 王韻香, *h.* Ch'ing-wei tao-jên 清微道人.
From Wu-hsi, Kiangsu. A Buddhist nun. Lived *c.*1800. Orchids. M, p.59.

Shina Nanga, II, 10. Orchids and Bamboos. Poems.

WEI HAO-LING 魏鶴齡.
Unrecorded. Probably a court-painter in the Ch'ien-lung period.

Li-tai, VI. Landscape. Signed.

WÊN TIEN 文點, *t.* Yü-yeh 與也, *h.* Nan-yün shan-ch'iao 南雲山樵.
Son of Wên Chên-hêng and a descendant of Wên Chêng-ming. B. 1633, d. 1704. Landscapes in the family tradition. Also pine-trees and bamboos. Q, I, 1. R, IV, 7. U, I, 2, 20. M, p.18.

T. T. Ma, Hongkong. A hilly Landscape with dry Trees and a Wanderer. Painted for Wen-tseng on his 60 years' birthday. Ten poems and a short colophon by the painter dated 1679.
Hui-hua kuan. River at the Foot of a Mountain; a bridge across the stream. Poem and colophon by the painter, dated 1687.
Shinchō 38. Two Men seated by a Lake. Short handscroll. Signed. Poem dated 1701.
Wu-mên p'ai ming-hua chi (Shên-chou album, 1924). Old Trees and cold Streams, after Wên Chêng-ming. Seal of the painter.
Ming-jên shu-hua, XXVI. Landscape. Signed. Poem, Colophon.
Ku-kung collect. Two leaves from an Album of Landscapes. Inscriptions and seal of the artist. *Cf.* Nanking Exhib. cat. 310.
Gems, I, 54. Autumn Grove after Rain. Inscription, signed.

WÊN TING 文鼎, *t.* Hsüeh-k'uang 學匡, *h.* Hou-shan 後山.
From Hsiu-shui, Chekiang. B. 1766, d. 1852. Connoisseur, collector. Landscapes, pines and stones; followed Wen Chêng-ming. M, p.19.

Ming-jên shu-hua, XII. The Plum-blossom Water Pavilion. Signed, dated 1820.
Ibid. XXI. Kuan-yin's empty Seat in the Mountains. Signed, dated 1823. A Sūtra copied by the painter.
Po-mei chi. Plum-tree at a Rock and Narcissi. Signed, dated 1824.
Ming-jên shu-hua, XI. A Man and a Boy with a *Ch'in* walking in high Mountains, after Wen Chia. Signed, dated 1841 (at 76).
Fei-tun lu hua-hui. A Twisted Pine-tree on Rocks. Signed, dated 1843.
Ming-jên shu-hua, XI. Travellers in Autumn Mountains, after Lu Shih-tao. Signed.

WÊNG LO 翁雒, *t.* Mu-chung 穆仲, *h.* Hsiao-hai 小海, second son of Wêng Kuang-p'ing 翁廣平.
From Wu-chiang, Kiangsu. B. 1790, d. 1849. Figures and portraits in early years, flowers, animals (especially turtles) and insects in old age. T. U, III, 2, 19. M, p.311.

Hamburg Exhib. 1949–1950. "White-headed Birds" in the wild Cherry and Peony Flowers. In the manner of Chao Ch'ang.

WU CHAO 吳照, *t.* Chao-nan 照南, *h.* Po-an 白菴.
Active during the late Ch'ien-lung period. Poet. Landscapes, figures; particularly famous for his orchids and bamboos. T. M, p.173.

Tomioka collect., Kyōto. Bamboo and Rock; the bamboo painted in red. Signed and dated 1804.
Ming-jên hsieh-chu. Bamboos. Eight-fold screen. Signed.

WU CH'I 吳琦, *t.* Yü-hsüan 玉鉉.
From Chekiang. Unrecorded.

British Museum (No.214). A Deer by a Tree and Magpies. Signed.

WU CH'I 吳祺, *t.* I-chü 以拒. According to the signature on the following painting, *h.* Hsüeh-yai tao-jên 雪崖道人.
From Ch'ien-t'ang, Chekiang. Active *c.*1750(?) Figures, followed Ch'ên Hung-shou. M, p.178.

Tokasha Shina Meigashū 36. Two Men seated under Pine-trees by a Waterfall in Mist. Signed, dated *chi ssŭ* (1749?)

WU HSI-TSAI 吳熙載, original name T'ing-yang 廷颺, *t.* Jang-chih 讓之, *h.* Wan-hsiang chü-shih 晚香居士.
From I-chêng, Kiangsu. B. 1799, d. 1870. Flowers. T, Add. I. M, p.177.

Nanga Taisei, Add. IV, 130. Willows and Lotus. Signed, dated 1839.
Nanga Taikan 8. Willows and Roses. Signed, dated 1859.
Ming-jên shu-hua, XII. Bamboos by a Rockery. Signed at 71 (1869).
Shên-chou, XVI. Wistaria and blossoming Shrubs. Signed.
Ming-jên shu-hua, XII. Orchids by a Rock over a Stream. Signed.
Ibid. XXI. Chrysanthemums and Cassia-flowers in a Pot. Signed.
Ibid. XXVI. Bamboos and Orchids by a Rock. Signed.
T'ai-shan ts'an-shih-lou ts'ang-hua, Ib. Bamboo and Blossoming-cherry by a Rock. Signed.
Ibid. Four Flower-paintings, forming a screen (?)
Ōmura, I, 6. Peach-blossoms. Fan-painting. Signed. Poem.
(See also Nanga Taisei, II, 78, 79 (Orchids and Bamboo), 192 (Chrysanthemums), 259; III, 207 (Plum); IV, 176–184 (Flowers); IV, 245 (Tree); V, 74, 87, 133, 185, 237 (Flowers and Fruits); VII, 208 (Portrait).)

WU HSIAO 吳綃, *t.* Su-kung 素公 and Ping-hsien 冰仙, *h.* P'ien-hsia 片霞.
Wife of a Mr. Hsü 許. Native of Suchou. Birds and flowers. M, p.170.

I-yüan chêng-shang, 5. Two white Birds on a Branch of a flowering Pear-tree in the Moonlight. Signed.

WU HSIN-LAI 吳心來, *t.* T'ien-shêng 田生, *h.* Wang-lu-tzŭ 望穭子.
From Hsieh-hsien, Anhui. Active *c.*1730–1750. Landscapes and figures. M, p.168.

S.c.t.k. hsü-pien, I. Landscape in the style of Wang Mêng. Poem. Signed.

WU HUAN 吳煥, *t.* Ming-hsien 銘仙.
From Suchou. Act. *c.* 1770 (?) Flowers and birds followed the Yüan masters. M, p.178.

Mo-ch'o pi-chi, vol.I. A Hawk on a Pine-tree. Signed, dated *i-yu* (probably 1765).
Sōgen 337. Two Cranes on a Rock. Signed, dated 1770(?)

WU HUNG 吳宏, *t.* Yüan-tu 遠度, *h.* Chu-shih 竹史.
From Chin-ch'i, Kiangsi; lived in Nanking. Active *c.*1670–1680. One of the "Eight Masters of Nanking". Landscapes. P, III, 13. Q, I, 1. R, III, 6. U, I, 2, 11. M, p.166.

Ming-jên shu-hua, X. River Landscape after a Yüan Master. Signed, dated 1672.

Hui-hua kuan. A View of the Swallow Cliff outside Nanking. Signed. Handscroll.

Chūgoku 7. Bamboo growing from behind a Rock. Poem, signed. Leaf in an album containing works of the eight Nanking masters.

Ibid. Landscape in the manner of Li Ch'eng. Poem, signed. Another leaf in the same album.

National Museum, Stockholm. Landscape in Winter. Signed. *Cf.* Sirén, *Later*, pl.186.

Ibid. Bamboos in Snow. Signed.

Hamburg Exhibition, 1949–1950. Landscape with a Waterfall, covered bridge and high buildings on the mountain slope. Ink and slight colour on satin. Signed.

WU I-LIN 吳一麟, *t.* Shêng-chêng 聖徵.

From Ch'ang-shu, Kiangsu. 18th century. Flowers and birds in the style of Ma Yüan-yü. M, p.179.

British Museum, No.260. Tree Peonies and a Kingfisher Bird.

WU JUNG-KUANG 吳榮光, *t.* Po-jung 伯榮, *h.* Ho-wu 荷屋, K'o-an 可盦, Shih-yün shan-jên 石雲山人 and many others.

From Nan-hai, Kuangtung. B. 1773, d. 1843. Poet and calligraphist. Landscapes after Wu Chên; birds and flowers after Yün Shou-p'ing. M, p.177.

S.c.t.k. hsü-pien, IX. Landscape after Wu Chên. Signed, dated 1827.

WU KÊN 吳艮.

Lady painter. Ch'ing period. Unrecorded.

Li-tai, V. The God of Longevity. Signed.

WU KUEI-CH'ÊN 吳規臣, *t.* Hsiang-lun 香輪, *h.* Fei-ch'ing 飛卿 and Hsiao-hsien 曉仙.

From Chin-t'an, Kiangsu. Lady painter. Pupil of the painter P'an I-chien (1740–1830). Flowers. T, XV, 15. M, p.175.

Compagnie de la Chine, Paris. Peony Flowers after Yün Shou-p'ing. Signed, dated 1830.

Po-mei chi. A Plum-tree, after Chao Mêng-chien. Signed.

WU LI 吳歷, *t.* Yü-shan 漁山, *h.* Mo-ching 墨井.

From Ch'ang-shu, Kiangsu. B. 1632, d. 1718. Landscapes in the style of Huang Kung-wang. Study-companion of Wang Hui. Became a Christian in 1682 under the name of Acunha. Served as a missionary in Chia-ting, Kiangsu, and was buried in the Jesuit cemetery in Shanghai. Q, I, 2. R, IV, 4. U, I, 1, 4. M, p.166.

Yūchikusai 12. Collecting Fungi. Signed, dated 1659. Poems by Ch'ien Ch'ien-i, Wu Wei-yeh and the painter.

Sōraikan, I, 53. Spring in Chiang-nan. Long handscroll. Signed. Poem dated 1666.

Nanga Taisei, Add. II, 34–43. Album of ten Landscapes. Signed, one dated 1666. Another inscription by the artist dated 1675.

Ōmura, II, 2. Landscape in Snow. Signed. Poem, colophon dated 1667. Poems by Wu Wei-yeh, Wang Shih-min and others. *Cf.* Chūgoku, V.

Takashima collect., Kugenuma. Landscape after Wang Mêng. Signed and dated 1670.

Liu 117. River Landscape after Chao Mêng-fu and Huang Kung-wang. Signed and dated 1670.

Ibid. 116. Stalks of Bamboo and a Clump of bare Trees, in the manner of Ni Tsan. Poem (written in Ni Tsan's calligraphic style), signed and dated 1673.

Shina Nanga, I, 59. Landscape. Signed. Poem, colophon dated 1673.

Yūchikusai 13. Cloudy Mountains. Signed, dated 1673. *Cf.* Shincho 14.

Ōmura, I, 10. In the Mist of the Woods and far from the Dust. Signed, dated on the same day as the preceding picture (1673). Dedicated to the same person.

Shi-O Go Un 31. Birds flocking after Snow over Mountains and River. After Li Ch'êng. Handscroll. Signed, dated 1673. *Cf.* Yūchikusai 14.

Ōmura, II, 4. Huts by a clear Stream. Signed. Poem dated 1674. *Cf.* Chūgoku, V.

Sōgen 279. Cloudy River Landscape, after Fang Ts'ung-i. Handscroll. Signed, dated 1674.

Kokka 266. A Mountain Abode, after a Yüan Master. Signed, dated 1674. *Cf.* Shincho 17; Pageant 798.

Contag, pl.16 (Chang Ts'ung-yü collect.) A Homestead in Wooded Mountains. The painter is seen playing the *ch'in*, as indicated in the poem, dated 1674. *Cf.* Liu 118.

Vannotti collect., Lugano. Landscape. Signed and dated 1674.

Contag, pl.15 (Chiang Ku-sun collect.) A Mountain River; leafy trees and small cottages. Poem dated 1675.

Shên-chou, IX. Mountains in Autumn. Signed. Long poem dated 1675. Also in Shina Nanga, III, 4.

I-shu ts'ung-pien, 16. View over a wide Water with Fishing-boats; Rocky Shore on the right. Handscroll. Signed, dated 1675.

Shi-O Go Un p.32. Steep Mountain rising above a River; pine-trees below. Ink and colours. Poem by the painter dated 1675. Also in Contag, pl.17.

Chūgoku, V. A Man in a Pavilion built over the River, shaded by Pine-trees. Signed and dated 1675.

Shên-chou, XVII. Deeply-creviced Mountains rising in winding Forms, trees and buildings in the valley below. Colophon by the painter, dated 1676. *Cf.* Shina Nanga, II, 7.

Chung-kuo ming-hua, 14. Two Homesteads on the opposite Shores of a wide River. Temple buildings in a pine-grove in the mountains. Handscroll. Inscription and poem by the painter, dated 1676.

Ibid. 19. A deep Gully between steep Cliffs; rushing water, two large pine-trees below. Inscription by the painter, dated 1676.

T'ien-ch'i shu-wu. A House on the River Shore. Signed, dated 1676.

Shên-chou, V. The Feng-o Mountain Study. Signed and dated 1677. Colophon by Wang Hui, dated 1703. *Cf.* Chung-kuo ming-hua, 16; T'ien-ch'i shu-wu.

Chang Ta-ch'ien cat. I, 37. An old Tree by a Rock. Signed and dated 1677.

Private collect., Hongkong. Scholars enjoying the Summer Breeze in open Garden Pavilions; bamboos and leafy trees along the river-shore. Ink-painting. Long handscroll. Signed and dated 1679.

H. C. Wêng, Scarsdale, N.Y. River View: small Houses along the rocky Shore, wooded Mountains. Short handscroll. Signed and dated 1680. *Cf.* Nanga Taisei, XVI, 62, 63(?)

Shanghai Museum. Autumn Landscape with spare Trees, rushing Water and Houseboats on the River. Long handscroll. Two inscriptions by the painter, one dated 1681. One colophon by Chang Ti.

Nanga Taikan 11. Mountain Dwellings under large Pines. Poem by the painter, dated 1681.

Chung-hua album, 1921. Twelve Landscapes, in the manner of Sung and Yüan Masters. Two are dated 1685. *Cf.* Nanga Taisei, Add. II, 44–55.

Chung-kuo, II, 70. A River at the Foot of overhanging Mountains. Temples in the valley in mist. After Wang Mêng. Poem dated 1693. *Cf.* Chung-kuo ming-hua, 3.

K. Sumitomo collect., Ōiso. View of a River-shore; green mountains and red trees. After Wang Mêng. Handscroll, signed and dated 1693. *Cf.* Sekai Bijutsu XX, text illus. 92.

Ōmura, II, 1. Landscape after Wang Mêng. Signed and dated 1696. *Cf.* Chūgoku, V.

J. P. Dubosc, Lugano. Landscape. Handscroll. Signed and dated 1699.

Private collect., Peking. The old Snow Man on Huang-shan. Long inscription by the painter, dated 1703. *Cf.* Sirén, *Later*, 223.

Metropolitan Museum (13.220.117). Landscape with a Scholar in a Hut. Inscription dated 1703. *Cf.* Bulletin, Dec. 1952.

Wên-ming album, 1917. Eight Landscapes in old styles, inscribed, the last dated 1706. Chūgoku, V.

Freer Gallery (58.13). (I-shu ts'ung-pien, 9.) Landscape after Wang Mêng. Poem by the painter, dated 1707.

Shên-chou ta-kuan, vol.7. Bamboo growing by a Stone. Signed.

Chung-kuo, II, 71. Pine-trees and Clouds on the South Mountain, after Wu Chên. Signed. *Cf.* Shina Nanga, I, 58.

Ibid. II, 72. A Lake in Spring, after Chao Ta-nien. Signed. Poem and colophon. *Cf.* Shina Nanga, I, 60.

Chung-kuo ming-hua, 16. Deeply-folded and topped Mountains rising above a River; small buildings between the cliffs. Illustration to a poem by Shên Chou.

Chung-hua album, 1921. Eight Landscapes with poem and colophon on each.

Shih-ku hsiao hsiang pu t'u-ts'ê (Wên-ming album). View over a River-shore, with Portraits of Wang Hui and the painter (?) Only the landscape by Wu Li. Signed. Colophon by the painter.

K.-k. shu-hua chi, I. The Nine Fungi. Signed.

Ibid. IX. Landscape after Wu Chên. Signed.

Ku-kung collect. (Photographs by Yen-kuang co., Peking, 1922). Ten Album-leaves: Landscapes after Sung and Yüan Masters. Colophon by Wang Tsuan. *Cf.* Chūgoku, V; Nanking Exhib. cat. 300.

Ibid. Ten Landscapes, reproduced in colour.

Hui-hua kuan. Mountain Stream; a high peak beyond and buildings on the rocky promontory. After Wu Chên.

Ibid. Mountain Landscape; a bridge leading over the stream; buildings and trees.

Ibid. Landscape Studies after old Masters. Eight album-leaves.

I-yüan chên-shang, 9. Green Mountains and White Clouds, after Chü-jan. Poem, signed.

Ibid. 10. Landscape in the manner of Wang Mêng. Inscription, signed.

Mei-chan t'ê-k'an, 42. Summer Mountains after Rain. After Wu Chên. Signed.

Nanking Exhib. cat. 301. A Mountain rising from a River; houses in the distance. Poem, signed.

Liu 115. Landscape in the manner of Huang Kung-wang Houses in a narrow Gorge, others above on a Plateau. Signed.

Chung-hua wên-wu chi-ch'êng, vol.IV, 398. A steep Cliff rising up from a River; a Boat with two Men below. After Chao Ta-nien. Large album-leaf.

Chang Ts'ung-yü cat. Steep Mountains, high peaks and trees below.

Lo Chia-lun, Taipei. A Mountain Gully. An intimate study from nature. Inscription by Chien Ju. Signed.

Kokka 237. Autumn Landscape. Signed. Poem.

Ibid. 594 (Abe collect.) Landscape.

Tōyō, XII. A solitary Pavilion under Pine-trees. Signed.

Shina Nanga, I, 57. Bamboos growing by a Rockery. Signed.

Ibid. I, 56. Wooded Mountain. After a part of Huang Kung-wang's Fu-ch'un picture.

Ibid. III, 8. A Pavilion in the Mountains, after Wu Chên. Signed.

Shi-O Go Un 33. Pines and Clouds on the South Mountain. Dedicated to Mrs. Ai. Signed. *Cf.* Chung-kuo, II, 71 and Chung-kuo ming-hua, 8.

Ibid. 34. View of a Village with a Boat returning Home, after Wu Chên. Signed. Also in Ōmura, I, 3; Chūgoku, V.

Shinchō 15. Lake in Autumn. Fan-painting. Signed. Poem.

Ibid. 16. Spring in the T'ien-t'ai Mountain, after Wang Mêng. Fan-painting. Signed.

Tōan, 50. A Pine-grove on a Mountain-slope. Album-leaf. Signed. Colophon.

Sōgen 278. Mountains in Autumn. Poem by the painter.

Ibid. 279. Cloudy Hills along Rivers. Sections of two different handscrolls.

Ibid. 280. A Man seated on a Rock under Pine-trees. Short handscroll. Signed.

Yūrintaikan, II. High Mountains and tall Trees; a Pavilion built over the Stream below.

Sōraikan, II, 73. Four leaves from an album of eight Landscapes. Poems and colophons by the painter.

Chūgoku, V. Bamboo growing beside a Rock. Two lines of poetry. Signed.

Contag, pl.18 (Ts'ao Yu-ch'ing collect.) Towering Hills and Pine-trees along a Mountain Stream. Poem by the painter.

C. C. Wang, New York. Reading Poetry before the Yellowing of Autumn. Signed. *Cf.* Cleveland Exhib. cat. 90.

Cleveland Museum of Art. Myriad Valleys and the Flavour of Pines. Signed. *Cf.* Cleveland Exhib. cat. 91.

Boston Museum. Mountain Landscape in Autumn. Signed. One of a series of ten fan-paintings.

British Museum (Add. No.8). Album of small Landscapes drawn with the hot stylus. Seals of the painter. Probably copies.

Vannotti collect., Lugano. Landscape in Ni Tsan's manner. The River winding between rocky banks. Short poem by the painter.

Ibid. Album of ten Pictures of Bamboo, Trees and Rocks. Poems, signed.

Formerly Hobart collection, Cambridge, Mass. A Homestead under Willows by a River. After a painting by a Sung artist. Handscroll.

J. P. Dubosc, Lugano. Bamboos by a huge Rock. Album-leaf. Short poem by the painter; signed.

Ibid. Landscape. Album-leaf. A short poem by the painter; signed.

W. Hochstadter, New York. Towering Mountains. Signed.

H. C. Wêng, Scarsdale, N.Y. A Mountain Retreat, after Wu Chên.

WU LIEN 吳漣, *t.* Ch'iu-i 秋漪.
Unrecorded. Probably 18th century.

British Museum, (No.241.) Lady and Children. Seals of the painter.

WU LI 吳履, *t.* Kung-chih-t'an 公之坦, *h.* Chu-hsü 竹虛 and other names.
A native of Chia-hsing, Chekiang. Active *c.*1790. Landscapes, figures, flowers. T. M, p.175.

Nanga Taisei, X, 198. A Man in a House at the Foot of steep Cliffs. Signed and dated 1790.

Chūgoku 8. "Reading the Tablet". Two men at a large table in an open pavilion; bare trees outside. Signed.

WU MOU 吳楙, *t.* Ch'ao-ying 朝英 and I-ch'üan 逸泉.
From Wu-hsi, Kiangsu. Active *c.*1750. Flowers. R, X, 13. U, III, 1, 13. M, p.169.

Ars Asiatica, I, pl.XLV. Peonies. Signed. Two lines of poetry, dated 1750.

WU NA 吳訥, *t.* Chung-yen 仲言.
From Hangchou. Landscapes after Lan Ying and flowers after Sun Ti. M, p.169.

Shina Meiga Senshū, III. Mountain Landscape after Tung Yüan. Album-leaf. Signed and dated *kuei-yu* (1693?)

WU PAO-SHU 吳寶書, *t.* Sung-yai 松崖, *h.* T'o-hsien 籜仙.
From Wu-hsi, Kiangsu. Granson of Wu Mou. Flowers, fruits, orchids and bamboos; also portraits of ladies. In his latter years, he liked to paint ink plum-blossoms. T. U, III, 2, 10. M, p.169.

Po-mei chi. Branches of blossoming Plum-trees. Signed, dated *wu-shên.* (1848?) *Cf.* Nanga Taisei, II, 256.

Wu Shan-t'ao 吳山濤, *t.* Tai-kuan 岱觀, *h.* Sai-wêng 塞翁.
From Hsieh-hsien, Anhui; lived at Hangchou. Chü-jên in 1639, and d. at 86. Landscapes after the Yüan masters. R, I, 19. U, I, 2, 15. M, p.165.

T'ai-shan album, series I. Seven sketchy Landscapes. Many inscriptions by the artist, one dated 1676.
Po-mei chi. A Twig of blossoming Plum-tree. Album-leaf. Signed, dated 1676.
T'ai-shan ts'an-shih-lou ts'ang-hua, III. Sketchy Tree by a low Hut. Signed.
Ibid. River View; tall trees in the foreground and an angler in a boat.
Hui-hua kuan. Spring Mountains with spare Trees and small Buildings. Ink and slight colour. Sketchy manner. Inscription by the painter.
Gems, I, 81. A deserted Pavilion in Autumn. Poem, signed.
Vannotti collect., Lugano. Two thin Pine-trees. Signed.

Wu Shih 吳時.
Unrecorded. 18th century (?)

Ku-kung, XXXIX. Landscape with Figures, illustration to two lines of a T'ang poem. Signed.

Wu Tan 吳丹, *t.* Chung-po 衷白.
From Nanking. Active 1672–1689. Landscapes. Q, II, 1. M, p.223.

Kokka 308. Landscape. Signed. Poem dated 1667.
Nanju 6 (Iwasaki collect.) The Plum Blossom Study. Signed, dated 1675. Also in Tōyō, XII; Pageant 885.
Freer Gallery (50.11). Landscape. Handscroll. Signed, dated 1675. Title written by Kung Hsien.
Shimbi, XV. Landscape after Ching Hao. Signed, dated 1676.
Boston Museum. Leafless Trees at the Foot of a misty Mountain. Signed, dated 1676.
S.c.t.k. hsü-pien, II. Bare Trees and a thatched Pavilion on a River-bank. Dated 1681.
Nanju 2. Angling on a quiet River. Signed, dated 1681. *Cf.* Pageant 884.

Wu T'ao 吳滔, *t.* Po-t'ao 伯滔, *h.* T'ieh-fu 鐵夫.
From Shih-mên, Chekiang. B. 1840, d. 1895. Landscapes. M, p.182.

Ming-jên shu-hua, XX. Plum-blossoms in a Vase, a Lamp, and a Pot with Grass. Signed. Poem dated 1876.
Wu Po-t'ao hsien-shêng shan-shui ching-p'in (No place or name indicated). An Album of twelve Landscape Studies. Signed.
Ōmura, I, 9. Landscape. Poem. Seal of the painter.
(See also Nanga Taisei, III, 215; IV, 146 and 248; VII, 142–144; X, 236, 237; Add. IV, 145–148.)

Wu Ting 吳定, *t.* Tzŭ-ching 子靜, *h.* Hsi-an 息菴.
From Hsiu-ning, Anhui. Active at the end of the 17th and beginning of the 18th centuries. Landscapes, followed the monk Hung-jen. Q, I, 2. M, p.171.

Nanga Taisei, XI, 242–251. Album of ten Landscapes after old masters, the last signed and dated 1688.
Bijutsu, XVII. Mountain Landscape. Fan-painting. Signed.

WU T'ING-K'ANG 吳廷康, *t.* Yüan-shêng 元生, *h.* Tsan-fu 贊府, K'ang-fu 康甫, Chin-chai 晉齋 and Ju-yün 茹芸.
From T'ung-ch'êng, Anhui. Active about the middle of the eighteenth century. Painted plum-blossoms and epidendrums. T. M, p.177.

S.c.t.k. hsü-pien, X. Epidendrums growing out from vertical Rock. Inscription by the painter. Also in Nanga Taisei, II, 81.

WU TZŬ 吳鼒, *t.* Chi-chih 及之 and Shan-tsun 山尊, *h.* I-an 抑菴 and Nan-yü shan-ch'iao 南禺山樵.
From Ch'üan-chiao, Anhui. B. 1755, d. 1821. Poet. Landscapes, followed Wang Yüan-ch'i; also flowers. M, p.175.

Fei-tun lu hua-hui. A Duck and some blossoming Plants, after Ch'ên Shun. Handscroll. Signed, dated 1815.

WU TZŬ 吳咨, *t.* Shêng-yü 聖俞.
From Wu-chin, Kiangsu. Active *c.*1860. Flowers and birds. T, Add. I.

Nanga Taikan 8. Peach-blossoms, Roses and Lilies by a Rock, after Ch'ên Shun. Signed, dated 1857.

WU WEI-YEH 吳偉業, *t.* Chün-kung 駿公, *h.* Mei-ts'un 梅邨.
From T'ai-ts'ang, Kiangsu. B. 1609, d. 1671. Famous as poet; wrote the descriptive poem called "The Nine Friends in Painting", referring to Tung Ch'i-ch'ang, Li Liu-fang, Yang Wên-ts'ung, Ch'êng Chia-sui, Chang Hsüeh-tsêng, Pien Wên-yü, Shao Mi, Wang Shih-min and Wang Chien. P, I, 4. Q, I, 1. R, I, 6. U, I, 1, 4. M, p.165.

Sōgen 232. Landscape with a Man on a galloping Horse, Signed, dated 1630. *Cf.* Sirén, *Later*, pl.177.
Lo Chia-lun, Taipei. Trees by a River; a Man in a Boat. Signed and dated 1631. *Cf.* Nanking Exhib. cat. 266.
Chung-kuo, II, 37. Man seated under Trees among steep Rocks. Signed, dated 1645. *Cf.* Chung-kuo ming-hua, 29.
Hua-chung chiu-yu (Yu-chêng album). Landscape. Signed, dated 1650. *Cf.* Nanga Taisei, X, 3, 1(?)
Ōmura, I, 12. Mountain Landscape, with Houses on the Shore of a River. Signed. Poem dated 1655. *Cf.* Chūgoku 5.
Kokka 251. Snowy Landscape. Signed, dated 1657.
Ku-kung collect. River Landscape. Album-leaf. Signed and dated 1658. *Cf.* Nanking Exhib. cat. 245.
Shina Nanga, II, 6. River Landscape. Album-leaf. Signed, dated 1666.
Shên-chou, XV. River-view with high Mountains, in the manner of Tung Yüan. Signed, dated 1667.
Shina Nanga, I, 23. High Mountains by a River. Signed, dated 1667.
Chang Ts'ung-yü cat. A broad River at the Foot of an overgrowing Mountain. Dated 1667.
Shên-chou, VI. A Man seated by a winding Brook. Signed.
Hui-hua kuan. Summer Days in the Mountains. Terraced rocks, a hut below. Signed?
Ōmura, I, 3. Chrysanthemums. Poem by the painter. *Cf.* Chūgoku, V.
Yūrintaikan, II. Small Landscape after Wang Shih-min. Handscroll. A long poem by the painter.
Nanga Taikan 2. Tall Trees and small Buildings on a rocky Ledge. Signed.
Nanga Taisei, Add. IV, 37. A View of the West Lake at Hangchou. Handscroll. Signed.
Musée Guimet, Paris. A Study among tall Trees at the Foot of a Mountain. Colophon by the painter.

WU WÊN-CHÊNG 吳文徵, *t.* Nan-hsiang 南薌.
From Hsieh-hsien, Anhui. Active *c.*1820. Landscapes, followed the four Yüan masters and the painters of the Northern school. Flowers in the style of Shen Chou. M, p.176.

Tōan 61. Landscape. Fan-painting. Signed, dated 1821.

WU YING-CHÊN 吳應貞, *t.* Han-wu 含五.
Lady painter. Native of Wu-chiang, Kiangsu. Flowers and portraits. Q, I, 3. M, p.170.

Hui-hua kuan. Lotus Flowers rising above the Water. Painted in *mo-ku* manner. Ink and colour on paper. Signed and dated 1780 (?).

WU YÜAN-K'AI 吳元楷, *t.* Hsin-shêng 辛生.
From Suchou. Pupil of Chai Chi-ch'ang and active in the middle of the 19th century. Flowers, epidendrum, rocks and landscapes. T. M, p.176.

I-yüan album. Twelve leaves with Studies of various Flowers. Signed and dated 1845.

WU YÜN 吳雲, *t.* Shao-fu 少甫, *h.* P'ing-chai 平齋 and many other names.
From Kuei-an, Chekiang. B. 1811, d. 1883. Famous collector. Landscapes, flowers and birds. M, p.181.

Kurokawa cat. 44. A Stalk of a Flower. Signed and dated 1846.

Nanga Taisei, Add. IV, 137. A Magnolia Bush and Orchids. Signed and dated 1876.

Musée Guimet (Dubosc collect.) River in the Mountains, a man walking over a bridge. After Huang Kung-wang. Album-leaf. Signed.

WU YÜN 吳雲, *t.* Yeh-ma 野馬 and Ch'iu-nan 秋南.
From Hsieh-hsien, Anhui. Poet and landscape-painter. M, p.181.

S.c.t.k. hsü-pien, VIII. A tall River-view. Signed.

YANG CHIN 楊晉, *t.* Tzŭ-hao 子鶴, *h.* Hsi-t'ing 西亭.
From Ch'ang-shu, Kiangsu. B. 1644, d. after 1726. Pupil and assistant of Wang Hui. Q, I, 3. R, VII, 14. U, I, 3, 6. M, pp.586–587.

Nanga Taikan 3. Nightfall in the Yen-hsüeh Pavilion. Signed. Bamboo Groves by Wang Hui. Poem and colophon by Yün Shou-p'ing, dated 1683.

Shina Nanga, III, 12. Landscape: The three Friends in the cold Winter. Painted together with Wang Hui and Wang Yün. Signed, dated 1694.

Hamburg Exhibition, 1949–1950. Bamboos, in the style of Wu Chên. Signed, dated 1696.

Nanga Taisei, XI, 253–261. An Album of Landscapes after old masters. Signed and dated 1700.

Nanking Exhib. cat. 317. Landscape in the manner of Tung Yüan. Signed and dated 1701.

Ming-jên shu-hua, XII. A Crow on a Branch of a blossoming Peach-tree. Signed, dated 1703.

Ōmura, II, 1 and 3. Two pictures from an Album of Flowers and Fruit-paintings. Signed, dated 1706. *Cf.* Chūgoku 7.

Ho Kuan-wu, Hongkong. Landscape after Shên Chou. Handscroll. Inscription dated 1710.

K.-k. shu-hua chi, XXVI. Plum-blossoms, Bamboos,

Orchids and Rocks. Signed, dated 1712.

Shina Meiga Senshū, II, 33 (*ex*-Nagao collect.) Leafless Trees, Bamboos and Rocks along a River. Part of a handscroll. Inscription by the painter, dated 1712.

Nanga Taikan 12. A Crow on a Branch of a blossoming Plum-tree. Signed, dated 1713.

Hobart collect., Cambridge, Mass. Studies of Flowers and Fruits. Four album-leaves. Signed, dated 1714.

Chūgoku VII. Portrait of the Connoisseur and Collector An I-chou in his Garden. Painted in conjunction with Wang Hui. Signed and dated 1715.

Shên-chou, XX. Illustrations to Ou-yang Hsiu's "Dirge of the Autumn Wind". Signed, dated 1717.

Chung-kuo ming-hua, 13. Buffaloes grazing on a low River-shore. Poem by the painter, dated 1717.

Ibid. 10. Three Magpies and Five Sparrows; a large pine and an old plum-tree by a rockery. Signed, dated 1721 (at 78).

K.-k. shu-hua chi, XVII. A Cow-herd. Signed. Poem dated 1724.

Fei-tun lu shan-shui. A Mountain Homestead after Rain. Signed, dated 1725.

Ming-jên shu-hua, XXV. Buffaloes in a Farmers' Village. Signed. Poem dated 1726 (at 83).

Ibid. X. Three Magpies on a Branch of a Willow. Signed. Poem. *Cf.* Shina Nanga, III, 11.

Ku-kung, XXXIII. Landscape. Fan-painting. Signed.

Chung-kuo ming-hua, 14 and 17. Four sections of a handscroll representing the Hundred Birds.

Shinchō 48. Frosty Trees and Rocks, in the manner of Ts'ao Chih-po and K'o Chiu-ssŭ. Handscroll. Signed. Colophon.

Boston Museum. A Spray of a Lichee-tree with Fruits. Signed. Colophons.

British Museum (Add. No.25). The Emperor Ch'ien-lung hunting. Long handscroll. Signed.

Ibid. Overhanging Rocks at a River-bank. Album-leaf. Signed.

Hamburg Exhibition, 1949–1950. The Eight Horses of the Chou emperor Mu-wang.

YANG CHOU 楊舟, *t.* Yü-wei 漁爲.

From P'u-t'ien, Fukien. Active *c.*1754. Famous for his pictures of deer. M, p.587.

Tokasha Shina Meigashū, 63, 64. A pair of pictures: 1. A Deer under a Pine-tree in Winter. 2. Two Deer under a Pine in Moonlight and a Monkey in the Tree. Signed, dated 1754.

G. Del Drago, New York. A Deer standing by a Pine-tree looking at the Moon. Signed.

YANG HSÜAN 楊鉉.

Not mentioned in the literature but known through the following picture.

Hui-hua kuan. Large River-views with Wooded Shore in the foreground and undulating Hills beyond. In the manner of Tung Yüan. Ink on silk. Large handscroll. Signed and dated 1644.

YANG PU 楊補, *t.* Wu-pu 無補 and Po-pu 白補, *h.* Ku-nung 古農.

From Ch'ing-chiang, Kiangsi; lived in Suchou. B. 1598, d. 1657. Led a hermit's life after 1644. Landscapes. P, III, 9. U, I, 2, 5. M, p.586.

Shên-chou, VII. Cottages by a River. Handscroll. Signed, dated 1648.

K.-k. shu-hua chi, XVI. Landscape. Signed, dated 1648.

Wu-mên p'ai ming-hua chi (Shên-chou album, 1924.) River Landscape. Signed. Colophon dated 1652.

I-yüan chen-shang, 10. A River Landscape; a man crossing a bridge to visit another. Signed, dated 1655.

YANG TA-CHANG 楊大章.

Court-painter *c.*1790. Figures and birds in Huang Ch'üan's style. S. M, p.587.

K.-k. shu-hua chi, XXXV. A white Eagle. Signed, dated 1791.

Li-tai, II. A Plum-tree, Bamboos and Narcissi. Signed.

Ku-kung, XLI. Looking at the Waterfall. Signed.

YANG WEI-TS'UNG 楊維聰, *t.* Hai-shih 海石.

From Hai-yen, Chekiang. Early Ch'ing period. Famous painter of fish. Q, I, 2. R, V, 24. M, p.586.

British Museum, (No.218.) Carp. Signed.

YANG YÜN-HUA 楊韞華, *h.* Chih-yün 稚雲.

From Suchou. B. *c.*1812, d. 1852. Plum-blossoms. M, p.591.

Chung-hua album. Twelve pictures of Plum-blossoms. Dated 1851.

YAO HSIEH 姚燮, *t.* Mei-po 梅伯, *h.* Yeh-ch'iao 野橋 and Ta-mei shan-min 大梅山民.

From Chên-hai, Chekiang; lived in Shanghai. B. 1805, d. 1864. Poet. Plum-blossoms, figures. M, p.291.

Nanga Taisei, VII, 206. An Arhat seated in a Root-chair. Signed and dated 1851.

Ming-jên shu-hua, XX. Tea-kettle, Branches of Plum-tree and Pine-tree, and a Fan. Signed.

Nanga Taisei, III, 207. Branches of flowering Plum. Signed.

YAO JO-I 姚若翼, *t.* Po-yu 伯右 and Han-yü 寒玉.

From Nanking. Poet. Painted plum-blossoms. R, III, 17. U, II, 1, 24. M, p.288.

Po-mei chi. Branches of Plum-blossoms. Signed. Poem. *Cf.* Nanga Taisei, III, 68.

YAO SUNG 姚宋, *t.* Yü-chin 羽金, *h.* Yü-ching 羽京.

From Hsin-an, Anhui. Active *c.*1700. Landscapes, figures, flowers and birds. Q, I, 2. R, X, 14. M, p.289.

S.c.t.k. hsü-pien, V. Tall Pine-trees in front of a Mountain Wall. In the manner of Hsiao Yün-ts'ung. Signed, dated 1707.

Musée Guimet, Paris. The poetical Gathering in the Western Garden. Fan-painting. Signed at 71.

Hobart collect., Cambridge, Mass. Mountain Landscape in colour, imitating pre-Sung model. Album-leaf.

Ibid. Terraced Mountains, Pine-trees, Temple Pavilion and Figures. Album-leaf.

J. P. Dubosc, Lugano. Album of Landscape-sketches.

YAO WÊN-HAN 姚文瀚.

Court-painter in the Ch'ien-lung period. Active *c.*1760. Figures. S. M, p.289.

K -k. shu-hua chi, VI. Pedlars. Signed.

K.-k. chou-k'an 3. Portrait of Wên-shu. Signed.

Metropolitan Museum (47.81.1–2). Portraits of the Emperors, after the paintings in the Nan-hsün hall of the Peking palace. Two albums. Signed.

YAO YÜAN-CHIH 姚元之, *t.* Po-ang 伯昂, *h.* Chien-ch'ing 廌青 and Chu-yeh-t'ing-shêng 竹葉亭生

From T'ung-ch'êng, Anhui. B. 1773, d. 1852. Figures and flowers. U, III, 2, 9. M, p.290.

Nanga Taisei, V, 43. A Pine-tree. Signed and dated 1823.

Shên-chou, XIII. A Lemon-tree and a blossoming Shrub. Signed, dated 1840.

YEH HSIN 葉欣, *t.* Jung-mu 榮木.

From Hua-t'ing, Kiangsu; lived in Nanking. Active *c.*1670. One of the "Eight Masters of Nanking". Landscapes, followed Chao Ling-jang. P, III, 17. R, IV, 22. U, II, 1, 21. M, p.576.

C. C. Wang, New York. Two album-leaves. Ink and light colours on paper. From a collective album painted in or about 1654. *Cf.* Cat. Exhibition of the Chinese Art Society, New York, March 1955, No.16.

Hamburg Exhibition, 1949–1950. Picking Chrysanthemums by the Eastern Hedge. Signed, dated 1655.

Chin-ling p'ai ming-hua chi (Shên-chou album, 1924). Two Pine-trees in Mist. Signed.

Chou Li-yüan 5. Two Men standing on a high Rock; another man approaching. Seal of the artist.

Ibid. 11. Two Lanterns on a rocky Ridge; a stream below. Seal of the artist.

Nanga Taisei, II, 66. Branches of flowering Plum. Album-leaf. Seals of the artist.

YEH TAO-FÊN 葉道芬, *t.* Hsiang-shih 香士.

From Chia-ting, Kiangsu. Active *c.*1850. Landscapes and figures; pupil of Ch'êng T'ing-lu. T. M, p.577.

Hamburg Exhibition, 1949–1950. Landscape in the style of K'o Chiu-ssŭ.

YEH TAO-PÊN 葉道本.

Unrecorded. Probably Ch'ing period.

Bijutsu, XVII. Cliffs and Trees. Fan-painting. Signed.

Ibid. XXII. The Nine Old Men from Shang-shan. Signed.

Ōmura, I, 12. A Lady in a Pavilion and a young Man on Horseback. Signed. *Cf.* Chūgoku, III.

Tōkyō National Museum. Chrysanthemums, Rock, a flowering Tree and a Bird. Signed and dated *hsin-hai*.

YEH T'AO 葉洮, *t.* Chin-ch'êng 金城, *h.* Ch'in-ch'uan 秦川.

Court-painter in the K'ang-hsi era. Landscapes. Q, I, 2. R. VIII, 23. M. p.576.

Kurokawa cat. 17. A River and Hills in Mist. Signed and dated 1671.

YEN HSIEN 嚴顯, *t.* Shih-fu 時甫,

From Kuangtung. Chü-jên in 1818. Poet. Landscapes, epidendrums and bamboos. M, p.729.

S.c.t.k. hsü-pien, II. Road along a Mountain Stream, a wanderer under large trees. In Sung style. Signed. *Cf.* Nanga Taisei, X, 118.

YEN KUAN 嚴冠, *t.* Ssŭ-hsiang 四香.

From Hangchou. Beginning of the 19th century. Ink plum-blossoms. T. M, p.729.

Po-mei chi. A Plum-tree in Bloom. Signed. Poem dated 1812.

YEN SHÊNG-SUN 嚴繩孫, *t.* Sun-yu 蓀友, *h.* Kou-wu yen-ssŭ 勾吳嚴四.
From Wu-hsi, Kiangsu. B. 1623, d. 1702. Scholar, poet. Landscapes, figures, flowers, birds, etc. Q, I, 2. R, VI, 1. U, I, 2, 13. M, p.728.

Chung-kuo, II, 128. Old Trees and Crows, after Ni Tsan. Signed. Poem dated 1666. *Cf.* Chung-kuo ming-hua 36.
Shina Meiga Senshū 23. Two Cranes. Signed, dated 1680.
Ming-jên shu-hua, III. Fishermen's Cottages by a River. Signed. Poem dated 1684. Poems by Kao Shih-ch'i and others.
Chou Li-yüan 8. Houses at the Foot of a Mountain. Album-leaf, signed.
J. Cahill, Wash., D.C. A Man walking with his Servant on a Lake-shore. Poem, signed. Inscription by K'ang Yu-wei.

YEN TSAI 嚴載, *t.* Ts'ang-p'ei 滄醅. Also known by the name of Yen Kuai 嚴怪 (Yen the Queer).
From Sung-chiang, Kiangsu. Active *c.*1700. Landscapes. Q, I, 2. R, VII, 8. U, III, 1, 2. M, p.728.

I-shu ts'ung-pien 13. Tall leafless Trees and high Mountain Peak rising above a misty River; a man in a boat on the water. Poem by the painter. *Cf.* Shina Nanga, II, 12.

YEN YÜ 嚴鈺, *t.* Shih-ju 式如, *h.* Hsiang-fu 香府.
From Chia-ting, Kiangsu. B. 1682; active as a court-painter *c.*1765. Landscapes. M, p.728.

Chūgoku 8. A Man in a Hut on a Promontory; a servant approaching. Album-leaf. Signed and dated 1758, "at age 77".
Shên-chou, IX. Landscape: A Stream winding at the Foot of a Mountain Ridge. Signed.

YIN HSI 尹錫, *t.* Huai-yüan 懷元, *h.* Hsi-ts'un 西邨.
From Hu-chou, Chekiang. 18th century. Landscapes, figures, flowers and birds. M, p.14.

Shinchō 54. Pines on a rocky Hill. Signed. Poem.

YIN SHU-PO 殷樹柏, *t.* Man-ch'ing 縵卿, *h.* Yün-lou 雲樓 and Lan-yün 嬾雲.
From Chia-hsing, Chekiang. B. 1769, d. 1847. Flowers in the style of Hsiang Mo-lin. M, p.310.

Ming-jên shu-hua, XI. A crowing Cock, after Shên Chou. Signed. Two lines of poetry.

YIN YEH 尹埜.
From Fêng-yang, Anhui. 18th century. Famous donkey-painter. Nicknamed Yin Lü (The Donkey Yin). Q, I, 2. M, p.14.

Shên-chou album, 1920. A Donkey Caravan. Handscroll. Seals of the painter.

YIN YÜAN-LIANG 殷元良.
From the Liu-ch'iu Islands. Active *c.*1748. Unrecorded.

Bijutsu Kenkyū, 47. Two Quails. Signed, dated 1748.

YING PAO 瑛寶, *t.* Mêng-ch'an 夢禪, *h.* Chien-an 間菴.
A Manchu. Active *c.*1800. Landscapes, flowers. Finger-painting. M, p.554.

British Museum (No.247). A Horse. Finger-painting. Signed. Colophon dated 1792.
Mizuta collect., Kyōto. Landscape with Autumn Colours, after Wang Mêng. Signed and dated 1796.
Ming-jên hsieh-chu. Bamboos at a Rockery. Signed, dated 1800.
British Museum, No.246. A seated Falcon. Finger-painting. Signed, dated 1805.

YO KAO 岳峼, *t.* Hao-t'ing 鶴亭.
From An-i, Shansi. Active *c.*1715. Figures, animals, birds and flowers. M, p.219.

Shên-chou album, 1926. Six pictures of Animals. Signed, dated 1715. In the same album, six landscape-pictures by Kao Fêng-han.

YU YIN 尤蔭, *t.* Kung-fu 貢父, *h.* Shui-ts'un 水村.
From I-chêng, Kiangsu. B. 1732, d. 1812. Poet. Bamboos, landscapes, flowers and birds. U, III, 2, 5. M, p.12.

Ming-jên shu-hua, XIII. A Branch of Bamboo and Narcissi in a Vase. Signed. Poem dated 1788. Also in Nanga Taikan, 11.
Po-mei chi. A blossoming Plum-tree. Signed, dated 1799.
Fei-tun lu hua-hui. Bamboos by a Rockery. Handscroll. Signed. Colophon dated 1806.
Nanga Taisei, I, 229. Orchids. Album-leaf. Signed.
British Museum (formerly Brener collect.) Fruits and a Brush-pot. Two large album-leaves. Lengthy inscriptions by the painter.

YÜ CHI 余集, *t.* Jung-shang 蓉裳, *h.* Ch'iu-shih 秋室.
From Hangchou. B. 1738, d. 1823. Figures, orchids and bamboos. T, VII, 1. U, III, 1, 18. M, p.119.

Shinchō 83. A Lady with a Looking-glass. Signed. Two lines of poetry dated 1803.
Shên-chou, XVI. A Lady with a Basket and a Hoe. Signed, dated 1810. *Cf.* Shina Nanga, I, 121.
Ibid. V. The Poetess Liu Ju-shih. Half-length. Signed.
Chung-kuo, II, 158. A Maid at her Loom. Signed. *Cf.* Chung-kuo ming-hua, 30.
Ming-jên shu-hua, XVII. A Lady with a Boy in the Garden. Signed. Two lines of poetry.
Chung-kuo ming-hua, 21. The Moon-fairy Chang O surrounded by whirling mist.

YÜ CHIH-TING 禹之鼎, *t.* Shang-chi 上吉 or 尙吉, *h.* Shên-chai 愼齋.
From Yang-chou, Kiangsu. B. 1647, d. *c.*1705. Court-painter in the K'ang-hsi period. Figures. Q, I, 2. R, XIII, 7. U, II, 2, 26. M, p.260.

Shên-chou ta-kuan, vol.9. Portrait of the Poet Sung Wang, *hao* Li-shang. He is seated on a mat, two young girls are standing behind. Signed and dated 1677. *Cf.* Shina Nanga, II, 6.
British Museum. A Woman warming her Cloths over a Brazier, attended by a maid carrying a candle. Signed and dated 1684.
Kokka, 761. A Scholar asking another how to write a Character. Handscroll. Signed and dated 1686.
Nanking Exhib. cat. 320. Portrait of Lan Ch'ien-shan seated on the Bank of a River. Handscroll. Signed and dated 1695.
Shên-chou, VIII. Portrait of Wan Yen seated on the Ground. Signed and dated 1696.

I-shu ts'ung-pien 11. The Poetess Liu Ju-shih seated on a Sofa under leafy Trees. Signed and dated 1696.
Hui-hua kuan. Portrait of a Man standing among Pine-trees. Handscroll. Signed and dated 1697.
British Museum (No.174). Pheasant and Convolvulus. Signed and dated 1699.
I-shu ch'uan-t'ung 12. Wang Yü-yang on a Donkey, searching for the first Plum-blossom of Spring. Signed and dated 1701.
N. Gashū 28. Landscape. Signed, dated 1703. *Cf.* Nanga Taisei, X, 52.
K.-k. shu-hua chi, XIII. Landscape after Wang Mêng. Signed. Colophon dated 1705.
Shên-chou ta-kuan, 14. Portrait of Wang Yüan-ch'i. Seated among Bamboo. Signed.
Shên-chou, IV. Portrait of the Poet Wang Shih-chên in a Pavilion. Signed.
Ibid. VII. The Poet Wu Wei-yeh seated by a winding Stream.
Ibid. XVIII. A Girl standing under a Tree: Tung Hsiao-wan, the Concubine of Mao Hsiang. Album-leaf. Signed.
K.-k. shu-hua chi, XXIX. Ladies. Seals of the painter(?)
Ibid. XXXIV. Ladies. Seals of the painter(?)
Hui-hua kuan. Portrait of Nan-lan Jung-jo seated on a Sofa. Colour on paper. Many inscriptions.
Ibid. A Woman seated under a Banana-plant. Ink on paper. Inscription by the painter. *Cf.* P'ang Yüan-chi Illus. cat. II.
Ibid. Evening Mist at the River-shore; a man and a boy admiring the view from a terrace. Moon in the sky. Ink on silk. Large handscroll.
Shanghai Museum. A Scholar's Homestead in a Garden; a man beside a bamboo-grove. Ink on paper. Handscroll.
Nanking Exhib. cat. 319. Portrait of Wang Yü-yang seated in a Bamboo-grove, holding a *Ch'in*. In the manner of Wang Mêng. Handscroll. Two lines from a poem by Wang Wei, signed.
Shina Nanga, II, 10. The Four Scholars. Signed. *Cf.* Shên-chou ta-kuan, 14.
Shinchō 40. Five Scholars in a Garden. Part of a scroll. *Cf.* Sekai Bijutsu Zenshū, 20, pl.54.
Nanga Taikan, 4. Man lying on a Rock.
Sōgen 282. Bamboos in Wind. Signed. *Cf.* Nanking Exhib. cat. 318.
Ibid. 283. A Man writing on a Fan under a Wu-t'ung tree. Signed.
Ars Asiatica, I, pl.XLII. Two Pine-trees. Signed. A fragment.
Boston Museum. A Lady on a white Horse, conducted by two attendants. Album-leaf. Signed.
British Museum (No.173). Playing Chequers. Signed.
National Museum, Stockholm. Portrait of the Painter Wang Hui. Signed.

Yü Ching-hsing 虞景星, *t.* Tung-kao 東臯.
From Chên-chiang, Kiangsu. Chin-shih in 1712. Poet, calligraphist. Landscapes in Mi Fei's style; also pine-trees. Q, II, 1. R, X, 2. M, p.563.

N. Gashū 27. Two Pine-trees, after Huang Ch'üan. Signed. Poem dated 1746. *Cf.* Nanga Taisei, V, 23.

Yü-fêng 輿風, *t.* of a man named Chü 駒, *h.* Hsüan-yün 懸雲 and Pan-ch'ao 半巢.
Unrecorded. Ch'ing period.

Kyūka, II. River Landscape. Album-leaf.

Yü Hsing 余省, *t.* Tsêng-san 曾三, *h.* Lu-t'ing 魯亭.
From Ch'ang-shu, Kiangsu. Served in the palace together with T'ang Tai and Chou K'un 周鯤 in the Ch'ien-lung period. Flowers and birds. Q, II, 1. R, IX, 19. M, p.118.

K.-k. shu-hua chi, XXXIV. Chrysanthemums. Signed, dated 1744.
Ku-kung, XXXII. An Orange-tree. Signed, dated 1745.
Li-tai, II. Flowers and Insects. Signed.
Ibid. III. Flowers and Birds. Signed.
Pageant 904. Blossoming Trees by a Stream. Album-leaf.

YÜ LING 俞齡, *t*. Ta-nien 大年.
From Hangchou. Active at the close of the 18th century. Famous for his pictures of animals, particularly horses. R, V, 28. M, p.283.

Private collect., Kyōto. Portrait of Wang Ping-ming seated on the Bank of a River, while a servant washes his horses. The portrait is by Wei Tzū-liang, the rest by Yü Ling. Handscroll, signed and dated 1758(?)
Robert Rousset, Paris. A Man riding on a Camel. Signed, dated 1792.

YÜ SHOU-PO 于壽伯, *t*. Hai-wu 海屋.
From Ch'ang-shu, Kiangsu. Probably Ch'ien-lung period. Flowers, birds. M, p.7.

Sōgen 365. Two white Pigeons and Tree-peonies by a Rock. Signed.

YÜ SUNG 余崧, *t*. Wei-yo 維嶽, *h*. Ch'iu-t'ing 秋亭.
From Suchou. 18th century. Portraits, flowers. M, p.119.

N. Gashū 37. Peach-blossoms and Ducklings, after T'ang Yin. Signed.
British Museum, No.259. Small Bird in blossoming Plum-tree. Signed.

YÜ TSUNG-LI 俞宗禮, *t*. Jên-i 人儀, *h*. Tsai-fan 在凡.
From Shanghai; lived in Suchou. Active *c*.1765. Landscapes, Buddhist and Taoist figures. M, p.284.

Nanju 21. Two Landscapes, illustrating Episodes from the Lives of 1. T'ao Yüan-ming and 2. Chang Ssŭ-kung. Second picture also in Tōyō, XII.

YÜ YÜAN 虞沅, *t*. Wan-chih 畹之 or Han-chih 翰之.
From Yang-chou; lived in Ch'ang-shu, Kiangsu. Active *c*.1715. Pupil of Wang Hui. Flowers and birds. Q, II, 1. R, VII, 5. U, II, 2, 17. M, p.563.

Kyūka, II. Chrysanthemums and a Bird. Signed, dated 1691.
Nanju 10. Autumn Flowers and two Birds, after a Yüan master. Signed, dated 1715. Also in Tōyō, XII.
Chung-kuo, II, 150. A Crow in Snow-covered Bamboos. Signed. *Cf*. Chung-kuo ming-hua, 33.
British Museum (No.224). Cock, Roses, and Hydrangea. Signed.

YÜAN CHIANG 袁江, *t*. Wên-t'ao 文濤.
From Chiang-tu, Kiangsu. Court-painter in the Yung-chêng period (1723–1735). Followed the Sung masters. Excelled as painter of architectual motifs. Q, II, 1. R, XI, 22. M, p.323.

Nelson Gallery, Kansas City. Pulling Carts over a Mountain Pass, after Kuo Hsi. Signed, dated *chia-hsü* (1694). *Cf.* Cleveland Exhib. cat. 89.
Sōgen 298. Boats in a Yangtse Gorge. Signed, dated *wu yin* (1698).
National Museum, Stockholm. Pulling Carts over a Mountain Pass, after Kuo Hsi. Signed, dated *ting-hai* (1707). *Cf.* Sirén, *Later*, pl. 170.
Kyūka, II. Travellers in the Mountains, after Kuo Hsi. Signed, dated *jên-ch'ên* (1712).
Sōgen 297. A Pavilion on Lu-shan. Signed, dated 1715.
Hamburg Exhibition, 1949–1950. Summer Palace in Spring. Broad ink manner. Signed, dated 1715.
Chicago Art Institute. Early Spring Landscape, with blossoming Plum-tree. Signed and dated 1717.
Tokasha Shina Meigashū 87. A Mountain Path in Szechuan: high mountains covered by leafy trees rising over a misty valley. Travellers gathered in an inn. Signed, dated 1718.
Kokka 584 (S. Kobayashi). Landscape with a Mansion. Signed, dated 1719.
Hamburg Exhibition, 1949–1950. The Wonderful View of P'êng-lai, the Island of Immortals in the East Sea. Signed, dated 1722.
Hui-hua kuan. Landscape-studies after old Masters. Eight album-leaves.
Ibid. P'êng-lai, the Island of the Immortals. Ink and bluish colour.
Tomioka collect., Kyōto. Mountain Landscape, with Pine-trees and Figures. Fan-painting. Inscription by the artist. *Cf.* Sekai Bijutsu Zenshū, XX, text illus. 98
Shinchō 64. Landscape. Signed.
Tokasha Shina Meigashū 86. Three Men by a steep Waterfall in a Mountain Gorge. Signed.
Boston Museum. Pavilion and Galleries in a Rock Garden. Signed.
Ibid. Pavilion under large Trees in a Rock Garden at the Foot of steep Mountains. Signed.
George Stout, Boston. Landscape after Kuo Hsi. Signed.
British Museum, Mountain Landscape with Pavilions. Signed.
Princeton (Du Bois-Morris collect.) Summer Palaces in the Mountains. Large decorative composition in six sections. Not signed, but in the manner of the painter.

YÜAN HSÜEH 袁雪, *t.* Wo-shêng 臥生.
From Suchou. Beginning of the Ch'ing period. Famous as seal-engraver; praised by Wu Wei-yeh. Unrecorded.

Tōyō, XI. Palatial Buildings among Snow-covered Mountains. One of a series of eight pictures. Signed.
Kyūka, II. Two album-leaves: 1. A Boat on a Stream in Snow. 2. A Fisherman's Cottage in Snow. Signed.
Shinchō 64. Travellers in the Mountains. Album-leaf. Two lines of poetry. Seal of the painter.

YÜAN NIEN 阮年, *t.* Hsia-shêng 遐生.
From Hangchou. 18th century. Ink bamboos, pupil of Chu Shêng (active *c.*1680–1735). R, VII, 23. M, p.117.

Ming-jên hsieh-chu. Bamboos at a Rockery. Signed.

YÜAN YAO 袁耀.
From Chiang-tu, Kiangsu. Active *c.*1744–1755. Nephew of Yüan Chiang. Also employed at the court. M, p.323.

Field Museum, Chicago. Lu-yeh t'ang, the Summer Residence of the Prime Minister P'ei Tu of T'ang (765–839). Signed, dated 1740.
British Museum (No.191). Spring Dawn at the Han Palace. Signed, dated 1744.
Boston Museum. The O-fang kung, the Palace of Ch'in Shih-huang-ti. Signed, dated 1744.
Shinchō 65 (Hashimoto collect., Takatsuki). Landscape. Signed, dated 1747.
Tokasha Shina Meigashū 85. Pavilions on Top of the Mountain of the Immortals. Signed, dated 1749.
Nanking Exhib. cat. 342. A large Landscape, with an ox-cart and mounted travellers fording a river to reach an inn. Signed and dated 1754.

Hamburg Exhibition, 1949–1950. Returning from the Hunting. Illustration to a poem by Wang Wu-kung. Handscroll. Signed, dated 1755.
Bijutsu, III. Mountains and Pavilion by a Stream. Signed.
Sōgen 299. Waterfall on Lu-shan.
Artibus Asiae, vol.5 (Düsseldorf). The Autumn Moon over a dewy Terrace. Signed.
Hui-hua kuan. Two Landscapes in Sung Style.
Boston Museum. Pavilions among Trees at the Foot of steep Mountains. Long handscroll. Signed.
Ibid. Steep Cliffs rising from a Stream; a pavilion on a promontory. Signed.
Ibid. Twelve pictures forming a continuous Garden Scenery. Signed.
Ibid. The Imperial Han Palace in a Garden. Long handscroll. Signed.
Lin Nan-hai, Kobe. A large Landscape. Signed.

YÜAN YING 袁瑛, *t.* Chin-hua 近華, *h.* Êrh-fêng 二峯.
From Suchou. Court-painter. Active 1765–1785. Landscapes, flowers. M, p.324.

K.-k. shu-hua chi, XXV. Landscape after Chao Tsung-han. Signed, dated 1776.

YÜAN YÜAN 阮元, *t.* Po-yüan 伯元 and Liang-po 良伯, *h.* Yün-t'ai 芸臺.
From Yang-chou, Kiangsu. B. 1764, d. 1849. Grand Secretary, given posthumous title Wên-ta 文達. Took part in the compilation of the Ch'ien-lung catalogue *Shih-chü pao-chi* 石渠寶笈. Flowers, trees and stones. M, p.117.

Sōgen 335. A blossoming Plum-tree. Signed, dated 1796.
Po-mei chi. A blossoming Plum-tree. Signed, dated *kuei-mao* (1843).

YÜN HSI 允禧. Prince Shên 愼郡王, *h.* Tzŭ-ch'iung tao-jên 紫瓊道人.
Twenty-first son of the emperor K'ang-hsi. Landscapes. Q, I. M, p.10.

K.-k. shu-hua chi, XVI. The quiet Mountains. Dated 1674. Poem by the painter copied by a courtier.
Ibid. XVIII. Landscape.
K.-k. chou-k'an 470–475, 498–510. Two albums of Landscapes. Signed.

YÜN-K'O 韻可. A monk, original name Huang 黃, *t.* T'ieh-chou 鐵舟, *h.* Mu-shih shan-jên 木石山人.
From Wu-ch'ang, Hupeh. 18th century (?) Landscapes, flowers and bamboos. U, III, 1, 27. M, p.719.

Tokasha Shina Meigashū 25. A Pavilion under bare Trees by a Mountain Stream, after Ni Tsan and Wang Fu. Poem by the painter.

YÜN PING 惲冰, *t.* Ch'ing-ju 清如, *h.* Hao-ju 浩如 and Lan-ling nü-shih 蘭陵女史.
A descendant of Yün Shou-p'ing. Active 1670–1710. She painted mainly flowers and fruits. Q, II, 2. R, XVI. M. pp.511–512.

Chung-kuo ming-hua, 15. A Collection of brightly-coloured Spring-flowers. Section of a handscroll.
Sōgen 357. Three Peonies by a Rockery, after Yün Shou-p'ing. Signed.
Hamburg Exhibition, 1949–1950. Cranes and Peonies.
J. Cahill, Wash., D.C. Chrysanthemums of many Colours growing by a Rock. Poem, signed.

YÜN SHOU-P'ING 惲壽平, original name Yün Ko 惲格, *t.* Chêng-shu 正叔, *h.* Nan-t'ien 南田, Yün-ch'i wai-shih 雲溪外史, Po-yün wai-shih 白雲外史, Tung-yüan ts'ao-i 東園艸衣 and other names.
From Wu-chin, Kiangsu. B. 1633, d. 1690. The greatest flower-painter of his time, imitated Hsü Ch'ung-ssŭ. Also landscapes. Q, I, 2. R, IV, 2. U, I, 1, 3. M, p.510.

Sōgen 263. River Landscape. Signed. Poem dated 1664.

K.-k. shu-hua chi, XXX. The Fu-ch'un Mountain, after Huang Kung-wang. Signed. Poem dated 1668.

Shi-O Go Un 35. Trees and Clouds on the Sung Mountain. Signed, dated 1669. Also in Ōmura, I, 11; Chūgoku 6.

Yūchikusai 27. Pine-tree and Plum-blossoms. Fan-painting. Signed. Colophon dated 1669.

Shên-chou, VI. Bamboos and Plum-blossoms in Snow. Signed, dated 1670. Also in Shina Nanga, II, 11.

Chung-kuo ming-hua, 14. The Fu-ch'un Mountains, in the manner of Huang Kung-wang. Section of a hand-scroll. Signed, dated 1670.

Shi-O Go Un 36. Landscape in Autumn. Handscroll. Signed, dated 1670.

T. T. Ma, Hongkong. Bamboo, Day-lily and Ling-chih by a Stone. After a Sung master. Poem by the painter dated 1670.

Yūchikusai 19. Landscape. Fan-painting. Signed, dated 1670.

Sōgen 261. An old Cedar, Bamboos, and Roses by a Rockery. Signed. Poem dated 1670.

Contag, pls.43, 44. Landscape-studies after old masters. Two album-leaves. Signed, dated 1670.

Kokka 268. River Scenery. Handscroll. Signed. Colophon dated 1671. Also in Yūchikusai 15.

Contag, pl.45 (Wu Hu-fan collect.) A solitary River in the Mountain, after Ts'ao Chih-po. Poem. Signed, dated 1672.

K.-k. shu-hua chi, XLIV. An old Cedar on the Yü-hsü Mountain. Signed. Colophon dated 1673.

Shinchō 19. Cloudy Mountains. Fan-painting. Signed. Colophon dated 1673. Also in Bijutsu Kenkyū 18.

Yūchikusai 28. Flowers. Fan-painting. Signed, dated 1675.

Chung-kuo ming-hua 3. Travellers in the Mountains; a man on muleback followed by his servant. After Tung Yüan. Album-leaf. Colophon by the painter dated 1675. Poem by Ch'ien-lung. Also in Shina Nanga, I, 43.

Princeton (Du Bois-Morris collect.) Monkeys by a Rockery, after Hsü Ch'ung-ssŭ. Signed, dated 1675.

W. Hochstadter, New York. Song of the Lily Flowers and Cypress Leaves. Poem and two seals of the artist; dated 1676. *Cf.* Cleveland Exhib. cat. 92.

S.c.t.k. hsü-pien, IX. Mountains along a River. Poem by the painter, dated 1677.

K.-k. shu-hua chi, XIX. Landscape after Tung and Chü. Signed, dated 1678.

Ibid. XVIII. The Five Pure Things. Signed. Colophon dated 1681.

Ibid. XLV. Scholar's Cottage among Trees; river landscape. Signed, dated 1682. Eight poems by the painter.

Ōmura, I, 12. Fishing-boats on a River in Autumn, after Ma Yüan. Signed, dated 1682. *Cf.* Chūgoku 6.

Shi-O Go Un 38. Peonies. Fan-painting. Signed. Poem dated 1683. Also in Yūchikusai 30.

Bijutsu Kenkyū 7. Fruits. Fan-painting. Signed, dated 1683.

N. Gashū 23. Plum-blossoms and Camellias, after Hsü Ch'ung-ssŭ. Signed. Poem dated 1683.

Shi-O Go Un 39 (Ōgawa collect., Kyōto). Rocky Cliffs at T'ien-ch'ih, after Wang Mêng. Handscroll. Signed. Poem, colophon dated 1684.

Contag, pl.46 (Hsü Chün-ch'ing collect.) Peach-blossoms in Spring Breeze, after Hsü Ch'ung-ssŭ. A leaf of an album of flower paintings. Dated 1684.

J. P. Dubosc, Lugano. Lotus. Handscroll. A short poem by the painter, signed and dated 1684.

T. T. Ma, Hongkong. A Branch of blossoming Plum-tree and two flowering Plants. Three poems by the painter, one dated 1685.

Shina Nanga, II, 2. Landscape after Chao Mêng-fu. Signed. Poem dated 1685.

Contag, pls.47, 48 (Li Tso-hsien collect.) Studies of Bamboo and flowering Shrub by a Stone. Two album-leaves. Dated 1685.

Ibid. pls.49, 50 (Li Tso-hsien collect.) Bamboos and dry Trees at a Rockery; Pine-trees leaning down from a Cliff. Two album-leaves. Dated 1685.

S.c.t.k. hsü-pien, XI. Branches of Plum-blossoms and

other blossoming Shrubs. Signed, dated 1685.

Kokka, 652 (Okura collect., Tōkyō) A Gourd, from an album of ten Flower and Fruit-pictures. Signed, dated 1685.

Ibid. Birds and Flowers. Signed.

Nanga Taisei, XVI, 64, 65. Landscape after Wang Mêng. Handscroll. Signed and dated 1685.

K.-k. chou-k'an 77, 88. Ten Landscape-studies on album-leaves, all with poems or colophons by Wang Hui. The first one dated 1685.

Yamaguchi collect., Ashiya. Bamboos on the low bank of a broad Water. Ink only. Short handscroll. Signed and dated 1685.

Nanga Taikan 12. Bare Trees and Bamboos by a Rock. Signed, dated 1686. Bamboos by Wang Hui. *Cf.* P'ang Yüan-chi Illust. cat. (1940) I.

Shên-chou, VII. Chrysanthemums. Signed. Poem dated 1686.

Ibid. XIX. Winding Stream at the Foot of a Mountain Ridge, after Tung Yüan. Poem by the painter, dated 1687.

Yün Nan-t'ien shan-shui hua-ts'ê (Yu-chêng album, 1922). Eight Landscape-sketches after old Masters, accompanied by eight inscriptions. Signed, dated 1687.

Gems, I, 72. A crowing Cock. Poem, signed and dated 1687.

Yūchikusai 18. Bamboo Shoots. Fan-painting. Signed, dated 1687.

Shi-O Go Un 40. Pine-trees by a River, after Wên Chêng-ming. Signed. Poem dated 1687. Also in Tōan, 52.

K. Sumitomo, Ōiso. Large Album containing twelve Paintings of Birds, Flowers and Landscapes after Sung Masters, most of them in colour. The last leaf in the style of Mi Fei is dated 1687. *Cf.* K. Sumitomo, II.

Kokka 304. Chrysanthemums, after Hsü Ch'ung-ssŭ. Signed. Poem dated 1688.

I-shu ch'uan-t'ung, II. Fragrant Peonies in Spring, after Hsü Ch'ung-ssŭ. Signed and dated 1688.

Shên-chou, XXI. Three Hares among Reeds, after Huang Ch'üan. Signed, dated 1689.

Kokka 546. Peonies. Fan-painting. Signed, dated 1689.

Sōgen 264. A Heron under Peony Flowers, after a Sung master. Signed. Poem dated 1689.

Palace Museum album, 1931. Ten Landscape-sketches. Inscriptions by Wang Hui; one of them dated 1705.

Shên-chou, II, III. Ten Pictures of Flowers from an album.

Ibid. III. Pine-tree and Stones, after Chao Mêng-fu. Signed. Colophon.

Ibid. VI. A Man in a Boat looking at the Plum-blossoms on the Shore. Signed. Poem.

Ibid. VII. Two Feng Birds on a Rockery and Tree Peonies. Signed. Two lines of poetry.

Ibid. XIV. River-view with Mountain Peaks rising through the Mist and Trees in the foreground. After Chao Ta-nien. Signed.

Ibid. XIV, XV. Landscape-studies, Mountains and running Waters. Four long album-leaves.

Shên-chou album, 1923. Ten Pictures of Flowers, some after old models.

Shên-chou ta-kuan, vol.6. Admiring the blossoming Plum-trees along the River. After T'ang Yin. *Cf.* Shên-chou, VI.

Ibid. vol.8. Travellers among wintry Mountains, after Kuo Hsi. Signed.

Chung-kuo, II, 74. A Study among Bamboo Groves. Signed. *Cf.* Chung-kuo ming-hua, 20.

Ibid. II, 75. Peach-blossoms. Signed. Poem.

Ibid. II, 76. A Cat watching a Butterfly. Signed. Poem.

Ibid. II, 77. Cock and Flowers, after a Sung master. Signed. Poem.

Ibid. II, 78. The Five Pure Things. Signed. *Cf.* K.-k. shu-hua chi, XVIII.

Ibid. II, 79. Chrysanthemums, after Hsü Ch'ung-ssŭ. Signed. Poem.

Chung-kuo ming-hua, 3. Bamboo and Wu-t'ung Trees, after Wang Fu. Signed.

Ibid. 13. Flowering Chrysanthemums growing on a Garden Rock. Signed. Poem by the painter.

Ibid. 28. Landscape after Tung Yüan. Inscription, signed.

Ibid. Branches of a blossoming Peach-tree. Inscription, signed.

Yu-chêng album, 1917. Twelve Pictures of Flowers and Landscapes.

Yün Wang shan-shui ho-ts'ê (Yu-chêng album, 1922). An Album of twelve leaves representing Landscapes after old masters. Painted together with Wang Hui.

Ch'ing-kung pi-ts'ang Nan-t'ien mo-hsi ts'ê (Yu-chêng album, 1923). Twelve leaves representing Landscapes after old Masters.

Yu-chêng album, 1925. Fourteen Pictures of Flowers and Landscapes.

Chung-hua album, 1918. Twelve Pictures of Flowers, Fruits and Birds.

Yün Nan-t'ien shan-shui ching-p'in ts'ê (Shên-chou album, 1926). Ten leaves representing Landscapes after old Masters.

Ming-jên shu-hua, IV. Bamboos and Chrysanthemums among Rocks by a Stream, after Liu Chüeh. Signed. Poem. Also in Shina Nanga Taikan, 1.

Li-tai, I. Wistaria Flowers. Signed.

Ibid. III. Flowers. Signed. Poem.

K.-k. shu-hua chi, XIII. Old Trees and Bamboos, after K'o Chiu-ssŭ. Signed.

Ibid. XVII. Trees and Bamboos, after Ni Tsan. Signed. Colophons.

Ibid. XXII. Lilies, after T'ang Yin. Signed. Poem.

Ibid. XXVII. The Plum-blossom Study, after Chao Mêng-fu. Signed.

Ibid. XXIX. Lotuses. Signed. Poem.

K.-k. chou-k'an, vol.VI, VII, 128–141. Ten Landscape Studies after old masters. Album-leaves. Colophons and poems by the painter. Signed.

K.-k. ming-shan chi, 2. Various Fan-paintings. For others, see K.-k. chou-k'an, Index (twenty-eight paintings); Nanga Taisei, VIII, 147–162.

Ku-kung collect. Two leaves from an album of Landscapes. Inscription, seals of the artist. *Cf.* Nanking Exhib. cat. 308.

Hui-hua kuan. Studies of Flowers, Plants and Trees. Colour on paper. Eight album-leaves.

Ibid. Long Branches of a blossoming Peach-tree. Inscription by the master. Slight colours on paper.

Ibid. Large Mountain-landscapes with rich Growth of Trees in the Crevices. A scholar's homestead on a terrace. After Huang Kung-wang. Ink and reddish colour on paper. Signed.

Shanghai Museum. Mountain Peak rising through the Mist; leafy trees below. Signed.

Gems, I, 71. Lotuses, after Hsü Ch'ung-ssŭ. Poem, signed.

Chang Ts'ung-yü cat. Trees on a rocky Shore. Signed.

Nanking Exhib. cat. 309 (formerly P'ang Yüan-chi). River Landscape, after Mi Fu-jên. Signed.

Liu 114. Bamboo and Flowers growing by a Rock. Signed.

P'ang Yüan-chi Illust. cat., 1940, IV. Landscape with a Waterfall, old Trees and Wistaria. Poem, signed.

Mei-chan t'ê-k'an, 43. Old Trees on steep Cliffs. Poem by the painter.

Mo-ch'ao pi-chi, vol.II. Irises and Narcissi by a Rockery at the Foot of a Pine-tree. Signed. Poem.

Yen-kuang album, Peking. Eight Album-leaves representing Landscapes after old masters.

S.c.t.k. hsü-pien, X. Peach-blossoms and white Pigeons, after Sung Master. Signed.

Chang Ta-ch'ien cat., IV, 38. *Hao-ming k'ung-shan t'u*: A Crane cries in the empty Mountain. Landscape-handscroll, painted for Wei Yin-chün who was retiring to the Chin-ching shan. Inscriptions by the painter and by Yün Jih-ch'u. Quotations from *Shih-ching* written by Ts'ai Yüan-ch'ên.

Lo Chia-lun, Taipei. A Scholar in his Study Pavilion among leafy Trees at Foot of a Mountain. After Wang Mêng. Bright colouring.

Contag, pls.35–40. Six Landscape-studies after Huang Kung-wang and other masters. Signed.

Kokka 292. 1. Chrysanthemums; signed. 2. Peonies; seals of the painter; poem. 3. Flowers; signed.

Ibid. 578 (T. Hashimoto, Tōkyō). An old Pine-tree.

Ibid. 586 (Y. Sakata, Tōkyō). Tree-peonies.

Ibid. 652 (Okura Shukokan). Flowers and Fruits.

Nanju 12. Endless Mountains and Streams, after Chü-jan. Signed.

Bijutsu Kenkyū 92 (Abe collect.) Flowers.

Shina Nanga, I, 40. A Man with a Staff among tall Pine-trees, after T'ang Yin. Album-leaf.

Ibid. I, 41. Cloudy Peaks and Waterfalls. Album-leaf.

Ibid. I, 42. Landscape. Album-leaf.

Ibid. I, 44 and 45. Two pictures of Flowers. Signed. Poems by Ch'ien-lung.

Ibid. I, 70. Landscape. Album-leaf. Signed. Poem.

Ibid. II, 7. Trees in Winter, after Li Ch'êng.

Po-yün wai-shih miao-p'in (Kobayashi, Kyōto, 1919). An album of ten leaves: Studies of Flowers and Plants. Each leaf with inscription by the painter.

Yün Nan-t'ien shan-shui ts'ê (Hakubundō (Kobayashi) album). Eight Landscapes after Chü-jan, Li Ch'êng, Ni Tsan and Huang Kung-wang.

Yamamoto Bunkadō album, 1931. Ten Pictures of Flowers.